WITHDRAWN

11718

WITHDRAWN

PN
4121
.M579
1967

MONROE
Principles and types of speech

WITHDRAWN

Illinois Central College
Learning Resource Center

PRINCIPLES AND TYPES OF SPEECH SIXTH EDITION

PRINCIPLES AND TYPES OF SPEECH

SIXTH EDITION

ALAN H. MONROE
Purdue University

DOUGLAS EHNINGER
The University of Iowa

SCOTT, FORESMAN AND COMPANY

Illinois Central College
Learning Resouce Center

11718

Library of Congress Catalog Card No. 67-16956

Copyright © 1935, 1939, 1949, 1955, 1962, 1967 by Scott, Foresman and Company, Glenview, Illinois 60025. All rights reserved.
Printed in the United States of America.
Regional offices of Scott, Foresman and Company are located in Atlanta, Dallas, Glenview, Palo Alto, and Oakland, N. J.

Preface

To the student

The primary purpose of *Principles and Types of Speech* is to help you become an effective speaker. In a democratic society, effective speech is extremely important. It is crucial in today's world that must—if it expects to survive—*talk* out rather than *fight* out its differences. Indeed, as Thomas Mann has one of his characters say in *The Magic Mountain,* "Speech is civilization itself. The word, even the most contradictory word, preserves contact—it is silence which isolates."

To help you become an effective speaker, this book explains and illustrates the general *principles* of speech composition and delivery and then relates them to special as well as basic *types* of speeches.

In presenting these principles and types, it draws upon modern research in communication theory, because one of its basic tenets is that effective speech *is* effective *communication.* And in the course of presenting the principles and types, it points up the fact that the study of speech is a humane discipline—that speech is, in fact, "civilization itself." The main emphasis of *Principles and Types of Speech,* however, is not on communication theory or on speech as a humane discipline. Although the authors believe that these emphases are important and useful, we are convinced that the primary purpose of a first course in public speaking should be to help students become effective speakers. Oh, then, someone may ask, this book is planned for a skills course? Yes, skills are certainly necessary for effective speech. But also necessary are self-confidence, knowledge, and, above all, integrity. To the development of these qualities, as well as to the development of skills, this book is devoted.

The approach. Principles and Types of Speech takes a functional approach to the development of effective speech. Because men speak primarily to communicate their ideas and feelings to others, audience analysis and adaptation are stressed throughout the book. In Part Two, for example, the principles of vocal and bodily delivery are treated not as ends in themselves but rather as means which the speaker employs to win a response from his listeners. Similarly, in Part Three the standard devices of speech composition—transitions, illustrations, motive appeals, and the like—are viewed as methods for evoking a desired audience reaction.

Throughout Parts Four and Five, audience analysis and adaptation continue to be emphasized. In Part Four, in order to emphasize the dynamic relation between speaker and listener, the conventional names for the divisions of a speech are replaced by terms which describe functionally the role that each division plays in achieving a desired goal. Thus, instead of introduction, body, and conclusion, a speech is viewed as a succession of *attention, need, satisfaction, visualization,* and *action* steps. Together, these steps form a *motivated sequence*—a sequence which, because it is patterned after the process men naturally follow in arriving at choices and decisions, motivates an audience to respond affirmatively to a speaker's purpose. Depending upon the general or specific response you hope to obtain from your listeners, you may use the motivated sequence in its complete form or may omit one or more of the steps. On some occasions, you may even discard it entirely in favor of a more traditional pattern of organization. When the motivated sequence is used, however—in class assignments and practice-speaking situations, for example—it will serve as a constant reminder that the purpose of a speech is to communicate and, in order to achieve cogent communication, you may adapt your ideas and proposals to the thought processes of your listeners.

Organization and development. Part One provides a perspective on the study of speech and offers directions for planning and presenting your first classroom talks. Part Two emphasizes speech delivery—the use of your body and voice to communicate your ideas and feelings to others. Part Three explains how to plan and organize your speeches, and Part Four shows you how to adapt the structure and style of your speech to a particular audience.

Part Five considers the purpose, content, organization, and delivery of the *basic* types of speeches (speeches to entertain, inform, convince, stimulate, and actuate) and the problems involved in answering questions and objections raised by listeners. Part Six relates these basic types to the *special* types of speeches (speeches of courtesy, good will, and tribute), and also provides general instructions for broadcasting a talk. Finally, Part Seven presents the elementary principles of discussion and conference method and of parliamentary procedure.

Each of these seven parts provides information on the speaking process, purposes, and situations and practical suggestions for applying this information. The authors hope that by relating these instructions to your speaking experiences in the classroom and elsewhere, you will progress toward the goal of effective speech—the goal for which this book was developed.

To the instructor

Although the general approach and content of earlier editions of *Principles and Types of Speech* have not been radically modified for this sixth edition, numerous substantial changes have been made. Extensive portions of the text have been rewritten for clarity and economy of expression. In addition, the new organization of the chapters accords more closely with the steps customarily followed in preparing a speech, thus clarifying and strengthening the logical relationship among the elements of the motivated sequence.

As part of the extensive reorganization of the book, five new chapters have been added. Four of these contain materials which earlier formed parts of other chapters and which now have been singled out for greater emphasis or for more comprehensive treatment. These four chapters are: Chapter 3, "First Steps in Preparation and Practice"; Chapter 11, "The One-Point Speech"; Chapter 14, "Selecting, Phrasing, and Arranging the Ideas Within the Speech"; and Chapter 24, "The Speech to Actuate." The material on listening, which previously was part of the Appendix, has been revised and expanded to form the fifth new chapter, Chapter 19, "Listening: Speaker-Audience Interaction." Moreover, Chapter 12, "Selecting the Basic Appeal," has been carefully aligned with current developments in the psychology of motivation.

To increase their efficacy as pedagogical aids, the "Problems" appearing at the ends of chapters have been reorganized and expanded into *(a)* "Problems" —for class discussion and/or individual investigation, and *(b)* "Speaking Assignments." "Suggestions for Further Reading" also have been supplied and will be found at the close of each chapter. And the lists of "Speeches for Collateral Study" have been updated and expanded.

Many new illustrative passages and examples have been supplied throughout the book, especially in the chapters on supporting material, the factors of attention, and the speech to entertain. Twenty-two new sample speeches, including several student speeches and a new discussion, have been added, bringing the number to twenty-eight in all.

Finally, the illustration program as a whole has been redeveloped and enlarged. One of its most interesting features is the addition of photographs of many of the speakers whose speeches are printed in the text. In some instances, it has been possible to show a photograph of the speaker in the process of delivering the actual speech, and in at least three instances to provide a photograph of the setting for the speech—see, for example, the speeches of Franklin Delano Roosevelt, Martin Luther King, Jr., and D. Elton Trueblood.

The authors have been pleased to receive various recommendations and suggestions from instructors who were acquainted with the book in its earlier editions. In more than a few instances we have heeded their criticisms and their recommendations. In particular, we are indebted to Professor John Bowers of the University of Iowa for calling our attention to a number of significant advances in psychological research as these relate to speech, for directing us to recent studies on the points in question, and for suggesting ways in which this research could be integrated with the text. And to all of our other colleagues and students who have provided us with useful ideas, to the speakers and publishers who have generously granted permission for the inclusion of their materials in these pages, and to past users of *Principles and Types of Speech,* we are pleased to acknowledge a special debt of gratitude.

If students using this sixth edition of *Principles and Types of Speech* learn more fully to appreciate the value of good speech and become themselves more effective speakers, the purpose of this book will have been fulfilled.

A. H. M.

D. W. E.

LIST OF ILLUSTRATIONS AND ACKNOWLEDGMENTS

Contents

PART FOUR: ADAPTING THE SPEECH TO THE AUDIENCE

PART SIX: SPECIAL TYPES OF SPEECHES

SAMPLE SPEECHES FOR STUDY AND ANALYSIS

CHARTS

PART ONE

FIRST PRINCIPLES AND PRELIMINARY PRACTICE

CHAPTER ONE

Essentials of effective speaking

Certain wise men of Laputa, as reported by Swift's hero Gulliver, were strangely intent upon improving their country's language and its utterance. Some proposed to simplify discourse by cutting polysyllables into monosyllables and by omitting verbs and participles. Others urged an even bolder scheme. They wished to abolish "all words whatsoever" on the ground that "every word we speak is in some degree a diminution of our lungs by corrosion, and consequently contributes to the shortening of our lives." In place of words, this second group of scholars urged that men carry about with them in large sacks all of the various objects to which they might wish to refer. "I have," writes the fanciful Gulliver, "often beheld two of these sages almost sinking under the weight of their packs, like pedlars among us; who, when they met in the streets, would lay down their loads, open their sacks, and hold conversation for an hour together; then put up their implements, help each other to resume their burthens, and take their leave."[1]

Broadly satirical though it is, Swift's illustration serves as a graphic reminder that because we use speech continually, we tend to forget how convenient it is as a means of communicating our ideas and wants to others. But were we forced to carry about with us all of the tangible things we might need to refer to during the course of a single day, we would soon come to realize the all-pervasive role that speech plays in our lives. Without words and the power to voice them, imagine how difficult if not impossible it would be to coordinate our activities, apply for a job, plan a trip, react to newspaper headlines, elect public officials, recite in class, or argue for a higher grade. Without the ability

[1]Jonathan Swift, *Gulliver's Travels* (Garden City, N.Y.: Doubleday & Company, 1945), pp. 186-187.

to speak, how could we dine with a friend or a client, discuss the relative merits of color television sets, defend the choice of the car we drive, inform our doctor of our aches and pains, explain our income tax return, choose a career, or marry a good mate? And of course our use of the telephone and radio would be entirely out of the question.

But while speech itself is important to us, mere talking is not enough; we also need to talk well—coherently, concisely, cogently. Let's think for a moment of all of the people we have met during the past twenty-four hours. Perhaps one or two stand out. Why? By what means did they etch themselves sharply upon our memory? Consider the five or six most influential men and women in our home community. Aren't most of them better-than-average speakers? In a democratic society like ours, the ability to express ideas is as essential as the capacity to have ideas. Even in our own circle of friends, the impression we make depends very largely upon the ease and vigor with which we talk, the tact with which we advance and defend our convictions, and the attractiveness of our speaking manner.

ATTRIBUTES OF THE ABLE SPEAKER

In speech, as in almost all human endeavor, successful achievement depends upon a combination of factors. Among these, we must count integrity, knowledge, self-confidence, and skill.

Integrity

More than two thousand years ago, the Greek philosopher Aristotle emphasized a truth that was then already old and widely recognized. Success as a public speaker, he said in his treatise *The Rhetoric*, depends upon more than a ready vocabulary, pleasing diction, and coordinated gestures. An effective speaker also must be an effective person. He must be intelligent and well informed, not only about his immediate subject but about human affairs in general; and he must possess a high degree of poise and self-control. But above all, if a man is to win acceptance for his ideas, he must be respected as a person of character and moral worth by those who hear him.

This emphasis upon character as an essential element in effective speaking has been echoed by major writers on the subject from Aristotle's time to our own. In order to communicate ideas to others, one must first express himself; and *self-expression* is a two-part term. It involves not only the mechanical processes of sound production and transmission but also—and inevitably—the expression of *something* by *somebody*. People never listen merely to a speech; they always listen to a *person* speaking. And because a man's words and manner mirror what he is, the *self* and the *expression* can never be divorced. Sometimes "What you are," as the old saying points out, "speaks so loudly that I cannot hear what you say."

The man who has a reputation for seeking the facts and speaking the truth will be listened to because people believe in his integrity. On the other hand, the man who is not respected can seldom, even with the strongest arguments or most subtle appeals, win lasting adherence to his views. People are quick to see through insincerity and to recognize a speaker for what he really is.

Traditionally, this persuasive force which resides in the character or reputation of the speaker has been called "ethical proof," after the Greek word *ethos*, meaning character. Of all the modes of persuasion, it is perhaps the strongest and most permanent, for when actions contradict words, we lose faith in what is said. A speaker of poor character may win a temporary success, but soon he becomes known as a person who seeks unfair personal advantage or who suppresses or warps evidence to prove his case, and his ability to convince an audience is lost. The currency of his speech has been recognized as counterfeit.

In order to be listened to and believed, then, you must have a deserved reputation for integrity. Effective speaking, of course, calls for the mastery of certain skills and technics, but first of all it requires that you develop as a judicious and responsible person. Learning to speak well is not an art to be mastered during the course of a single semester nor to be comprehended completely within the covers of any textbook, no matter how long or profound. It is a task which requires prolonged and persistent effort.

Knowledge

When Daniel Webster was asked how he was able to prepare his famous reply to Senator Robert Y. Hayne on such short notice, he replied that the ideas came to him like thunderbolts which he had only to reach out and seize, white hot, as they went smoking by. But this store of "thunderbolts" was not an accident. Over many years a constant study of law, politics, and literature had filled Webster's mind with an abundant supply of facts, illustrations, and arguments. When faced with a specific speaking situation, he had merely to call these forth.

You, too, will find it important to read widely and carefully to broaden your background of knowledge and understanding. Through such study, your speaking will grow in depth and maturity. You need not, however, wait until you have reached middle age before you dare to speak in public. The very process of selecting and organizing materials for a speech often clarifies your thoughts, and the background you already have, when carefully considered and supplemented by additional study, will provide sufficient material for practice speeches.

As you grow in skill and confidence, you will want to reach out beyond immediate and familiar topics—to learn and to speak about subjects in new fields. In particular, you may want to investigate topics related to the business or profession you intend to enter, since most of your speeches after college will deal with ideas and developments pertinent to your chosen field. Why not begin now to correlate your vocational objective with your development as a speaker by occasionally talking on such subjects? The more you learn about them at this time, the better you will be able to speak intelligently about your profession in years to come.

But even a thorough knowledge of your own field is not sufficient. If you wish to become a well-rounded speaker, you must know about more than this single subject. It is important to keep abreast of current events by reading at least one daily newspaper and by listening to authoritative news broadcasts. You also should develop hobbies or interests outside your profession. Do you enjoy the theatre? See as many plays as possible; study the development of drama from ancient to modern times; read about recent trends in costume design, make-up, lighting, and scenery. Do you like good literature? Find out as much as you can about current books and authors while you also continue to study the classics. In short, try to become well informed on current events and on at least three or four subjects outside your vocational emphasis. Remember, too, that in order to relate your ideas to persons who do not have your specialized knowledge, you will need a variety of illustrative material. This also may be acquired by wide reading and careful listening. Perhaps you will want to build up a file of pertinent notes and clippings. In speaking, as in any other activity, there is no substitute for knowledge that is thorough and varied.

Self-confidence

What traits characterize a poised and self-confident speaker? Among other things, he has an erect but comfortable posture; easy movements free of fidgeting or jerkiness; direct, eye-to-eye contact with his listeners; earnestness and energy in his voice; and an alertness of mind which enables him to adapt his remarks to the demands of the occasion.

Many factors help determine the degree of nervousness a speaker may feel—including the amount of sleep he had the night before and the quantity of mince pie he ate for dinner.[2] The observance of the following simple rules, however, should help increase your poise and self-control.

Pick an interesting subject. Have you ever noticed how a shy youngster loses his bashfulness when you get him to talk about what really interests him: his new telescope, the rabbit his dog was chasing, or the racing car he is building for the soapbox derby? The more a speaker thinks about his subject and the less he thinks about himself, the less self-conscious he becomes. Choose, therefore, material in which you are vitally interested; avoid topics to which you yourself are indifferent. Don't talk about something merely because you think it might make a good subject for a speech; select a topic that will make you want to speak out—an idea that you are eager to communicate to others. On such a subject you will be able to talk more freely and confidently.

Know your subject thoroughly. Compare your feelings if called on to recite *(a)* when you have thoroughly studied your lesson and *(b)* when you are unprepared. The man who is thoroughly familiar with his subject always is more confident than the one who is not. But how can you gain an adequate knowledge of a subject? There are two ways: *(1)* you may study in order to find out more about your subject than anyone in your audience will know; or *(2)* you may pick a subject from your own experience—one concerning which your knowledge is broad, direct, and personal. Normally, for your first few speeches, you should choose subjects you already know about; but for later speeches you should select subjects that require more research. In neither case, however, should you choose too broad a subject. You will feel more confident if you talk about living conditions on the campus or in your home town—situations with which you are familiar—than if, with a smattering of information obtained from hasty reading, you try to discuss the American standard of living.

Learn thoroughly the sequence of ideas you intend to present. As long as the highway is straight or the turns are clearly marked, the motorist is confident of reaching his destination; but if he gets off on a lonely, unmarked road, he is less certain of his direction and hesitates

[2]For a review of current theories concerning the causes of stage fright, see Theodore Clevenger, Jr., "A Synthesis of Experimental Research in Stage Fright," *Quarterly Journal of Speech,* XLV (April 1959), 134-145.

at every turn. Similarly, you will feel more confident if you have the direction of your speech firmly in mind—if you have memorized completely the sequence in which your main ideas are to be presented. Do not, however, memorize your speech word for word. When you do this, you usually concentrate on the words rather than on the ideas; hence, if you forget one phrase, you are likely to lose the entire sequence of your talk and to break the line of communication you have established with your listeners.

Speak as often as you can. The first time a person drives a car or flies an airplane, he is tense and unsure of himself; but with each successful attempt, his confidence grows. In the same way, each speech you deliver will strengthen your poise and self-assurance. Try to speak as often as you can. Soon you will find that the principles of good speech have become so much a part of you that you will observe them automatically, while repeated exposures to audiences of different sizes and types will remove most of the dread such groups now hold for you.

Focus your attention on your audience. In any kind of speaking, your purpose is to communicate ideas or feelings to someone else. When you step up to a soda fountain and ask for a coke, you do not worry about how you are standing, sitting, or speaking. You are concerned only that the clerk understands you correctly. This same goal—to be sure that you are understood fully—should dominate your efforts in public speaking. So concentrate on the individuals in your audience; watch to see if they are getting your point. If not, say it over again in a different way or explain it more completely; but be thinking of them and talking to them while you are doing it.

Of course, there are times when you need to be concerned with your speaking manner; everyone has his weak points, and nearly everyone can improve by drills designed to correct them. As you proceed with your course of study, you will want to single out one or two faults at a time and devote detailed practice to eradicating them. But practice in private. When you are before the audience, forget about yourself as much as possible; think only about getting your listeners to understand or to agree with you.

Use physical activity to reinforce your ideas. Properly employed, bodily movement has two important functions: it helps you communicate, and it tends to dissipate your nervousness and tension. Physical activity, however, must not be superimposed or aimless; it must be integrated with the ideas and the mood of your speech and must help you secure the audience response you want.

Normally, the speech-making event generates nervous energy; harness this energy and make it work *for* you. Just as the runner is tense before the gun is fired to start the race, so the speaker who stands before an audience justifiably feels nervous strain. But the athlete's nervousness disappears almost at the instant the race begins and his muscles "go into action," and the speaker usually can accomplish the same result by moving purposefully in relation to his audience and gesturing appropriately to project his ideas. Such activities help to stimulate energetic thought and expression. If you reinforce what you say with bodily movements and with gestures of your hands and arms, you will speak more vigorously and will feel greater assurance and confidence. Walk from one part of the platform to another as you turn to a new idea; go to the blackboard and draw a diagram or write down the points you want the audience especially to remember; show your listeners the object you are talking about and demonstrate how it is used; imagine you are on the scene you are describing and use your arms and hands to point out where each object is located. In this way you will increase your own confidence and also add meaning and vitality to what you say.

Remember that some nervous tension is both natural and good for you. As we have noted, it is normal, even desirable, for the speaker to be "keyed up" to a degree. Even in the deepest sleep our muscles are never completely relaxed; they invariably have a certain amount of tension which physiologists call "muscle tonus." When we are awake, this tonus is higher; and it increases when we are keyed up and preparing to do something important. Naturally, then, when we stand up to talk to a group of people, the tonus of our muscles will rise, and we will literally be more alive. Much of the sparkle and alertness that we admire in good speakers comes from this physical verve and energy. Therefore, if you experience some tension before you start to speak, regard this as a good sign; it means that there is little chance of your making a dull and listless speech. Instead of worrying because you feel keyed up, be happy that your nerves and muscles are alive enough to put vigor into your speaking.

Never allow yourself to give up. Each time you meet a situation and master it, the more confident you become; each time you acknowledge yourself beaten or evade an issue, the harder you will find it to face the next time. In your first few speeches avoid setting yourself too difficult a task, and do not select subjects that are abstract or complex;

but once you have begun to work on a suitable topic, go through with the job. Confidence, like muscles, develops by overcoming resistance.

Skill

Although success as a speaker depends upon much more than a ready tongue, a flexible voice, and appropriate gestures, these are of great importance. Combined with integrity, knowledge, and self-confidence, skill in delivery increases a speaker's effectiveness by helping him reveal to best advantage his inner traits of mind and character.

Obviously, you already have developed considerably in many of the skills necessary for good delivery—fluency, control of the voice, and purposeful use of the body. For the past sixteen to twenty years you have been speaking many thousands of words every day. As a result, you are able to express yourself far more capably and explicitly now than you were at the age of five or six; your vocabulary is larger, and you are better able to put your ideas into words. Through training and practice, your control of voice and body also has advanced steadily since babyhood. But over the years you may have developed bad speech habits as well as good ones; moreover, no matter how skilled a speaker is, further improvement is always possible. The task which lies before you as you begin a course in public speaking, therefore, is twofold. It consists, first, of correcting whatever bad speech habits you may have unthinkingly acquired; and, second, of developing further the desirable skills and habits you already possess. As you work at this twofold task day by day, your effectiveness as a public speaker gradually will increase. Eventually new skills and correct habits will become fixed—so much a part of you that you do not even need to stop to think about them; then you will find speaking a rewarding as well as an enjoyable and stimulating experience.

The conversational mode. In practicing to gain skill in the use of your voice and body, however, you must take care not to develop artificiality. The best type of public speech is based upon the desirable elements of conversation, stepped up to meet the demands of the larger audience situation.

Good public speaking, like good conversation, is distinct and lively. It is free of artificial effects and is decidedly informal. Yet it commands attention and is forceful because of the speaker's earnest desire to communicate important ideas to others. In fact, many effective public speakers seem merely to be conversing energetically with the audience. A large audience and the peculiar acoustics of an auditorium may require increased volume and more pronounced inflectional patterns, but the speaker should retain the essential spirit of sincere and animated conversation.

Physical behavior on the platform. Just as the natural pattern of conversation furnishes the ideal basis for a speaker's vocal delivery, so a natural, unobtrusive use of the body furnishes the ideal basis for that part of delivery which an audience sees rather than hears—for what might be termed bodily delivery or the speaker's physical behavior on the platform.

When a friend is trying to communicate an important idea to you in conversation, you seldom are aware of how he is standing, the position of his head, the slant of his shoulders, or the gestures and facial expressions he is using to help convey his thoughts. All of these significant aspects of bodily delivery are completely natural and hence completely unobtrusive. But put your friend on a platform in front of an audience and ask him to communicate the same idea to a group of one, two, or three hundred persons. Unless he has had some training or experience as a public speaker, one of two things may happen: *(a)* he will "freeze" into a tense and rigid posture with his hands held stiffly at his sides or clasped hard together and with his face immobile and expressionless; or *(b)* he will assume a completely artificial or exhibitory manner, marked by those exaggerated traits of posture, gesture, and facial expression that we call oratorical.

Obviously, neither the rigid, expressionless delivery nor the exaggeratedly oratorical delivery is desirable; for the speaker who speaks in either of these two ways draws attention away from his ideas and centers it upon his manner of expressing them. When the members of an audience are more aware of how a speaker looks than of what he says, they will probably neither understand nor believe his ideas. Therefore, the important guiding principle for your physical behavior on the platform, as well as for the use of your voice, is to be natural. Concentrate on the ideas and arguments you wish to communicate; present these in such a way that the audience's attention is always focused upon your speech rather than upon your delivery.

THREE BASIC RULES

As your first step toward becoming a good speaker, resolve now to be guided always by three basic rules which summarize much of what has been said in this chapter:

1. Have something important to say.
2. Want someone else to understand or believe it.
3. Say it as simply, meaningfully, and directly as you can.

The more experienced you become in speaking, the more you will come to understand the reasons underlying these rules and to appreciate their importance.

Problems

1. Describe in detail the part that speech plays in carrying on the work of one or more of the following: a college or university, a commercial air line, a manufacturing plant, an insurance company, a newspaper.
2. Give two or three examples from your own experience of men who have exerted influence over others because of their strong personal or ethical appeal.
3. With the aid of your instructor, select for detailed study a speech that has become important historically. Prepare to answer as accurately and completely as possible these questions concerning it:
   a. What had the speaker done prior to the delivery of the speech to establish listener confidence in his personal integrity?
   b. How did the speaker bring his general background of knowledge and experience to bear in developing the subject?
   c. What specific skills of voice, language, and body did the speaker employ to help achieve his end? (In the case of voice and body, you will, of course, have to depend on reports of observers.)
4. Attend a speech or lecture given by some prominent person in your community—possibly a minister, teacher, or public official—and in so far as possible, attempt to answer the questions asked in Problem 3.
5. Compare two nationally known persons whom you have recently heard speak on television as to knowledge of their subject matter, self-confidence before the audience, and skill in vocal and bodily delivery.
6. Analyze as carefully as you can some situation other than a speaking occasion in which you were highly tense and nervous, such as your first day in the army or on a new job, before an important final examination, or while participating in an athletic contest. To what extent do you believe the causes of nervousness discussed in this chapter also applied in this nonspeaking situation? Did you try any of the corrective or alleviative measures suggested in this chapter? With what success? Did you try any other ways of reducing or eliminating your tensions?
7. Which would you say is the more important in determining how a speech will be received by an average audience: the speaker's knowledge of his subject matter or his skills in delivery? Defend your answer.

Speaking assignment

1. Be prepared to participate actively in a general class discussion on the following subject: Things that I like (or dislike) in a public speaker.

As various likes and dislikes are mentioned by members of the class, your instructor may want to list them in two separate columns on the blackboard. At the close of the discussion, help him sum up by attempting to draw a general picture of those traits or qualities in a speaker to which the majority of your class would respond favorably and those traits or qualities to which the majority would respond unfavorably.

Suggestions for further reading

Kenneth Anderson and Theodore Clevenger, Jr., "A Summary of Experimental Research in *Ethos*," *Speech Monographs*, XXX (June 1963), 59-78.

Aristotle, *Rhetoric*, 1356a, "The Character of the Speaker as a Means of Persuasion"; 1378a, "A Certain Character in the Speaker."

Virgil L. Baker and Ralph T. Eubanks, *Speech in Personal and Public Affairs* (New York: David McKay Co., Inc., 1965), Chapter VI, "Speech as a Civilizing Force," and Chapter VII, "Speech and the Pursuit of Ideas."

Hugh Blair, *Lectures on Rhetoric and Belles Lettres*, ed. Harold Harding (Carbondale: Southern Illinois University Press, 1964), Lecture XXXIV, "Means of Improving in Eloquence."

Ernest G. Bormann, "Ethics of Ghostwritten Speeches," *Quarterly Journal of Speech*, XLVII (October 1961), 262-267.

Cicero, *De Oratore*, Book I.

Theodore Clevenger, Jr., "A Definition of Stage Fright," *Central States Speech Journal*, VII (Fall 1955), 26-30.

Milton Dickens, Francis Gibson, and Caleb Prall, "An Experimental Study of the Overt Manifestations of Stage Fright," *Speech Monographs*, VII (March 1950), 37-47.

Howard Gilkinson, "A Questionnaire Study of the Cause of Social Fears among College Speech Students," *Speech Monographs*, X (1943), 74-83.

Louis Lerea, "The Verbal Behavior of Speech Fright," *Speech Monographs*, XXIII (August 1956), 229-233.

Richard Murphy, "Preface to an Ethic of Rhetoric," *The Rhetorical Idiom*, ed. Donald C. Bryant (Ithaca, New York: Cornell University Press, 1958), pp. 125-143.

Quintilian, *Institutio Oratoria*, XII. 1, "The Orator Must Be a Good Man."

Edward Rogge, "Evaluating the Ethics of a Speaker in a Democracy," *Quarterly Journal of Speech*, XLV (December 1959), 419-425.

Karl R. Wallace, "An Ethical Basis of Communication," *The Speech Teacher*, IV (January 1955), 1-9.

CHAPTER TWO

Speech: Its nature and functions

Before studying the principles of public speaking in detail, you should first gain some insight into the social and psychological foundations upon which speech rests. What are the nature and functions of speech? Of what parts does the act of oral communication consist? How are belief and behavior determined? From what sources may we gain knowledge concerning speech and its role in society? At first these questions may seem remote from your present interests. Even a brief consideration of them, however, will help you understand the importance of many of the specific rules and directions you will be given in subsequent chapters.

THE SOCIAL FUNCTION OF SPEECH

One way to obtain a better understanding of the nature of speech and its functions in society is to study the various theories concerning the origin and development of language. Some scholars, for example, believe that automatic cries of alarm, screams of pain, snarls of rage, and other emotional expressions formed the basis of language. As human beings recognized these sounds and discriminated among them, a means of communication evolved. Gradually language systems developed, employing sounds and written symbols as words to represent thousands of meanings.

A different theory is that as men found it necessary to work or fight together in groups for their common good, they discovered the utility of audible signals in coordinating their efforts. For example, in lifting or pulling heavy objects, they would grunt with the effort, and this rhythmic grunt became the signal for all to pull together. A third theory suggests that language began with man's attempt to imitate the sounds of nature (like the child saying "choo-choo" for train) in order to tell about his experiences; and still another theory holds that meaningful articulation resulted from the movements of the tongue, jaw, and lips which accompanied changes in facial expression. Of course, none of these theories can be proved because we have no records of primitive ages; but a study of the known history of languages and of certain elements common to all language systems lends partial credence to at least some of them.

While the beginnings of human speech are lost in antiquity, the development of speech in children is observable and well understood. Starting with simple, emotional cries of hunger, pain, and pleasure, the child soon reaches the "babble" stage—that is, he plays with sounds, making all sorts of noises apparently just for the fun of it. He gradually finds that certain of these noises produce reactions; his mother responds to some of his sounds but not to others. When he associates a given sound with the response it secures and begins to use the sound consciously to obtain this response, he has discovered a "word." His parents, meanwhile, talk to him, and he notices similarities between their sounds and his own; through *imitation,* and with encouragement from his parents, he learns additional words and their meanings. Later, he puts words together into simple sentences ("Bobby bye-bye," etc.), and gradually he uses more complex phrases as his thoughts and actions become more complex.

Speech, therefore, develops in the child for the same reason that language developed in the race—in order to meet a social need. The child at first cries and gurgles merely to express his own emotions, but as his mastery of vocal sounds improves, he discovers how to use these sounds *to get responses from other people.* As he grows older, he uses speech on the playground and in the schoolroom, at home and at the store, in the club, and at work. But he always uses it to communicate with someone else, and through this communication he adjusts himself to his environment and his environment to himself.

Because speech is a means of human adjustment, it is a distinctively social tool. Thanks to our speech, we are not isolated individuals,

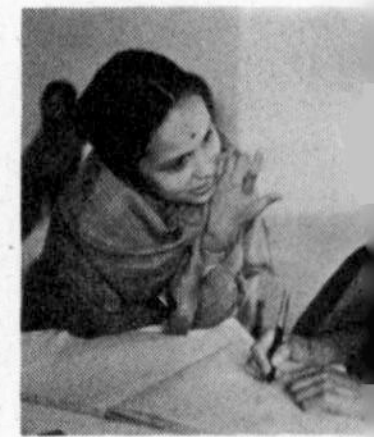

enslaved by the forces of nature. We can join others to make discoveries, impart knowledge, and secure cooperative action; we can develop great industrial enterprises and political organizations, and we can hold these enterprises and organizations together and direct their activities.

Finally, by learning to think, to speak, and to write in language symbols, we can speed up the rate of our own development, both individually and as a race. In his book *Human Destiny*, Pierre Lecomte du Noüy, the biologist, points out:

> The incomparable gift of the brain, with its truly amazing powers of abstraction, has rendered obsolete the slow and sometimes clumsy mechanisms utilized by evolution so far. Thanks to the brain alone, man, in the course of three generations only, has conquered the realm of air, while it took hundreds of thousands of years for animals to achieve the same result through the processes of evolution. . . . Thousands of young dogs and cats and tens of thousands of chickens and other animals have been run over on the roads since the invention of automobiles. This will continue for a long time, simply because the experience of the parents who have survived by chance cannot be transmitted to the young for lack of speech and tradition. Articulated speech alone has already considerably shortened the time necessary for certain adaptations. What we call the education of young children can be considered as an extraordinarily quick short-cut, replacing the biological process of adaptation, and obtaining in one generation results better than those which required ages amongst the animals at the cost of innumerable deaths.[1]

Because speech is a social tool designed for the communication of ideas from one person to another, we must be careful to distinguish it from mere self-expression. We must not think of speech as a subjective outpouring of ideas and feelings; rather, we must think of it in its functional setting as a means of transmitting thoughts, attitudes, and emotions—as something that goes on *between a speaker and a listener.* If we do this, we shall be less concerned with what speech *is* than with what speech *does;* its form and beauty will be important to us only in so far as they aid in securing the responses we seek from others.

THE NATURE OF THE SPEECH ACT

What chain of events is involved in the process of oral communication; what happens when one person speaks to another?

[1](New York: Longmans, Green, 1947), pp. 120-122.

Figure 1

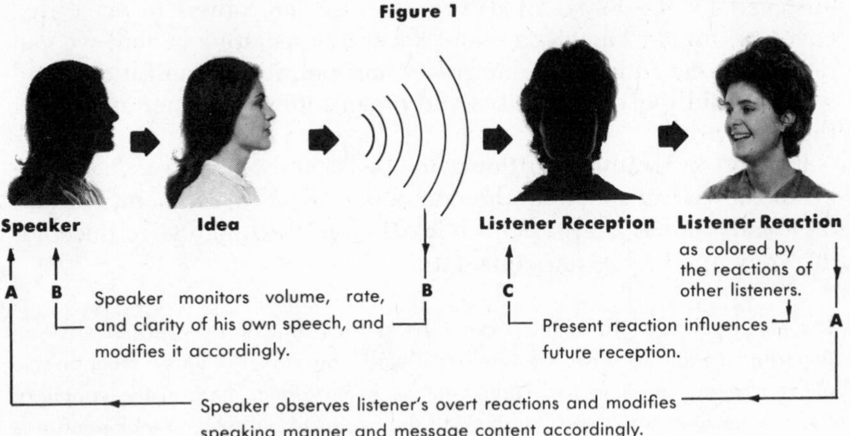
Speaker
Idea
Listener Reception
Listener Reaction
as colored by the reactions of other listeners.
A
B
Speaker monitors volume, rate, and clarity of his own speech, and modifies it accordingly.
B
C
Present reaction influences future reception.
A
Speaker observes listener's overt reactions and modifies speaking manner and message content accordingly.

Speech as a circular response

First and most important, we must realize that the act of speaking is not a one-way process, but involves a series of interacting elements. The sound of your voice reaches your own ears as well as your listener's and causes you to talk louder, perhaps, or more slowly. Your listener reacts to your message by changes in facial expression or bodily posture, and in so doing sends meaningful signals to you as a speaker. Finally, because of what psychologists call "social facilitation," the reactions of an individual in an audience are influenced by the reactions of those sitting about him. If his neighbors seem to be enjoying or believing what you say, he, too, is apt to enjoy or to believe; if, however, they are reacting negatively, the chances are greater that he also will fail to respond as you desire. In Figure 1, the influence which a listener's reactions have on the subsequent behavior of the speaker is indicated by line A. Line B represents the influence the speaker has on himself as he monitors his own speech; and line C suggests that a listener's reaction to an idea, as colored by the reactions of those about him, determines how he will receive ideas presented later in the message. The interactions described here are most obvious, of course, in the give-and-take of conversation and group discussion. They are equally present in the public speaking situation, however; and unless the speaker is aware of them, he seldom will be able to communicate effectively.

The communication chain

Because interaction between speaker and listener is continuous, communication is a circular process which contains no true starting or stopping points. For the sake of simplicity, however, let us break the communication chain into arbitrary segments and describe it as if its various elements always appeared in a regular sequence. This sequence—eight steps in all—is illustrated in Figure 2. (1) We begin with a speaker who has an idea which he wishes to communicate to a listener. How he arrived at the idea is itself a complex process which would take many pages to describe.[2] This process, however, is of no concern to us at the moment; nor are we interested in why the speaker wants to transmit his idea to another person. We begin at the point where he has the idea and desires to tell it. (2) In order to communicate, the speaker must translate the idea into language symbols of some kind: words, phrases, sentences—in English or some other language. As yet, however, these language symbols are mental concepts only; they have not emerged from the speaker's mind. To make these symbols audible, (3) nerve impulses from the central nervous system must actuate and control the complex systems of muscles used in speech—the breathing muscles, the muscles of the larynx and jaw, the tongue, the lips, etc.; and (4) these muscles must react in a coordinated movement to produce the proper sounds.

Now, however, these sounds are no longer words and sentences; they are merely disturbances in the molecules of air surrounding the speaker, a wave pattern of compressed and rarefied particles of gas. (5) The outward movement of these wave patterns through the air now transmits the sounds made by the speaker until they strike the eardrums of a listener. (The use of telephone or radio, of course, introduces additional steps by changing sound waves to electronic waves and back again to sound waves.) (6) In the ear of the listener, the waves of compressed and rarefied air are again translated into nerve impulses and (7) are carried to the brain by the auditory nerve. When this happens, the listener has "heard" the sounds, but he has not yet understood the speaker. As a final step, therefore, (8) he must recognize these nerve impulses as language symbols—words and sentences—and he must attach a meaning to this series of symbols. Thus, what the listener hears arouses thought and feeling in him.

From the foregoing description and Figures 1 and 2, it is easy to see why speakers are so often misunderstood by those who hear them. A break or distortion *anywhere* along the chain of events which link the speaker's mind with the listener's mind will result in an idea

[2]See, for example, John W. Riley, Jr., and Matilda White Riley, "Mass Communication and the Social System," *Sociology Today*, American Sociological Society, R. K. Merton *et al.* (New York: Basic Books, 1959), p. 577; and Bruce H. Westley and Malcom S. MacLean, Jr., "A Conceptual Model for Communications Research," *Audio-Visual Communication Review*, III (1955), 9.

Figure 2

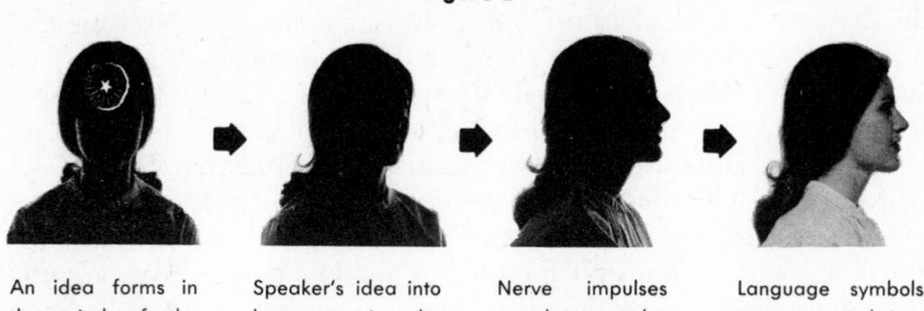

An idea forms in the mind of the speaker → Speaker's idea into language in the speaker's mind → Nerve impulses travel to muscles used in speech → Language symbols are converted into sounds

different from the one intended. Poor choice of language by the speaker (step 2), poor articulation (steps 3 and 4), interfering external noise (step 5), partial deafness (steps 6 and 7), possession of an inadequate vocabulary or misinterpretation of the meaning by the listener (step 8)—a break at any of these points will result in an incomplete or distorted message. Similarly, a break in the chain of signals which the listener sends back to the speaker or which the speaker sends to himself (see Figure 1) will impair the communication process. In view of these facts, the wonder is not that we sometimes misunderstand one another, but that we ever understand at all.

Speech as habit

If each step in the process of oral communication required conscious effort on the part of the speaker and listener, talking to another person would be slow and painfully laborious. In spite of its complexity, however, for most of us communication is easy, natural, and spontaneous. This is because so much of the act of speaking or of listening to the speech of others is automatic. By practice, we have reduced most of the total process to the level of habit. When we see a certain animal, the word *cat* automatically occurs to us; and if we wish to talk about that animal, habit has established appropriate neuromuscular patterns which cause our speech mechanism to produce the sounds of the word *cat* without conscious effort. Even the sentence structure we use and, to some extent, the arrangement of our larger units of thought are influenced by our established habits of thinking and speaking. As the various steps in the act of speaking become habitual through practice, speaking grows easier for us. By

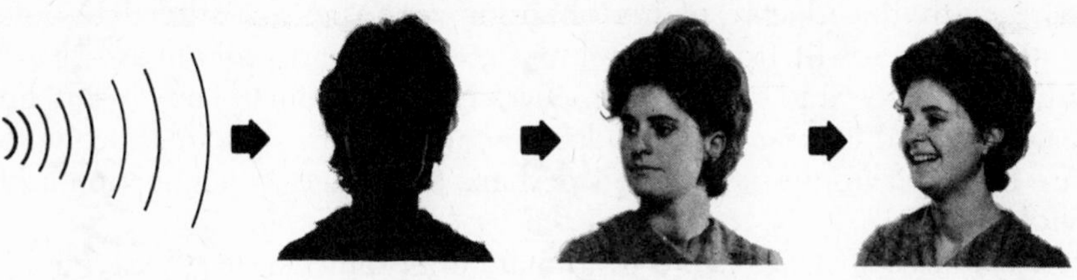

Sounds are carried as a wave pattern in the air

Sound waves strike the eardrums of the listener

Nerve impulses travel to the listener's brain

Speaker's phrase becomes idea in listener's mind

Notice that unless each step in the communication chain is present, the process of communication breaks down at some point; and the idea cannot be transmitted from the mind of the speaker to the mind of the listener.

the same token, however, the more our speech becomes fixed by habit, the less conscious we are of it *regardless of whether our habits are good or bad.* Practice makes permanent—but not necessarily perfect. As students of speech, we may profit by examining our speaking habits to see whether they contribute to the clarity with which our ideas are transmitted or whether they distort or impair communication.

THE BASES OF BELIEF AND ACTION

Throughout his history man has inquired with never-failing interest into the causes of his own beliefs and actions. Why do we accept one conclusion and reject another? Why do we choose a first alternative over a second? What forces move us to action, and why do we select the particular course of action that we follow?

As a result of these inquiries, many theories of human behavior have been formulated, theories varying widely in detail and emphasis. On one fundamental, however, they are in essential agreement. Man, they teach us, is *both a thinking and a feeling animal.* Some of his beliefs and actions are based largely, if not entirely, on reasoned judgments; others are almost exclusively the result of feeling or emotion; still others are "mixed" in the sense that reason and emotion each play an important part—sometimes a contradictory part—in their formation.

Man's rational beliefs and actions are perhaps best represented by his work in science and scholarship. In these areas he makes a conscious attempt to exclude desire and feeling from his investigations and to develop tests which bring his judgments into close accord with the "facts" of his environment. Man's irrational beliefs and actions result from his impulses, drives, and prejudices—those blind motives and desires which may cause him to buy what he cannot afford, to fear what he does not understand, to hate those who are different from him, or even perhaps to engage in mob action and violence.

Most of us strive to avoid irrational beliefs and actions, but we find it difficult always to be rational. Consequently, many of the decisions which direct our daily behavior, both as individuals and as members of society, are of the "mixed" variety. They have in them some measure of rational judgment, but they are grounded in irrational wants and desires.

The relative roles of reason and emotion in determining our "mixed" beliefs or actions have long been disputed. Some philosophers have contended that man is essentially a rational being—that it is this quality which distinguishes him from other animals. Cynics have gone to the opposite extreme and have argued that man's drives and desires exercise almost complete dominance over his beliefs and actions. Today, many psychologists adhere to the so-called "field theory" of behavior, which holds that

> instincts, drives, and motives merely supply the going power or energy for most acts and perhaps determine the general direction of action. The specific acts are an outgrowth of the dynamic interplay of environmental factors and such organismic factors as attention, perception, learning, urgency of wants, and so on.[3]

From the welter of theories concerning human behavior may be drawn two conclusions of great significance to the public speaker: (1) The speaker who would interest and inform, let alone persuade his hearers, must be mindful that man is both a rational and an irrational animal. Seldom can he achieve his end by appealing to man's rational nature alone or to his irrational nature alone. In the first case, the speaker's material will lack the warmth and compulsion upon which interest, and consequently learning, depend; in the second, it will lack the sound explanations and cogent reasonings which are necessary to produce lasting conviction. (2) Whether man's judgments are rational or emotional, they are largely bound up with language. When we objectively reason our way to a conclusion, we manipulate words as the *names* of objects in order to save ourselves

[3]Wayne C. Minnick, *The Art of Persuasion* (Boston: Houghton Mifflin, 1957), pp. 27-28.

the trouble of manipulating the objects themselves. On the side of emotion, civilized man has largely substituted words for deeds, the language symbol for the overt action. We become angry when we are struck by a word just as if we were struck by a fist, and we strike back in the same way; when lovers are separated, words of endearment and affection may take the place of caresses. Indeed, as some present-day philosophers suggest, language is but an extension of physical behavior, a form of symbolic action.

Because of the close relationship between language and thinking and language and behavior, the speaker who does not think clearly cannot hope to lead his audience to a rational judgment; the speaker who does not use language in a way that will touch his listeners personally cannot hope to appeal to their feelings and sentiments.

SOURCES OF KNOWLEDGE ABOUT SPEECH

Thus far in this chapter we have examined the social function of speech, the nature of the speech act, and the bases of belief and action. From what sources do we derive our knowledge of these matters and our information about speech in general?

For the most part, the body of facts and principles that compose the field of speech come from seven sources: *a priori* assumptions, expert opinion, direct observation, historical evidence, pictures and recordings, experimental studies, and inferences drawn from other fields of knowledge.

A priori assumptions

Many rules and principles of speech are "intentional" or *a priori;* that is, they have been chosen deliberately to represent a certain purpose or point of view. Consider the following statements: *(a)* "Speech is a tool for transmitting ideas from one person to another"; and *(b)* "Speech is a means of self-expression." If you accept statement *(a)*, the effectiveness of speech will be determined by how well it communicates; but if you accept statement *(b)*, the effectiveness of speech will be measured by the beauty and precision with which it is uttered. According to *(b)*, you could make an excellent speech all by yourself with no one to listen; but according to *(a)*, your perfectly worded and delivered speech will be useless unless someone else hears it and understands what you mean. Yet neither statement in itself can be proved to be true or false. Each merely represents an attitude or preference—an *a priori* assumption on the part of the person who holds it.

Few *a priori* assumptions concerning speech or anything else will be accepted by everyone. Each individual must determine the aims and values to which he adheres and then make the assumptions that are consistent with them. However, most students of speech, including the authors, agree with the first assumption *(a)* stated above. Therefore, they use it consciously as the basis for many of the principles stated in later chapters.

Expert opinion

The fact that a great many people make a certain assumption does not prove it to be correct, and even experts can be wrong in their opinions. Nevertheless, when there is substantial agreement on a principle among those who have devoted careful study to it, or when those who have used a given method agree on its value, there is at least a presumption that they are right. Many of the principles and methods included in the study of speech derive their validity from expert opinion. Adaptations of statements by Aristotle and Quintilian, for example, are found in modern textbooks. The successful application of these principles over so long a period is evidence of their essential soundness. Until proof to the contrary is presented, they may be regarded as reliable and applied with confidence.

Direct observation

A great deal can be learned about speech simply by observing others speak, analyzing the methods they use, and noting the results. Most of us make such observations in a random fashion all of the time. By going about our observations systematically, we can improve the soundness of our judgments. We may select in advance the type of speaking we wish to study and the aspects of speech we intend to concentrate on; we may devise a standard form for recording our observations so that their bearing upon the principle or method we are studying can be summarized and a judgment reached.

Two mistakes should be avoided in making observations of this sort. First, one must be careful not to project preconceived ideas onto his observation. It is always easy to see what we *expect* to see. While an observer cannot entirely divorce himself from his observation, he can guard against undue subjectivism. The other mistake consists in jumping to the conclusion that what is observed in one or a few instances is necessarily typical. What is effective speaking in the United States Senate may not be effective in a business conference, or what is appropriate speech in an informal bull session may not be appropriate in a conversation with the dean. If the mistakes of subjectivism and unwarranted generalization are avoided, a great deal can be learned about speech by observing it directly.

Historical evidence

Men and women have been speaking for a long time. Although the speakers and speeches of past ages cannot be observed directly, a careful study of the available historical materials discloses many interesting and important facts. The written reports of contemporary observers give us information about the great orators of the past—about their lives, their manner of speaking, and the influence they exerted. Biographical sources explain the influence of environment and education upon these men and describe the working methods and habits of mind that made them effective. The annals and newspapers of an earlier day contain the texts of many of their addresses.

The study of rhetoric as the art or science underlying effective speaking is centuries old. In fact, the first known treatise on the subject, written by a Sicilian Greek named Corax, dates from approximately 470 B.C. In the ancient world, the philosopher Aristotle, the orator-statesman Cicero, the critic called Longinus, and the great Roman schoolmaster Quintilian produced significant works upon the subject. Among the works of modern writers and theorists the contributions of George Campbell, Richard Whately, Charles Woolbert, and James Winans are particularly to be noted. These men, however, represent only a small, select sample of the thousands of scholars who over the centuries have devoted their best efforts to exploring the sources and conditions of successful oral discourse. By studying their writings one not only may learn much which still can be applied in practice; but, what is even more important, he may gain an appreciation of the aesthetic, ethical, and epistemological foundations upon which effective speaking rests.[4]

Pictures and recordings

In studying the speakers and speeches of earlier centuries we must depend entirely upon written sources. For speeches made in more recent times, written information may be supplemented by photo-

[4]See Aristotle, *Rhetorica*, tr. W. Rhys Roberts (New York: Modern Library, 1954); Cicero, *De Oratore*, tr. E. W. Sutton and H. Rackham, 2 vols. (Cambridge: Harvard University Press, 1948); pseudo-Longinus, *On the Sublime*, tr. W. Rhys Roberts (Modern Readers' Series, New York: Macmillan, 1930); Quintilian, *Institutio Oratoria*, tr. H. E. Butler, 3 vols. (New York: Putnam's, 1933); George Campbell, *The Philosophy of Rhetoric*, ed. Lloyd Bitzer (Carbondale, Ill.: Southern Illinois University Press, 1963); Richard Whately, *Elements of Rhetoric*, ed. Douglas Ehninger (Carbondale, Ill.: Southern Illinois University Press, 1963); Charles Woolbert, *The Fundamentals of Speech* (New York: Harpers, 1920); James A. Winans, *Public Speaking* (New York: Century, 1915).

graphs, recordings, newsreels, and video tapes. These materials are available not only for national and international leaders, but often for less well-known persons as well. Together they provide information such as we can never hope to recapture concerning speakers of the past. Posture, movements, gestures, pronunciation, vocal tones—all these may now be studied, together with a modern speaker's organization, proofs, and language.

Experimental studies

Certain aspects of speech may be subjected to experimental investigation by an observer who controls not only his observation but also the phenomenon studied. In order to simplify and narrow his inquiry and to rule out complicating influences, the experimenter sets up conditions under which he permits or causes the speech act to occur. Often he uses instruments or apparatus to secure accurate and objective data and to measure his results. An increasing amount of knowledge about speech is being gathered in this way, including information about such widely different problems as how the vocal folds vibrate, what effect emotion has on the voice, how important humor is in influencing opinion, how to organize a talk most effectively, and what sorts of materials best command a listener's attention.

Experimental evidence may provide us with highly reliable information about many aspects of speech. We must remember, however, that the controls necessary for conducting an experiment often tend to destroy the spontaneity with which people talk in normal situations. A person whose thoracic movements are being recorded by a pneumograph may not speak quite the same into a microphone in a laboratory as he does before a live audience and without this apparatus around his chest. We must be careful, therefore, not to overextend the conclusions reached in experimental situations.

Inferences drawn from other fields of knowledge

Perhaps no other field of study draws so heavily from related areas of knowledge as does the field of speech. Indeed, it is sometimes suggested that the discipline we call Speech is merely a cluster of related problems concerning the communication act, all of which depend for their solution upon data supplied by neighboring arts and sciences. It is like the hub of a wheel, from which spokes radiate in many directions. The physiologist gives the student of speech information about how the vocal apparatus works. The physicist helps him understand the characteristics of sound waves. The psychologist gives him insight into the nature of memory and emotion. The linguist

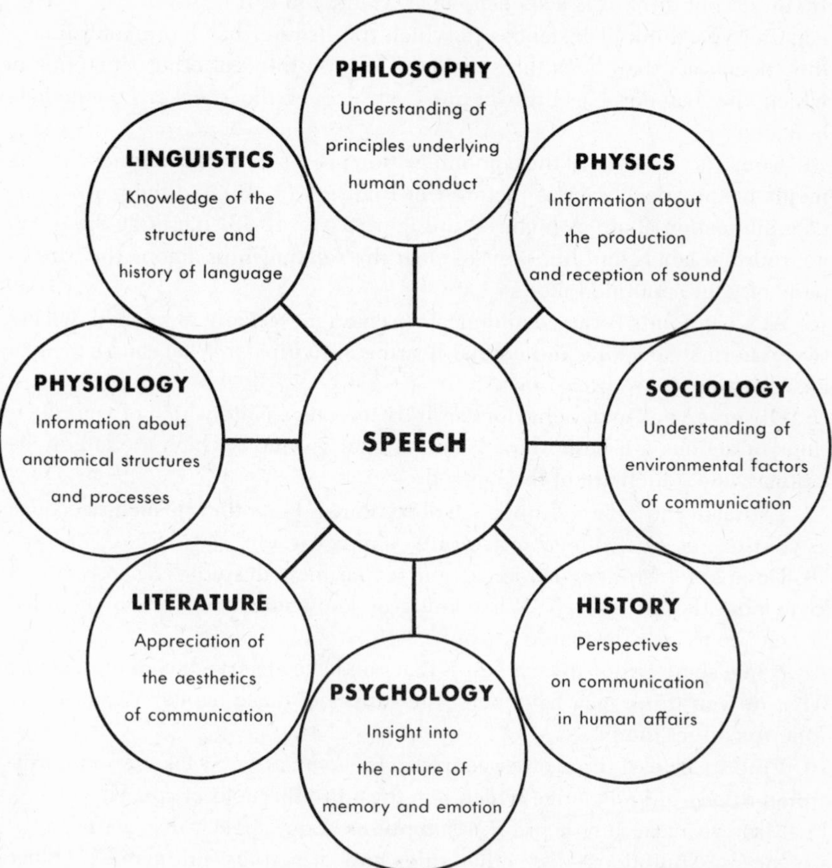

teaches him about the structure and history of language. The philosopher, historian, sociologist, and student of literature all provide information which leads to a fuller understanding of human communication. As you read further, you will find that many of the principles set forth in this book are based upon inferences drawn from these fields.

Problems

1. It has been said that speech "binds men together" in time as well as in space. What do you think this statement means? Do you agree? Can you think of instances in which speech tends to separate or isolate men?

2. A man stands in the middle of an open field and loudly expresses his opinions concerning the administration in Washington, though there is no one

present to hear him. Would you call this a speech? If so, why? If not, why not? If you do not think it is a speech, what would you call it?

3. Can you think of instances in which the listener has more control over the speech act than does the speaker? Can you think of other situations in which the listener has little or no control over the speaker's immediate behavior?

4. Construct a model of the communication process which combines the elements of the speech act as pictured in Figure 1 (p. 16) and the parts of the communication chain as pictured in Figure 2 (pp. 18-19). Through the use of appropriate labels and lines, make clear the relationships among the various parts of your combined model.

5. At what points is the communication chain most likely to break down between normal-speaking and normal-hearing individuals? What can be done to guard against these breakdowns?

6. Observe your own behavior carefully for a day. Note which of your decisions or actions are based largely on rational grounds, which are largely irrational, and which are of the "mixed" variety.

7. Estimate the relative influence of reason and emotion in such decisions as your choice of a college, a fraternity, a new car, etc.

8. Compare historical evidence and experimental studies as sources of knowledge about speech. What kinds of knowledge does each provide? Which seems more valuable to you?

9. Name some faulty speech habits that you have observed in other persons. What do you think may have been the causes of these habits? What can be done to correct them?

10. Find in at least three other courses which you are now taking some principle or body of knowledge which is relevant to the field of speech.

11. May we make any *a priori* assumptions about speech that we wish, or are these assumptions—like other rules and principles—ultimately subject to empirical testing and verification? Explain and illustrate.

Speaking assignments

1. Drawing upon sources suggested in the reading list below or by your instructor, investigate at some length one or more of the following subjects. Report your findings informally, either while sitting in your seat or standing before the class, as your instructor stipulates.

How speech and language originated
How a baby learns to talk
Language among animals
Nonverbal communication
Speech as a means of social control

2. Together with several of your classmates, investigate the concept of social facilitation, as developed in H. Kelley and J. Thibaut, "Experimental Studies of Group Problem Solving and Process," *Handbook of Social Psychology* II, Gardner Lindzey, ed. (Cambridge, Mass.: Addison-Wesley Publishing Co., Inc., 1954), pp. 747-752. Read also some of the sources suggested by Kelley and Thibaut. Then hold a class discussion in which you consider the ideas you have encountered and apply them to the public speaking situation.

Suggestions for further reading

David K. Berlo, *The Process of Communication* (New York: Holt, Rinehart & Winston, Inc., 1960), Chapter I, "Communication: Scope and Purpose," and Chapter II, "A Model of the Communication Process."

Douglas Ehninger and Wayne Brockriede, *Decision by Debate* (New York: Dodd, Mead & Co., 1963), Chapter XIII, "The Nature and Sources of Belief."

Jon Eisenson, J. Jeffery Auer, and John V. Irwin, *The Psychology of Communication* (New York: Appleton-Century-Crofts, 1963), Chapter II, "The Oral Code and Its Origin"; Chapter X, "Communication among Animals"; Chapter XII, "The Development of Speech in the Child: First Sounds to First Words"; Chapter XIII, "Language Development in the Child."

Henry L. Ewbank, Sr., A. Craig Baird, W. Norwood Brigance, Wayland M. Parrish, and Andrew T. Weaver, "What Is Speech?—A Symposium," *Quarterly Journal of Speech*, XLI (April 1955), 145-153.

Harvey Fletcher, *Speech and Hearing in Communication* (New York: D. Van Nostrand Co., Inc., 1953).

Wendell Johnson, *People in Quandaries* (New York: Harper & Row, Publishers, 1946).

Daniel Katz, "Psychological Barriers to Communication," *Annals of the American Academy of Political and Social Science*, CCL (March 1947), 17-25.

Grace Andrus de Laguna, *Speech: Its Function and Development* (New Haven, Conn.: Yale University Press, 1927). Reissued by Indiana University Press, Bloomington, 1963.

Susanne K. Langer, "The Origins of Speech and Its Communicative Function," *Quarterly Journal of Speech*, XLVI (April 1960), 121-134.

Richard Murphy, "The Speech as Literary Genre," *Quarterly Journal of Speech*, XLIV (April 1958), 117-127.

Norman Thomas, "Random Reflections on Public Speaking," *Quarterly Journal of Speech*, XL (April 1954), 145-151.

CHAPTER THREE

First steps in preparation and practice

Having explored briefly some of the social and psychological foundations upon which speech rests, you now are ready to begin practicing to develop your own speech skills. How should you go about preparing your first speeches? What sort of subjects should you select? How should you organize them? How may you best fix the ideas of a speech in your mind and practice delivering them? In later chapters of this book you will encounter specific principles and will consider at length the problems and processes involved in speechmaking. The recommendations presented here are intended to provide a starting point—a core of correct habits and procedures which you will later be able to develop and refine.

METHODS OF SPEAKING

First, what method of speaking should you use? As you may have already observed, a speech may be (1) *impromptu,* (2) *memorized,* (3) *read from manuscript,* or (4) *extemporized.*

An *impromptu speech* is a speech delivered on the spur of the moment. No specific preparation is made; the speaker relies entirely on his general knowledge and skill. The ability to speak impromptu is useful in an emergency, but its use should be limited to emergencies. Too often the moment arrives without the spur. Whenever possible, therefore, it is better to plan ahead rather than risk the rambling, incoherent speech which the impromptu method so often produces.

A *memorized speech,* as its name implies, is written out word for word and committed to memory. A few speakers are able to use this

The manuscript speech, appropriate on occasions when exact wording is required, places special demands on the speaker. In particular, it requires careful preparation and practice in delivery, because the speaker cannot afford to concentrate unduly on the manuscript while giving the speech; his attention must be directed as much as possible to his listeners. Note evidence of close attention to manuscript preparation in this photo of President Lyndon B. Johnson delivering a State of the Union Message to Congress. Anyone who plans to read a speech may find here several tips for manuscript preparation. For example, some words are underlined for stress, and lines are widely spaced for easy readability. Also, the speech is typed on only one side of the paper, and is held in place by a three-ring binder, which not only supports the manuscript but keeps its pages from becoming scattered.

method effectively, but usually memorization results in a stilted, inflexible presentation. The speaker either is excessively formal and oratorical or he tends to hurry through his talk, saying words without thinking of their meaning. Besides, with this method it is difficult to make the changes so often needed to adapt a speech to audience reactions; and, as a result, communication is seriously hampered.

Like the memorized speech, the *read speech* is written out. When extremely careful wording is required—as in the President's messages to Congress, or in the presentation of scientific reports, where exact, concise exposition is required—the read speech is appropriate. Many radio and television speeches also are read from manuscript because of the strict time limits imposed by broadcasting schedules. Viewed as a specialized skill useful in certain kinds of speaking situations, the ability to read a speech effectively is, therefore, important. But this method should not be resorted to upon occasions when the read speech is neither useful nor necessary. No matter how skilled a speaker may be, in reading his speech he almost inevitably sacrifices some of the freshness and spontaneity that are vital to effective oral communication.

The *extemporaneous speech* takes a middle course between the memorized or read speech and the speech that is delivered impromptu. It is planned and outlined in detail, and sometimes a complete draft is written out, but the words are not committed to memory. Instead, working from his outline, the speaker practices the speech aloud, expressing himself somewhat differently each time he goes through it. He uses his outline to fix the order of ideas in his mind and practices various wordings to develop flexibility of expression. If the extemporaneous method is used carelessly, the result will resemble an impromptu speech—a fact which sometimes leads to a confusion of these two procedures. A proper use of the method, however, will produce a speech which is as clear and well organized as a memorized one and at the same time more vigorous, flexible, and spontaneous. With few exceptions, the talks you deliver in your speech class probably will be extemporaneous.

THE SEVEN ESSENTIAL STEPS IN SPEECH PREPARATION

Whether your speech is to be memorized, read, or extemporaneous, the process of preparation will be much the same and will involve seven tasks or steps:

Steps	Stage
1. Selecting and narrowing the subject 2. Determining the purpose 3. Analyzing the audience and occasion	Surveying the problem
4. Gathering material 5. Making an outline 6. Wording the speech	Building the speech
7. Practicing aloud	Oral practice

These steps need not always be performed in exactly this sequence. Sometimes you will be given your subject by the group or individual who invites you to speak, and you therefore may begin with the problem of determining a suitable purpose. On other occasions you will begin with a certain purpose in mind—say to entertain your audience—and will select a subject accordingly. As you gain experience in preparing and presenting speeches you may be able to dispense with one or more of the steps entirely. For the present, however, and especially for your class talks, you should perform all of the steps suggested and take them up in the given order.

Selecting and narrowing the subject

When you are free to choose the subject of your speech, begin by reviewing your own interests and knowledge. If possible, choose a subject you have learned about through personal experience or about which you can discover more than your audience already knows. Select subjects in which you are vitally interested and about which you have fresh or original ideas. You will find that you not only will speak better on such subjects, but will have more poise and self-assurance when discussing them.

Remember, too, to narrow your subject so that it fits within the time limits you have been assigned. You owe it to your audience not to exceed them. More importantly, you will find that if you adapt your material to a predetermined time limit, you will generally make a better organized and more compelling speech. One of the commonest faults of beginning speakers is to select a topic too broad to be treated adequately in the time available.

When, therefore, you have settled upon a general subject, select some particular aspect or segment of it for your speech—no more than you can make clear or convincing in the time that you have. For a four- or five-minute speech, instead of discussing "How we can promote highway safety" tell "How seat belts save lives"; instead of explaining "How a big city newspaper operates" tell "How local news is gathered." The narrower your subject, the more fully you can explain or prove the essential points and the more interesting you can make your speech by including many illustrative facts and stories.

Determining the purpose of the speech

Too often a speaker arises to "say a few words" with no clear idea of his purpose in speaking. When this happens, his own time as well as that of his hearers usually is wasted. It is not enough to center your speech in a well-defined subject, you also must have clearly in mind the exact reaction or response that you want from your audience. You may wish them to *understand* a term or concept, to *believe* a proposition, to *take some definite action,* or merely to sit back and *enjoy* themselves. Frame your purpose into a clear, concise statement, such as the following: "Specific purpose: to explain the difference between *de jure* and *de facto* recognition." "Specific purpose: to prove that the sales tax is regressive." "Specific purpose: to secure contributions to the campus charity drive." "Specific purpose: to share with the audience some of my misfortunes as a baseball umpire."

Think of each speech as an instrument for winning a definite response from your listeners. Once determined, your purpose should constantly be a guide to the selection and organization of the ideas and facts that compose your speech.

Analyzing the audience and the occasion

A good speech not only reflects the interests and enthusiasms of the speaker, but is closely adapted to the audience and to the occasion on which it is given. Avoid topics which, though they may seem simple and clear to you because of some special experience or study, are too technical for the majority of your listeners. Also guard against imposing your own interests and enthusiasms upon others. The fact that you are an avid student of the social life of the Middle Ages or of Shakespeare's versification does not guarantee that other people will automatically share these interests.

Finally, if your talk is to be delivered as part of a speech course, make certain that it fulfills the assignment you have been given. Each of the speeches your instructor assigns will have a definite goal—to teach you how to organize ideas, to prove a point, to maintain interest, and the like. Always keep this goal in mind. Do not deliver a speech to inform when you are supposed to give a speech to persuade; do not support your argument with explanation and examples when you have been told to use statistics.

Gathering the material

Having completed your survey of the problem by considering the subject, purpose, audience, and occasion, you are now ready to begin building your talk. Ordinarily you will start by drawing together what you already know about the subject and deciding tentatively what ideas you want to include. Nearly always, however, you will find that what you already know is not enough. You will need to gather additional information—facts, illustrations, stories, and examples—with which to develop your speech. Some of this information may be acquired through interviews and conversations with persons who know something that you do not know about the subject. Other materials will be gathered from newspapers, magazines, books, and government documents, or will come from radio or television programs. No matter how much time and labor may be involved, do your research thoroughly. Good speeches grow out of a full and deep knowledge of a subject, and are packed with the facts, figures, and examples which only long and careful study can produce.

Making an outline

Early in your preparation you will want to make a preliminary list of the points to be included in your speech and to indicate very tentatively the arrangement of the central ideas. A complete outline, however, cannot be drawn up until all of the necessary material has been gathered. When this material is at hand, you should set down in final order the main points you expect to make, together with such subordinate ideas as are necessary to explain or to prove these points.

Later you will learn a number of specific patterns by which the ideas in a speech may be arranged. You will learn, too, the form which a complete and systematic outline should take. For the present, remember two simple but important rules: (1) arrange your ideas in a clear and systematic order; and (2) preserve the unity of your speech by making sure that each point is directly related to your specific purpose.

Notice in the abbreviated outline below how the speaker covers the duties of the various members of a school theatre staff. Observe also that instead of wandering off into a vague discussion of the nature of drama or of the value of dramatic training, he holds strictly to his announced purpose of explaining to his audience the job of each staff member. Such clarity of organization and unity of subject matter will make his speech easy to understand and remember.

Specific purpose: To explain the duties of a school theatre staff.

I. The staff backstage sees that a play is suitably staged.
    A. The stage manager is responsible for:
        1. Building the set
        2. Painting the set
        3. Setting up the scenes on stage
        4. Shifting scenes between acts
        5. Storing the set after the performance
    B. The chief electrician has charge of:
        1. Arranging the lights
        2. . . . etc.
    C. The property manager . . .
    D. The costume mistress . . .
    E. The make-up chairman . . .

II. The auditorium staff takes care of things "out front":
   A. The ticket manager . . .
   B. The chief usher . . .

Summary: (important points)

Wording the speech

If your speech is to be extemporaneous, talk it through several times under your breath, with your outline before you, and compose your sentences orally in a variety of ways until you find the most effective manner of stating them. At this point, if your speech is to be read from manuscript or delivered from memory, commit it to writing, being careful that each word and each sentence express exactly the idea you wish to convey.

Practicing aloud

You now are ready for the final step in preparation—practicing aloud. For extemporaneous speeches, most speakers find it best to take their outlines and, in the privacy of a room, to talk their speeches through aloud. You should do this several times until you have the sequence of ideas clearly in mind. Then lay aside your outline and think through your speech silently, point by point, until you are sure the ideas are fixed in your memory. Finally, try to talk through the entire speech aloud without looking at the outline. The first time through you may omit a good deal or interchange ideas, but do not let this worry you. Go over the speech again and include what you left out. Continue doing this until the ideas come in an orderly fashion and the words flow easily. Throughout this practice, preserve a mental image of the audience you expect to face. Decide whether the situation you will confront can best be handled by a vigorous, lively presentation or by a quiet, dignified one; whether your manner should be light or serious; whether the occasion calls for straight talk or a tactful approach. Above all, practice making your manner of speaking seem personal; remember that you will be speaking *to* people, not *at* them.

If your speech is to be read, make yourself so familiar with your manuscript that you will be able to take in each sentence at a glance, and therefore can maintain close eye contact with your listeners. When reading or speaking from memory, practice also to make your speech sound conversational and spontaneous. Nothing detracts from effective delivery quite so much as a speech pattern that seems to be "canned" or artificial.

The amount of oral practice you will need depends largely on your ability, experience, and knowledge of the subject. You should not practice a speech so often that you become stale, but you must be sure that you have the material well in mind. As a general rule, the less experience you have had in speaking, the more oral practice you will require. Students are inclined to practice too little rather than too much.

It is hard to force the development of a speech; good speeches, like stout trees, must grow over a period of time. Therefore, begin thinking about your subject and the desired audience response as soon as you know you are to speak. In this way you can best utilize your background of knowledge and fill in the gaps with additional material. Work on the speech as frequently as possible, even if only for a few minutes at a time. Your confidence will increase in direct proportion to your mastery of your material. To postpone beginning the preparation even of a classroom speech until the night before it is to be given is folly.

SAMPLE SPEECH AND OUTLINE

The following speech and accompanying outline were prepared by Miss Linda Crowell, at the time of her speech a junior at the University of Iowa. Miss Crowell's assignment was similar to Speaking Assignment 4 at the end of this chapter. The students in a beginning public speaking class were asked to present a three- or four-minute talk on a subject of interest to them and their classmates, and to supplement their own knowledge of the subject with information drawn from at least three printed sources.

Miss Crowell chose to talk on poor penmanship not only because she long had been interested in the subject, but also because (1) it was simple enough for an inexperienced speaker to handle with ease and confidence; (2) it was potentially interesting and important to her listeners; and (3) it could be covered adequately in the short time she had to speak. This was her specific purpose: "To get my listeners to recognize the value of good handwriting."

In order to keep within the time limit and to preserve the unity of her speech, Miss Crowell chose to deal with only two aspects of the problem: (1) the results or effects of poor penmanship; and (2) its causes. She developed each of these topics in a clear and orderly fashion, and was careful to complete her remarks on the first before proceeding to the second. Thus, she avoided jumping back and forth between her points or making her talk a stringing together of unrelated ideas. Moreover, by dealing first with the effects of the problem and then with its causes, she followed a logical order which the audience could easily grasp and remember.

Miss Crowell opened her speech by stating the problem with which she was concerned, and aroused interest in her subject by a series of concrete references to "mother's shopping list . . . sister's homework papers," etc. The use of the word *we* three times in the first paragraph made the audience feel involved in the problem and helped establish a friendly bond between speaker and listener. Through the body of the talk, Miss Crowell presented a number of interesting examples and preserved a natural, conversational style of expression. Her concluding idea made a strong personal appeal to the members of the audience by showing that good handwriting is important for everyone and necessary for satisfactory human relations.

On the whole, Miss Crowell's speech is a good example of what an imaginative student can do in developing a simple subject into an interesting talk. Practicing on subjects such as this will enable you to attempt more difficult and complex topics with confidence.

POOR PENMANSHIP[1]

Linda Crowell

Something has happened to people's longhand lately. Either the art of penmanship is dying or everyone has started using a new language and no one has bothered to tell me about it! We boast the highest literacy rate in history, yet we can't make out our mother's shopping list, our little sister's homework papers,

[1]Presented January 1963. Supplied through the courtesy of Miss Crowell and Mr. Paul Newman, her instructor.

what a waiter scribbles on our dinner check, or our own class notes. We are always in a hurry, so we write in a rapid scrawl to save time. But often it takes more time than we have saved to figure out what we have written!

Mistakes due to poor penmanship are the cause of much lost time and money. The Handwriting Foundation, established by the leading pen and pencil manufacturers, estimates that illegible penmanship costs businessmen approximately a million dollars *a week* in scrambled orders, lost time, missent deliveries, clerical mistakes, and inventory foul-up. In a regional office of a large oil company, a card-punch operator misread a poorly written number and fed the wrong figures into her machine. Two thousand incorrect invoices shot out the other end. Illegibility on a national scale piles up astonishing statistics. Each day thousands of carelessly addressed letters end up in the dead-letter bins of our post offices. Each year as many as 400,000 taxpayers wait for refunds because the government is unable to read their tax returns.

The cost of bad handwriting to the college student is also greater than we might imagine. Transport, telephone, and other industries turn down thousands of job applicants because their handwriting is poor. In a survey of several hundred personnel directors, the Handwriting Foundation discovered that 88 per cent regarded legible writing as an important factor in selecting a job applicant. As many as 29 per cent used legibility as one of the criteria for promotion.

We have not always been a nation of scrawlers and scratchers. John Hancock signed the Declaration of Independence in a bold Spencerian hand, underlined with yards of loops and the curlicues of a broken bedspring. Spencerian writing gave way early in this century to the "Palmer method"—a system of endless muscular movements, of dashes, ovals, and "push-pulls." In the 1930's, the age of depression, teachers of penmanship largely disappeared. Good writing was thought to be a frill that could be eliminated from the curriculum. Today most children are taught to print in the first and second grades before being led in the third or fourth into the script form of writing. Most schools give only fifteen to twenty minutes a week to formal instruction in penmanship. The wisdom of shifting from print to script is widely questioned since many people revert to printing in some form in their later years. But whatever form is used, in the modern world writing has become a tool rather than an end product. The result is a handwriting like the trail of a wounded flea—a crazy, rapid scrawl.

The fact that people in a hurry write in a rapid scrawl has led to the belief that the busier and more successful you are, the more illegible your handwriting may become. Suppose young John Hancock was hired by a business firm today. He starts as an office boy. [Speaker writes example of Hancock's signature on board.] After a year he is promoted to mail room superintendent [example of signature]. Then he is promoted to office manager [example of signature]. When he is promoted to vice-president in charge of sales he initials the office memos [example]. But when he becomes president he immediately turns his correspondence over to a secretary to sign for him while he goes out and plays golf.

We all have illusions of grandeur. We can easily imagine ourselves in an executive position, with a secretary to attend to our writing and correspondence. Perhaps we pretend that we *already* have an acceptable "executive scrawl." This attitude makes it easier for us to ignore our bad handwriting. But we can find other excuses too. The trend toward automation reduces the necessity for writing. The click of card-punching, calculating, dictating, and duplicating machines is heard everywhere—doing our work for us. Such sentimental events as birthdays and appendectomies are taken care of—*for* us—by formal greeting cards. We say "Roses are blue, we're thinking of you," or "Here's a little note of cheer to hurry up and get well, dear." Our Christmas cards come with our names already engraved on them. When the old folks have a wedding anniversary, we call the telegraph office and send form 31-B or telephone them collect to offer congratulations.

As more and more of our writing is done for us, the automation-bent world asks, "Why do we need better penmanship?" The penman has an answer that cannot be refuted. Perhaps machines will become foolproof; maybe the day will come when nobody who orders "shirts" gets "shorts." But handwriting is still a medium of good manners, and no machine can substitute for that. In a personal exchange the flow of affection, thanks, even of anger, is better conveyed by hand. There are times when we need to talk personally to our friends on paper, in our own handwriting, be it good or bad. There are times when it would be in the worst possible taste to type or to dictate a message. Legible communication—of the hand as well as of the heart and mind—is at these times essential.

Sources

Josef Berger, "The Lost Art Of Handwriting," *New York Times Magazine* (February 19, 1961), 43.

Corey Ford, "Excuse This Hasty Scrawl," *Saturday Evening Post* (August 6, 1955), 25.

Robert O'Brien, "Moving Finger Writes—But Who Can Read It?" *Saturday Review* (July 18, 1959), 8-10.

Now that you have read Miss Crowell's speech, study the outline that she submitted at the time of its delivery. Note how she distinguished between her major ideas and her subordinate ideas and the factual material by which these major ideas were supported or developed. Note also the systematic way in which the various points are numbered or lettered and the uniform pattern of indentation. Attention to details such as these is the first step toward successful outlining.

POOR PENMANSHIP

I. Something has happened to people's longhand lately.
   A. We have the highest literacy rate in the world, but much of what we write is illegible.
   B. Because we are in a hurry, we write in a scrawl.
II. The costs of poor penmanship are high.
   A. Illegible writing costs business approximately a million dollars a week.
   B. Thousands of letters end up in the dead-letter bins each day.
   C. About 400,000 tax refunds are delayed annually.
   D. Applicants for jobs and for promotions lose out because of poor penmanship.
III. Our interest in penmanship has changed over the years.
   A. John Hancock wrote a bold Spencerian script.
   B. Spencerian writing gave way to the Palmer method.
   C. During the 1930's penmanship was almost eliminated from the school curriculum.
   D. Today most children are taught to print before they are taught to write.
   E. Writing now is regarded as a tool rather than as an end product.
IV. Some people believe that illegible handwriting is a mark of success.
   A. As the office boy moves up, his writing becomes worse.
      1. As a vice-president he initials memorandums.
      2. As president his letters are signed by a secretary.
   B. This belief causes us to downgrade the importance of penmanship.
V. We find other excuses for bad handwriting, too.
   A. Card-punching, dictating, and duplicating machines do our work for us.
   B. Greeting cards come already engraved.
   C. Telegrams are sent by code number.
VI. Handwriting is important because it is still a medium of good manners.
   A. Personal sentiments and emotions are best conveyed by handwriting.
   B. Typewritten messages often are in poor taste.

OTHER OPPORTUNITIES FOR PRACTICE

Most college students are called upon to speak not only in their speech courses, but in many other courses and situations as well. Here, too, are excellent opportunities for practice.

In the next few pages are some brief suggestions to use in presenting oral reports or engaging in class discussions, whether the course is speech or some other subject. By following these suggestions, you will improve your speaking skills in these situations, and also form habits that will help you progress more rapidly in your speech course itself.

Oral reports

Most of the oral reports you are required to present in typical classroom situations fall into one of four categories. They concern (1) some outside reading you have done, (2) a special laboratory experiment you have conducted, (3) a situation, condition, or event you have observed at first hand, or (4) the results of an investigation carried out by a study committee for which you are spokesman.

The purpose and content of *reports on outside reading* will vary, depending upon the nature of the material to be presented. In a book report for a class in history the author's style may be unimportant, but in a book report for a class in literature it may be a major consideration. Whatever the subject matter, it is usually desirable to follow the organization the author himself used in his book or article. Your job is to convey his ideas to the class as clearly and accurately as you can, and ordinarily you can do this best by following his own pattern of presentation. This does not mean that you can or should reproduce in detail all of the ideas and evidence which the original book or article contains. Your job as a reporter is to condense the material, selecting only the most important of the author's ideas, or to reduce the whole to a convenient summary or précis. You also may need to interpret points which are unclear or difficult and to evaluate the worth of the material. In any event, your report should faithfully reproduce the author's ideas, and it should make clear how the book is related to the work of the academic course for which you have prepared it.

The *report of a laboratory experiment* may most conveniently follow the actual sequence of the experiment you conducted. Hence, you would begin such a report by stating the problem you set out to investigate. Then you would review briefly the previous research on this problem, state the hypotheses you selected for testing, outline the testing procedure employed, and discuss the nature and significance of the results. In reports of this sort, you may find visual aids such as diagrams or models especially useful, or you may wish to repeat the experiment before the class for purposes of demonstration. (For information on the selection and use of visual aids, see pages 172-178.)

Like a laboratory experiment, the *systematic observation of an event or condition* follows a well-planned method of investigation. Therefore, in a report of the observation, you may reproduce the steps in the inquiry and then state your conclusions. In reporting on the flow of traffic on a city's streets, for example, you might tell when, where, and how certain traffic counts were made, why particular streets or intersections were chosen for study, etc. Then you would offer your conclusions or recommendations. In reporting an event such as a speech at a mass meeting, you might tell in a systematic fashion what you observed about the speaker, the speech, the audience, the room or auditorium, etc. Then you could evaluate the performance in terms of these factors.

In a *report of the results of a committee investigation,* you should make clear what the committee as a whole decided and not what you as its spokesman may think. Of course, if opinion is split, you should give the minority as well as the majority view; and if the committee could not reach a conclusion, you should state this fact frankly. As in all reports, a systematic order of presentation is important; in many cases this may be a summary of the deliberations by which the committee reached or failed to reach a decision.

Reports, no less than speeches, should be carefully prepared and clearly and attractively presented. For suggestions concerning preparation and presentation, review those given on pages 30-35. Finally, plan to save time for questions and comments. Since your object is to present information and ideas that will be useful to your audience, you will want to make sure that everyone has an opportunity to question you about your report.

Classroom discussion

Discussion procedures in the classroom vary from answering rapid-fire questions posed by the instructor to giving fairly long explanations or comments. Often, instead of conducting a formal recitation period, your instructor will outline a problem and ask the class to discuss its solution. In some classes, you may speak sitting down; in others, standing at the blackboard or before the class. In every instance, however, these rules will apply:

Be prepared. There is no substitute for knowledge. If you study your assignments daily, you will have little trouble.

Act alert. Sit or stand erect; even when you are not speaking, avoid a slouched position. Keep awake, mentally as well as physically.

Listen to what is being said and keep close track of the discussion. Don't plan what you will say next while another member of the class is talking. Effective listening is important if you are to follow the course of the discussion and keep your own comments pertinent.

Talk loudly enough to be heard. Do not mumble or swallow your words; remember that everyone should be able to hear you. If what you say is not worth being heard, don't say it at all. But if you are asked a question, at least answer, "Yes," "No," or even "I don't know," with alertness and vigor.

Do not remain silent when you have something worthwhile to say. Avoid giving the impression that the discussion is not worth your time or that the subject is boring. At least show interest by your facial expression and posture; and, if possible, express that interest by participation. Ask sensible questions and add useful comments whenever you can.

Speak to the point; do not ramble. In most discussions time is valuable. Don't waste it by saying something unimportant or by using five minutes to express an idea that could be stated in one. Be definite. Avoid vague statements, uncertain opinions, and equivocal answers. Do not stretch the facts, but be as complete and precise as possible in giving information.

Do not try to show off. Sarcasm, flamboyant statements, the continuous suggestion that "I know it all"—all of these will irritate your listeners. Do not efface yourself completely—self-assurance is desirable —but avoid the appearance of arrogance.

Accept criticism with dignity. Avoid curt or irritated replies to criticism. If you think the criticism justified, accept it graciously; if not, refute it politely or ignore it. Above all, remember that you are part of a group and that every member of it has as much right to consideration as you have.

You now have concluded your introductory look at the field of speech and have gained some notion of the principles and skills upon which effective speaking depends.

You have learned that the good speaker is one who has something worthwhile to say, wants others to understand or believe it, and speaks clearly, concisely, and purposefully toward that end. You have examined in summary form the physical, physiological, and psychological basis upon which oral communication depends. And, finally, you have formulated some preliminary procedures to be followed in preparing and presenting a speech.

While only a brief discussion of these concepts and procedures has been possible here, the perspective gained should pave the way for your subsequent study of more complex problems and methods, and point you in the proper direction so far as the development of your own speaking abilities is concerned. Part Two considers in detail such pertinent matters as the speaker's physical behavior on the platform, his vocal projection and variety, and his articulation and pronunciation, by which he makes his speech intelligible. Parts Three and Four, in turn, deal with the basic processes of preparing and organizing a speech and adapting it to the audience for which it is intended. In Parts Five and Six the basic and special types of speeches are described, and the special problems of presiding over meetings and adapting speech to radio and television are discussed. Finally, in Part Seven attention is given to various methods for organizing group discussions and conferences and to the rules of parliamentary procedure.

Throughout the book you will find numerous written and oral assignments designed to increase your knowledge of the principles of good speech and to improve your skill as a communicator. As your background of information about speech grows and as your skill as a speaker develops, you will come to find the speechmaking experience a pleasant one and to appreciate more fully its importance as part of your daily life.

Problems

1. This chapter has given you suggestions for communicating orally as a participant in discussion, as a maker of oral reports, and as a classroom speaker. Discuss the importance of these skills in classes other than your speech class.
2. Analyze your background of knowledge and interests as a speaker:

a. List (1) your principal curricular and extracurricular interests, (2) your hobbies and enthusiasms, and (3) the business or profession you intend to enter. Indicate how much you already know about this business or profession firsthand and how much you know as a result of reading or talking with others.

b. Make a list of subjects connected with your interests or your vocational objective—subjects about which you think you know enough to give a good speech, or subjects upon which you would like to speak but need more information.

c. List several social, economic, or political principles which you believe in and would be willing to defend.

d. Select from your lists five or six topics upon which you might talk in class during the semester, and narrow each down to where it could be handled in a four- or five-minute speech.

3. Gather as much information as you can concerning the vocational and avocational interests of the other members of the class. Record this data in a systematic fashion and use it as a guide to the selection of the subjects upon which you will speak during the semester and as an aid in adapting these subjects to your hearers.
4. Compare the seven steps of speech preparation given in this chapter with

the steps involved in writing a descriptive or critical essay. In what respects are the processes similar? How do they differ? Which one do you think is more difficult to perform well? Why?

5. Take critical notes on any class discussion in which you participate during the next few days. Which student best exemplified the principles of discussion set forth in this chapter? In what ways were these principles violated by various members of the class? As objectively as possible, rate your own performance in the discussion.

Speaking assignments

1. Using source materials suggested by your instructor, gather information on the methods of speech preparation employed by one or more of the great orators of history—Franklin Roosevelt, Woodrow Wilson, Abraham Lincoln, Lord Chatham, etc. Report your findings to the class in an informative talk that is as interesting and also as fact-laden as you can make it. (The instructor will coordinate the assignment so that each member of the class studies a different speaker or group of speakers.) At the close of the reports compare the different methods described and attempt to construct a master list of procedures common to all of the orators discussed.

As an alternative to the above assignment, let different members of the class interview some professor or person in the community who does a great deal of speaking, and report his advice concerning the process of speech preparation.

2. Following suggestions on pages 31-35, prepare and deliver a two-minute extemporaneous speech in which you introduce yourself to the class. Cover briefly such topics as the following: where you come from, your major in college, your vocational objective, your extracurricular activities, your hobbies, trips you have taken, jobs you have held, etc.

3. Following the same suggestions for preparation and delivery, present a two-minute speech in which you illustrate from your own experience the truth of some well-known adage or proverb.

4. Again following the same suggestions for preparation and delivery, but supplementing your own knowledge with information gained from at least three printed sources, present a three- or four-minute speech on one of the topics listed below, or on a similar topic. Narrow your speech by selecting the one or two aspects of the subject that you think would be most interesting to your classmates.

Foreign sports cars
Today's headline story
Sailing as a hobby
Low-budget motion pictures
Highway safety
The new comedians
Our city government
An unusual new product

Suggestions for further reading

Carroll C. Arnold, Douglas Ehninger, and John C. Gerber, *The Speaker's Resource Book,* 2nd ed. (Glenview, Illinois: Scott, Foresman and Co., 1966), "Student's Handbook of Public Speaking," pp. 293-299.

Virgil L. Baker and Ralph T. Eubanks, *Speech in Personal and Public Affairs* (New York: David McKay Co., Inc., 1965), Chapter III, "Making Your First Speeches."

Waldo W. Braden and Mary Louise Gehring, *Speech Practices* (New York: Harper & Row, Publishers, 1958), Chapter II, "How Speakers Prepare Their Speeches."

W. Norwood Brigance, *Speech: Its Techniques and Disciplines in a Free Society,* 2nd ed. (New York: Appleton-Century-Crofts, 1961), Chapter III, "First Steps in Managing Ideas," Chapter IV, "First Steps in Managing Yourself," Chapter VIII, "The Seven Lamps of Planning a Speech."

W. Norwood Brigance, "What Is a Successful Speech?" *Quarterly Journal of Speech Education,* XI (November 1925), 372-377.

Donald C. Bryant and Karl R. Wallace, *Fundamentals of Public Speaking,* 3rd ed. (New York: Appleton-Century-Crofts, 1960), Chapter IV, "The First Speeches."

G. Jack Gravlee, "Franklin D. Roosevelt's Speech Preparation During His First National Campaign," *Speech Monographs,* XXXI (November 1964), 437-460.

Robert N. Hall, "Lyndon Johnson's Speech Preparation," *Quarterly Journal of Speech,* LI (April 1965), 168-176.

Charles A. McGlon, ed., "How I Prepare My Sermons: A Symposium with the Assistance of Harry Emerson Fosdick, Joseph M. Dawson, Ralph Sockman, Vincent J. Flynn, Joseph Rauch, and Edgar DeWitt Jones," *Quarterly Journal of Speech,* XL (February 1954), 49-62.

Kurt Tucholsky, "How to Make a Bad Speech," *Today's Speech,* IV (September 1956), 31-32.

Milton J. Wiksel, "How to Make a Speech," *Today's Speech,* VIII (April 1960), 5-8.

Russel Windes, Jr., "Adlai E. Stevenson's Speech Staff in the 1956 Campaign," *Quarterly Journal of Speech,* XLVI (February 1960), 32-43.

PART TWO

COMMUNICATING IDEAS VOCALLY AND BODILY

CHAPTER FOUR

Bodily behavior on the platform

The effectiveness of your speaking depends upon both what you say and how you say it. Without solid content you will not have anything worth communicating; without effective delivery you cannot convey your thoughts clearly and vividly to others. Just as a pitcher can give a ball direction and power by the way he throws it, so a speaker can give his speech strength and vitality by the manner of his delivery.

Effective delivery does not depend upon applying mechanically a predetermined set of rules; it comes from practice under the direction of a competent instructor who can help you smooth out rough spots and develop points of strength. This chapter and the two that follow provide suggestions to help you avoid falling into undesirable habits that later may be difficult to correct; they also explain certain principles that will help you derive maximum benefit from your instructor's comments.

Since in the usual speaking situation the audience both sees and hears the speaker, a consideration of delivery involves two basic elements: the speaker's *physical behavior on the platform* (the subject of the present chapter), and his *use of the voice* (the subject of Chapters 5 and 6).

The importance of physical or bodily delivery is apparent. People in an audience read meanings into a speaker's facial expression, into the way he stands and walks, and into what he does with his head, arms, shoulders, and hands; and an audience will attach significance to these physical manifestations whether they are intentional or unintentional. Often a slight shrug of the shoulder or an expressive movement of the hand is more revealing than a hundred words. Moreover, listeners are quick to perceive any discrepancy between a

"People in an audience read meanings into a speaker's facial expression, into the way he stands and walks, and into what he does with his head, arms, shoulders, and hands. . . ."

Although he possesses an extraordinarily expressive voice, Senator Everett M. Dirksen of Illinois does not rely on voice alone to convey his meaning. In this series of photographs he reveals the important part that is played by visual aspects of delivery—facial expression, bearing, and arm and hand movements.

speaker's actions and his ideas. Vigorous ideas expressed in a languid manner or trivial ideas propounded with great force or dignity produce an unconvincing if not ludicrous effect. Finally, since the speaker is seen before he is heard, it is through visual rather than auditory impressions that the audience makes its initial estimate of his sincerity, his friendliness, and his energy.

CONTACT WITH THE AUDIENCE

From the very beginning and continuing throughout his speech the speaker must make the members of his audience feel that he is talking to each of them personally. Listeners are repelled by a speaker who seems unaware of their identity as individuals. They value a sense of close personal relationship, such as exists in an informal conversation.

Nothing is quite so important in establishing personal contact with an audience as the simple device of looking at individuals directly. For this reason, reading a speech or even glancing at notes too frequently reduces this feeling of interpersonal communication and almost invariably detracts from a speaker's effectiveness. Obviously, it is impossible to look at each member of the audience at the same time. Therefore, do as you would in an informal conversation: pick out one person and talk directly to him for a few seconds, looking him in the eye as you do so; then shift to someone else. Be careful, moreover, to pick out people in various parts of the audience and to stay with each one long enough to avoid the appearance of simply wagging your head.

To achieve good audience contact, however, you must do more than merely look at your listeners; you also must have an earnest desire to *communicate*. Sometimes it is possible to look a person directly in the eye and yet have him believe that your mind is miles away. In order to combat this impression, concentrate intently on both your subject and your listeners. Study individual reactions as evidenced by facial expression, bodily posture, and similar indications to make sure you are maintaining a circular response. Make it evident to each person in your audience that you are interested in him as an individual and are eager to have him understand or believe the ideas you are presenting.

POSTURE

Posture also is of prime importance in speech delivery. How do you stand when you talk to people? Are you erect? comfortable? alert? Does your position seem natural or does it call attention to itself because it is awkward or unusual? There is no one best way to stand when delivering a speech, but there are several errors which you should avoid. Do not hide behind the speaker's table; stand beside it or leave it altogether. Avoid letting the weight of your body fall on your heels; instead, let it fall on the balls of your feet. Avoid bouncing up and down or swaying from side to side. Stand so that you are comfortable without being slouchy, erect without being stiff. Give the impression that you are awake and "on your toes." Show the assurance of one who is in command of the situation and of himself.

MOVEMENT

The eye instinctively follows moving objects and focuses upon them. A speaker can, therefore, often awaken a sleepy or inattentive audience by the simple expedient of moving from one part of the platform to another. If your movement is natural, easy, and purposeful, it will help you hold attention, maintain interest, and convey your thoughts more clearly.

How much movement about the platform is desirable? How often should you change your position? The answer is to follow your natural impulses. Move about when you feel a desire to do so. Obviously, you should try to make your physical activity as meaningful and as pertinent to your speech as possible and avoid continuous and aimless pacing back and forth. But you also should avoid standing glued to a single spot throughout your entire speech. If you are earnestly trying to communicate an important idea to your listeners, sooner or later you will feel the desire to move. It will, for instance, seem natural to change your position as a means of letting your hearers know that you have finished one idea and are ready to start another, or to step forward as a means of stressing an important point.

Remember also that the way you walk to the platform and the way that you leave it are important. Instead of ambling up to the speaker's stand in a slovenly, meandering fashion, move briskly and purposefully. Let your manner suggest confidence; do not tiptoe timidly, as though you were afraid the audience might see or hear you. Once in position, do not begin your speech immediately. Take time to compose your thoughts and to look at your listeners; *then* begin to talk. When you have finished speaking, do not rush or sidle to your seat. Pause long enough at the end of your talk to let your final words take effect; then walk off in a relaxed but dignified way, still keeping your eyes on your listeners. The total effect of a speech may be ruined by an awkward or poorly timed entrance or exit.

GESTURES

In addition to moving about on the platform, you can use gestures to clarify or to emphasize the ideas in your speech. By gestures we mean *purposeful* movements of some part of the body—head, shoulders, arms or hands—to reinforce or to demonstrate what you say. Fidgeting with coat buttons or aimlessly rearranging books or papers on the speaker's table are not gestures; they are not purposeful, and they detract rather than add to the ideas you are expressing.

A simple experiment will show you how important gestures are to communication. Try to give directions for finding a place several blocks distant and notice how necessary it is to point the way and to show turns by movements of the arms or head. Or observe two persons in a heated argument and notice how often their hands come into play to emphasize the points they are making.

Besides their usefulness in clarifying and stressing ideas, gestures also are valuable in helping to hold the listener's attention. Just as we watch the speaker who moves about rather than the one who remains rooted in a single spot, so we listen with greater attention to the speaker who gestures appropriately. Unless a speaker compensates for his lack of gestures in some other way, listeners respond sluggishly and apathetically to him and his message. On the other hand, a physically active speaker stimulates lively attention and interest.

In emphasizing the importance of gestures, we are not implying that you should simulate or pretend a forceful, dynamic delivery if such a manner is uncharacteristic of you. The impulse to make gestures always should come from *within* and should be a natural response to or reinforcement for the ideas you are communicating. Do not decide in advance that at a certain place in your speech you are going to point your finger at the audience and a moment later shake your fist. If gestures are to be effective, they must spring naturally from an inner state of earnestness, enthusiasm, or emotion. At home or in your room, practice gesturing all you please—the more the better—until you can feel the easy swing, the abandon, and the punch of it; but when you stand before an audience, do not consciously force your arms or head to move. If you have practiced sufficiently and are genuinely concerned with communicating important ideas to others, gestures will come naturally as part of your total speaking pattern.

Gestures of the hands and arms

A speaker should understand the common types of hand and arm gestures and the kinds of ideas which each type tends to convey. Basically, such gestures fall into two classes, *conventional* and *descriptive*.

Conventional gestures. Six basic movements of the hands and arms are used so extensively by speakers that people recognize almost automatically the meanings they are intended to convey. Consequently, these gestures have become a kind of universal sign language.

1. *Pointing.* When a speaker wishes to indicate a position or show a direction, or when he wishes to call attention to an idea or object, he often will point with his index finger. He may, for example, point at a map hanging on the wall as he says, "This map is already out of date because the boundaries keep changing so rapidly." Or, as he says, "The argument rests upon this single principle . . . ," he may point at the stand or table in front of him as if the principle actually were there in tangible form. When making an accusation or issuing a challenge, a speaker also frequently will point his finger at the audience or at some imaginary person on the platform beside him.

2. *Giving or receiving.* If you were to hand someone a sheet of paper or to hold out your hand to accept one given to you, the palm

would face upward. This same movement is often used by speakers when they are presenting a new idea to the audience or are requesting support for a proposal they are advancing. Such a gesture indicates, "This is the information I have discovered," or "The ideas I am holding before you deserve your attention," or "I appeal to you to give me your help in this matter." No other conventional gesture is used quite so often as this one because of the wide variety of purposes it may serve. Sometimes it is even combined with the pointing gesture described above—the idea is, as it were, held out in one hand while the other hand directs attention toward it.

3. *Rejecting.* If a dog with dirty paws were to jump up on you, you would push him to one side with your hand. In the same way, speakers often express disapproval or rejection of an idea. They use a sweeping movement of the hand with the palm downward to reinforce such statements as "That proposal is absolutely worthless," "We must put that idea out of our heads," or "It can't be done that way."

4. *Clenching the fist.* This gesture expresses strong feeling, such as anger or determination. Raised and brandished, the clenched fist often symbolizes challenge or defiance. It is used to emphasize such statements as "We must fight this to a finish!" or "He's the worst scoundrel in the world!"

5. *Cautioning.* If you wished to calm an angry or excited friend, you might do so by putting your hand lightly on his shoulder. A similar movement of the hand, as if on an imaginary shoulder, is used by speakers to caution listeners against arriving at too hasty a judgment or against losing their tempers. This gesture often is employed to strengthen such statements as "Don't take this thing too seriously" or "If you'll just keep quiet a moment, I think I can make the point clear." By using this gesture, the speaker attempts to check his hearers' thoughts and get them ready to listen to another idea.

6. *Dividing.* When speakers wish to indicate the separation of facts or ideas into different parts, they will sometimes be observed to move their hands from side to side with the palm held vertical. This kind of cutting-and-separating gesture says, in effect, "Part of the great crowd stood on this side of the river, part on the other," or "In these days of national and international tension, we must not, on the one hand, be radical in our ideas, nor, on the other, ultraconservative."

These, then, are six basic movements of conventional gesturing. From what has been said about them, however, do not infer that they are set and invariable. No two persons will make these movements

"Conventional gestures . . . have become a kind of universal sign language . . . however, do not infer that they are set and invariable. No two persons will make these movements in exactly the same way or on exactly the same occasions."

POINTING: Interesting variations of the pointing gesture are displayed in these photos of (left to right, top to bottom) Charles De Gaulle, Billy Graham, Vanessa Redgrave, Lyndon B. Johnson, a soapbox orator, and J. Roscoe Miller.

GIVING OR RECEIVING: Sammy Davis, Jr., Marshall McLuhan, and Charles De Gaulle provide individual variations of gestures in this classification.

CLENCHING THE FIST: Billy Graham emphasizes a point. ● DIVIDING: James E. Webb makes a distinction. ● REJECTING: Alec Douglas-Home reveals his attitude toward an idea.

CAUTIONING: Danny Kaye and an auctioneer at a county sale demonstrate cautioning gestures.

". . . gesturing is likely to be a continuous process rather than an isolated entity; frequently one gesture will begin almost before the previous one has stopped. . . ."

As Helena Zhahiecki Lopata, Roosevelt University sociologist, discusses a subject, the effect of her gestures is one of continuity and blending.

in exactly the same way or on exactly the same occasions. Nor could they even if they wanted to, for a gesture is not an imitated movement but a personal and highly individualized form of expression, always best when it is spontaneous. Moreover, gesturing is likely to be a *continuous* process rather than an isolated entity; that is, frequently one gesture will begin almost before the previous one has stopped so that the overall effect is one of continuity and of blending. Finally, remember, it is the movement of the hand and arm rather than the final position they assume that emphasizes the speaker's ideas. Practice alone will make your use of conventional gestures smooth and effective, and this practice will be most valuable when it is guided by the suggestions and criticisms of your instructor.

Descriptive gestures. The movements just discussed carry meaning primarily by custom, convention, or symbolic relationship; but other movements of the head and body may directly describe or imitate the idea to be communicated. The speaker may describe the size, shape, or action of an object by movements of his hands and arms. He may show how vigorous a punch was by striking the air with his fist, the height of a younger brother by holding out his hand, the speed of an automobile by a quick sweep of his arm, and the details of a complicated movement by performing the movement itself. Because of their spontaneous and image-evoking nature, descriptive gestures cannot be cataloged precisely. Useful hints may be obtained, however, by watching other speakers, and your own originality will suggest many possibilities. Merely ask yourself, "How can I best make this idea clear to my audience?" Then use any descriptive movements or gestures that occur to you, so long as they are reasonably dignified and in good taste.

Gestures of the head and shoulders

Shrugging the shoulders and shaking the head have the same implications in public speech that they have in conversation, and here—as elsewhere—are frequently used to help clarify an idea or gain emphasis. Like arm gestures, moreover, such motions should not be planned or executed consciously. Unless they spring from a genuine desire to communicate more effectively, they appear artificial or awkward, and impair rather than enhance the speaker's message.

Facial expression and impersonation

For many years psychologists have studied how facial expressions convey thoughts and feelings. Everyone's own experience will attest that such expressions often speak as eloquently as words. When natural and unplanned, they reveal sincere convictions and deep feelings. If you are well disposed toward your audience, are interested in the subject of your talk, and are enthusiastic about speaking, your face will reflect your attitude and will help emphasize the ideas you express orally.

Sometimes a speaker may want to vivify an illustration or story by acting and talking as if he himself were the person involved. In such cases his posture, movements, gestures, and facial expression combine to create a composite picture of the individual in the story. His shoulders droop or he develops a slight limp; his hand trembles as he knocks on the door, and his face shows surprise at what he sees when the door opens—together, these actions portray a character and tell what the character is doing. Such detailed imitation or "acting out" of a point, however, should be done only infrequently and with the greatest caution. Too vivid or dramatic a presentation may center the attention of the audience on the action rather than on the idea being expressed, and thus defeat its purpose. Moreover, it is essential that audience contact be maintained and that one's dignity as a speaker be preserved. Use such imitation when you think it to be the clearest and surest way of communicating the point you have in mind, but always use it with good judgment and restraint.

CHARACTERISTICS OF GOOD GESTURES

Although you can perfect your gestures only through practice, practice will yield better results if you keep these characteristics of good gestures in mind: relaxation, vigor and definiteness, and proper timing.

Relaxation

When your muscles are strained or tense, you have difficulty expressing yourself naturally, and awkward or jerky gestures result. As we mentioned earlier, one of the best ways to break your tension is to move about—to take a few easy steps or unobtrusively to rearrange your notes or papers. To avoid stiffness and awkwardness during your first few minutes in front of the audience, make a conscious effort to relax your muscles *before* you start to speak.

Vigor and definiteness

Good gestures are alive and vigorous. Put enough force into them to make them convincing. A languid shaking of the fist is a weak support for a threat or challenge; an aimless or hesitant movement of the arm confuses rather than clarifies. Be energetic, yes; but be selective, too. Do not pound the table or saw the air constantly; exaggeration of minor points is ludicrous. Vary the force and nature of your gestures, but in the main be vigorous enough to project your conviction and enthusiasm.

Timing

The comedian gets many laughs from his audience by timing his gestures improperly. If, for example, you make a gesture after the word or phrase it was intended to reinforce already has been spoken, the result will be ludicrous. The stroke of the gesture—that is, the shake of the fist, the movement of the finger, or the break of the wrist—should fall exactly on, or should slightly precede, the point that is being emphasized. If you practice making gestures until they have become habitual and then use them spontaneously as the impulse arises, you will have no trouble synchronizing them effectively. Poor timing is the result of an attempt to use "canned" or preplanned gestures.

ADAPTING PHYSICAL BEHAVIOR TO THE SUBJECT AND THE AUDIENCE

Just because a certain type of speech delivery is effective with one subject or with one audience, you must not assume that it will suit all subjects and audiences. As observation will show, good speakers vary their physical behavior according to the size and character of the audience they are addressing and the nature of the ideas they are communicating.

The size of the audience

Generally speaking, the larger the audience, the larger and more pronounced the speaker's gestures will have to be. What might seem to be a wild swing of the arm to a small audience close to the speaker appears quite appropriate to an audience of several hundred. Conversely, little gestures of the arms or slight changes in facial expression, while effective in conversation, seem weak and indefinite to a large group of listeners.

The nature of the subject and the occasion

Subjects on which feelings run strong or which require great and immediate decisions usually motivate speakers to more vigorous bodily action than do subjects which are less moving or crucial. Moreover, occasions such as memorial services or dedications call for dignity of movement as well as of expression, while political meetings or pep rallies require more varied and enthusiastic activity. Therefore, adjust your speaking manner to both subject and occasion. But in doing this, let your movements and gestures conform to your own personality as a speaker and as an individual. Remember that your best speaking always is done when you are most fully and naturally yourself.

In summary, then, if you wish to enhance your skill as a speaker, maintain meaningful contact and rapport with your listeners; assume an alert, yet comfortable posture; move purposefully about the platform; use vigorous, clear, and well-timed gestures; let your facial expression be mobile and responsive; and adjust your movements and gestures to the size and nature of the audience you are addressing and to the subject on which you are speaking.

THE IMPORTANCE OF PRACTICE

As a student speaker, your immediate task is to learn to move about the platform freely and to gesture frequently. Begin by moving several times during each speech you give and by gesturing as often as possible. For the time being, let yourself go. If a classmate tells you that you are pacing aimlessly or using too many gestures, make sure that he does not really mean that your movement or gestures lack sufficient variety. Instead of cutting down on the amount of activity, vary it more. Later, after you have learned to move easily and naturally, you may want to use fewer gestures and to move less often—to become more selective. Until you are completely loosened up and at home in the public speaking situation, however, move and gesture freely and frequently. Proper movement and gestures must be practiced until they are habitual and natural. Then they may be forgotten while you are speaking. They will be more or less automatic in their obedience to impulse, and effective in clarifying or reinforcing your ideas.

SPECIAL PROBLEMS OF THE MANUSCRIPT SPEECH[1]

When a speaker reads a speech from manuscript instead of speaking extemporaneously or from memory, he faces certain problems of bodily or physical delivery. (1) Because he must look at his manuscript frequently, he finds it difficult to maintain close eye contact with his listeners; (2) because his manuscript usually is lying on a speaker's stand or table, his movement about the platform is restricted; and (3) because he is reproducing ideas previously thought out and written down, he tends to have little or no impulse to reinforce the expression of his ideas with arm and hand gestures.

Eye contact

In order to maintain the best eye contact that is possible under the circumstances, follow these suggestions:

1. Bring to the platform a cleanly typed, triple-spaced copy of your manuscript, free of inked-in changes or additions. Interlined modifications and corrections are difficult to follow easily and may lead to embarrassing pauses or misstatements.
2. Divide your speech into many short paragraphs rather than a few long ones. As you raise your eyes from the manuscript, glance at the audience, and then return your attention to the page, the indentations at beginnings of paragraphs will make it easier for you to catch your place quickly.
3. Place your manuscript near the top of the speaker's stand or podium; or if you are holding it in your hand, keep it near eye level.

[1]For suggestions concerning physical delivery when presenting visual aids see pages 172-178.

This will shorten the arc between the words on the manuscript and the eyes of your listeners and will make it much easier for you to look at the audience frequently without losing your place.

4. Practice reading your speech until by looking at the first few words of a sentence you are able to recall the remainder of it. In this way, you will only need to glance at your manuscript in order to catch the sentence as a whole and can spend most of your time looking at your audience. Do not, however, memorize the speech in its entirety. This not only will be a waste of time, but will seriously detract from the spontaneity and naturalness of your delivery.

Movement

Although your movements will be restricted, you can still move from one side of the speaker's stand to the other or can shift your position slightly from time to time. Even short moves will help you hold the attention of your listeners and "paragraph" your speech. In those few situations where, because of a microphone or television camera, you cannot move about at all, you must compensate for the lack of movement by more animated facial expression, by head and shoulder gestures, and by increasing the variety and color in the use of your voice.

Gestures

Many or free-swinging gestures usually seem inappropriate when you are reading a speech from manuscript, nor in all probability will you feel the impulse to make them. A few, more restrained gestures may be quite in order, however, especially if they are of a descriptive nature. Strive as earnestly as you can to get your audience to understand or to believe the ideas you are presenting. When you feel an impulse to use your hands, arms, shoulders, or head to help convey a point, let your body respond easily and naturally. Ordinarily, under these circumstances you will feel impelled to make at least a few gestures during the course of a long and vigorous manuscript speech. Moreover, you will be sure that your gestures will seem natural and appropriate to your listeners.

Exercises

1. Imagine yourself in one of the situations described below, and react spontaneously with whatever physical behavior your impulse suggests. Speak out also if you feel impelled to do so.

   a. Someone has fired a gun just behind you.

   b. A child just ahead of you steps into the path of a fast-moving automobile.

c. Someone has just slapped your face.

d. Someone shouts to warn you of a heavy object about to fall on the exact spot where you are standing.

e. You are marooned on an island and are trying to catch the attention of men on a passing ship.

f. A mob is bent on destruction; as the crowd goes past, you try to turn it in another direction.

2. Holding your elbows well out from your body, keeping your wrists flexible, and using a great deal of energy, do the following exercises in sequence:

a. Shake your arms and hands vigorously as if trying to get something loose from your fingers. Do this with your arms far out at the sides, up over your head, and out in front of you. Continue until all stiffness is eliminated.

b. While you are shaking your hands and arms, begin repeating the alphabet over and over—not in a monotonous rhythm but as if you were actually talking in highly emotional language. Continue this "talking" while proceeding with Exercises c, d, e, and f.

c. Let one hand at a time fall to your side and continue shaking the other.

d. Gradually change from merely shaking your arm and hand to making varied gestures; that is, point your finger, reject the idea, drive home a point, etc. During this change be sure to preserve the vigor and complete abandon of your arm movements.

e. Select a partner. Harangue each other by repeating the letters of the alphabet loudly and as though you were greatly excited. Keep up a vigorous flow of gestures all the while. Both of you "talk" and gesticulate at the same time.

f. In a group of four or five, all talking simultaneously, harangue the rest of the class in the same way you did your partner in Exercise e above. See which speaker can keep the attention of the class away from the others in the group.

3. Try to communicate the following ideas silently by means of physical action alone. You will need to use descriptive as well as conventional gestures.

a. "Get out of here!"

b. "Why, Tom (or Mary)! I haven't seen you for ages!"

c. "If we're going to get what we want, we'll have to fight for it, and fight hard!"

d. "Quiet down a little, won't you? Give him a chance to explain."

e. "Come here a minute, Jim, will you?"

f. "Every penny I had is gone."

g. "Now, the first thing to remember is this: . . ."

4. Convey to the class without words a clear picture of each of the following:

a. A nervous pedestrian crossing a street through heavy traffic.

b. An irate motorist changing a tire on a hot day.

c. A mother getting dinner and setting the table while trying in vain to keep the two-year-old out of mischief.

d. A Christmas shopper trying to carry too many parcels, some of which slip out of his grasp.

e. A panhandler asking several different people for a coin for a cup of coffee.

Problems

1. Go to hear some speaker on the campus or in your community. Then write a brief report on your observations regarding his platform behavior. Before you go, make a brief outline of the suggestions and warnings contained in this chapter and check the speaker's physical behavior for these points while he is talking. Note both strong and weak qualities in the speaker's contact with the audience, as well as his posture, movements, and gestures. Observe particularly those statements he emphasizes with gestures, and the particular gestures he uses for emphasis.

2. Attend a motion picture or a play or watch a drama on television and report on the physical behavior of the actors. Comment on such questions as these:

a. What impression of the character was conveyed by the actor's posture and manner of walking?

b. How was movement used to help hold attention?

c. What special meanings were conveyed by facial expression and by movements of the head or shoulders?

d. What conventional and descriptive gestures were especially effective?

e. Did you notice any relationship between comedy effects and awkward, poorly timed gestures? Explain.

f. Would the gestures which the actors used have been appropriate in a speech? Why or why not?

Speaking assignments

1. Make a two- or three-minute speech explaining to the class how to do something, such as driving a golf ball, kicking a football, bowling, doing a sleight-of-hand trick, playing a musical instrument, or cutting out a dress. Use movement and gestures to help make your ideas clear. Do not use the blackboard or previously prepared diagrams.

2. Make a short speech describing some exciting event you have witnessed —an automobile accident, a rocket launching, a militant civil rights march, a touchdown play, a streetcorner brawl. Use movement and gestures to make the details clear and vivid. Try to make your description so colorful that your

listeners will tend to project themselves into the situation and to see it as clearly as if they were actually witnessing it. Remember that to succeed in doing this you will need to imagine yourself in the situation while you describe it; you must feel the excitement yourself in order to communicate it to others.

3. Give a three- or four-minute speech on some subject that arouses your fighting spirit—dishonesty, cruelty, unnecessary red tape, campus injustices, unsympathetic officials or teachers, unfair requirements or restrictions, the denial of civil liberties, biased newspaper reporting, or dangerous demagogs. Choose a subject that makes you genuinely angry, excited, or indignant. Let yourself go vocally and physically in denouncing the institution or practice. Be careful, however, to back up what you say with facts; do not pointlessly rant and rave, or merely air a prejudice. You may make a point as strongly as you like, provided you are able to prove it. Remember to frame a specific purpose and to choose materials suitable to secure the desired response from your listeners.

Suggestions for further reading

Martin P. Anderson, Wesley Lewis, and James Murray, *The Speaker and His Audience* (New York: Harper & Row, Publishers, 1964), Chapter XIV, "The Communicative Personality: Physical Behavior."

Marguerite Battye, *Stage Movement* (London: Herbert Jenkins Ltd., 1954).

W. Norwood Brigance, *Speech: Its Techniques and Disciplines in a Free Society,* 2nd ed. (New York: Appleton-Century-Crofts, 1961), Chapter XVI, "Being Seen."

John Waite Bowers, "The Influence of Delivery on Attitudes toward Concepts and Speakers," *Speech Monographs,* XXXII (June 1965), 154-158.

Delwin Dusenbury and Franklin H. Knower, "Experimental Studies of the Symbolism of Action and Voice—I: A Study of the Specificity of Meaning in Facial Expression," *Quarterly Journal of Speech,* XXIV (October 1938), 424-436.

Paul Heinberg, "Relationships of Content and Delivery to General Effectiveness," *Speech Monographs,* XXX (June 1963), 105-107.

Ray Nadeau, "Delivery in Ancient Times: Homer to Quintilian," *Quarterly Journal of Speech,* L (February 1964), 53-60.

Jurgen Ruesch and Weldon Kees, *Nonverbal Communication* (Berkeley: University of California Press, 1956).

Richard Whately, *Elements of Rhetoric,* ed. Douglas Ehninger (Carbondale: Southern Illinois University Press, 1963), pp. 339-390, "Of Elocution, or Delivery."

Charles Woolbert, *Fundamentals of Speech* (New York: Harper & Brothers, 1920), Chapter VI, "Total Bodily Action and the Speaker," and Chapter VII, "Gesture and the Audience."

CHAPTER FIVE

Improving voice quality

After long experience in public life, Benjamin Disraeli, the British statesman, declared, "There is no index of character so sure as the voice." It is true that we often tend to judge a person by his voice. A woman whose tones are sharp and nasal may be thought of as a shrew. A man whose voice is harsh or guttural may be regarded as crude and rough. A thin, breathy voice, characterized by the frequent use of upward inflections, may suggest a lack of conviction or decisiveness.

The conclusions we draw from vocal characteristics, of course, are sometimes incorrect. But whether correct or not, such judgments are important to the speaker because they color his listeners' attitudes toward what he is saying. Sometimes a speaker's voice may be the most important single factor in determining the impression his hearers form of him as a person; frequently it is among the major factors.

In addition to projecting a desirable image, a good voice enables a speaker to make what he says more interesting and meaningful. Have you ever listened to a child at a church or school program rattle off a poem with so little expression that, even though you heard his words, you could not get their full meaning? On the other hand, can you recall a play-by-play account of some football or baseball game broadcast by a skilled sports announcer? Did not the clarity and vividness of his description depend largely upon the way he used his voice?

How can you as a speaker acquire an effective voice? As in bodily delivery, improvement results chiefly from practice. But here again unintelligent practice may do more harm than good; repeatedly doing the wrong thing merely fixes a bad habit more firmly. To make practice worth while, you should first understand something about the mechanics of voice production. Also you should be acquainted with the characteristics of a good voice and with methods by which these characteristics may be developed. In this chapter, in addition to describing in simple terms the nature of the vocal mechanism, we shall discuss the elements of voice quality and suggest some ways in which quality may be improved. In the next chapter we shall consider how the voice may be used to communicate different kinds of ideas and feelings. Each chapter is accompanied by a variety of exercise and practice materials. These exercises, together with the directions and criticisms of your instructor, will help you move purposefully toward your goal of developing an effective speaking voice.

THE MECHANICS OF SPEAKING

Strictly speaking, there is no such thing as a *speech*, or *vocal, mechanism.* We shall use the term, however, to include those parts of the body which are used in the speaking process.

All the muscles, bones, cartilages, and organs used in speaking have other functions which are biologically more important than producing the voice. The tongue, for example, even though a vital part of the speaking mechanism, is more important in eating. The vocal folds protect our lungs from irritants in the atmosphere and help to regulate the airflow. The very fact that speaking is a secondary function of these organs makes doubly important a program of vocal training, for though we were able at birth to breathe, we had to learn to speak. In the process, many of us did not learn to speak well. We may have established bad habits of articulating; we may have formed the habit of straining our throats as we speak, or of grouping our words into short, jerky units. But even though we may have inadequate speech habits, or bad ones, we all have learned in childhood how to use these organs together in some form of speaking. Let us therefore forget for the present their primary biological functions and consider them in combination as a single mechanism—the instrument of speech. This instrument may be divided into two major parts: the *voice-producing mechanism,* including the motor, the vibrator, and the resonators; and the *articulatory mechanism,* including the tongue, teeth, lips, jaw, and the hard and soft palates.

The voice-producing mechanism

The motor. The motor part of the speech mechanism is essentially a pump for compressing air. It consists of *(a)* the *lungs,* which contain spaces for the air; *(b)* the *bronchial tubes,* which converge into the windpipe or *trachea,* out of which the compressed air is released; *(c)* the *ribs* and other bones, cartilages, and tissues which serve to hold the motor in place and give leverage for the application of power;

11718

Figure 1

THE VOICE AS A WIND INSTRUMENT

This diagram shows how the speaking mechanism is similar to a wind instrument. The motor compresses the air in the lungs, as shown by the arrows; this compressed air is sent through the vibrator, which first produces the speech sound; the speech tone next enters the resonators of the throat, mouth, and head to be amplified and modified in quality; finally, the tone is affected by the articulatory mechanism, which alters the quality further and serves also to produce the consonant sounds.

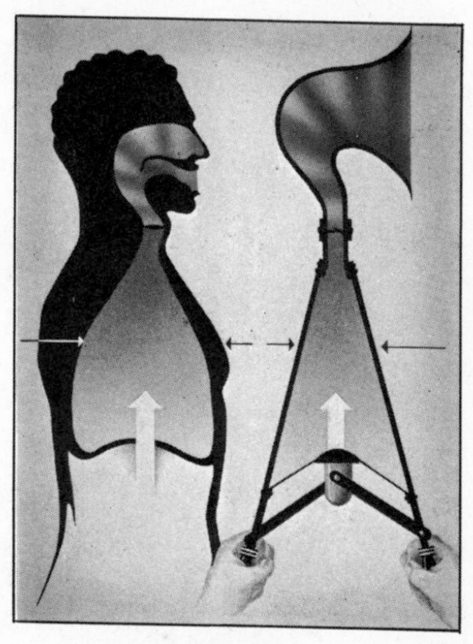

and *(d)* the *muscles,* which alternately expand and contract the area occupied by the lungs, thus first allowing air to enter and then compressing it for expulsion. To detail the large number of muscles used in the breathing process would be beyond the scope of this book. It should, however, be noted that the human air pump works in two ways: Certain muscles draw the ribs down and in when we exhale, so as to squeeze the lungs after the fashion of a bellows, while others—the strong abdominal muscles—squeeze in below to exert pressure up against the bottom of the lungs after the manner of a piston. This double action also is exerted when we inhale: One set of muscles pulls the ribs up and out to expand the horizontal space, while the diaphragm—a layer of muscles and flat tendon tissue—expands the vertical space by lowering the floor of the chest cavity; this two-way expansion creates a suction, so that air rushes into the lungs. Thus, both inhaling and exhaling involve two coordinated actions: moving the ribbed walls of the chest, and raising and lowering its floor.

The vibrator. The air compressed in the lungs during exhalation is directed through the trachea into the *larynx,* which contains the main vibrating unit. The larynx is situated at the upper end of the trachea and is attached above and below by muscles which shift it up and down. The larynx itself consists of a group of small cartilages joined so that they can move as if on joints like the bones of the arm. The position of these cartilages can be changed by a number of small muscles which are delicately intertwined. Within the larynx, stretched

THE VOCAL MECHANISM
(anatomy involved in speech)

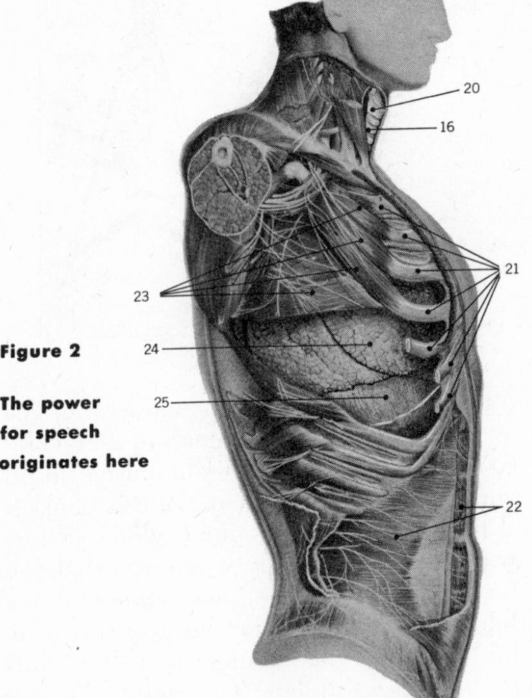

1. Sinuses
2. Nasal cavity
3. Hard palate
4. Upper lip
5. Upper teeth
6. Tongue
7. Lower lip
8. Lower teeth
9. Lower jaw
10. Soft palate
11. Base of the tongue
12. Epiglottis
13. Thyroid cartilage
14. Vocal fold
15. Cricoid cartilage
16. Trachea (windpipe)
17. Esophagus
18. Pharynx (throat)
19. Vertebrae
20. Larynx
21. Rib bones (numbers 6, 7, and 8 cut away)
22. Abdominal muscles
23. Chest muscles
24. Lungs
25. Diaphragm
26. Base of epiglottis
27. Glottis
28. Arytenoid cartilage

Figure 2

The power for speech originates here

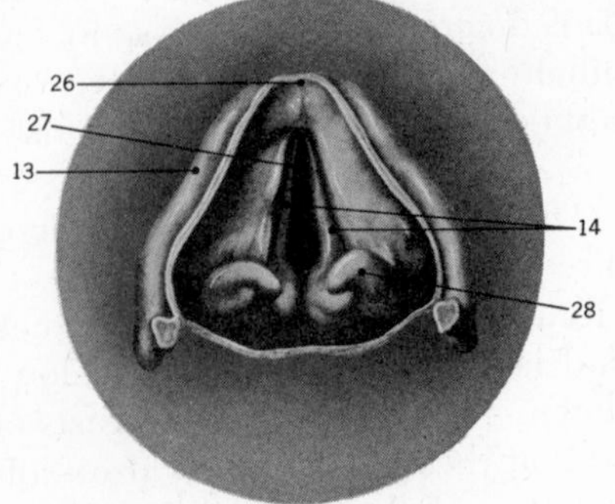

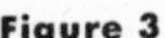

Figure 3

The vocal folds
(laryngoscopic view of the vocal folds in relaxed position at normal breathing)

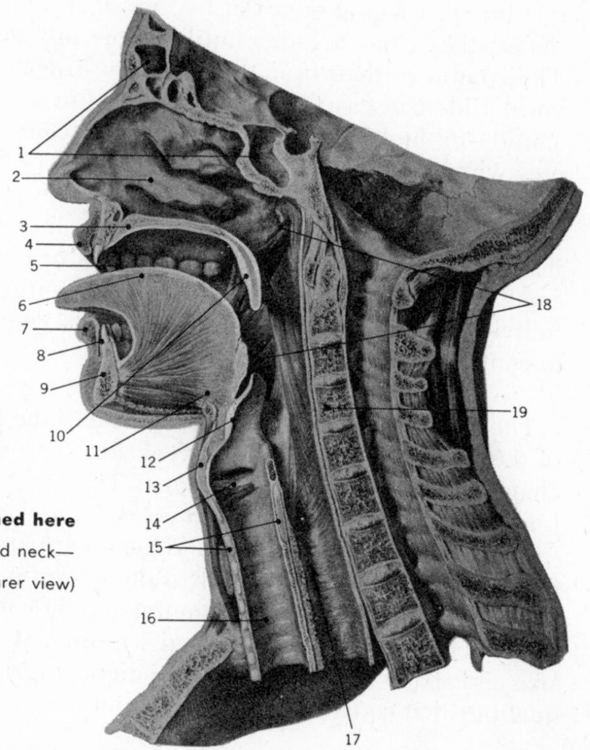

Figure 4

Speech sounds are formed here

(sagittal section of the head and neck—tongue drawn out for clearer view)

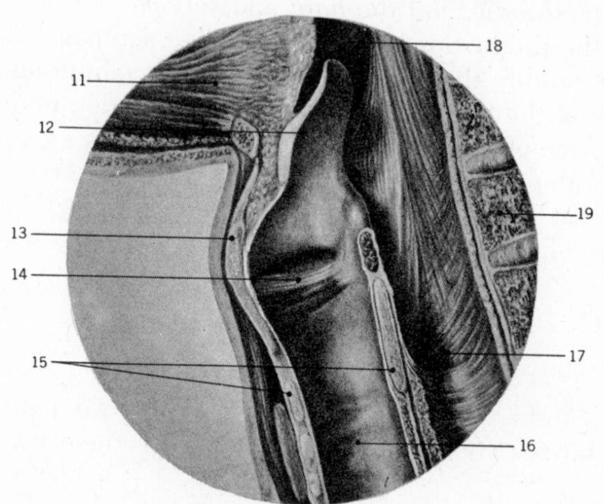

Figure 5

Detail showing structure of the larynx

between the cartilages, are the *vocal folds*. The *folds* are the tendonous inner or facing edges of two muscles. When sound is to be produced, they come together until there is only a tiny slit between them. The compressed air from the lungs, pushing against and between the vocal folds, causes a vibration which results in sound. The pitch of this sound—its highness or lowness on the scale—depends on the muscles which control the tension and length of the folds. The position of the larynx as a whole is adjusted to a proper relation with the air cavities above by the action of the larger outside muscles which hold it in place. The action of these two sets of muscles, particularly the small internal ones, is primarily automatic—they cannot be controlled individually. But we can operate these laryngeal muscles as a group to control pitch.

The resonators. The sound produced in the larynx by the vibration of the vocal folds is thin and weak. It is resonated by a group of air chambers in the head and throat. The principal resonators of the human voice are the upper part (or *vestibule*) of the *larynx*, the throat *(pharynx)*, the *nasal cavities*, and the *mouth*. (See the Figures on page 69.) These resonators act much as do the resonating parts of a musical instrument: they amplify the sound; and they modify its quality, making it rich and mellow or harsh or whining. Moreover, changes in the size and shape of some of these chambers result in the different tone qualities that constitute the vowel sounds.[1]

The articulatory mechanism

The *tongue, lips, teeth, jaw*, and the *hard* and *soft palates* act as modifying agents in the production of speech sounds. (See page 69.) By moving them we modify the size and shape of the mouth and, therefore, the quality of the tone. Another important function of the modifiers is the formation of consonant sounds—the stops, hisses, and other interruptions in the steady flow of vowel sounds that serve to make words out of what would otherwise be mere vocal tones. Precision and sharpness of articulation come from the proper use of these modifiers.

VOICE QUALITY

The basic component of a good voice is a pleasing quality. Quality sometimes is referred to as "timbre" or "tone color." It is the overall

[1]By definition, vowels are resonant speech tones produced by the vibration of the vocal folds, amplified in the pharyngeal and oral resonators, and not significantly obstructed by the modifiers.

impression which the voice makes upon a listener as being harsh, mellow, nasal, thin, or resonant. Just as the quality of tone produced by one violin differs from that produced by another, so does the quality of one voice differ from another. Everyone, however—depending upon the size, shape, and state of health of his vocal mechanism—has what is for him a best or optimum quality. This quality results when a proper balance is preserved between oral and nasal resonance, and when excessive tension and breathiness are avoided. (See Figures on page 69.)

Let us consider a few of the more common types of poor voice quality and see what may be done to remedy them.

Thin, weak voices lack carrying power. More often found in women than in men, this type of voice is faint and lacks body. A number of causes may combine to produce such a voice: the muscles of the tongue and palate may be so inactive that inadequate use is made of the resonating cavities; the pitch level may be too high—even a falsetto—so that the lower resonances are not used (something like this happens when you tune out the lower partials on your radio or hi-fi set); or the power given to the voice by the breathing muscles may be inadequate. Of these causes, the latter two are the most common. If your voice is thin, try lowering your pitch and at the same time talk a little louder. Open your mouth wider, especially on the vowel sounds *ah, oh,* and *aw,* in order to increase the size of the oral cavity and improve its resonating effect. For practice, say *bound* as if projecting the word from deep in your chest and bouncing it upon the back wall of the room.

Huskiness and harshness may result either from tension in the throat or from the pressure of too much air against the vocal folds. An irritated or diseased condition of the throat sometimes creates the same effect. If a throat examination fails to disclose any pathological condition, the huskiness often can be lessened or eliminated by proper breathing and relaxation. Let the neck muscles become slack; then say a word such as *one, bun, run,* very quietly, prolonging it until it becomes almost a singing tone. Work at this until the tone is clear and free of all breathiness; if you have trouble, use less breath. When the tone seems clear, gradually increase the volume until you can produce a strong tone without tension or huskiness.

Nasality, contrary to popular notion, is more often the result of too little nasal resonance, rather than too much; that is, the nasal passages are not sufficiently open. Say *button* or *mutton.* Notice what happens to your soft palate. Did you feel it tighten up just before the production of the *t* sound and then relax to allow the *n* sound to be emitted through the nose? For consonant sounds such as *t* and *p*, the palate has to close tight; but if this tension is continued during the production of vowel sounds, a flat quality is likely to result. To correct this difficulty, begin by working on those sounds which must be produced through the nose—*m-m-m-m* and *n-n-n-n*. Hum these sounds, prolonging them until you can feel the vibration in your nose. At the same time, keeping the lips closed, drop the jaw somewhat and let the sound reverberate in the mouth cavity. When you can feel a "ringing" sensation in both mouth and nose, open your lips and let the *m* become an *ah* thus: *m-m-m-m-m-a-a-ah*. You should still feel some vibration both in the mouth and nose; continue until you do. Once you recognize the sensation of nasal resonance, try the same exercise with other vowel sounds (*m-m-m-m-m-o-o-oh*, *n-n-n-n-n-ee-ee-ee*, etc.). You will be wise, however, to have your instructor listen to you because, though the chances are slight, it is possible to relax the palate too much so that you give the tone an excess of nasal resonance.

EFFECT OF EMOTION ON VOICE QUALITY

Changes in quality are closely related to a speaker's emotions and state of mind. Therefore, if you are sincere in what you are saying, your voice ordinarily will change of its own accord to suit your feeling. Never attempt to vary the quality of your voice artificially, or you almost certainly will lose the direct, conversational speech pattern that insures maximum contact with your audience. Feel deeply, and let your voice ring out without restraint. You will find that it responds to your thoughts and feelings automatically—not in an artificial way but with the subtle and varied shadings which will carry conviction to your listeners.

In order to develop a more pleasing voice, learn to control your breathing and to relax your throat. Let your voice respond naturally to the ideas and moods you wish to communicate. Practice under the supervision of your instructor and with special concern for your own individual problems.

Exercises

TO IMPROVE CONTROL OF BREATHING

1. Practice expelling the air from your lungs in short, sharp gasps; place your hand on your abdomen to see that there is a sharp inward contraction of the muscle wall synchronous with the chest contraction on each out-going puff.

a. Then vocalize the puffs, saying "Hep!—Hep!—Hep!" with a good deal of force.

b. In the same way, say "bah, bay, bee, bo, boo," with staccato accents and considerable vigor.

2. Fill your lungs; then exhale *as slowly as possible* until the lungs are empty. Time yourself to see how long you can keep exhaling without a break. (Note that the object here is not to see how much air you can get into the lungs but how slowly you can let it out.)

a. Filling your lungs each time, vocalize the outgoing breath stream first with a long continuous hum, second with an *oo* sound, and then with other vowel sounds. Be careful not to let the sound become "breathy"; keep the tone clear.

b. Place a lighted candle just in front of your mouth and repeat the series outlined above. The flame should just barely flicker.

3. On the same breath alternate the explosive and the slow, deliberate exhalations outlined in the two preceding problems. Practice until you can shift from one to the other easily, both in silent breathing and in vocalized tones.

TO INDUCE RELAXATION OF THE THROAT

4. Repeat the following sequence several times in succession:

a. Turn your head slowly and tensely to the right as far as possible; to the left; backward; forward. In each direction, *stretch.*

b. Break the tension, letting your head fall inertly forward on your chest; let your jaw drop open and your eyes close; move your jaw from side to side with your hand to be sure your jaw muscles are relaxed; let your facial muscles become lax as if you were asleep.

c. With your muscles in this relaxed condition, allow your head to roll around slowly, making a complete rotation in each direction; repeat two or three times.

d. Keeping your eyes closed and your neck and jaw muscles as relaxed as possible, raise your head easily to an upright position and then yawn with your mouth open as wide as possible.

e. While your mouth is thus open, inhale deeply and exhale quietly two or three times; then intone "a-a-a-ah" very quietly.

f. Each time nodding your head forward quietly and without tension, say "m-m-a-a-ah" several times slowly.

g. Keeping the same degree of relaxation, count aloud slowly from one to twenty and then continue in the same relaxed manner, repeating several times:

And may there be no moaning of the bar,
  When I put out to sea.

Tennyson

TO IMPROVE THE QUALITY OF TONE

5. Intone the following words quietly at first, then louder, and louder; try to give them a ringing quality; put your fingertips on your nose and cheekbones to see if you can feel a vibration there. Avoid breathiness.

one	home	tone	alone	moan
rain	plain	mine	lean	soon
ring	nine	tong	moon	fine

6. Read aloud the following passages in as clear and resonant tones as you can produce. Be sure that you open your mouth wide enough and that you use only enough air to make the tones vibrate. Do not force the tone. If you notice any tension in your throat or harshness in your voice, go back to the preceding exercises until the tension and harshness disappear.

Roll on, thou deep and dark blue Ocean, roll!

Byron

Alone, alone, all, all alone,
Alone on a wide, wide sea!
And never a saint took pity on
My soul in agony.

Coleridge

The day is cold and dark and dreary;
It rains, and the wind is never weary;
The vine still clings to the moldering wall,
But at every gust the dead leaves fall,
And the day is dark and dreary.

Longfellow

I have raised my head,
And cried, in thraldom, to the furious wind,
"Blow on!—This is the land of liberty!"

Knowles

God of our fathers, known of old,
Lord of our far-flung battle-line,
Beneath whose awful Hand we hold
Dominion over palm and pine—
Lord God of Hosts, be with us yet,
Lest we forget—lest we forget!

Kipling

SELECTED PASSAGES FOR FURTHER PRACTICE.

Some of these selections are included because of the emotional tone they portray; others because of the vocal control they require. All of them, however, call for a clear, resonant quality for the best expression. Study them first for their meaning so that you are sure you understand what the author is saying. Then absorb the feeling; allow yourself to follow the mood of the writer. Finally, read the passages aloud, putting as much meaning and feeling into the expression as you can.

from THE CONGO[2]

Fat black bucks in a wine-barrel room,
Barrel-house kings, with feet unstable,
Sagged and reeled and pounded on the table,
Pounded on the table,
Beat an empty barrel with the handle of a broom,
Hard as they were able,
Boom, boom, BOOM,
With a silk umbrella and the handle of a broom,
Boomlay, boomlay, boomlay, BOOM.

Vachel Lindsay

from THE MAN WITH THE HOE[3]

Bowed by the weight of centuries he leans
Upon his hoe and gazes on the ground,
The emptiness of ages in his face,
And on his back the burden of the world.
Who made him dead to rapture and despair,
A thing that grieves not and that never hopes,
Stolid and stunned, a brother to the ox?
Who loosened and let down this brutal jaw?
Whose was the hand that slanted back this brow?
Whose breath blew out the light within this brain?

Edwin Markham

from THE BARREL-ORGAN[4]

There's a barrel-organ carolling across a golden street
  In the City as the sun sinks low;
And the music's not immortal; but the world has made it sweet
And fulfilled it with the sunset-glow;

[2]Reprinted with permission of The Macmillan Company from *The Congo and Other Poems* by Vachel Lindsay. Copyright The Macmillan Company, 1914, renewed 1942 by Elizabeth C. Lindsay.
[3]Copyright by the author and used by permission.
[4]From "The Barrel-Organ" in *Collected Poems* by Alfred Noyes. Copyright 1906, 1934 by Alfred Noyes. Published by J. B. Lippincott Company.

And it pulses through the pleasures of the City and the pain
  That surround the singing organ like a large eternal light;
And they've given it a glory and a part to play again
  In the Symphony that rules the day and night.

Alfred Noyes

from APOSTROPHE TO THE OCEAN

Roll on, thou deep and dark blue Ocean, roll!
  Ten thousand fleets sweep over thee in vain;
Man marks the earth with ruin—his control
  Stops with the shore;—upon the watery plain
  The wrecks are all thy deed, nor doth remain
A shadow of man's ravage, save his own,
  When for a moment, like a drop of rain,
He sinks into thy depths with bubbling groan,
Without a grave, unknelled, uncoffined, and unknown.

Byron

DEATH, BE NOT PROUD

Death, be not proud, though some have called thee
Mighty and dreadful, for thou art not so;
For those whom thou think'st thou dost overthrow
Die not, poor Death; nor yet canst thou kill me.
From rest and sleep, which but thy picture be,
Much pleasure; then from thee much more must flow;
And soonest our best men with thee do go—
Rest of their bones and souls' delivery!
Thou'rt slave to fate, chance, kings, and desperate men,
And dost with poison, war, and sickness dwell;
And poppy or charms can make us sleep as well
And better than thy stroke. Why swell'st thou then?
One short sleep past, we wake eternally,
And Death shall be no more: Death, thou shalt die!

John Donne

WIND IN THE PINE[5]

Oh, I can hear you, God, above the cry
  Of the tossing trees—
Rolling your windy tides across the sky,

[5]From *Covenant with Earth* by Lew Sarett. Edited and copyrighted 1956 by Alma Johnson Sarett. Gainesville: University of Florida Press.

And splashing your silver seas
Over the pine,
To the water-line
Of the moon.
Oh, I can hear you, God,
Above the wail of the lonely loon—
When the pine-tops pitch and nod—
Chanting your melodies
Of ghostly waterfalls and avalanches,
Swashing your wind among the branches
To make them pure and white.

Wash over me, God, with your piney breeze,
And your moon's wet-silver pool;
Wash over me, God, with your wind and night,
And leave me clean and cool.

Lew Sarett

GOD'S GRANDEUR

The world is charged with the grandeur of God.
It will flame out, like shining from shook foil;
It gathers to a greatness, like the ooze of oil
Crushed. Why do men then now not reck his rod?
Generations have trod, have trod, have trod;
And all is seared with trade; bleared, smeared with toil;
And wears man's smudge and shares man's smell: the soil
Is bare now, nor can foot feel, being shod.

And for all this, nature is never spent;
There lives the dearest freshness deep down things;
And though the last lights off the black West went
Oh, morning, at the brown brink eastward, springs—
Because the Holy Ghost over the bent
World broods with warm breast and with ah! bright wings.

Gerard Manley Hopkins

BY THE BIVOUAC'S FITFUL FLAME

By the bivouac's fitful flame,
A procession winding around me, solemn and sweet and slow—but first I note
The tents of the sleeping army, the fields' and woods' dim outline,
The darkness lit by spots of kindled fire, the silence,
Like a phantom far or near an occasional figure moving,

The shrubs and trees (as I lift my eyes they seem to be stealthily watching
  me),
While wind in procession thoughts, O tender and wondrous thoughts,
Of life and death, of home and the past and loved, and of those that are far
  away;
A solemn and slow procession there as I sit on the ground,
By the bivouac's fitful flame.

Walt Whitman

from FERN HILL[6]

Now as I was young and easy under the apple boughs
About the lilting house and happy as the grass was green,
  The night above the dingle starry,
      Time let me hail and climb
  Golden in the heydays of his eyes,
And honoured among wagons I was prince of the apple towns
And once below a time I lordly had the trees and leaves
      Trail with daisies and barley
  Down the rivers of the windfall light.

And as I was green and carefree, famous among the barns
About the happy yard and singing as the farm was home,
  In the sun that is young once only,
      Time let me play and be
  Golden in the mercy of his means,
And green and golden I was huntsman and herdsman, the calves
Sang to my horn, the foxes on the hills barked clear and cold,
      And the sabbath rang slowly
  In the pebbles of the holy streams.

All the sun long it was running, it was lovely, the hay-
Fields high as the house, the tunes from the chimneys, it was air,
  And playing, lovely and watery
      And fire green as grass.
  And nightly under the simple stars
As I rode to sleep, the owls were bearing the farm away,
All the moon long I heard, blessed among stables, the nightjars
  Flying with the ricks, and the horses
      Flashing into the dark.

Dylan Thomas

[6]Dylan Thomas, *The Collected Poems of Dylan Thomas.* Copyright 1953 by Dylan Thomas. Reprinted by permission of New Directions Publishing Corporation, J. M. Dent & Sons, Ltd., London, and the Trustees of the copyright of the late Dylan Thomas.

DOOM IS DARK AND DEEPER THAN ANY SEA-DINGLE[7]

Doom is dark and deeper than any sea-dingle.
Upon what man it fall
In spring, day-wishing flowers appearing,
Avalanche sliding, white snow from rock-face,
That he should leave his house,
No cloud-soft hand can hold him, restraint by women;
But ever that man goes
Through place-keepers, through forest trees,
A stranger to strangers over undried sea,
Houses for fishes, suffocating water,
Or lonely on fell as chat,
By pot-holed becks
A bird stone-haunting, an unquiet bird.

There head falls forward, fatigued at evening,
And dreams of home,
Waving from window, spread of welcome,
Kissing of wife under single sheet;
But waking sees
Bird-flocks nameless to him, through doorway voices
Of new men making another love.

Save him from hostile capture,
From sudden tiger's spring at corner;
Protect his house,
His anxious house where days are counted
From thunderbolt protect,
From gradual ruin spreading like a stain;
Converting number from vague to certain,
Bring joy, bring day of his returning,
Lucky with day approaching, with leaning dawn.

Wystan Hugh Auden

Problems

1. Make a fairly detailed drawing of one or more parts of the speech (or hearing) mechanism. Label the various muscles, bones, and cartilages. (A good set of drawings may be found in Giles W. Gray and C. M. Wise, *The Bases of Speech*, 3rd ed. [New York: Harpers, 1959]. Also consult the appropriate sections of Gray's *Anatomy*.)

[7]Copyright 1934 and renewed 1961 by W. H. Auden. Reprinted from *The Collected Poetry of W. H. Auden* by permission of Random House, Inc., N.Y., and Faber & Faber, Ltd., London.

2. Make a tabulation of the muscles used in inhaling, exhaling, raising and lowering the larynx in the throat, changing the position or tension of the vocal folds, manipulating the jaw, tongue, soft palate, and lips. (Refer to the sources listed in Problem 1.)
3. Be prepared to describe briefly each of the following: How we breathe; how the vocal folds produce sound; how the voice is resonated; the production of consonant sounds; the production of vowel sounds.
4. Demonstrate for the class the vocal quality which results when the muscles of the throat and neck are tense and tight. Then demonstrate the improved sound that comes when these muscles are relaxed. Tighten and relax the muscles alternately while sustaining the *a* sound in *father*.
5. Discuss the role that our hearing plays in improving voice quality. How might you go about improving the voice quality of someone who is hard of hearing? Your instructor will suggest appropriate sources of information on this subject.
6. Drawing upon sources suggested by your instructor, investigate the problem of speech defects. When should speech be considered defective? What are the common types of speech defects? What segments of the population are most likely to suffer from them? Which defects are caused by abnormalities in the speech mechanism? Which may occur even though the speech mechanism is completely normal? What are some of the methods by which speech defects may be treated? Is the prognosis for the correction of most defects good or bad? What can society as a whole do to help the speech-defective individual? Report your findings orally or in writing. (One member of the class may be assigned to investigate each of the questions listed above, and to report his findings as part of a general class discussion of speech defects.)
7. For several consecutive broadcasts, listen to a popular figure on radio or television—a newscaster, sports announcer, the announcer who handles the commercial "messages," etc. Take careful notes on what you consider to be good about his voice and how he uses it and also on what you consider to be faults or deficiencies in his voice. Compare your notes with those made by the other members of the class to see if you can arrive at a common agreement on the desirable and undesirable aspects of the voice in question.
8. Compare the human speech mechanism with the comparable mechanism in *(a)* a fish, *(b)* a sheep, and *(c)* a higher ape. What, if anything, does your comparison suggest about why man learned to speak and these animals did not?

Suggestions for further reading

Virgil A. Anderson, "A Modern View of Voice and Diction," *Quarterly Journal of Speech,* XXXIX (February 1953), 25-32.

John W. Black and Wilbur E. Moore, *Speech: Code, Meaning, and Communi-*

cation (New York: McGraw-Hill Book Company, 1955), Chapter II, "The Mechanisms of Speech," and Chapter III, "The Sound of Speech."

William H. Canfield, "A Phonetic Approach to Voice and Speech Improvement," *Speech Teacher,* XIII (January 1964), 42-46.

Donald H. Ecroyd, "A Rationale for the Teaching of Voice and Diction," *Speech Teacher,* VIII (September 1959), 256-259.

Donald H. Ecroyd, Murray L. Halfond, and Carol Chworowsky Towne, *Voice and Articulation: A Handbook; Voice and Articulation: Programed Instruction; Voice and Articulation: Recorded Exercises* (Glenview, Illinois: Scott, Foresman and Company, 1966).

Giles W. Gray and C. M. Wise, *The Bases of Speech,* 3rd ed. (New York: Harper & Row, Publishers, 1959), Chapter III, "The Physiological Basis of Speech," and Chapter IV, "The Neurological Basis of Speech."

Donald E. Hargis, "Some Basic Considerations in Teaching Voice," *Speech Teacher,* XII (September 1963), 214-218.

Ward Rasmus, "Voice and Diction: Historical Perspective," *Quarterly Journal of Speech,* XLVII (October 1961), 253-261.

Norma Schneiderman Rees, "Measuring and Training Pitch Discrimination Ability in Voice Improvement," *Speech Teacher,* XI (January 1962), 44-47.

Harold M. Scholl, "A Holistic Approach to the Teaching of Voice Improvement," *Speech Teacher,* X (September 1961), 200-205.

Roy Edward Tew, "Rating of Vocal Characteristics," *Speech Monographs,* XXIII (March 1956), 26-30.

CHAPTER SIX

Using the voice: Communicating ideas and feelings

Although a pleasing quality is basic to effective vocal delivery, it does not in itself constitute good speech. If a speaker is to communicate his ideas and feelings to others, he must meet two additional requirements: first, his speech must be easily intelligible; and, second, his voice must be flexible enough in pitch, force, and rate so that it responds readily to the various shades of thought or feeling he wishes to convey. In this chapter we shall consider how these desirable characteristics may be attained.

INTELLIGIBILITY

The intelligibility or understandability of speech normally depends upon five separate but related factors: (1) the overall level of volume or loudness, (2) the duration of sounds within individual syllables, (3) the choice and sequence of words, (4) the distinctness with which sounds are articulated, and (5) the standard of pronunciation that is observed.

Adjusting the loudness level

Probably the most important single factor in intelligibility is the loudness level at which you speak as related to the *distance* between you and the listener and the amount of *noise* that surrounds him.[1]

[1]The term *loudness* is here used synonymously with *intensity* because the former term is clearer to most people. Technically, of course, loudness, a distinct function in the science of acoustics, is not strictly synonymous with intensity. To explain the exact relation between the two terms is beyond the scope of this book, since the explanation involves many complicated psychophysical relationships. For a full discussion of the relationship, see *Hearing: Its Psychology and Physiology* by Stanley S. Stevens and Hallowell Davis (New York: Wiley, 1938), p. 110 ff.

Obviously, the farther away your listener is, the louder you must talk for him to hear you well. All of us make this loudness-level adjustment unconsciously when projecting our voices over extreme distances; when we call to someone a block away or across a field, we have learned that we must shout in order to be heard. What we often forget is that the same principle also applies to shorter distances. You must realize that your own voice will always sound louder to you (unless you are deaf) than to your listeners—even if they are only ten or twenty feet away—since your own ears are closer to your mouth than are the ears of your listeners.

The sound of your voice diminishes rapidly as it travels from you; and if it were not reflected from surrounding surfaces, listeners only a short distance away would hear but a fraction of its initial loudness.[2] This fact explains why it is important to hold a microphone or the mouthpiece of a telephone fairly close to your mouth or, if the microphone is of a type which picks up sounds at a greater distance, why you should be careful not to vary your distance from it. The effects of distance on the loudness of your voice cannot be too rigidly stated, however, since there are a number of modifying factors which also help determine the volume level at which you must talk; these include the surface of the walls—whether acoustically treated or made of smooth plaster—the number of people present, and the sound-absorbency of their clothing.

In addition to distance, the amount of surrounding noise with which you must compete has an effect on the required loudness level. It is important to realize that even in normal circumstances some noise always is present. For example, the noise level of rustling leaves in the quiet solitude of a country lane (10 decibels[3]) is louder than a whisper six feet away. The noise in empty theatres averages 25 decibels, but with a "quiet" audience it rises to 42. In the average factory a constant noise of about 80 decibels is likely to be maintained. This is just about the same level as very loud speaking at a close range.

How can you determine the proper strength of voice to use in order to achieve sufficient loudness for the distance and noise conditions of a particular speech situation? While apparatus is available to meas-

[2]The loudness of your voice—strictly speaking, its intensity—varies inversely with the square of the distance it travels from your lips. (Expressed mathematically, $I \propto 1/D^2$.) Therefore, if it were not reflected from the walls and ceiling, your voice would be only one sixteenth as loud twelve feet away as it is at a distance of three feet; and the listener fifty feet away would hear only a very tiny fraction of the original sound.

[3]Loudness is expressed in *decibels* (dbs.). Within certain acoustic limits, one decibel is roughly equal to the smallest difference in loudness which the ear can detect. Standard measurements for loudness are at distances of three feet unless otherwise noted.

ure the intensity of sounds accurately, most of us do not have it and would not want to carry it around with us if we did. You can, however, use your eyes to see if those auditors in the back row appear to be hearing you; or, even better, you can *ask* if they are able to hear you. Get your instructor's advice on this point also. Ask your friends to report on the loudness of your voice as you talk in rooms of various sizes and under varying noise conditions. Listen to the sound of your voice so that you can begin to correlate your own vocal sensations with their reports. You will soon learn to gauge the volume you must use in order to be heard.

The proper loudness for talking into the microphone of a public address system introduces a different problem. Here the loudness of your voice will be affected by the type of microphone, the amplifying system, and the loud-speaker. No invariable rule can be given, since equipment varies widely. It is important, however, to try out the equipment before you are scheduled to speak. Ask the technician in charge to advise you and find out what signals he will use to tell you to talk louder or to move farther away from the microphone.

Syllable duration

The second factor that affects a listener's ability to understand what you say is the duration of sound within the syllables you utter. Generally, a slower rate of speaking is more easily understood than a fast one, but merely slowing down is not enough. As we shall explain more fully later in this chapter, the rate of your speech depends on two elements: quantity, or the duration of the sound within a syllable, and pause, or the silent interval between sounds. Experimental evidence seems to show that the intelligibility of speech—how much the listener hears accurately—depends more on syllable duration than on the overall rate of speaking. Thus a slow staccato utterance is not much more intelligible than a faster staccato utterance, but talking at a moderate rate while prolonging the sounds uttered improves intelligibility markedly.

This does not mean that everything you say should be spoken in a slow drawl; it *does* mean, however, that a rapid, "machine-gun" utterance often is hard to understand and should, therefore, generally be avoided. When the momentum of a fast-moving narrative is more important to your purpose and your listeners than exact comprehension of every word you say, naturally you will want to speak with more speed. But when you want to be sure your listeners understand precisely what you are saying on some important point, take time to dwell on every significant word long enough to be sure it will be heard and understood.

Syllable duration is of especial importance when you are talking in a large hall, when you must be heard above a great deal of noise, or when the acoustics of the room produce a noticeable echo effect. Speakers who address mass meetings held out-of-doors, or who make announcements at a banquet where there is a clatter of dishes, have found that they must stretch out their syllables if they are to be understood. Even unaccented syllables (such as *-ing* in *going*) are drawn out longer than usual. The ringmaster at a circus or the announcer at a prize fight is not just trying to be different when he sings out, "L-a-a-d-i-e-s and ge-e-n-tle-m-e-en"; he has learned through experience that he has to prolong the sounds if they are to be understood. Similarly, pilots, in talking on the airplane intercom and in radioing the control tower, have found that sustained and slightly drawn-out syllables are much more easily understood above the noise of the engine. You will find the same thing true in talking over the telephone in a noisy office or shop.

Practice, then, until you can prolong your syllables without losing the rhythm and emphasis of your sentences; but be careful not to overdo it when neither noise nor distance requires you to do so.

Choice and sequence of words

This is not the place to discuss the choice of words in terms of their rhetorical or persuasive value; that subject will be covered in Chapter 18. We are concerned here with the *sounds* which words contain, and with the errors in understanding which occur because one word is mistaken for another. Experiments have shown that the word *fox* is more than twice as hard to understand as *dog* and that six times as many errors of recognition are made on the word *nuts* as on *limeade.* And if the listeners in these experiments have never heard of foxes or nuts, the percentage of error is even greater since strange words usually are harder to understand than familiar ones.

The English language contains many words with different meanings but the same, or very similar, sounds: words such as *one* and *won, for* and *four, sick* and *six,* and the like. Moreover, the acoustic difference between certain individual sounds often is too small for clear differentiation if all the other sounds in the word are the same. Thus it may be hard to understand the rapid utterance of such a phrase as "nine fine swine."

Careful articulation and lengthening the duration of syllables will help reduce misunderstandings of this sort. Especially when you talk on unfamiliar subjects requiring the use of terms—particularly technical terms—which are strange to your listeners, you must talk more slowly, prolong your syllables, and articulate more carefully.

Wherever possible, try also to choose words that cannot be mistaken in context. In particular, be careful about using similar sounding words close together in sentences where the meaning of the first word may influence the meaning of the second. The story is told of a reporter who interviewed a farmer by telephone and reported in his newspaper that the farmer had just purchased "2008 pigs." The farmer had actually told him that he had bought "two sows and eight pigs." A difference of only one sound resulted in an error of 1998 hogs. Although errors of this magnitude do not often occur, a listener is frequently confused about a certain word or sentence until something is said later in the discussion to clarify the point, and in the meantime the effectiveness of the intervening remarks may have been reduced. Be careful, therefore, to think of words in terms of the way they *sound* and not only of the way they look in print. Remember, it is what the listener thinks he hears that counts.

Distinctness of articulation

Besides increasing the loudness of utterance, giving individual syllables greater duration, and selecting words with attention to their sound as well as their sense, the speaker may improve the intelligibility of his speech by exercising greater care in articulation.

Good articulation is chiefly the job of the jaw, tongue, and lips. Only by using the muscles which manipulate these members with skill and energy can you achieve crisp, clean-cut speech. Some oriental people move their jaws very little in speaking; in their language so much of the meaning is conveyed by variation in pitch that scarcely any jaw movement is necessary. In English, however, failure to open the jaws adequately is a serious fault because meaning is largely conveyed by consonant sounds, and these cannot be made effectively unless the tongue is given enough room to move vigorously. Even the vowel sounds are likely to be muffled if the jaws are kept immobile. As you talk, therefore, remember to move your jaws freely.

The tongue has more to do with the distinct formation of speech sounds than does any other organ. Even when the jaw is opened adequately, the sounds produced cannot be sharp if the tongue lies idle or moves sluggishly. All the vowels depend partly on the position of the tongue for their distinctive qualities. Try saying "ee, ay, ah, aw, oor" and notice how the highest point of the tongue changes its position. A great many consonant sounds, such as *d*, *th*, *ch*, *g*, and *k*, also depend upon the active movement of the tongue.

The lips, too, are important to distinct speech. If they are allowed to become lazy, the result will be a mumbled articulation, particu-

ARTICULATORS IN THE FORMATION OF CERTAIN SOUNDS

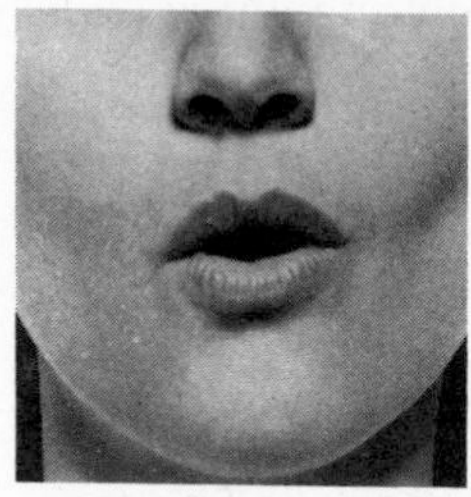

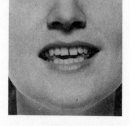

rose

cheese

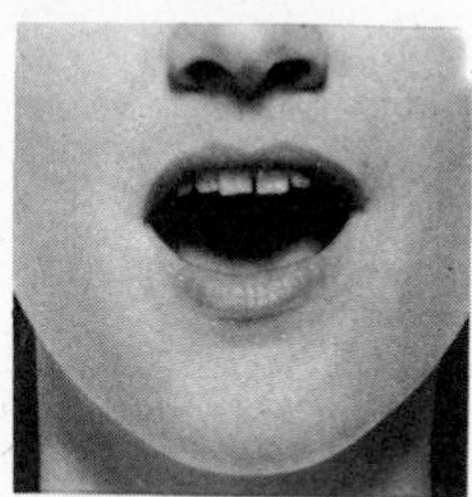

father

Contrasting movements, especially of the lips and jaw, produce and distinguish each of these vowel sounds from the others: the o in *rose*, ee in *cheese*, and *a* in *father*.

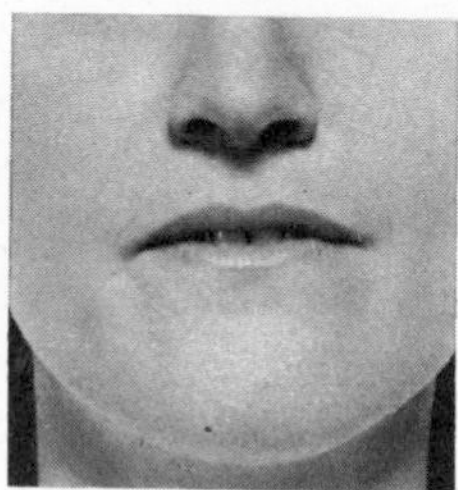

veil

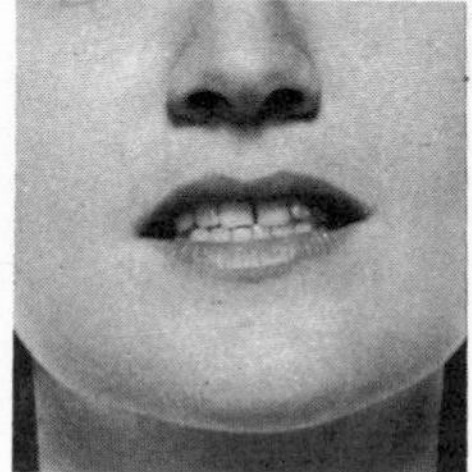

see

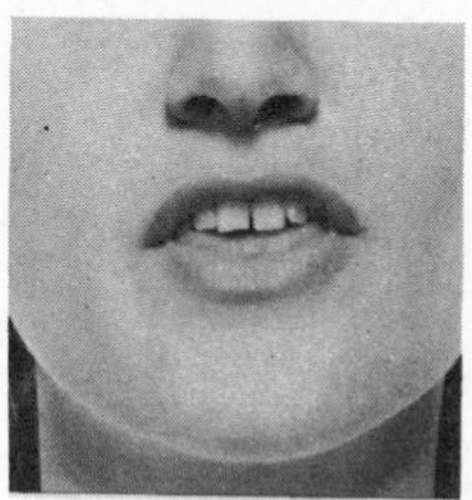

thing

Note characteristic positioning of the articulators—particularly of the lips, tongue, and teeth—for proper formation of these sounds: *v* in *veil*, *s* in *see*, and *th* in *thing*.

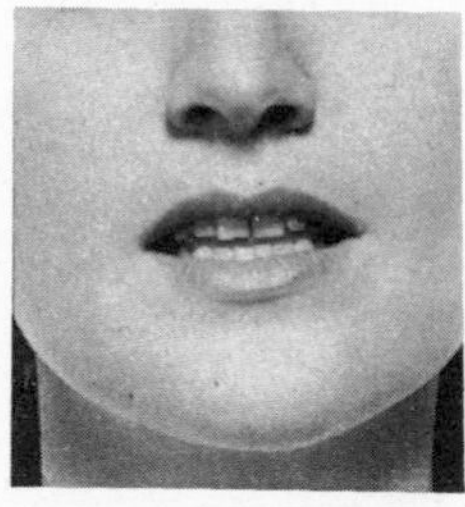

lead

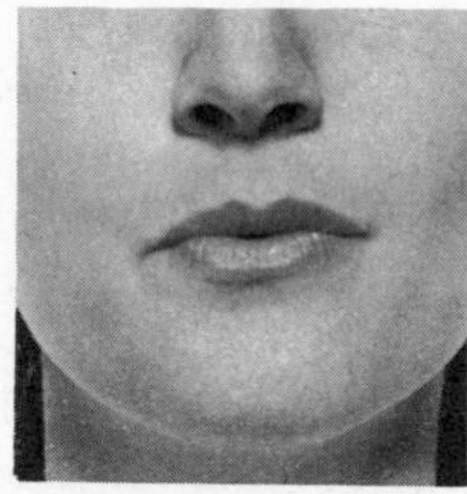

wear

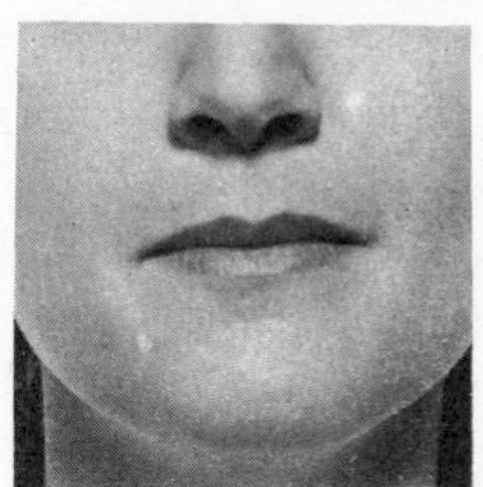

man

Note modifications in the position of the lips and tongue for the formation of sounds represented by the *l* in *lead* and *w* in *wear*.

Prominent use of the articulators is required for formation of *m* in *man*.

larly of such sounds as *p*, *b*, *m*, and *f*, which demand vigorous lip action. Of course, when one talks directly into a microphone, violent and explosive utterance of consonant sounds should be avoided. But in ordinary speaking, and especially in public speaking, most of us should use our lips more decisively to cut and to mold the sounds we make.

Finally, a great deal of indistinctness could be avoided if speakers took time enough to get each sound out clearly instead of jumbling successive sounds together. Take time to speak distinctly; as your jaw, tongue, and lips develop greater flexibility and precision, you can speed up. For the present, though, avoid rushing.

Briefly, then, when you are talking, open your jaw wide; move your lips energetically; use your tongue vigorously; and don't speak too fast. Practice the exercises for distinctness which are given at the end of this chapter, and see that the results of this practice are carried over into your daily conversation. It is possible to be so precise that you seem affected, but the chances are that your fault lies in the other direction. Nothing will create so much unconscious respect for you as a person as crisp and precise speech.

Acceptable pronunciation

The fifth factor that contributes to the intelligibility of vocal utterance is adherence to an accepted standard of pronunciation. If you fail to pronounce words acceptably, your listeners will not be able to grasp easily and quickly the meaning or significance of what you say. Even if your words are recognized, any peculiarity of pronunciation is almost sure to be noticed by some of the people in your audience; and the mistake not only may distract their attention from your thought but may discredit your knowledge and authority as a speaker.

It is sometimes difficult to know what pronunciation is acceptable, because standards differ. Ordinarily, the best criterion is the usage of the educated people of your own community. For most words, a dictionary provides a helpful guide; but dictionaries can become outdated and for this reason should not be followed too slavishly. Moreover, most dictionaries do not take sufficient notice of regional differences in dialect. A native of Louisiana pronounces words differently from a man who lives in Montana, and the speech of a Chicagoan is easily distinguished from that of a Bostonian. The standard of an up-to-date dictionary, modified to agree with the usage of educated people in your community, should, therefore, be the basis of your pronunciation.

A common fault of pronunciation is to misplace the accent in words

—to say "genu-*ine*," "*de*-vice," "the-*ay*-ter," "pre-*fer*-able," instead of the more accepted forms, "*gen*-uine," "de-*vice*," "*the*-ater," "*pref*-erable." Other errors arise from the omission of sounds (as in the pronunciation "guh'mnt" for *government*), from the addition of sounds ("athalete" for *athlete*), and from the substitution of sounds ("set" for *sit*). The way words are spelled is not always a safe guide to pronunciation, for English words contain many silent letters (of*t*en, i*s*land, mor*t*gage), and many words containing the same combinations of letters require different pronunciations (b*ough*, r*ough*, thr*ough*; call*ed*, shout*ed*, gasp*ed*). In addition, the formality of the occasion exerts considerable influence; many omissions acceptable in conversation become objectionable in formal address. In television and radio broadcasting, careful pronunciation is particularly important. Because network programs are seen and heard throughout the nation, they tend to minimize regional differences in pronunciation and to foster a common standard across the country. In general, however, what is good pronunciation elsewhere is also good "on the air."

Do not be so labored and precise as to call attention to your pronunciation rather than to your ideas, but do not take this admonition as an excuse for careless speech. Avoid equally pronunciation that is too pedantic or too provincial. Use your ears; listen to your own pronunciation and compare it with that of educated people in your community and with that of speakers on television and radio. If your pronunciation is faulty, keep a notebook in which you list the words you mispronounce, and practice the acceptable pronunciation frequently.

FLEXIBILITY

Speech that is easily intelligible may yet be dull to listen to; moreover, it may fail to communicate to the audience the full measure of thought and feeling which the speaker wishes to convey. In fact, this often happens when the speaker's voice is not flexible enough to express the fine shades of meaning and emotion upon which accurate and pleasing expression depend.

How may your voice be varied so as to become more colorful, and at the same time to communicate your meaning more fully and precisely? How can you make important ideas stand out from those that are less significant? How can you build a climax in delivery to support a climax in thought or argument? These are some of the questions with which we shall be concerned as we discuss in order the "vocal fundamentals" of rate, force, pitch, and emphasis.

Rate

Most persons speak between 120 and 180 words a minute; however, a uniform rate is not maintained with clocklike regularity. In normal speech, the speed of utterance corresponds to the thought or feeling the speaker is attempting to transmit. Weighty, complex, or serious ideas tend to be expressed more slowly; light, humorous, or exciting matters more rapidly. Observe how fast the sports announcer talks when he is describing a completed forward pass or a quick double play; in contrast, observe the slow, dignified rate at which a minister reads the wedding or burial service. A temperamentally excitable person tends to talk fast all of the time, while a stolid person characteristically talks in a slow drawl. However, the enthusiastic but poised individual who is in complete command of his material and of the speaking situation *varies* his rate, using this variation to convey the intensity of his convictions and the depth of his feelings. He tells a story, lays out facts, or summarizes an argument at a lively pace; but he presents his main ideas and more difficult points slowly and emphatically so that their importance may be fully grasped by the listener.

Two elements determine a speaker's rate. These are *quantity*, or the length of time used in the actual utterance of a sound within a word; and *pause*, or the cessation of sound between words. If one says "ni-i-ine fo-o-o-our three-ee-ee," he is using long quantity; if he says "nine four three," he is using short quantity. Similarly, one may say "nine . . . four . . . three," using long pauses, or "nine/four/three," using short pauses. The longer the quantity or pause or both, the slower the overall rate; the shorter the quantity or pause or both, the faster the rate.

Quantity. Quantity is usually associated with the mood or sentiment expressed. If you were to say the opening lines of the Gettysburg Address ("Four score and seven years ago, our fathers brought forth on this continent a new nation . . .") with sharp staccato quantity, the result would be absurd; such serious and dignified sentiments customarily call forth sustained tones. On the other hand, imagine listening to the following play-by-play account of a basketball game delivered in a slow drawl: "Jones passes to Schmidt . . . he's dribbling down the floor . . . back to Jones . . . back again to Schmidt . . . over to Lee . . . and it's in! Another basket for . . ." Like the game itself, such a description needs snap; short quantity provides it.

A good way to develop sensitivity to quantity values is to practice reading aloud selections in which some particular mood or sentiment prevails or in which there is a definite shift from one mood to another.

A number of the passages of poetry and prose at the end of this chapter are useful for this purpose. Notice when studying them that vowel sounds are usually longer than consonant sounds, and that some consonant and vowel sounds are longer than others. The word *roll,* for example, contains sounds that are intrinsically longer than those in *hit.* Many words suggest their meaning by the duration of the sounds they contain: compare *flit* with *soar, skip* with *roam, dart* with *stroll.* Writers know this and use such words, either consciously or because of an unconscious sensitivity to these values, to help convey their feelings. By absorbing the sentiments or emotions expressed in the practice selections and then reading them aloud, you can develop a sensitivity to quantity values, and thus increase the expressiveness of your voice.

Pause. Pauses punctuate thought. Just as commas, semicolons, and periods separate written words into thought groups, so pauses of different lengths separate spoken words into meaningful units. The haphazard use of pauses when you are speaking or reading a speech from manuscript, therefore, is as confusing to the listener as the haphazard use of punctuation in printed matter is to the silent reader.

Be sure that your pauses come between thought units and not in the middle of them. Moreover, when reading a speech aloud remember that written and oral punctuation differ; not every comma calls for a pause, nor does the absence of punctuation always mean that no pause is required. In extemporaneous speaking, pauses tend to fall naturally between thought groups. Here, as in the read speech, however, it is important to set off one idea from another clearly and definitely.

Often a pause may be used for emphasis. Placed immediately after an important statement, it suggests to your audience, "Let this idea sink in." A pause before the climax of a story sometimes helps to increase suspense; a dramatic pause introduced at the proper moment may express the depth of your feeling more forcefully than words.

Many speakers are afraid to pause. Fearing they will forget what they want to say or that silence will focus attention on them personally, they rush on with a stream of words or vaguely vocalize the pause with *and-er-ah.* These random and meaningless syllables not only draw attention away from the ideas being expressed, but also are extremely annoying to the listener. Remember that a pause seldom seems as long to the audience as it does to the speaker and that the ability to pause for emphasis or clarity is an indication of poise and self-control. Do not be afraid to pause whenever a break in utterance will help clarify an idea or emphasize an important point. Concentrate on the thought or emotion you are trying to convey and let your voice respond accordingly. But above all, when you do stop, stop completely; do not fill in the gap with *er, uh,* or *um.* These intrusive vocalizations defeat entirely the purpose of a pause.

Force

As we already have suggested, it is a basic responsibility of any speaker to use adequate vocal force—to talk loudly enough to be heard easily. A certain amount of force also is needed, however, if the speaker is to give an impression of confidence and vigor. Talking too softly suggests that you are not sure of yourself or that you do not believe deeply in what you are saying. On the other hand, continuous shouting wears out an audience and dissipates attention. With force, as with rate, variety should be your guiding consideration.

The force with which you speak may be varied either in degree or in form. *Degree* refers to the *amount* of force applied: a whisper or an undertone is uttered with a low degree of force; a shout with a high degree. *Form,* on the other hand, refers to the *manner* in which force is applied: whether abruptly and explosively, or with a gradual swell. The relative amount of force applied to different syllables in a word, or to different words in a phrase, is called *stress.* Stress, of course, also is obtained by a change of pitch or rate. But since stressing a sound usually makes it louder, we may conveniently consider stress as a third type of force variation.

Degree. Force is varied in degree primarily in order to gain emphasis. Either by increasing the loudness of a word or phrase or by pointedly reducing its loudness, you may make that word or phrase stand out as if it had been underscored. Moreover, changing the degree of force is an effective way to reawaken lagging interest. A drowsy audience will sit up quickly if you suddenly project an important word or phrase with sharply increased energy. Remember, however, that the effect is produced not so much by the force itself as by the *change* in degree; a sharp reduction may be quite as effective as a sharp increase.

While you are practicing to develop variety in force, observe what happens to the pitch and quality of your voice. The natural tendency for most speakers is to raise their pitch when they try to increase their loudness; you probably have noticed that when you shout, your voice is keyed much higher than when you speak in a conversational tone. This happens because the nerves which control the speaking mechanism tend to diffuse their impulses to all of the muscles involved, and the resulting general tension is likely to produce a higher pitch as well as more force. Sometimes this tension is so great that it creates a harsh quality at the same time. A little practice, however, will enable you to overcome this tendency. Just as you have learned to wiggle one finger without moving the others or to wink one eye without the other, so you can learn to apply force by contracting the breathing muscles without tightening the muscles of the throat and thus unnecessarily raising the pitch of your voice. A good way to begin is by repeating a sentence such as "That is absolutely *true!*" Hit the last word in the sentence with a greater degree of force and at the same time lower your pitch. When you are able to do this, say the entire sentence louder, and LOUDER, and *LOUDER*, until you can shout it without your pitch going up, too. As you practice, sustain the tone, use a long quantity, and try to maintain a full resonance. By learning to control the force of your voice, you will do much to make your speaking more emphatic and to convey to your audience an impression of power in reserve.

Form. The manner, or form, in which force is applied generally indicates the underlying attitudes or sentiments of the speaker. If force is applied gradually and firmly, in what is called the *effusive* form, it suggests deep but controlled sentiment; generally, effusive force is used to express grandeur, dignity, reverence, and similar attitudinal qualities. When the *expulsive* form is used, force is applied firmly but more rapidly and energetically; this form is used to express decisiveness, vigor, and earnestness. Sudden or *explosive* force suggests violent or uncontrolled feeling; it is associated with extreme anger, sudden fear, or other strong emotions that burst out abruptly.

Obviously, the form of force one uses is closely related to the quantity or duration of the words spoken. The effusive form, for example, demands longer quantity than the explosive form. Thus the elements of quantity and force combine in the expression of feeling. Here again, to acquire skill in expressing feelings through the different forms of force, practice reading aloud passages of prose or poetry laden with these feelings, first absorbing the mental attitudes and then giving free play to their expression. The selections at the end of the chapter will be useful for this practice, and your instructor can give you helpful criticism and advice. Only by a certain amount of conscious drill can you develop sufficient flexibility and control over your voice to provide these feelings with a free and appropriate means of expression. Remember, however, that the form of force you use should be the natural response to an inner feeling; sheer vocal manipulation is bound to sound artificial and hollow.

Stress. To be understood, a word must be accented correctly and according to accepted standards of pronunciation. Consider the change of meaning produced by shifting the stress from one syllable to the other in the word *content.* The rules of stress, however, are by no means inflexible when words are used in connected speech. Emphasis and contrast often require the shifting of stress for the sake of greater clarity. For example, notice what you do to the accent in the word *proceed* when you use it in this sentence: "I said to proceed, not to recede." Many words change considerably in sound when they are stressed; especially is this true of short words such as pronouns, articles, and prepositions. If you are speaking normally, you will say, "I gave 'im th' book." But if you stress the third word, or the fourth one, you will say, "I gave *him* th' book," or "I gave 'im *the* book." In short, the requirements of contrast and emphasis, as well as the conventional rules of accent, influence the placing of stress in words.

Pitch

Just as singers' voices differ, some being soprano or tenor and others contralto or bass, so do people in general vary in the normal pitch level at which they speak. Except when you are impersonating a character to embellish a story or an anecdote, it is best to talk in your normal pitch range; otherwise there is danger of straining your voice. Fortunately, you will find that there is considerable latitude within your normal range. In fact, few beginning speakers take advantage of the possibilities their normal range offers; instead, they tend to hit one level and stay there. Nothing improves the animation and vivacity of speech so much as effective pitch variation. At this point, therefore, we shall discuss not only the *key,* or general level of pitch, but also changes in pitch—both the abrupt changes called *steps,* and the gradual changes called *slides.* We will note, too, how *melody patterns* emerge from these variations.

Key. The general pitch level, or key of the voice, varies considerably from person to person. Nearly everyone, however, can easily span an octave, and many people have voices flexible enough to vary more than two octaves without strain. Within this range, the key-level at which you habitually speak may create a very definite impression of you as a person. Ordinarily, a pitch that is continuously high suggests weakness, excitement, irritation, or extreme youth, while a lower key-level suggests assurance, poise, and strength. For this reason, your customary pitch normally should be in the lower half of your natural range. In particular, be careful, when you are applying increasing degrees of force, not to let your voice get out of control, going to a higher and higher key until it cracks under the strain. If you feel tension, pause for a moment and lower your pitch. At times, of course, you will be excited, and your voice naturally will rise to a high key to match your emotion. Remember, however, that a somewhat restrained emotion makes a more favorable impression on an audience than does emotion which has gone completely out of control.

Steps and slides. In connected speech, pitch is, as we have suggested, changed in two ways: by steps and by slides. For example, suppose someone has made a statement with which you agree and that you answer by saying, "You're exactly right!" The chances are that you will say it something like this:

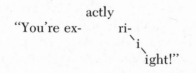

actly
"You're ex- ri-
i
ight!"

Notice that a complete break in pitch level occurs between the first and second syllables of the word *exactly.* This abrupt change in pitch is what we mean by a *step.* On the word *right,* however, a more gradual pitch inflection accompanies the production of the sound. Such a continuous change of pitch within a syllable is a *slide.* Both steps and slides may go upward or downward, depending on the meaning intended. Slides also may be double, the pitch going up and then down or vice versa, as when one says,

o
o o
"O oh!"

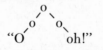

to express the meaning, "I didn't realize that!"

In general, an upward step or slide suggests interrogation, indecision, uncertainty, doubt, or suspense, while a downward inflection suggests firmness, determination, certainty, finality, or confidence. Thus if you were to say, "What shall we do about it? Just this . . . ," a rising inflection on the question would create suspense, while a downward inflection on the last phrase would indicate the certainty with which you were presenting your answer. A double inflection, as indicated by the example above, suggests a subtle conflict or contradiction of meaning, and is frequently used to express irony or sarcasm, or to convey innuendo. Steps and slides are primarily useful in carrying thought content rather than in expressing emotional tone or color. By mastering their use, you will be able to make your meaning clearer and more precise.

All this does not mean that when you arise to speak you should say to yourself: "This sentence requires an upward inflection," or "I shall use a step between these two words and a slide on that one." Such concentration on the mechanics of utterance would destroy communicative contact with your audience. Rather, in private and in class exercises, practice reading aloud selected passages which require pitch inflection, until the habit of flexibility grows on you. Then, when you speak in public your voice will respond more or less automatically to the ideas and moods you wish to convey.

Melody patterns. In all kinds of speech the rhythm and swing of phrase and sentence weave themselves into a continuous pattern of changing pitch. As the thought or mood changes, this melodic pattern changes also. The use of a monotonous melody pattern, however, is just as deadly as staying in one key all of the time. Beware, therefore, of seesawing back and forth in a singsong voice. Avoid also the tendency of many inexperienced speakers to end every sentence with an upward inflection. Assertions tend to become questions when so uttered, and you may sound doubtful even though you feel certain. A downward inflection at the close of each sentence is almost as bad, for it suggests an intolerance or dogmatism to which most listeners react unfavorably. If you can develop flexibility of pitch inflection, your melody pattern normally will adjust itself to the thought and mood you intend to express. Be careful, however, not to get into a vocal rut, unconsciously using the same pattern for everything you say.

Emphasis

Obviously, all forms of vocal variety help provide emphasis. Any change of rate, or of force, or of pitch serves to make the word, phrase, or sentence in which the change occurs stand out from those which precede or follow it. This is true regardless of the direction of the change; whether the rate or force is increased or decreased, whether the pitch is raised or lowered, emphasis will result. And the greater the amount of change or the more suddenly it is effected, the more emphatic will the statement be. Furthermore, emphasis is increased by pause and contrast: a pause allows the audience to get set for or to think over an important idea; contrast makes the idea seem more important than it otherwise would.

Two warnings, however, should be given: avoid *over*emphasis, and avoid *continuous* emphasis. If you emphasize a point beyond its true value or importance, your audience will lose faith in your judgment; if you attempt to emphasize everything, nothing will stand out. Be judicious. Pick out the ideas that are really important and give them the emphasis they deserve.

Vocal climax

Frequently a speaker expresses a thought or feeling that rises steadily in power until it reaches a point where the strongest appeal is made. Such climaxes of thought or feeling require climactic use of vocal expression. Roughly, there are two methods of expressing vocal climax. The first involves increased vocal power; the second, decreased vocal power coupled with increased feeling or emotion. The first method requires that each successive thought unit, whether it be a word, phrase, or sentence, be said with a successive increase in force, with a more rapid rate, with a higher level of pitch, or with any combination of these changes. When the second method is used, the force is successively decreased, the rate slowed down, or the pitch lowered; but coupled with these changes is an increasing intensity of feeling expressed by the speaker's movements, gestures, facial expression, and by the emotion evident in his voice. Notice that the second method involves much more than merely letting the voice run down; the power is there, but it is kept under control—the audience is made to sense the tremendous strength of feeling which the speaker is holding in check. The first method is easier and more frequently used; the second requires more skill but is often more effective.

There are times when these two types of climactic emphasis may be combined or contrasted. The speaker may build a climax of vocal power and then swing rapidly and positively into one of emotional intensity; or he may show an increased intensity of controlled emotion followed by a climax of vocal power. When such a shift of direction is motivated by genuine feeling and enough time is allowed to develop the climactic movement in each direction, the contrasting swing gives an added momentum to the second climax that can rarely be achieved by moving in one direction alone. You must be careful if you use this method, however, not to make the shift too sudden or the climactic "climb" too short. Give the climax time enough to build, and keep it building steadily.

Some immature speakers attempt too many climaxes in a single speech. As a result, the effect of climax is lost by repetition. One good climax has more power to move an audience than several mediocre ones, and frequently even more than several consecutive good ones. Save your vocal climaxes for the places where they will be most effective, usually near the end of the speech or at the ends of major thought units.

Beware also of anticlimax. When successive stages of climactic power begin to follow one another, audiences expect them to continue until the peak of interest has been reached. If before the true climax of thought or feeling is attained, the added increments of vocal power begin to lessen or the climactic movement stops, the audience feels let down. Start slowly enough, or quietly enough, or at a low enough level of pitch, so that you can keep on building until the high point in composition has been reached. Furthermore, after a vigorous and effective climax has been attained, pause or shift your manner of speaking and your mood completely. Above all, don't say the same thing over in a cooler or less impassioned way.

The effective use of vocal climaxes requires considerable skill. To develop this skill, select climactic passages from the speeches of great speakers and practice reading them aloud or speaking them from memory. Digest the meaning and the mood of the passage before you begin to speak, in order to get the feel of it; then use all the power and control you have to communicate the passage effectively.

IMPORTANCE OF PRACTICE

In this chapter we have suggested ways in which you can make your speech more intelligible and have reviewed the standard of pronunciation to which you should adhere. In addition, we have pointed out the importance of having a voice that is flexible as well as clear, and have shown how flexibility depends upon a proper use of rate, force, pitch, and emphasis. Do not assume that you will be able to master in a day or a week all of the vocal skills that have been described. Take time to review and digest the ideas presented; above all, practice the exercises which are given in the following pages. Return to these exercises again and again, even after you have mastered them, so that your skills will not become rusty through disuse. Remember that any vocal skill, before it can be natural and effective with an audience, must be so much a habit that you are able to forget about it completely when you stand up to speak.

Exercises

TO TEST THE INTELLIGIBILITY OF YOUR SPEECH

1. The following lists of phonetically balanced words are taken from tests constructed by the Psycho-Acoustic Laboratory of Harvard University.[4] They may be used in class to test whether your speech is intelligible to others. Your scores will not be so accurate as if these tests were conducted under scientifically controlled conditions, but they will provide a measure of the relative intelligibility of your speech as compared with your classmates' and will show you what happens under various conditions. Proceed with the test as described on pages 100-101.

A		B		C	
bat	muff	at	muss	aid	map
beau	mush	barn	news	barge	nap
change	my	bust	nick	book	next
climb	nag	car	nod	cheese	part
corn	nice	clip	oft	cliff	pitch
curb	nip	coax	prude	closed	pump
deaf	ought	curve	purge	crews	rock
dog	owe	cute	quack	dame	rogue
elk	patch	darn	rid	din	rug
elm	pelt	dash	shook	drape	rye
few	plead	dead	shrug	droop	sang
fill	price	douse	sing	dub	sheep
fold	pug	dung	slab	fifth	sheik
for	scuff	fife	smite	fright	soar
gem	side	foam	soil	gab	stab
grape	sled	grate	stuff	gas	stress
grave	smash	group	tell	had	suit
hack	smooth	heat	tent	hash	thou
hate	soap	howl	thy	hose	three
hook	stead	hunk	tray	ink	thresh
jig	taint	isle	vague	kind	tire
made	tap	kick	vote	knee	ton
mood	thin	lathe	wag	lay	tuck
mop	tip	life	waif	leash	turn
moth	wean	me	wrist	louse	wield

[4]Printed also in *Hearing and Deafness* by Hallowell Davis, pp. 475-476.

D		E		F	
awe	nab	ache	muck	bath	neat
bait	need	air	neck	beast	new
bean	niece	bald	nest	bee	oils
blush	nut	barb	oak	blonde	or
bought	our	bead	path	budge	peck
bounce	perk	cape	please	bus	pert
bud	pick	cast	pulse	bush	pinch
charge	pit	check	rate	cloak	pod
cloud	quart	class	rouse	course	race
corpse	rap	crave	shout	court	rack
dab	rib	crime	sit	dodge	rave
earl	scythe	deck	size	dupe	raw
else	shoe	dig	sob	earn	rut
fate	sludge	dill	sped	eel	sage
five	snuff	drop	stag	fin	scab
frog	start	fame	take	float	shed
gill	suck	far	thrash	frown	shin
gloss	tan	fig	toil	hatch	sketch
hire	tang	flush	trip	heed	slap
hit	them	gnaw	turf	hiss	sour
hock	trash	hurl	vow	hot	starve
job	vamp	jam	wedge	how	strap
log	vast	law	wharf	kite	test
moose	ways	leave	who	merge	tick
mute	wish	lush	why	move	touch

a. Choose one of the fifty-word lists above and rearrange the words on a sheet of paper in some different and random order. (Subsequent students should use different lists to avoid immediate repetition.)

b. Stand in a corner of the room with your back to the class and read aloud one word at a time, saying, "Number one is——." Then pause long enough for your classmates to write it down (3-5 seconds) before going to the next word.

c. The rest of the students will write down in a numbered column the words they understood you to have said.

d. To determine your score, add together the number of words understood correctly by each listener and divide this total by the number of listeners times fifty (the number of words spoken); the result will be your percentage of intelligibility on this test.[5]

[5]Dr. Davis says, "It is a very convenient property of these lists that the volume at which 50% of the words is correctly understood is a little above that at which we can easily understand ordinary connected speech." *Ibid.*, p. 151.

e. Repeat this test, using a different list, under each of the following conditions:

1) Listeners' ears plugged with cotton (in order to simulate distance).

2) Relatively loud phonograph music playing while the list is read.

2. A somewhat more difficult test may be conducted in a manner similar to that described in Problem 1 with the word series listed below.[6] Listeners should keep their books closed while listening to the speaker and writing down the words they understand him to say. In this test the speaker should read four words consecutively—long pause; read four more—long pause; etc., until he has completed one of the series. Score as in Problem 1.

a. Three, flap, switch, will——resume, cold, pilot, wind——chase, blue, search, flight——mine, area, cleared, left.

b. Iron, fire, task, try——up, six, seven, wait——slip, turn, read, clear——blue, this, even, is.

c. Nan, flak, timer, two——course, black, when, leave——raise, clear, tree, seven——search, strike, there, cover.

d. List, service, ten, foul——wire, last, wish, truce——power, one, ease, will——teeth, hobby, trill, wind.

e. Flight, spray, blind, base——ground, fog, ceiling, flame——target, flare, gear, low——slow, course, code, scout.

f. Tall, plot, find, deep——climb, fall, each, believe——wing, strip, clean, field——when, chase, search, select.

g. Climb, switch, over, when——this, turn, gear, spray——black, flare, is, free——runway, three, off, red.

h. Thing, touch, marker, sleeve——find, top, leave, winter——skip, free, have, beach——meet, aid, send, lash.

i. Try, over, six, craft——green, victor, yellow, out——trim, X-ray, ramp, up——speed, like, believe, sender.

j. Dim, trip, fire, marker——wave, green, rudder, field——climb, to, plot, middle——speed, like, straight, lower.

k. Smooth, mike, four, catch——strip, park, line, left——leg, wheel, turn, lift——time, baker, orange, look.

l. Wake, other, blue, been——size, wish, black, under——field, down, empty, what——ship, strip, land, fire.

m. Leg, on, strip, leave——ground, trip, plot, area——speed, blue, will, ramp——wheel, blind, sector, nan.

[6]From a test used by Gayland L. Draegert in an experiment reported in *Speech Monographs,* XIII, 50-53. With noise interference, military personnel averaged 38.2% of the words understood correctly in the initial test, and 46.3% after training. For scientific purposes, this test is not so accurate as the list in Problem 1 or a similar test developed by C. Hess Hagen at Waco, Texas, Voice Communication Laboratories, which is described in OSRD Report No. 5414, issued by the Office of Technical Services, Department of Commerce. For classroom purposes, however, it is sufficiently accurate for determining relative intelligibility among members of a group.

n. Tail, when, through, at——climb, off, tower, rain——time, gear, cloud, pass——loaf, three, crash, direction.

o. Station, left, reply, read——final, blue, field, out——wind, west, marker, fire——tower, ground, gear, time.

p. Sighted, toward, finder, search——red, blind, each, weather——tall, after, while, wide——close, hole, mark, signal.

q. Neat, warm, beam, where——side, leader, bell, map——view, face, trap, well——seem, feed, clutch, vine.

r. Circle, beach, up, that——port, even, catch, pad——reach, heat, break, safe——still, put, enter, iron.

s. Chamber, wait, hair, open——wind, keep, sector, free——light, home, take, will——base, eleven, headphone, by.

t. Service, flat, have, on——bay, wait, fade, cold——tire, horn, bill, sad——feel, cave, set, limit.

TO DEVELOP AN ADEQUATE DEGREE OF LOUDNESS AND SYLLABLE DURATION

3. Practice saying the words in the above lists with a voice loud enough—
   a. to be barely understood (score below 50%) in a quiet classroom.
   b. to be perfectly understood in a quiet classroom.
   c. to be understood in a quiet classroom with your listeners' ears plugged with cotton (to simulate distance).
   d. to be understood above the noise of two, three, or four other students who are all reading aloud from different pages of the textbook.
4. Practice saying the words in the lists above with varying degrees of syllable duration under the conditions listed in the problem above.
5. Devise variations of these conditions with whatever recording or public address systems are available to your class.
6. Prepare sentences requiring precise understanding of the component words and practice saying them with the loudness and syllable length required for:
   a. a small group in a small room
   b. a class in a fairly large lecture room
   c. an audience in your college auditorium
   d. a crowd in your football stadium

Here are a few sample sentences to use:

"Just ten minutes from now, go in single file to room 316."

"In 1985, the population of Panama may be one and two fifths what it was in 1948."

"Hemstitching can be done by machine operation, using strong thread."

"Oranges, nuts, vegetables, and cotton are raised on the Kingston ranch."

TO INCREASE DISTINCTNESS OF ARTICULATION

7. Stretch the muscles of articulation:

a. Stretch the mouth in as wide a grin as possible; open the mouth as wide as possible; pucker the lips and protrude them as far as possible.

b. Stretch out the tongue as far as possible; try to touch the tip of the nose and the chin with the tongue tip; beginning at the front teeth, run the tip of the tongue back, touching the palate as far back as the tongue will go.

8. With vigorous accent on the consonant sounds, repeat "pah, tah, kah" several times. Then vary the order, emphasizing first *pah,* then *tah,* then *kah.* In the same way, practice the series "ap, at, ak" and "apa, ata, aka." Work out additional combinations of this sort, using different combinations of consonants and vowels.

9. Experiments have shown that the words grouped in fours below are easily mistaken for one another under conditions of noise interference.[7] Practice articulating them distinctly and precisely. Then with your back to the class and with three or four other students creating a noise by reading aloud from the textbook at the same time, read down one column or across one row, choosing one word at random out of each four. Announce before you start which column or row you are going to read from, pause briefly after each word, and have other members of the class put a check by the word they understood you to say. (Used in this way, the following list is not an accurate *test* of intelligibility, but it should provide interesting material for practice.)

	A	B	C	D	E	F
1	system pistol distant piston	firm foam burn term	banner manner mother batter	puddle muddle muzzle puzzle	carve car tarred tired	offer author often office
2	heave heed ease eve	detain obtain attain maintain	scream screen green stream	porch torch scorch court	fable stable table able	cross cough cloth claw
3	roger rupture rapture obscure	pure poor tour two	petal battle meadow medal	vision bishop vicious season	bubble tumble stumble fumble	thrown drone prone groan

[7]Taken from answer sheets for standardized tests developed by C. Hess Haagen, printed in *Intelligibility Measurement: Twenty Four-Word Multiple Choice Tests,* OSRD Report No. 5567 (P.B. 12050), issued by the Office of Technical Services, Department of Commerce, p. 21.

	art	sponsor	game	cape	texture	eye
4	heart	spotter	gain	hate	lecture	high
	arch	ponder	gage	take	mixture	tie
	ark	plunder	gang	tape	rupture	hide
	comment	exact	made	process	glow	single
5	comic	retract	fade	protest	blow	jingle
	cannon	detract	vague	profess	below	cycle
	carbon	attack	may	possess	low	sprinkle
	bumper	cave	pier	divide	kitchen	baker
6	number	cake	pierce	devise	mission	major
	lumber	cage	fierce	define	friction	maker
	lover	case	spear	divine	fiction	banker
	gale	glamour	ward	leap	second	rich
7	jail	slimmer	wart	leaf	suction	ridge
	dale	swimmer	wash	lease	section	bridge
	bail	glimmer	war	leave	sexton	grip
	danger	enact	hold	crater	seaport	joy
8	feature	impact	old	traitor	keyboard	going
	nature	relax	ode	trainer	piecework	join
	major	intact	hoed	treasure	eastward	dawn

10. Make a list of as many tongue twisters as you can find and practice saying them rapidly and precisely. Here are a few short examples to start on:

a. She sells sea shells on the seashore.

b. National Shropshire Sheep Association.

c. "Are you copper-bottoming them, my man?" "No, I'm aluminuming 'em, mum."

d. He sawed six long, slim, sleek, slender saplings.

e. Dick twirled the stick athwart the path.

f. Rubber baby-buggy bumpers.

g. "B—A, Ba; B—E, Be;
B—I, Bi; Ba Be Bi;
B—O, Bo; Ba Be Bi Bo;
B—U, Bu; Ba Be Bi Bo Bu!"

11. Read the following passages aloud in a distinct and lively fashion; move the tongue, jaw, lips, etc., with energy:

To sit in solemn silence in a dull, dark dock
In a pestilential prison, with a lifelong lock,
Awaiting the sensation of a short, sharp shock,
From a cheap and chippy chopper on a big black block!

Gilbert and Sullivan

"You are old," said the youth, "and your jaws are too weak
  For anything tougher than suet;
Yet you finished the goose, with the bones and the beak—
  Pray, how did you manage to do it?"
"In my youth," said his father, "I took to the law,
  And argued each case with my wife;
And the muscular strength which it gave to my jaw
  Has lasted the rest of my life."

Lewis Carroll

  How does the water
Come down to Lodore?
  My little boy ask'd me
  Thus, once on a time;
And moreover he ask'd me
To tell him in rime.

  The cataract strong
  Then plunges along,
  Striking and raging
  As if a war waging
Its caverns and rocks among;
  Rising and leaping,
  Sinking and creeping,
  Swelling and sweeping,
Showering and springing,
  Flying and flinging,
  Writhing and whisking,
  Spouting and frisking,
  Turning and twisting,
  Around and around . . .

And rushing and flushing and brushing and gushing,
And flapping and rapping and clapping and slapping,
And curling and whirling and purling and twirling,
And thumping and plumping and bumping and jumping;
And dashing and flashing and splashing and clashing;

And so never ending, but always descending,
Sounds and motion forever are blending,
All at once and all o'er, with a mighty uproar,
And this way the water comes down at Lodore.

Robert Southey

TO ENCOURAGE ACCEPTABLE PRONUNCIATION

12. Make a list of words which you have heard pronounced in more than one way. Look them up in the dictionary and come to class prepared to defend your agreement or disagreement with the dictionary pronunciation. Here are a few words on which to start:

abdomen	creek	gauge	indict	route
acclimated	data	gesture	inquiry	theatre
advertisement	deficit	grievous	recess	thresh
alias	drowned	humble	research	vagary
bona fide	forehead	idea	roof	yacht

PASSAGES WHICH REQUIRE CAREFUL SPEECH TO CONVEY THEIR MEANING

13. The whole meaning of each of the passages below depends on a clear understanding of the words and phrases used in it. Be sure you understand the significance of an entire passage before you begin practice on it. Practice reading it as you would before a small, quiet audience; then as you would need to do if the audience were large or there were considerable noise interference. Remember that *exaggerated* precision, loudness, syllable duration, etc., beyond the amount clearly required for easy intelligibility under the actual situation will sound artificial and is not good speech. (In a similar way, practice again the passages at the end of Chapter 5.)

from THE WAR SONG OF THE SARACENS[8]

We are they who come faster than fate: we are they who ride early or late:
We storm at your ivory gate: Pale Kings of the Sunset, beware!
Not on silk nor in samet we lie, not in curtained solemnity die
Among women who chatter and cry, and children who mumble a prayer.
But we sleep by the ropes of the camp, and we rise with a shout, and we tramp
With the sun or the moon for a lamp, and the spray of the wind in our hair.

James Elroy Flecker

from ESSAY ON SELF-RELIANCE

A foolish consistency is the hobgoblin of little minds, adored by little statesmen and philosophers and divines. With consistency a great soul has simply

[8]From *Collected Poems* by James Elroy Flecker. Reprinted by special permission of Martin Secker & Warburg, Ltd., London.

nothing to do. He may as well concern himself with his shadow on the wall. Speak what you think now in hard words and tomorrow speak what tomorrow thinks in hard words again, though it contradict everything you said today—"Ah, so you shall be sure to be misunderstood."—Is it so bad, then, to be misunderstood? Pythagoras was misunderstood, and Socrates, and Jesus, and Luther, and Copernicus, and Galileo, and Newton, and every pure and wise spirit that ever took flesh. To be great is to be misunderstood.

Emerson

from THE SEA AROUND US[9]

For the sea as a whole, the alternation of day and night, the passage of the seasons, the procession of the years, are lost in its vastness, obliterated in its own changeless eternity. But the surface waters are different. The face of the sea is always changing. Crossed by colors, lights, and moving shadows, sparkling in the sun, mysterious in the twilight, its aspects and its moods vary hour by hour. The surface waters move with the tides, stir to the breath of the winds, and rise and fall to the endless, hurrying forms of the waves. Most of all, they change with the advance of the seasons. Spring moves over the temperate lands of our Northern Hemisphere in a tide of new life, of pushing green shoots and unfolding buds, all its mysteries and meanings symbolized in the northward migration of the birds, the awakening of sluggish amphibian life as the chorus of frogs rises again from the wet lands, the different sound of the wind which stirs the young leaves where a month ago it rattled the bare branches. These things we associate with the land, and it is easy to suppose that at sea there could be no such feeling of advancing spring. But the signs are there, and seen with understanding eye, they bring the same magical sense of awakening.

Rachel L. Carson

Problems

1. Make a set of drawings which show the positions of the various parts of the articulating mechanism—tongue, lips, jaw, and soft palate—in the production of different vowel and consonant sounds. (Consult such books as Giles W. Gray and C. M. Wise, *The Bases of Speech,* 3rd ed. [New York: Harpers', 1959] and Ida C. Ward, *The Phonetics of English* [Cambridge, England: Heffner, 1939] for diagrams from which to work.)

2. Rate one of your friends or professors on the intelligibility of his speech. Pay particular attention to the factors of intelligibility mentioned in this chapter: allover level of loudness, distinctness of articulation, etc. Which factors do you think are particularly important in accounting for the fact that this person's speech is or is not readily intelligible?

[9]Rachel Carson, *The Sea Around Us,* Oxford University Press, 1961, pp. 28-29.

3. Do you know anyone whose speech is easily intelligible but also dull and colorless? What would you say causes this lack of color? Is it principally due to the absence of variation in pitch, to poor emphasis, or to some other factor?
4. Make a list of all of the methods you can think of for emphasizing an important idea through the use of the voice. Compare your list with those drawn up by the other members of the class.
5. A good dictionary always contains as part of its front matter an explanation of the principles followed in determining the pronunciations it records. Study the explanations contained in several of these dictionaries and write a short paper reporting your findings.
6. Observe critically the speech patterns of someone whom you would consider a good speaker—a radio or television announcer, a minister, a professional lecturer, etc. What use does this individual make of the "vocal fundamentals" of rate, force, and pitch to convey ideas and emotions to his listeners? To what extent is his speaking effectiveness dependent upon how he uses his voice rather than on his bodily delivery or his ideas and arguments? Is there any way in which his vocal delivery could be improved? Would some of the technics he employs be good ones for you to use also? Why or why not?

Speaking assignments

1. Let selected members of the class present a series of oral reports dealing with the general subject of Regional Variations in American English. (One student may discuss Southern speech, another General American, etc.) In building each report consider word selection and usage as well as the characteristic pronunciation pattern. Employ maps and diagrams to show the various speech areas, sound positions, and the like. Your instructor will suggest appropriate sources of information; or you may consult such a book as Charles Kenneth Thomas, *An Introduction to the Phonetics of American English* (New York: Ronald, 1947), Chapters XXI and XXII.
2. Present a short lecture-recital built around several of the poems or prose selections included in the exercises at the end of this chapter (or similar ones). Choose poems or selections which together develop a common theme or idea. Work out suitable introductory and transitional remarks, and also an appropriate conclusion. In reading each poem or selection, vary your rate, force, and pitch so as to express as fully as possible the meaning and mood intended by the author. In addition, pay particular attention to the intelligibility of your speech.

Suggestions for further reading

David W. Addington, "The Effect of Mispronunciations on General Speaking Effectiveness," *Speech Monographs*, XXXII (June 1965), 159-163.

Virgil L. Baker and Ralph T. Eubanks, *Speech in Personal and Public Affairs* (New York: David McKay Co., Inc., 1965), Chapter XX, "Speech Manuscript Reading."

John W. Black, "Speech Intelligibility: A Summary of Recent Research," *Journal of Communication,* XI (June 1961), 87-94.

John W. Black and G. C. Tolhurst, "The Relative Intelligibility of Language Groups," *Quarterly Journal of Speech,* XLI (February 1955), 57-60.

Arthur J. Bronstein, *The Pronunciation of American English* (New York: Appleton-Century-Crofts, 1960).

Charles F. Diehl, Richard C. White, and Kenneth W. Burk, "Rate and Communication," *Speech Monographs,* XXVI (August 1959), 229-232.

Ray Ehrensberger, "An Experimental Study of the Relative Effectiveness of Certain Forms of Emphasis in Public Speaking," *Speech Monographs,* XII (1945), 94-111.

Grant Fairbanks, *Voice and Articulation Drillbook,* 2nd ed. (New York: Harper & Row, Publishers, 1960).

Herbert W. Hildebrandt and Walter W. Stevens, "Manuscript and Extemporaneous Delivery in Communicating Information," *Speech Monographs,* XXX (November 1963), 369-372.

Ralph R. Leutenegger, *The Sounds of American English: An Introduction to Phonetics* (Glenview, Illinois: Scott, Foresman and Company, 1963).

C. K. Thomas, *Handbook of Speech Improvement* (New York: The Ronald Press Company, 1956).

Gordon L. Thomas, "Oral Style and Intelligibility," *Speech Monographs,* XXIII (March 1956), 46-54.

Mark Twomey, "Attitudes of Americans Toward Pronunciation," *Speech Teacher,* XII (September 1963), 204-213.

PART THREE

PREPARING THE SPEECH

CHAPTER SEVEN

Determining the subject and the purpose of a speech

In Chapter 3 we discussed briefly the seven essential steps in speech preparation: (1) selecting and narrowing the subject, (2) determining the purpose, (3) analyzing the audience and the occasion, (4) gathering material, (5) making an outline, (6) wording the speech, and (7) practicing aloud. In this chapter and in the twelve that follow we shall discuss these steps in greater detail and also consider other matters which the speaker must keep in mind when preparing a talk.

To begin with, we return to the initial problem of selecting a suitable subject and determining the response that is to be sought from the audience.

THE SUBJECT

Beginning speakers frequently experience great difficulty in selecting a suitable speech subject. Sometimes they choose a topic on which they have no background of knowledge or experience; often they select a subject without due attention to the needs and interests of their audience or to the amount of time necessary to develop it adequately. To avoid these mistakes and to make the selection process more direct and systematic, observe the following guidelines:

Select a subject about which you already know something and can find out more. In speech, as elsewhere, there is no substitute for knowledge that is thorough and authoritative.

Select a subject that is interesting to you. If you are not interested in what you are talking about, you will find preparation a dull task, and your speaking is likely to be listless and ineffective.

Select a subject that will interest your audience. The more interest your listeners already have in the subject, the less you will have to worry about holding their attention when you speak. A subject may be interesting to an audience for one or more of the following reasons:

1. It vitally concerns their health, happiness, prosperity, or security.
2. It offers a solution to a recognized problem.
3. It is new or timely.
4. There is conflict of opinion concerning it.

Select a subject that is neither above nor below the intellectual capacity of the audience. A talk about the value of a savings account in the local bank would be appropriate for an audience of grade school children, but a discussion of the complex workings of the Federal Reserve System would not. On the other hand, do not underestimate the knowledge or capacity of your listeners by selecting a subject that makes you seem to be talking down to them.

Select a subject that you can discuss adequately in the time at your disposal. In a five-minute speech, do not attempt to discuss "The Causes and Results of the Russian Revolution." Instead, describe the organization of a typical collective farm or explain the role of Lenin in bringing the Revolution to reality.

Even though you are assigned a subject, you may still need to limit it, to select some aspect of the topic that you can discuss effectively within the time limits you have been given.

THE TITLE

Closely related to the subject of the speech is its *title.* The subject identifies the content of the speech: the problem to be discussed, the objects or activities to be described. The title is the specific label given to the talk—usually announced by the chairman—for the purpose of arousing the audience's interest. Hence, it is a sort of advertising slogan—a catchword, phrase, or brief statement which epitomizes the subject and spirit of the speech in an attractive or provocative form. When Ernest A. Jones, president of MacManus, John & Adams, Inc., discussed the effects of advertising techniques on modern man, he titled his speech "The Man with the Split-Level Head." A college orator, deploring the lack of personal interaction between teachers and students, called her speech "Walking Wounded." Another student, insisting that equality must encompass *all* areas of our society—personal as well as economic and political—

chose the title "What Color Is Justice?" A third labeled his denunciation of the tendency to condone successful crime "The Eleventh Commandment."

What, then, are the requirements of a good title? There are at least three: it should be *relevant;* it should be *provocative;* it should be *brief.* To be relevant, a title must be pertinent to the subject or to some part of the speaker's discussion of the subject. The relevancy of the title "The Eleventh Commandment" was made clear when the speaker pointed out that the commandments "Thou shalt not steal" and "Thou shalt not kill" had been supplemented by a new one, the eleventh, "Thou shalt get away with it." In this example, notice that while the title was not a prosaic statement of the subject, it clearly was pertinent to the idea the speaker sought to convey. People do not like to be misled by a speaker's title any more than they enjoy false advertising.

To be provocative, a title should make the audience sit up and listen. Sometimes the subject of the speech is of such compelling interest that a mere statement of that subject is provocative enough. In most instances, however, the speaker must find a more vivid or unusual phrasing. Of course, care must be taken not to give away the entire content or message of the speech in the title, to provide too much advance information. Especially if the audience is hostile to his purpose, the speaker must avoid wording his title in such a way as to make that purpose too obvious. To entitle a speech for a fraternity group "Why Fraternities Should Be Abolished" is provocative enough, but undiplomatic in the extreme.

Finally, the title of a speech should be brief and simple. Imagine the effect of announcing as a title, "The Effects on Non-Target Classmates of a Deviant Student's Power and Response to a Teacher-Exerted Technique." Such a title can only be excused when the discussion is a technical one to be presented before a professional audience that has a specialized interest in the subject. Here the precise denotation of the subject matter may be important. Even so, the title should be as short and as quickly comprehensible as possible.

Usually the phrasing of the title can best be left until the speech has been completely built. To devise a title that is both relevant and provocative will be much easier after the central ideas of the talk are developed. The phrasing of titles has been discussed in this chapter because of its close relation to the subject and purpose of the speech and not because it is to be settled early in the process of speech preparation.

Regardless of the subject or title, the aim of every speech is *to get a reaction from the audience.* This purpose must never be lost sight of, for it lies at the basis of the entire process of speech preparation and leads directly to the question: What different *kinds* of reactions may a speaker seek from his hearers?

THE GENERAL ENDS OF SPEECH

There can be no doubt that the reaction sought by the after-dinner speaker at a social banquet differs materially from that sought by a legislator urging the adoption of a bill, or that both of these desired responses differ from the response a college professor seeks when he addresses a class. The first speaker wants his audience to *enjoy* themselves; the second wants them to *act,* to vote "aye"; the third wants them to *understand.*

Writers on practical speaking, from the classical period to the present, have grouped speech purposes into a few fairly definite types, and for the last two centuries have classified them according to the kind of reaction the speaker seeks from his listeners. Many such classifications, varying in scope and detail, have been used. The following one, listing five general ends of speech, will be found quite usable:

THE FIVE GENERAL ENDS OF SPEECH

General End	*Reaction Sought*	*Class of Speech*
1. To Entertain.	Interest and Enjoyment	Recreative
2. To Inform.	Clear Understanding	Instructive
3. To Convince.	Belief (intellectual agreement)	Persuasive
4. To Stimulate.	Inspiration (emotional arousal)	Persuasive
5. To Actuate.	Definite Observable Action	Persuasive

A general end, as the term is used here, denotes the broad category or type of audience response which a speaker desires. Merely because your purpose falls within one of the five general ends, however, it does not always follow that you will be unconcerned with the others. You will sometimes need to entertain during a speech to inform; you usually must inform in order to secure belief; and you will need to convince or stimulate in order to win a response of action. But one of these five general ends will be your major objective, and the others only contributory. For this reason you must take care that the contributory purposes do not detract from the central objective of the speech—that they are included only when they advance the principal aim, and only to the extent that they do so. The following discussion treats each general end in its capacity as a *primary* aim.

To entertain

The general end of your speech will be to entertain when your chief concern is to cause your audience to enjoy themselves. This is a frequent purpose of after-dinner speeches, but is by no means limited to such speeches. Although the popular travel lecturer, for example, may present informative material of a striking and unusual character, his primary aim is to entertain his audience; if he creates an understanding of the subject, it is contributory to his larger objective. There are, in fact, many occasions when your legitimate object in speaking is to generate enjoyment and delight for your audience, to afford them pleasure, to give them "a good time." On these occasions you may depend chiefly on humor, or you may merely present interesting anecdotes or curious bits of information. In any event, avoid heavy discussion and controversial issues; and if you do present facts and figures, offer them in a verbal setting or context that is unique and exceptional, something unlikely to be anticipated by your listeners. Always, in achieving a desired goal in speaking, you will find that vividness and originality of statement will play an important part; but in speaking to entertain, they take on added significance.

To inform

More than ever before—in this age of electronics, automation, and increasingly complex technologies of all kinds—we are under compulsion to inform and to be informed. When, as a speaker, you try to clarify a concept or a process for your audience, when you endeavor to define terms and relationships, or strive in other ways to widen the range of your auditors' knowledge, the object of your speech will be to inform. This is the purpose of the foreman who is showing a workman how to operate a new machine, of the teacher lecturing to his class, or of the county farm agent explaining the results of tests carried on at an agricultural experiment station. What has been said, however, does not mean that clear explanation is useful only in a speech to inform. In a speech to convince, for example, a speaker can rarely persuade his audience to believe a proposition until he has first made the proposition completely clear to them. But in a speech in which the speaker aims to inform, he does not want to urge any particular belief or advise any particular action; his purpose is only to have his audience understand and to provide them with the information needed for this understanding. To achieve this end, he must relate his ideas to the existing knowledge of his listeners; he must be sure that the structure of his speech is clear in order to encourage greater retention of the information by his listeners; and he must present an abundance of concrete examples and specific data so that his leading ideas will be clear, colorful, and timely.

To convince

The general end of your speech will be to convince when your purpose is to influence or alter the beliefs or attitudes of your audience. Many speeches have this as their general end. Political speakers urge their constituents to believe in the platforms and performances of their respective parties; attempts are made to create belief in the superiority of certain products, principles, or forms of government; philosophical hypotheses are debated pro and con. But in all these cases, if the general end is only *to convince* (and not to actuate through conviction), no overt act or performance is requested of the audience. They are merely asked to agree with the speaker.

Many times, in fact, listeners are incapable of taking definite action because the authority for action lies with some other person or group. But they can form opinions by which to judge and sometimes change the actions of those who are in authority. For example, a great many public speeches are made to the electorate, even in non-election years, about the foreign policy of the administration. The actual authority for controlling this policy lies with the President and with Congress, yet speakers outside the administration attempt to influence the beliefs of the ordinary citizen. Why? Because these beliefs, through the influence they can exert upon public opinion, ultimately will affect the government's foreign policies and help shape the nation's future course of action abroad. The immediate purpose of the speakers, however, is not to prompt performance, not to gain action in the form of voting, but to win agreement in belief. Later, of course, the candidates for President and Congress will talk on these same subjects in an attempt to actuate—to urge, to impel people to exert a direct influence on foreign policy by voting in the fall elections. In the first case, the speaker's purpose is merely to convince the audience; in the second, to secure action based upon conviction.

The essential characteristic of a speech to convince is that it attempts to prove something; hence, it is usually filled with arguments supported with facts, figures, and examples. New situations are related to old beliefs, and evidence is presented to substantiate the speaker's assertions. In this way an attempt is made to establish or change the convictions of the audience.

To stimulate

Your general end will be to stimulate when you are trying to inspire, to arouse enthusiasm, or to deepen a feeling of awe, respect, or devotion on the part of your listeners. Speeches commemorating great events, such as Memorial Day or Veterans Day, and those given at rallies, pep sessions, and as keynotes to conventions usually have stimulation as their general end. Instead of attempting to change the attitudes or beliefs of the audience, the aim is to strengthen and revivify existing beliefs. Rarely, therefore, does the speaker try to prove anything. Instead, his speech is filled with striking statements, vivid descriptions, and strong emotional appeals. Rededication and renewal rather than specific performance are demanded of the audience.

To actuate

The aim of your speech will be to actuate when you wish your audience to perform some definite overt act. This performance may be to vote "yes" or "no," to contribute money, to sign a petition, to form a parade and engage in a demonstration; or it may be any one of a hundred other types of observable public actions. Underlying and prompting this behavior, however, will be strong belief, aroused emotion, or both. For this reason the development of the speech which aims at producing action follows closely the methods suggested for speeches which aim to convince or to stimulate. Sharply distinguishing the actuating speech, however, is the fact that it goes *beyond* the other two; in it you openly ask your audience to perform some particular act—usually an overt act—at a specified time and place. The relationship between the speech to convince or stimulate and the speech to actuate may be diagramed as follows:

When the general end of a speech is *to actuate,*
the speaker's purpose is

To stimulate (and/or) *To convince*	in order *to actuate:*	to cause the auditors to engage in some definite, observable behavior

THE SPECIFIC PURPOSE

In addition to a clearly defined general end or goal, a good speech also must have an immediate and specific purpose.

The specific purpose necessarily falls within the general one and states exactly what it is that the speaker wishes the audience to enjoy, understand, believe, feel, or do. The following examples will illustrate the relationship between the subject, the general end, and the specific purpose of various sorts of speeches:

1. *Subject:* The Trials and Tribulations of a College Dramatic Season.

   General end: To entertain.

   Specific purpose: To share with the audience some of the humorous situations that arose in the casting and production of the season's four plays.

2. *Subject:* Man in Space.

   General end: To inform.

   Specific purpose: To help the audience understand some of the medical problems involved in space travel.

3. *Subject:* Built-in Automotive Safety.

   General end: To convince.

   Specific purpose: To persuade the audience that car manufacturers should be required by law to design and build safer vehicles with less speed potential and smaller size.

4. *Subject:* American Heroes—Then and Now.

   General end: To stimulate.

   Specific purpose: To remind the audience of inspirational examples of some of the courageous men who have dedicated their lives to preserve freedom—both in the past and in the present.

5. *Subject:* Health Insurance for College Students.

   General end: To actuate.

   Specific purpose: To get members of the student council to vote in favor of the group policy offered to the student body by the ABC Health Insurance Company.

Additional examples of a specific speech purpose might be:
To induce the audience to
—laugh at the absurdities of puppy love (entertain).
—understand how safety matches are made (inform).

—believe in public ownership of electric utilities (convince).

—renew their adherence to the basic principles of democracy (stimulate).

—vote for Jones for congressman on November 4 (actuate).

Selecting the specific purpose

If we think of communication as a circular response, we will realize immediately that the selection of the specific purpose of a speech depends not only upon the speaker's own aims or wishes, but also upon the nature of the audience and the speaking occasion. In choosing and framing the specific speech purpose, therefore, you should keep the following factors in mind:

Authority or capacity of the audience. To demand of a group of college students that they "abolish all required courses" would be foolish; they do not have the authority to take this action because curricular requirements are in the hands of the faculty. But students do have the right and the ability to bring pressure on the faculty toward this end. A more logical and positively framed demand would be "petition the faculty to make all courses elective." Limit your request to something that is within your listeners' range of authority. Do not ask them to do something which they would be unable to do even if they wanted to.

Existing attitude of the audience. A group of striking workmen who believe that they are badly underpaid and unfairly treated by their employer probably would be hostile to the suggestion that they return to work under their present conditions; but they might approve submitting the dispute to arbitration by some disinterested person whose fairness and judgment they respect. An audience hostile to the speaker's point of view might, as a result of only one speech, be convinced that "there is something to be said for his side of the question"; but the speaker would probably find it impossible to persuade them to take positive action. Your purpose, in short, must be adjusted not only to the authority but also to the attitudes of your listeners. Do not ask them for a response that you cannot expect from persons with their feelings or beliefs.

The occasion. To ask people to contribute money to a political campaign fund might be appropriate at a pre-election rally, but to make such a request at a church dinner would be decidedly out of place. The celebration of a football victory is hardly the occasion on which to seek an understanding of Einstein's theory. The members of a little theater association would not want to engage in a discussion of finances between the acts of a play, though they might respond to a brief announcement urging their attendance at a business meeting where the budget would be discussed. Be sure, then, that your purpose is adapted to the mood or spirit of the occasion on which you are to speak.

Personal or ultimate aim of the speaker. Suppose that an assistant vice-president of an electronics company is presenting a reorganization plan to his executive committee or board of directors. His immediate purpose is to secure the adoption of his plan; but his ultimate aim may be to increase his own reputation, authority, or salary. Keeping this in mind, he may modify his proposal somewhat, or he may strive to get someone else to urge its adoption so that the responsibility for it will not be entirely his own. Failure to consider one's ultimate, as well as immediate, aim can sometimes be disastrous. For example, a campaign was started to raise funds for a union building for the student body of a large university. At a mass meeting of the senior class the members were asked to sign pledges to contribute a specified amount each year after graduation. High-pressure methods were used, and the students were even told that they would not be allowed to leave the meeting until they had signed. The next morning the college paper announced that the senior class had pledged itself 100 per cent—the immediate purpose had been attained. But less than a third of these signers ever paid any money; so much opposition was created by the high-pressure methods that it became difficult to secure money from anyone else; and as a result, the entire project was delayed for several years. Do not try to get from the audience an immediate positive response which will have a negative effect upon your ultimate objective.

Time limit of the speech. You may be able in a few sentences to induce a hostile majority to postpone action until a later time, but you almost certainly will need a much fuller discussion in order to dislodge their fixed feelings and convictions. Similarly, if your subject is complex, you may be able to inform your audience about your proposal in a fifteen-minute speech—i.e., enable them to understand it—but you may require much more time *to convince* them of its desirability. In an hour you probably can provide an audience with an understanding of the basic structure of the United Nations, with its various committees and agencies; but if you have only five minutes, it would be better to limit your effort to emphasizing the importance of one or two agencies and suggesting how to find out more about them. Do not, in sum, attempt to secure a reaction which is impossible to win in the time available.

Using the specific purpose as a guide

If you keep the foregoing factors in mind as you determine the specific purpose of your speech, your preparation will be off to a sound start. Moreover, a properly selected and limited purpose will serve as a useful guide throughout the remaining stages of your preparatory process. Write out your specific purpose in a clear, simple sentence and fix that sentence firmly in your mind. Whenever you encounter a fact or idea that will help advance you toward your goal, work it into your outline; otherwise, forget about it, no matter how interesting or attractive it may be. By thus using a carefully framed purpose as the criterion for determining the relevance or irrelevance of possible speech materials, you can make certain that your talk will have unity and coherence, and that everything you say will be directed toward the precise response that you seek.

SUBJECT CATEGORIES

As we said earlier in this chapter, the beginning speaker often has difficulty in selecting a suitable speech subject. If you find yourself in this situation, it may be helpful for you to study the following list of subject categories. These categories are not speech subjects, but are types or classes of material in which speech subjects may be found. To find a suitable subject, consider them in terms of your own interests and knowledge, the interests of your audience, and the nature of the occasion on which you are to speak.

PERSONAL EXPERIENCE

1. Jobs you have held
2. Places you have been
3. Military service
4. The region you come from
5. Schools you have attended
6. Friends and enemies
7. Relatives you like—and dislike

PUBLIC AFFAIRS

Foreign Affairs

1. Foreign-policy aims
   a. What they are
   b. What they should be

2. The implementation of policy aims
3. History of the foreign policy of the United States (or of some other nation)
4. Responsibility for our foreign policy
5. Ethics of foreign policy decisions
6. How foreign policy affects domestic policy

Domestic Affairs

1. Social problems
    a. Crime
    b. The family
        (1) and divorce
    c. Of cities
    d. Of rural areas
    e. Of races and ethnic groups
    f. Of juveniles or the aged
    g. Traffic accidents
2. Economic problems
    a. Federal fiscal policy
    b. Economically deprived persons and areas
    c. Fiscal problems of state and local governments
    d. Taxes and tax policies
3. Political problems
    a. Powers and obligations of the federal government
    b. Relations between federal government and the states
    c. Problems of state and local governments
    d. Parties, campaigns, and nominating procedures
    e. The courts and court procedures
        (1) Delays in justice
        (2) The jury system
    f. Congress vs. the President
    g. Democracy as a form of government—advantages and disadvantages
    h. Careers in government

THE ARTS

1. Painting, music, sculpture
2. Literature and criticism
3. Theatre, cinema, and the dance
4. Government support of the arts
5. The artist as a person
6. History of an art form
7. Censorship of the arts

EDUCATION

1. Proper aims of education
2. Recent advances in methods and teaching materials
3. The federal government and education
4. Courses and requirements
5. Grades and grading
6. Athletics
7. Extracurricular activities
8. Meeting the demand for education
9. Fraternities
10. Student marriages

MASS MEDIA

1. Radio, television, and film
2. The press
3. Censorship of mass media
   a. To protect public morals
   b. For national security
4. Used for propaganda purposes at home or abroad
5. Ways to improve mass media
6. Effects on children

SCIENCE

1. Recent advances in some branch of science
2. Science as method
3. Pure vs. applied research
4. Government support of science
5. History of science
6. Science and religion
7. Careers in science

BUSINESS AND LABOR

1. Unions
   a. Benefits and/or evils
   b. Regulation of unions
   c. "Right to work" laws
2. Government regulation of business
3. Ethical standards of business practice
4. Advertising in the modern world
5. Training for business
6. Careers in business
7. Blue-collar and white-collar status

8. Wages: hourly, weekly, or annually?
9. A guaranteed lifetime income

PERSISTENT CONCERNS

1. "The good life"—what and how
2. Man and God
3. Beauty
4. The ideal society
5. Happiness—what it is and how to attain it
6. Parents and children
7. The tests of truth
8. Love
9. The causes of marriage

In this chapter we have pointed out the importance of selecting a suitable subject and of defining the general and specific purposes of your talk. Moreover, we have suggested why these tasks should constitute the first two steps in your preparation. At the outset of your work on a speech, therefore, ask yourself the following questions and do not proceed until the answers are clear in your mind. Remember also that no one of these questions can be answered without simultaneous consideration of the others.

1. What subject shall I talk about, and to what aspect of that subject shall I limit myself?

2. What general end shall I try to attain? Shall it be one of entertainment, information, conviction, stimulation, or actuation?

3. What specific response shall I seek from my audience? What is it exactly that I want them to enjoy, understand, believe, feel, or do?

Finally, after you have finished building your speech in detail, ask yourself also this fourth question:

4. How shall I phrase the title of my speech so that when it is announced, my audience will want to hear what I have to say?

Problems

1. Describe briefly some situation from your own experience in which a speech to entertain would have been appropriate. Do the same for each of the other types of speeches—i.e., the speech to inform, the speech to convince, the speech to stimulate, and the speech to actuate. Compare the situations you describe with those offered by other members of the class, and

make as complete a list as you can of all the various kinds of occasions on which each type of speech might be used.

2. Select a subject with which you are familiar. (This subject may be drawn from your major in college, from work experience, from travel, from your hobby, etc.) Assume that during the course of the semester you will be required to present three five-minute speeches on this subject—one to entertain, one to inform, and one to convince. Select and frame a specific purpose for each speech. Then repeat the experiment, but this time assume that in each case you will be presenting a fifteen-minute speech to a local service club. Let the other members of the class criticize the appropriateness of your choices.

3. Read five printed speeches. (See, for example, such books as *Representative American Speeches,* edited by Lester Thonssen; *The Speaker's Resource Book,* edited by Carroll Arnold, Douglas Ehninger, and John Gerber; or recent issues of the magazine *Vital Speeches.)* Try to determine the general and specific purpose of each speech and to evaluate how well the specific purpose was fulfilled.

4. Attend with other members of your class some public lecture, speech, or sermon that is given in your community. See if you can agree as to the speaker's general and specific purpose. Discuss also whether he made that purpose clear; and if not, suggest how he might have done so.

5. During a round of classroom speeches, jot down what you believe to be the specific purpose of each speech. At the close of the round, question the speakers to see if you have interpreted their purposes accurately. In cases where the majority of the class failed to grasp the speaker's purpose, decide who was chiefly at fault—the speaker or the listeners.

Speaking assignment

1. Select a subject with which you are well acquainted and about which you could say many different things. Write out the specific purposes of four or five speeches which you would like to give on this subject. Select from among these the topic and purpose that seem to you to be best adapted to the interests of your classmates, and deliver a five-minute speech on your selection. At the close of your speech, read aloud the specific purposes you have rejected, and let your classmates and instructor evaluate your choice.

Suggestions for further reading

Aristotle, *Rhetoric,* 1358b-1359a.

George Campbell, *The Philosophy of Rhetoric,* ed. Lloyd Bitzer (Carbondale: Southern Illinois University Press, 1963), pp. 1-7.

Giles Wilkeson Gray and Waldo W. Braden, *Public Speaking: Principles and Practice,* 2nd ed. (New York: Harper & Row, Publishers, 1963), Chapter XIII, "Selecting a Speech Goal."

James H. McBurney and Ernest J. Wrage, *The Art of Good Speech* (Englewood Cliffs, N.J.: Prentice-Hall, Inc., 1953), Chapter V, "Subjects for Speaking."

Glen E. Mills, *Composing the Speech* (Englewood Cliffs, N.J.: Prentice-Hall, Inc., 1952), Chapter II, "Speech Purposes."

Arthur Edward Phillips, *Effective Speaking* (Chicago: Newton, 1908), Chapter II, "The General Ends."

Loren Reid, *Speaking Well* (Columbia, Mo.: Artcraft Press, 1962), Chapter II, "Choosing Subject and Purpose."

Paul L. Soper, *Basic Public Speaking,* 3rd ed. (New York: Oxford Book Co., Inc., 1963), Chapter III, "Selecting the Speech Subject and Aims."

CHAPTER EIGHT

Analyzing the audience and the occasion

Talking to hear one's own voice may help to bolster courage on a dark night, but it is not to be confused with talking with the aim of communicating ideas to others. Often speakers forget this important fact. They become so engrossed in their own interests, so impressed by ideas that seem important to them, that they forget they are talking to people whose interests and attitudes may be different from their own. One of the most important lessons you can learn as a speaker is to see things from the standpoint of your listeners. You must continually ask yourself, "How would I feel about this proposal if I were in their place?" "Would this argument sound reasonable to me if I had had their experiences?" "Would this story interest me if I were the same age as they are?"

Besides knowing as much as possible about your hearers, you should also know as much as possible about the occasion on which your speech is to be delivered. What is the purpose of the gathering before which you are to appear? What rules and customs will prevail? What will precede and follow your speech? What will the physical conditions and surroundings be? These and similar questions must be explored early in the preparation process.

In this chapter we shall lay out a method for analyzing audiences and speaking occasions. In Chapter 16, after more has been said concerning the structure and content of a speech, we shall consider the problem of adapting explanations and appeals to different sorts of audience attitudes and to different occasions.

AUDIENCE TYPES AND ATTITUDES

How can you go about finding out what you need to know concerning the audience you will address? The best way, of course, is to ask direct questions of the chairman or of other persons who will be among your listeners. Sometimes, too, you can gain useful information from speakers who have appeared before the group at an earlier date or from individuals who are acquainted with many of the audience members. If none of these methods is practicable, you must *infer* the probable interests and attitudes of your listeners from whatever information you can gather concerning their education, occupation, age, special interests or biases, and similar determinants. When you must draw inferences in this way, consider the following factors:

General data

The size of the audience. As we emphasized earlier, your vocal and physical delivery should be adapted to the size of the audience: the larger the audience, the greater the need for broad gestures and movement, for an adequate degree of loudness, and for distinctness in articulation. Also the larger the audience, the greater the diversity of attitudes and opinions which are likely to be represented, and therefore the more general and comprehensive your appeals must be.

The age of those making up the audience. It is important to know whether the members of the audience are of the same age level or of widely divergent ages. Age not only affects one's ability to understand but determines how far back a person's experience runs. For example, the events of World War II are only second-hand experiences to persons under thirty. In general, also, older persons are less impulsive and more conservative than younger ones; and both groups tend to be somewhat skeptical, even contemptuous, of the values and attitudes of the other.

The sex of members of the audience. Is it a mixed audience or are all of the same sex? Men and women differ in their interests and often in the way they approach a problem or difficulty. Their response to intellectual and emotional appeals will ordinarily vary somewhat, also.

The occupation of the members of the audience. Occupation tends to suggest the interests and types of knowledge people will have. A talk directed to a university faculty, therefore, must differ from one offered to a labor union. In addition, a fair index of income level can be gained from a knowledge of the audience's principal occupation —information which becomes especially significant if one's speech is to involve economic or social considerations, either directly or indirectly.

The education of those in the audience. Both formal education and that education which comes from experience are important. A Chicago cab driver may not have a broad formal training, but his knowledge of the ways of human nature and of the conditions in that city may be profound. Remember, therefore, to consider both schooling *and* experience.

Membership in social, professional, and religious groups. Membership in special groups often indicates both interests and prejudices. The Rotary Club, Knights of Columbus, Sigma Chi, Forest Hills Tennis Club, Young Republican Organization, American Association of University Women—what do these organizations mean to you? They should represent types of people, points of view, interests, and special abilities. Whenever you find that a sizable part of your audience is affiliated with some special group, you will have gained a valuable clue to their motivations and interests.

Audience's knowledge of the subject

Either through the accumulation of general data or through some special information which you may have discovered, you should be able to infer how much the members of your audience already know about the subject of your speech. Will they understand technical terms without explanation? Will an elementary discussion seem boring or trivial? What facts will be new, and what ideas and arguments will your listeners be likely to dismiss as "the same old stuff"? For a speaker to imply by his remarks that he thinks his listeners ignorant or for him to assume a condescending manner toward them is not only bad manners and bad judgment, it is a serious barrier to communication. An almost equally bad policy is to talk over their heads. Try as well as you can to gauge the knowledge and understanding of the audience, and adapt your remarks accordingly.

Audience's primary interests and desires

Any speaker should be concerned about the primary interests and desires of his listeners. In analyzing your audience, ask yourself: What do these people want or value most, and in what are they chiefly interested? How are their wants and desires related to my subject and the purpose of my speech? These questions are of such importance that they will be considered in detail in Chapter 12.

Audience's fixed attitudes and beliefs

As soon as a child begins to receive impressions of his environment, he starts to form opinions and attitudes toward the persons and objects that compose or influence it. These opinions and attitudes may be modified by later experience; but by the time the infant has grown to adulthood, some of them, through habit and repetition, have become the bases for firmly held beliefs and predictable conduct. Many people, for example, are convinced of the value of science; others (though they may not admit it openly) believe in hunches, jinxes, and the like. A man may have a set opinion concerning a governmental threat to his privacy, or the law of supply and demand, or the values of a liberal education. Such proverbs as "Honesty is the best policy" and "Spare the rod and spoil the child" are traditional ways of stating the fixed beliefs held by many members of our society. Of course, the speaker should—if he can—determine whether these convictions are held heart-deep or skin-deep. For instance, a minister speaking from his pulpit or a lawyer addressing a jury must constantly make analyses of this kind.

The speaker who knows what settled beliefs and attitudes lie at the basis of his hearers' thinking can avoid arousing needless hostility and often can use these beliefs as pegs upon which to hang an argument or a proposal. If he can show how his idea coincides with one already established in the minds of his audience, or how his proposition accords with one of their existing principles, the acceptance of his view will practically be assured.

Attitude of the audience toward the speaker

If your general diagnosis of the audience has been accurate and comprehensive, you are ready to assess your listeners' probable attitude toward you and your subject. Ask yourself first what will be their attitude toward you personally and toward your qualifications to address them. In this connection, at least two determinants must be considered: *(a)* their *friendliness* toward you and *(b)* their *respect* for you or your knowledge of the subject. These two components of audience attitude may vary widely and sometimes in ways that are quite inconsistent. For instance, a father who may love his small son deeply may not respect his childish judgments. On the other hand, the son may have the greatest respect for the judgment of his teacher but yet may dislike her intensely. Respect and friendliness are two different things, and they both must be taken into account.

Adaptation to personal hostility. When your analysis predicts that your audience will be hostile toward you, your first job as a speaker is to try to alter this attitude. Obviously, this will be easier to accomplish if respect for you and your knowledge is high. In any case, try in some way to establish common ground with your auditors. This often can be done by one or more of the following methods:

1. By showing a friendly attitude toward your listeners.
2. By maintaining an attitude of fairness, modesty, and good humor.
3. By pointing out your own agreement with some of the cherished hopes or beliefs of your auditors.
4. By referring to experiences which you hold in common with them.
5. By using humor that is pertinent and in good taste, especially when it can be employed at your own expense.

Adaptation to an attitude of condescension. The thing *not* to do when an audience has a condescending attitude toward you is to assume a conceited or antagonistic manner yourself. Of course, you must appear self-confident, but this confidence must be tempered with a large measure of modesty. Gain the respect of your hearers by the soundness of your thinking and your obvious knowledge of the facts. Avoid saying "I think that . . ."; instead, present the evidence which makes such a conclusion apparent. If you have occasion to call attention to your own accomplishments, do so in a matter-of-fact, unassuming way. Remember that real personal worth does not advertise itself but rather is made evident by its accomplishments.

Attitude of the audience toward the subject

Although, as we have suggested, audiences sometimes are hostile or condescending, ordinarily they are either *interested* in a subject or are *apathetic* toward it. Apathy is usually present when they see no connection between a topic and their own needs or affairs. If your diagnosis indicates that this will be the case, you will need to show your hearers that a significant and perhaps unsuspected relationship *does* exist between what you have to say and their lives, their fortunes, or their happiness. Conceding that they may not have been *aware* of this relationship or connection, proceed quickly and skillfully to *make* them aware of it. Develop, emphasize, and dramatize the association. Arouse their curiosity in some novel aspect of your subject. Utilize all the methods that you can for holding attention. Of course, you should not neglect doing these things even if your audience already is interested. Regardless of the nature of your audience, you must strive to develop and sustain their interest. But when an audience is apathetic, you will find that even more effort is required to hold their attention.

Audience attitude toward speaker purpose

If, with no preliminaries at all, you told the audience the specific purpose of your speech, what would their attitude toward it be?

Would they approve, disapprove, or reserve judgment? The answer indicates the meaning of the phrase "attitude toward purpose." This does not mean the attitude you hope to have implanted by the end of your speech but rather the attitude which exists before you begin. Since an audience seldom is an homogeneous group, many different shades of opinion usually will be represented. Therefore, generally it is best to determine the *predominant* attitude and to adapt your speech principally to it, while at the same time making allowances for any marked variations you expect on the part of the minority. The following outline suggests some of the attitudes which may prevail toward a speaker's purpose.

POSSIBLE ATTITUDES TOWARD THE PURPOSE

I. When the general end is *to entertain* or *to inform:*
  A. The audience's attitude toward the purpose will be governed largely by their attitude toward the subject.
  B. Hence, it will be one of the following:
    1. Interested.
    2. Apathetic.

II. When the general end is *to convince, to stimulate,* or *to actuate:*
  A. The audience's attitude toward the purpose will be governed largely by their attitude toward the specific feeling, belief, or action that is urged.
  B. Hence, it will be one of the following:
    1. Predisposed to respond as desired.
    2. Favorable but not aroused.
    3. Apathetic.
    4. Interested in the situation but undecided what to think or do about it.
    5. Interested in the situation but skeptical of the *proposed* belief, attitude, or action because of
      a. doubts concerning its workability or soundness, and/or
      b. fears of its possible bad effects, and/or
      c. a preference for some other belief, attitude, or action.
    6. Firmly opposed to any change from the present situation.

The attitudes listed in Section I of this outline are closely related to the audience's attitude toward the subject, which has already been explained. The six attitudes listed in Section II require brief illustration. Let us assume that property taxes in your college community are high and that fraternity property is tax-exempt. Under these conditions, suppose your purpose were to start a movement for the removal of this exemption so that fraternity houses would be placed on the assessment sheet. Members of a local Committee to Increase Revenue by Taxing the Fraternities would agree with you in advance and would only need to be given directions as to how to proceed. An audience of local property owners (provided they were not fraternity alumni) most likely would be favorable, but they would need to be aroused before they would take any concerted action. Nonfraternity students ordinarily would form an apathetic audience because they would not see how the proposal affected them one way or the other. The university administration and faculty probably would be interested in the situation because of its connection with both students and community but might be undecided whether or not to support the plan (excepting, of course, those persons who were influenced by owning property themselves or were fraternity alumni). Property owners who were also fraternity alumni or sympathizers would be interested in the situation and desirous of some way to relieve themselves of the heavy property tax, but they would probably be opposed to this particular way of doing it because of their fraternity connections. Student fraternity men, on the other hand, would be openly hostile to any change from a situation under which they were obtaining a distinct advantage. If, therefore, you were to know what proportion of your audience represented each of these groups, you could form a fairly good estimate of its initial response to you and to the ideas you will be advancing.

Having determined the prevailing attitude or combination of attitudes which your audience probably will have toward your purpose, you will need to adjust the structure and content of your speech accordingly, and also perhaps your manner of delivery so as to adapt to that situation. We shall defer a fuller discussion of the problem of adaptation, however, until Chapter 16, when you will have a better understanding of how a speech is constructed and of the materials which compose it.

AUDIENCE ORGANIZATION

In addition to forming an accurate estimate of the type of people you will be talking to and of their probable attitude toward you and your subject, you also should attempt to determine the degree or level of organization which the audience possesses.

In his book *The Psychology of the Audience*, H. L. Hollingworth has pointed out five such levels.[1] Some audiences—for example, those

[1](New York: American Book Co., 1935), pp. 19-32.

". . . determine the degree or level of organization which the audience possesses."

Study these six audiences and try to match each of them with a label descriptive of its degree or level of organization. Use H. L. Hollingworth's classification, which includes five specific levels of audience organization: chance gathering, passive audience, selected audience, concerted gathering, and organized group. FROM TOP LEFT, CLOCKWISE: Participants in a university seminar being held outdoors; a serious group filling a large auditorium to capacity; students in a science lecture hall; a sidewalk audience gathered around a speaker at a campus demonstration; the Ohio State football team listening to the athletic director, Woody Hayes; and a smiling audience in evening clothes.

which gather about a pitchman at a county fair—are entirely *chance gatherings* in the sense that any passer-by who cares to do so may stop for a few moments to listen. Such audiences display no homogeneity as to either type or attitude and do not even come together because of a previous interest in the speaker or his subject. Moreover, it is probable that during the course of the pitchman's "speech" some persons will leave and others arrive, so that at the close he may be addressing quite a different group than he was at the beginning.

Distinguished from this chance or "pedestrian" gathering is a second level or kind of group which Hollingworth calls *the passive audience.* This consists of persons who have voluntarily assembled for the "common but passive" purpose of hearing a speech or lecture that has been advertised and is open to the public. Hence, unlike the chance or "pedestrian" audience, its members at least have enough interest in the speaker or subject to take the trouble to attend.

Third, Hollingworth places *the "selected" audience,* the group that is especially invited to attend a closed or semiclosed meeting because they are known to have previous interest in the subject that is to be considered. Fourth is *the "concerted" gathering,* the audience which has an "active purpose, with sympathetic interest in a mutual enterprise, but with no clear division of labor or rigid organization of authority." A college class intent upon understanding the ideas in a professor's lecture or a group of specialists at a scientific meeting where a new discovery is being discussed would be typical examples. Fifth and finally, says Hollingworth, there is *the "organized" group* such as the military unit or the athletic team in which the division of labor is fixed and the lines of authority rigidly established. This group not only exists for a specific purpose which all of its members recognize, but through choice or necessity obeys the commands of an established leader.

There are two reasons why it is important for a speaker to consider the level of organization inherent in his audience. First, for obvious reasons this level may be a factor in determining the attitude which his listeners display toward him and his subject, since a "concerted" audience is more inclined to be friendly than a "passive" one, while an "organized" group may be either friendly or hostile, depending upon whether it is a voluntary or involuntary gathering. Second, and even more importantly, such knowledge informs the speaker of the point at which he must begin in his effort to win understanding or acceptance for his view. Must he be concerned with catching the attention and arousing the interest of his hearers, or may he turn at once to the task of convincing or directing them? The speaker's responsibilities at the various levels of audience organization are summarized by Hollingworth in this way:[2]

SPEAKER'S RESPONSIBILITIES FOR VARIOUS AUDIENCE-LEVELS

Pedestrian Audience	*Passive Audience*	*Selected Audience*	*Concerted Audience*	*Organized Audience*
Attention	. . . . . .	. . . . . .	. . . . . .	. . . . . .
Interest	Interest	. . . . . .	. . . . . .	. . . . . .
Impression	Impression	Impression	. . . . . .	. . . . . .
Conviction	Conviction	Conviction	Conviction	. . . . . .
Direction	Direction	Direction	Direction	Direction

AUDIENCE REACTIONS DURING THE SPEECH

No prior analysis of an audience is proof against mistaken judgment. Moreover, the audience's attitude may change even while you are speaking. For these reasons, it is important to keep a close watch on the reactions of your listeners when your subject is announced and throughout your entire speech. The way your hearers sit in their seats, the expressions on their faces, such audible reactions as laughter, applause, shifting about, or whispering—all these are vivid symptoms of their attitude toward you, your subject, or your purpose. If you are wise, you will develop a keen sensitivity to these signs and learn to adapt your remarks accordingly.

SAMPLE ANALYSIS OUTLINE

"I am convinced by my own experience, and by that of others," said Henry Ford, "that if there is any secret of success, it lies in the ability to get the other person's point of view and to see things from his angle as well as your own."[3] A systematic method for finding out the other fellow's point of view has been presented in this chapter. Your task now is to practice applying this method in specific speaking situations. Examine carefully the sample analysis outline which follows and notice how this particular speaker used facts at his disposal to draw a clear picture of the audience he would face.

[2]*Ibid.*, p. 25.

[3]From *Strategy in Handling People* by E. T. Webb and J. J. B. Morgan (Chicago: Boulten, Pierce, 1931), p. 76.

I. *Subject:* Representation on the Student Senate.

II. *Title:* "Neglected Men—and Women!"

III. *General End:* To actuate.

IV. *Specific Purpose:* To get the members of the Student Senate to approve a constitutional amendment increasing the number of Senators from the Independent Student Association.

V. *Specific Audience:* Student Senate, Purdue University.

VI. *Audience Diagnosis:*

A. Size: About thirty persons.

B. Sex and Age: Men and women, 19-23 years old.

C. Occupation: College students representing wide variety of interests and educational objectives.

D. Knowledge of the subject:

1. A general knowledge of the provisions of the Senate constitution and the present system of student representation.
2. A limited knowledge of the dissatisfaction among some independent students toward the present system of representation.
3. Specific knowledge of the problem which a few have derived from conversations with the speaker and other students.

E. Primary Interest: Their own educational objectives and problems, including campus organizations and activities.

F. Fixed Attitudes:

1. Political: Believe in the principle of equal representation for all.
2. Professional: Strong desire for success in their chosen professions; believe that participation in civic affairs will contribute to that success and will bring personal prestige.
3. Economic: Most of them are economically dependent upon parents or some other outside source of income and tend not to classify groups or organizations on this basis.
4. Religious: Attitudes probably unimportant in consideration of this subject.

G. Attitude toward subject: Interested because of their concern about all issues presented to the Senate.

H. Attitude toward speaker: Personally friendly—a fellow member of the Senate.

I. Attitude toward purpose: Most listeners will be interested in the situation but hostile to the proposed change. They believe existing methods are satisfactory and may fear the loss of influence or prestige.

VII. *Level of Organization:* Organized. Audience has an established power structure, and hence is capable of carrying out any action agreed upon.

VIII. *Proposed Adaptation to the Audience:*

A. Introduce the subject by referring to the Senate's responsibility to treat all student groups fairly.
B. Use visual aids to show inequities of the present apportionment of representatives.
C. Primary appeal: To their pride in fulfilling their civic responsibility by giving equal representation to all students.

THE SPEAKING OCCASION

At the outset of this chapter we emphasized the importance of studying in advance not only the audience for which a speech is designed but also the occasion on which it is to be delivered, and we suggested four questions by which the nature of a speaking occasion may be probed (p. 128). Let us now consider each of these questions briefly as the final step in our analysis.

1. *What is the purpose of the gathering?* Are you to address the regular meeting of an organized group, an audience that has come together for the specific purpose of hearing your talk, or a chance or pedestrian gathering? Are people interested in learning more about your subject, in taking some positive action concerning it, or have they perhaps come to heckle or embarrass you? Are your subject and purpose in line with the reason for the meeting, or are you merely seizing the occasion to present some ideas which you think are important? Are you one in a series of speakers which the audience has heard over a period of weeks or months? If so, how does your subject relate to those subjects which already have been discussed?

2. *What rules or customs will prevail?* Will there be a regular order of business or a fixed program into which your speech must fit? Is it the custom of the group to ask questions of the speaker? Do the listeners expect a formal or an informal speaking manner? Will it be necessary to extend gracious or complimentary remarks to some person or persons or to display respect or reverence for some traditional concept? A knowledge of these facts will help you avoid feeling out of place and will prevent you from arousing antagonism by some inappropriate word or action.

3. *What will precede and follow your speech?* At what time of day will your speech be given? Immediately after a heavy meal? After a long and tiring program? Just before the principal address or event of the evening? What other items are on the program? What is their tone or character? All these things will, of course, influence the interest the audience may have in your talk. In some instances

you will be able to use the other events on the program to increase interest or belief in your own remarks; sometimes they will work against you. In any event, you must always consider the effect which the program as a whole may have on your speech.

4. *What will the physical conditions—the audience-speaker environment—be?* Will your speech be given out-of-doors or in an auditorium? Is it likely to be hot, cold, or comfortable? Will the audience be sitting or standing; and if sitting, will they be crowded together or scattered about? In how large a room will the speech be given? Will a public-address system be used? Will you be seen and heard easily? Are there likely to be disturbances in the form of noise or interruptions from the outside? These and similar environmental factors have an effect on the temper of the audience, their span of attention, and the style of speaking you will find necessary.

Problems

1. Select a subject concerning which you have more than a passing knowledge. (This subject may be drawn from your major in college, from summer work experience, from your hobby, etc.) Assume that you have been asked to discuss some aspect of this subject before each of three different audiences: (1) a luncheon club made up of local business and professional men, (2) a group of undergraduate students from a nearby girls' college, and (3) the members of the fifth-grade class in a rural elementary school. In each case you have fifteen minutes for your talk.

Keeping in mind the type and the probable attitude of the persons you will be addressing, select a suitable aspect of your general subject for each audience and determine what the general and specific purpose of each speech will be. Also outline briefly the main points or ideas you would plan to present. Be ready to defend the particular subject and purpose, and also the leading ideas you have selected for presentation to each group.

2. Using as a model the sample audience-analysis outline on pages 138-139, make a similar analysis of your own speech class for one or more of the following subjects:

Students' ratings of their instructors' effectiveness should be forwarded to the Dean's office annually.

The peacetime draft should be abolished.

Women should choose a career rather than marriage.

Chemistry: Its contributions to a better life for everyone.

The traditions of our college.

Veterans' Day: What it should mean to you.

Censorship of our college newspaper.

3. How would you rank the following factors in terms of their importance in determining audience interests: predominant sex, educational level, region of the country in which the audience lives, occupation, age? Compare your ranking with those made by the other members of the class and attempt to reach a consensus.

4. Why is it important to distinguish between the attitude the audience displays toward the speaker and the attitude it displays toward his subject?

5. Come to class ready to discuss the general topic, "The Ideal Physical Arrangements for a Public Speech." Consider such factors as the following: the size of the room in relation to the size of the audience; the arrangement of the chairs around the speaker's stand; the type of chairs in which the audience sits; the distance between speaker and audience; the advisability of positioning the speaker on a platform that raises him above the level of his listeners; the acoustics; the lighting arrangements (house lights dark, spotlight on speaker, etc.); the ventilation; and the decoration of the room in relation to the subject of the speech.

6. If, as a result of analysis, you find that your audience will be heterogeneous—that is, will contain persons of many different ages, occupations, educational levels, etc.—how should you plan to adapt your remarks? Should you attempt to find a subject or approach broad enough to be of interest to all? Should you try to speak to the majority of your listeners and forget the rest? Should you divide up your subject in such a way that different parts or aspects of it will appeal to different segments of your audience? Be prepared to defend your answer.

7. Discuss some of the special problems involved in speaking to a chance or "pedestrian" audience, and suggest ways in which these problems might be solved.

8. At the beginning of this chapter we said that one of the most important lessons a speaker can learn is to see things from the standpoint of his listeners. Does this mean that you should never talk about subjects in which your listeners are uninterested in advance of your speech or that you should never present ideas and points of view with which they disagree?

9. Estimate the probable attitude of the members of your speech class toward each of the following speech situations:

	SPEAKER	SUBJECT	PURPOSE
A.	The instructor.	Preparation of class work.	To get students to spend more time in preparing speeches.
B.	A visiting student from England.	Life at Oxford.	To secure appreciation of the difference between English and American customs.

c. A senior.	Athletic rally.	To urge attendance at a rally to be held that evening.

Speaking assignment

1. Present to the class a five-minute speech on a subject of your choice. As an aid to subject selection, study the list of subject categories found on pages 122-125. In addition to the usual subject-matter outline, turn in to the instructor an audience-analysis outline similar to the one found on pages 138-139.

Suggestions for further reading

Aristotle, *Rhetoric*, 1388b-1391b, "Types of Character; the Young; the Elderly; the Prime of Life; Character as Modified by Fortune; the Influence of Wealth; the Influence of Power."

Jon Eisenson, J. Jeffery Auer, and John V. Irwin, *The Psychology of Communication* (New York: Appleton-Century-Crofts, 1963), Chapter XVI, "Psychology of Public Address." See esp. pp. 273-286.

Albert L. Furbay, "The Influence of Scattered Versus Compact Seating on Audience Response," *Speech Monographs*, XXXII (June 1965), 144-148.

George Gallup, *A Guide to Public Opinion Polls* (Princeton, N. J.: Princeton University Press, 1948).

L. S. Harms, "Listener Judgments of Status Cues in Speech," *Quarterly Journal of Speech*, XLVII (April 1961), 164-169.

H. L. Hollingworth, *The Psychology of the Audience* (New York: American Book Co., 1935), Chapter II, "Preliminary Analysis"; Chapter III, "Types of Audiences"; Chapter IV, "A Typical Situation."

Charles W. Lomas, "Churchill's Concept of His Audiences," *Western Speech*, XXII (Spring 1958), 75-81.

Bruce L. Smith, Harold Lasswell, and Ralph D. Casey, *Propaganda, Communication, and Public Opinion* (Princeton: N. J.: Princeton University Press, 1946).

Richard Whately, *Elements of Rhetoric*, ed. Douglas Ehninger (Carbondale: Southern Illinois University Press, 1963), Part Two, Chapter III, "Of the Favourable or Unfavourable Disposition of the Hearers or Readers Towards the Speaker or Writer, and His Opponent."

Elmo C. Wilson, "The Measurement of Public Opinion," *Annals of the American Academy of Political and Social Science*, CCL (March 1947), 121-129.

CHAPTER NINE

Speech materials: Sources, records, and classification

For most speeches you will need to find out more about the subject than you already know, and for all speeches you will need to review your information and to classify it. It is the purpose of this chapter to suggest the various sources from which speech materials may be drawn and to explain a practicable method for recording and classifying them.

THE SOURCES OF SPEECH MATERIALS

Personal experience

A good way to begin your search for speech materials is to jot down on a piece of paper everything you already know about the subject as a result of personal experience or observation. Then, in so far as possible, add to this list by further observations or personal experimentation. As we already have emphasized in Chapter 7, you can expect to speak best about those things which you know best; and you know best those things which you have actually seen, touched, tasted, smelled, heard, or done. Even when your direct experience with the subject cannot appropriately be cited in your speech, it will provide the perspective or insight that invariably makes for greater clarity and vividness of expression. In short, make personal experience and observation your first and, whenever possible, your principal source of speech materials.

Interviews

Beginning speakers often fail to realize that vast amounts of authoritative information may be gathered merely by asking questions of the right persons. If, for example, you expect to talk on interplanetary navigation, what better and more convenient source of information could there be than a member of your college's astronomy department? Or if you are to discuss a problem in national or international affairs, why not talk first with a trained political scientist? Nearly all faculty members are willing to talk with you on questions pertaining to their special fields of interest. In your town or community also, you usually will find one or more experts on nearly any topic you choose to speak about. Of course, you must avoid being bothersome or pushy in approaching these persons, and you must respect their time and schedules. But brief interviews, properly arranged for, frequently can yield invaluable factual data; and, what is even more important, they can be a source of authoritative interpretations and opinions.

To save the time of the person you interview and to insure getting the specific information you desire, make an appointment in advance, and prepare for the meeting by writing down the questions you particularly want answered. During the interview itself, remember that your purpose is to obtain facts and judgments from the expert, not to argue with him by expressing your own views. If your opinions are asked for, state them, of course; but do so as briefly and as objectively as possible. At the same time, make sure that you understand the meaning and significance of the expert's remarks and make careful mental notes of his major ideas or arguments. Immediately after the interview, reduce these to a written record; and if you plan to quote him directly, give him an opportunity to verify the accuracy and completeness of the statements you attribute to him.

Even if an interview provides you with no facts or opinions that you can quote directly in your speech, it probably will give you a broader outlook on the problem and will suggest new sources of information. Do not, however, always limit yourself to interviews with experts. Sometimes it also is important to find out what the proverbial "man on the street" thinks. Information derived from this source not only may be used in your speech itself, but often will provide you with guidelines for adapting your ideas to the persons in your audience.

Letters and questionnaires

If it is impossible to talk with an expert directly, you can sometimes obtain information through correspondence. If you write to an expert, however, be sure that you make clear exactly what information you want and why you want it. Moreover, be reasonable in your request. Do not expect the expert to spend hours or days gathering facts for you; and, above all, do not ask him for information that you yourself could find if you were willing to search for it. Write only after you have exhausted all other resources available to you.

When there is controversy on some point and you want to get a cross section of the varying opinions, send a questionnaire to a number of people and compare their answers. This method is valuable but has been somewhat overused. As a result, many people who would answer a personal letter will throw a questionnaire, particularly a long one, into the wastebasket. Make your questions as easy to answer as possible, and keep the list of questions brief. Always enclose a stamped, self-addressed envelope for the reply. If you can find out a man's name and title, address him personally instead of mailing your questionnaire, for example, to "The Head of the Economics Department, X—— University."

Even in those cases, however, where the substance of your speech comes from questionnaires, interviews, and personal experience, it usually will have to be supplemented by *printed* data. The most abundant source of speech materials, of course, is printed matter —newspapers, magazines, and books.

Newspapers

Newspapers obviously are a useful source of information about events of current interest. Moreover, their feature stories and accounts of unusual happenings provide a storehouse of interesting illustrations and examples. You must be careful, however, not to accept as true everything printed in a newspaper, for the very haste with which news is gathered sometimes makes complete accuracy impossible. Your school or city library undoubtedly keeps on file copies of one or two highly reliable papers such as *The New York Times*, *The Observer*, or the *Christian Science Monitor*, and also provides a selection from among the papers of your state or region. If your library has *The New York Times*, it probably has the published index to that paper; and by using it, you can locate accounts of men and events from 1913 to the present. Another useful and well-indexed source of information on current happenings is *Facts on File*, issued weekly since 1940.

Magazines

An average-sized university library subscribes annually to some 8,000 magazines and periodicals. Among those of general interest, some—such as *Time*, *Newsweek*, and *U. S. News and World Report*—summarize weekly events. *The Atlantic* and *Harper's* are representative of a group of monthly publications which cover a wide range of subjects of both passing and permanent importance. Such magazines as *The Nation*, *Vital Speeches of the Day*, *Fortune*, *The Reporter*,

Information relating to specific aspects of speech as a field of study are contained in a variety of professional journals, prominent among which are these: *Educational Theatre Journal, Journal of Broadcasting, Central States Speech Journal, Journal of Speech and Hearing Disorders, Television Quarterly, Speech Monographs, The Journal of Communication, Western Speech, Today's Speech, Quarterly Journal of Speech, The Speech Teacher,* and *The Southern Speech Journal.* As a student of speech, you should find such journals especially useful. Your library may have some or all of them, as well as others in the same or related subject-matter areas.

and *The New Republic* contain comment on current political, social, and economic questions; discussions of popular scientific interest appear in *Popular Science, Scientific American,* and *Popular Mechanics Magazine.* For other specialized areas, there are such magazines as the *Tulane Drama Review, Field and Stream, Saturday Review, Better Homes and Gardens, Today's Health, National Geographic Magazine,* and *American Heritage.*

This list is, of course, merely suggestive of the wide range of materials to be found in periodicals. When you are looking for a specific sort of information, use the *Readers' Guide,* which indexes most of the magazines you will want to refer to in preparing a speech. Look in this index under various topical headings that are related to your subject. Similar indexes also are available for technical journals and publications.

Professional and trade journals

Nearly every profession, industry, trade, and academic field has one or more specialized journals. Such publications include: *The*

Annals of the American Academy of Political and Social Science, American Economic Review, Quarterly Journal of Speech, Journal of the American Medical Association, Journal of Applied Psychology, AFL-CIO American Federationist, Trade Unionist, Coal Age, Educational Theatre Journal, and others. These journals contain a great deal of detailed and specialized information in their respective fields.

Yearbooks and encyclopedias

The *Statistical Abstract of the United States* is the most reliable source of comprehensive data on a wide variety of subjects ranging from weather and birth rates to coal production. It is published by the federal government and is available in most libraries. Also useful as a source of facts and figures is the *World Almanac and Book of Facts.* Encyclopedias such as the *Britannica* and *Americana,* which attempt to cover the entire field of human knowledge in a score of volumes, are valuable chiefly as an initial reference source or for information on subjects which you do not need to explore deeply. Refer to them for important scientific, geographical, literary, or historical facts, and also for bibliographies of authoritative books on a subject.

Special documents and reports

Various government agencies—state, national, and international—as well as many independent organizations publish reports on special subjects. Among government publications, those most frequently consulted by speakers are the reports of Congressional committees or those of the United States Department of Labor or of Commerce. Reports on agricultural problems, business, government, engineering, and scientific experimentation are issued by many state universities. Such endowed organizations as the Carnegie, Rockefeller, and Ford Foundations, and such groups as the Foreign Policy Association, the League of Women Voters, and the United States Chamber of Commerce also publish reports and pamphlets.

Books on special subjects

There are few subjects suitable for a speech upon which someone has not written a book. As a guide to these books, use the subject-matter headings in the card catalog of your library.

General literature

Wide reading in general literature provides a speaker with a wealth of illustrations and literary allusions which frequently can be used to illuminate an idea. Quick sources of apt quotations are Bartlett's

Familiar Quotations, H. L. Mencken's *A New Dictionary of Quotations on Historical Principles from Ancient and Modern Sources,* Arthur Richmond's *Modern Quotations for Ready Reference,* George Seldes' *The Great Quotations,* and Burton Stevenson's *The Home Book of Quotations.*

Biography

Detailed accounts of the lives of famous persons often furnish material for illustrating or amplifying ideas: The *Dictionary of National Biography* (deceased Britishers), the *Dictionary of American Biography* (deceased Americans), *Who's Who* (living Britishers), *Who's Who in America, Current Biography,* and similar collections which contain biographical sketches are useful in locating facts about famous people and in finding the qualifications of authorities whose testimony you may wish to quote.

Radio and television broadcasts

Lectures, debates, and the addresses of leaders in business and government frequently are broadcast over radio and television; and many of these talks later are mimeographed or printed by the stations or by the organizations that sponsor them. Usually copies may be secured upon request. If no manuscript is available and you are taking notes as you hear the broadcast, listen with particular care in order to get an exact record of the speaker's words or meaning. Just as you must quote items from other sources accurately and honestly, so you are obligated to respect the remarks someone has made on a radio or television broadcast and to give that person full credit.

Obviously, you will not have to investigate all of these sources for every speech. Your personal experience often will provide you with adequate knowledge, or you will need to locate only a few additional facts. Usually, however, a search among several outside sources will provide you with material that will make your speech more authoritative and interesting. Even though laborious at first, a careful investigation of these sources will be doubly valuable because you will be learning how to skim rapidly through a mass of material to pick out the important facts and ideas. This skill is valuable not only in preparing speeches, but in every type of work where research into printed materials is required.

RECORDING THE MATERIAL

Have you ever begun to tell a story only to find that it has slipped your mind entirely? Or have you ever tried in vain to recall an important date or name? Since it is impossible to remember everything you read or hear, you must have some method for recording potential speech materials. Moreover, it is important that you *record immediately* any data which you think may later prove useful. All too often, to recover a fact or idea after a period of days or weeks, you must engage in a long and laborious search, and sometimes you lose the fact or idea forever.

A few persons prefer to keep their notes in notebooks, but for most research purposes notebooks are not so efficient as cards. Cards of various sizes may be utilized (4 x 6 are recommended), and a few should be carried in your pocket or brief case for use whenever you encounter an idea you wish to preserve. Completed cards may be kept permanently in a classified file and are easy to sort and rearrange when you begin to organize your speech. Moreover, figures or quotations which you wish to present to your audience verbatim may be read directly and unobtrusively from the card itself.

In preparing note cards observe the following rules:

Place in the upper left-hand corner a subject heading which accurately labels the material recorded on the card. Such a heading will greatly facilitate the process of sorting and selection when you begin to prepare your speech.

Note in the upper right-hand corner the part or section of your speech in which the information on the card probably will be used. Will it help to develop or illustrate the problem with which you are concerned? Will it prove the soundness of the solution you propose? Will it point to certain benefits or advantages to be gained from acting according to your recommendations? If it is not possible to decide upon the proper classificatory label during the early stages of your speech preparation, leave the space blank to be filled in later.

Put only one fact or idea, or a few closely related facts or ideas, on each card. Unless you follow this rule, you will not be able to sort and to classify the data properly, or to have at hand the specific information needed in developing a particular part of your talk.

Indicate verbatim quotations by quotation marks. In the first sample card (p. 150), the note is a direct quotation and therefore carries quotation marks. Use direct quotations when they are sufficiently brief or when they state facts or ideas so clearly or forcefully that you probably will want to reproduce the original wording in your speech. Condense or paraphrase longer or less important statements, but in doing so be sure to preserve the author's meaning.

Responsibilities of the Press[1]	(classification) Problem: Presumption of Guilt

"In law, the accused is presumed innocent until proved guilty. The press pays formal obeisance to this principle but frequently betrays it in practice. In a variety of ways, news stories tend to convey presumption of guilt. If the police announce that the accused has confessed, the press usually accepts the assertion as proof of guilt, even though the confession may later turn out to be false. If no confession is mentioned but the police provide a lengthy chronicle of what the accused is supposed to have done, the newspaper account usually reads like a statement of fact rather than merely an elaboration of the charge. The occasional qualifying phrase 'as the police allege' or 'the police charge that' is likely to be lost on the average reader."

Irwin Ross, "Trial by Newspaper," The Atlantic CCXVI (September 1965), 64.

Congressional Apportionment[2] (card 1)	(classification) Changes in Representation by States

State	1950 Census	1960 Census	State	1950 Census	1960 Census
Ala.....	9	8	Ind.....	11	11
Alaska..	1	1	Iowa....	8	7
Ariz....	2	3	Kan.....	6	5
Ark.....	6	4	Ky......	8	7
Calif...	30	38	La......	8	8
Colo....	4	4	Me......	3	2
Conn....	6	6	Md......	7	8
Del.....	1	1	Mass....	14	12
Fla.....	8	12	Mich....	18	19
Ga......	10	10	Minn....	9	8
Hawaii..	1	2	Miss....	6	5
Idaho...	2	2	Mo......	11	10
Ill.....	25	24	Mont....	2	2

(Continued on card 2)

The World Almanac and Book of Facts for 1965, ed. Harry Hansen (New York World Telegram and Sun, 1965), p. 47.

[1]Irwin Ross, "Trial by Newspaper," *The Atlantic*, CCXVI (September 1965), p. 64. Copyright © 1965, by The Atlantic Monthly Company, Boston, Mass. Reprinted with permission.

[2]*The World Almanac and Book of Facts for 1965*, ed. Harry Hansen (*New York World Telegram and Sun*, 1965), p. 47.

Note at the bottom of the card the exact source from which the information is drawn. This point cannot be stressed too strongly. Often you will want to recheck a note for accuracy or completeness, or you may be called upon to verify the facts you cite. For both of these reasons it is important that you have an exact record of the source from which the information was drawn.

CLASSIFYING MATERIAL

When you first begin to gather material, a simple topical method of classification usually is satisfactory. Group the cards together according to the apparent similarity of the headings which you have placed in the upper left corner. But as the number of cards increases, you will need a more systematic method. Here are a few possible methods:

Chronological. You may classify your material on the basis of the time to which it refers—by years, by months, or by its relation to some fixed event.

Causal. This method divides material relating to the causes of a phenomenon from material relating to its effects.

Problem-solution. Here the facts about a *problem* are put into one group, and the descriptions of the various *solutions* and the evidence which supports them are put into another.

Location. When this method is used, the material is divided according to the localities, countries, states, or other space units to which it refers.

Begin by classifying your notes according to one of these methods or a similar one. Then as the material in any category becomes bulky or unwieldy, subdivide that class.

The value of classifying your material as you gather it is twofold. First, you can see at a glance what sort of information you lack and, in this way, can make your further investigations more purposeful. Second, the organization of the material into a speech is made much simpler if the material is in some form of reasonable order before the actual organizing process begins. If you follow a systematic method of ordering and preserving speech materials over a period of time, you will have a steadily growing mass of readily available information at your disposal, not only for the speech you are currently preparing but also for future use.

The gathering, recording, and classifying of the materials for a speech comprise no small part of the total task of speech preparation. Therefore, you will do well to begin your research early enough so that you will have plenty of time to digest the information, organize it, and practice presenting it in its finished form.

Problems

1. Visit your college library and list the following:

a. Five yearbooks or compilations of statistical data.

b. Four encyclopedias, with some indication of the sort of information in which each specializes.

c. Three technical or scholarly journals relating to your present or proposed major in college.

d. Two indexes to periodical literature other than the *Reader's Guide*.

e. Five biographical dictionaries.

f. Two standard atlases of the world.

g. Two reference works that list books in print.

2. Examine carefully selected cards in the card catalog of your library, and answer the following questions:

a. How many times is each book listed in the catalog, and *how* is it listed?

b. What information about the author is contained on the catalog card?

c. What information does the card give you about the book itself?

3. Without the help of the reference librarian, answer the following questions and name the sources in which you found the answers:

a. How many miles of interstate highways have been completed to date?

b. What was the size of the American expeditionary force in Europe during World War I? During World War II?

c. Where did the governor of your state attend college?

d. How many hits were collected by the baseball team that won the World Series in 1964?

e. How did the senators from your state vote on the last military appropriations bill?

f. Who is the author of *Men and Machines?*

g. How many articles on trade with Africa were published during the first four months of 1966?

h. How much does your state government contribute to the support of the schools in your community?

i. What are five recent books on corporation finance?

4. Select a subject of some substance and scope on which you would like to give a classroom speech in the future.

a. Outline all the pertinent information you already have on this subject.

b. Indicate what first-hand observations you could make concerning it.

c. List persons whom you could interview on the subject, and decide what questions you would ask each.

d. Devise a sample questionnaire on the subject and indicate the groups or individuals to whom it might be sent.

e. Prepare a bibliography of printed materials on the subject, including (a) five references taken from a periodicals index, and (b) five books found in the card catalog of your library.

5. Read selected articles or books on a subject of your choice; and, following the samples on p. 150, prepare five or six note cards, at least one of which presents statistics, one a direct quotation, one an indirect quotation, and one an illustration or example.

6. On slips of paper write three questions beginning, "Where would you go to find out about ________?" Put these questions in a hat with those submitted by your classmates and take turns drawing them out to be answered.

7. Evaluate radio and television newscasts and public service programs as sources of speech materials. What advantages do they have over printed sources? What disadvantages? What special rules or cautions should be observed when gathering materials from these sources?

8. Practice gathering speech materials through interviews, as follows: Select five or six persons in your speech class who because of work experience, travel, service in the armed forces, hobbies, or other personal involvement have acquired a considerable amount of knowledge concerning a certain subject. Interview these individuals, following the suggestions set forth in this chapter. Make sure that you have a series of questions, planned in advance; that you interpret correctly the information you are given; that you record it accurately; and that you subsequently verify any statements which you might want to quote verbatim.

Speaking assignment

1. Prepare a five-minute speech on any subject that you believe will be of interest to your classmates. (Review Chapter 8, "Analyzing the Audience and the Occasion.") In this speech, use material gathered from personal experience, from interviews, and from printed sources. In addition to the usual outline, hand to your instructor properly prepared note cards on which you have recorded the material gathered in interviews and from printed sources.

Suggestions for further reading

Ella V. Aldrich, *Using Books and Libraries*, rev. ed. (New York: Prentice-Hall Inc., 1946).

Jacques Barzun and Henry P. Graff, *The Modern Researcher* (New York: Harcourt, Brace and World, Inc., 1957). See esp. Part Two, "Research."

Walter Van Dyke Bingham and Bruce Victor Moore, *How to Interview*, 4th ed. (New York: Harper & Row, Publishers, 1959), Chapter I, "First Principles"; Chapter II, "Learning How to Interview"; Chapter XV, "Conclusions about Interviewing."

Douglas Ehninger and Wayne Brockriede, *Decision by Debate* (New York: Dodd, Mead & Co., 1963), Chapter IV, "Obtaining Information: Personal Knowledge, Contacts with Experts"; Chapter V, "Obtaining Information: Printed Sources"; Chapter VI, "Recording and Filing Information."

R. C. Oldfield, *The Psychology of the Interview* (London: Methuen, 1951).

Harry W. Robbins and Robert T. Oliver, *Developing Ideas into Essays and Speeches* (New York: Longmans, Green & Co., Ltd., 1943), Chapter IV, "Gathering Primary Materials."

CHAPTER TEN

Supporting the main points

Human beings, especially when they are members of an audience, find it difficult to understand abstract ideas, bare and unadorned. Nor will they easily believe a proposition or act upon a proposal without stimulation or proof.

Suppose, for example, that the purpose of your speech is to explain to an audience why "'bad' money drives out 'good' money," or to prove that "Military training teaches tolerance and cooperation." How would the average listener react to each of these statements upon first hearing it? In the former instance, he would be almost certain to think, "I do not understand this assertion; please explain it." In the latter, he probably would think, "I doubt or disbelieve this statement; prove it." These reactions would not arise because the hearer was dull or obstinate, but because he was unable to comprehend an abstract and ambiguous statement and honestly reluctant to accept any proposition without some notion of the evidence and reasoning which underlie it. Materials which provide the explanation and proof upon which understanding and belief rest are called *supporting materials.* Their purpose is to clarify, to amplify, or to establish the major points or contentions of your speech.

Without supporting material, the thoughts you present may be as well organized as the bones in a skeleton, but they will be equally bare and unappealing. The forms of support are the flesh and blood which bring your ideas to life. The thought-skeleton of your speech must be there to give it unity and coherence, but it is the meat which you put upon that skeleton that gives it body and warmth and reality for your audience. You must round out your points with such facts and examples as will make them clear and vivid—with verbal material that is concrete and specific—and when appropriate, with visible support, such as charts, diagrams, and models.

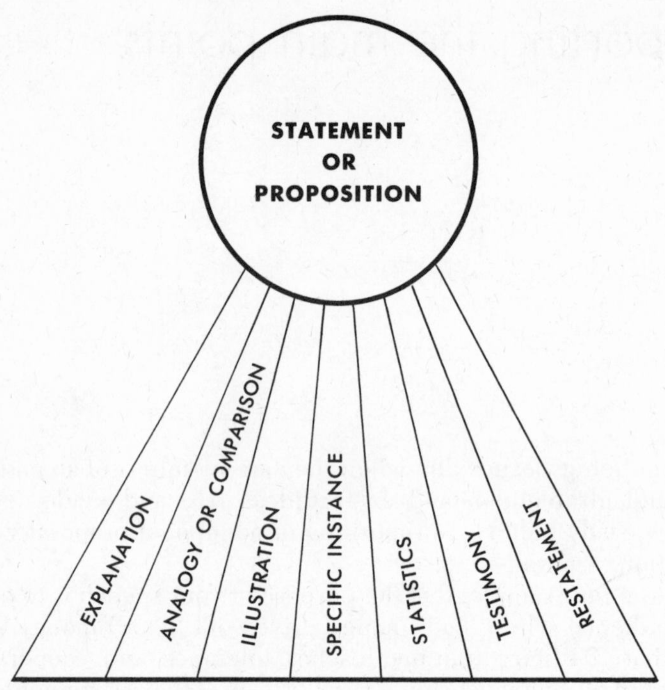

THE FORMS OF VERBAL SUPPORTING MATERIAL

In general, there are seven forms of verbal support which may be used to develop the ideas in a speech:

1. Explanation
2. Analogy or comparison
3. Illustration (detailed example)
   a. Hypothetical illustration
   b. Factual illustration
4. Specific instances (undeveloped examples)
5. Statistics
6. Testimony
7. Restatement

Often two or more of these forms are combined, as when figures or examples are used within an illustration, or the testimony of an expert is offered to add weight to a restatement. As you consider the following explanations of these seven types of material, notice that the first three (explanation, comparison, and illustration), though they sometimes may be employed as proof, are primarily useful in making an idea clear and vivid; while the next three (instances, statistics, and testimony) have as their principal function establishing and verifying the truth or importance of a point which the speaker wishes to prove. Restatement, as we shall learn, serves both purposes.

Explanation

By definition, an explanation is an expository or descriptive passage, the purpose of which is to make a term, concept, process, or idea clear and intelligible. It may also set forth the relation between a whole and its parts. Usually explanation involves exposition alone, but sometimes other forms of supporting material also may be used.

In a speech at the University of Portland, Mortimer J. Adler explained his conception of a liberal education, first by breaking it down into its parts, and then by giving examples of liberal studies:

Liberal education means two things essentially. On the side of the liberal arts, it means all the basic skills of the mind—the skills of reading and writing and speaking and listening, observing, measuring, and calculating; the skills essential to all forms of learning; the skills required for all forms of communication. And on the side of substance, liberal education means the humanities, which centuries ago would have been called "humane letters." By that, one does not just mean poetry or history, but even more philosophy and theology, and even the natural and social sciences when these are studied with a humane rather than a technical interest.

Let me explain this one step further. The humanities, as the word itself should suggest, represent the permanent and universal features of human life and society, which stem from the constancy of human nature itself—the powers and aspirations of man. Hence philosophy and theology are central and must be central in any humanistic education. As Cardinal Newman has taught us all, to be basically liberal, education must be through and through philosophical and theological.[1]

Definition and authority, as well as examples, were used by Mrs. Lauralee Peters, a student at the University of Kansas, to explain "totalitarianism":

To understand totalitarianism it is necessary for us to understand the unique aspects of a totalitarian state which make it different from other forms of government. J. A. Piekalkiewicz, professor of political science at the University of Kansas, has devoted considerable research and writing to the problem of

[1]Mr. Adler's address, delivered on January 13, 1963, is reprinted in *Town and Gown,* Alumni Magazine of the University of Portland (January 1963).

defining totalitarianism. It is, he says, a system in which the group or party in control claims to have a complete and comprehensive plan or idea to answer all problems of a political, social, and economic nature in a given society. They claim to have, that is, a monopoly on truth, and their monopoly includes the exclusion of all alternative solutions and all differing points of view. The solutions they have are total and comprehensive, and the control they exercise over the people and the institutions of society is total and complete.

This definition, I think, helps us understand the unusual nature of the totalitarian state. Totalitarianism, for its existence, demands not only concentration of power in the hands of the government, but that this power be unlimited. Governmental power must be unlimited in two respects. First, it means complete government control of school curricula, newspapers, magazines, public and private utterances of individuals; in short, all aspects of social and intellectual life. This control is maintained through extensive police forces with the power to eliminate any deviation or suspected deviation from the "official line." Second, there must be present a single-minded ideology which is all-encompassing in nature and to which devotion can be demanded of the people. The devotion is demanded not only to the ultimate ends of the society, but also to any means which the regime might employ. This is illustrated aptly by Arthur Koestler in his novel, *Darkness at Noon,* in which the central character is liquidated, not because he disagreed with the *end* of the Russian state under Stalin, but with certain minor aspects of the *means* being employed. Modern-day examples of the existence of such conditions include Hitler's Germany, Mussolini's Italy, and the Communist regime, particularly under Stalin. Another example of the totalitarian state which points to these characteristics is that of Paraguay under the rule of the Jesuits. Here was a state in which unlimited power was given to a government which possessed an all-encompassing ideology, in the form of the church, which demanded allegiance of the people.[2]

In explaining the problem created by an unfavorable balance of payments in the international market, James F. Oates, Jr., Chairman of the Board of the Equitable Life Assurance Society, depended chiefly on statistics:

But let me first review, very briefly, the problem we face with our balance of payments. For seven years, 1958 through 1964, the United States has continuously had a deficit in its international payments accounts. As you know, this means simply that the United States has, during each of these years, spent, loaned, or invested abroad more than foreigners have purchased, loaned, or invested in this country. The total accumulated deficit during these seven years

[2]Lauralee Peters, "What Is Totalitarianism?" *Contemporary American Speeches,* ed. Wil A. Linkugel, R. R. Allen, and Richard L. Johannesen (Belmont, Calif.: Wadsworth, 1965), pp. 70-71.

amounted to $21 billion computed on the conventional basis. This deficit was financed by exporting roughly $7 billion of gold and $14 billion of dollar claims. The U.S. gold stock is now down to $14 billion, and outstanding dollar claims in the hands of foreigners exceed $30 billion.

Our failure to correct the deficit has opened to question the very integrity of the U.S. dollar, its role as a reserve currency, and the continued survival of the free world monetary system. So far this year we have lost $1.5 billion of gold. Unless this outflow is stopped, there will come a time when we can no longer provide gold for dollars at a rate of $35 per ounce.[3]

Valuable as explanation is in making ideas clear, two cautions must be observed in its use: First, *do not allow your explanations to become too long or involved;* and, second, *do not talk in vague or abstract terms.* Many an audience has been put to sleep by a long-winded explanation filled with unimportant or irrelevant details or by one conducted in language so vague and general that it was almost impossible to follow. Keep your explanations simple, brief, and accurate; combine them with other forms of supporting material so as to make each idea concrete and specific. This is a good rule to follow in all forms of communication, written as well as oral.

Analogy or comparison

In an analogy or comparison, similarities are pointed out between something which is already known, understood, or believed by the audience and something which is not. Thus, in part at least, we may explain the game of cricket by comparing it with baseball, or tell how a thermostat works by comparing it with a simple temperature thermometer.

At times also we may clarify an idea by comparing it with something which, though quite different in nature, yet exhibits similar characteristics or relationships. Tyler Dennett, former President of Williams College, quoted a Massachusetts statesman who once described the difference between a democracy and a dictatorship as follows:

It is the difference between a raft and a yacht. On the yacht you are safe if you have a good captain as dictator. On the raft your feet are wet all the time, but you never sink.[4]

William C. Marquis, in a speech explaining some of the advantages a small business has over a large one, used this analogy:

[3]James F. Oates, Jr., "Thinking Ahead in Federal Tax Policy," *Vital Speeches of the Day*, XXXII (December 1, 1965), 107.

[4]Tyler Dennett, "Democracy as a Factor in Education," *Vital Speeches of the Day*, III (May 15, 1937), 461.

On major matters [a] big business moves with a ponderous slowness. It's like a huge ocean liner. It can turn, but the turning takes time and then more time. Usually there have to be three or four busy little tugs alongside to warp the giant into home port.[5]

The rapid rate at which new information is accumulated in the modern world and the rapid rate at which that information becomes outmoded were described by Peter G. Peterson, President of Bell and Howell, by referring to a flooded river:

In the space age, the flow of knowledge is as relentless and in a real sense as uncompromising as this spring's Mississippi River. It imposes on us the stiff and, in many ways, new requirement that we not merely adjust but that we *anticipate* the future.[6]

Still another analogy of the same type appears in a speech in which Albert Wass de Czege, a Hungarian writer, urged an American audience to preserve their freedom by accepting their responsibilities:

If you want to live in your own home, you have to take care of the roof, paint the walls, watch for termites, and repair whatever needs to be repaired. If you are too lazy to do all that, you can live in an apartment, and in this case someone else will do all these things for you. However, the one who owns the building in which you decide to live will have the right to tell you what kind of pets you can have, how many children, and what colors you can use to paint your rooms.

The same is true about your country. You can keep it a private home that suits your needs, your own way of life. Or you can concentrate it into a huge apartment house in which the government will tell you how to live, as is done in the communist dominated countries. It is entirely up to you.[7]

Although analogies which compare things that are unlike—yachts with governments, businesses with ocean liners, knowledge with rivers, and so forth—may be excellent means of clarifying a point or making it vivid, they are of decidedly limited value as proof. For this purpose it always is better to employ comparisons of *like* phenomena—to argue, for example, that a system of one-way traffic on the downtown streets of City X would relieve congestion and promote safety because such a system has had these effects in City Y, or that

[5]"What Is a Small Business Man?" *Vital Speeches of the Day*, XXXII (October 15, 1965), 22.

[6]"Help Wanted," *Vital Speeches of the Day*, XXXI (September 15, 1965), 725.

[7]"The Golden Key to America," *Vital Speeches of the Day*, XXVI (February 15, 1960), 267

a longer orientation period would improve the academic performance of freshmen students at College A because it has done so at College B. Note how a comparison of like phenomena—in this case two state universities—was used to prove one of the points advanced in a student speech by George Gruner:

To show that an active and effective student government would help to reduce disciplinary problems at Iowa, we may refer to the experience of the university I attended before transferring here last fall—a school which, like Iowa, has between 15,000 and 16,000 students and which is a publicly supported state institution.

Prior to reconstituting student government as a vital and responsible force, the office of the dean at my former university handled more than 600 disciplinary cases each year. After putting new responsibility and authority into the hands of the students themselves, however, this number was cut by more than half, and the number of merely trivial or nuisance offenses decreased by about two-thirds. The dean himself attributed this reduction chiefly to the new sense of pride which a revitalized student government had given the students in their school.[8]

Because it attempts to base a conclusion on a single parallel instance, an analogy which is thus used as proof must meet a rigid test. And this is that the instances compared must be *closely similar in all essential respects.* Whether giving more authority to student government at Iowa would have the effect predicted, for instance, would depend upon the extent to which Iowa actually did resemble Mr. Gruner's previous school in size, composition of student body, administrative structure, and similarly pertinent elements. Clearly, you could not infer that what worked in a small denominational college also would work in a large state university or that an effect achieved in a select private school also would be obtained in an institution whose student body was more varied. Do the similarities between the items or classes compared outweigh any differences that might be relevant to the conclusion you are drawing? This is the question that always must be asked when you attempt to use an analogy as proof for a contention or claim.

Illustration

An illustration is a detailed example of the idea or statement to be supported. It is the narration of an incident to bring out the point you

[8] "Let's Revitalize Student Government," delivered in an advanced public speaking course at the University of Iowa, March 14, 1966.

are trying to make. Sometimes an illustration relates the results obtained elsewhere from adopting an actual proposal the speaker advocates; sometimes it describes in detail a case *typical* of the general conditions the speaker wishes to emphasize. Note its two principal characteristics: the illustration is narrative in form—it tells a story; and the details of the story are vividly described.

There are two principal types of illustrations: hypothetical and factual. The former tells a story which *could* happen; the latter tells what *actually has happened.*

A *hypothetical illustration,* though it is an imaginary narrative, must be consistent with the known facts; it must be reasonable. The following is such an illustration:

> Let's put ourselves in the other fellow's place. If you got no satisfaction out of your job as employer, if you had no pride in the sense of accomplishment, if you didn't feel yourself a vital part of a dynamic organization, all the pay you would get would be money. Take away all those things that make up your compensation, and every one of you would demand that your pay be doubled, because money would be all that was left.
>
> Out in your shop a man comes to work at 7 A.M. He doesn't know too much about his job and almost nothing about his company or how his work fits into it. He works 8 hours and goes home—with what? His pay and nothing more. Nobody (except the union steward!) took much if any notice of him. Nobody complimented him if he did do well because nobody except a foreman *knows* whether or not he did well, and he realized *that* fact. Nobody ever flattered him by asking his opinion about something. In millions of cases nobody ever told him the importance of his work.
>
> At night he goes home to his family and neighbors—unimportant, with nothing to boast about or even talk about. And the union calls a meeting to discuss a grievance—that workman can get up on his feet and sound off while people listen, he can be an officer with a title, he can boast to his family and friends how he "gave those big shots of the company what-for!" A strike vote is exciting!—Being a picket is important!—He gets looked at and talked about; he wears a badge!
>
> Again let's be honest. If you and I were in that worker's situation, wouldn't we do pretty much what he's doing?[9]

The hypothetical illustration is used principally to make an abstract explanation more vivid and concrete. It is particularly useful in ex-

[9]Charles J. Stilwell, "Effective Leadership for Better Employee Relations," *Vital Speeches of the Day* (December 15, 1947), 157.

plaining a complicated plan. Instead of merely outlining the details, you take some hypothetical person, yourself or a member of the audience, and envision him going through the process or living and working under the plan. Note in the above example how the speaker leads his listeners to put themselves in the workman's place.

As a means of gaining clarity the hypothetical illustration is useful because the speaker may tell his story as he wants; as proof, however, it is of doubtful value simply because it is hypothetical.

A factual illustration, as we have said, is a narrative that describes in detail a situation or incident that has actually occurred. It is one of the most telling forms of support a speaker can use. Because details are brought into the story, the incident is made clear and vivid to the listeners; because the incident actually happened, the illustration frequently has high persuasive value. In the factual illustration which follows, note particularly the vividness of the imagery and the personal tone created by the use of direct discourse:

> Today, man-made law is in conflict with natural law. . . . I met Ed Davis, our guide, on vacation after I had studied engineering at Columbia University. Impressed with scientific methods, I tried to substitute them for the art of angling. They caught me no fish. Finally, Ed dug down in his tackle box and produced a small yellow, low-wing wooden monoplane with a metal propeller that would spin. He had hung a triple hook where the tail-skid belonged and had soldered a swivel to the prop shaft. Now, as he snapped this to my wire leader, he grinned and remarked, "Try this. It's about time to give 'em something comical!" With that he tossed the contraption over the side.
>
> As I trolled it astern, the propeller chugged like the churning screw of an empty tramp steamer riding high in ballast. And, believe it or not, a huge muskellunge, one that must have previously ignored many lures scientifically designed to imitate live bait, rose up and hit that yellow monoplane. When, after a long battle, the fish lay stretched out in the bottom of our canoe, I expressed my amazement to Ed. Pausing to choose his words, Ed vouchsafed another truth germane to our subject. "It ain't how a bait looks to you and me that counts," he said. "It's how it looks to the fish."[10]

In developing his point that a large part of the success of any business rests on a genuine understanding of human relationships, Jack I. Straus, Chairman of R.H. Macy and Company, drew upon this factual illustration to generate a strong sense of reality for his listeners:

[10]Eugene E. Wilson, "The New Role of the Engineer," *Vital Speeches of the Day*, XIII (November 1, 1946), 61.

Not long ago I received a complaint from a college professor's wife in Athens, Georgia. Our Davison division has a store there. It seems that this customer and her husband had gotten their signals mixed, and both had bought an item that they had wanted, so one was returned for credit. I remember the price very well —$5.09. Instead of getting the credit, she was billed for $10.18. She paid $5.09, expecting the credit for the other on her next bill. P. S. She never got the credit so she started a correspondence that I am sure must have cost us at least $150 in labor, overhead, postage, and executive time. Finally, six months later, she sent the correspondence to me—the whole big bundle of it.

You can be sure that by the time any complaint gets to me, the customer is really hot. This one was exasperated almost to tears.

The minute I read her letter I phoned our division headquarters and said: "Pay the lady her $5.09 and apologize to her. Don't bother about the facts of the case now. But when you have apologized, check all the facts and I'll bet you will find we made a mistake." They did as I suggested and sure enough we had made the mistake. We had not credited the item which had been returned.

But even if we had been right, what had we to gain by battling a customer—particularly on a university campus that provided most of our customers for our Athens store?

I say if we are right and the customer is wrong but we can't convince her, settle the matter promptly in her favor. Sure there are deadbeats, but they're part of the cost of doing business. We could have paid off fifty questionable claims and still saved money in this case.[11]

Three considerations should be kept in mind when choosing a factual illustration to support an idea. *First, is it clearly related to the idea?* If you have to labor to show its connection, the illustration will be of little use. *Second, is it a fair example?* An audience is quick to notice unusual circumstances in an illustration; and if you seem to have picked only the exceptional case, your example will not prove convincing. *Third, is it vivid and impressive in detail?* The primary value of an illustration is the sense of reality which it creates. If this quality is absent, the advantage of using an illustration is lost. Be sure, then, that your illustrations are pointed, fair, and vivid.

Specific instance

A specific instance is an undeveloped illustration or example. Instead of describing a situation in detail, you merely refer to it pointedly and succinctly, in passing. When time prevents the development of an illustration to clarify an idea or to show the seriousness of a

[11]Jack I. Straus, "Wanted: Concern for the Customer," *Vital Speeches of the Day*, XXXII (December 1, 1965), 110.

problem, you sometimes may achieve the same result by mentioning a succession of instances which are already more or less known to the audience. Thus the impact is a kind of cumulative one. Speaking before the Inter-American Defense College, C. Langdon White, Professor of Geography at Stanford University, used specific instances to remind his listeners of some of the difficulties in our relations with Latin America:

The road to good neighborliness [with Latin America] is strewn with a number of obstacles, obstacles that are partly geographic and partly human. I submit here a few of the more obvious and significant differences between us:

1. Difference in language
2. Difference in race
3. Difference in religion
4. Differences in stage of economic development
5. Differences in our legal systems
6. Differences in our ideas of democracy (except perhaps on paper)
7. Differences in our attitude toward manual work
8. Differences in standard of living . . .
9. Differences in per capita annual wage: $400 average for Latin America, $2,450 for U.S. (1963)
10. Differences in rate of literacy

These differences form a chasm, a *cultural chasm*, that is not easy to bridge. As a result of the differences listed, we tend to irritate each other; in a slangy sense, we just do not see eye-to-eye.[12]

In a speech entitled "Without a Word," Miss Laura Ann Wilbur, a student at Mississippi Southern College, employed specific instances as follows:

Look briefly with me at our United States today, and see, as I have seen, how our freedom of speech is being lost.

In Colorado, a teacher was advised to discontinue a study of the Mexican laborers in beet-sugar fields because the subject was "too controversial." Fearing the criticism of local businessmen, a home economics teacher dropped a project in which her pupils tested certain nationally advertised brands of household appliances. An English teacher found it wise to remove John Steinbeck's books from the literature course. A biology teacher was forbidden to continue use of the film "Human Growth." At an Illinois college, teachers became suspect when they recommended that their students read Karl Marx in

[12]C. Langdon White, "Anglo-America and Latin America: Can They Become Better Neighbors?" *Vital Speeches of the Day*, XXIX (October 1, 1963), 746.

order to understand the philosophies of Communism, and *Mein Kampf* to understand Fascism better.

Teachers find themselves under suspicion when they discuss Russian authors in World Lit classes, even though many of these writers died before Marx was born. Professors of history, economics, political and social science must be careful if, when, and how they discuss Russia.

In Galesburg, Illinois, an alderman was irked because a college political science class was doing field research on the operation of the city government. The discussions he stirred up placed several members of the college faculty under suspicion of "Communistic leanings" by the townspeople. . . .

The principal of a Rhode Island high school suspended one of the student clubs which called itself the "UNESCO Thinkers." Why? Why? Because a denominational paper had charged UNESCO itself (not the student club) with being under "atheistic control."

. . . .

These are just a few examples, but they begin to show us the conditions existing in the United States today.[13]

If the names, events, or situations cited by the speaker are well known to his listeners, specific instances may provide strong support for a claim or contention. To an American audience, for example, the assertion that a poor boy may become President can be supported merely by mentioning the names of Andrew Jackson, Abraham Lincoln, and Herbert Hoover. On subjects with which the audience is not familiar, however, or on subjects concerning which people have marked differences of opinion, it is well to supplement specific instances with more fully developed examples or illustrations.

Statistics

Not all figures are statistics; some are merely numbers. Statistics are figures used to show *relationships* among things: to point out increases or decreases, to emphasize largeness or smallness, or to show how one phenomenon affects another. Statistics are impressive because, when properly gathered and analyzed, they constitute "facts" which help to convince the audience of the truth or justice of the speaker's claims. Moreover, they enable one to cover a great deal of ground in a short time. Note how much information concerning the national economy is packed into the following paragraph of a speech by Paul W. McCracken:

[13]Excerpt from a speech entitled "Without a Word" by Laura Ann Wilbur in *Speech Practices* by Waldo W. Braden and Mary Louise Gehring. Copyright © 1958 by Waldo W. Braden and Mary Louise Gehring. Reprinted by permission of Harper & Row, Publishers.

When . . . the statisticians close the books on 1965, the facts are going to make exceedingly good reading. The year's national output will probably be just short of $670 billion, showing a gain of more than 6½ per cent over that for 1964. The persistently rising demand for output has opened up job opportunities more rapidly than the normal growth of the labor force, and the unemployment rate dropped well below 5 per cent for the first time since 1957. In fact, we have now moved into the zone of reasonably full employment. The length of the work week, one measure of pressures in the labor market, was at least 41 hours during most of the year, substantially above the 40.3 hours that prevailed, on the average, in the full employment years of 1955-1957. The unemployment rate for married men is now back to 2 per cent, or about the same level as in the mid-1950's. The help-wanted index computed by the N.I.C.B., one of the unfortunately few statistics on the number of jobs seeking people, has advanced sharply and is now 20 per cent higher than a year ago. And labor shortages are being mentioned with increasing frequency as a limitation to further increases in operating rates.[14]

Masses of figures or unusually large or small figures often are difficult for an audience to comprehend. Therefore, whenever possible they should be translated into more immediately understandable terms, terms which are concrete and specific rather than abstract and general. In the following passage, Hugh L. Dryden, Deputy Administrator of the National Aeronautics and Space Administration, used a number of comparisons to show how large a building is required to house the Saturn V manned lunar rocket:

The Vertical Assembly Building will be one of the largest structures on earth. According to present plans, the high-bay area will be 524 feet tall, about as tall as the Washington Monument, or only 58 feet less than the Gulf Building in Pittsburgh. It will be almost as wide and long as it is tall, 448 by 513. The height of the door is 456 feet, tall enough to permit a 41-story building to slide through. Its total volume will be about 128 million cubic feet, more than twice that of the Merchandise Mart in Chicago and 1⅔ times the volume of the Pentagon Building in Washington. Four space vehicles may be assembled in this building at the same time, protected from salt air and hurricane winds.[15]

[14]Paul W. McCracken, "The Outlook for 1966," *Vital Speeches of the Day*, XXXII (October 15, 1965), 16.

[15]"The U.S. Space Program," address at the annual dinner meeting of the Pittsburgh Post, The Society of American Military Engineers, April 2, 1963. Text supplied by National Aeronautics and Space Administration.

During the course of an interview on the same subject of lunar exploration, Dr. Warren Weaver attempted to provide some notion of the huge amount of money which the United States is spending to land a man on the moon. To establish his point, he cited how many other things could be done with the $30 billion now earmarked for that purpose:

> With that $30 billion we could give every teacher a 10 per cent raise for 10 years; endow 200 small colleges with $10 million each; finance the education through graduate school of 50,000 scientists at $4,000 a year; build 10 new medical schools at $200 million each; build and endow complete universities for more than 50 developing countries; [and] create three new Rockefeller Foundations with $500 million each.[16]

Finally, to help his audience conceive of the immense age of the earth, Richard Carrington, a science writer, gave the readers of the *Milwaukee Journal* this comparison:

> If the earth's history could be compressed into a single year, the first eight months would be completely without life, the next two would see only the primitive creatures, mammals wouldn't appear until the second week in December, and no *homo sapiens* until 11:45 P.M. on Dec. 31. The entire period of man's written history would occupy the final 60 seconds before midnight.[17]

Other ways of making statistics more readily understandable include stating very large figures in round numbers (say "nearly 4,000,000," rather than "3,984,256"), breaking totals down on a per capita basis, writing figures on the blackboard as you discuss them, pointing to prepared charts or graphs on which the data are presented, handing out mimeographed material summarizing the statistics you are presenting, and slowing down your rate of delivery. When effectively and honestly interpreted, statistics are invaluable in explanation or proof. You always strive, however, to make them intelligible. Moreover, you must take care to avoid the misuses and fallacies to which they are prone. Remember that an average can be a deceiving figure, since it tells us little or nothing about any one of the individual items upon which it is based. Remember, too, when drawing comparisons, that the units compared must actually be of the same sort; and that in order to establish a trend, figures must cover a rea-

[16]Cited by Arthur Krock of *The New York Times* News Service, in the *Des Moines Register*, December 1, 1965, p. 10.

[17]*Des Moines Register*, September 16, 1965, p. 6.

sonably long period of time. There is an old saying to the effect that figures don't lie, but liars figure. Never let this be said of you.

Testimony

When a speaker cites verbatim the opinions or conclusions of others, he is using *testimony*. Sometimes testimony is used merely to clarify or explain an idea; at other times it is intended to supply proof for a point.

In the following passage from a speech entitled "National Security," Governor Nelson A. Rockefeller used testimony to explain and reinforce an idea:

> If we are to preserve democracy, our political leaders must be candid rather than clever.
>
> They must be responsive to the people—and they must have the courage to give the people the bad news as well as the good.
>
> The American people are not afraid.
>
> They want to know the facts.
>
> The Scripps-Howard newspapers have a slogan that puts it very well:
>
> "Give light, and the people will find their own way."
>
> This is the great privilege and right of which you as members of the press are the guardians for the American people.
>
> It is our mutual obligation to the people and to our free, democratic society, to make certain that the light shines clearly for all to see.[18]

Additional examples of testimony used to clarify or explain may be found in speeches by Robert T. Oliver and Arthur J. Goldberg. In commenting on the difficulty of communicating with persons whose cultural backgrounds and value systems are different from our own, Professor Oliver said:

> We can communicate with people in another culture only in terms that make sense to them. Prime Minister Nehru, on his visit to America in 1950, made the same point a bit more explicitly, and cogently enough to merit quotation. "If we seek to understand a people," he said, "we have to put ourselves, as far as we can, in that particular historical and cultural background. . . . One has to recognize that . . . countries and peoples differ in their approach and their ways, in their approach to life and their ways of living and thinking. In order to understand them we have to understand their way of life and approach. If we wish to convince them, we have to use their language as far

[18]Presented at the annual dinner of the New York State Publishers Association, January 29, 1963. Text supplied by Governor Rockefeller.

as we can, not language in the narrow sense of the word, but the language of the mind."[19]

In explaining an important aspect of American foreign policy during a plenary session of the United Nations' Assembly, Ambassador Goldberg summed up his remarks in this way:

So what we seek for our own people in a Great Society at home, we seek for all mankind. President Johnson, I think, has said this very well, and I quote him: "We seek no fidelity to an iron faith, but a diversity of belief as varied as man himself. We seek not to extend the power of America but the progress of humanity. We seek not to dominate others but to strengthen the freedom of all people."[20]

All testimony, of course, should meet the twin tests of *authoritativeness* and *audience acceptability*. In addition, when used to prove a statement, rather than merely to explain or to clarify, testimony also should satisfy, in so far as possible, four more specific criteria:

1. The training and experience of the person quoted should qualify him as an authority. He should be an expert in the field to which his testimony relates.
2. Whenever possible, the statement of the authority should be based on first-hand knowledge.
3. The judgment expressed must not be unduly influenced by personal interest. The authority must not be prejudiced.
4. Your hearers must recognize that the man quoted actually is an authority. They must respect his opinion.

The following passage from a student speech on water fluoridation employs testimony as proof. Observe that the speaker, Neal Luker, of the University of Iowa, chose as his authority a presumably unbiased expert in a position to know the facts at first hand, and that he was careful to state the authority's full title for his listeners:

Summing up experiments too numerous to mention and representing the best current professional opinion on fluoridation is the following statement by Dr. Nicholas Leone, Chief of Medical Investigation for the National Institute of Dental Research: "We know without question or doubt that one part per

[19]"Culture and Communication," in *The Speaker's Resource Book*, ed. Carroll C. Arnold, Douglas Ehninger, and John Gerber, 2nd ed. (Glenview, Illinois: Scott, Foresman, 1966), p. 21.

[20]"A Society for All Men," *Vital Speeches of the Day*, XXXII (November 1, 1965), 35.

million fluoride in water supply is absolutely safe, is beneficial, and is not productive of any undesirable systemic effect in man."[21]

When citing testimony, avoid the tendency to use big names simply because they are well known. A movie star may be famous for her beauty and appeal, but her opinion on the nutritive value of a breakfast food is less reliable than the opinion of your physician. The most reliable testimony always comes from subject-matter experts whose qualifications your listeners recognize and respect.

Restatement

This last form of support gains its strength from the power of repetition to clarify or to persuade. Advertisers realize the persuasive power of repetition and spend hundreds of thousands of dollars to say the same thing over and over in magazines, on billboards, over the radio, and on television. Teachers, clergymen, and other speakers frequently repeat ideas in the hope that if they are not understood the first time, they will be the second or third. The possible danger, of course, is that such reiteration will become monotonous. Restatement, as we use the term here, however, is not mere repetition; it consists of *saying the same thing over one or more times,* but saying it each time *in a new and different way.* In the example of a factual illustration given earlier in this chapter, the speaker introduced his point by asserting that "man-made law is in conflict with natural law," and closed by quoting the guide as saying, "It ain't how the bait looks to you and me that counts. It's how it looks to the fish." The same idea is being expressed, but in different words.

In a speech entitled "Lights upon the Horizon," which he delivered to the Economics Club of Chicago on December 16, 1937, President Herbert Hoover used multiple restatement to clarify the term "economic middle class":

By the economic middle class I take it that you mean all the people who have to support themselves. You mean the people who have sacrificed years of devotion to learn to do their jobs skillfully. They are the creative people. They are the people who want to get forward. They are the quiet, decent people who are busy keeping things going. They seldom appear in the press except when they die.[22]

[21]"Water Fluoridation," presented in an advanced public speaking class at the University of Iowa, May 13, 1963. Quotation taken from *Water Fluoridation: Facts, Not Myths* by Louis I. Dublin (Public Affairs Pamphlet No. 251), p. 15.

[22]Quoted in Robert T. Oliver, *Training for Effective Speech* (New York: Cordon, 1939), p. 110.

Note also how President Franklin D. Roosevelt used restatement to clarify and to gain emphasis in a "fireside chat" on his controversial plan to "pack the Supreme Court":

> Last Thursday I described the American form of Government as a three-horse team provided by the Constitution to the American people so that their field might be plowed. The three horses are, of course, the three branches of government—the Congress, the Executive, and the Courts. . . . Those who have intimated that the President of the United States is trying to drive that team, overlook the simple fact that the President, as Chief Executive, is himself one of the three horses.
>
> It is the American people themselves who are in the driver's seat.
>
> It is the American people themselves who want the furrow plowed.
>
> It is the American people themselves who expect the third horse [the Supreme Court] to pull in unison with the other two.[23]

These, then, are the seven forms of verbal support. Select them judiciously; use them generously but discerningly. Avoid abstract, unsupported statements. Do not depend solely upon assertions of your own opinions. Express your views, by all means; but amplify and develop them by using explanation, comparison, illustration, instances, statistics, testimony, and restatement.

THE USE OF VISIBLE SUPPORTING MATERIAL

Thus far we have discussed only the *audible* materials which may be used to explain or to prove a point—what you can *say* about it. Equally important, sometimes even more important, are the *visible* materials which you can use for the same purposes. These materials, which include maps, diagrams, charts, pictures, small working models, and even demonstrations with full-scale equipment, may make your presentation more effective. For instance, if you are explaining how to use a complicated camera, your instructions will be much clearer if you take an actual camera, show your listeners the parts that require adjustment, and demonstrate how to use it in taking different kinds of pictures. Sometimes equipment for demonstration is not available or is too big to bring into the room where the speech is to be made. Small-scale models are then very useful. Model airplanes, for example, are widely used to teach aerodynamics. Similarly, in explaining a flood-control project, a large map of the area would be helpful. The operation of a device, apparatus, or machine

[23]*Vital Speeches of the Day*, III (March 15, 1937), 349.

and the assembly of its interrelated parts can be made clearer by showing pictures or diagrams of the important pieces. Statistical data can often be clarified by column graphs or "pies"—circles cut into segments to show proportions. Slides and movies also are extremely useful.

Types of visual support

The following list suggests the kinds of visual aids which the thoughtful and imaginative speaker can use to support and enhance his ideas:

The object itself (for example, a metronome or a walkie-talkie). The speaker, of course, may supplement the object with diagrams showing its internal parts or its functioning.

Models, either small-scale models of large objects (a model racing car) or large-scale models of small objects, are useful when it is impossible to show the original. A working model has the added advantage of showing the operation of a device or apparatus, as well as its basic design.

Slides require projection equipment, and the darkened room obscures the speaker, but they usually add interest and promote understanding.

Movies require more equipment than slides but have the advantage of showing action.

Maps should be large enough to be seen easily and should emphasize those details which relate to the point being made.

Blackboard drawings should be completed before the audience assembles. Be sure that the chalk marks are heavy enough to be seen by the entire group.

Graphs. Bar graphs show the relationship of two sets of figures. *Line* graphs show two or more variable facts. *Pie* graphs show percentages by a circle divided proportionately. *Pictorial* graphs show relative amounts by size or number of symbols.

Diagrams. Cut-away diagrams of an object show its inner workings as well as its external aspects. Diagrams which allow for a *three-dimensional view* are especially helpful.

"These [visible] materials, which include maps, diagrams, charts, pictures, small working models, and even demonstrations with full-scale equipment, may make your presentation more effective."

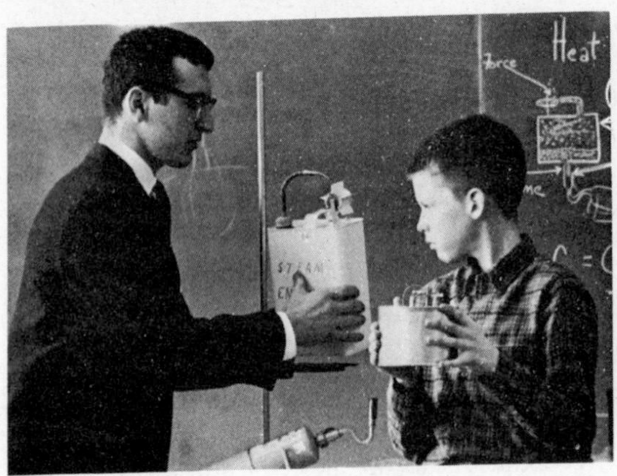

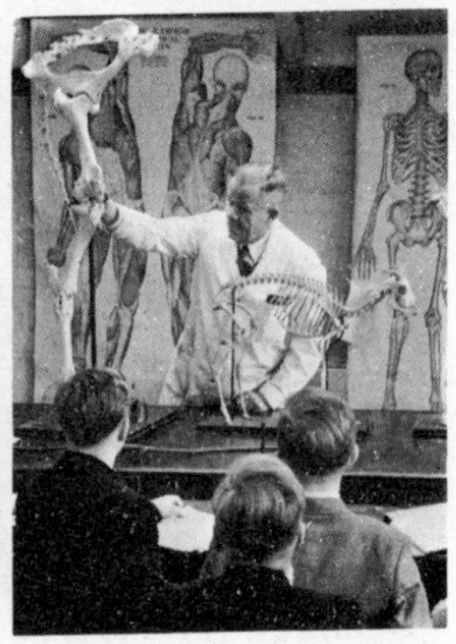

These pictures afford a sampling of the many kinds of visible supporting materials that can be used to make ideas clearer or more interesting. THIS PAGE, CLOCKWISE: A map, a globe, and a relief map are used in a televised dialog; skeletons and anatomical charts are used by an instructor; and homemade equipment and a blackboard diagram are used in a demonstration of force exerted by steam. OPPOSITE PAGE, CLOCKWISE FROM UPPER LEFT: A line chart showing relationships between and trends in prices of major nondurable commodities is used at a press conference by Arthur M. Ross, Commissioner of the Bureau of Labor Statistics; a model of crystal structure is discussed in a televised lecture on physics; a simple diagram is used in a student speech to depict types of radioactive decay; and a cutaway drawing of a plant stem is projected from a transparency onto a screen by an overhead projector.

CONSUMER PRICE INDEX
NONDURABLE COMMODITIES
120
115
110
105
100

beta
gamma

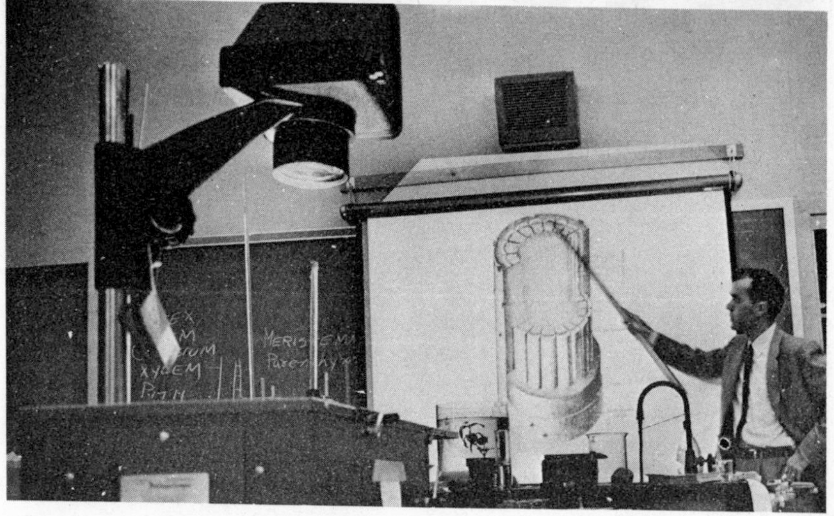
XYLEM
Pith

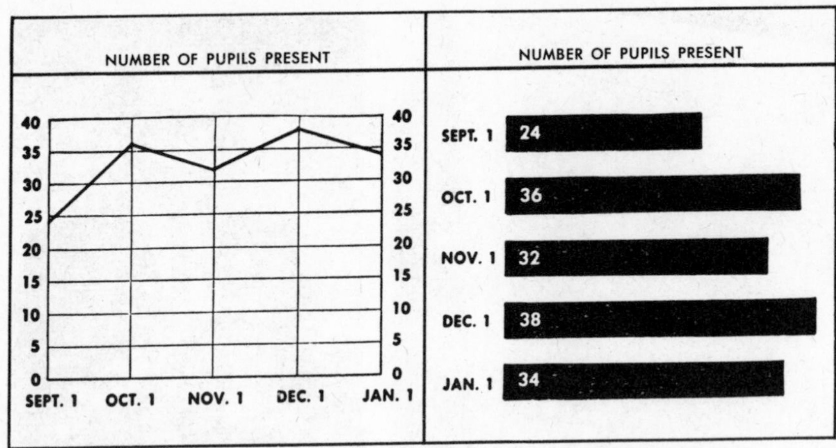

Line graph **Horizontal bar graph**

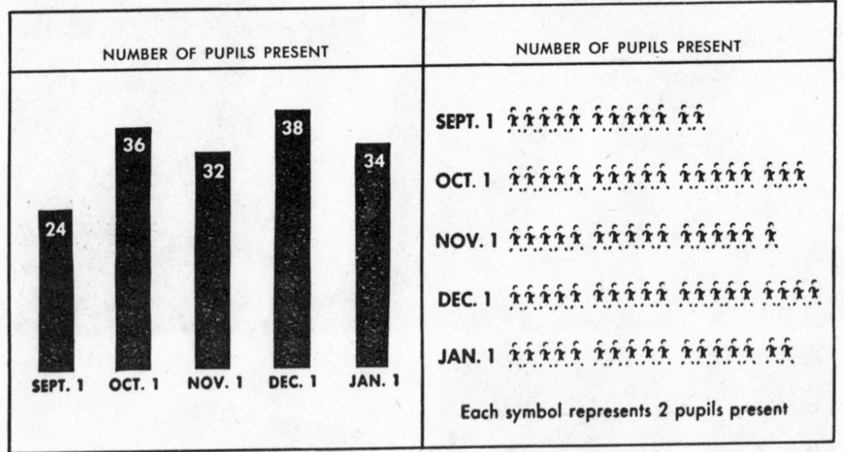

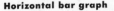

Vertical bar graph **Picture graph**

The four graphs on this page, by Pictograph Corporation, demonstrate not only the rudiments of graph preparation but also the presentation of the same set of facts by various types of graphs. A line graph, a horizontal and a vertical bar graph, and a picture graph present the same example, which pertains to a record of class attendance at a certain school on the first day of five consecutive months. (On September 1, 24 students attended; on October 1, 36; on November 1, 32; on December 1, 38; and on January 1, 34.)

When your purpose in speaking is to indicate trends established by specific figures, or to illustrate the relationships between them, you may employ graphs similar in basic plan to these. Certain variations are, of course, possible. Before constructing your graphs you may wish to consult available references in your library. Some useful sources are included in the list of suggested readings at the end of this chapter.

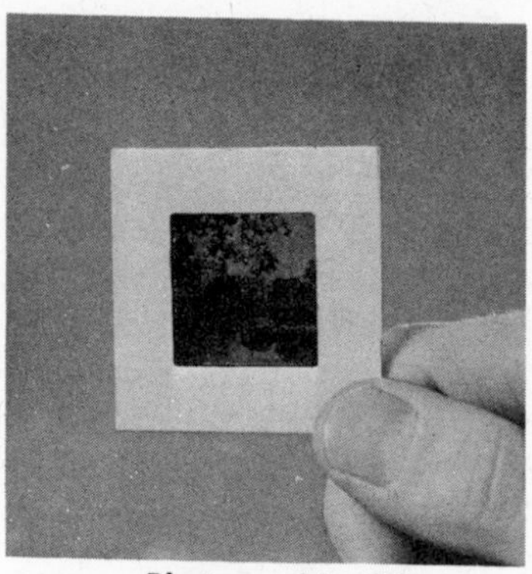

Photographic slide

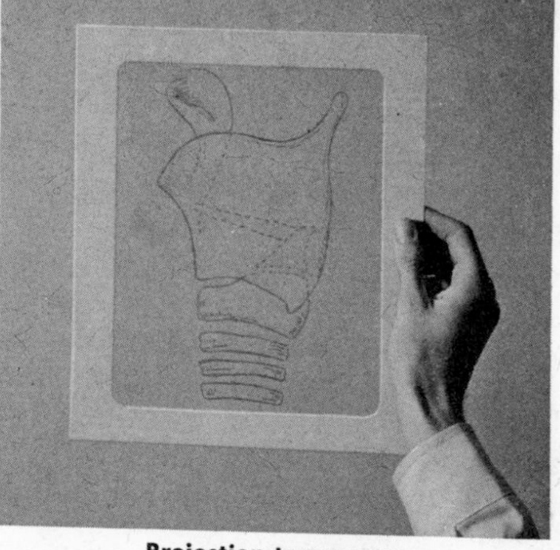

Projection transparency

Slides and transparencies can give an added measure of clarity and concreteness to your speeches. In the illustrations are a 35-mm. photographic slide, to be used with slide-projection equipment, and an 8×10-in. projection transparency for use with an overhead projector. (The diagram on the transparency is of the laryngeal cartilages and topmost tracheal rings.)

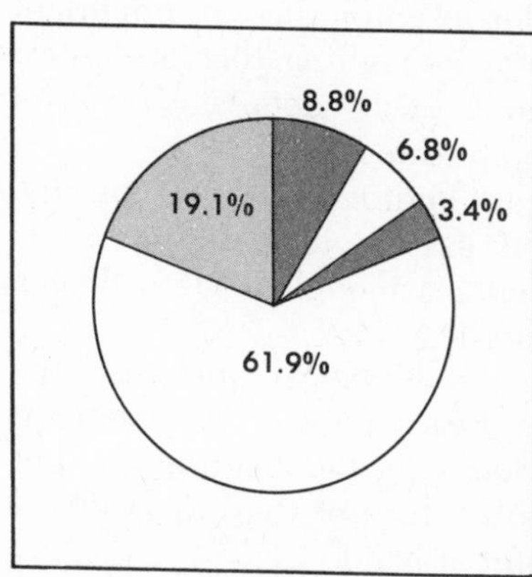

Circle graph

The circle graph, also called a pie chart, shows proportions—the relation of parts to the whole. The example shows percentages of the sum of $2 billion, supposed to be the cost of education in a hypothetical country. In this example the percentages include: general control, 3.4; instruction, 61.9; maintenance and auxiliary agencies, 19.1; capital outlay, 8.8; and interest, 6.8. Sometimes in such graphs the segments are marked with specific sums or amounts instead of percentages, and may carry identifying labels as well.

Organization chart

Lines of authority can be clearly delineated in an organization chart, as in this chart depicting the kind of central organization that might be suitable for the school system of a large city.

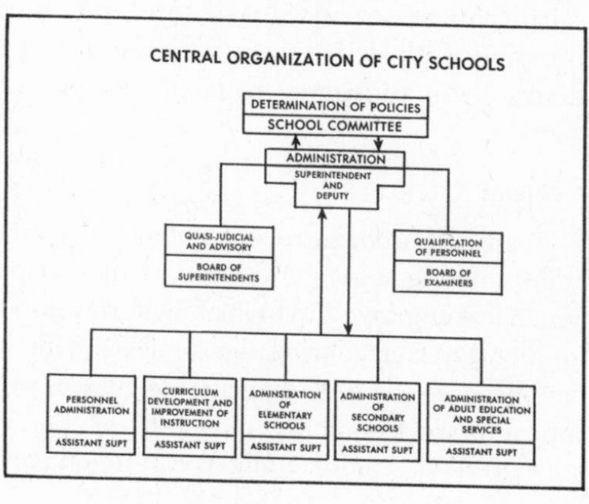

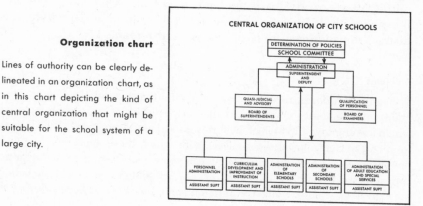

Organization charts illustrate the parts and structure of an organization.

Guides for using visual aids

In using visual support for your speeches, be sure that you:

1. Choose objects and materials that are relevant. The purpose of visual aids is to make an idea more graphic for your audience; irrelevant materials distract the viewers' attention from the point you are discussing.
2. Prepare the displays before giving the speech. Check to see that you have all the needed equipment, that blackboard diagrams are complete, and that papers and books are arranged so that they will be easy to handle. Practice using the visual aids as you rehearse your speech itself.
3. Keep charts, graphs, and diagrams simple and clear. Use ink in heavy broad lines and possibly in color to emphasize an important fact or feature. Make the displays large enough so that the entire audience can see them easily. Omit unnecessary details. A series of simple charts is better than a single complicated one.
4. Place the object material where your audience can see it easily. Stand well to the side of the display and use a pointer to indicate its different parts or aspects. When showing a model or other object, hold it so that your hands do not obscure it.
5. Use your visual aids at the proper psychological moment in the speech. If your timing is faulty and the showing of the visual support is not closely coordinated with the discussion, the chain of thought will be broken, and the visual aids will interrupt the continuity of the speech instead of clarifying the point at hand.
6. Have the display visible only when it is in use. Keep it covered until you are ready for it, and put it out of sight when you have finished with it. If it can be seen when it is not in use, it will tend to distract the audience from the rest of your remarks.

Problems

1. Read half a dozen recent speeches in *Vital Speeches of the Day* or some other suitable source and tabulate the various forms of supporting material which are employed. Which of the forms is used most frequently? Which least frequently? Considering the subjects with which these speeches deal and the purposes at which they are aimed, can you explain why some of the forms appear more frequently than others? For anthologies of recent speeches see Carroll C. Arnold, Douglas Ehninger, and John Gerber, *The Speaker's Re-*

source Book, 2nd ed. (Glenview, Illinois: Scott, Foresman, 1966); Wil A. Linkugel, R. R. Allen, and Richard L. Johannesen, *Contemporary American Speeches* (Belmont, Calif.: Wadsworth, 1965). A number of recent speeches also are included in Goodwin Berquist, *Speeches for Illustration and Example* (Glenview, Illinois: Scott, Foresman, 1965).

2. With the aid of your instructor, locate a number of speeches delivered before 1800. Compare the forms of supporting material used in those speeches with the forms found in the speeches studied in Problem 1. In what respects, if any, are they different? How does the frequency of occurrence among the various forms compare with that found in the recent speeches? What, if anything, can you conclude from this comparison concerning changes in the use of supporting material over a period of time?

3. Re-examine critically the forms of supporting material which you located in Problem 1. Find instances in which a given form of support seems to be appropriately and effectively used, and instances in which it is inappropriate or poorly developed. Rewrite the latter passages so as to improve them.

4. During the next several rounds of classroom speeches, list and evaluate the forms of supporting material used by each speaker. In doing this, be certain to keep in mind whether the purpose of a given speech is to explain and clarify a point or to establish a claim or conclusion. At the close of each day's speaking, see how well the members of the class agree as to which forms of supporting material were employed and how effectively they were used.

5. Review in your mind various courses which you have taken in high school or college. What use was made of visible supporting materials in presenting the subject matter of these courses? Were the visible materials effectively used? Did the instructor take full advantage of the possibilities which such aids offered? How could his use of them have been expanded or improved?

Speaking assignment

1. In an interesting little book entitled *How to Lie with Statistics* (New York: Norton, 1954), Darrell Huff explains some of the tricks and fallacies in statistical proof and tells how to guard against them. Read Huff's book and present to the class an oral report on the subject "Pitfalls in Statistics." Use appropriate visual aids as an integral part of your presentation. (If time allows, various students may be assigned separate chapters of Huff's book, and a series of reports presented.)

Suggestions for further reading

Martin P. Anderson, Wesley Lewis, and James Murray, *The Speaker and His Audience* (New York: Harper & Row, Publishers, 1964), Chapter XIII, "Visual Aids to Communication."

Russell L. C. Butsch, *How to Read Statistics* (Milwaukee: The Bruce Publishing Company, 1946).

Lionel Crocker, "Make the Illustration Linger," *Today's Speech,* IV (January 1956), 3-5.

Lionel Crocker, *Public Speaking for College Students* (New York: American Book Company, 1941), Chapter XIII, "The Illustration."

Kenneth G. Hance, David C. Ralph, and Milton J. Wiksell, *Principles of Speaking* (Belmont, Calif.: Wadsworth Publishing Co., Inc., 1962), Chapter IV, "Materials of Development," and Chapter V, "Materials of Experience."

Darrell Huff, *How to Lie with Statistics* (New York: W. W. Norton & Company, Inc., 1954).

A. L. Long, "Recent Experimental Investigations Dealing with Effectiveness of Audio-Visual Modes of Presentation," *Educational Administration and Supervision* (February 1945), 65-78.

Rudolf Modley and Dyno Lowenstein, *Pictographs and Graphs: How to Make and Use Them* (New York: Harper & Row, Publishers, 1952).

Walter A. Wittich and Charles F. Schuller, *Audio-Visual Materials: Their Nature and Use,* 2nd ed. (New York: Harper & Row, Publishers, 1957).

Hans Zeisel, *Say It with Figures,* 4th ed. (New York: Harper & Row, Publishers, 1957).

CHAPTER ELEVEN

The one-point speech

In the preceding pages we have considered the substantive elements which the speaker may use to explain or to prove the major ideas of his speech. In all likelihood, however, unless his subject is an extremely complex one, he will not use all seven forms of support in developing each major point in his outline. To substantiate his first point he may, for example, employ explanation, definition, hypothetical illustration, and comparison; for his second, he may use specific instances, statistics, and testimony; for his third, factual illustration, analogy, and restatement. In general, his selection will be governed by the criteria of appropriateness, variety, and cogency.

There are many occasions when the purpose of a speech is to clarify only one idea or to prove one simple point. When this is the case, the structure of your talk should be uncomplicated, and the forms of support should all bear directly upon the concept you wish to establish.

How, then, should you organize and develop a one-point talk? What forms of support may be used to explain or to develop your idea?

SELECTING THE POINT

The first step, of course, is to decide upon the exact point you wish to explain or to prove. Frame this idea into a short, simple sentence, to be sure that you really have only one point in mind; for example, "A good truck driver must be relaxed." Focus on this single point throughout your speech; do not wander off onto some other idea.

With your purpose determined, assemble the supporting material best suited to achieving it and arrange this material in such a way that it will be easy for the audience to understand and to follow. Keep clearly in mind whether you are trying to explain and clarify an idea or whether, on the other hand, you are attempting to prove a contention.

THE USE OF SUPPORTING MATERIAL TO EXPLAIN

If the purpose of your speech is to explain an idea, first state that idea simply; next bring in your supporting material, using especially explanation, comparisons, and illustrations, as well as any visual or auditory aids that may be available; finally, restate the idea you have explained. This arrangement may be outlined as follows:

1. State in a short, simple sentence the idea to be explained.
2. Make it clear
   a. by explanation, comparisons, and illustrations;
   b. by using maps, diagrams, pictures, or models.
3. Restate the idea you have explained.

Under (2) above, the auditory and visual materials may be presented separately or together. That is, you may tell your listeners and then show them; or you may show them while you are telling them. The following outline for a one-point speech illustrates how supporting material may be assembled to make an idea clear.

WHAT IS A DEMOCRATIC COMMUNITY?

I. The essence of a democratic community is the control of the government by those governed. — *Statement*
   A. This means that the people have authority to: — *Explanation*
      1. Make the laws under which they live.
      2. Select public officials to administer these laws.
   B. Suppose a group of students were to plan a cooperative housing unit in the democratic way. — *Hypothetical illustration*
      1. They would get together to discuss it.
      2. They would decide where the unit would be located.
      3. They would agree how much each student should contribute to the cost.
      4. In case of disagreement, they would reach a compromise or abide by the vote of the majority.
      5. One of them would be selected to collect the money and pay the bills.
      6. They might elect a small committee to enforce the agreed-upon rules and regulations.
      7. Each student would have a voice in deciding what these rules and regulations should be.
   C. If, however, one student took it upon himself to decide all these questions, the unit would not be *democratic*, regardless of how efficiently it might be run. — *Comparison with B*
   D. Compare these cases of civic communities:

Comparison of specific instances

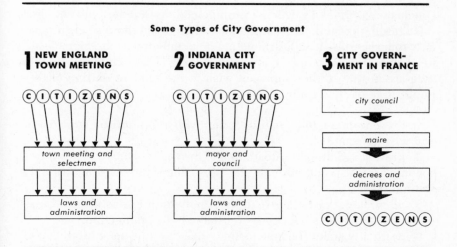

1. In New England, towns are governed by town meetings.
   a. All qualified residents are allowed to speak and to vote directly on current problems.
   b. Public officials are selected by vote of the citizens.
2. Indiana cities are governed by representatives of the people.
   a. City ordinances are made by the city council, whose members are elected by the voters.
   b. Administrative officials are elected.
3. In France, a city council selects a chief executive or *maire*.
   a. The *maire* exercises extensive police powers independently of the council and is solely responsible for the conduct of the city adminstration.
   b. The *maire* is directly accountable not to the people, but to the prefect of the *departement* in which the city is located—i.e., to an official of the national government.

Diagram

E. This diagram will show why civic communities in New England and Indiana are democratic, and why those in France are not. (Arrows show the direction of governmental control.)

Some Types of City Government

1 NEW ENGLAND TOWN MEETING

C I T I Z E N S

town meeting and selectmen

laws and administration

2 INDIANA CITY GOVERNMENT

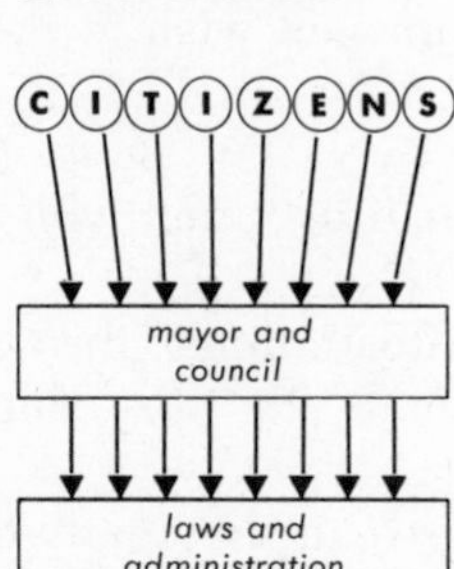

3 CITY GOVERNMENT IN FRANCE

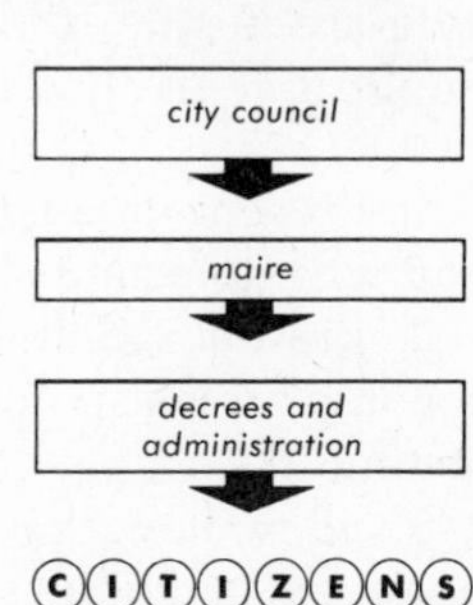

Restatement

II. Democracy, as Lincoln said of the United States, is government "by the people."

THE USE OF SUPPORTING MATERIAL AS PROOF

There are two common methods of assembling the forms of support to establish the proof for a statement: the didactic method and the method of implication.

In using the *didactic method,* you state your conclusion first, then present the support or proof, and finally restate your conclusion. As the old parson explained, "I tell 'em what I'm goin' to tell 'em; I tell 'em; then I tell 'em what I told 'em." This is perhaps the clearest and most obvious method of assembling the supporting material. It may be outlined as follows:

1. State the point to be established.
2. Make it clear by explanation, comparisons, or illustrations.
3. Support it by additional factual illustrations, specific instances, statistics, or testimony.
4. Restate your point as the conclusion.

In using the *method of implication,* you present the facts first and then state the conclusion which is based upon those facts. In other words, the conclusion or judgment comes near the end of the speech, and is stated only *after* the evidence which supports it has been presented. This procedure, sometimes called the "natural" method of argument, coincides more nearly with the way in which we reach conclusions ourselves when uninfluenced by another person. For this reason, the method of implication, though not quite so clear or so easy to use as the didactic arrangement, is sometimes more persuasive to an audience. It is, in fact, almost the only plan to use with listeners who are hostile to the point you wish to present. An outline of this implicative method follows:

1. Present an analogy or illustration which *implies* the conclusion you wish to establish.
2. Present additional illustrations, instances, statistics, and testimony which point strongly to this conclusion without directly stating it.
3. Show how these facts lead inevitably to this conclusion; use as much explanation as necessary to establish the connection.
4. Explicitly state the conclusion which has thus been established.

Notice again that regardless of which of these two methods you use, the first three forms of support (explanation, comparison, and illustration) are primarily useful in making an idea clear and vivid, while the next three (instances, statistics, and testimony) have the function of establishing and verifying the truth or importance of a claim. Restatement, of course, serves both to clarify and persuade, as well as to assist the memory. As you study the sample speech outline below, note that the didactic method is being used. By omitting the general statement at the beginning, however, this outline also would illustrate the method of implication.

INSTRUCTION BY TELEVISION

I. Classroom instruction by television is effective. — General statement

 A. Suppose you were to have this experience in your English literature class: — Hypothetical illustration
  1. When you enter the room, there is a television set rather than an instructor in front of the class.
  2. On TV, however, you see the department's best teacher for the course you are taking.
  3. In other rooms, other classes are watching the same telecast.
   a. The students in each class can see and hear the lecturer and the teaching materials being used.
   b. The students in each class can obtain individual assistance when necessary.
  4. You will learn as much about English literature as you would in a conventional class.
   a. Tests on appreciation of literature show this.
   b. Tests on comprehension of literature demonstrate the same result.
 B. Television has been used successfully in the Hagerstown, Maryland, public schools. — Factual illustration
  1. Mathematics classes at nearly every grade level participated.
  2. Teachers, student ability, and other variables were controlled so that television was the only major difference in method.
   a. About half of the classes received instruction by television.
   b. The other half received regular instruction.
  3. The students who received television instruction

scored as high or higher on tests than those who had regular instruction.

C. This experience has been repeated in a number of cases: — Specific instances
   1. Miami University of Ohio reported that students in TV sections and those in regular classes did equally well in subject-matter learning.
   2. The city of Chicago found similar results for high school physics and algebra.
   3. In Cincinnati, high school chemistry classes taught by TV were ahead of other classes.

D. A special committee headed by Arthur E. Traxler, of the Educational Records Bureau, and supported by the Fund for the Advancement of Education reported figures that clearly show the effectiveness of television instruction. — Statistics
   1. Experiments involving almost 27,000 students were conducted in several cities.
   2. Of 110 comparisons made in this study, 68 or over 60% showed that the groups instructed by television achieved higher scores than the other groups.

E. On the basis of studies such as these, experts have expressed their views. — Testimony
   1 Leslie P. Greenhill, associate director of the Division of Academic Research and Services for Pennsylvania State University, stated in the *National Education Association Journal:*
      a. "Results of TV research show that when the same teacher teaches in each situation, televised instruction is equivalent in effectiveness to face-to-face instruction."

F. Just as training films have assisted in teaching millions of men and women in the armed forces, so television can be useful in the classrooms of our schools. — Analogy

II. Subjects can be effectively taught by television. — Restatement

Not all one-point speeches will require as many different forms of support as were used in this sample outline. Moreover, as we emphasized at the outset, most one-point speeches are briefer. This sample was given to show how a number of different types of support might be combined to achieve a single purpose.

SAMPLE SPEECH

In the following speech by Clarence Yurk, a student at the University of Wisconsin-Milwaukee, a single idea or point is impressed upon the audience through a series of striking examples. When you have learned to develop one point in this way, you will be ready to attempt speeches in which a number of different ideas must be put together into an integrated whole.

LOST: FOUR FRIENDS[1]

Clarence Yurk

In the last four years I have lost four friends.

During January of this year a friend of mine was driving on a highway late at night. Out of the darkness a car sped toward her. Her car was involved in a head-on collision and Gladys was killed. I lost a friend.

Four years ago a friend of mine scored thirty-eight points against Green Bay West in a high-school basketball game. That was on a Friday night. Two nights later the car in which he was riding slammed into a tree at ninety miles an hour. John was cut in half, and I lost another friend.

Two years ago Susie Hinz was killed. As usual, her mother picked her up after school and, as usual, they took the same side road home. They lived in the country. On that road they came upon a railroad crossing they had crossed a thousand times. However, on that particular day, because they had crossed the railroad crossing a thousand times and there wasn't a train scheduled for that time anyway, they started across the tracks without looking. A train smashed into their car at seventy miles an hour, dragging their car over a hundred feet. Susie was killed. I lost another friend.

All three of these accidents were a result of some form of carelessness. Let's go back over them again. As I said, Gladys was killed in a head-on collision. That means that either one or both of the cars involved crossed the centerline of the highway. One or both drivers were guilty of negligence.

John was killed in a car traveling at ninety miles per hour. Need I say more? That was foolishness.

Susie was killed because of inattentiveness. Had either she or her mother bothered to look before crossing those tracks they'd probably be alive today.

By this time you've probably guessed what I'm getting at. I'm talking to you about the age-old theme of "Drive Carefully." Oh, I know, you're probably saying, "Now look, Clarence, I heard this sermon a thousand times. What do

[1]The text of this speech appears on pp. 13-14 of Goodwin F. Berquist, Jr., *Speeches for Illustration and Example* (Glenview, Illinois: Scott, Foresman, 1965). Used by permission of Clarence Yurk and of Goodwin F. Berquist, Jr.

you expect me to do?" There's *no reason* why you and I as college students should ever be guilty of negligence, foolishness, or inattentiveness. *Think* when you get behind the wheel of your car. If I can leave you with just one thought today, it's that. I want you to think when you drive. I don't know why it is, but a man can spend his whole day on the job thinking, or a college student can spend hours in a library, thinking, but when he gets into his car at night he completely forgets to think and relies entirely on natural instinct. A car is a two thousand-pound battering ram. That "tin lizzy" out there, or whatever affectionate name you've given it, kills more people in one year than we lost during the whole Korean conflict. *Think* when you drive. Always expect the unexpected. The shortstop for the Milwaukee Braves always expects the next play to come to him. That way he stays on his toes. You, too, should be on your toes when you drive. Always expect the unexpected. Always think.

Perhaps you've noticed by now that I said I lost four friends in four years and I've only told you about three. This afternoon I'm going to Sheboygan to attend a funeral. One of my best friends was killed in an auto accident on Tuesday. Gene was twenty-five, married, and had a seven-months-old son. What am I going to say to his wife?

Four friends in four years. At that rate, if I live to the age of seventy, I'm going to lose forty-five more friends. My definition of a friend is someone I know and like. *You* are all my friends.

Problems

1. List five general subject-areas on which you would like to speak. For each of these areas, first frame a specific purpose suitable for a one-point speech on this subject and then a specific purpose suitable for a longer and more complex talk. Be ready to defend your choice of purposes and to tell why each is suitable for one-point development or for a longer talk.
2. Name some of the circumstances under which you probably would choose to organize a one-point speech according to the didactic pattern and then some of the circumstances under which you would select the method of implication. Include among these circumstances the nature of the subject, the attitude of the audience, the time available, etc.
3. Prepare a short paper analyzing the sample speech at the end of this chapter. Comment on its pattern of development, the forms of support used, and its general effectiveness or impact.

Speaking assignments

1. Following the suggestions offered in this chapter, prepare to present in class a two- or three-minute one-point speech to inform, to convince, or to entertain. For possible subjects study the list of subject categories on pp. 122-125.

2. Present to the class a five-minute one-point speech, the purpose of which is to explain or clarify a term, concept, process, plan, or proposal. Use at least three different forms of supporting material in developing your ideas and employ at least one chart, diagram, map, picture, or other visual aid. Your speech will be judged on the following points: (1) adequacy of supporting material; (2) appropriateness of supporting material, both as to type and to substance; (3) effectiveness with which the supporting material is developed.
3. Present to the class a five-minute one-point speech, the purpose of which is to win acceptance for a claim or conclusion. Again use at least three different forms of supporting material and one visual aid. Your speech will be judged on the criteria set forth in Assignment 2.

Suggestions for further reading

Donald C. Bryant and Karl R. Wallace, *Fundamentals of Public Speaking*, 3rd. ed. (New York: Appleton-Century-Crofts, 1960), Chapter IV, "The First Speeches," esp. pp. 49-53.

Wilbur E. Gilman, Bower Aly, and Loren D. Reid, *Speech Preparation* (Columbia, Mo.: Artcraft Press, 1946), Chapter V, "Composing the Speech," esp. pp. 94-104.

Donald E. Hargis, "The Forms of Support," *Western Speech*, XIV (March 1950), 18-22.

Arthur Jersild, "Modes of Emphasis in Public Speaking," *Readings in Speech*, ed. Haig Bosmajian (New York: Harper & Row, Publishers, 1965), pp. 130-139.

Loren Reid, *Speaking Well* (Columbia, Mo.: Artcraft Press, 1962), Chapter IV, "Organizing: The Short Speech."

Wayne N. Thompson, *Fundamentals of Communication* (New York: McGraw-Hill Book Company, Inc., 1957), Chapter IX, "The Development of an Idea."

CHAPTER TWELVE

Selecting the basic appeal

The most carefully constructed speech is likely to fail unless it contains an appeal to the people who hear it. Before going further, therefore, we must pause to consider the motives which generate and direct so much of human behavior and to point out why a knowledge of these motives is important to the speaker.

THE CONCEPT OF MOTIVES

Someone tells me that the only way I can find a job and provide for my family is to join the union; so I pay my dues and join. I am assured that membership in a fraternity will enhance my social prestige on campus and help me get into activities; so I become interested. My bed is warm and the room is cold; so I decide to "cut" my eight o'clock class; but recalling that I must pass a quiz at nine o'clock or fail the course, I brave the cold and shiver into my clothes at eight-thirty. In each instance some latent force has spurred me toward a certain sort of goal-directed behavior.

Depending upon their point of view, psychologists in earlier years called such action-tendencies by different names: instincts, emotions, prepotent reflexes, purpose- or wish-fulfilling impulses, etc. Today the most common term for them is *motives.*

There have been many arguments about the number of motives and whether they are inborn or acquired. With the details of these arguments we are not concerned here. It is important for us, however, to note two facts which are commonly agreed upon: (1) that much human behavior is goal-directed in the way we have just described; and (2) that while in some instances such behavior may be set into motion by the individual's own physiological or psychological needs, in others it may be triggered by aspects of the environment in which he finds himself.

CLASSIFICATIONS OF MOTIVES

Motives have been classified in various ways, and no two lists agree entirely. Of late, however, it has become popular to distinguish between "biological" and "psychological-social" motives, or between what are sometimes called "maintenance" (homeostasis-oriented) and "actualization" tendencies. In addition, greater importance is being attached to such social drives as the need for participation and belonging, "competence" in relation to one's environment, achievement, group approval, and the like.

Two well-known classifications of human needs cited by psychologists are those by Maslow and Prescott. Maslow's list follows:

1. Body needs—basic "tissue" needs for food, water, sleep, air, etc.
2. Safety needs—for protection from harm or injury.
3. Needs for love and belonging—for warmth, status, acceptance, approval.
4. Needs for adequacy—security, self-esteem, self-enhancement, competence.
5. Needs for self-fulfillment—broader understanding and appreciation.[1]

Prescott's list, on the other hand, consists of only three items:

1. Physiological needs—for essential materials and conditions, for a certain rhythm of activity and rest, and for sexual activity.
2. Social needs—for affection, belonging, and likeness or "conformity" to others.
3. Ego-integrative needs—for contact with reality, harmony with reality, progressive symbolization, increasing self-direction, a fair balance between success and failure, and the attainment of selfhood.[2]

Obviously, the motives represented in these lists vary in strength among different individuals. One man may value self-enhancement more than the avoidance of harm or injury; another may care more for self-fulfillment than for social acceptance or approval. Regardless

[1]A. H. Maslow, *Motivation and Personality* (New York: Harpers, 1954), pp. 80-106.

[2]D. A. Prescott, *Emotion and the Educative Process* (Washington, D.C.: American Council on Education, 1938), pp. 110-124.

of such variations, however, motives play an exceedingly important role in shaping human behavior.

But while motives often underlie and impel behavior, the cause-effect relation is not always a direct and simple one. The complexity of human life and the customs and mores of the society in which it is lived may prevent their immediate fulfillment. As a result, there develops a variety of indirect or "manifest" needs—needs which may represent certain aspects or segments of a given motive, or in some cases a combination of two or more motives. These indirect or "manifest" needs provide the grounds for what we shall here call *motive appeals.*

MOTIVE APPEALS

Because human wants, as shaped by the environment, are infinite in number, any attempt to enumerate them must of necessity be incomplete and contain some items which overlap. The following list of "motive appeals" as drawn up by the psychologist Henry A. Murray in his book *Explorations in Personality* has, however, come to be widely accepted:

To do one's best, to be successful, to accomplish tasks requiring skill and effort, to be a recognized authority, to accomplish something important, to do a difficult job well.	Achievement
To get suggestions from others, to find out what others think, to follow instructions and do what is expected, to praise others, to accept leadership of others, to conform to custom.	Deference
To keep things neat and orderly, to make advance plans, to organize details of work, to have things arranged so they run smoothly without change.	Order
To say clever and witty things, to have others notice and comment upon one's appearance, to say things just to see the effect upon others, to talk about personal achievements.	Exhibition
To be able to come and go as desired, to say what one thinks about things, to be independent of others in making decisions, to do things without regard to what others may think.	Autonomy
To be loyal to friends, to participate in friendly groups, to form strong attachments, to share things with friends, to write letters to friends, to make as many friends as possible.	Affiliation

To analyze one's motives and feelings, to understand how others feel about problems, to judge people by why they do things rather than by what they do, to predict others' behavior.	Intraception
To have others provide help when in trouble, to seek encouragement from others, to have others be kindly and sympathetic, to receive a great deal of affection from others.	Succorance
To argue for one's point of view, to be a leader in groups to which one belongs, to persuade and influence others, to supervise and direct the actions of others.	Dominance
To feel guilty when one does something wrong, to accept blame when things do not go right, to feel that personal pain and misery do more good than harm, to feel timid and inferior.	Abasement
To help friends when they are in trouble, to treat others with kindness and sympathy, to forgive others and do favors for them, to show affection and have others confide in one.	Nurturance
To do new and different things, to travel, to meet new people, to have novelty and change in daily routine, to try new and different jobs, to participate in new fads and fashions.	Change
To keep at a job until it is finished, to work hard at a task, to work at a single job before taking on others, to stick at a problem even though no apparent progress is being made.	Endurance
To engage in social activities with the opposite sex, to be in love with someone of the opposite sex, to be regarded as physically attractive by those of the opposite sex.	Heterosexuality
To attack contrary points of view, to tell others off, to get revenge for insults, to blame others when things go wrong, to criticize others publicly, to read accounts of violence.[3]	Aggression

MOTIVE APPEALS USEFUL TO THE PUBLIC SPEAKER

A similar list of motive appeals, drawn with a particular eye to the needs of the public speaker, might include these items:

[3]Henry A. Murray, *Explorations in Personality* (New York: Oxford, 1938; and New York: Psychological Corporation, 1954). Adapted by permission. Copyright 1954 © 1959, The Psychological Corporation, New York. All rights reserved.

1. Acquisition and saving.
2. Adventure.
3. Companionship.
4. Creativity.
   a. Organizing.
   b. Building.
5. Curiosity.
6. Destruction.
7. Fear.
8. Fighting.
   a. Anger.
   b. Competition.
9. Imitation.
10. Independence.
11. Loyalty.
    a. To friends.
    b. To family (parental or filial love).
    c. To social groups (school spirit, civic pride).
    d. To nation (patriotism).
12. Personal enjoyment.
    a. Of comfort and luxury.
    b. Of beauty and order.
    c. Of pleasant sensations (tastes, smells, etc.).
    d. Of recreation.
    e. Of relief from restraint (sprees, protest marches, etc.).
13. Power and authority
14. Pride.
    a. Reputation.
    b. Self-respect.
15. Reverence or worship.
    a. Of leaders (hero worship).
    b. Of traditions or institutions.
    c. Of a deity.
16. Revulsion.
17. Sexual attraction.
18. Sympathy.

Do not be disturbed by the fact that in the foregoing lists certain wishes or desires may appear to work at cross-purposes—fear against the drive for adventure, personal enjoyment against the desire for power and authority, etc. Remember that the human being himself is an inconsistent and changeable animal who, at different times, pursues quite different ends or goals. Later in this chapter, we shall suggest a number of ways in which this difficulty may be avoided. For the present, let us consider in greater detail each of the motive appeals included in the foregoing list.

Acquisition and saving

Most of us like to earn money, to keep it, and to spend as little of it as we can in order to acquire the other things we want. Bargain basements are filled with people trying to get as much as possible at the lowest price. But this want also extends to many things besides money. Stamp collecting, the keeping of dance programs or photo albums, the gathering of art treasures or rare books, and similar hobbies are forms of the same tendency.

Adventure

Nearly everyone likes the thrill of mild danger—the adventure of diving beneath the surface of the sea, of scaling a mountain, or of exploring strange lands and cities. Youngsters rarely climb the safest tree; roller coasters coin money because of the thrills they provide; some motorists drive as fast as possible even if they don't have to "get there quickly." When acquisition and adventure are combined —as in most forms of gambling, from slot machines to stock speculation—they provide especially powerful motivation.

Companionship

A few people prefer to be hermits, but most of us like company. We cross the street to stroll with a friend rather than to walk alone. We go to parties, join clubs, write letters to absent relatives, and prefer to live in dormitories or fraternity houses. Even in our beliefs and opinions we tend to go along with the crowd, while the most humdrum work becomes more bearable if others are sharing it with us.

Creativity

We like to be able to say, "I made this myself." The urge to create shows itself in many ways: in inventions, books, buildings, business organizations, and empires. In addition to the creative *arts* (painting, music, sculpture, etc.), this tendency takes two more general forms: *building* with physical objects, such as bricks, steel, or wood; and *organizing* human beings into working units—political parties, business firms, athletic teams, and the like. This desire, for instance, lies behind many campus and civic activities.

Curiosity

Children tear open alarm clocks to find out where the tick is, and adults crowd the sidewalks to watch a celebrity pass by. But curiosity is not mere inquisitiveness or "nosiness," as is sometimes implied; it provides the motivation of the experimental scientist, the scholar, and—when curiosity is coupled with a love for adventure—of the explorer. Without curiosity, life would be dull and static.

Destruction

In most of us there seems to be an occasional impulse to tear down, to break, to cut to pieces, to destroy. Perhaps this urge arises from the desire to show our superiority over what we destroy and thus to expand our ego, or it may arise from a desire to free ourselves from social and cultural restraints. In any event, we all are destroyers at times. Build a block house for a baby, and he knocks it down. Let someone present a theory or an argument, and someone else delights in tearing it to pieces. There is always a crowd at a fire, and one of the reasons is the swift and awesome destruction by the flames. Nor is this tendency entirely antisocial; after all, the old must be destroyed before the new can take its place. The agitator who shouts "Down with" a practice or institution may be disliked by many of us, but he sometimes performs a valuable service.

Fear

Fear has both positive and negative effects. It may prevent us from doing things that bring peril, or it may make us act to protect ourselves against that peril. If the other man is bigger than I am, I may hesitate to attack him, but I may go home and put a lock on the door to keep him out. Physical injury, however, is not the only thing we fear. We also are afraid of losing our jobs, our property, our friends. Especially do we fear the unknown, the dangerous power of what is strange or hidden. This is one reason for stage fright. As practice makes us familiar with the situation of confronting an audience, this fear diminishes.

Fighting

Usually men fight because their *anger* has been aroused by some opposing force or person. We become angry at people who cheat or insult us, challenge our ideas or values, destroy our property, or interfere with our rights or efforts. The form in which we fight back against these intrusions may vary all the way from physical attack to subtle gossip, but it normally has for its purpose protecting our safety or restoring our self-esteem in the face of attack. Because society frowns on assault and battery, we generally tend to use more civilized and legal methods of responding—social ostracism, court action, and the like. But show any man that he is being cheated, insulted, or threatened, and he will likely become angry and fight back in one way or another.

The impulse to fight, to struggle, also takes another form of expression in modern society, and this is *competition.* We enjoy matching wits and muscles against antagonists, even though we are not angry with them, for the sheer pleasure of the struggle or for the sake of demonstrating our superiority. Participation in games is based on this tendency, and many people argue or debate just for this reason. Business and scholastic rivalry are manifestations of the element of competition. The prevalent use of the phrase "We *beat* them" to indicate the winning of such competitive engagements suggests the "fighting" nature of the effort.

Imitation

People tend to imitate others, both consciously and unconsciously. When a new term or expression appears on the campus, everyone begins to use it. But slang is not the only thing we imitate. We copy the dress, attitudes, actions, and even the pronunciations of other persons, especially of those we admire or respect. Tell someone how a famous person does a thing or how he attained his success, and your hearer is likely to want to imitate that individual.

Independence

In spite of the tendency to imitate or conform, we do not like to lose our independence: we do not like to be *forced* to imitate. A woman's dress must be in style, but at the same time it must not be exactly like any other dress—it must be unique. We do not like to be bossed about, to have to attend class, or to be prohibited from acting as we like. If you can make your hearer feel he is doing something of his own volition, he will be much more likely to do it than if the act is forced upon him. Workmen have quit their jobs; members have resigned from clubs; nations have engaged in revolutions—all to maintain independence of action.

Loyalty

The sentiment of loyalty, based upon the individual's tendency to identify himself with other persons or groups, sometimes provides very strong motivation. The strength of an appeal to this motive will vary, of course, with the degree to which the individual has become identified with such groups or persons. Hence, a man's loyalty to his family is usually stronger than his loyalty to his college. A few of the more important types of loyalties are:

Loyalty to friends. We do more for persons to whom we are affectionately attached than for chance acquaintances or strangers. People resent slurs upon their friends and are more likely to believe in the opinion of their associates than in those of strangers.

Loyalty to family. Sometimes family loyalty is referred to as *parental love or filial duty.* Brothers may fight with one another, but let an outsider attack one of them, and their differences are forgotten in a common loyalty to each other. Men buy life insurance to protect their wives and families; mothers give freely of their time and strength for the good of their children; the pleasure of a campus visit from mother or father is a very real one.

Loyalty to social groups. Such terms as school spirit, civic pride, and club morale typify this expression of loyalty. Let someone challenge the status of a fraternity, and those who belong to it rise to its defense; let some group begin an undertaking, and its loyal members immediately tend to give that undertaking their full support.

Loyalty to nation: patriotism. Loyalty to our country and its institutions is instilled in all of us throughout our lives. Schools, books, newspapers, moving pictures, and civic celebrations constantly remind us of this loyalty. We depend upon our government for our safety, and we support it when our support is demanded. In prosperous and peaceful times, loyalty to political parties or sectional interests may be stronger than this larger loyalty; but when danger—economic or military—threatens, patriotic sentiment reasserts itself in the great majority of the population.

Because appeals to loyalty are so easily made, they are often overdone. After too much repetition, they lose their force and become nothing but rubber-stamped expressions. Especially avoid such trite and soporific phrases as "the constitushun uv our grea-a-a-t Republic!" When used sparingly and sincerely, the appeal to loyalties is powerful; but it must not become monotonous or shallow.

Personal enjoyment

Man's pleasures are many and varied, and he usually will act to prevent their being curtailed or to increase the facilities for enjoying them. Some types of pleasures universally enjoyed are:

Enjoyment of comfort and luxury. Most people prefer to sit on a soft chair rather than on a hard one. If a man can afford it, he gets a reservation in a sleeping car rather than sit up all night on a coach;

he takes a cab instead of a crowded bus. What pleasure there is in stopping at a luxuriously appointed hotel with impeccable dining-room service! One reason why people work hard to earn money is to enjoy the comfort and luxury it will buy for them.

Enjoyment of beauty and order. Most of us like to have things clean and neat, even if we may not always want to expend the effort to keep them so. In the beauty of autumn foliage, in the cadence of the surf, or in the creation of a skilled artist there is an esthetic pleasure that cannot be paralleled. But even a neat outline, an orderly boiler room, or a well-pressed suit contributes to one's esthetic pleasure. More than one customer has bought an automobile because of its luxurious appointments and beautiful body lines rather than because of its economy or mechanical excellence.

Enjoyment of pleasant sensations. Sights, sounds, smells, tastes, and feelings which gratify the sensory organs—the eyes, the ears, the nose, the palate, and the rest—give special pleasure to most people. Obviously, the pleasures listed in the two preceding paragraphs are closely associated with this type, since they also are sensory in nature. But sensory pleasure exists even without beauty or luxury; it is more direct in its appeal. Regardless of the comfort, luxury, beauty, or orderliness of the environment in which it may be served, the *taste* of roast turkey on Thanksgiving gives pleasure. The smell and taste of a pipe filled with rare tobacco or of a bowl of steaming tomato soup are further evidence.

Enjoyment of recreation. Who does not like to relax and to play? Crowded golf courses, the steady stream of tourists to vacation spots, the popularity of certain television programs, and the enormous sale of paperback novels give an overwhelming answer. Everyone enjoys breaking away from his regular work and engaging in interesting activities which have no serious purpose. Show your audience the *fun* they will have in doing a certain thing, and the impulse to do it will grow strong.

Enjoyment of the relief from restraint. Have you ever listened to the laughter and shouts of children when they are dismissed from school on Friday afternoon? Similarly, college students appreciate a holiday because it is a relief from the restraints of hard study and regular class attendance. Note also the joyous attitude of the person who has just been allowed to break away from a rigid diet. The tendency to seek relief from restraint is prevalent in almost everyone.

Power and authority

Most people like to exert influence over others. Men have given up lucrative positions to enter government service at a much smaller salary. Why? Among other reasons, because their power over others may be increased thereby and the principles they believe right can be more easily established. Few persons will refuse election or appointment to an office that gives them a measure of authority. Show your audience the additional power your proposal will bring to them or to the group or nation to which they belong. For many men, self-advancement means not only an increased income but also an increase in power and authority. Together these two appeals may become exceedingly persuasive.

Pride

One of the most powerful single appeals that can be made is to pride, especially when you are dealing with young people. A varsity letter has little intrinsic value, but an unbelievable amount of work will be done to earn one. Election to an honorary society has more importance to the average student than a cash award. But the influence of pride is not limited to the young; from childhood to old age, we are extremely careful to protect our egos.

Pride, it should be observed, manifests itself in two ways: in *reputation* and in *self-respect*. Of these two, the desire for self-respect is the more fundamental, but in many practical situations the desire for a good reputation has a more tangible appeal. Reputation is the estimate others have of you; self-respect is the opinion you wish to have of yourself. For most of us, it is difficult to have one without the other. To influence an audience, then, show them what effect your idea will have upon their reputation, but be careful not to suggest something incompatible with their self-respect. In particular, beware of reciting the praise of some person whom your listeners regard so unfavorably that to accept your praise of him would be to lower their self-respect. Nor can the appeal to pride be too obvious: oily compliments can evoke a negative reaction.

Reverence or worship

There are times when all of us are aware of a sense of our own inferiority in relation to a superior person or thing. This sentiment shows itself in a feeling of humility and a willingness to subordinate ourselves. It takes three common forms: *hero worship*, or the deep admiration of other persons; *reverence for traditions and institutions;* and *worship of a deity*, whether it be conceived religiously or as a philosophical concept.

The first of these, hero worship, is more common in children; but it sometimes exists in adults, especially in their admiration of business, political, or social leaders whose personal qualities have made a strong impression on them. Toward certain traditions and institutions also we have a strong feeling of reverence: we sit quietly and with bared heads at a funeral; the national anthem brings us to our feet; we consider democracy worth fighting for. The feeling of worship for a deity has come down to us through the ages. It shows itself formally in religious exercises; but even the man who rejects formal religion is awestruck when he gazes at the immensity of the heavens or feels the full fury of a storm. He may call himself Christian, Jew, Buddhist, Mohammedan, or atheist—but his feeling of reverence is nonetheless real. The wise speaker respects the heroes, traditions, and religious attitudes of his audience and avoids the antagonism which opposition to them may bring. At times an appeal to reverence or worship may add an enormous force to arguments or proposals.

Revulsion

Just as a fragrant flower garden attracts people, so the odors of a dump heap repel them. Just as there is enjoyment in pleasant sensory experiences, so unpleasant ones may evoke disgust or loathing. By showing the unpleasant conditions in a city's slums, you may create sentiment to clean them up; if you can induce people to become disgusted with graft and corruption in public office, they will vote against those who allow it; by picturing the undesirable results of a proposal, you may turn people against it. While doing these things, however, you must beware of rendering your descriptions so gruesome that your speech itself becomes revolting. Tact is required to make a description of repulsive conditions vivid enough to be impressive without, at the same time, offending the good taste of your listeners.

Sexual attraction

Men strive for the attentions of women, and women seek to attract men. The importance of this force in human life needs no emphasis here. Whenever a proposal will make us more attractive in the eyes of the opposite sex or will remove an obstacle to that attraction, that proposal gains our support. The taboos that society has placed upon sexual matters require that the speaker use extreme care in referring to them. Vulgar stories in particular are revolting to most audiences. However, the appeal to sexual attractiveness itself, when used with tact and good taste, is strong and, in addition, serves to strengthen other appeals the speaker may employ.

Sympathy

Just as we are likely to identify ourselves with the groups to which we belong or aspire to belong, so we tend to see ourselves in the plight of those who are unfortunate. This feeling of compassion for the unhappy or the unlucky, which we here call sympathy, makes us want to help them. We pause to aid a blind man or to question a crying child. We give money to feed people whose homes have been ravaged by flood, earthquake, or fire. As a speaker, you may influence your audience by arousing in them the sentiment of sympathy or pity. To do so, however, remember that you must make it easy for them to identify themselves with the unfortunate ones, to put themselves in the other fellows' shoes. You cannot accomplish this with statistics and abstractions; you must describe sympathetically and compassionately the individuals to whom you refer, and you must depict their plight vividly.

USING MOTIVE APPEALS

The sentiments or desires just discussed are some of those to which appeals may be made in an effort to influence the thinking or action of an audience. Remember, though, that these appeals are not always made singly but often are combined. In fact, you have probably noticed in many of the examples above that some appeal other than the one being illustrated was also present. Suppose you were urging students to attend college. You might tell them that doing so would enable them to "get ahead" in the world more quickly and easily. But what else is involved in this statement? There is, of course, a desire for greater income, the power of higher positions, and the pride of a recognized station in life; all these—acquisition, power, pride—are combined into the one pattern called "getting ahead." Or let us take another common experience; suppose you were going to buy a suit or a dress. What would influence your decision to purchase it? One thing would be its price—*saving;* another would be its comfort and appearance—the *pleasure* to be derived from beauty or luxury; another consideration would be its style—*imitation;* or its individuality of appearance—*independence;* and finally, a combination of these items would make an appeal to *pride:* Would other people think the clothing in good taste; would they envy your selection? Some of these desires might be stronger that others, and some might conflict with each other, but all of them would affect your choice, and you would buy whichever suit or dress made the strongest appeal to these desires.

Because motive appeals are so closely related, it is usually a good idea to use them in combination rather than singly when building a speech. On the other hand, however, too great a variety may dissipate the effect at which you aim. Usually it is best to select the two or three appeals which you think will have the greatest effect on your audience and concentrate on these, allowing other appeals to be secondary or incidental. Be sure also that you do not inadvertently use conflicting appeals—for instance, urging your audience to do something because of the *adventure* involved while describing it so vividly that they come to *fear* the act or its consequences. To avoid this, select as the main points of your speech arguments that contain basic appeals and examine them for clarity and consistency.

For example, a student who was urging his classmates to participate in interclass athletic contests chose the following as the main points of his speech:

1. Concentrated study without exercise will make your mind stale and ruin your grades *(fear).*
2. By playing with others you will meet new friends *(companionship).*
3. Interclass competition may lead to a place on the varsity teams *(power* and *pride).*
4. You will have a great deal of fun playing *(enjoyment of recreation).*

In the complete development of his speech, this student made incidental appeals to imitation through examples of those who had previously engaged in interclass sports; he stimulated the desire for competition; he suggested that participation would signify loyalty to the class, but the principal appeal was made to those few motives which were incorporated in his main points.

In most cases, you should not attempt to motivate your audience too directly or obviously, for to do so almost certainly would result in resistance. You should not say, "I want you to *imitate* Jones, the successful banker," or "If you give to this cause, we will print your name so that your *reputation* as a generous man will be known to everybody." Instead, you must make your appeals effective through the suggestion of these results as carried in the descriptions and illustrations you use. Remember, too, that people generally are ashamed to acknowledge publicly certain motives which privately may be very powerful, such as the appeal to greed, fear, imitation, or pride. Therefore, when these appeals are used in a public speech, they must be carefully framed and supplemented by other appeals which people are publicly willing to admit as the cause of their action.

APPEALING TO FIXED ATTITUDES AND OPINIONS

The choice and phrasing of your motive appeals always should be adapted to the beliefs and attitudes of your listeners. Either as the result of personal experience or because of repeated assertions by parents, teachers, respected friends, or accepted authorities, people tend to develop strong opinions concerning many aspects of their environment. They are "for" or "against" labor unions, civil rights, military preparedness, professional athletics, fraternities; they consider policemen, politicians, nurses, flyers, lawyers, and Frenchmen as good or bad, unreliable or trustworthy, ignorant or intelligent; they like or dislike popular music, flashy clothes, mathematics, and traveling on buses. Crystallized attitudes and opinions of this sort are usually based on a combination of wants; but over a period of time, the underlying motivation is submerged, and the specific attitude or opinion becomes the dominating influence. With respect to any particular subject, therefore, you must consider not only the controlling motives of your audience and the more universal types of motive appeals, but also the specific attitudes and opinions into which these motives have developed. By associating your ideas and proposals with the positive attitudes of your audience and by avoiding negative associations, you can make your appeals stronger and more direct.

Problems

1. Clip from a popular magazine ten advertisements which contain one or more motive appeals. Name each appeal, tell why you think it was selected to sell this particular product, and evaluate its effectiveness. Note that a motive appeal may lie in a picture as well as in the text of an advertisement, or that picture and text may be used to reinforce each other.
2. In your opinion, which motive appeals are best adapted to persuading an audience of young persons? Of older persons? Of men? Of women? Defend your answers.
3. Name some motive appeals that might well be combined to strengthen a persuasive effort. Then name several motive appeals which, if combined, would work against each other.
4. Under what conditions would you consider a motive appeal to the wants or desires of listeners a perfectly ethical and legitimate means of persuasion? Under what conditions would you say that such an appeal is unethical? In answering, consider the subject matter of the speech and the situation in which it is made, as well as the nature of the appeal itself.
5. Assuming your speech class to be the audience, which motive appeals do you think would best support each of the following propositions? Which

motive appeals probably would be most effective if you were opposing these same propositions?

Fraternities and sororities should be abolished.
Books and magazines should be censored to protect public morals.
The United States should disarm unilaterally.
Attend the movies regularly.
Eat less and live longer.

6. If a speaker with whom you disagree attempts to persuade through the use of motive appeals, how do you think the effect of that persuasion may best be combatted? By presenting motive appeals which work at cross-purposes with his (fear against self-enhancement, etc.)? By explaining to the audience the appeals with which he is trying to move them? By presenting evidence and arguments to the contrary? Why do you answer as you do?
7. To what extent are the motives of men conditioned and shaped by the cultures in which they live, and to what extent are their motives the same regardless of culture? For example, are the motives of the Chinese Communist significantly different from those of the democratic American? The motives of the Buddhist different from those of the Christian? How does one's answer to this question affect his theory and practice of public speaking?

Speaking assignment

1. Present a three- or four-minute speech in which, through the combined use of two or three related motive appeals, you attempt to persuade your audience to a particular belief or action. (For example, combine Adventure, Companionship, and Personal Enjoyment to persuade them to take a conducted group tour of Europe; or combine Sympathy and Pride to elicit contributions to a charity drive.)

At the conclusion of your speech, let an assigned member of the class attempt to determine which motive appeals you were using. If there is any question about what these appeals were, explore with him and the other members of the class the reasons why they were not made clear. Consider also after each speech how the motive appeals could have been sharpened and strengthened.

Suggestions for further reading

Robert Bostrom, "Motivation and Argument," *Perspectives on Argumentation*, ed. Gerald R. Miller and Thomas R. Nilsen (Glenview, Illinois: Scott, Foresman and Company, 1966), pp. 110-128.

Judson Brown, *Motivation of Behavior* (New York: McGraw-Hill Book Company, 1961).

John Dollard, Neal E. Miller, Leonard W. Doob, O. H. Mowrer, and Robert R. Sears, *Frustration and Aggression* (New Haven, Conn.: Yale University Press, 1939).

R. Barry Fulton, "Motivation: Foundation of Persuasion," *Quarterly Journal of Speech,* XLIX (October 1963), pp. 295-307.

Murray A. Hewgill and Gerald R. Miller, "Credibility and Fear-arousing Communications," *Speech Monographs,* XXXII (June 1965), pp. 95-101.

Eugene Knepprath and Theodore Clevenger, Jr., "Reasoned Discourse and Motive Appeals in Selected Political Speeches," *Quarterly Journal of Speech,* LI (April 1965), pp. 152-156.

D. C. McClelland, J. W. Atkinson, R. A. Clark, and E. L. Lowell, *The Achievement Motive* (New York: Appleton-Century-Crofts, 1953).

C. E. Osgood and P. H. Tannenbaum, "The Principle of Congruity in the Prediction of Attitude Change," *Psychological Review,* LXII (1955), pp. 42-55.

Floyd L. Ruch, *Psychology and Life,* 7th ed. (Glenview, Illinois: Scott, Foresman and Company, 1967), Chapter IX, "Observation and Action," and Chapter XI, "Motivation and Drive."

Randall C. Ruechelle, "An Experimental Study of Audience Recognition of Emotional and Intellectual Appeals in Persuasion," *Speech Monographs,* XXV (March 1958), pp. 49-58.

Donald K. Smith and Robert L. Scott, "Motivation Theory in Teaching Persuasion: Statement and Schema," *Quarterly Journal of Speech,* XLVII (December 1961), pp. 378-383.

Otis M. Walter, "Toward an Analysis of Motivation," *Quarterly Journal of Speech,* XLI (October 1955), pp. 271-278.

CHAPTER THIRTEEN

Choosing material that will hold attention

In the preceding chapter we examined the various types of appeals which a speaker may use to motivate his listeners to belief or action. In this chapter we shall see how he may hold attention on the ideas and arguments he wishes to present.

Attention is a great deal like electricity: we don't know exactly what it is, but we do know what it does and what conditions bring it about. A baseball fan is sitting in the bleachers. The count is three and two. The pitcher settles himself on the rubber, winds up, and sends a fast ball sizzling over the plate. The umpire bawls, "Strike three! Yer out!" Only then does the spectator lean back, take a long breath, and notice what has been going on about him: the man who has been thumping him on the back, the sack of peanuts he has dropped, the threatening clouds that have suddenly darkened the sky, the hornet buzzing around his ankles. What has happened? We say that this spectator was unaware of his surroundings because his attention was focused on the game. Those things to which he was paying attention controlled his thought and action so completely that everything else was forced into the background.

THE NATURE OF ATTENTION

Dr. Floyd Ruch, professor of psychology at the University of Southern California, suggests that, psychologically, attention may be looked upon as having three interrelated aspects: (1) an adjustment of the body and its sense organs, (2) clearness and vividness in consciousness, and (3) a set toward action.[1] Thus, during attention, posture is

[1]From *Psychology and Life*, 7th ed., by Floyd L. Ruch (Glenview, Illinois: Scott, Foresman and Company, 1967), pp. 295-296.

adjusted and the sense organs are "aimed at" the stimulus in order to receive impressions from it more readily. Just as the robin cocks its head to listen for the worm underneath the sod, so people lean forward and turn their eyes and ears toward the object which captures their attention. You have only to call your friend by name, and he will turn toward you in order to attend to your remarks. By gaining the attention of your audience, then, you increase their capacity to hear what you say because they will have adjusted themselves physically to listen.

Of greater importance to the speaker, however, is the second characteristic of attention—the fact that when we attend to a stimulus it becomes clearer and more vivid in our consciousness, while other equally strong stimuli seem to get weaker or to fade out altogether. This explains why the spectator at the ball game was unaware of so many of the things going on about him as long as his attention was focused on the game. Every moment of our lives innumerable stimuli impinge on our senses. We can hear the wind whistling, the birds calling, or the trucks rumbling; the temperature is warm or cold; a hundred different sights are before our eyes. Why don't we notice them all? It is because of the selective nature of attention. As we attend, some stimuli become strengthened and our awareness of them increases, while other stimuli recede and become less influential. If you as a speaker can catch and hold the attention of your audience, the ideas you express will make a clearer and more vivid impression on them, while distracting sights and sounds or conflicting ideas will tend to fade into the background.

Finally, as we noted above, a set toward action accompanies attention. We have a tendency, while attending to a series of stimuli, to "get set" to do something about them. Thus the driver of an automobile who pays attention to highway signs is *ready* to steer his car around a curve or to stop at an intersection. Similarly, assuming that what you say makes sense and contains the proper motive appeals, the closer your audience pays attention to you, the more likely they will be to act as you suggest. As they listen, they will tend to "get set" to think or act as you propose and will be more disposed to do so without wavering or hesitation. It has been said that *what holds attention tends strongly to determine action.* Certainly, speakers who do not secure the audience's attention rarely get the action they desire, and the most influential speakers are those who command the attention of their listeners.

We must not assume, however, that paying attention is entirely a spontaneous and involuntary reaction of the audience, governed solely by what the speaker says. Many times we must force ourselves to concentrate on something which in itself does not attract us. A student, for example, may compel himself to focus his attention on a textbook assignment in spite of the distractions around him or to listen attentively to a dull classroom lecture because he is required to pass the course. Necessity or strong motivation often leads us, as members of an audience, to exert this type of conscious effort in order to focus our minds on stimuli which are not attention-provoking in themselves.

Psychologists refer to attention which results from such conscious effort as *voluntary* or *forced* attention, as distinguished from the *involuntary* or *effortless* attention paid to things which are striking or engaging in themselves. Audiences sometimes force themselves to listen to a speaker out of mere politeness or respect for his prestige or position. More often, however, such voluntary attention results from the audience's feeling that the subject is important to them. If, therefore, your topic lacks natural or immediate interest, early in your speech make its importance so clear that your listeners will exert a voluntary effort to concentrate.

The very fact that voluntary attention requires conscious effort by the listeners, however, also makes it tiring to them. As the psychologists say, "It is accompanied by a mass of strain sensations" resulting, ultimately, in fatigue and boredom. Unless you want to tire your audience or to risk having their interest wane as you go on, you cannot, therefore, depend on voluntary attention alone. Desirable as it is to give your listeners a reason at the start for paying voluntary attention, it is also your task to see that as soon as possible their attention becomes effortless and involuntary. By using speech material which employs one or more of the factors of attention discussed below, you can make it easier for your audience to listen to you and to focus attention on what you have to say. In this way, voluntary attention on their part will become involuntary, effortless, and sustained; and your ideas will be left sharply impressed upon their minds.

THE FACTORS OF ATTENTION

How, then, can you capture and hold the attention of an audience? In Chapters 4 and 6 we pointed out how purposive movement about the platform, varied and vigorous gestures, and an animated vocal delivery contribute to this end. Obviously, your general reputation as a speaker and the degree of prestige accorded you by your listeners also are important. But here we are concerned with the content of the speech itself. What type of arguments or ideas tend more than others to command attention and hence to generate response? The *factors of attention*—those qualities of subject matter which usually capture the spontaneous attention of an audience—may be listed as follows:

1. Activity or movement
2. Reality
3. Proximity
4. Familiarity
5. Novelty
6. Suspense
7. Conflict
8. Humor
9. The vital

These qualities, of course, overlap; and frequently two or more are combined to capture and hold attention, but for convenience let us consider them separately.

Activity

If you were standing on the sidewalk and two cars of the same make, model, style, and color were in your view, one parked at the curb and the other speeding down the street at sixty miles an hour, which one would you look at? The moving one, of course. Your speech likewise must move. Stories in which something happens have this quality. The more active or animated the ideas and events you talk about, the more intently people will listen. Instead of describing the structure of a machine, tell how it works—get the wheels turning, the parts moving, the pistons pounding; show what happens step by step.

Moreover, your speech *as a whole* should move. Nothing is so boring as a talk that seems to get nowhere. Foreshadow your destination; set up some signposts pointing toward your goal. Make the movement of your speech clear to your audience by indicating when you are done with one point and are ready to advance to the next. Don't spend too much time on any single idea; keep pressing forward.

Reality

The earliest words a child learns are the names of objects and of tangible acts related to them. This interest in reality—in the immediate, the concrete, the actual—persists throughout life. The abstract proposition $2 + 2 = 4$ may be true, but it holds little interest. Instead of talking abstract theory, talk in terms of people, events, places, tangible circumstances. Use pictures, diagrams, and charts; tell not what happened to "a certain prominent physician of this city," but to Dr. Fred Smith, who lives at 418 Paine Street; use all the forms of support possible; make your descriptions specific and vivid. Remember always that individual cases are more real than general classifications; actual names and places more fascinating than vague allusions.

Proximity

A direct reference to someone in the audience, to some object near at hand, to some incident which has just occurred, or to the immediate occasion on which the speech is being made usually will command attention. A reference to some remark of the preceding speaker or of the chairman has the same effect. The next time an audience starts dozing while you are speaking, try this: use a hypothetical illustration in which you name some person in the audience as the supposed chief character. Not only that man but everyone else as well is almost sure to wake up and listen.

Familiarity

Some things which are not near at hand at the moment are, nonetheless, familiar to us because of the frequency with which we meet them in our daily lives. Thus, knives and forks, rain, automobiles, shaving, classes, and a host of other common objects and events are closely built into our experiences. Because they are so much a part of us, familiar things catch our attention. We say, "Ah, that is an old friend." But, as with old friends, we become bored if we see too much of them and nothing else. The familiar holds attention only when it is introduced in connection with something unfamiliar or when some fresh or unknown aspect of it is pointed out. Stories about Lincoln and Washington, for example, are interesting because we are familiar with their characters; but we don't like to hear the same old railsplitter or cherry tree tales unless they are given a new twist or application.

Novelty

An old newspaper proverb has it that when a dog bites a man, it's an accident; when a man bites a dog, it's news. In other words, we tend to pay attention to that which is new or unusual. This would appear to be the reverse side of the familiarity coin. Airplanes fly daily the hundreds of miles from Chicago to Paris, but there is nothing in the papers about them unless one of them happens to crash, disappear, or set a speed record. Even missile launchings have begun to lose their novelty, and man's exploration of space commands less attention than it did a few years ago. Nevertheless, the factor of novelty, if judiciously used, can be a potent force in arousing the attention of an audience; and in selecting his materials, the speaker will do well to give careful consideration to two special types of it: the novelty of *size* and the novelty of *contrast*.

Size. Objects that are extremely large or extremely small attract our attention. People often are startled into attention by large figures, especially if they are much larger than commonly supposed or than numbers with which they are familiar. In an address given at the University of Virginia, Henry W. Grady remarked, "A home that cost three million dollars and a breakfast that cost five thousand are disquieting facts." Notice, however, that mere size alone is not sufficient; the size must be unusual or startling in comparison to that which we expect or are already familiar with. Reference to a truck costing six thousand dollars or a bridge worth three million would hardly be striking. The New Yorker pays no attention to the skyscrapers, but the newcomer gets a cramp in his neck from gazing up at the Empire State Building.

Contrast. At a formal dance, evening clothes pass unnoticed; but let a student come to class so dressed and he immediately becomes the center of amused attention. He would have been equally conspicuous had he gone to the dance in sport clothes. Obviously, impropriety of this sort is not recommended for the speaker; but contrast need not necessarily be achieved through dress or conduct. How much more compelling the facts mentioned by Grady in the quotation above become when he throws them in contrast with others: "Our great wealth has brought us profit and splendor, but the status itself is a menace. A home that cost three million dollars and a breakfast that cost five thousand are disquieting facts to the millions who live in a hut and dine on a crust. The fact that a man . . . has an income of twenty million dollars falls strangely on the ears of those who hear it as they sit empty-handed with children crying for bread."[2]

In utilizing the materials of novelty, be careful not to inject elements that are so different or unusual that they are entirely unfamiliar. Remember that your audience must at least know what you are talking about, or their attention will soon waver. It is the proper combination of the new and the old, of the novel and the familiar, that accomplishes the best results. Novelty may gain attention, but it will not necessarily hold it.

Suspense

Much of the fascination of a mystery story arises from uncertainty as to who committed the crime. If the reader were to be told at once

[2]From an address before the Literary Societies of the University of Virginia by Henry W. Grady, June 25, 1889.

who killed the murdered man and how and when the deed was done, probably the rest of the book never would be read. An effective advertisement began in this way: "The L. J. Smithson Co. had been writing its balance in the red for two years, but last year it paid a dividend of twelve per cent." This statement was accompanied by a picture of a dividend check. Immediately the reader wondered, "How did they do it?" and he was impelled to read on into the body of the ad to find out. Few people go to see what they know will be a one-sided football game; the outcome is too certain. But the suspense of an evenly matched game draws a crowd. Hold the attention of your audience by pointing out results the cause of which must be explained (like the dividend mentioned above) or by calling attention to a force the effect of which is uncertain. Keep up the suspense in the stories you use to illustrate your ideas. Mention some valuable information that you expect to divulge later in your speech but that first requires an understanding of the point you are now making. Make full use of the factor of suspense, but remember two things: *(a)* Don't be so vague or mysterious that your listeners lose all hope of solving the riddle; give them a large enough taste to make them want to hear more. *(b)* Make sure the situation is important enough to the audience so that the suspense matters; attention is seldom drawn by uncertainties which are trivial.

Conflict

The opposition of forces compels attention—especially if the listeners identify themselves with one of the contending sides. In a sense, conflict is a form of activity; but it is more than that—it is also a clash or struggle between competing desires or actions. Often conflict suggests uncertainty; but even when there is little doubt of the outcome, the combat itself draws attention. Dog fights, election contests, the struggle of man with the adverse elements of nature and disease—all these have an element of conflict within them, and people become interested when the conflicts are vividly described. For the same reason, controversial issues are of more interest than those agreed on; and a vigorous attack upon some evil force—be it crime, graft, or a personal opponent—will draw more attention than a quiet analysis, though it is not always so effective or enduring. Describe a fight, show vividly the opposition between two factions, or make a verbal attack yourself, and people will listen to you. Be cautious, however, of sham battles: if you set up straw men and knock them down, the reality—and hence the effectiveness—of your speech may be totally destroyed.

Humor

Laughter indicates enjoyment, and people pay attention to that which they enjoy. Few things, in fact, will hold an audience as well as the judicious use of humor. It provides relaxation from the tension which other factors of attention often create and thus prevents fatigue while still retaining control over the thoughts of the listener. Various types of humor and recommendations concerning their use will be discussed in Chapter 20. For the present, however, be sure to observe these two requirements:

Relevancy. Beware of wandering from the point under discussion. The joke or anecdote must reinforce rather than detract from the idea you are developing.

Good taste. Avoid humor on occasions where it would be out of place, and refrain from using those types of humor which might offend the sensitivities of your listeners.

The vital

Finally, people pay attention to those things which affect their lives or health, their reputations, property, or employment. If you can show a man that what you say concerns him or his family directly, he nearly always will consider your discussion vital and will listen intently. In a larger sense, the satisfaction of any desires based on the primary motives of human behavior discussed in Chapter 12 becomes a matter of vital concern to most people. Even a danger to someone else's life attracts the listeners' attention because of their tendency to identify themselves with others. If the other eight factors of attention are important in speaking, this one is indispensable. Always make your comments and recommendations concern matters which are vital to the existence, well-being, and satisfaction of your audience.

These nine factors of attention should be your constant guides in selecting the ideas for a speech. Given adequate support in the manner described in the preceding chapters, your speech will be effective in proportion to its conscious and proficient employment of these factors.

SAMPLE SPEECH

A graduate of John Marshall Law School and Chicago's Loyola University, The Honorable Edith S. Sampson, Circuit Court Judge of Cook County, Illinois, has been active in public life for most of her adult years and has served in numerous posts. Admitted to the Illinois Bar in 1927, she has been a referee in the Juvenile Court of Cook County and an assistant corporation counsel for the City of Chicago, and is the first Negro woman in the United States to become an elected judge.

The following address was delivered by Judge Sampson at the 100th Annual Commencement ceremonies at North Central College, Naperville, Illinois, on May 30, 1965—an occasion on which an honorary LL.D. degree was conferred on her. Note how the speaker has employed a number of the factors of attention—especially humor, familiarity, and the vital. Observe also how the easy conversational style of the speech and its close adaptation to the audience help to sustain attention and interest.

CHOOSE ONE OF FIVE[3]

Edith S. Sampson

This degree that you have bestowed upon me out of your magnificent kindness is not just an honor. It's outright flattery—and I love it. Recognizing that it's impossible adequately to express my gratitude, I shall take the coward's way out and not even try.

Let me, instead, talk briefly to these graduates who have won their degrees the hard way instead of by the simple expedient of traveling from Chicago to Naperville.

[3] *Vital Speeches of the Day*, XXXI (August 15, 1965), 661-663. Reprinted by permission.

You graduates have every right to expect penetrating words of profound wisdom from an LL.D., even when the doctorate is honorary.

You look for too much, of course, if you ask that I settle all affairs, both international and domestic, in anything under an hour. But I surely ought to be able to handle either one or the other of the side-by-side package without imposing too great a strain on your patience and your posteriors.

I should be able to untangle the enigma of Vietnam for you in 10 minutes and solve the Dominican problem in another 5. This would still give me, within a 20-minute limit, ample time to pronounce with authority on the assorted crises in the U.N., NATO, the Organization of American States, the Congo, Laos, Cambodia, Malaysia, Indonesia, India, and Pakistan.

Or, if I were to talk about the domestic scene, I should be able to sum up for you my definitive solutions to the problems of interracial relations, poverty, urban renewal, mass transportation, education—both higher and lower—organized crime, juvenile delinquency, the balance of payments, labor-management controversy, and what's to become of those dreadful people in Peyton Place.

If you wanted an analysis of the current state of art, literature, music, drama, and philosophy, you would naturally have to give me another ten minutes.

Unfortunately, though, I am going to have to disappoint you, and I can only hope that you survive the sharp shock of disillusion. The degree that I've been given, precious as it is to me, did not endow me with instant wisdom.

As a result, I've been forced to fall back on a substitute for the all-revealing address that is your due today.

It's worse than that, really. Compounding what is already an offense, I'm going to present to you a multiple-choice test—the last of your college career.

The only consolations that I can offer in presenting the test are that it involves no bluebooks, you may consult texts freely, the test is self-scoring, and you have a lifetime at your disposal now to complete it.

This exam will be proctored, though. The proctors will be two—the community in which you live and, hardest taskmaster of all, your inner self.

The question: What do you do with your college education now that you have it—and now that it is beginning to become obsolete even as you sit here?

Choose one of five possible answers.

Choice One:

Put your diploma in a convenient drawer and close the drawer. Put whatever textbooks you've accumulated in a bookcase and close the bookcase. Put your mind to the dailiness of earning a satisfactory livelihood and close your mind.

I should warn you that it will take a bit of doing to follow this course with the rigor that it deserves.

You will have to take care not to read anything except, in the case of men, the sports pages or, in the case of women, columns of household hints.

You'll have to choose your friends with extreme care to make sure that you don't rub up against any stimulating personalities.

You'll have to build your own defenses against a world of complex realities that will insist on trying to intrude on you at the most inconvenient times.

But it can be done. I've known college graduates who have achieved it. They've wrapped themselves in an apathy so thick that they're in position to say in all truth, "No opinion," to any Gallup or Roper pollster who might question them on any subject.

It's a choice that's available to you. *Choice one.*

Choice Two:

Go forth into that waiting world, carefully assess the prevailing opinions, and then conform.

Forget this theoretical nonsense they've been feeding you here at North Central. What do professors and assistants and associates and instructors know about the real world anyway? Academics, all of them.

You'll have your degree. That certifies you're educated. Let it go at that.

This choice gives you more latitude than choice one.

You can scan the whole of the daily newspaper, as long as you make certain it's a newspaper that agrees with you and all other right-thinking citizens on all critical issues.

You can keep *Time* or *Newsweek, Life* or *Look* on the coffee table.

You can subscribe to the *Reader's Digest* and had better read at least some of it for conversational purposes.

You are even permitted, if you take this choice, to buy two books a year as long as you make sure they're best best-sellers. Reading the books is optional.

You don't have to be nearly so selective in making friends if you go this route instead of the first one. Just avoid the kooks—although that's easier said than done when what prevailing opinion recognizes as unmistakable kooks come in bewildering variety. But with a little caution you can easily manage.

After all, about 80, perhaps 85, per cent of the people with whom you'll come in contact fit nicely in this choice-two category. It isn't that they're particularly talented at blending into the background. They are the background.

You, too, can be a pillar-of-society conformist. No strain, no pain.

Well, almost no pain. The anguish of those moments in your middle age when you lie sleepless at 2 A.M. or 3 and wonder whatever happened to all your bright ambitions of college days—that anguish and those moments don't count too much.

Most of the time you can be comfortable with choice two, and who could ask for more than that?

One footnote at this point: Don't worry that your college degree will set you apart and make it impossible for you to be a really thorough-going conformist.

That was a slight danger in my day, but it's none at all now.

Ever since people have come to recognize the dollars-and-cents value of a college diploma as a passport to employment, more and more people have been going to college. Only the bigoted, narrow-minded people hold a degree against a person today, and the ranks of the conformists are filled with those who have had campus and even classroom exposure. B.A.'s, B.S.'s, masters, doctors—they can all live in the ticky-tacky houses.

Choice Three:

Refuse to relax into the commoner forms of conformity. Find yourself, instead, a clique of the elite, an "in" group, and conform yourself to it.

You might imagine, from that bare description of this choice, that this would be a difficult thing to do. It isn't at all.

There are just two requisites.

First, you must have a specialty of your own, some one field—or, better, part of a field—in which you're expert. It might be something in the arts—music before Vivaldi, for instance, or the epic poetry of Afghanistan. On the whole, though, it's better if your specialty is a little more practical, intellectual but money-making.

Then to the specialty, whatever it is, you add a dedication to everything that is advance guard and an amused contempt for everything else that isn't.

One thing you can't have if you go the third-choice way—at least not today—and that's a conviction that human beings and the history they have made and are making are important. Nothing is important really—nothing, that is, except your one staked-out small field of specialization.

A James Reeb is beaten to death for daring to assert in action the dignity of man. A Mrs. Liuzzo is shot, killed after the Selma to Montgomery march. Too bad.

But someone suggests that "The Cabinet of Dr. Caligari" isn't really such great shakes as a movie. This is monumental heresy. Tie him to the stake and put a torch to the faggots.

You must preserve the proper hierarchy of values, you see.

If you join the sort of "in" group I have in mind, your reading becomes constricted again, I'm afraid.

You mustn't read the daily papers, or at a minimum you mustn't admit it if you do. The Sunday *New York Times*, on occasion, can be tolerated, but no more than tolerated.

You may not read *Life*, *Look*, *Time*, *Newsweek*, or the *Reader's Digest*, not to mention such unmentionables as *Better Homes and Gardens* or *Family Circle*. Nothing more popular than *Scientific American*.

No best-sellers, of course—that goes without saying. It's much better to criticize Saul Bellow without having read *Herzog* all the way through, although you should read enough to be able to say it nauseated you so much you couldn't finish it.

This constriction of your reading is rather unfortunate in one way, really. You can't read things like the *New Republic*, or the *National Review*, or *Commentary*, or *Foreign Affairs*, or the *Bulletin of the Atomic Scientists*, or the *Reporter*, or anything of the sort. Those all deal with political and social and economic matters, you see, and an "in" conformist who attached importance to such matters would be drummed out of the corps. Serve him right.

Choice Four:

Choice four, though, offers an alternative for those who cannot erase their political-social-economic consciousness.

Join an extremist group.

There is real effort involved in this at the very beginning. You have to study the various groups that present themselves and make your initial commitment.

The beauty of this choice, though, is that once you've made it, you can turn off your thinking and let yourself be carried by the forward surge of what is obviously a significant movement.

Say you link yourself to the far right.

Your enemies are immediately identified for you—Negroes, Jews, and Communists. Communists are easy to recognize—they're all the people who don't agree with you.

You know immediately what to oppose—fluorine in the water supply, income taxes, aid to foreign nations, the Supreme Court, movements for mental health, and any squeamishness about dropping nuclear bombs at will or whim.

You know immediately what to support—anything that the leaders of your group find good and pleasing, although unfortunately they find little that's either.

Say you link to the far left.

Your enemies are immediately identified for you—capitalists, the poor misled sheep of the middle class, and Fascists. Fascists are easy to recognize—they're all the people who don't agree with you.

You know immediately what to oppose—all business corporations, no exceptions; all Trotskyites; all deviationists; all revisionists; all efforts to help established governments resist Communist revolt.

You know immediately what to support—anything that the leaders of your group find good and pleasing, which is whatever the men in Moscow have smiled upon for the day.

What is so attractive about this choice four is that it requires no mental effort of you beyond the initial effort of making your selection. Yet it provides a wide-open emotional release that isn't possible with any of the first three choices.

With choice four you can convince yourself that every action you perform has world-molding significance. In sharp contrast to the choice-three people, choice-four people are convinced that everything is important because everything links somehow to the cause.

Choice Five:

And then, finally, there's CHOICE FIVE. It's hard to state this one. About as close as I can come to it is this: Hang loose, but stay vibrantly alive.

This one's strenuous. This one's demanding.

Choice five would demand of you that you consider today's graduation no more than a pause to catch your breath before continuing the life-long job of education.

It would demand of you that you be your own unique best self. And there is no higher demand than that.

Choice five entails wide-ranging reading and deep-probing thought.

It calls for a contradictory thing—a mind that is constantly open to new facts that dictate change but at the same time is resolutely committed to what seems best at any given point of time.

It calls for human involvement, a compassionate concern for everyone on this fast-shrinking little planet of ours and for the generations to come.

It calls for the resolute rejection of all stereotypes and insists on the thoughtful examination of even the most widely held assumptions that are too easily taken for granted.

If only choice five involved only one thing or the other—thought or action—it would be ever so much easier. It doesn't, though. It involves both.

And as if that weren't bad enough, this choice usually brings with it a certain amount of inner ache, because this way is a lonely way.

Those who make choice four are caught up in a wave of fervent enthusiasm that is all the more compelling because there's so little of the rational in it. They have the company of their Birchite brothers or their Communist comrades.

Those who make choice three clump together with others of their kind to exchange small coins of comment about existentialism and Zen, the hilarious glories of Busby Berkley movies and the charm of Tiffany lamp shades.

Those who make choice two are protected by the great crowd of which they've so willingly, gladly made themselves an anonymous part, no different from every other anonymous part.

Those who make choice one deliberately dull their sensitivities. They are cud-chewing content to join the boys at the bar of a Saturday night or the girls at the bridge table Wednesday afternoon. They vegetate.

But those who make choice five are never fully comfortable.

They are nagged at by their realization that they could be wrong.

They're prodded by their recognition that they've still so much more to learn and even more than that to understand.

They're made restless by their knowledge that no matter how much they do, there's still ever so much more left to be done.

Choice-five people have to live constantly with an acceptance of the fact that there are no simple answers in this world because there are no simple questions.

This makes life exciting for them, challenging, at least intermittently rewarding. But comfortable? No.

I would not urge choice five on any of you graduates. It asks so much of you.

Any of the other four will see you through to age 60 or 65, retirement, and a modest pension. They might easily do better than that and make you rich. In dollars, that is.

Five is there, though—one of the multiple choices on the test.

If any of you in this class of '65 makes that fifth choice, I wish you'd let me know about it. You I'd like to know better than I possibly can just by having made a speech here.

You I would treasure even above the LL.D. with which North Central College has so graciously honored me—and that, you can believe me, is saying a great deal.

Problems

1. Think back over your experiences of the past three or four days and select half a dozen objects or events to which you have paid sustained attention during that time—classroom lectures, books or magazine articles, television programs, etc. To which of these things did you pay attention effortlessly or involuntarily? On which was your attention voluntary or forced? What elements in the first group especially attracted you? What elements in the second group militated against the sort of effortless attention you paid to the items in the first group? How could some of the materials in the second group of objects and events have been reworked so as to make them more intrinsically interesting?
2. Perform the following experiment. Have the instructor place a small white chalk dot on an otherwise clean blackboard. Then have the members of the class attempt to pay attention only to that dot for one minute. At the end of this time, discuss the results of the test. Was anyone able to pay attention to nothing but the dot, or did attention keep wandering to other matters? What does this test suggest concerning the nature of attention and the obligations of the public speaker who hopes to hold it throughout his speech?
3. Find in the sample speeches printed in this book or in recent issues of *Vital Speeches of the Day* examples of at least seven of the nine factors of attention.
4. Study television commercials and magazine advertisements to discover some of the methods which advertisers use to capture the attention of the public. Which of these methods would be useful to the public speaker?

5. Select three or four speech subjects which you believe would have little natural interest for your classmates. Suggest how, through the use of the factors of attention or similar devices, these subjects might be rendered more interesting to them.
6. Select from a recent issue of *Vital Speeches of the Day* or some other appropriate source a speech which you think is not as interesting as it could or should be. Without changing the major ideas materially, rework the speech so as to make it more interesting. Introduce new illustrative material, reorganize the various points, vitalize the style, work in suitable factors of attention, etc. Do not, however, make the speech much, if any, longer as a result of these alterations; and, as already indicated, do not make substantive changes in the ideas expressed. Assume that you are revising the speech either for presentation in class or for a particular audience which you specify.
7. Assess the relative importance of varied, animated, colorful delivery and of intrinsically interesting subject matter in capturing and holding the attention of the average audience.

Speaking assignments

1. Let selected members of the class investigate the subject of attention as it is discussed in current textbooks in psychology, and relate their findings to the class in a series of ten-minute reports. Observe the rules for good reporting as set forth on pp. 40-41.
2. Present a three- or four-minute speech throughout which you attempt to hold the attention of the audience at as high a peak as possible. Select a subject which in itself has great interest value and use all of the methods and devices discussed in this chapter to enhance its interest still further.
3. As a variation of the preceding assignment, deliberately stack the cards against yourself. Again present to the class a speech throughout which you attempt to hold attention at the highest peak possible, but this time select a subject which has little or no natural interest for your audience and strive to make it as interesting and attention-commanding as you can.

Suggestions for further reading

H. L. Hollingworth, *The Psychology of the Audience* (New York: American Book Company, 1935), Chapter V, "Securing an Audience," and Chapter VI, "Holding an Audience."

Wayne Minnick, *The Art of Persuasion* (Boston: Houghton Mifflin Company, 1957), Chapter III, "Getting and Holding Attention."

David C. Phillips, *Oral Communication in Business* (New York: McGraw-Hill Book Company, 1955), Chapter IV, "How to Make Oral Communication Interesting."

Rollin W. Quimby, "How D. L. Moody Held Attention," *Quarterly Journal of Speech,* XLIII (October 1957), pp. 278-293.

Floyd L. Ruch, *Psychology and Life,* 7th ed. (Glenview, Illinois: Scott, Foresman and Company, 1967), Chapter IX, "Observation and Action."

Howard W. Runkel, "How to Select Material That Will Hold Attention," *Today's Speech,* VIII (September 1960), pp. 13-14.

John L. Vohs, "An Empirical Approach to the Concept of Attention," *Speech Monographs,* XXXI (August 1964), pp. 355-360.

James Winans, *Public Speaking* (New York: Century House, Inc., 1915), Chapter III, "Principles of Attention"; Chapter IV, "Attention of the Speaker to His Topic"; Chapter VI, "Attention of the Audience—Interest."

CHAPTER FOURTEEN

Selecting, phrasing, and arranging the ideas within the speech

In the seven preceding chapters we have considered the analytical aspects of speech preparation and have discussed the various kinds of materials out of which speeches are built. Moreover, we have seen how these materials may be employed to explain or support a single point. Most speeches, however, contain more than one idea. Therefore, we must now turn our attention to the problems involved in selecting, phrasing, and arranging ideas in these more complicated types of speeches. With this information before us, we may then consider how to begin and end a speech (Chapter 15), how to adapt what we say to the thought processes of our listeners (Chapter 16), and how to cast our ideas into proper outline form (Chapter 17).

SELECTING THE MAJOR IDEAS

First, then, what rules or principles should we follow in selecting the major points or ideas which we wish to present to our listeners?

Here, as in so many other aspects of speechmaking, common sense should be our guide. If a speech is to be successful, its major ideas should be (1) few in number, (2) of equal scope or importance, and (3) should cover all aspects of the specific subject with which the speech is concerned.

Keep major ideas few in number

Even the most intent and earnest listener has limited powers of attention and memory. Therefore, if a speaker attempts to develop too many different ideas within a speech, the chances are strong that many of them will either be forgotten or will pass unnoticed. Most audiences would be appalled by a speaker who announced: "This morning

I am going to discuss with you fifteen important aspects of our trade with foreign nations," or "I am going to give you twenty-three reasons why the United States should withdraw from the United Nations." Select at most three or four ideas or arguments, and group the rest of your material as subpoints under these major headings. Then if the subpoints are forgotten, at least the chances are good that the audience will go away with the crucial considerations fixed in their minds. Dwell on each major idea long enough so that your listeners have a fair opportunity to grasp and consider it; reiterate this idea at several different points in your speech. Wise speakers always limit severely the number of major ideas or arguments which they attempt to communicate.

Keep major points of equal scope or importance

Do not make the mistake of the student who argued against the abolition of tariffs on the grounds that such action would (1) threaten American manufacturers with a flood of cheap foreign goods, (2) mean a significant loss of revenue to our government, and (3) necessitate the rewriting of the syllabus used in the beginning economics course at his college. The last point was so obviously trivial in relation to the other two that he not only wasted precious minutes which might have been used to better effect, but actually made his entire speech appear ludicrous.

Cover all essential aspects of the subject

The major ideas of a speech should cover all important facets of the subject being discussed. In so far as they fail to do so, the information which the speech presents is incomplete, or the arguments which it develops are less convincing than they might otherwise be. If a proposal has significant economic implications as well as social and political ones, be sure to include this fact. If the history of a subject is important to understanding it, do not pass this over. When your speech is finished, all aspects of the subject which are relevant to your purpose should have been thoroughly explored. As we have urged, limit severely the number of major points or arguments you desire to communicate; but once you have limited them, be sure to treat each one as fully as the purpose of your speech and the nature of the occasion require.

PHRASING THE MAJOR IDEAS

The major ideas in a speech always should be stated clearly and emphatically. While illustrations, arguments, and facts constitute the bulk of what you say, the statement of your main points ties these details together and points up their significance. Good speakers take particular pains to phrase their main points in such a way that the meaning will be clear, persuasive, and easily remembered by their listeners. To achieve this result, keep in mind four characteristics of good phrasing: *conciseness, vividness, motivational appeal,* and *parallelism.*

Conciseness

State your major ideas as briefly as you can without impairing their meaning. Use the fewest words possible. A simple, straightforward declaration is better than a complex one. Avoid clumsy modifying phrases or distracting subordinate clauses. State the essence of your idea in a short sentence which can be modified or elaborated as you subsequently present the supporting material, or phrase your point as a simple question to which your detailed facts later will provide the answer. For example, "Our state taxes are too high" is better than "Taxes in this state, with one or two exceptions, are higher than present economic conditions justify." The second statement may present your idea more completely than the first, but it contains nothing that your supporting material should not clarify anyhow, while its greater complexity makes it less crisp and emphatic.

Vividness

Wherever possible, use words and phrases that are colorful and provoke attention. If the wording of your major ideas is dull and lifeless, you cannot expect them to stand out and to be remembered. Since they *are* the main points, they should be phrased so that they *sound* that way. They should be the punch lines of your speech. Notice how much more vivid it is to say, "We must turn these rascals out!" than to say, "We must remove these incompetent and dishonest men from office." Remember, of course, that vivid phrasing can be overdone. The sober presentation of a technical report at a scientific meeting does not require the colorful language needed at a political rally; on the other hand, neither does it justify the ponderous, trite, and sterile jargon too often employed. Keeping in mind the nature of your subject and the occasion on which you are speaking, avoid equally a superficial and exaggerated vividness that seems merely to be straining for effect and a lifeless, dull wording that lacks strength or color.

Motivational appeal

Whenever possible, word your major ideas so that they appeal to the wants and desires of your listeners. Review the factors of attention listed in Chapter 13 and the motive appeals discussed in Chapter 12. Try to phrase your main points so that they rivet the attention of your listeners and impel them toward the belief or action you desire. Instead of saying, "Chemical research has helped improve medical treatment," say, "Modern chemistry helps the doctor make you well." Rather than asserting, "Travel by air is fast," declare, "Travel by air saves time." Remember that you not only are speaking about something, but *to* somebody. Your major ideas should be phrased so that they appeal to your hearers and remain linked to their thinking.

Parallelism

Try to use the same sentence structure or similar phrasing for each point. Since your major ideas represent coordinate units of your speech, word them so that they sound that way. Avoid unnecessary shifts from active to passive voice or from questions to assertions. Whenever possible, use prepositions, connectives, and auxiliary verbs which permit a similar balance, rhythm, and direction of thought. Avoid wording a series of main points in this way:

I. The amount of your income tax depends on the amount you earn.
II. Property tax is assessed on the value of what you own.
III. You pay sales taxes in proportion to the amount you buy.

Phrase them like this:

I. The amount you earn dictates your income tax.
II. The amount you own controls your property tax.
III. The amount you buy determines your sales tax.

Note that part of each statement in the series above ("The amount you . . . your . . . tax") has been repeated, while the rest of the statement changed from point to point. Repetition of key words is often used in this way to intensify the parallelism. Similarly, in discussing the industrial value of aluminum, you might say:

I. Aluminum is strong.
II. Aluminum is light.
III. Aluminum is cheap.

Parallelism of phrasing—together with conciseness, vividness, and motivational appeal—will help make your major ideas stand out forcefully.

ARRANGING THE MAJOR IDEAS

When you get up to speak, an immediate and persistent problem will be to remember what you planned to say; and nothing will help you quite so much as having the major ideas of your speech arranged in a systematic sequence so that one leads naturally into the next. Moreover, your audience will follow your thoughts more easily and grasp them more firmly if the pattern of your speech is clear. As is sometimes said, to hold the interest of your audience you must *"let your speech march!"* Your listeners should not get the impression that you are wandering aimlessly from point to point; you must make it evident to them that your ideas are closely related to one another and are "marching" toward completeness in a unified and orderly manner. There are several ways of selecting and arranging the points of a speech so as to accomplish this result.

Time sequence

Begin at a certain period or date and move forward or backward in a systematic way. For example, the climate of a region may be discussed by considering the conditions which exist in the spring, summer, fall, and winter, respectively; methods for refining petroleum, by tracing chronologically the development of the refining process from the earliest attempts down to the present; the manufacture of an automobile, by following the assembly-line process from beginning to end. A time sequence may be appropriate to your subject no matter what your purpose in the speech may be. As in each of the instances above, however, it is often the most effective means of determining and arranging the major ideas in a speech to inform. Here is an example of time order used in an informative talk:

THE EARLY HISTORY OF TEXAS

I. Until 1822, Texas was under Spanish colonial rule.
II. From then till 1835, Texas remained a part of the Mexican Republic.
III. For the next ten years, Texas was an independent nation.
IV. In 1845, Texas became one of the United States.

Space sequence

Arrange your material from east to west, from bottom up, from right to left. The density of population, for example, may be discussed according to geographical areas; the plans of a building may be considered floor by floor; or the layout for a city park may be explained by proceeding from entrance to exit. Different aspects of a problem or a solution also are sometimes arranged according to a space sequence. The following example shows a problem analyzed according to this spatial or "geographic" method:

OUR DECLINING SALES

I. New England sales have dropped 15 per cent during the past year.
II. The Gulf States sales have dropped 10 per cent.
III. The Great Lakes area sales have dropped 20 per cent.

Cause-effect sequence

While a cause-effect sequence may be used to arrange the ideas in a speech to inform (as in explaining the relationship between a past and present event), it is more commonly found in speeches to convince or to actuate. When you discuss certain forces and then point to the results these forces will produce, or when you describe conditions or events and then show what forces created them, you are dealing with causal relationships. Thus you might first describe a community's zoning ordinances and, second, try to prove that present conditions (good or bad) are the effect of those regulations. The number of individuals who commit crimes after they have served prison sentences can be reported, and then their criminal actions attributed to certain major causes—ineffective methods of rehabilitation, public misunderstanding, or others. A cause-effect argument may be arranged as follows:

THE RISING COST OF LIVING

I. Each year the cost of living increases. (A, B, C, etc.: cite examples and statistics.)
II. The causes of the increase are: (A, B, C, etc.: list and explain causes.)

Problem-solution sequence

Sometimes the major ideas of a speech may best be arranged according to a two-fold plan: the description of a problem (or related problems) and the presentation of a solution (or solutions) to it. Thus you might describe the problems involved in building the Mackinac bridge connecting the Upper and Lower Peninsulas of Michigan, and then explain how the problems were solved. Usually, however, this type of arrangement is applied to problems facing the immediate audience for which you wish to present a solution. For example, you might point to declining interest in an important campus activity and then try to convince your listeners that they should adopt one or more ways of reversing this trend. It is also possible to apply this method to discussions of future contingencies: for example, one could outline the problems to be faced by the American school system after twenty more years of increasing population, and then present suggested solutions. When this type of sequence is used with a multiple problem or solution, each of the two main divisions of your discussion must itself be arranged in an orderly way; and you may use one of the other sequences—time, space, or cause-effect—for this purpose. Here is an example of how one speaker employed the problem-solution sequence:

CONTROLLING CRIME

I. The problem of crime is constantly growing more serious.
   A. Serious offenses are more common.
   B. Juvenile crimes have increased alarmingly.
II. We must meet this problem in three ways:
   A. We must begin a crime-prevention program.
   B. We must strengthen our police force to insure speedy arrests.
   C. We must free our court procedure from politics.

Special topical sequence

Certain types of information are best presented in divisions which already are familiar to the audience. For example, financial reports customarily are divided into assets and liabilities. Institutions or agencies are described as clusters of related departments—for example, legislative, executive, and judicial. Objects or processes are explained as a series of parts or functions. Policies are considered in terms of advantages and objections, or of problems and solutions. A special topical order for a speech on democratic government, for example, might take this form:

DEMOCRATIC GOVERNMENT IS BEST

I. It guarantees legitimate freedom to the individual.
II. It reflects the will of the majority.
III. It deepens the citizen's feeling of responsibility.

Similarly, your points may be arranged to answer a series of questions known to be present in the minds of the audience. It would be foolish to diffuse the answers to these questions by adopting a different partition of the subject.

The fact that one of the above sequences may have been chosen for the major ideas of a speech does not prevent the use of another sequence for arranging the *subordinate* points. On no condition, however, should you shift from one method to another in ordering the main points themselves. The following outline will illustrate how two or more methods may be combined in ordering the main and subordinate points of a speech:

MAJOR INDIAN TRIBES OF THE WEST

I. Southwest.
  A. Apache.
    1. Early history.
    2. Contacts with explorers and settlers.
    3. Present conditions.
  B. Navaho.
    1. Early history, etc. (Develop chronologically, as above.)
  C. Pueblo.
II. Pacific coast.
  A. . . . etc.
III. Northwest.
  A. . . . etc.

Notice that in this outline the space sequence has been used for the main headings; the special topical sequence for the subpoints, A, B, and C; and the time sequence for the sub-subpoints, 1, 2, and 3.

ARRANGING SUBPOINTS AND SUPPORTING MATERIAL

After you have put the major ideas of your speech into a suitable sequence, you must decide how to arrange the subpoints and supporting material so that the *internal* structure of each of the principal units of your talk has orderliness and substance.

Subordinating the subpoints

A "string-of-beads discussion," in which everything seems to have equal weight—tied together, as it usually is, by "and-uh," "and next," "and then," "and so"—lacks contrast and purposeful movement and soon grows tiresome. If you emphasize everything, nothing will stand out as important. Regardless of how well you have chosen, arranged, and worded your major ideas, they will be lost unless your subpoints are properly subordinated to them. Therefore, avoid listing subpoints as if they were main points, and avoid listing under a main point items that have no direct relation to it. Here are some forms of subject matter that are commonly subordinate:

Parts of a whole. Frequently a major idea concerns an object or a process which consists of a series of component parts; the subpoints then take up and treat the parts in order. For example, the grip, shaft, and head may be discussed as the parts of a golf club; or the number of churches in England, Scotland, Ireland, and Wales may be cited as subtotals of the aggregate number of churches in the British Isles.

Lists of qualities or functions. When the main point describes the general nature of an object, process, or concept, the subpoints often list the qualities which contribute to that nature. If the main point suggests the purpose of some mechanism, organization, or procedure, the subpoints may list the specific functions it performs. Thus timbre, pitch, and loudness are qualities under which the nature of sound may be discussed; or the purpose of a police department may be made clear by citing its various duties or functions.

Series of causes or results. If you use the cause-effect sequence to arrange your major ideas, you will often find that neither cause nor effect is single. Each of the separate several causes and results will then constitute a subpoint. Even when another type of sequence is used for the major ideas, a list of causes and results often forms the subitems under this point. The causes of a crop failure, for instance, might be listed as drought, frost, and blight; or the results of proper diet could be given as greater comfort, better health, and longer life.

Items of logical proof. In a speech to convince or to actuate, the subpoints should always provide logical proof of the idea they support. Often they consist of reasons or of coordinate steps in a single process of reasoning. When this is the case, you should be able to connect the major idea and subpoints with the word "because" (major idea is true, *because* subpoints a, b, c, etc., are true); and, in reverse, you should be able to use the word "therefore" (subpoints are true; *therefore* main point is true). Here is an example of this type of subordination: Strikes are wasteful, because *(a)* workers lose their wages, *(b)* employers lose their profits, and *(c)* consumers lose the products they might otherwise have had.

Illustrative examples. Many times the main point consists of a generalized statement for which the subpoints provide a series of specific illustrative examples. This method may be used both in exposition and in argument, the examples constituting clarification or proof respectively. Thus the general statement that fluoride helps reduce tooth decay might have as its subpoints a series of examples citing the experience of those cities which have added fluoride to their drinking water.

These are by no means all of the categories of subordinate items, but these common types should serve to illustrate the general principle of subordination. Remember also that the same principle applies to further subordination under subpoints. In longer and more detailed speeches you may have sub-subpoints and even sub-sub-subpoints. Do not let the process of subordination become too intricate or involved; but however far you go, keep your system of subordination clear and consistent.

Arranging coordinate subpoints

Usually there will be two or more subpoints under every major idea in your speech. Besides being subordinate to the major idea, these subpoints should be coordinate with each other. In what sequence, then, should they be arranged? Generally it is best to list them according to one of the types of arrangement given at the beginning of this chapter. Choose the sequence—time, space, causal, problem-solution, or topical—that seems most appropriate. You may want to use one of these sequences for the items under one major idea and a different sequence for those under another, but do not shift from one sequence to another *within* the same coordinate series. Above all, be sure that you do employ some kind of systematic order; don't crowd items in haphazardly just because they are subordinate points.

Supporting subpoints

The importance of supporting material was emphasized in Chapter 10. The general rule is: *Never make a statement of a major point or a significant subpoint in a speech without presenting at least one of the forms of support to clarify, illustrate, or prove it.* Too often, speakers think that if they have set down several subpoints under every major idea, they have done enough. The fact is, however, that you can subdivide ideas all day without doing any more than add detail to the *structure* of your speech. The *substance* of what you say lies in the figures, illustrations, facts, and testimony introduced. The manner in which such material is used to support a point was fully discussed in connection with the one-point speech (Chapter 11) and need not be repeated here. While you may not always need as much support for each subpoint in your talk as was suggested there, remember that the more you have, the stronger the point will be.

We have now considered some of the methods for the logical and coherent arrangement of ideas within a speech. Even with a thorough grasp of these methods, however, few persons can sit down with a mass of material and work out a suitable arrangement at first try. Test your general plan by putting your ideas into several different sequences. See which one seems to fit your material most naturally and best enables you to observe the rules for the selection and phrasing of major ideas. Time spent in this task will be of inestimable benefit not only in enabling your hearers to follow you more easily but also in helping you remember what you want to say.

A PRACTICAL EXAMPLE

For a practical example of how the methods and procedures described in this chapter may be applied, let us suppose that as the most important speech of the semester you are asked to prepare a fifteen-minute talk on some subject in which you are particularly interested. You decide to talk about the Federal Bureau of Investigation because you have already read a good deal about its activities and because you know a special agent of the FBI who can give you information that is not available in the usual printed sources. Your broad topic, then, is:

THE FBI

However, in fifteen minutes you will not be able to tell all that you know or can find out about the FBI. Therefore, recalling what you learned in Chapter 7 about limiting a subject, you ask yourself what information will be most interesting and useful to your listeners. After careful consideration, you decide to discuss the history and services of the FBI. The history, you think, will be interesting and also will emphasize the achievements of the Bureau, while the discussion of its services will show the various ways in which it contributes to law enforcement. Because of the time limit, however, you realize that you must sketch the history briefly and select for discussion only the more important of the FBI's services. Therefore you limit your topic as follows:

THE FBI

(Restricted to a brief review of its history, achievements, and major areas of service.)

Selecting and arranging the major ideas

In determining the limits of your subject, you have already made a preliminary selection of the major ideas to be covered in your speech. Now you set these points down on paper to see how they may be modified and fitted into a proper sequence. Your list may look something like this:

1. Origin and history of the FBI.
2. Purpose and functions of the FBI.
3. Activities of the FBI.
4. Famous cases the FBI has solved.

This itemization covers what you want to say, but the order does not please you, and at several points the subject matter overlaps. Conceivably, a time sequence could be used for the speech as a whole, and information about the FBI's activities could be brought in as part of the story of its development; but this would result in a great deal of repetition and also would tend to subordinate certain ideas about the Bureau's achievements which you especially wish to emphasize. After further consideration, therefore, you decide to use a topical sequence suggested by the nature of the material you want to cover:

1. Purposes of the FBI.
2. Its origin and history.
3. Its areas of service.

Under this arrangement, you find that what you wish to say about the FBI's major activities can be included in a discussion of its purposes, and its famous cases can be included in a discussion of its history. You also decide that recounting its history before you highlight some of its services will make for a more natural and logical development of the subject.

Working out the subheads

With the principal ideas of the speech thus chosen and arranged, your next task will be to phrase these points so that they express clearly and attractively the meaning you wish them to convey, and to place under each head the subordinate ideas by which it is to be explained or supported. Then you will need to check your work carefully to be sure (1) that you have included all the points you want to cover, (2) that you have not unbalanced your discussion by expanding unimportant items too greatly or skimping on important ones,

(3) that you have followed the principles of systematic arrangement and subordination, and (4) that you have assembled enough substantiating material in the form of illustrations, comparisons, statistics, and other forms of support. When this is done, the result should resemble the following:

OUR FBI: SERVANT TO THE NATION

(Limited to a brief review of the FBI's purposes, history, and services.)

I. The FBI is the permanent investigative arm of the Department of Justice.
  A. It is charged with investigating violations of all federal criminal statutes, except those delegated to other agencies.
    1. It must gather evidence in cases to which the United States is or may become a party.
    2. It must apprehend "public enemies."
  B. The FBI also is charged with protecting the internal security of the United States.
    1. It must apprehend foreign espionage agents.
    2. It must guard against sabotage and other subversive activities.
  C. Another of its purposes is to assist state and local law-enforcement agencies.
    1. It does this by helping identify known or suspected criminals.
    2. It does this by providing technical laboratory services.
    3. It does this by offering training to local police officials.
II. The FBI has a history of service to the nation.
  A. The early years of the FBI were marked by decisions important to its development.
    1. In 1908 it was founded by Attorney General Charles J. Bonaparte.
    2. In 1924 J. Edgar Hoover was appointed director by Attorney General Harlan Fiske Stone.
      a. Hoover reorganized the FBI along present lines.
      b. Hoover inaugurated policies which are still in effect.
  B. During the late 1920's and early 1930's, the prestige of the FBI grew rapidly.
    1. The FBI's campaign against the illegal liquor traffic of the Prohibition era aroused favorable publicity.
    2. Congress passed bills increasing its power.
      a. In 1932 Congress passed the federal kidnaping statute.
      b. In 1934 Congress passed the federal Bank Robbery Act.
      c. In 1934 Congress also passed legislation authorizing FBI agents to carry guns and make arrests.
    3. These bills enabled the FBI to increase its effectiveness.

a. In 1933 all kidnaping cases referred to the FBI were solved.
b. In 1934, FBI agents ended the careers of three notorious criminals —John Dillinger, Arthur ("Pretty Boy") Floyd, and Lester Gillis (alias "Baby Face" Nelson).

C. International developments leading up to the entry of the United States into World War II brought the FBI additional responsibilities.
1. It kept watch over the activities of enemy aliens residing in the United States.
2. It apprehended many foreign espionage agents.
3. It supervised the security of defense plants.
4. It was instrumental in developing a Pan-American intelligence force.

D. In the postwar era the FBI turned to important new problems.
1. It investigated communist activity within the United States.
2. It made detailed loyalty checks on prospective employees of the Atomic Energy Commission and other federal agencies.

III. The FBI provides important cooperative services.

A. The FBI Laboratory makes available the latest scientific methods of crime detection.
1. It is staffed by experts in firearms identification, serology, spectrography, metallurgy, explosives, hair and fiber analysis, and handwriting identification.
2. It maintains large reference collections useful in identifying tire treads, paint samples, etc.
3. It provides cost-free services to state and local law-enforcement agencies.

B. The Identification Division is the famous "fingerprint division" of the FBI.
1. It has more than 150 million sets of fingerprints on file.
a. Approximately 23 million of these are of known or suspected criminals.
b. The remainder are those of members of the armed forces or of other law-abiding citizens who voluntarily submitted to fingerprinting.
2. The fingerprints serve various purposes.
a. Those of known or suspected criminals help in the apprehension of lawbreakers.
b. Those of law-abiding citizens are used to identify missing persons and accident victims.

C. Educational services, in addition to training FBI agents, take several forms.
1. The FBI Academy, established in 1935, provides a twelve-week course for selected police personnel.
2. The FBI cooperates in police training schools and institutes.

3. FBI agents participate in annual conferences with state and local police officers.
4. Two FBI publications dispense information to law-enforcement agencies.
   a. The *Law Enforcement Bulletin* is a general medium for the exchange of ideas.
   b. The *Uniform Crime Reports* give statistical analyses of local crime on an annual and semiannual basis.

Problems

1. Indicate the type of arrangement (time, space, cause-effect, problem-solution, or special topical sequence) which you think would be most suitable for a speech on each of the following subjects. Be prepared to defend your choice.

The campus parking situation
Facilities of the college library
The fraternity tradition
Why farmers are leaving the farm
Censorship of the press
Preparing for a final examination
Our city government
The development of the modern corporation
Stamp collecting as a hobby
Principles and policies of public taxation

2. Select three of the preceding subjects (or three similar ones) and work out the major ideas of a speech on each. In phrasing these ideas, observe the rules given on pages 225-227. Try to select subjects which in your judgment require different types of arrangement.
3. Choose one of the following subjects (or a similar subject) and develop it according to three different types of arrangement. Your instructor will tell you whether to confine the development to major ideas or to include subordinate ideas and supporting material.

The great American novel
Careers in engineering (law, medicine, etc.)
Computers and "thinking machines"
Slum clearance
Photographing the moon
Political problems of Southeast Asia
The Head Start program

Reapportionment of state legislatures
The "art" film
The "paperback revolution"
Our federal court system
The modern newspaper

4. As you listen to the next group of speeches delivered in class, try to determine the major ideas and the type of arrangement employed by each speaker. After the speeches have been delivered, see whether the class can agree on (1) the type of arrangement employed, (2) the suitability of this arrangement to the speaker's subject and purpose, and (3) the faithfulness with which the chosen pattern was adhered to.

5. Read at least two speeches in *Vital Speeches of the Day* or some other suitable source. Be prepared to discuss (1) whether, in stating his major ideas, the speaker adhered to the rules set forth on pages 225-227; and (2) different ways in which the speaker arranged the subordinate material under his major ideas.

Speaking assignment

1. Choose one of the subjects listed below (or a similar subject of which your instructor approves). After completing the necessary research, prepare a five-minute classroom speech on this topic. Select one of the patterns for arranging the major ideas outlined in this chapter and follow it consistently. Pay particular attention also to the ordering of your subpoints. Are they coordinated with one another? Do they properly belong to the major idea under which they are placed? After your speech, ask for comments from the class on the method of arrangement which you employed and upon your handling of the subheads.

The Dead Sea Scrolls
Pop art
The British system of broadcasting
Measuring public opinion
The decline of the movies
Christmas (or any holiday) in foreign lands
Advances in anesthetics
Playing the stock market
The juke-box business
Our crowded colleges
Responsibilities of the college newspaper (radio station)
The future of the laboring man
Cigarettes and your health

The detective story as literature
Practical photography

Suggestions for further reading

Jacques Barzun and Henry F. Graff, *The Modern Researcher* (New York: Harcourt, Brace & World, Inc., 1957), Chapter XI, "Organizing: Paragraph, Chapter, and Part."

Waldo W. Braden and Mary Louise Gehring, *Speech Practices* (New York: Harper & Row, Publishers, 1958), Chapter III, "How Speakers Organize Their Speeches."

Gilbert S. Macvaugh, "Structural Analysis of the Sermons of Dr. Harry Emerson Fosdick," *Quarterly Journal of Speech*, XVIII (November 1932), 531-546.

Ralph A. Micken, *Speaking for Results* (Boston: Houghton Mifflin Company, 1958), Chapter VII, "Selection and Arrangement of Points."

Glen E. Mills, *Composing the Speech* (Englewood Cliffs, N.J.: Prentice-Hall, Inc., 1952), Chapter XI, "Arranging Materials."

Donald E. Sikkink, "An Experimental Study of the Effects on the Listener of Anticlimax Order and Authority in an Argumentative Speech," *Southern Speech Journal*, XXII (Winter 1956), 73-78.

Eugene E. White, *Practical Speech Fundamentals* (New York: The Macmillan Company, 1960), Chapter XII, "Organizing the Body."

CHAPTER FIFTEEN

Beginning and ending the speech

Too often speakers devote all of their time to preparing the main ideas they wish to present and give little or no attention to planning effective introductions and conclusions. True, the development of your major ideas deserves the greater share of your preparation time and must be worked out before you can sensibly plan how to lead into them or how to tie them together at the end. But it is folly to leave the opening and closing to the inspiration of the moment. The impact of your speech will be greater if you plan in advance how to catch your listeners' attention at the outset and how to conclude your remarks clearly and vigorously. In this chapter we shall first discuss various ways of beginning a speech and then a number of ways of closing it. Finally, we shall see how the beginning and ending may be integrated with the main body of the talk.

BEGINNING THE SPEECH

The audience's interest must be maintained throughout a speech; but at the beginning your principal task is to capture it. Therefore, your opening remarks should be built on one or more of the factors of attention discussed in Chapter 13. Nowhere in your speech is there a greater need for novelty, reality, activity, or humor. But mere attention is not enough; you also must gain the good will and respect of your listeners. In many situations your reputation or the chairman's introduction will create a favorable attitude toward you, and when this is the case you need only be sure to start your talk in a confident but tactful manner. When, however, you are confronted by hostility, distrust, or skepticism, you must immediately take steps to overcome this handicap. This can be done by establishing common ground with your audience in the manner described in Chapter 8 (see pp. 131-132), or by conceding whatever you can to their point of view.

Another important function of the introduction is to indicate the specific topic you wish to discuss and to lead your hearers easily and naturally into a consideration of it. A good introduction, therefore, has three goals: *to win attention, to gain good will and respect,* and *to pave the way for the body of your speech.*

To attain these results speakers frequently use one or more of the following devices:

1. A reference to the subject or problem
2. A reference to the occasion
3. A personal greeting or reference
4. A rhetorical question
5. A startling statement of fact or opinion
6. A quotation
7. A humorous anecdote
8. An illustration

Reference to the subject or problem

When you are sure that your audience already has a vital interest in the problem or subject you are to discuss, it often is enough merely to state your topic succinctly and then plunge immediately into your first main point. The very speed and directness of this approach suggest an eagerness to present your ideas and to press for understanding or belief. For example, a speaker began a talk to college seniors with this sentence: "I'm going to talk to you about jobs: how to get them and how to keep them." Such an appeal is both brief and forthright. In a speech delivered before the Detroit Economic Club, William A. Allen, President of the Boeing Company, also began by referring to his subject:

> In talking to you, or I would rather say with you, I have a question that I would like to explore, more than to answer. It is a fairly large question: How can we retain the advantages of private enterprise in major projects which, because of their scope or for other reasons, require government participation?[1]

Similarly, Mrs. Lauralee Peters, a student at the University of Kansas, began a speech entitled "What Is Totalitarianism?" by referring directly to the concept she was attempting to explain:

[1]"The Public-Private Enterprise," *Vital Speeches of the Day,* XXXII (December 1, 1965), 112.

In the early 1930's a new word was coined in the language of the political scientist. Used at first to describe the changes occurring in Hitler's Germany and Stalin's Russia, the term *totalitarianism* soon enjoyed widespread usage. As with any complex term, however, its usage by laymen and newsmen looking for a convenient label has led to a dilution of its meaning. In the American press, for example, the term *totalitarianism* is applied to virtually anything which doesn't reek of democracy. Dictators, communists, strong military leaders and the like are all labeled totalitarian. In view of the present easy use, if not misuse, of this term, it is my purpose to attempt to arrive at some understanding of what the term *totalitarianism* actually means.[2]

Although a reference to the subject is a good way to begin a speech when the audience is friendly toward the speaker or already is interested in the subject he is going to present, it is of doubtful value when listeners are hostile or apathetic. For a hostile audience, such a beginning lacks the elements of common ground and ingratiation upon which acceptance depends; nor does it in itself contain the curiosity-provoking qualities desirable in the opening of a speech to an apathetic audience. When used in the latter situation, therefore, it must be combined with one of the factors of attention (see pp. 209-214) or with other material specifically designed to arouse interest. How this may be done is illustrated by the opening of a speech delivered by Father Theodore M. Hesburgh, President of the University of Notre Dame:

I wish to address you this evening on the subject of science and man. It is a fair assumption that the majority of this audience knows much more about science and technology than I do. This being so, one might wonder why I do not drop the first part of my title of science and man. This is why: I shall not pretend to make any startling revelations in the field of science and technology; but I do want to consider this twin reality in conjunction with man and his actual world. What I have to say may not be popular, but then I never have found this to be a good reason for not saying something that should be said. Anyway, most statements that are popular and safe are also generally dull. This you should be spared.[3]

Reference to the occasion

Speeches may sometimes best be begun by referring to the occasion which prompts their delivery. Robert F. Goheen, President of Prince-

[2]*Contemporary American Speeches*, ed. Wil A. Linkugel, R. R. Allen, and Richard L. Johannesen (Belmont, California: Wadsworth, 1965), p. 70.

[3]*Representative American Speeches, 1962-1963*, ed. Lester Thonssen (New York: Wilson, 1963), p. 57.

ton University, began his remarks in this way at a convocation called to mark the opening of a new academic year:

> Long-held and most fitting custom has brought us together this morning—members of the Trustees, the faculty, students, administrators, neighbors, and friends—to mark the opening of the academic year in a service of worship. I follow custom, too, in directing my remarks particularly to those undergraduates who have freshly joined the University.[4]

Similarly, on October 18, 1964, President Johnson began a nationwide radio-television address by referring to the events which had occasioned it:

> My fellow Americans: On Thursday of last week, from the Kremlin in Moscow, the Soviet government announced a change in its leadership. On Friday of last week, Communist China exploded a nuclear device on an isolated test site in Sinkiang. Both of these events make it right that your President report to you as fully and as clearly and as promptly as he can. This is what I mean to do this evening.[5]

Personal greeting or reference

At times, a personal word from the speaker serves as an excellent starting point. This is particularly true if the speaker occupies an important position and has considerable prestige in the eyes of the audience. Dr. Grayson Kirk, President of Columbia University, began a speech at the centennial celebration of the University of Denver, with this paragraph:

> It is a pleasure to be in Denver once more, to visit again this university where I taught one happy summer, and to have the opportunity to renew so many longstanding and precious friendships. Actually, I tend, in retrospect, to associate this institution with one of the major changes in the direction of my life. It was here that I enjoyed my last full-time teaching—though I did not know it at the time—because immediately after my return from that pleasant summer here I was invited to become Provost of Columbia, a decision that, once made, brought my teaching days to a close. Now that I am here again, who knows but that when I go back to New York there might be a strong campus opinion developed in favor of my return to teaching. If this

[4]"The Library and the Chapel Stand Side by Side," *Representative American Speeches, 1964-1965*, ed. Lester Thonssen (New York: Wilson, 1965), p. 113.
[5]*Representative American Speeches, 1964-1965*, p. 46.

should be the case, then I think I ought to come back here and start where I left off in 1949.[6]

A personal reference of a somewhat different type was used by General Eisenhower to open a speech in Detroit in 1952, when he was campaigning for the Presidency:

Ladies and gentlemen, I think sometimes my military training may not have been as thorough as it could have been, because one of the principles of military life is never to be surprised. I am touched, astonished, and surprised this morning, and I expect it is due to deliberate intent on the part of my associates, now normally labeled as political advisers.

They get some inkling of the way I get tired of my own voice, and so I think they conceal from me at times that I am expected to battle again with one of these microphones.

In any event, as you know, I am scheduled for two talks here today. For a simple fellow like myself, that is quite a chore.[7]

As long as such a personal reference is modest and sincere, it may establish good will as well as gain the attention of the audience. Beware, however, of apologizing. Avoid saying, "I don't know why the chairman picked me out to talk on this subject when others could do it so much better," or "The man who was to speak to you couldn't come, and so at the last minute I agreed to speak, but I haven't had much time to get ready." Apologetic beginnings of this sort defeat their own purpose by suggesting that your speech is not worthy of attention. Be cordial, sincere, and modest, but not apologetic.

Rhetorical question

Often a speech may be opened with a question which prompts the audience to seek an answer in their own minds, thus stimulating them to think about the subject which the speaker is about to develop. A student began his discussion of the fire hazards of the building in which his class was being held by asking, "What would you do if a fire should break out downstairs while I am talking and the stairway should collapse before you could get out?" Questions of this kind are especially effective if they impinge upon some vital concern of the audience or if they set forth some unusual or puzzling problem. Note this opening which Dr. Charles Malik, former President of the

[6] "Responsibilities of the Educated Man", *Vital Speeches of the Day*, XXX (May 15, 1964), 471-474.

[7] *The New York Times*, June 15, 1952. Reprinted in *Speeches for Illustration and Example*, ed. Goodwin Berquist (Glenview, Illinois: Scott, Foresman, 1965), p. 193.

General Assembly of the United Nations, used in a speech on July 6, 1962, before the Virginia State Bar Association. After briefly greeting the audience and announcing his theme, he asked four rhetorical questions which stimulated the thinking of his listeners and prepared them for the body of the talk:

It is a great pleasure, I assure you, to address this distinguished group of American citizens who have dedicated their lives to the determination and realization of justice. One of the eternal truths that has been poignantly brought home to all thinking men in this critical age is that justice is much deeper than mere legal justice between individuals. There is such a thing as "silent injustice" which ravages the lives of men. Is it just that man may be a permanent prey to fear and anxiety and ignorance? Is it just that tyranny remains rampant over whole sections of the globe? Is it just that some people appear to be born unto slavery, so that, so far as we can now see, they will never be free? And above all, is it just that those who know better, those who are blessed with an abundance of mind and means, those whom history has chosen to say the decisive word today, both in utterance and in action, appear to be hesitant, uncertain, complacent, soft, dazed, divided in counsel, paralyzed in will? Justice is much deeper than legal justice: there is the justice of the mind, there is the justice of the spirit, there is the justice of history, and above all there is the justice and righteousness of God.[8]

Employing the same approach more briefly and directly, Dick Montgomery, a student at the University of Iowa, opened a classroom speech on the subject of the trimester plan with two rhetorical questions:

How would you like to graduate from college in three years? How would you like to be able to get out into the world and begin earning money while gaining valuable experience a year sooner than is now possible? You could do this if Iowa adopted the trimester plan.[9]

Startling statement

Another effective method of opening a speech has been called by H. A. Overstreet "the shock technic."[10] It consists of jarring the audience into attention by a startling statement either of fact or of opinion.

[8] "Silent Injustice: A Radical Awakening Is Needed," *Vital Speeches of the Day*, XXIX (November 1, 1962), 37.

[9] Presented in May, 1963. Text supplied by Mr. Montgomery and his instructor, Mr. Donovan Ochs.

[10] *Influencing Human Behavior* (New York: Norton, 1925), p. 120.

To see how a statement of fact may be used for this purpose re-read the first few paragraphs of the student speech by Clarence Yurk printed on pages 187-188. A startling statement of opinion was used by Clarence Darrow, the famous trial lawyer, to open a lecture to the prisoners in Cook County Jail in Chicago:

> If I looked at jails and crimes and prisoners in the same way the ordinary person does, I should not speak on this subject to you. The reason I talk to you on the question of crime, its cause and cure, is because I really do not in the least believe in crime. There is no such thing as a crime as the word is generally understood. I do not believe there is any sort of distinction between the real moral condition of the people in and out of jail. One is just as good as the other.[11]

More briefly, Alfred E. Smith once began a speech before the New York League of Women Voters by saying, "I have repeatedly said that the State of New York to a certain extent is the victim of its own growth."[12]

Whether startling statements are used as the sole method of beginning a speech or are combined with other methods, unusual phrasing plays an important part in catching the audience's attention.

Quotation

Frequently a speaker gains attention at the beginning of his speech by citing a quotation which aptly states the theme he wishes to develop. Observe how this method was used by Senator J. W. Fulbright of Arkansas in a speech entitled "Education and Public Policy":

> George Bernard Shaw wrote that "we have no more right to consume happiness without producing it than to consume wealth without producing it." In our affluent society we are blessed with both continually rising production and continually rising consumption of material wealth. At the same time, we are not keeping pace in the production of those human resources that make for quality and creativity in our lives. In these areas—the vital areas of the public happiness—we have begun to live off our intellectual capital, trying to consume more happiness than our efforts are producing.[13]

[11]From "Address to Prisoners in Cook County Jail," in *Attorney for the Damned*, ed. Arthur Weinberg (New York: Simon and Schuster, Inc., 1957), p. 3. Reprinted with permission of the publisher.
[12]*Modern Speeches*, ed. Homer D. Lindgren (New York: Crofts, 1930), p. 490.
[13]*Representative American Speeches, 1964-1965*, ed. Lester Thonssen (New York: Wilson, 1965), pp. 157-158.

Miss Judith Kinnamon, a junior at the University of Iowa, also employed a quotation as a means of opening a speech in which she advocated the removal of legal restrictions to interracial marriages:

> At the turn of this century, a novelist thoughtfully wrote of our land: "What is the glory of Rome and Jerusalem, where all nations and races come to worship and look back, compared with the glory of America, where all races and nations come to labor and look forward!"
>
> Today, we have made significant progress toward equality for all peoples in education and employment opportunities and in judicial impartiality; but by a strange paradox, we are overlooking a situation which derides the very ideals of justice which we seek. For as long as eighteen states maintain laws against interracial marriage, all minority groups will remain second-class citizens.[14]

If it is to make an effective opening, a quotation *(a)* must be germane to the central idea or theme of the speech, *(b)* must, if possible, be strikingly or memorably phrased, and *(c)* must not be too long or involved. When, however, it meets these requirements, it provides a particularly useful means for getting a speech started easily and quickly.

Humorous anecdote

Another way to begin a speech is to tell a funny story or relate a humorous experience. Be sure, however, that the story or experience you recount will amuse the audience and that you can tell it well. If your opening falls flat, your speech will be off to a poor start. Also be sure that the anecdote emphasizes the central point of your talk. A joke or story that is unrelated to your subject wastes valuable time and channels the attention of your listeners in the wrong direction. Most important of all, be sure that what you say is in good taste. Not only do questionable or "off-color" stories violate the accepted rules of social behavior, but they may seriously undermine the respect which the members of the audience have for you.

A humorous anecdote which meets the requirements stated above was used by Miss Janice Caldwell to open a classroom speech entitled "Education by Remote Control":

> A story was told me several months ago by Dr. Jack F. Padgett, my former philosophy professor, and the head of the department at Simpson College.

[14] "What Color Is Justice?" Delivered at the seventy-fourth annual contest of the Northern Oratorical League, held at Northwestern University, April 8, 1965.

Settling himself on the edge of his desk, he related the tale of a professor at a large state university in our own Middle West, who, busy with his many lecture tours, research projects, and writing activities, went to his department head in extreme consternation. It seemed that the poor professor was just too busy to teach his one class a week. Therefore, he asked for and was granted permission to tape-record all of his lectures.

Toward the end of the term the professor arrived back on the campus and decided to visit his class to see how his plan was working. He walked into the room to find his tape recorder in the middle of the room . . . and twelve little tape recorders around it.

Whether this story is true or not, it does raise an important question—a question which you and I as college students are directly concerned with: Are our professors teachers?[15]

Illustration

Real-life incidents, stories taken from literature, and hypothetical narratives may be used to start a speech. Be sure, however, that the illustration is interesting in itself and that it is closely connected with the central idea of the speech that is to follow. Miss Sally Ann Webb, a student at Southeast Missouri State College, used this illustration to open a speech criticizing our tendency to "stereotype" people on the basis of one past error or mistake:

In the local newspaper of my community recently, there was a story about a man named —— ———. He lived in a small town about forty miles from my home. He had served five years in the Missouri State Penitentiary for passing bogus checks. When he returned to his family, Mr. ——— couldn't find a job. Everyone knew he was an ex-con, and everyone knew that ex-cons aren't to be trusted. Finally in what was described as calm desperation, he walked into a local barbershop where he was well known, pulled a gun, and took all the money the barber had. Up to this point it had been a fairly routine robbery, but then something unusual happened. Mr. ——— didn't try to get away. He got into his car, drove slowly out of town, and waited for the highway patrol. When they caught him, he made only one request. He turned to the arresting patrolman and said: "Would you please ask that the court put my family on welfare just as soon as possible?"

To the people of Clarkston, Missouri, —— ——— wasn't to be trusted because he was an ex-con. . . .[16]

[15]Presented at the University of Iowa, May 1963. Text supplied by Miss Caldwell and her instructor, Mr. Paul Newman.

[16]"On Mousetraps," in *Winning Orations* (Evanston, Ill.: The Interstate Oratorical Association, 1963), p. 31.

Employing a somewhat more complicated pattern, Joel L. Swabb, a student at Muskingum College, combined a series of illustrations to begin a speech in which he attacked the activities of some of the spokesmen for "the far right":

The time is 3 A.M. The place, the home of a Protestant minister in Phoenix, Arizona. The minister awakens to the ringing of his telephone. He wonders what member of his congregation is in need of his help at this early hour. The voice on the other end of the line is hard and determined, "Are you a communist?"

The time is 11 A.M. A school teacher in Pittsburgh, Pennsylvania, sits behind her desk opening the morning mail. She has just received a letter from a friend in New York, a copy of *Time* magazine, and a plain white mailing envelope with no return address. A quick slip of the letter opener and she is greeted with the bright red exclamation, "Communist!"

It is now evening. The dinner plates have been removed and the President's light-touch speech before the Washington Press Corps is receiving its final ovation. In scanning the audience our eyes come to rest upon one man who is obviously not amused. The ovation dies and a tablemate nudges him with his elbow, asking at the same time for his reaction. He replies in a methodical, serious tone of voice: "I regard him as a very dangerous man."

These incidents are typical of the all-encompassing wrath of the arch conservative, the far right, or as Archibald MacLeish put it, "the Irresponsibles." It is not because they deplore softness toward communism that they have derived this title but because, as J. Edgar Hoover stated, "They are merely against communism without being for any positive measures to eliminate the social, political, and economic frictions which the communists are so adroit at exploiting."[17]

These, then, are eight useful ways of beginning a speech. Sometimes one method may be used alone; at other times, it is better to combine two or more of them. Notice, for example, how Professor Lester Thonssen brings together an illustration, a personal reference, and a reference to the occasion in opening a commencement address at Huron College:

In his essay on "The Anthropology of Manners," Edward T. Hall, Jr., tells of a tribesman who came to a prearranged spot in Kabul, the capital of Afghanistan, to meet his brother. But he couldn't find him. So he left, giving instructions

[17]"The Irresponsibles," first-place oration in the Interstate Oratorical Contest, held at Northwestern University, April 1963. Text supplied by Mr. Swabb and his instructor, Professor James Golden.

to the local merchants where he might be reached if his brother showed up. Exactly a year later, the tribesman returned to the same place in Kabul, and sure enough, there was his brother. It seems that the brothers had agreed to meet in Kabul on a certain day of a certain month at a particular place, but they failed to specify the year.

My plans have been like those of the tribesman. Often I've agreed to meet friends on a return to the campus at commencement time, but the year was never definitely set. Now thirty-two years after graduation—a disturbingly grim statistic—I'm honored and privileged to keep an appointment on this important occasion in the life of a fine institution.[18]

Whatever method or methods you use to begin a speech, remember that while gaining attention is your main task, you must also lead the minds of your listeners easily and naturally into your subject. Remember, too, that you must gain the good will and respect of the audience and that this will sometimes require establishing a common ground of interest or understanding.

ENDING THE SPEECH

The principal function of any method used to end a speech is to focus the thought and feeling of the audience on the central theme developed during the course of the talk. If you present a one-point speech, that point must be restated at the end in a manner which will make your meaning clear and forceful.[19] If your speech is more complex, you must bring its most important ideas together in a condensed and unified form or else suggest the action or belief to which these ideas lead. In addition to bringing the substance of the speech into final focus, a good ending should leave the audience in the proper mood. If you expect your listeners to express vigorous enthusiasm, you must stimulate that feeling by the way you close. If you want them to reflect thoughtfully on what you have said, your conclusion should encourage a calm, judicious attitude. Decide whether the response you seek requires a mood of serious determination or good-humored levity, of warm sympathy or cold anger, of thoughtful consideration or vigorous immediate action; then plan to end your talk in such a way as to create that mood. Finally, remember that the end of a speech should convey a sense of completeness and finality. Nothing annoys an audience so much as to think the speaker has finished only to have him go on again. Avoid false endings. Tie the threads together so that

[18]From *Representative American Speeches, 1958-1959* (New York: Wilson, 1959), pp. 132-133.
[19]See Chapter 11, "The One-Point Speech," pp. 181-189.

the pattern of your speech is brought to completion, deliver your concluding sentence with finality—and then stop. If you bring the central theme into sharp focus, create the proper mood, and close with decisiveness, you will be more likely to achieve the purpose for which you speak.

Some of the methods most frequently used by speakers to end a speech involve the use of:

1. Challenge or appeal
2. Summary
3. Quotation
4. Illustration
5. Inducement
6. Personal intention

Challenge or appeal

When using this method, the speaker openly appeals for belief or action, or reminds his listeners of their responsibilities in furthering a desirable end. Such an appeal should be vivid and compelling, and should contain within it a suggestion of the principal ideas or arguments which have been presented in the speech. Note how James E. Webb, head of the National Aeronautics and Space Administration, closed a speech to the Department of Elementary School Principals of the National Education Association:

> And, finally, achievement of our goals in space will demand the highest scholastic efforts and intellectual accomplishments in virtually every field of study.
>
> Space is, indeed, a new and challenging frontier, but it is a frontier of the intellect—one which challenges brain, not brawn, with creative intelligence, our greatest weapon.
>
> Your elementary schools have a vital role as mankind moves toward the conquest of space.[20]

Robert J. Wert, Vice Provost and Dean of Undergraduate Instruction at Stanford University, also presented a challenge or appeal in concluding an address delivered at an honors convocation at Los Angeles State College:

[20]Address at Annual Meeting of the Department of Elementary School Principals, National Education Association, Oklahoma City, Oklahoma, April 1, 1963. Text supplied by National Aeronautics and Space Administration.

In conclusion, I believe that many of us are going to be disturbed about various crises in colleges and universities during the next decade. The college has become one of society's most valued and essential institutions. As such, it should be criticized. As such, it will be attacked. I urge that each of us, in his own way, should learn more about the aims and functions of colleges so that we can better understand what they do and how well they do it. The future of this state and of our country rests squarely upon the character and quality of our colleges and universities. If this is true, students, faculty members, administrators, trustees, alumni, and the general public must work cooperatively, moderately, and constructively to understand our colleges and help them move successfully through what will certainly be a period of trauma, travail, and excitement.[21]

Summary

In a summary conclusion, the speaker reviews the main points of his speech and draws whatever inferences may be implicit in the material he has presented. In a speech to inform, a summary ending is nearly always appropriate since it helps to impress upon the listeners those ideas which you especially want remembered. In a speech to convince, a summary conclusion provides a final opportunity to reiterate the principal arguments you have presented.

D. Brainerd Holmes, Director of the Office of Manned Space Flight of the National Aeronautics and Space Administration, used this summary to conclude an informative talk before the American Rocket Society:

Let me conclude, then, by reiterating a few of our basic concepts.

We believe it was necessary to carefully evaluate all feasible mission modes and select the best of these upon which to concentrate our efforts.

We believe that the lunar orbit rendezvous mode is best.

We believe that we must obtain the very best efforts of the very best people we can find, both in Government and industry, if we are to achieve our national goal.

We believe that our organizational concepts and management techniques must be no less excellent than our technical efforts.

We believe that with constant attention to these concepts, and with the hard work and dedication of the people involved, we will be able to carry out our responsibility to our country to be second to none in man's conquest of space.[22]

[21] "The Restless Generation and Undergraduate Education," *Representative American Speeches, 1964-1965*, ed. Lester Thonssen (New York: Wilson, 1965), p. 156.

[22] Address before the American Rocket Society, Cleveland, Ohio, July 17, 1962. Text supplied by National Aeronautics and Space Administration.

Another example of a summary-type conclusion is furnished by Dr. John H. Fischer, Superintendent of Public Instruction for the City of Baltimore, in a speech discussing the problems of racial desegregation in the public schools:

To summarize, then, briefly what I have tried to say about the educational problems of desegregating schools:

1. The focus of sound teaching is always on the individual, for education is an intensely personal matter, having its principal effect always within the person.

2. If we are to achieve good education, we must respect the individuality of each student, relating his instruction to his background, his needs, his possibilities.

3. To achieve equality of opportunity within the whole of our culture, it may be necessary to offer those who are handicapped by their history or their current situation not merely equal, but compensatory educational opportunity.

4. In organizing education many considerations are important, many characteristics are relevant, but racial differences in themselves are not. In the administration of schools, therefore, the manipulation of pupils on purely racial grounds is irrelevant and improper.[23]

Quotation

A quotation may be used to end a speech if it bears directly on the central idea of the talk or strongly suggests the attitude or action the speaker wishes his listeners to take. U Thant, Secretary-General of the United Nations, used a quotation to such purpose in a speech entitled "Some Major Issues before the United Nations." The speech was delivered March 5, 1963, to the Economic Club of New York City.

What is most needed in these tense times is the will to compromise. In human affairs, no one group is 100 per cent right and another 100 per cent wrong. In international relationships, pure white and pure black are rare. That is why every international agreement represents a compromise of some kind, except where the terms are dictated.

To my knowledge one of the wisest mottoes for every one of us is enshrined in the UNESCO Charter. It says, "Since wars begin in the minds of men, it is in the minds that the defenses of peace have to be constructed."

There is no peace in the world today because there is no peace in the minds of men.[24]

[23] "Educational Problems of Segregation and Desegregation of Public Schools," *Representative American Speeches, 1962-1963*, ed. Lester Thonssen (New York: Wilson, 1963), p. 121.

[24] *Vital Speeches of the Day*, XXIX (April 1, 1963), 364.

A variation of the method was employed by President Johnson when he concluded a nationwide radio-television address by quoting what he himself had said in an earlier speech:

> Almost eleven months ago, at a still more fateful hour, just after I had assumed the presidency, I spoke to all of the Congress and to our people of the purpose of America. Let me close tonight by repeating what I said then:
>
> "We must be ready to defend the national interest and to negotiate the common interest. This is the path that we shall continue to pursue. Those who test our courage will find it strong, and those who seek our friendship will find it honorable. We will demonstrate anew that the strong can be just in the use of strength; and the just can be strong in the defense of justice."[25]

Illustration

Just as an illustration which epitomizes your leading ideas may be used to open a speech, so may an illustration of this sort be used at the close. Dr. Samuel B. Gould, President of the Educational Broadcasting Company, concluded a speech to the students and faculty of Hunter College as follows:

> Whatever the career and whatever the task, it deserves what is best and finest in us. . . . B. J. Chute, the writer, tells a wonderful story about a small child who watched a sculptor working on a slab of marble. Day after day, the child watched and the sculptor worked. And then, at last, there came a day when the child drew his breath and looked at the sculptor in amazement and said, "But how did you know there was a lion in there?"
>
> To know there is a lion in one's mind, and finally to produce it—that is success. That is the flavor for our daily bread, the closest we shall ever come to human happiness.[26]

In concluding a speech to the Linn County Veterans' Council of Albany, Oregon, Senator Robert F. Kennedy also used an illustration:

> The challenge of the future requires not panic but power, not doubt but deeds.
>
> During the Korean War a young American was called out of the ranks by his Chinese captors and they said to him, "What do you think of General George C. Marshall?"

[25]"An Address to the Nation," *Representative American Speeches, 1964-1965* (New York: Wilson, 1965), p. 51.

[26]"A Flavor for Our Daily Bread," *Representative American Speeches, 1964-1965* (New York: Wilson, 1965), p. 128.

He said, "I think General Marshall is a great American."

The Chinese knocked him to the ground with the butt of a rifle. They picked him up and said, "What do you think of General George C. Marshall now?"

He said, "I think General Marshall is a great American."

This time there was no rifle butt because in their own way they had classified him as brave.

Today, all of us have been called out of the ranks to be questioned and, in the months ahead, we too must give the affirmative answer. I have no doubt that we will.[27]

Inducement

Sometimes a speech may be concluded by quickly reviewing the most important ideas presented in the body of the talk and then supplying one or two additional reasons for accepting the belief or taking the action proposed. Observe how these two elements of summary and added inducement are combined in the conclusion of a classroom speech by Miss Linda Mast, urging use of seat belts in cars:

All in all, you will find that buying seat belts for your car and using them is a worth-while investment. As I have shown, they are a great aid in saving lives and preventing serious injuries; having them in your car may enable you to pay less insurance; and wearing them will make travel more comfortable and enjoyable. The few arguments which may be raised against seat belts do not outweigh their advantages, but only show how indifferent most people are to their own safety and well-being. Even if you are willing to take chances with your own life, however, you owe this additional security to your family and friends. Install seat belts in your car today![28]

In a speech advocating increased American aid to improve higher education in foreign countries, Vice-President Hubert Humphrey closed by suggesting that such a policy also might contribute to the larger goal of world peace:

I ask you for your consideration of this proposal. If you will give it your thoughtful criticism and your intelligent support, we may be able to help our country take another long step toward a more balanced and vital foreign policy and eventually a stable, just, and serene peace.[29]

[27]Text supplied by the Department of Justice.

[28]Presented at the University of Iowa, January 15, 1963. Text supplied by Miss Mast and her instructor, Mr. Donovan Ochs.

[29]"College Teaching in Today's World," *Vital Speeches of the Day,* XXV (April 15, 1959), 413.

Personal intention

A statement of the speaker's personal feeling or of his intention to act as his speech recommends is particularly valuable when his prestige with the audience is high, but sometimes it may also be used in other circumstances as well. The most famous example of this method of closing a speech, perhaps, is the phrase attributed to Patrick Henry: "As for me, give me liberty or give me death!" The personal-intention type of conclusion was also used by the British Minister of Science, Viscount Hailsham (Quintin Hogg), in an address in which he called for adherence to democratic ideals despite obstacles existing in the world today:

> For my part and on behalf of my country I pledge myself despite all disappointments and undeterred by criticism and ingratitude to maintain these ideals and pursue the goal which we have set before us.[30]

In a speech urging members of the class to donate blood for American service men in Vietnam, Robert J. Walker, a student at the University of Iowa, concluded by thus expressing his own intention to do so:

> Therefore, without harm or inconvenience to ourselves, we can help our fellow Americans who are wounded in Vietnam. I urge you to go to the infirmary this afternoon, where through the cooperation of the inter-fraternity council all the necessary arrangements have been made. I myself intend to be there at 1:30. Won't you join me?[31]

FITTING THE BEGINNING AND END TO THE MAIN STRUCTURE

As we stated earlier in this chapter, you usually should work out the main points of your speech in considerable detail before devising a method of starting and finishing it. If you prepare your opening and closing first, the chances are that they will stand as independent units unrelated to the substance of your remarks or that the joints between them and the body of your speech will be awkward and strained. On the other hand, by preparing them after your major ideas have been chosen and developed, it is possible to fit them in smoothly and to make your speech as a whole a closely knit logical and psychological unit.

[30]"The Toast of Democracy," presented January 22, 1963 at the Center for Study of Democratic Institutions. *Vital Speeches of the Day*, XXIX (March 1, 1963), 304.

[31]Delivered in a beginning course in public speaking, January 17, 1966. Text supplied by Mr. Walker.

Starting and ending the one-point speech

For a short one-point speech, you may start with a simple reference to your subject or the point you plan to present. Then, after citing the supporting material in detail, you may close with a summary, a challenge, or an appeal. In a somewhat longer one-point speech, or in one before an audience whose attitude precludes an opening that is quite so forthright, you may need to use one of the other methods. You might begin, for instance, with an illustration, a quotation, or even a personal statement, thus leading more gradually into the statement of your central idea. Likewise, the close may be developed with a quotation, illustration, or statement of personal intention. The structure of the body or substance of the speech will remain unchanged, but your method of leading up to it and of pressing your point home at the end will have been adapted to your audience, subject, and purpose.

Speeches having a more complex structure

For a speech that contains several major ideas a direct reference to the topic is more difficult, and therefore you generally will employ one or more of the other methods to get your speech under way. Once you are started, however, your major points may be mentioned, and then taken up one by one.

In Chapter 14 we considered various patterns for developing the body of a talk and the principles to be followed in outlining it. When the opening and closing are added to this section, your completed outline should look something like this:

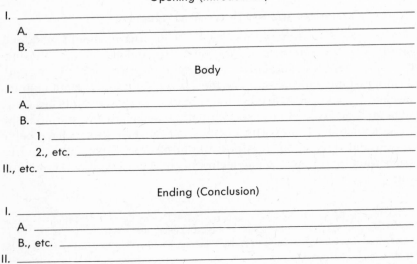

Opening (Introduction)

I. ____________________
   A. ____________________
   B. ____________________

Body

I. ____________________
   A. ____________________
   B. ____________________
      1. ____________________
      2., etc. ____________________
II., etc. ____________________

Ending (Conclusion)

I. ____________________
   A. ____________________
   B., etc. ____________________
II. ____________________

A beginning and ending for the speech on the FBI, outlined in Chapter 14 (pp. 236-238), might take the following form:

Opening

I. Recently a group of high-school students was asked to identify ten government agencies from their initials.
   A. Sixty per cent correctly identified the FCC as the Federal Communications Commission.
   B. Seventy-five per cent knew that the ICC was the Interstate Commerce Commission.
   C. One hundred per cent correctly named the FBI as the Federal Bureau of Investigation.

II. These same students were then asked to write a paragraph telling something about the history and activities of the FBI.
   A. Only five students were able to say anything about its history.
   B. Less than half could list its principal activities and areas of service.

III. Could we score better than these high-school students?
   A. Do we know why the FBI was founded?
   B. Do we know how it developed?
   C. Do we know all of the ways it serves us?

IV. In the next few minutes I will give you answers to these and similar questions.
   A. My aim is to inform you concerning the FBI's purposes, history, and services.
   B. I also hope to give you a deeper appreciation of the FBI's importance in your life and mine.

Ending

I. Remember, then, that the FBI does more than engage in thrilling gun battles with criminals.
   A. It is a group of highly trained professionals whose investigations are essential to the operation of the Department of Justice.
   B. It has a distinguished record of expanding service to the nation since its founding in 1908.
   C. It provides valuable services to local law-enforcement agencies in the areas of crime detection, identification, and education.

II. Truly, the FBI is the servant of our nation.

In the next two chapters, we shall discuss how to adapt the basic plan or structure of a speech to the mental habits of listeners. As we do so, we shall introduce terms which describe the opening and closing of a speech more accurately—terms which reflect the psychological functions which these parts of the speech perform. But we shall also see that despite this difference in terminology, the methods of beginning and ending which we have just described remain useful and may be fitted smoothly into those plans of speech organization which take into account the customary patterns of human thought and action.

Problems

1. Select fifteen or twenty speeches from recent issues of *Vital Speeches of the Day*, *Representative American Speeches*, or some other likely source. Classify the various ways in which these speeches begin and end. Are certain types of beginnings and endings used more frequently than others? Do some types seem to be more common in speeches to inform, and others more common in speeches to convince? What types appear most frequently in speeches delivered on special occasions—anniversaries, dedications, etc.? How often are several different methods of opening and closing a speech combined? Which types most commonly enter into such combinations?
2. Select ten of the beginnings and endings cataloged in Problem 1. Evaluate these in terms of their suitability *(a)* to the speaker's purpose, *(b)* to the subject matter of the speech, and *(c)* to the nature and attitude of the audience (in so far as you are able to determine them). Which of the beginnings and endings could have been improved? How?
3. After listening to one or more of the following types of speeches, evaluate the beginning and ending which the speaker used:

   a. A classroom lecture
   b. A church sermon
   c. A television address
   d. Remarks made at a fraternity or dormitory council meeting

   In reporting your evaluation, supply sufficient information about the speaker and speaking situation so that a person who was not present could understand why you evaluated a particular beginning or ending as you did.
4. Work out at least two alternative means for beginning and ending a talk to members of your speech class on one of the following subjects:

The R.O.T.C. program
Career opportunities
"The Ugly American"
Pay television
Theatre of the Absurd
The Peace Corps
Legislative reapportionment
The emerging nations
Primitive culture
City planning
Medicare
Foreign exchange students

5. Assume that you are to address an audience of local businessmen on the subject you worked with in Problem 4. Adapt your opening and closing accordingly.

Speaking assignments

1. Select a subject toward which the members of your speech class probably will hold one of the attitudes described on page 132—favorable but not aroused, apathetic, interested but undecided, hostile to any change, etc. Prepare a five-minute speech addressed to this subject, and plan an opening specifically adapted to the probable audience attitude.
2. Present a five-minute speech on a subject of interest to the members of your speech class. Conclude it with an ending designed to leave the audience in one of the following frames of mind:

 a. Thoughtful or reflective
 b. Emotionally aroused or excited
 c. Determined to take the action you propose

Suggestions for further reading

Aristotle, *Rhetoric,* 1414b-1415a, "The Proem or Introduction," and 1419b-1420b, "The Epilogue."

Donald C. Bryant and Karl R. Wallace, *Fundamentals of Public Speaking,* 3rd ed. (New York: Appleton-Century-Crofts, 1960), Chapter X, "Introductions, Conclusions, and Transitions."

Quintilian, *Institutio Oratoria,* IV. 1, "The Prooemium or Exordium."

Richard Whately, *Elements of Rhetoric,* ed. Douglas Ehninger (Carbondale: Southern Illinois University Press, 1963), pp. 168-174, "Of Introductions and Conclusions."

Eugene E. White, *Practical Public Speaking,* 2nd ed. (New York: The Macmillan Company, 1964), Chapter VIII, "Developing the Introduction of the Speech," and Chapter IX, "Developing the Conclusion of the Speech."

PART FOUR

ADAPTING THE SPEECH TO THE AUDIENCE

Adapting the speech organization to the audience: The motivated sequence

Making an outline

Wording the speech

Listening: Speaker-audience interaction

CHAPTER SIXTEEN

Adapting the speech organization to the audience: The motivated sequence

We have seen how to select, phrase, and arrange the major ideas within a speech (Chapter 14) and have considered various ways to begin and close a speech (Chapter 15). These are important aspects of speech composition, but one of the most important still remains to be discussed: how best to adapt the structure of a speech to the thought processes of an audience.

A speaker cannot ram ideas down people's throats. Instead of trying to force his listeners to conclusions against their wills, he must lead their thinking so that they will respond in a way in accord with his specific purpose. To succeed in this undertaking, the speaker must build his speech with his audience constantly in mind and must plan the structure of his speech so that its sequence of points corresponds to the way people habitually arrive at understanding or belief or a decision to act.

THE LISTENER'S MENTAL PROCESSES

On first consideration, you might suppose that a listener's mental processes would vary according to the type of response the speaker asks him to make—that enjoyment or entertainment calls for thought patterns different from those used in understanding, and that belief requires patterns which are different from both. The fact of the matter, however, is that *the mental processes involved in making various sorts of responses differ not so much in kind as in completeness.* When the only reaction asked of a listener is that he enjoy himself, all that he needs to do is to give attention to what the speaker says. The listener's attention is still necessary when the speaker's object is to inform, but now the listener must also become conscious of a need or desire to acquire new knowledge and must understand and absorb the information the speaker presents. Finally, let us suppose that a speaker wishes to obtain a response of overt action—to induce a hearer to do something: sign a petition, make a contribution, join a protest march, vote for a specific candidate on election day. In this case, if the speaker's speech is to succeed, the hearer not only must pay attention, recognize a need, and understand a proposal but also must be convinced of the soundness and desirability of the recommended action and must be spurred on to perform it. In short, the mental processes of a listener as related to each of the general ends of speaking are not actually different; instead, they are *cumulative*, their scope or complexity being determined by the nature of the responses required of the listener.

THE MOTIVATED SEQUENCE

Finally, it should be observed that despite listeners' individual differences of temperament and ability, their thought processes in responding to various sorts of specific purposes on the part of the speaker are surprisingly uniform—so uniform, in fact, that they provide a practical basis for a standard pattern of speech organization. We shall call this pattern the *motivated sequence: the sequence of ideas which, by following the normal processes of human thinking, motivates an audience to respond to the speaker's purpose.*

As we shall see, the speaker may, if he chooses, use the motivated sequence as the backbone for all types of speeches, modifying it only by omitting or lengthening certain ones of the steps. For the moment, however, let us examine a magazine advertisement in which all of the steps are employed. This advertisement appeared in the January 1966 issue of *Fortune Magazine* and was entitled "Motivated Men Made America Great." Here, in part, is the text:

1. The beginnings of Abraham Lincoln's greatness can be found in his boyhood desire to learn. . . . With less than a year of formal education, "Honest Abe" overcame the obscurity of a bleak frontier environment to become a self-taught lawyer, a universally respected national leader, and our country's "Great Emancipator". . . .

. . . .

2. Countries need motivated men. Companies do too, especially when their success depends on the extra effort of individual salesmen and entire sales organizations.

. . . .

3. We help fill this need for companies in all industries.

ABRAHAM LINCOLN
Motivated Men Made America Great
Abraham Lincoln
The beginnings of Abraham Lincoln's greatness can be found in his boyhood desire to learn. His greatness grew as he continued to gain the knowledge he sought. It was fully achieved when his wise and compassionate leadership reunited a nation that had been divided by secession and then torn by history's bloodiest civil war.
Lincoln became the sixteenth President of the United States by dedicating himself to serving others. He thought of himself as a common man and, during terms as an Illinois Legislator and in the House of Representatives, he championed the causes of other common men. Kindness, patience, humor and understanding were characteristics that dominated his personal life and his public career.
With less than a year of formal education, "Honest Abe" overcame the obscurity of a bleak frontier environment to become a self-taught lawyer, a universally respected national leader, and our country's "Great Emancipator." He was motivated by an unshakable belief in the rights of others and equality for all. In pursuing his beliefs, Lincoln re-established the principles of union and democracy that make America great.
Countries need motivated men. Companies do too, especially when their success depends on the extra effort of individual salesmen and entire sales organizations. We help fill this need for companies in all industries.
Maritz is the only company in the United States engaged exclusively in the business of motivating men to sell. As specialists, we offer complete sales motivation services including planning, program promotion, administration and follow-through. All are offered in conjunction with distinctive merchandise and glamorous travel awards. The combination causes salesmen to work harder, more intelligently, and more successfully. Their increased productivity improves sales and profits for the clients we serve.
Your Maritz Account Executive can tell you how we can help you develop new markets, open new territories, promote particular products, and achieve more sales with a sales motivation program designed to meet your company's specific needs. We suggest you contact him. He offers you the exclusive services of the leader in the field of sales motivation.
Motivating men to sell your product is our business
MARITZ INC.
M

Maritz is the only company in the United States engaged exclusively in the business of motivating men to sell. As specialists, we offer complete sales motivation services including planning, program promotion, administration and *follow-through.* All are offered in conjunction with distinctive merchandise and glamorous travel awards.

. . . .

4. The combination causes salesmen to work harder, more intelligently, and more successfully. Their increased productivity improves sales and profits for the clients we serve.

. . . .

5. Your Maritz Account Executive can tell you how we can help you develop new markets, open new territories, promote particular products, and achieve more sales with a sales motivation program designed to meet your company's specific needs. We suggest that you contact him. He offers you the exclusive services of the leader in the field of sales motivation.[1]

Notice that this advertisement has five distinct steps: (1) the reader's *attention* is caught; (2) he is made to feel a definite *need;* (3) he is shown a way in which this need can be *satisfied;* (4) the benefits of purchasing the Maritz service are *visualized;* and (5) *action* in the form of contacting a representative of the Maritz agency is called for.

[1]From "Motivated Men Made America Great," *Fortune Magazine* (January 1966), 5. Used by special permission of Maritz, Inc.

The steps in the motivated sequence

To each of these steps we shall assign a name indicative of its function:

1. Attention
2. Need
3. Satisfaction
4. Visualization
5. Action

With the names of these steps in mind, study the *Fortune* advertisement again in terms of the following analysis:

1. *Attention.* Using the interest factor of "the familiar," as explained in Chapter 13 (p. 211), attention is caught by a brief description of Lincoln's strong motivation to succeed.
2. *Need.* A direct statement asserts that businesses, like countries, need motivated men.
3. *Satisfaction.* Because it specializes in all phases of motivation, the Maritz agency says it is well qualified to meet this need and can, therefore, ensure satisfaction.
4. *Visualization.* Benefits in the form of harder working salesmen and greater sales and profits are pictured.
5. *Action.* The reader is asked to contact a Maritz account executive.

The motivated sequence applied to persuasive speeches

Let us now consider a speech which, like the advertisement we have just examined, has *actuation* as its general end. The speech was broadcast on January 27, 1940, from the Metropolitan Opera House during a matinée performance of *Lohengrin.* The speaker, General David Sarnoff, Chairman of the Radio Corporation of America, sought to elicit popular support for the Saturday afternoon broadcasts of the Metropolitan Opera.

Observe that General Sarnoff's speech, like the Maritz advertisement, consists of five steps. It (1) calls attention to the subject by mentioning a few striking facts, (2) points out the pressing need for funds to maintain the Metropolitan Opera program, (3) explains how popular subscription could provide these funds, (4) visualizes the personal pleasure of helping maintain the opera, and (5) appeals for direct action in the form of contributions from the listeners.

ASKING SUPPORT FOR THE METROPOLITAN OPERA[2]

David Sarnoff

[1. *Attention step.*] This is the ninth consecutive year in which the National Broadcasting Company, through the miracle of radio, has been privileged to bring the Metropolitan Opera into the homes of America. On Christmas Day in 1931, the nation-wide radio audience heard the first of these programs, a performance of "Hansel and Gretel," direct from the stage of this historic opera house. Since then, every single week of the New York season of the Metropolitan, for nine years, one of the great operas—performed by great artists—has been broadcast to you.

The American system of broadcasting has made it possible for radio listeners everywhere to hear the world's finest opera week after week, without having to pay a cent for the privilege.

But over this same period of nine years, the National Broadcasting Company has paid directly to the Metropolitan Opera Association one million dollars for the privilege of bringing grand opera to its radio audience. This has been an important and necessary source of income to the Metropolitan. The National Broadcasting Company will continue to pay the Metropolitan Opera for the opportunity to broadcast these programs to you.

[2. *Need step.*] Today the Metropolitan faces a critical financial situation, if grand opera of the first rank is to continue in America. As a member of the Board of Directors of the Metropolitan Opera Association, I have been asked

[2]From *NBC Presents*, February 1940, Vol. II, No. 5.

to explain this situation to the radio audience. As a radio man, who knows from experience how widespread in America is the appreciation of grand opera, I have taken upon myself an even greater responsibility. I have told the management and the artists of the Metropolitan that I have full faith in the willingness of the opera's national radio audience to help them.

You who constitute this vast audience may not realize what an important part you play in the operation of the Metropolitan today. While you cannot see the other millions who are gathered around their radios, all of you, together, form the greatest opera audience in the history of the world. It is estimated that this afternoon in the United States alone, more than 10,000,000 people are listening to this inspiring performance of "Lohengrin." This famous old building on Broadway has ceased to be a local opera house. It is now the nation's opera—the People's Opera—your opera.

Many of you may not know that this historic house is not owned or controlled by the company which produces the opera—that is, the Metropolitan Opera Association. The time has now come when the future of the opera, and its ability to advance as a national institution, demands permanent ownership of a house, supported by the general public, and serving broad public interests.

The Metropolitan Opera Association has an option on the opera house, which in its terms requires $500,000 in cash. It faces the problem of taking up this option by May 31, 1940, and maintaining opera in the present house, or of working out other plans which will insure the continuance of opera in some other appropriate location. An additional $500,000 is needed to carry out plans for essential improvements, and for the advancement of the Metropolitan Opera as a national music center.

[3. *Satisfaction step.*] The Metropolitan Opera Association therefore has undertaken a campaign to seek $1,000,000 from public-spirited citizens, including radio listeners, in gifts both large and small. The Directors of the Metropolitan have made a public announcement of the need and purposes of this campaign, and the details have been published in newspapers throughout the country.

I have been asked to serve as Chairman of the Radio Division of this campaign, and I am happy to announce that Mrs. August Belmont and Miss Lucrezia Bori have consented to serve with me as Vice-Chairmen. Their deep interest and great service to the Metropolitan over a period of many years is well known throughout the United States.

I believe that there are many radio listeners who will be willing and happy to contribute a small sum to help insure the continuance of the Metropolitan Opera. I therefore earnestly appeal to all of you who can afford to do so, to send one dollar directly to the Metropolitan Opera Association, as your contribution toward helping preserve in America the world's finest opera.

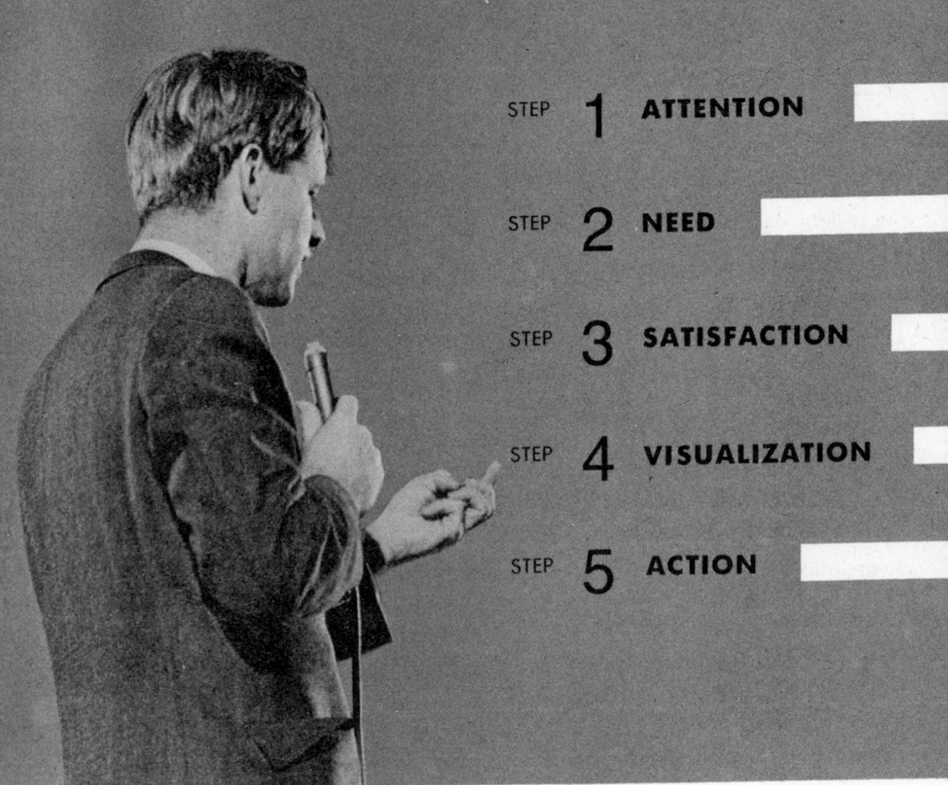

These five steps make up the complete motivated sequence, a method that helps a speaker achieve the response he seeks when facing an audience. The basic plan may be used in almost all types of public speeches, and may be modified to fit the general end of a particular talk.

[4. *Visualization step.*] Please ask yourself this question: "If I knew that I could not hear another Metropolitan Opera on the radio unless I gave one dollar, would I give it?"

I am sure your answer will be "yes," because I feel certain that you want Metropolitan Opera to go on. Surely you want to see continued an American institution which has won a reputation all over the world; an unchallenged reputation for its interpretation of the great beauty that lies in the operas of the world's great masters.

[5. *Action step.*] The Metropolitan Opera asks you who are its friends to express that friendship now in a practical way. We ask for one dollar from each listener who can afford to give it. Naturally, larger gifts will be most welcome.

I particularly ask the organized listening groups in schools and clubs and

homes throughout the country to help make this campaign a success, and thereby to insure the continuance of the Metropolitan Opera.

Remember that the steps in the motivated sequence will not be of equal length in every speech, nor will they have the same development. Each situation must be handled separately. Sometimes one or more of the steps may be developed very briefly or may be omitted entirely because the attitude of the audience does not require them. For instance, if your listeners already realize that a need exists—that something must be done—you do not have to expand the need step; you may merely remind your listeners of the nature of the problem and show them how your proposal will remedy it.

In its complete form, as used for persuasive speeches (those to convince, stimulate, or actuate), the motivated sequence, then, consists of five steps.[3]

THE MOTIVATED SEQUENCE APPLIED TO PERSUASIVE SPEECHES

General ends: to convince, to stimulate, to actuate.

Step	**Function**	**Audience response**
1. Attention step.	Getting attention.	"I want to listen."
2. Need step.	Showing the need: describing the problem.	"Something needs to be done (decided, or felt)."
3. Satisfaction step.	Satisfying the need: presenting the solution.	"This is what to do (believe, or feel) to satisfy the need."
4. Visualization step.	Visualizing the results.	"I can see myself enjoying the satisfaction of doing (believing, or feeling) this."
5. Action step.	Requesting action or approval.	"I will do (believe, or feel) this."

These five steps again are illustrated in the following outline which a student drew up for a persuasive speech on fire prevention:

FIRE PREVENTION AT HOME

Attention step

I. If you like parlor tricks, try this:
   A. Place a blotter soaked in turpentine in a jar of oxygen.
   B. The blotter will burst into flames.

[3]For a more detailed discussion of these steps in persuasive speeches see pp. 411-418.

II. If you have no oxygen jar around the house, try this:
   A. Place a well-oiled mop in a storage closet.
   B. In a few days the mop will burst into flames.

Need step

I. Few homes are free from dangerous fire hazards.
   A. Attics with piles of damp clothing and paper are combustible.
   B. Storage closets, containing cleaning mops and brushes, are dangerous.
   C. Basements are often filled with dangerous piles of trash.
   D. Garages attached to houses are a danger spot.

Satisfaction step

I. To protect your home from fire requires three things:
   A. A thorough cleaning out of all combustible materials.
   B. Careful storage of such hazards as oil mops, paint brushes, etc.
      1. Clean them before storage.
      2. Store them in fireproof containers.
   C. A regular check to see that inflammable trash does not accumulate.
II. Clean-up programs show practical results.
   A. Clean-up campaigns in Evansville kept insurance rates in a "Class 1" bracket.
   B. A clean-up campaign in Fort Wayne helped reduce the number of fires.

Visualization step

I. You will enjoy the results of such a program.
   A. You will have neat and attractive surroundings.
   B. You will be safe from fire.

Action step

I. Begin your own clean-up campaign now.

Ordinarily you will use all five steps of the motivated sequence only when your general end is *to convince, to stimulate,* or *to actuate.* When your general end is *to entertain,* you usually will omit steps two through five; when your general end is *to inform,* you usually will omit steps four and five.

The motivated sequence applied to informative speeches

The speech to inform requires only three steps: attention, need, and satisfaction—the need step showing the audience why the information to be presented is important to them and the satisfaction step meeting the need by supplying the information itself.

THE MOTIVATED SEQUENCE APPLIED TO INFORMATIVE SPEECHES

Step	**Function**	**Audience response**
1. Attention step.	Getting attention.	"I want to listen."
2. Need step.	Demonstrating the need to know.	"I need information on this subject."
3. Satisfaction step.	Presenting the information itself.	"The information being presented helps me understand the subject more satisfactorily."

Here is how a student organized an informative speech, using these three steps:

ROW—THROW—GO

Attention step

I. Holiday deaths by drowning are second only to auto accidents.

Need step

I. Every person should know what to do when a call for help is heard.
   A. This information may help you save a friend.
   B. This information may help you save a member of your family.

Satisfaction step

I. Remember three important words when someone is drowning: row, throw, go.
   A. Row: Look for boat.
      1. You can well afford to take a little time to look for a means of rowing to the rescue.
         a. Look for a boat.
         b. Look for a canoe.
         c. Look for a raft.
      2. Rowing to the rescue is always the wisest way.
   B. Throw: Look for a life buoy.
      1. See if you can locate something buoyant to throw to the person in distress.
         a. Look for a life buoy.

b. Look for an inflated inner tube.
c. Look for a board.
d. Look for a child's floating toy.
2. You can throw an object faster than you can swim.
C. Go: As a last resort, swim out to the drowning person.
1. Approach the victim from the rear.
2. If you are grabbed, go under water.
3. Clutch the person's hair.
4. Swim for shore.

II. Remember when you hear the call for help:
A. Look first for something in which to row.
B. Look for something buoyant to throw the victim.
C. Swim out only as a last resort.

The motivated sequence applied to entertaining speeches

And, finally, the speech to entertain may consist entirely of an expanded attention step, with the other four steps omitted.[4]

THE MOTIVATED SEQUENCE APPLIED TO ENTERTAINING SPEECHES

Step	Function	Audience response
1. Attention step.	Getting attention and retaining interest through entertainment.	"I want to listen, and I'll continue listening because I'm enjoying myself."

The outline below illustrates how an entertaining speech may be developed:

A TOAST TO THE APPLE

Attention step

I. The apple should be our national fruit.
A. Adam and Eve started our life of joy and confusion because of an apple.
B. Apples saved the lives of our favorite childhood characters.

[4]For an alternative method of developing a speech to entertain, see Chapter 20, and also the chart on page 277.

1. The third little pig in the *Three Little Pigs* was saved from the wolf by an apple.
2. Alex in the *Bear Story* was saved from starvation by eating the apples growing on the sycamore tree.

C. Apples are the symbol of our early education.
1. "A was an apple pie; B bit it; C cut it."

D. Apples enter into our courtship songs.
1. We sing to our sweetheart, "I'll Be with You in Apple Blossom Time."
2. We then serenade her with, "In the Shade of the Old Apple Tree."
3. We warn her, "Don't Sit Under the Apple Tree with Anyone Else But Me."

E. Our own health may depend upon an apple.
1. As the proverb says, "An apple a day keeps the doctor away."

F. Johnny Appleseed is rightfully a national hero.

II. So here's to the apple—our national fruit!

From what has been said thus far, it is apparent that these motivational divisions of a speech are functional in nature: that is, each part or step has a particular duty to perform in directing the mental processes of the listener. The ideas and supporting material in each step, therefore, must be sufficient in amount and quality to achieve the purpose of that step. Moreover, the number of steps and the particular function of each must be modified to suit the general end of the speech. The chart on the following page summarizes the ways in which the motivated sequence is adapted to each of the general ends. Study the chart carefully before going further. You will then be ready to consider in greater detail how each step in the motivated sequence may be developed.

THE ATTENTION STEP

As a speaker, your first task is to *gain attention,* but merely gaining attention is not enough; you also must gain *favorable* attention, and you must direct it toward the major ideas in your speech. Since the methods for gaining and directing attention were explained in the preceding chapter, we shall merely list them here:

1. Reference to the subject
2. Reference to the occasion
3. Personal greeting
4. Rhetorical question
5. Startling statement
6. Quotation
7. Humorous anecdote
8. Illustration

Review these eight methods of beginning a speech and examine the examples on pages 242 to 251. Frequently you will use only one

ADAPTATION OF THE MOTIVATED SEQUENCE TO THE GENERAL ENDS

Type of speech	**Instructive**	**Persuasive**			**Recreative**	
General end	TO INFORM	TO CONVINCE	TO STIMULATE	TO ACTUATE	TO ENTERTAIN	
Reaction sought	*Understanding* (Clarity)	*Belief* (Intellectual)	*Inspiration* (Emotional Arousal)	*Specific action* (Observable)	*Interest and diversion* (Enjoyment)	
Attention step	Draw attention to the subject.	Draw attention to the need.	Draw attention to the need.	Draw attention to the need.	(A) Draw attention to an interesting idea. Keep interest in it alive by a series of illustrations, anecdotes, and a humorous treatment: relate these to things in which the audience is already interested. Organize as a one-point speech. Stop while interest is still high. Omit last four steps of the motivated sequence.	(B) Draw attention to an absurd problem and entertain by an exaggerated treatment of it, thus burlesquing the entire motivated sequence as used in a serious persuasive speech; present the discussion in mock seriousness, with marked and obvious exaggeration.
Need step	Show why the listeners need a knowledge of the subject; point out what problems this information will help them meet.	Present logical evidence to prove the existence of a situation which requires that something be decided and upon which the audience must take a position.	Increase the feeling that the need is vital; create emotional dissatisfaction with present situation through the use of striking facts and illustrations.	Combine methods outlined in the two preceding columns, to show the need for action.		
Satisfaction step	Present information to give them a satisfactory knowledge of the subject as an aid in the solution of these problems; begin and end this presentation with a summary of the main points presented. (Normal end of the speech.)	Get the audience to believe that your position on this question is the right one to take, by using logic and evidence as proof.	Briefly state the heightened emotional attitude (enthusiasm, reverence, etc.) required of the audience.	Propose the specific action required to meet this problem; get the audience to believe in it by presenting logical evidence (as in the speech to convince).		
Visualization step	Sometimes: briefly suggest pleasure to be gained from this knowledge.	Briefly stimulate favorable emotion by projecting this belief into imaginary operation.	By means of vivid description, picture the results such an attitude will bring, especially the emotional satisfaction to be gained by the audience.	Picture the results which such action or the failure to take it will bring; use vivid description (as in the speech to stimulate).		
Action step	Sometimes: urge further study of the subject.	Arouse determination to retain this belief (as a guide to future action if need should arise).	Request the audience to actually assume this attitude, or express the assumption that they already have.	Urge the audience to take definite action.		

method to develop this step in your speech, but you may combine two or more methods. Speakers almost always make a reference to the subject to point up whatever other methods they employ. Except in the speech to entertain, however, the attention step is only a means to an end, not an end in itself. When speaking to inform, convince, stimulate, or actuate, be sure that your attention step leads naturally into the rest of your talk.

THE NEED STEP

The kind of need step you develop will vary with the purpose of your speech (and, as we shall see in later chapters, with the audience's attitude toward that purpose).[5] For example, speeches to persuade often urge a change in existing conditions. In such speeches, the need step attempts to create dissatisfaction with existing conditions in order to convince the audience that those conditions should be changed. In its campaign strategy, the political party out of power makes use of a need step of this sort, because it is concerned with condemnation—the pointing out of flaws and failures. Speeches to inform, on the other hand, require a need step in which the listeners are made to feel the limited scope of their knowledge of the subject to be discussed and are helped to realize how important information on this subject is to them.

As we have seen, the ideas and points of view expressed in the need step will vary according to the purpose of the speech. Furthermore, the structure of this step will vary according to the nature of the material to be presented. Detailed suggestions for making the necessary adaptations are offered in the chapters on the basic types of speeches (Chapters 20-24). The following pattern of development, however, has general usefulness. It includes these elements: (1) *Statement*—a clear, concise statement of the problem. (2) *Illustration*—one or more detailed examples which illustrate it. (3) *Ramification*—additional examples, statistical data, testimony, and other forms of support to show the problem's extent and seriousness. (4) *Pointing*—a convincing demonstration of how the need directly affects the people addressed—their health, happiness, security, or interests.

Let us put this method of development in outline form so that its essential structure is clear:

1. *Statement.* State the need (the specific problem or the importance of the information to the audience).
2. *Illustration.* Relate one or more incidents to illustrate the need.

[5]See Chapters 22, 23, and 24.

3. *Ramification.* Employ as many forms of support as are required to make the need convincing and impressive.
4. *Pointing.* Show the importance of the need to your audience.

You will notice how similar this structure is to that of the one-point speech described in Chapter 11, pages 181 to 189. Many need steps, if taken by themselves, are really one-point speeches; that is, they point out one thing—need. Develop your need step, then, just as you would a one-point speech. If the method just described seems inappropriate, use the didactic method or the method of implication, described on page 184, depending upon the attitude of the audience toward your purpose.

Some needs, of course, are complex and consist of more than one main aspect. In this case, you can develop each of these aspects separately and then draw them together to show their interrelation. The result will be similar to a series of one-point speeches related to one another and tied together at the end.

Although it is usually desirable, it is not always necessary to use all four of the structural elements of statement, illustration, ramification, and pointing to develop the need step. You should always use the statement and the pointing, but you can omit the illustration and the ramification, depending upon the amount of detail you require to impress the particular need on the audience. But regardless of whether you use the complete fourfold development, only part of it, or some other structure, you will find that the need step is one of the most important in your speech because through it your subject is related to the vital concerns and interests of your audience.

THE SATISFACTION STEP

As we have said, the purpose of the satisfaction step is to enable the audience to understand the material the speaker has chosen to explain or to induce the audience to agree that the belief or action the speaker proposes is the correct one. The structure of this step differs somewhat, however, depending on whether the purpose of the speech is instruction or persuasion. For this reason the satisfaction step for the instructive speech and the satisfaction step for the persuasive speech are discussed separately in the following paragraphs.

In speeches to inform

When your purpose is to inform—to give the audience a clear understanding of some subject—the satisfaction step will constitute the bulk of your speech, and will present the information that was outlined as necessary in the need step. The development of this step usually involves: (1) *an initial summary*, (2) *detailed information*, and (3) *a final summary.*

The *initial summary* gives a brief preview of the information you expect to present, and usually consists of an enumeration of the main points around which you will group your facts. In this way you make the direction of your discussion clear in advance. Obviously, the main points listed in this initial summary should parallel the order in which you intend to discuss them, or you will give your audience a false lead. When it is properly used, the initial summary serves as an excellent guidepost.

Next, the *detailed information* is presented; the main points mentioned in the initial summary are considered in turn, and the detailed facts and explanations relating to them are grouped around these points in an orderly fashion. Some consistent order of discussion, such as the time sequence, space sequence, etc., is used. (See pp. 228-231 in Chapter 14.) This will insure that your speech moves along in a definite direction, and that your audience does not get lost.

The *final summary* recapitulates the main points you have discussed, with the inclusion of whatever important conclusions you have made clear in relation to them. It is similar to the initial summary in structure, but it is usually longer.

Thus the development of the satisfaction step as used in informative speeches may be outlined as follows:

1. *Initial summary.* Briefly state in advance the main points you intend to cover.
2. *Detailed information.* Discuss in order the facts and explanations pertaining to each of these main points.
3. *Final summary.* Restate the main points presented, together with any important conclusions you have made.[6]

If presented as outlined above, your information will tend to be clear and coherent.

In persuasive speeches

When the purpose of a speech is to convince or to actuate, five elements may be included in the satisfaction step: (1) *Statement.* Briefly

[6]For a fuller discussion of these parts of the satisfaction step in a speech to inform, see Chapter 21.

state the attitude, belief, or action you wish the audience to adopt. (2) *Explanation.* Make sure your proposal is understood. Often diagrams or charts are useful here. (3) *Theoretical demonstration.* Show how the solution logically meets the problem pointed out in the need step. (4) *Practical experience.* Give actual examples showing that this proposal has worked effectively or that this belief has been proved correct; use facts, figures, and the testimony of experts to demonstrate this conclusion. (5) *Meeting objections.* Forestall opposition by showing how your proposal overcomes possible objections which might be raised against it.

As was the case with the elements in the need step, not all of the elements in the satisfaction step are required in every speech. Nor must these elements always appear in the same order. For instance, objections can sometimes best be met by answers scattered throughout the satisfaction step, at whatever points the questions arise. For developing the satisfaction step in speeches to convince or to actuate, however, the first four elements—statement, explanation, theoretical demonstration, and practical experience—form a convenient and effective sequence:

1. Briefly state the attitude, belief, or action you propose.
2. Explain it clearly.
3. Show how in theory it will meet the need.
4. Cite examples from practical experience to explain it and to show its soundness. Supplement these examples with facts, figures, and the testimony of experts.[7]

Parallel development of need and satisfaction steps

In some of your speeches, your need step may have two or more important aspects. To give each of these aspects sufficient emphasis and to make your discussion clear, you can develop the need and satisfaction steps in a *parallel* order. First present one aspect of the need and show how your proposal or information satisfies it; follow this same procedure with the second aspect, then the third aspect, and so on. This method weakens the cumulative effect of the motivated sequence, but the additional clarity often makes up for the loss.

These two skeleton outlines, developed for the subject "Structural Safety in Airplane Design," illustrate the normal order and the parallel order.

[7] In speeches to stimulate, Steps 1 and 2 are appropriate, but Steps 3 and 4 are unnecessary.

NORMAL ORDER

Attention step

I. I recently witnessed several interesting and frightening test flights.
   A. Vivid description of test flights.
   B. Vivid description of accidents.

Need step

I. The body design of a new airplane may have serious faults.
   A. Parts in the wing structures may be too heavy.
   B. The structures may not be strong enough to withstand strain.
II. The engine design of a new airplane may have serious faults.

Satisfaction step

I. Test flights throw light on how the body design of a new airplane can be improved.
   A. They show up defects in the wing structures.
   B. By putting extra strains on the airplane, they indicate the strength of the structures.
II. Test flights throw light on how the engine design of a new airplane can be improved.
   A. They indicate engine reliability.
   B. They reveal general engine performance under great strains.

Visualization step

I. Through the help of test flights, there should be tremendous development in airplane engine and body design in the near future.

Action step

I. Increased expenditures for test flights are thoroughly justified.

PARALLEL ORDER

Attention step

I. I recently witnessed several interesting and frightening test flights.

Need and satisfaction steps
(First aspect)

I. Airplane body design.
   A. The body design of a new airplane may have serious faults.
      1. Parts in the wing structures may be too heavy.
      2. The structures may not be strong enough to withstand strain.
   B. Test flights throw light on how the body design can be improved.

1. They show up defects in the wing structures.
2. By putting extra strains on the airplane, they indicate the strength of the structures.

(Second aspect)

II. Airplane engine design.
  A. The engine design of a new airplane may have serious faults.
  B. Test flights throw light on how the engine design of a new airplane can be improved.
    1. They indicate engine reliability.
    2. They reveal general engine performance under great strains.

Visualization step

I. Through the help of test flights, there should be tremendous development in airplane design and body design in the near future.

Action step

I. Increased expenditures for test flights are thoroughly justified.

Whether you use the normal order or the parallel order, you will always need to develop support for your statements.

THE VISUALIZATION STEP

The visualization step is used only in speeches to convince, stimulate, or actuate. Speeches to entertain or to inform, as we have seen, ordinarily achieve their main purpose in the earlier steps of the motivated sequence. (See chart on p. 277.)

The function of the visualization step is to intensify desire: to help motivate the audience to believe, feel, or act. In order to do this, it projects them into the future. Indeed, this step might also be called the "projection" step, for its effectiveness is determined by the vividness with which it pictures the benefits of believing or acting as the speaker proposes. The visualization step may be developed in one of three ways: by projecting a picture of the future that is *positive*, by projecting one that is *negative*, or by projecting first a negative picture and then a positive picture in order to show *contrast*.

The positive method

When using the positive method, describe conditions as they will be in the future if the solution you propose is carried out. Provide concrete descriptions. Select some situation which you are quite sure will arise in the future, and picture your audience in that situation actually enjoying the safety, pleasure, pride, etc., which your proposal will have produced.

The negative method

When using the negative method, describe adverse conditions that will prevail in the future if the solution you propose is *not* carried out. Graphically picture for your audience the danger or unpleasantness which will result. Select the most striking problems or deficiencies pointed out in the need step and demonstrate how they will continue unless your proposal is adopted.

The method of contrast

The method of contrast combines the positive and negative methods. Use the negative development first, visualizing the *bad* effects of failing to adopt your proposal; follow this with the positive development, visualizing the *good* effects of adopting your proposal. By the immediate contrast, both the bad and the good effects are made more striking and intense.

Whichever of these methods you use, remember that the visualization step must stand the test of *reality.* The conditions you picture must at least be probable. In addition, you must actually *put the audience into the picture.* Use vivid imagery: make your listeners see, hear, feel, taste, and smell.[8] The more vividly real you make the projected situation seem, the stronger will be the reaction of your audience.

The following example of a visualization step, developed by a student in a speech urging the use of fireproof materials in home construction, uses the method of contrast:

> But suppose you do build your home of the usual kindling wood: joists, rafters, and shingles. Some dark night you may awake from your pleasant sleep with the smell of acrid smoke in your nostrils, and in your ears the threatening crackle of burning timbers. You will jump out onto the cold floor and rush to wake up the household. Gathering your children in your arms, you will hurry down the stairs—if they are not already in flames—and out of doors. There you will watch the firemen chop holes in your roof, pour gallons of water over your plaster, your furniture, your piano. You will shiver with cold in spite of the blazing spectacle, and the plastic minds of your children will be indelibly impressed with fright. No fire insurance can repay your family for this horror, even though it may pay a small part of the financial loss.

[8]See Chapter 18, pp. 321-325, for a discussion of imagery.

How much better to use safe materials! Then throughout the long winter nights you can dig down under the warmth of your bedclothes to sleep peacefully in the assurance that your house cannot burn, and that any fire which catches in your furnishings can be confined to a small space and put out. No more the fear of flying sparks. Gone the danger to your wife and children. Sleep—quiet, restful, and secure in the knowledge that the "burning horror" has been banished from your home.[9]

THE ACTION STEP

The action step, like the visualization step, occurs only in persuasive speeches. Its function is to translate the desire created in the visualization step into overt action or into a definitely fixed attitude or belief. There are many methods for developing the action step, but the six most frequently used are fully described and illustrated in Chapter 15 as "methods of ending a speech." They are:

1. Challenge or appeal
2. Summary
3. Quotation
4. Illustration
5. Inducement
6. Personal intention

For suggestions on developing the action step, review pages 251-257, where these six ways of ending a speech are described. Be sure to keep the action step short. Someone has given the following rule for public speaking: "Stand up; speak up; shut up!" So far as the action step is concerned, we may modify this rule in this way: "Clinch your major ideas; finish your speech briskly; and sit down."

The motivated sequence, then, consists of five steps which correspond to the natural thought processes by which people come to understand, to believe, and to act. Speeches constructed on this organic basis are not automatically assured of success, but they are more likely to accomplish their communicative intention than those put together without regard for how the listener himself thinks, reasons, and reacts. There are, of course, other ways of organizing a speech. For instance, in the chart on page 286, you may wish to study the relationship between the *steps* of the motivated sequence and the *divisions* traditionally designated as *Introduction, Body,* and *Conclusion.* The purpose of this chapter has been to explain the psychological principles upon which motivational structuring is based and to suggest why each of its steps is important in terms of

[9]From a student speech by James Fulton.

THE RELATIONSHIP BETWEEN THE STEPS OF THE MOTIVATED SEQUENCE AND THE TRADITIONAL DIVISIONS OF A SPEECH

General ends	**Introduction**		**Body or discussion**		**Conclusion**	
To entertain	*Attention Step* Illustration or statement of the idea or subject.		*Attention Step* (continued) Further illustration or ramification of the idea or subject.		*Attention Step* (concluded) Final illustration, quotation, or restatement of the idea or subject.	
To inform	*Attention Step* Provoke curiosity in subject.	*Need Step* Show its relation to the listeners: why they need to know.	*Satisfaction Step* 1. Initial summary, outlining points to be covered to satisfy this need.	2. Detailed discussion of points in order.	*Satisfaction Step* (concluded) 3. Final summary: a recapitulation of the main points and of important conclusions.	
To convince	*Attention Step* Direct attention to basic elements of the proposition.		*Need Step* Demonstrate that a need for decision exists and lay down criteria for judgment.	*Satisfaction Step* State the proposition and evidence to induce belief in it and its benefits.	*Visualization Step* Briefly make its desirability vivid through imagery.	*Action Step* Restate the proposition and recapitulate the reasons for belief.
To stimulate	*Attention Step* Stimulate attention and direct it to—		*Need Step* Present the conditions, objects, subject, which demand an emotional reaction from audience.	*Satisfaction Step* Briefly state attitude desired.	*Visualization Step* Bring about climax of emotional stimulus by picturing desired attitude.	*Action Step* Restate the attitude desired or challenge to audience.
To actuate	*Attention Step* Direct attention to—		*Need Step* Present conditions showing a need for action.	*Satisfaction Step* State proposed action and prove its workability and benefits.	*Visualization Step* Picture future conditions as a result of the action taken.	*Action Step* Appeal for or demand the specified action.

Note: Not everything listed above is always included. The chart is used merely to show the relationship between the two methods of organization.

the listener. In later chapters we shall consider in detail the various ways in which the motivated sequence may be adapted to different kinds of speeches and speechmaking situations.

Problems

1. In a book entitled *How We Think* (Boston: Heath, 1933), the philosopher John Dewey said that when a person reasons his way through a problem systematically or "reflectively," he characteristically does five things: (1) defines or delimits the problem, (2) analyzes the problem, (3) thinks of possible solutions, (4) makes a preliminary evaluation of these solutions by reasoning, and (5) verifies the most likely solutions empirically. After reading Dewey's more detailed descriptions of these steps in reflective thinking, compare them with the steps in the motivated sequence as explained in this chapter. To what extent are the two processes alike? To what extent are they different? How do you account for the similarities and differences?
2. Defend orally or in writing (1) the logical validity and (2) the psychological validity of the motivated sequence. That is, point out why both logically and psychologically *attention* must begin the sequence, why *need* must precede *satisfaction, action* follow *visualization*, etc. Would any other order of these same steps have equal logical and psychological validity?
3. Find in *Vital Speeches of the Day* or elsewhere two persuasive speeches (i.e. to convince, to stimulate, or to actuate) organized according to the motivated sequence. Indicate the points in each speech at which the various steps begin. Are the need and satisfaction steps arranged according to the formulas suggested on pages 278 and 279-281? Is the positive, negative, or method of contrast used to develop the visualization step? Are any of the devices listed in this chapter (pp. 276 and 285) used in the attention and action steps? If not, how are these steps developed?
4. How might either of the two speeches studied in Problem 3 be differently organized? Would such an alternative organization be preferable to the motivated sequence? Why or why not?
5. Find in *Vital Speeches of the Day* or elsewhere a speech to inform which is not organized according to the motivated sequence. Rewrite this speech so that it conforms to the threefold pattern of attention, need, and satisfaction. (If the speech does not contain suitable material for the attention and need steps, supply it out of your own invention; but in adding it, be careful not to alter the original subject matter or purpose.)
6. Supposing your speech class to be the audience, select a specific purpose for a persuasive speech (i.e., a speech to convince, stimulate, or actuate). Then prepare a five-sentence outline of a speech designed to obtain this response—one sentence for each step in the motivated sequence. In writing these sentences, follow the rules for stating the major ideas of a speech as

outlined in Chapter 14. Let the other members of the class evaluate your effort.

7. Using the motivated sequence as a pattern, construct an outline for a speech urging support of a proposed reform in college life or administration, or in municipal, state, or national affairs. Prepare three different visualization steps for this speech—one using the positive method, one the negative method, and one the method of contrast. Also prepare three different action steps—one using inducement, one using a statement of personal intention, and one using any one of the other four methods. (See p. 285 for a listing of the different types of action steps.) Which type of visualization step and which action step appear to be most effective for this particular speech? Why?

Speaking assignment

1. Present in class a six-minute persuasive speech on one of the following subjects or on a similar subject upon which you and your instructor have agreed in advance. Build your speech on the pattern furnished by the motivated sequence. Develop a strong need directly related to the interests and desires of your listeners. Show through reasoning and examples how your proposal will satisfy this need. Use the positive, negative, or contrasting method to build the visualization step. Close with a direct appeal for belief or action.

The sale of cigarettes should be controlled by law.
Go to church every Sunday.
Exercise to help your heart.
All college students should take at least three years of science (or mathematics, foreign language, etc.).
We should have a national repertory theatre.
Good books are a permanent source of satisfaction and pleasure.
Solve the problem of race relations.
How can we improve the quality of television programs?
We can conquer urban blight.
Give a fair deal to the farmer.
Remove the threat of strikes.
Improve college teaching.

Suggestions for further reading

Hugh Blair, *Lectures on Rhetoric and Belles Lettres*, ed. Harold Harding (Carbondale: Southern Illinois University Press, 1965), Lecture XXI, "Conduct of a Discourse in All Its Parts," and Lecture XXXII, "Conduct of a Discourse—the Argumentative Part, the Pathetic Part, the Peroration."

W. Norwood Brigance, *Speech: Its Techniques and Disciplines in a Free Society,* 2nd ed. (New York: Appleton-Century-Crofts, 1961), Chapter VII, "The Architecture of Persuasion."

Columbia Associates in Philosophy, *An Introduction to Reflective Thinking* (Boston: Houghton Mifflin Company, 1923).

John Dewey, *How We Think* (Boston: D. C. Heath and Company, 1933).

James H. McBurney and Kenneth G. Hance, *Discussion in Human Affairs* (New York: Harper & Row, Publishers, 1950), Chapter VI, "The Steps in Reflective Thinking."

Otis M. Walter and Robert L. Scott, *Thinking and Speaking* (New York: The Macmillan Company, 1962), Chapter VIII, "Thinking and Speaking about Problems"; Chapter IX, "Thinking and Speaking about Causes"; Chapter X, "Thinking and Speaking about Solutions."

CHAPTER SEVENTEEN

Making an outline

In Chapter 14 we studied how to select, phrase, and arrange the major ideas of a speech. In Chapters 15 and 16 we surveyed methods for beginning and ending speeches and examined the means of adapting our remarks to the natural thought processes of our listeners. Let us now turn to the problem of translating our speech plan into acceptable outline form.

There are several reasons for developing a good outline.[1] For one thing, it lays out before you the entire structure of your speech so that you can see whether you have fitted the various parts together appropriately, whether you have given each element sufficient emphasis, and whether you have included all necessary elements. It also enables you to check the adequacy of your supporting material. If you have failed to support any of your major points or have used only one type of support throughout your speech, your outline will reveal these deficiencies. Finally, an outline helps you fix firmly in your mind the ideas you wish to communicate to your listeners and the order in which you wish to present them. By reading over your outline repeatedly, you can memorize the pattern or "geography" of your speech, with its major headings and developmental material, so that as you stand before your audience you will be able to recall how your speech "looks" as well as what it says. Most persons find this visual map or pattern a highly useful aid to memory.

In this chapter, we shall consider, first, the requirements of a good outline; second, the different types of outlines and how to prepare them; and, third, the technic of testing an outline by drawing up an analytical or technical plot of the speech.

[1]See Chapter 3, pp. 33.

REQUIREMENTS OF GOOD OUTLINE FORM

The amount of detail and the type of arrangement you will use in an outline will depend on your subject, your analysis of the speaking situation, and your previous experience in speech composition. But regardless of these factors, any good outline should meet certain basic requirements:

1. *Each unit in the outline should contain only one item or statement.* This is essential to the very nature of outlining. If two or three items or statements are run together under one symbol, their structural relationship does not stand out clearly. Notice the differences in the following examples:

Wrong

I. Our city should conduct a campaign against the thousands of flies that infest it every year, breeding everywhere and buzzing at every kitchen door, because they spread disease by carrying germs and contaminating food, and because they can be eliminated easily by killing them with insecticides and preventing their breeding by cleaning up refuse.

Right

I. Our city should conduct a campaign against flies.
   A. Thousands of flies infest the city every year.
      1. They breed everywhere.
      2. They buzz at every kitchen door.
   B. Flies spread disease.
      1. They carry germs.
      2. They contaminate food.
   C. Flies can be eliminated easily.
      1. Widespread use of insecticides kills them.
      2. Cleaning up refuse prevents their breeding.

2. *The items in the outline should be properly subordinated.* Those statements or facts that are listed as subpoints under a larger heading should actually be subordinate to it in meaning and not of equal or greater importance. Moreover, an item should not be included as a subpoint unless it has a direct connection with the main point under which it appears. Each subordinate point should directly and logically support or amplify the larger heading beneath which it stands.

Wrong

I. Radio is a direct benefit to humanity.
   A. It has saved many lives at sea.

II. It makes easier the spreading of news.
III. Present broadcasting methods are not as good as they might be.
 A. There are too many stations cluttering the air.
  1. Programs are becoming worse.
  2. There are too many disk-jockey programs and high-pressure sales talks.
 B. This is true even though a great many criminals have been tracked down by means of radio.

Right

I. Radio is a direct benefit to humanity.
 A. It has saved many lives at sea.
 B. It makes easier the spreading of news.
 C. It has aided in tracking down a great many criminals.
II. Present broadcasting methods are not as good as they might be.
 A. There are too many stations cluttering the air.
 B. Programs are becoming worse.
  1. There are too many disk-jockey programs.
  2. There are too many high-pressure sales talks.

3. *The logical relation of the items in an outline should be shown by proper indention.* The greater the importance or scope of a statement, the nearer it should be placed to the left-hand margin. If a statement takes up more than one line, the second line should be indented the same as the beginning of the statement.

Wrong

I. Shortening the college course to three years is not necessary.
 A. Provision is already made for students who are unable to spend four years in college.
 B. Other parts of one's educational career can be cut short with less loss than would result from this proposal.
  1. The preparatory-school course could be shortened.
  2. The course in professional school could be shortened.

Wrong

I. Shortening the college course to three years is not necessary.
A. Provision is already made for students who are unable to spend four years in college.
B. Other parts of one's educational career can be cut short with less loss than would result from this proposal.
1. The preparatory-school course could be shortened.
2. The course in professional school could be shortened.

Right

I. Shortening the college course to three years is not necessary.
   A. Provision is already made for students who are unable to spend four years in college.
   B. Other parts of one's educational career can be cut short with less loss than would result from this proposal.
      1. The preparatory-school course could be shortened.
      2. The course in professional school could be shortened.

4. *A consistent set of symbols should be used.* One such set is exemplified in the outlines printed in this chapter. But whether you use this set or some other, be consistent; do not change systems in the middle of an outline. Items of the same logical importance should have the same type of symbol *throughout*, and those which differ in their logical importance should *not* have the same type of symbol. Thus:

Wrong

I. There is a need for better traffic regulation.
   II. Figures show the extent of traffic-law violations:
      A. 300,000 motorists were arrested in New York last year.
      2. $1,000,000.00 was paid in fines last year by New York motorists.
         I. This is more than the total paid in all England, Scotland, and Wales.
         a. This amount would buy about 400 new automobiles at $2500 each.

Right

I. There is a need for better traffic regulation.
   A. Figures show the extent of traffic-law violations:
      1. 300,000 motorists were arrested in New York last year.
      2. $1,000,000.00 was paid in fines last year by New York motorists.
         a. This is more than the total paid in all England, Scotland, and Wales.
         b. This amount would buy about 400 new automobiles at $2500 each.

TYPES OF OUTLINES AND HOW TO PREPARE THEM

There are two principal types of outlines, each of which fulfills a different purpose—the *full-content* outline and the *key-word* outline. The former helps make the process of speech preparation more systematic and thorough; the latter serves as an aid to memory in the early stages of oral practice.

The full-content outline

As its name implies, a full-content outline represents the complete factual content of the speech in outline form. The components of the speech or the steps in the motivated sequence are set off in separate sections. In each of these sections, the major ideas are stated; and under them—properly indented and marked with the correct symbols—is put all the material used to amplify and support them. *Each major idea and all of the minor ones are written down in complete sentences* so that their full meaning and their relation to other points are made completely clear. After each piece of evidence or supporting material, the source from which it was obtained is indicated, or these sources are combined in a bibliography at the end of the outline. Thus, when the outline has been completed, not only the speaker but any other person can derive a clear, comprehensive picture of the speech as a whole simply by reading the outline. The only thing lacking is the specific wording to be used in presenting the speech and the visible and audible aspects of the speaker's delivery. The purpose of this type of outline is obvious. By bringing together all the material you have gathered and by stating it completely and in detail, you ensure thoroughness in the preparation of your speech.

A full-content outline requires much effort. It cannot be written offhand even by a person who has had a great deal of experience; the beginner should allow plenty of time for developing one. You can keep the time to a minimum, however, if you go about the task systematically.

1. *Begin by setting down the subject of your speech, the general end, the specific purpose, and the probable audience attitude toward the purpose.* (See Chapters 7 and 8 for detailed instructions.)

2. *Next, block out a skeleton plan of your outline.* This plan will be a sort of blueprint to be filled in later; it will not contain the actual material of the speech but will merely indicate its structure. The nature of this skeleton plan will depend upon the general end that you choose. If you employ the motivated sequence, a speech to entertain normally will contain only an attention step and will follow the method of a one-point speech (see pp. 181-189). Hence your skeleton plan will look something like this:

Subject: ____________________.
General end: To entertain.
Specific purpose: ____________________.
Probable audience attitude: ____________________.

Attention step

I. (Statement of the central entertaining idea) __________.
  A. (Illustration) __________.
    1. (Detail) __________.
    2. (Detail) __________.
    3, 4, etc. __________.
  B. (More support) __________.
  C. (More support) __________.
  D, E, etc. __________.
II. (Restatement of central entertaining idea) __________.

If your object is to inform, your skeleton plan will contain attention, need, and satisfaction steps. In each step there will be one or more main points; and these, in turn, will require amplification and support very much as if they were one-point speeches. Your skeleton plan may therefore be somewhat like this:

Subject: __________.
General end: To inform.
Specific purpose: __________.
Probable audience attitude: __________.

Attention step

I. (Opening statement) __________.
  A. (Support) __________.
    1, 2, etc. (Details) __________.
  B. (Support) __________.
II. (Statement or restatement) __________.

Need step

I. (Statement of need for information) __________.
  A. (Main supporting statement) __________.
    1, 2, etc. (Support) __________.
  B. (Main supporting statement) __________.
  C, D, etc. __________.
II. (Pointing statement relating to audience) __________.
  A, B, etc. (Support) __________.
III. (Summary statement) __________.

Satisfaction step

I. (Statement of subject, including preliminary summary).
  A. (Statement of first main division of subject) __________.
    1. (Support) __________.
      a. (Detail) __________.

b. (Detail) ______________________________________.
2. (Support) ______________________________________.
B, C, etc. (Statements of other main divisions of subject) __________.
II. (Summary statement) __________________________________.
A, B, C. (Recapitulation of main points) ____________________.

If you follow the motivated sequence when your purpose is to convince, to stimulate, or to actuate, your skeleton plan will provide for all five steps—attention, need, satisfaction, visualization, and action:

Subject: ____.
General end: To convince (stimulate, actuate) ____________________.
Specific purpose: ____.
Probable audience attitude: __________________________________.

Attention step

(Same form as for speech to inform; see p. 295.)

Need step

I. (Statement of need: the problem) ____________________________.
(The form used here will depend upon the specific purpose of the speech and the nature of the material. One common development includes supporting detail, pointing, and summary: the same form as for the speech to inform; see p. 295.)

Satisfaction step

I. (Statement of idea or plan proposed) _________________________.
A. (Explanation) _______________________________________.
1, 2, etc. (Details) ___________________________________.
B. (Main supporting statement) _____________________________.
1. (Support) ____.
a, b, etc. (Details) _________________________________.
2, 3, etc. (Support) __________________________________.
C, D, etc. (Main supporting statements) ______________________.
II. (Summary statement) ___________________________________.

Visualization step

I. (Statement of negative projection) _________________________.
A, B, etc. (Support of details) ____________________________.
II. (Statement of positive projection) __________________________.

Action step

I. (Statement of action requested) ____________________________.
A, B, etc. (Support or recapitulation) _________________________.
II. (Restatement or appeal) ________________________________.

Do not regard the preceding examples as rigid models; they are intended merely to illustrate possible skeleton plans for each of the basic types of speeches when developed according to the motivated sequence. The number of major ideas and the details of support will, of course, vary from speech to speech and cannot be determined in advance. For any particular speech, however, begin, as we have done here, by laying out a skeletal plan of its general structure. Details and modifications can come later.

3. *The next step is to fill in your skeleton plan with the actual ideas and materials you expect to present.* Be sure that your statements of these ideas help to perform the functions required of that part of the speech in which they are used; that is, in the attention step see that they are designed to secure attention; in the need step, to emphasize the necessity for understanding or action, and so on. Apply the principles of arrangement—of proper sequence, coordination, and subordination—studied in Chapter 14. At this stage, an outline for a speech to actuate might look like this:

OUR PLENTY IS NOT SO PLENTIFUL

Attention step

I. A fertile land area as big as Connecticut becomes silt.
II. Importance to your future.

Need step

I. Principles vital to conservation.
   A. Economy.
   B. Foresight.
   C. Preserving balance of nature.
II. Past disregard of these principles.
   A. Waste.
   B. Lack of foresight.
   C. Balance of nature ignored.
III. Summary.

Satisfaction step

I. Establish threefold program.
   A. Planned valley programs.
   B. Modern conservation methods.
   C. Scientific research.
II. Program follows vital principles.
   A. Economy.

B. Foresight.

C. Regard for balance of nature.

III. Past success of these measures.

Visualization step

I. If plunder continues—

A. Exhaustion of raw materials.

B. Drastic food and water shortages.

C. Weakening national defenses.

II. Plan will prevent catastrophe.

Action step

I. Delay no longer.

II. People must realize the problem.

III. You tell others about the danger.

4. *Finally, fill in this rough draft with detailed support;* then revise, reword, and rearrange the statements in your outline so that the result is both logical and persuasive. Each item should be phrased as a complete sentence, and its logical relation to superior and subordinate points should be carefully tested. If you find that you lack support for some of the statements you have included, either omit them or obtain the evidence you need. Thus your outline will continue to change until it has reached its final form. Then it will perhaps resemble in completeness and validity of arrangement the full-content outline below.

Notice the thoroughness of treatment which is obtained by developing an outline in full-content form.[2] Even though there are a number of defensible plans different from the one the speaker uses here, you cannot read through his outline without being at least partially convinced by the soundness of what he says. Any good full-content outline for a persuasive speech should have this effect on the reader.

Sample of a full-content outline

OUR PLENTY IS NOT SO PLENTIFUL

Attention step

I. The ground under our feet is not as solid as we think.

A. Each year a billion tons of earth are washed down the nation's rivers in the form of eroded soil.

[2]Students who have studied elsewhere the making of briefs or logical outlines, in contrast to rhetorical outlines for persuasive speeches, will observe that the full-content outline, especially when based on the motivated sequence, is really a combination of the two.

1. This is a fertile land area equivalent to the state of Connecticut.

II. Do you know that our most vital natural resources are being seriously depleted while demands for them are doubling or tripling?
   A. Hans H. Landsberg reports that by 2000 A.D. our need for industrial energy and metals will be tripled; for lumber, nearly tripled; and for farm products and fresh water, nearly doubled.
   B. At projected levels of future consumption, our crude oil reserves will last less than 50 years.
   C. By the end of this century we will be consuming forest products faster than they can be replaced.
   D. Every day we lose more water than we use—an average of 19 billion gallons—by evaporation from open storage areas alone.

III. You may be directly affected by this drastic depletion of resources.
   A. Conservationists warn of increasing difficulty in obtaining food, energy, and materials.
      1. Diminishing supplies of wood, coal, and oil will mean less fuel for your home.
      2. Evaporation, erosion, and sedimentation will create serious scarcities of food and water.
   B. Shortages will create higher costs.
   C. Depletion of resources can endanger our country's defense.

IV. You need to know how a national catastrophe can be prevented.

Need step

I. Three principles are vital to any conservation program:
   A. We must make the most of what we have.
   B. We must renew whatever resources we can.
   C. We must preserve the balance of nature.

II. In the past, these "musts" have been ignored.
   A. Irreplaceable metals and oils have been wasted.
      1. Petroleum and petroleum products have been mercilessly exploited.
         a. Estimates of the amount of known crude oil supplies left unrecovered in the developed oil fields range as high as 83 per cent.
         b. As late as 1948, losses of gas in well drilling and extraction processing in Texas alone were greater than the entire volume of gas shipped out of that state.
      2. Copper mines have been abandoned before the ore was exhausted.
         a. It is now too expensive to reopen the water-filled shafts.
         b. We are being forced to import more and more copper.
      3. Stuart Chase says that the avoidable waste in mining coal in the United States is 35 per cent, compared to 5 to 10 per cent in Europe.
   B. Principles vital to conservation have been too long ignored.

1. Early settlers, like some Americans of more recent times, looked upon America as inexhaustibly wealthy, with resources to squander.
    a. When cotton fields became sterile, farmers simply moved to new land.
    b. Within 50 years after the pioneers moved into the Western states in the nineteenth century, 700 million acres of grass west of the Mississippi had been destroyed.
    c. Later, over-expansion of crop acreages to capitalize on high prices denuded much of the Great Plains and led to the Dust Bowl of the 1930's.
    d. Up to now, lumber companies assumed a never-ending supply of high-grade timber.
2. This lack of foresight set in motion a vicious cycle of spoilage:
    a. With the forests went the protective soil covering of decayed leaves and pine needles.
    b. Rain and melted snow rushed down the hillsides instead of being gradually absorbed by this cover.
    c. Precious topsoil was carried away by the surging waters.
        i. The torrents eroded gullies in the farmlands.
        ii. The silt thus formed polluted the water supply.

C. Even today we continue to disregard the interrelation of natural resources.
1. Baltimore taxpayers are paying for the poor farming methods in the upper river valleys of Maryland:
    a. Sediment from the farms clogs the harbor.
    b. Over the years, the city has paid more than 17 million dollars to dredge 111 million cubic yards of sediment.
2. What happened in Decatur, Illinois, is another glaring example:
    a. In 1922, Decatur built a two-million-dollar dam across the Sangamon River.
    b. By 1946, silt had deprived the reservoir of 26 per cent of its capacity.
    c. The city had not taken heed of the shift to intertilled crops in the watershed area.
        i. Corn and soybeans had replaced hay, grass, and grain.
        ii. Lack of close-growing crops had increased erosion at the rate of 4000 tons annually for each average farm.
    d. Decatur was forced to invest more money to re-establish its water supply.
3. Mighty Lake Mead above Hoover Dam has been filling with 137,000 acre-feet of sediment annually since this world's third largest artificial lake and the dam were completed in 1936.

III. It is high time we fully observed the principles vital to conservation.

Satisfaction step

I. A threefold program is the only way to meet the urgent need:

A. We must establish programs for river valleys.

B. We must observe modern forestation and farming practices.

C. We must support programs of scientific research.

II. Such programs satisfy the three "musts" for effective conservation:

A. By establishing valley programs, we can restore and maintain the balance of nature.

1. Forests should be restored in watershed areas.

a. Such watershed erosion-control would prevent floods.

b. Such a program would also reduce downstream sediment significantly, as shown by the 33 per cent reduction in the Lake Waco, Texas, watershed, and the 78 per cent reduction in the Lake Newman, Georgia, watershed.

2. Below watershed areas, dams should be constructed.

a. They would prevent floods in the lower valley.

b. They would maintain water supply.

c. They would furnish electric power.

3. Below the dams, land can be reclaimed for cultivation.

a. Arid land can be made productive by irrigation.

b. Fertility can be maintained by growing the proper crops.

B. By applying modern methods of forestry and farming, we can produce more and still replenish the land.

1. According to an NEA report, 70 million acres can be cleared, drained, or irrigated to make productive farmland.

2. The quality of the soil can be improved.

a. Crop rotation would prevent excessive erosion and restore nitrates.

b. Proper fertilization would increase productivity.

3. Reforestation can supply the necessary lumber and soil protection.

C. With programs of scientific research, we can extend our valuable mineral resources.

1. The most efficient methods of extracting and refining can be worked out.

2. New mines and oil fields can be located.

3. Synthetics can be developed for the time when we run out of natural resources.

III. Specific results already obtained guarantee the success of such an overall program.

A. Harnessing the Colorado River has resulted in benefits for the whole valley.

1. Hoover Dam has conquered the floods which once threatened the Imperial and Yuma valleys.

2. Farmers in these valleys now irrigate their lands.

3. Navigation above and below the dam has been extended and improved.
4. According to the Department of the Interior, the dam produces electrical energy at the rate of $4\frac{1}{3}$ billion kilowatt-hours a year.
   a. By May 31, 1987, the end of the 50-year repayment period, Hoover Dam will have returned twice the entire Boulder Canyon power production allocation of $130 million.
   b. The dam returns more than $290,000 to the United States Treasury each month.

B. Startling results have been achieved from farming with modern conservation methods.
   1. In a study reported by the NEA, the average annual increase for 4 million acres under conservation was 36 per cent.
      a. Farmers grew 1,300,000 more bushels of corn on 32,000 fewer acres.
      b. Their average income was $4.90 per acre higher than that of other farmers.

C. Scientists and engineers have made important contributions to conservation and development of resources.
   1. Chemical film coatings have been developed to lessen evaporation from water surfaces in open storage areas.
   2. The Bureau of Mines has developed a way to make potassium, formerly imported from Germany, out of potash rock.

Visualization step

I. If we don't stop destructive practices now, catastrophe can result.
   A. In some instances, industry will decline for lack of raw material. (Description of ghost town)
   B. Although the chance of a killing famine in the U.S. is remote, certainly food or water shortages are grim possibilities.
   C. Weakened economy can lower our resistance to possible enemy invaders.

II. By developing valley projects, by renewing the soil and forests, and by supporting further scientific research, we can abolish those threats to our nation's welfare.

Action step

I. A unified conservation program demands the immediate cooperation of us all.
   A. We don't want water shortages, dust storms, and floods.
   B. We don't want our children to be the victims of our wasteful practices.
   C. We must provide wisely and courageously for the future.

II. Action will come only when enough people are made aware of the problem.
III. You must help others understand the problems we share.

Bibliography

"After a Hundred Years," *The Yearbook of Agriculture*, 1962. U.S. Department of Agriculture (Washington: Government Printing Office, 1962).

Clawson, Marion; Held R. Burnell; Charles H. Stoddard. *Land for the Future* (Baltimore: The Johns Hopkins Press, 1960).

Duerr, W. A. *Fundamentals of Forestry Economics* (New York: McGraw-Hill Book Company, 1960).

"Farmer's World," The Yearbook of Agriculture, *1964.* U.S. Department of Agriculture (Washington: Government Printing Office, 1964).

Golzé, Alfred R. *Reclamation in the United States* (Caldwell, Idaho: The Caxton Printers, Ltd., 1961).

Landsberg, Hans H. *Natural Resources for U.S. Growth* (Baltimore: The Johns Hopkins Press, 1964).

Natural Resources: A Summary Report. Committee on Natural Resources; Publication 1000, National Academy of Sciences (Washington: National Research Council, 1962).

Parson, Ruben L. *Conserving American Resources*, 2nd ed. (Englewood Cliffs, N.J.: Prentice-Hall, Inc., 1964).

Schurr, Sam H.; Bruce C. Neschert with Vera F. Eliasberg; Joseph Lerner; Hans H. Landsberg. *Energy in the American Economy, 1850-1975* (Baltimore: The Johns Hopkins Press, 1960).

"Valleys and Hills: Erosion and Sedimentation," *Yearbook of Agriculture, 1955.* U.S. Department of Agriculture (Washington: Government Printing Office, 1955).

Vetter, C. P. "Sediment Problems in Lake Mead and Downstream on the Colorado River," *Transactions of the American Geophysical Union*, Vol. XXXIV, No. 2, April, 1953.

Full-content outlines for speeches to entertain or to inform will differ from the one above because they will not contain all five steps in the motivated sequence. In all other details of form and content, however, they will be just as complete. Here is an outline for an informative speech on the subject of urban renewal:

URBAN RENEWAL

Attention step

I. Do you know how big the slum problem has become?
   A. Seventy per cent of our population now lives in urban areas.
   B. Fifteen to 17 per cent of city dwellers live in slum areas.
   C. About 20 per cent of the larger U.S. cities today consist of slum areas.
II. Do you know that attempts to solve the slum problem are costing you and your fellow citizens millions of dollars?
III. Do you know that the proposed solutions—comprehensively referred to as urban renewal—may prevent your own community from becoming a slum?

Need step

I. Information about urban renewal is important to everyone.
   A. Slums are expensive.
      1. Real estate tax revenues are disproportionately low.
         a. In tax appraisals, too much consideration is given to the dilapidation of slum structures and not enough to the high value of the land they stand on.
         b. Tax levies also are not in proportion to the high earnings of slum property.
         c. Tax collections are not pressed hard enough.
      2. Municipal service costs to slum areas are disproportionately high.
         a. Police, fire, health, and welfare costs comprise 45 per cent of the city's total.
         b. Part of the expense can be laid to sanitation and structural problems caused by lax building-code enforcement.
         c. Welfare costs are high because of social problems, largely due to poor or inadequate education.
   B. Slums are dangerous.
      1. Disease rates are high.
         a. As much as 50 per cent of the city's disease occurs in slum areas.
         b. Although TB has been declining in the nation as a whole, it has started increasing again in the cities.
            i. Comparing TB rates for 1962 and 1963 shows the disease was up 50 per cent in Akron, 46.8 per cent in Fort Worth, 39.3 per cent in Dallas.
            ii. New York City had a 1962-to-1963 increase of 12 per cent, with the greatest rise in the slums.
      2. Delinquency and crime rates are high.
         a. Fifty-five per cent of the city's juvenile delinquency occurs in slum areas.
         b. Forty-five per cent of the city's major crimes occur in slum areas.
         c. Fifty per cent of the city's arrests are made in slum areas.
   C. Slums are cruel.
      1. Children's lives are stunted or warped.
      2. Elderly people finish out their lives in misery.
      3. Adults of all ages are trapped and hopeless.
II. Urban renewal is aimed not only at destroying slums but at preventing their development.
III. Information about urban renewal is important to you personally.
   A. As a city business or professional man, you know that your livelihood may be affected by the prevalence of slums.
   B. As a city or suburban homeowner, you should realize that your community is never entirely free from the encroachment of slums.

C. As the head of a household, you must protect yourself, your wife, and children from dangers associated with slums and blighted areas.

Satisfaction step

I. This discussion will provide information about the development of urban renewal, its financing, and one example of its work.
   A. Urban renewal has been speeded up through federal legislation.
      1, 2, etc. (Details)[3]
   B. Urban renewal projects are sponsored cooperatively by the federal government and the community.
      1, 2, etc. (Details)
   C. Chicago's urban renewal work includes a huge redevelopment program.
      1, 2, etc. (Details)

II. Remember that urban renewal is of grave concern to the nation as well as to the community involved.
   A. It has been stimulated by federal legislation.
   B. It is being supported partly by various forms of federal aid and partly by the community.
   C. Projects like Chicago's are dramatic evidence of what can be done.

Bibliography

Anderson, Martin. *The Federal Bulldozer: A Critical Analysis of Urban Renewal, 1949-1962* (Cambridge, Mass.: M. I. T. Press, 1965).

Highlights of the Housing and Urban Development Act of 1965. Committee on Banking and Currency, House of Representatives (Washington: Government Printing Office, 1965).

Hunter, David R. *The Slums: Challenge and Response* (London: Collier-Macmillan, Ltd., 1964).

Johnson, Thomas F.; James R. Morris; Joseph G. Butts. *Renewing America's Cities* (Washington, D.C.: The Institute for Social Science Research, 1962).

"Poverty Blamed for Rise in Urban Tuberculosis," *Science Newsletter*, Vol. 86, No. 2, July 11, 1964, p. 18.

Scientific American, September, 1965. (The entire issue is devoted to the problems of metropolitan areas.)

Von Eckardt, Wolf. "The Case for Building 350 New Towns," *Harpers*, December 1965, pp. 85-94.

Weaver, Robert C. *The Urban Complex* (Garden City, N.Y.: Doubleday and Company, 1964).

The key-word outline

After you have constructed your speech and written out a full-content outline for it, you are ready to begin your oral practice. The key-word outline is an excellent aid to memory in such practice. This

[3]Details of the information presented by the speaker have been omitted here and below.

outline has the same indentation and the same symbols as the full-content outline, but it boils down each statement to a key word, phrase, or brief sentence that can be more easily remembered. By reading a key-word outline through repeatedly from beginning to end, you will be able to fix the ideas of your speech firmly in mind and to recall them readily as you stand before the audience. Of course, to ensure accuracy, you may read specific quotations or figures from note cards.

The following key-word outline is based on the full-content outline beginning on page 298.

Sample of a key-word outline

OUR PLENTY IS NOT SO PLENTIFUL

Attention step

I. The ground is not as solid as we think.
  A. One billion tons of rich soil are washed away annually.
    1. A fertile area the size of Connecticut.
II. Know danger to our natural resources?
  A. Needs are doubling and tripling.
  B. Oil exhausted by 2000 A.D.
  C. Forests cannot keep up with lumber demand.
  D. 19 billion gallons of water lost daily.
III. Shortages of fuel, food, water may affect you directly.
  A. Conservationists warn of increasing shortages.
    1. Less wood, coal, oil mean less fuel.
    2. Evaporation, erosion, sedimentation mean less food and water.
  B. Shortages create higher costs.
  C. Resource depletion spells danger to national defense.
IV. Know how to prevent catastrophe.

Need step

I. Three principles of conservation: economy, renewal, preserving nature's balance.
II. Past disregard.
  A. Metals and oils wasted.
    1. Petroleum exploited.
      a. Eighty-three per cent crude oil unrecovered.
      b. Texas loss of gas exceeded shipments.
    2. Copper mines abandoned.
      a. Water-filled shafts.

        b. Forced to import.
    3. Chase on avoidable coal waste.
  B. Vital conservation ignored too long.
    1. Early settlers.
      a. Cotton fields abandoned.
      b. Vast grasslands denuded.
      c. Over-expanded crop acreages: Dust Bowl.
      d. Timberlands not replanted.
    2. Vicious cycle of spoilage:
      a. Fewer forests meant less soil covering.
      b. Less protection, less water reserve.
      c. Water eroded precious topsoil.
        i. Torrent-eroded gulleys.
        ii. Silt-polluted water.
  C. Interrelation ignored.
    1. Example of Baltimore.
      a. Harbor clogged.
      b. Costly dredging.
    2. Example of Decatur.
      a. Two-million dollar dam.
      b. Capacity lowered 26 per cent.
      c. Unheeded shift to intertilled crops.
        i. Cover crops not planted.
        ii. Erosion greatly accelerated.
      d. Forced greater investments in water supply.
    3. Lake Mead filling with huge sediment deposits.
III. Must observe principles now.

Satisfaction step

I. Threefold program.
  A. River-valley programs.
  B. Reforestation, farming practices.
  C. Scientific research.
II. Programs satisfy "musts."
  A. Valley programs restore balance.
    1. Reforestation restores watersheds.
      a. Watersheds prevent floods, erosion.
      b. Flood-control reduces sedimentation.
    2. Construction of dams.
      a. Prevents flooding.
      b. Maintains water supply.
      c. Furnishes electric power.
    3. Land reclamation.

a. Irrigation.
b. Suitable crop-growing.

B. Modern forestry and farming.
1. Seventy million acres reclaimable—NEA.
2. Improved soil quality.
a. Crop rotation.
b. Proper fertilization.
3. Reforestation: lumber, soil.

C. Scientific research.
1. Efficient extraction and refining.
2. New mines, oil fields.
3. Synthetics.

III. Previous results insure success.
A. Colorado valley benefits.
1. Hoover Dam prevents floods.
2. Water for irrigation.
3. Navigation extended.
4. Four and one-third billion kw.-hrs. of energy.
a. Original costs repaid twice over.
b. Pays Treasury Dept. $290,000 per month.

B. Results of modern farming practices.
1. Yield increased 36 per cent—NEA.
a. More corn—fewer acres.
b. Higher income per acre.

C. Scientific-engineering advances.
1. Film coatings prevent evaporation.
2. Potassium from potash rock.

Visualization step

I. No change—irreparable damage.
A. Industrial decline.
B. Food and water shortages.
C. Weakened economy—reduced resistance to invasion.

II. Threefold program can prevent national catastrophe.

Action step

I. Unified program demands individual cooperation.
A. We don't want shortages, dust storms, floods.
B. We don't want children to be victims of waste.
C. We must provide for future.

II. People must be aware of the problem.

III. Help others understand danger and urgency.

THE TECHNICAL PLOT

When your full-content outline is completed, you should examine it minutely to discover possible gaps or other weaknesses. In making such an analysis, you will find that *a technical plot* of your speech is most helpful. Lay your completed full-content outline beside a blank sheet of paper; and on this sheet, set down symbol for symbol and line for line a statement of the technical devices you have employed in developing your speech plan. Where you have used statistics in the content outline, write the word *statistics* in the outline of the technical plot, together with a brief statement of their functions. In like manner, indicate all of the various forms of support, attention factors, forms of imagery (p. 322), motive appeals, and methods of development.

The outline of the technical plot is a testing device. It can help you determine whether your speech is sound structurally, whether there is adequate supporting material, whether you have overused certain forms of support, and whether the appeals you make are well adapted to the audience and the occasion. Many speeches, of course, do not need to be tested so thoroughly; and experienced speakers often can make this kind of analysis without writing a complete technical plot. For the beginner, however, there is no more effective method of testing the actual structure and technics of his proposed speech. The following sample is a technical plot of the full-content outline developed on pages 298-303.

Sample of a technical plot

OUR PLENTY IS NOT SO PLENTIFUL

Attention step

I. Startling statement of fact.
   A, 1. Statistics to support statement.
II. Rhetorical question, appeal to fear.
   A, B, C, D. Specific instances, novelty and contrast.
III. Statement relating subject to audience.
   A, B, C. Detailed application to audience; vital attention factor.
IV. Summary restatement relating subject to audience.

Need step

(Developed to show need for change)

I. General statement of standards by which situation is to be judged.
   A, B, C. Statements enumerating these standards, based on motive appeals of saving, preservation of the race, organizing, fear.

II. General statement of the need.
  A. Statement relating need to first standard; appeal to saving.
    1. Statement of fact for support.
      a, b. Testimony and statistics referring to specific instances.
    2. Specific instance.
      a, b. Description of effects.
    3. Testimony referring to a specific instance, statistics.
  B. Statement relating need to second standard; appeal to preservation of the race, organizing.
    1. Statement of fact by way of explanation (historical reference).
      a, b, c, d. Examples.
    2. Factual illustration.
      a, b, c. Cause-and-effect sequence to develop illustration.
        i, ii. Further effects for ramification.
  C. Statement relating need to third standard; appeal to organizing, fear.
    1. Factual illustration used as support.
      a, b. Specific instance, statistics as support.
    2. Another factual illustration used as support.
      a. Statement of fact.
      b. Statistics as support.
      c. Statement of fact.
        i. Specific instance as explanation.
        ii. Statistical effect.
      d. Conclusion based on preceding statements.
    3. Additional support, statistics.

III. Summary: restatement of general need.

Satisfaction step

(Developed to secure belief in plan proposed)

I. General statement of proposed plan.
  A. Statement explaining first part of plan.
  B. Statement explaining second part of plan.
  C. Statement explaining third part of plan.

II. General statement that plan meets need in terms of standards which have been set up.
  A. Statement that first part of plan meets third standard; appeal to saving, organizing.
    1, 2, 3. Enumeration of results of projected plan.
    1a, 2a, 2b, 2c. Further effects.
    1b. Futher effect, statistically evolved.
    3a, 3b. Explanation.

B. Statement that second part of plan meets second standard; appeal to saving, preservation of the race.
   1. Testimony, statistics.
   2. Statement of fact as support.
      a, b. Specific methods as explanation.
   3. Explanation of the way plan meets standard.

C. Third part of plan meets first standard; appeal to saving.
   1, 2, 3. Enumeration of projected results.

III. Statement indicating successful operation of plan; appeal to imitation.
   A. Specific instance of successful operation of first part of plan.
      1, 2, 3. Statements of fact for ramification.
      4. Testimony, statistics.
         a, b. Further statistics for additional proof.
   B. Instance of successful operation of second part of plan.
      1, 1a, 1b. Testimony and statistics referring to a specific instance of operation.
   C. Statement projecting success of third part of plan.
      1, 2. Specific instances for ramification.

Visualization step

(Developed by method of contrast; combining negative and positive projections of future conditions)

I. Projection of future conditions with present defects unremedied.
   A. Specific instance of consequence; appeal to saving, fear.
   B. Another specific consequence; appeal to fear, preservation of the race.
   C. A third specific consequence; appeal to patriotism, fear.

II. Projection of future conditions with proposal adopted; appeal to pride, organizing, patriotism.

Action step

I. Statement emphasizing urgency of need.
   A. Specific restatement of present need.
   B. Statement underlining future need; appeal to sympathy and preservation of the race. (Parallel structure of A and B for emphasis.)
   C. Statement foreshadowing appeal to action; restatement of inherent theme of speech.

II. Statement of condition for action to meet the need.

III. Personal appeal for audience action.

OUTLINES FOR ANALYSIS AND PRACTICE

The only way to develop skill in outlining is to examine critically the outlines prepared by other speakers and to prepare outlines of your own. Several problems to provide this kind of practice are suggested at the end of this chapter, and two outlines are also presented here for your study and criticism. Examine them carefully, noting both their good and bad points. Apply to each one the previously designated tests for a good outline—concise phrasing of main points and subpoints, proper subordination, correct indentation, and consistency of symbol usage—and determine whether its structure is clear and its content adequate. The first outline was prepared by Charles C. Higgins at Purdue University for a speech explaining gas-turbine engines to a group of engineering students.

HOW A GAS-TURBINE ENGINE OPERATES

OUTLINE	*TECHNICAL PLOT*
I. Power is the master of time and distance.	Attention step:
A. Today, distance is measured in time units. 1. Last Sunday morning, I rode downtown on a bus in 18 minutes. 2. Later that same day, a P-80 from the Air Show flew the same distance in 8 seconds.	Arouse interest by striking comparison.
B. But speed depends on driving power. 1. Why can the P-80 go so fast? 2. Because of its powerful gas-turbine engine.	Direct attention toward the subject.
II. You engineering students should learn all you can about gas turbines.	Need step:
A. As future engineers, you may need to apply gas-turbine power to the units you design. B. Your personal car or plane may be powered by a gas turbine in the future.	Pointing—the importance of the subject to this audience.
III. Consider the main parts of the gas turbine from front to rear: the compressor, the combustion chamber, and the turbine rotor.	Satisfaction step: Initial summary.
A. The compressor squeezes the air into the combustion chamber. 1. The compressor may have one of two possible arrangements:	Detailed information in space sequence.
a. The centrifugal compressor has a single rotor with blades shaped to take the air in at the center of the rotor and fling it outward into a collector ring connected to the combustion chamber.	Details on first main topic: Use drawings to show difference between two types.
b. The axial compressor uses a number of rotors	

(usually 7 to 11) composed of many windmill-like blades which decrease in size toward the combustion chamber.

i. The air is thus compressed by the large number of blades and the decreasing size of the rotors and blades.

B. The combustion chamber mixes and burns fuel with the compressed air.

Second main topic developed by detailed explanation: Two types shown by diagrams and pictures.

1. Combustion chambers may be arranged in one of two ways:
   a. The centrifugal compressor usually requires a number of small radially arranged chambers which are connected to the collector ring.
   b. The axial compressor feeds the air into a single large combustion chamber, which is the type used when streamlining and weight are most important.
2. Fuel is mixed with the air at the front opening of the combustion chamber.
3. The rear exit of the combustion chamber varies according to the combustion chamber used.
   a. The small radially arranged chambers have individual exits leading to the turbine rotor.
   b. The large combustion chamber of the axial turbine has only one outlet leading to the turbine rotor.

C. The turbine rotor absorbs energy from the hot, expanding gases that come from the combustion chamber.

Third main topic explained in detail: Show two types with drawings.

1. The turbine may have one of two forms:
   a. The turbine rotor is only large enough to drive the compressor if jet propulsion is to be used.
      i. The energy absorbed by the rotor must be small in this case to leave as much for the jet as possible.
   b. The turbine rotor is a very large multistage affair if the power is to be used in driving machines by means of a shaft.
      i. The rotor must be large enough to remove all of the energy possible from the expanding gases.

IV. Remember these things about the gas turbine:

Final summary:

A. The compressor, combustion chamber, and turbine rotor are placed one behind the other in that order.
   1. The compressor packs the air in.
   2. The combustion chamber expands the air.
   3. The turbine rotor absorbs the energy of the expanded air or passes it to the jet.

   Restatement of three main topics.

B. Each component may have one of two internal arrangements.

   Reiterate two alternate types.

C. All three components in assembled form produce the tremendous power of the gas-turbine engine.

   Concluding statement.

The following outline was prepared by Herschel Womble of the University of Denver for a speech to an audience presumed to consist of the directors of a museum. The purpose of the speech was to raise money for an anthropological expedition.

WHY AND HOW TO EXPLORE SOUTH AMERICA

OUTLINE	*TECHNICAL PLOT*
I. Parts of South America have never been explored anthropologically. A. The Highlands of Eastern Brazil comprises the largest blank spot on the map. 1. Inaccessible. 2. Hostile natives. B. Has never been explored by an anthropologist.	Attention step: Direct attention to basic elements of problem; define. Narrow the question. Use historical data.
II. The problem is how to get to the area. A. Highland rivers are hard to navigate by boat. B. There are no roads. C. Native packers offer labor problems.	Need step: Show causes of problem. Show why it exists.
III. An air expedition is the only practicable way to explore this territory. A. Amphibian planes can find landing places in various parts of territory. B. The party could protect themselves. 1. They could carry machine guns and automatic rifles. 2. They could easily fly away if the going was too hot. 3. They would not be in the hands of native crews or porters. C. A great deal of territory could be covered in a short time and at less expense than by other methods.	Satisfaction step: Show that this plan is the best solution; explain the plan. Demonstrate that it removes causes of the problem.

1. Preliminary exploration could be finished in six months.
2. The cost would be $75,000.

D. Other air explorations have succeeded. — Examples of operation.

1. The Southwest has been mapped in this way.
2. Explorers' flights over Yucatan furnish added examples of the effectiveness of this method.

IV. This expedition will bring scientific light to what is now darkness. — Visualization step: Make results more vivid.

A. Native life can be studied.

1. Their language.
2. Their customs.

B. Archeological finds are likely.

1. No doubt some artifacts will be found for the museum shelves. — Project them into future.
2. Possibly we will find something the equal of the Chichen Itzá or Cuzco.

C. The expedition will bring prestige to this museum.

V. Finance this expedition. — Action step: Request definite action: Specific means by which individuals can help.

A. Give all you can from your treasury.

B. Approach all those you are connected with and ask them to make up the difference necessary to put this expedition in the field.

Problems

1. Select three speeches printed in this book, in *Representative American Speeches,* in *The Speaker's Resource Book,* in *Vital Speeches of the Day,* or in some other suitable source. Make a full-content outline of each of these speeches (exclusive of indicating the sources from which the material is drawn or preparing a bibliography). Which of the three speeches was easiest to outline? Which was most difficult? How do you account for this difference? How might the speech which was most difficult to outline be reworked so that it would fall into good outline form more readily?
2. During the next round of speeches in class, try making a key-word outline of each talk as it is given. After the speech, compare your outline with the one the speaker himself drew up.
3. Make a key-word outline of a speech or lecture which you attend with the other members of your class. Compare the various outlines which are thus drawn up and, as a group, work out what you would consider to be the best possible outline of the speech in question.
4. Make a technical plot for each of the speeches outlined in Problem 1 or for three similar speeches. Using the technical plot as a guide, evaluate each

speech on the following factors: (1) adequacy of supporting material, (2) variety of supporting material, (3) use of the factors of attention, (4) use of motives, (5) correctness of subordination.

5. Working with a short outline on some subject with which you are familiar, show: (1) the correct subordination of points; (2) the correct use of indentation; and (3) the correct use of symbols.

6. Rearrange the following points and subpoints in proper outline form; use correct symbols and indentations.

Make Reading Your Hobby
Low cost rental libraries are numerous.
Reading is enjoyable.
It may lead to advancement in one's job.
Books contain exciting tales of love and adventure.
Many paperback books cost only 50 to 75 cents.
People who read books are more successful socially.
Reading is profitable.
One meets many interesting characters in books.
Nearly every town has a free public library.
Through books, one's understanding of men and the world is increased.
The new and stimulating ideas found in books bring pleasure.
Reading is inexpensive.

Speaking assignment

1. Prepare for presentation in class a five- to seven-minute speech on a subject of your choice. As part of your preparation, draw up a full-content outline of your speech and also a complete technical plot. Hand the outline and technical plot to your instructor at least a week before you are scheduled to speak. He will correct these materials and return them to you with suggestions for improvement. Following his suggestions, carefully rewrite both the outline and the technical plot and hand the improved versions to him just before you present your speech.

Suggestions for further reading

A. Craig Baird and Franklin H. Knower, *General Speech,* 3rd ed. (New York: McGraw-Hill Book Company, 1963), Chapter V, "Organization and Outlining."

Charles S. Mudd and Malcolm O. Sillars, *Speech: Content and Communication* (San Francisco: Chandler Publishing Company, 1962), Chapter VIII, "Outlining."

Porter G. Perrin, *Writer's Guide and Index to English,* 4th ed. (Glenview, Illinois: Scott, Foresman and Co., 1965) 47-52, 448-449, 720-723.

Edward D. Re, *Brief Writing and Oral Argument,* 2nd ed. (Dobbs Ferry, N. Y.: Oceana Publications, Inc., 1957).

Paul L. Soper, *Basic Public Speaking,* 3rd ed. (New York: Oxford University Press, 1963), Chapter V, "Outlining the Speech."

John F. Wilson and Carroll C. Arnold, *Public Speaking as a Liberal Art* (Boston: Allyn & Bacon, Inc., 1964), Chapter IX, "Disposition: Outlining."

CHAPTER EIGHTEEN

Wording the speech

An outline sets forth the structure of a speech and the material to be used in supporting that structure, but it does not provide a complete or finished talk. The problem of phrasing the ideas in vivid and compelling language and of making clear and graceful transitions from one point to another still confronts you. We are not concerned in this chapter with your method of preparing a speech for delivery —whether you write it out and memorize it or work it out orally through continued practice (see Chapter 3, pp. 28-30); but we are concerned with the *wording* you finally employ. Therefore, we shall consider some of the principles that underlie the effective use of words and shall offer specific guidance for their selection and arrangement.

ACCURACY OF MEANING

Precise meaning can be expressed only if words are carefully chosen. The man who tells the hardware clerk that he has "broken the hickey on his hootenanny and needs a thing'ma-jig to fit it," expresses his meaning vaguely; but his vagueness is only a little greater than that of the orator who proclaims, "We must follow along the path of true Americanism." The sentiment obviously is to be admired, but just what does this statement mean? Remember that words are only symbols which stand for meanings and that your listener may attach to a symbol a meaning different from the one you intend. *Democracy*, for example, does not mean the same thing to a citizen of the United States that it does to a citizen of Soviet Russia. An *expensive* meal to a college student may seem quite moderate in price to a wealthy man. A mode of travel that was *fast* in 1867 seems painfully slow a century later. The *United States* today is not the same as it was in the days of George Washington—in area, in population, in industry, or even in much of its governmental structure. Nor, for that matter, are all the members of a general class alike: Frenchman A differs from Frenchmen B and C; one Chevrolet may be old and rusty, another is new and shiny. Students of general semantics[1] continually warn us that words in themselves are not objects or qualities or operations, but only *symbols* for these things. Many grave errors in thinking and communication arise from treating words as if they were the actual conditions, processes, or objects to which they refer, and accordingly fixed and timeless in meaning.

If, therefore, you think there is the least chance that your audience may misinterpret what you say, define your words in more concrete or immediate terms.[2] Notice, for example, how Elliott V. Bell in the following passages makes clear what he means by *structural unemployment* and *fiscal policy:*

> "Structural unemployment" is just another name for what we used to call technological unemployment except that it has a broader meaning. It means not merely the unemployment that results when, for example, a textile plant is fitted out with labor-saving machinery and hand-workers are displaced by automation. It also means what happens when the old textile plant in New England is abandoned and the new automated plant is erected in North Carolina. It means what happens when homes and factories switch from coal to oil. Coal miners in West Virginia or Pennsylvania lose their jobs. Even if there are unfilled jobs elsewhere, the miners may not be able or willing to move away and learn new skills. . . .
>
> "Fiscal policy" is a term that is often used and seldom defined. By it I mean all of the taxing, spending, and borrowing operations that the Government conducts—all of the ways in which the Federal Establishment puts money into the national economy or takes money out of it.[3]

A speaker concerned about how his audience may interpret his remarks will, in definitions and elsewhere, choose words which express the exact shade of meaning he intends to convey. Although dictionary definitions are not sure guides to the meaning which any particular listener will attach to a word, they do represent the com-

[1]For a more extended treatment of this subject, see *Language Habits in Human Affairs* by Irving J. Lee (New York: Harper, 1941); *People in Quandaries* by Wendell Johnson (New York: Harper, 1946); *Putting Words in Their Places* by Doris B. Garey (Glenview, Illinois: Scott, Foresman, 1957); and *Words and Things* by Roger Brown (Glencoe, Illinois: The Free Press, 1958).

[2]A discussion of various methods of definition will be found on pp. 379-381.

[3]"Economic Outlook," *Vital Speeches of the Day*, XXVII (June 1, 1961), 499-500.

monly accepted usages stated as precisely as possible. The careful speaker, therefore, will refer to his dictionary constantly to verify or correct his choice of words. He will note and observe in his speech the distinctions dictionaries make among related words, such as *languor, lassitude, lethargy, stupor,* and *torpor.* He may even use a book of synonyms (such as Roget's *Thesaurus*) in an attempt to select words which exactly express his meaning. For example, among the synonyms for the verb *shine* are: *glow, glitter, glisten, gleam, flare, blaze, glare, shimmer, glimmer, flicker, sparkle, flash, beam.* The English language is rich in subtle variations of meaning. To increase the precision of your expression, make use of this variety in your choice of words.

SIMPLICITY

No matter how accurately a word or phrase may express a speaker's meaning, it is useless if the audience cannot understand it. For this reason, expression not only must be exact, but must be clear and simple. "Speak," said Lincoln, "so that the most lowly can understand you, and the rest will have no difficulty." This rule is as valid today as when Lincoln uttered it; and because modern audiences as created by the electronic media are vaster and more varied than any Lincoln dreamed of, there is even more reason for contemporary speakers to follow it. Say "learn" rather than "ascertain," "*after-dinner* speech" rather than "*postprandial* speech," "large" rather than "elephantine." Never choose a longer or less familiar word when a simpler one will do. As the Roman teacher Quintilian said, "Speak not so that you will be understood, but so that you cannot possibly be misunderstood."

In particular, choose words that are short and concrete over those that are longer and more abstract. Herbert Spencer illustrates the importance of this advice in his *Essay on Style* by comparing two sentences:

(1) "In proportion as the manners, customs, and amusements of a nation are cruel and barbarous, the regulations of their penal code will be severe." —How much better to have said—

(2) "In proportion as men delight in battles, bullfights, and combat of gladiators, will they punish by hanging, burning, and the rack."

Billy Sunday, the famous evangelist, has given us another example of the same point:

> If a man were to take a piece of meat and smell it and look disgusted, and his little boy were to say, "What's the matter with it, Pop?" and he were to say, "It is undergoing a process of decomposition in the formation of new chemical compounds," the boy would be all in. But if the father were to say, "It's rotten," then the boy would understand and hold his nose. "Rotten" is a good Anglo-Saxon word and you do not have to go to the dictionary to find out what it means.[4]

Use short words; use simple words; use words that are concrete and specific; use words whose meaning is obvious at once.

APPROPRIATENESS

A third requirement is that your language be appropriate to the subject on which you are speaking and to the situation in which your speech is delivered.

Serious or solemn occasions call for diction that is restrained and dignified; light or joyful occasions, for diction that is informal and lively. Just as you would never use slang in remarks at a funeral service or in a speech dedicating a church or memorial, so you should never phrase a humorous after-dinner speech in a heavy or elevated style. Suit your language to the spirit and tone of the occasion; be dignified and formal when formality is expected and light and casual when informality is called for. The good speaker is one who can sense what the situation requires, and can vary his style accordingly.

IMAGERY

We receive our impressions of the world around us through our senses of sight, smell, hearing, taste, and touch. In order to get an audience to experience the object or state of affairs you are describing, you must, therefore, appeal to their senses. But you cannot punch them in the nose, scatter exotic perfume for them to smell, or let them taste foods which are not present. The only senses through which you as a speaker can reach them *directly* are the visual and the auditory: they can see you, your movements and your facial expressions, and they can hear what you say.

Despite this limitation, however, you can *indirectly* stimulate all of the senses by using language that has the power to produce imagined sensations in a listener, or which causes him to recall images he has previously experienced. The language of imagery falls into

[4]Quoted in *Essentials of Style* by J. R. Pelsma (New York: Crowell, 1924), p. 193.

seven classes, or types, each related to the particular sensation that it seeks to evoke.

THE TYPES OF IMAGERY

The seven types of imagery are:

1. Visual (sight)
2. Auditory (hearing)
3. Gustatory (taste)
4. Olfactory (smell)
5. Tactual (touch)
   a. Texture and shape
   b. Pressure
   c. Heat and cold
6. Kinesthetic (muscle strain)
7. Organic (internal sensations)

Visual imagery

Try to make your audience actually "see" the objects or situations you are describing. Mention size, shape, color, movement, and the relative position of one part or element to another. Notice how C. P. Snow uses visual imagery to emphasize his point that we should help people in the underdeveloped countries "live as long as we do and eat enough." He says:

We are sitting like people in a smart and cozy restaurant and we are eating comfortably, looking out of the window into the streets. Down on the pavement are people who are looking up at us, people who by chance have different colored skins from ours, and are rather hungry. Do you wonder that they don't like us all that much? Do you wonder that we sometimes feel ashamed of ourselves, as we look out through that plate glass?[5]

Auditory imagery

Make the audience hear not only what you say but also the sounds which you are describing. Example:

As we stepped inside the power plant at Niagara, the roar of the mighty cataract was still in our ears, and it was some moments before we could hear any other sound at all. Then we began to hear the steady, high-pitched whine

[5]From "The Moral Un-Neutrality of Science," *Representative American Speeches: 1960-1961*, ed. Lester Thonssen (New York: Wilson, 1961), p. 53.

of the dynamos and, as the men below us moved around, the quiet patting of rubber-soled shoes against cement.

Note that sounds vary in loudness, pitch, and rhythm, as well as in quality. By calling attention to these details, you can create a vivid auditory image.

Gustatory imagery

Help your audience imagine the taste of what you are describing. Mention its saltiness, sweetness, sourness, or its spicy flavor. Observe how Charles Lamb in his "Dissertation upon Roast Pig" describes that delicacy:

There is no flavor comparable, I will contend, to that of the crisp, tawny, well-watched, not over-roasted, *crackling,* as it is well called—the very teeth are invited to their share of the pleasure at this banquet in overcoming the coy, brittle resistance . . . the tender blossoming of fat . . . the lean, not lean, but a kind of animal manna—or, rather, fat and lean so blended and running into each other, that both together make but one ambrosian result . . . too ravishing for mortal taste.

Olfactory imagery

Make your audience smell the odors connected with the situation you describe. Do this not only by mentioning the odor itself but also by describing the object that has the odor or by comparing it with more familiar ones. Example:

As he opened the door of the old apothecary's shop, he breathed the odor of medicines, musty, perhaps, and pungent from too close confinement in so small a place, but free from the sickening smell of stale candy and cheap perfume.

Tactual imagery

Tactual imagery is based upon the various types of sensation that we get through physical contact with an object. Particularly it gives us sensations of *texture and shape, pressure,* and *heat and cold.*

Texture and shape. Enable your audience to feel how rough or smooth, dry or wet, or sharp, slimy, or sticky a thing is. The following example is from H. G. Wells' *The Time Machine:*

While I stood in the dark, a hand touched mine, lank fingers came feeling over my face. . . . I felt the box of matches in my hand being gently disengaged, and other hands behind me plucking at my clothing.

Pressure. Phrase appropriate portions of your speech in such a way that your auditors sense the pressure of physical force upon their bodies: The weight of a heavy trunk borne upon their backs, the pinching of shoes that are too tight, the incessant drive of the high wind on their faces. Example:

As he pulled himself down foot by foot toward the bottom, he felt the water pressing against him until the enveloping squeeze was all that he could stand.

Heat and cold. This is sometimes called "thermal" imagery. Example:

After the night spent with icy spray whipping over me from the prow of the boat, the warmth of the morning sun and the steaming hot cup of coffee which the steward brought me were welcome indeed.

Kinesthetic imagery

Kinesthetic imagery relates to muscle strain and movement. Phrase portions of your speech in such a way that your audiences may feel for themselves the stretching and tightening of their tendons, the creaking in their joints:

Had it been an ordinary trapdoor, we could have pushed it open with no effort at all. As it was, the three of us braced ourselves firmly, but heave and shove as we might, we could not budge it. Our muscles became great hard knots; the sweat stood on our foreheads; it seemed as though our backs would break with the effort. But not a fraction of an inch would it move.

To emphasize his point that the networks had foolishly "been spending their time trying to bat down the arguments" on what to do about broadcasting, LeRoy Collins, Undersecretary of Commerce, made use of kinesthetic as well as other kinds of imagery in the following story:

Once, down in South America, I went to a bullfight. After the bull was turned into the arena, a series of efforts were made to agitate and weaken him.

The picadores came on horseback, driving their barbed sticks into the big neck muscles and causing the bull to charge in pain and frustration.

Then, another group came after him. They were the banderilleros with their torturous barbs. And the bull got more of the same treatment.

Finally, the matador came with a red cape. The slowly exhausting bull charged with all his remaining strength after the elusive man with the sword. But when all his strength was gone and the huge neck muscle had been weakened from the barbs, the bull's head lowered, and the matador could, with apparent ease, drive the keen steel through the shoulder blades to the heart.

Broadcasting is getting a lot of barbs in the neck muscle at this point.

Are we going to exhaust ourselves by thrashing around with defensive movements?[6]

Organic imagery

Hunger, dizziness, nausea—these are a few of the feelings organic imagery calls up. There are times when an image is not complete without the inclusion of specific details relating to these inward feelings. Be careful, however, not to offend your audience by making the picture too revolting. A fine taste is required to measure the detail necessary for vividness without making the image so gruesome that it becomes either disgusting or grotesque. Observe the use made of organic imagery by H. G. Wells:

That climb seemed interminable to me. With the last twenty or thirty feet of it a deadly nausea came upon me. I had the greatest difficulty in keeping my hold. The last few yards was a frightful struggle against this faintness. Several times my head swam, and I felt all the sensations of falling. At last, however, I got over the well-mouth somehow and staggered out of the ruin into the blinding sunlight.

USING IMAGERY

These, then, are the seven types of imagery: *visual, auditory, gustatory, olfactory, tactual, kinesthetic,* and *organic.* Victor Alvin Ketcham called them "The Seven Doorways to the Mind," doorways which the speaker must open with his words if he expects his audience to understand or believe him. As Professor Ketcham pointed out, *people differ in the degree to which they are sensitive to different types of imagery.*[7] The public speaker is wise, therefore, to employ as many types as possible.

In the example which follows, notice how the different types of imagery have been combined to create a vivid picture:

I was lately taken by a friend, with whom I was staying in the country, to a garden party. . . . The day was hot, and I was uncomfortably dressed. I found myself first in a hot room, where the host and hostess were engaged in what

[6]"Speech to the Directors of the National Association of Broadcasters." *Ibid.,* p. 183.

[7]From "The Seven Doorways to the Mind," in *Business Speeches by Business Men,* ed. William P. Sandford and W. H. Yeager (New York: McGraw-Hill Book Company, 1930).

is called receiving. A stream of pale, perspiring people moved slowly through, some of them frankly miserable, some with an air of false geniality, which deceived no one, written upon their faces. "So pleasant to see so many friends!" "What a delightful day you have for your party." Such ineptitudes were the current coin of the market. I passed on into another room where refreshment, of a nature that I did not want, was sadly accepted. And I passed out into the open air; the garden was disagreeably crowded; there was "a din of doubtful talk," as Rossetti says. The sun beat down dizzily on my streaming brow. I joined group after group, where the conversation was all of the same easy and stimulating character, until I felt sick and faint . . . with the "mazes of heat and sound" in which my life seemed "turning, turning." . . . I got away, dizzy, unstrung, unfit for life, with that terrible sense of fatigue unaccompanied by wholesome tiredness, that comes of standing in hot buzzing places. . . . As I went away, I pondered sadly upon the almost inconceivable nature of the motive which could lead people to behave as I had seen them behaving, and resolutely to label it pleasure.[8]

In the speech at the end of this chapter Ann Bogaard also uses imagery to vivify the ideas she develops.

In employing imagery you should be aware of three considerations: (1) the difference between produced and reproduced images, (2) the principle of reference to experience, and (3) the importance of detail in creating accurate and vivid word pictures.

Produced and reproduced images

There are two types of images: one based on the memory of a single experience, the other produced by putting together in a new pattern the details of several different experiences. If I describe the football game which you attended yesterday, I may be able to *reproduce* a fairly complete image of the experience which you had; if, however, I describe a cricket match—a sport which you have never seen—by putting together details of clothing, action, and sound which you have experienced in other circumstances, I can *produce* a new image in your mind. Of the two types, new (or produced) images obviously are the harder to create. In drawing them, take time to picture each part of the object or scene fully and to show exactly how it relates to the whole. When carefully developed, however, produced images can become vivid and can stimulate the imaginations of the listeners almost as well as reproduced ones.

[8]From "Sociabilities," an essay by Arthur Christopher Benson. Printed in *From a College Window* (G. P. Putnam's Sons, N. Y., 1907).

The principle of reference to experience

Words as symbols are effective in direct proportion to the strength of the experiences with which they are associated. Some words create stronger images than others; for example, *wrench* is more vivid than *pull* simply because stronger sensations have been associated with it. For the man who has never seen a *dirigible*, the word creates at best an indistinct picture; you must use language with which he is familiar or make comparisons to experiences which are common to him. Notice, for example, how much more vivid the image becomes when you say that the dirigible is like a "huge, elongated football, painted silver, moving slowly through the air."

The principle of detail

Remember, finally, that while you can speak only one word at a time, a large number of different and detailed sensations normally are received simultaneously. If you are to create a vivid image, you must take time to describe all aspects of an object or event. The importance of details in making ideas vivid has been noted by Barbara W. Tuchman, the historian:

> At a party given for its reopening last year, the Museum of Modern Art in New York served champagne to five thousand guests. An alert reporter for the *Times*, Charlotte Curtis, noted that there were eighty cases which, she informed her readers, amounted to 960 bottles or 7,680 three-ounce drinks. Somehow through this detail the Museum's party at once becomes alive; a fashionable New York occasion. One sees the crush, the women eyeing each other's clothes, the exchange of greetings, and feels the gratifying sense of elegance and importance imparted by champagne—even if, at one and a half drinks per person, it was not on an exactly riotous scale. All this is conveyed by Miss Curtis' detail."[9]

Observe also how the Atlanta editor, Henry W. Grady, used details to create a picture of the defeated Confederate soldier in the following passage from his famous address, "The New South":

> Let me picture to you the footsore Confederate soldier, as, buttoning up in his faded gray jacket the parole, which was to bear testimony to his children of his fidelity and faith, he turned his face southward from Appomattox in April, 1865. Think of him as, ragged, half-starved, heavy-hearted, enfeebled by wounds and exhaustion—having fought to exhaustion—he surrenders his

[9]Copyright © 1965, by Harper's Magazine, Inc. Reprinted from the July 1965 issue of *Harper's Magazine* by permission of the author's agent.

gun, wrings the hands of his comrades in silence, and, lifting his tear-stained and pallid face for the last time to the graves that dot the old Virginia hills, pulls his gray cap over his brows and begins the slow and painful journey.[10]

LOADED WORDS

Many words—even some of the shortest and simplest ones—contain within themselves not only a denotative or dictionary meaning but, in addition, an aura of implied or connotative meaning. Because such words are thus "loaded," they have a strong effect on the reactions of an audience. Observe the different responses that you yourself make to the following: *man, fellow, guy, person, savage, cheapskate, piker, chiseler, sportsman, father, dad, baron, miser, dictator.* Although each of these words denotes a human being, what different types of human beings they suggest and how strongly some of them convey approval or disapproval!

Because of the responses which they can call up, loaded words must be used with caution. When employing them, be sure you can answer these two questions affirmatively: Does the audience understand the meaning I intend to convey? Do I have sound facts and reasoning to support my position so that the words I use are justified? Select words which will add vividness to your speaking, but take care to employ them accurately and fairly.

Meaning derived from associations

Many words become "loaded" as a result of experiences with which they are associated. After the repeal of national prohibition, for example, places where liquor was sold came to be called *taverns* in order to avoid the unpleasant mental image associated with the old saloon. The word *politician* suggests to many people a scheming, dishonest man, making promises which he does not expect to keep and uttering pious platitudes while he secretly accepts illegal pay from "special interests"—a picture repeatedly painted by cartoonists and novelists and by opposing politicians. Yet the intrinsic meaning of the word denotes only one who is occupied in the management of public affairs or who works in the interest of a political party.

Since different people have different experiences, the connotation of a related word may vary greatly, and you must be tactful in adapting it to your particular audience. Shoe clerks, for example, tell a woman: "Madam, this foot is slightly smaller than the other," instead of "That foot is bigger than this one." Observe in the following

[10]Delivered at a New England Society Dinner in New York City, December 22, 1886.

example how Dr. Ernest Tittle, in his description of words as such, uses words freighted with meaningful associations:

> There are colorful words that are as beautiful as red roses; and there are drab words that are as unlovely as an anaemic-looking woman. There are concrete words that keep people awake; and there are abstract words that put them to sleep. There are strong words that can punch like a prize-fighter; and weak words that are as insipid as a "mama's boy." There are warm, sympathetic words that grip men's hearts; and cold, detached words that leave an audience unmoved. There are warm, sympathetic words that lift every listener, at least for a moment, to the sunlit heights of God; and base words that leave an audience in the atmosphere of the cabaret.[11]

Meaning derived from the sound of the word

Some words gain a particular value from the very sounds they contain. Such words as *hiss, crash, rattle, slink, creep, bound, roar* suggest by their sound their exact meaning. The poems of Edgar Allan Poe and of Vachel Lindsay abound in words of this kind—*clanging, tinkle, mumbo-jumbo.* As H. A. Overstreet has said, "There are words that chuckle; words that laugh right out; words that weep; words that droop and falter."[12] A proper appreciation of the sound values of words will help make your speaking clearer and more vivid.

TRITENESS

Words and expressions which are powerful or vivid in themselves may be rendered ineffective and colorless by overuse. A once powerful phrase is stripped of its significance by thoughtless repetition and serves only to display a lack of originality in the person who uses it. Thus, when one says that he "sat down to a sumptuous repast placed on a table loaded with delicacies," he not only is violating the rule of simplicity but is using worn-out phrases as well. The words *gorgeous, fabulous, terrific,* and others have been so overworked that they have lost their original effectiveness. Figures of speech in particular are likely to become trite; avoid such expressions as "slept like a log," "dead as a doornail," and "pretty as a picture." On the other hand, beware of grotesque combinations and mixed metaphors. The speaker who described a dump heap as a "picturesque eyesore" was original but ludicrous, as was the man who remarked that "The years roll on,

[11]From a commencement address by Ernest F. Tittle, delivered at the Northwestern University School of Speech, June 1924. Reprinted in full on pp. 453-461.

[12]From *Influencing Human Behavior* by H. A. Overstreet (New York: Norton, 1925).

drop by drop." Note in contrast the appropriateness of this figurative statement by Justice Learned Hand:

> Liberty lives in the hearts of men and women. When it dies there, no constitution, nor court, nor law can save it.[13]

Note also the strength and freshness of Yale President A. Whitney Griswold's comparison of the free mind and the unfree mind:

> The mind that is unfree, the mind that is possessed, the mind that is indoctrinated or forced does not learn. It copies. Discovery is the true essence of learning. The free mind travels while the unfree simply looks at the maps. The unfree mind locks the doors, bars the shutters, and stays at home.[14]

SLANG

Slang words and phrases may on certain occasions be both acceptable and effective. They can add succinctness and color. In fact, when a slang phrase is inherently precise or vivid, it may eventually become standard usage. Usually, however, slang is only temporary and weak. College slang especially tends to become trite and to substitute one word for a variety of more specific and effective ones. A young woman, for example, is "cool" or "neat," but so is a football game, a chocolate soda, a dance, a class lecture, or a pair of shoes. To use slang for a particular effect is permissible, but to use it merely to avoid the search for more precise words is slipshod and results in weak or meaningless expressions.

CONNECTIVE PHRASES

Unlike written compositions, material which is spoken cannot be divided into units by paragraph indentations or by underlined headings. Instead, the relationships between the points of a speech must be made clear by the wording itself.

Preliminary and final summaries are useful in mapping out for the audience the road you intend to follow and in reviewing your speech at its close. (See Chapter 15, pages 253-254; and Chapter 21, pages 376-379.) But you must also set up signposts as you go along to assist your audience in following you. For this purpose, you will find a

[13]Quoted in a speech "The Bold Go Toward Their Time," by William C. Lang, printed in *Vital Speeches of the Day*, XXVII (March 15, 1961), 333-334.
[14]*Ibid.*

variety of connective phrases useful. The following list contains some of the more common ones:

Not only . . . but also . . .
In the first place. . . . The second point is . . .
In addition to . . . notice that . . .
More important than all these is . . .
In contrast to . . .
Similar to this . . . is . . .
Now look at it from a different angle . . .
This last point raises a question . . .
You must keep these three things in mind in order to understand the importance of the fourth . . .
What was the result of this . . . ? Just this: . . .

Clarity often depends upon the effectiveness of a speaker's connective phrases. Expand your list of such phrases and use them to make easy, smooth transitions from one point to another.

BUILDING A VOCABULARY

In order to choose words that are accurate, clear, appropriate, and vivid, a speaker must have a large and constantly growing vocabulary. Wide reading, close observation of the language used by cultured people, even the systematic attempt to "use a new word every day" —all of these methods are helpful in vocabulary development. It is equally important, however, to put into active use the vocabulary you already possess. Most people know the meanings of ten times as many words as they actually use. Work to transfer the words in your recognition vocabulary to your active vocabulary. Effective speakers are noted not for the large number of words they use but for the skill with which they combine the simple words of the average man's vocabulary to state even complicated ideas vividly and precisely.

SAMPLE SPEECH

Examine the use of language and imagery in the following classroom speech by Miss Ann E. Bogaard, a sophomore at the University of Iowa. How well do you think Miss Bogaard met the criteria of accurate, simple, appropriate, and vivid expression? What criticisms do you have of this speech? What changes, if any, would you make in the development of her central idea? in her choice of words and images?

YOU—A SPONGE?[15]

Ann E. Bogaard

Suppose it's raining outside and you want to collect rain water, so you go out with a ketchup bottle; it's obvious that you're not going to collect much rain. You'd have much better luck with a wide-mouthed jug or even a basin.

This afternoon I'm going to persuade you—NOT to be a ketchup bottle, not even to be an ordinary basin; but I'm going to persuade you to be a sponge in a basin.

All of us are constantly in the "rain" of ideas, impressions, sights, sounds, personalities, and happenings. We are bombarded with these things simply because we are alive and because we are part of a complex world. Now let's get on with specifically what I mean by a "sponge."

A basin is a container that holds something; the world is a basin. A sponge in a basin absorbs the material or the something that the basin contains; *I* am a sponge! Not only do I absorb from my environment, but under the slightest pressure of being squeezed—if I am a real sponge—I will release and give back part of what I absorbed.

The *what* of being a sponge is mainly this: being an individual with an open mind that is flexible and receptive to change—not a mind that is restricted to the narrow dimensions of a bottleneck. Suppose the farmer had been a ketchup bottle, stubbornly resisting the changes in industrialization and mechanization. Where would we be today? But the farmer was a sponge, applying change and progress for the benefit of mankind.

Now that you know what a sponge is, let's ask the question, "Why a sponge?"

There are two basic reasons why I want to be a sponge. The first reason is that by being a sponge, I can benefit myself. I have to live with myself; and,

[15]Presented August 3, 1965. Supplied through the courtesy of Miss Bogaard.

therefore, I want to be fit to live with myself. I exist as a miracle and so do you. If this miracle is going to be a sponge, I must first understand and learn about *me*. I must know myself and to mine own self be true. The second reason logically follows: by being a sponge, others will benefit. Charity, kindness, love, sympathy, and knowledge for and of my brother can lead to nothing but understanding and peace. The oppressed, the downtrodden, and the destitute of this world can *live*, if *I* will be a sponge.

Maybe I've already persuaded you to be a sponge, but I'm not going to stop now. I want you not only to think like a sponge, but to act like a sponge. We've talked about the "what" and "why" of being a sponge; now comes the most difficult part: "how" to be a sponge.

Let's take a few examples and ask a few questions. If the questions seem to prick your conscience a bit, let them. We are all college students; are you a ketchup bottle in class, or a sponge? Most of us are members of a religious community; do you put on your suit of piety for an hour on Sunday morning, or do you wear your religion every day of the week? You are a member of a family; what do you give to your family which helps make "house" a "home," or is home just a place where you eat and sleep?

A sponge is an active participant in life, not just a spectator on the sidelines. He gives of himself, he shows emotion, he expresses himself, and he stands for something! A sponge must be trained to be aware, conscious, and observant, and at the same time be open and receptive.

Being a sponge is an abstract concept—a concept which has no charts, facts, or figures to back it up, but I believe in this concept with all my being. What about you there, standing in the rain? Are you a ketchup bottle? Do you stand there with your umbrella up, shielding and protecting you from the rain? Or is there the possibility that now you'll be a sponge with me?

Problems

1. As an exercise in choosing language that is appropriate for different speech situations, study the following groups of words and decide whether the individual words or phrases are (1) appropriate for any speech situation, (2) appropriate for informal speech situations, (3) appropriate for formal situations:

hoggish, greedy, gluttonous
drunk, intoxicated, soused, inebriated, tight, blotto, pie-eyed
falsehood, whopper, lie, fib, misrepresentation, untruth
crabby, ill-tempered, cross, quarrelsome, grouchy
savory, appetizing, delicious, tasty, scrumptious
laughable, funny, amusing, ludicrous, hilarious, killing
a capricious elderly man, a queer old duck, a nutty old character, an eccentric old man, a strange old fellow, a crazy old geezer

2. List two or more meanings for each of the following words:

fast	right	slip
fair	top	cut
race	hot	dope

Add to this list at least ten other multiple-meaning words.

3. Find a shorter and simpler word to express each of the following:

maintain	designate	culmination
escalate	perturbation	tenacious
partition	holistic	funereal
investigation	tautology	preferential

4. Make a list of ten neutral words or expressions. Then for each word in this list find *(a)* a "loaded" synonym which would cause listeners to react favorably toward the object or idea mentioned and *(b)* a "loaded" synonym which would cause them to react unfavorably toward the same object or idea. (Example: neutral word, "old"; complimentary synonym, "mellow"; uncomplimentary synonym, "senile.")
5. Pick out five "loaded" words or phrases in the speech by Ann Bogaard, pp. 332-333, and indicate whether each carries a favorable or unfavorable connotation. What would be a neutral synonym for each of these loaded terms?
6. Read a recent issue of *Vital Speeches of the Day* to find *(a)* passages that illustrate particularly good word choice (i.e., passages in which the words are accurate, simple, and appropriate), and *(b)* instances of the skillful use of connective words and phrases.
7. Read one or more speeches by each of the following: Edmund Burke, Daniel Webster, Abraham Lincoln, and Adlai Stevenson. Compare the wording in these speeches, giving special attention to *(a)* accuracy of word choice, *(b)* simplicity, *(c)* appropriateness, *(d)* imagery, and *(e)* the use of loaded language.
8. Expand the list of connective phrases given on page 331 until you have twenty or more.
9. Tell what connective phrase you might use *(a)* to join a major idea with a subordinate one, *(b)* a less important idea with a more important one, *(c)* two ideas of equal importance, *(d)* ideas comparable in meaning, and *(e)* contrasting or opposing ideas.
10. Using varied and vivid imagery, describe orally or in writing one of the following:

Sailboats on a lake at sunset
Goldfish swimming about in a bowl
Traffic at a busy intersection
Sitting in the bleachers at a football game in 15° weather
The hors d'oeuvre table at an expensive restaurant

The city dump
A symphony concert

11. List the examples of imagery to be found in Dr. Tittle's address, pages 453-461.

12. Describe orally in class a personal experience or an event you have recently witnessed—for example, a traffic accident, the crucial moment in a basketball game, a memorable meal, big city noises. Employ vivid imagery in an effort to stimulate your listeners to relive this experience or event with you.

Speaking assignment

1. Using either the pattern for a one-point speech as described on pp. 181-186 in Chapter 11 or the entire motivated sequence as described in Chapter 16, write a four- to six-minute speech to be presented from manuscript. Revise the manuscript several times to be sure that (1) the words and expressions you choose are accurate, simple, and appropriate; (2) that wherever possible you have employed live and vivid imagery, (3) that you have used loaded words skillfully but ethically, (4) that you have avoided trite expressions, and (5) that your connective phrases are clear and graceful. In presenting the speech, observe the rules for reading a speech from manuscript as described on pp. 29-30 and 34 in Chapter 3.

Suggestions for further reading

Martin P. Anderson, Wesley Lewis, and James Murray, *The Speaker and His Audience* (New York: Harper & Row, Publishers, 1964), Chapter XII, "Style in Speaking."

Virgil L. Baker and Ralph T. Eubanks, *Speech in Personal and Public Affairs* (New York: David McKay Company, Inc., 1965), Chapter XVI, "Language in Speech."

James I. Brown, *Programmed Vocabulary: Steps Toward Improved Word Power* (New York: Appleton-Century-Crofts, 1964).

Stuart Chase, *Power of Words* (New York: Harcourt, Brace and World, 1954).

Donald K. Darnell, "The Relationship Between Sentence Order and Comprehension," *Speech Monographs*, XXX (June 1963), 97-100.

Rudolf Flesch, *The Art of Plain Talk* (New York: Harper & Row, Publishers, 1946).

J. Middleton Murray, *The Problem of Style* (Oxford University Press, 1925), esp. Chapters I, IV, and VI.

Thomas Nilsen, "The Use of Language," in Horace Rahskopf's *Basic Speech Improvement* (New York: Harper & Row, Publishers, 1965), pp. 318-336.

I. A. Richards, *The Philosophy of Rhetoric* (New York: Oxford University Press, 1936), Chapter III, "The Interinanimation of Words," and Chapter V, "Metaphor."

Herbert Spencer, "The Philosophy of Style," in *Essays on Rhetoric*, ed. Dudley Bailey (New York: Oxford University Press, 1965), pp. 147-172.

William Strunk, Jr., and E. B. White, *The Elements of Style* (New York: The Macmillan Company, 1959).

Gordon L. Thomas, "Oral Style and Intelligibility," *Speech Monographs*, XXIII (March 1956), 46-54.

CHAPTER NINETEEN

Listening: Speaker-audience interaction

By following the principles of speech composition and delivery explained in the preceding chapters, a speaker may do much to increase the effectiveness with which he transmits or communicates his ideas to others. But because communication is a circular rather than a one-way process, its effectiveness also requires activity on the part of the listener.[1]

Basically the listener has three tasks:

1. To translate sound waves into nerve impulses,
2. To recognize these nerve impulses as language symbols, and
3. To assign to each impulse an appropriate sense or meaning.

This, however, is only the barest beginning. If the ideas communicated are to be of maximum service to himself and to the society of which he is a member, the listener also must make a concerted effort to understand what he hears. He must decide whether the speaker's recommendations are useful and his conclusions true. He must judge whether contentions are fairly stated and adequately proved. Finally, if he is to enjoy or appreciate the speaker's ideas, he must relate them to his own standards of taste and discrimination. Because of these varied obligations, the listener has a task just as demanding as that of the speaker; and because communication is a circular process, the ability to listen well is just as important as the ability to speak well.

RESEARCH IN LISTENING

In recent years considerable research has been devoted to the problem of listening; and while there still is a great deal we do not know

[1]For a description of the communication process and its circular nature, see pp. 16-19.

about it, a number of firmly established facts already have emerged. Listening, as we know, is among man's most important activities. Day in and day out, the average person spends far more time listening than he does in the other communicative processes of reading, writing, or speaking. Moreover, just as individuals differ in their ability to read, or to run and to jump, so do they differ in their ability to listen well. Most important of all, however, research has shown that—barring an organic disfunction—listening ability can be improved through properly guided practice, and that any particular act of listening can be made more productive if the listener will bring to it a correct physical adjustment and a proper mental attitude.[2]

THE NATURE OF LISTENING

Just as research has taught us more about listening in general, so has it changed our conception of the listening process. We have been made more conscious of the fact that good listening is not merely a passive soaking up of the speaker's words or arguments, no matter how complete or perfect this assimilation may be. Rather, it is an active effort to derive meaning from all aspects of the communication situation—from the speaker's tone of voice, movements, gestures, and facial expression, as well as from the words he utters. In addition, it includes interpretation and appraisal—a constant and critical consideration of the ideas presented, the materials by which these ideas are supported or explained, the purposes which motivate them, and the language in which they are expressed. In short, good listening is *comprehensive;* but, even more importantly, it is *creative.* Such activity is the listener's positive contribution to the communication act—the role that he plays in the transaction which occurs when the ideas of one person are thoughtfully received and evaluated by another.[3]

THE CHARACTERISTICS OF GOOD LISTENING

Good listening, authorities agree,[4] has two basic characteristics. First, it is purposeful; and, second, it is objective.

[2]See, for example, Colin Cherry, *On Human Communication* (New York: Wiley, 1957), p. 276; Charles E. Irwin, "Motivation in Listening Training," *Journal of Communication,* IV (Summer 1954), 42-44; Paul W. Keller, "Major Findings in Listening in the Past Ten Years," *Journal of Communication,* X (March 1960), 29-38; Paul T. Rankin, "The Importance of Listening Ability," *English Journal,* XVII (October 1928), 623-630.

[3]Ralph G. Nichols and Thomas R. Lewis, *Listening and Speaking* (Dubuque, Iowa: Brown, 1954), p. 1.

[4]See, for example, Ralph G. Nichols, "Factors in Listening Comprehension," *Speech Monographs,* XV (1948), 154-163; Walter W. Stevens, "How Well Do You Listen?" *Adult Education,* XII (Autumn 1961), 42-46.

Purposefulness

The good listener, like the good speaker, has a specific purpose which he wishes to achieve by participating in the communication process. It may be to learn—to acquire new information and points of view; it may be to judge or evaluate the worth of the ideas and arguments presented; it may be simply to enjoy himself. Although one of these purposes is usually primary, good listening often includes all three. Under no circumstances, however, is the good listener passive and indifferent; he has a reason for listening, and therefore approaches the listening situation with a positive rather than a negative attitude. He listens because he wants to, not because he has to.

In order to achieve his purpose, whenever possible the good listener prepares himself in advance for the speech or lecture he is going to attend. He studies the topic to be discussed, finds out what he can about the speaker and his beliefs, and investigates the group or organization by which the talk is sponsored. When he arrives at the place where the speech is to be given, he seats himself where he can see and hear easily, and throughout the program remains alert both physically and mentally. Finally, when the talk is over, he reviews what was said, discusses the ideas with his friends or if possible with the speaker himself, and studies the subject further. In this way, he is able to receive maximum benefit in return for the time and effort he has expended.

Objectivity

Although he has a definite purpose in listening, the good listener does not allow this purpose to affect the objectivity and emotional neutrality which he preserves throughout the listening experience. Instead of judging the probable worth of the speaker's ideas and arguments in advance, he withholds evaluation until the talk is finished; for he realizes that a weak beginning may be followed by a strong ending, and that points which at first may appear trivial or irrelevant take on new meaning and significance when the speaker has further developed them. Above all, he does not make the listening experience an exercise in fault-finding by constantly looking for weak points in the speaker's arguments or gaps in his reasoning. He listens critically, but he also listens sympathetically, realizing that when the talk is over, there will be plenty of time to consider its defects and to answer either orally or in his own mind the points that do not hold up under scrutiny. His purpose at the moment is to derive the greatest possible benefit from the speaker. Toward this end he strives to maintain an open, objective attitude throughout the communicative exchange.

GUIDES TO GOOD LISTENING

As we have already said, listening ability can be improved by practice. Practice, however, will be more profitable if it is based upon a set of proven guides. In the following paragraphs, we will suggest some ways of improving comprehension, appreciation, and evaluation. Actually, all three are involved to some extent in effective listening. For instance, if you were listening to a class lecture, your primary goal would probably be full *comprehension* of the lecturer's remarks. But you would undoubtedly be more likely to achieve that goal if you fully *appreciated* the humorous narratives with which the lecturer enlivened and amplified his points, and if you *evaluated* his ideas carefully by testing their truth and validity against what you had already learned about the subject. However, you will probably understand the total process of good listening better if you consider separately the suggestions for comprehension, appreciation, and evaluation.

Comprehension

Purpose. If your primary purpose in listening is to learn new facts or to understand more clearly terms and ideas which now seem vague or confused to you, begin by focusing on that purpose. This is highly important. As we have already suggested, in order to derive full benefit from a speech, you must approach the listening situation with a clearly defined and properly framed purpose.

Preparation. Next, if the listening experience is an important one —if a semester grade or employment, for example, depends upon it—prepare yourself carefully in advance by (1) reviewing what you already know concerning the subject, and (2) acquiring as much additional knowledge as you can through reading and discussion.

During the speech or lecture itself, do the following:

1. *Identify the speaker's major or leading ideas, and concentrate closely on each as it is expressed.* Every well-composed talk, as we pointed out earlier (pp. 228-231), consists of one or more major ideas and the details of amplification or proof by which these ideas are developed. Unless you take care to identify each major idea as it is stated and to separate it from the developmental material that is associated with it, you may fail to grasp the speaker's dominant thesis or point of view and may carry away from the listening experience nothing more than a confused mass of data.

Besides identifying each major idea as such, you should concentrate closely on each idea as it is stated. Such concentration not only will help you grasp its full scope and significance, but also will increase your chances of remembering it later.

2. *Identify the structure or pattern according to which the major ideas are arranged.* In Chapter 14, various patterns for arranging the major ideas of a speech were described. Ask yourself if the speaker is ordering his material in a time, space, causal, or topical sequence. By ascertaining his pattern and keeping it in mind as his talk develops, you will be able to follow his explanations more easily and to remember his main points more accurately and fully.

3. *Examine critically the details by means of which the major ideas are developed or supported.* As you identify each major idea and observe how it fits into the pattern of the speech as a whole, note also the materials by which this idea is exemplified or supported. What additional light is thrown on the idea by the illustrations or comparisons which the speaker supplies? Does this piece of explanation or that set of statistics point up some implication or inference that you have previously overlooked? Do certain of the speaker's quotations confirm or throw doubt on the idea as originally presented? Are the scope, pertinence, and importance of the idea significantly modified by the supporting data? By asking questions such as these, you will find that your comprehension of the idea and its place in the speech is greatly increased.

4. *Relate the major ideas to your own previous knowledge.* In most instances your understanding will be enhanced if you make an active effort to relate what you hear to what you already know. As each major idea is presented, therefore, put it into the context of your present knowledge. Use the idea to add to that knowledge, or to refine and qualify it. Do not listen, as it were, in an intellectual vacuum, but with a constant awareness of the terms and relationships you already know about. Make the new an active and integral part of the old; do not view it as something different and unrelated.

Appreciation

If the speaker's purpose is to entertain rather than to inform or persuade, your purpose as a listener may be simply to derive enjoyment from his speech. Under such circumstances you usually can increase your pleasure and appreciation by following these suggestions:

1. *Relax physically and mentally.* Sit in a comfortable, relaxed position. In so far as possible, free your mind from other interests and from vexing problems and worries.

2. *Cultivate a receptive attitude.* Do not spoil your pleasure by being too analytical or hypercritical. This does not mean that you

should be completely undiscriminating, but that you should view the speaker in a warm and friendly light and should anticipate with pleasure the talk he is going to present.

3. *Use imagination and empathy.* Instead of holding back, enter into the spirit of the occasion freely and fully. Give your imagination enough play so that you can join with the speaker in reliving the events or experiences he relates. If you can imagine yourself a participant in the situations described, their vividness will be enhanced and your pleasure in the speech will grow accordingly.

Evaluation

When you listen to comprehend, your primary purpose is to understand and remember what the speaker said. When you listen to appreciate, your primary purpose is to enjoy yourself or to be stimulated by the experience. When, however, your primary aim is to judge or evaluate the ideas presented, you must analyze critically not only the ideas themselves but also the evidence and reasoning by which they are supported. You must recognize which appeals are logical or fact-centered, and which are merely emotional; and you must look beneath the flourishes of style or expression to consider the intrinsic worth of the speaker's views.

Therefore, when the purpose of your listening is to judge the value of the ideas or arguments presented, proceed as follows:

1. *Evaluate the speaker's analysis of the problem.* As you listen, ask yourself whether the speaker has recognized all aspects or facets of the problem, and whether he has correctly judged the scope and importance of each. Ask, too, whether the proposal he advocates is a practicable and desirable method of meeting the problem.

2. *Evaluate the speaker's reasoning.* Is the speaker's reasoning sound, or does it contain flaws and fallacies? Does he generalize too hastily from his evidence? Does he advance as causes factors which really are not causes? Are his analogies fair and pertinent?

3. *Evaluate the evidence.* Does the speaker base his views upon facts or does he present unsupported assertions backed only by vivid phrases and a positive or aggressive manner of delivery? If he does present facts, does he do so fairly, or is his evidence partial and biased?

4. *Evaluate the speaker's emotional appeals.* Does the speaker try to make emotional appeals do the work of sound reasoning? Are his appeals justified by the subject and developed with restraint and good taste? Does he seem to be speaking with deep feeling and genuine conviction, or does his manner suggest that he is an opportunist or "rabble rouser"?

5. *Evaluate the speaker's use of language.* Is the speaker more interested in rounded sentences than in solid ideas? Does he try to make language do the work that should be done by facts and figures? Are his recommendations so general that they could mean anything to the listener? Do loaded words and name-calling take the place of valid arguments?

Listening as a student of speech

In addition to comprehending, appreciating, and evaluating a speaker's ideas, you have the special task, as a student of speech, of studying his manner and method. By doing so, you can develop your ability to judge good speaking and at the same time note ways to improve your own speech.

To analyze a speech thoroughly, you would have to consider many points—in fact, nearly all the topics covered in this book. Obviously, that would be a long and difficult task. Begin, therefore, by trying something less comprehensive. Each time you hear one of your classmates speak, center your attention on only a few closely related aspects of his talk—preferably on those matters which have been stressed in the particular assignment he is fulfilling. Later you will be able to make your analyses more complete, and to judge more points at a time.

A convenient guide to use in criticizing speeches is the chart of common errors printed inside the back cover of this book. Remember, however, that your critical analysis of a speech should not be limited merely to pointing out defects or weaknesses. Both you and the speaker can learn much about good speaking by giving attention also to the strong points of the speech.

If your instructor asks you to evaluate one of the speeches given in class, divide your criticism into three steps. *First,* point out what was good about it. Even the very worst efforts usually have something good about them. *Second,* tactfully suggest how the speech might have been improved. *Third,* indicate one or two specific things the speaker should work on the next time.

Do not hesitate to offer thoughtful criticism when it is invited. In a situation where all are trying to learn together, the objective comments of fellow students are seldom offensive. Learn also to accept criticism with good grace. After all, hearing and heeding the comments of your hearers is one of the best ways to improve your speaking.

Problems

1. Make an objective analysis of yourself as a listener. Note both your strong and your weak points. Are you objective in your attitude? Are you able to pay

close attention over a period of time? Are you usually alert physically and mentally? When you have completed your analysis, lay out a specific program for improving your listening ability. In doing this, consult again the suggestions for constructive listening set forth in this chapter and examine such additional sources as your instructor may suggest.

2. Attend a speech or lecture held on the campus or in the community. Attempt to determine (1) the speaker's specific purpose, (2) his major headings, and (3) the nature and adequacy of his supporting material. Compare your findings with those of others in your class who attended the same talk.

3. List various factors in the physical surrounding which make good listening difficult—distracting noises, uncomfortable temperature or humidity, unsatisfactory seating arrangements, etc. Tell what you as a speaker or program chairman can do to eliminate such problems.

4. At the next speech or lecture you attend, seat yourself where you can observe closely the reactions of various members of the audience as they listen to the ideas presented. How many appear to listen intently throughout the talk? How many seem to let their attention wander or not to listen at all? What cues or signs of a physical nature lead you to conclude that some persons are listening more intently or more consistently than others?

5. During a round of classroom speeches, make an outline of each talk as it is delivered. Pay particular attention to setting off the major ideas from the supporting material and to following the rules for proper subordination. (See Chapter 17, "Making an Outline.") As a test of your listening ability, compare your outlines with those drawn up by the speakers themselves.

Speaking assignment

1. Present a five-minute speech to inform on one of the topics suggested at the close of Chapter 21, or on a similar topic. Prepare a short list of true-false or completion-type questions covering your most important ideas. At the conclusion of the speech, have the members of the class take this test as a measure of their listening skill. (You may, if you wish, include questions on the structure or development of the speech as well as on the ideas presented.)

Suggestions for further reading

Martin P. Anderson, Wesley Lewis, and James Murray, *The Speaker and His Audience* (New York: Harper & Row, Publishers, 1964), Chapter 7, "The Role of Listening in Communication."

Wendell Johnson, *Your Most Enchanted Listener* (New York: Harper & Row, Publishers, 1956).

Paul W. Keller, "Major Findings in Listening in the Past Ten Years," *The Journal of Communication*, X (March 1960), 29-38.

Ralph Nichols, "Do We Know How to Listen? Practical Helps in a Modern Age," *Speech Teacher,* X (March 1961), 118-124.

Ralph Nichols, "Factors in Listening Comprehension," *Speech Monographs,* XV (1948, No. 2), 154-163.

Ralph Nichols and Leonard A. Stevens, *Are You Listening?* (New York: McGraw-Hill Book Company, 1957).

Doris Niles, "Teaching Listening in the Fundamentals Course," *Speech Teacher,* VI (November 1957), 300-304.

Wesley Wiksell, "The Problem of Listening," *Quarterly Journal of Speech* (December 1946), 505-508.

PART FIVE

BASIC TYPES OF SPEECHES

The speech to entertain

The speech to inform

The speech to convince

The speech to stimulate

The speech to actuate

Answering questions and objections

CHAPTER TWENTY

The speech to entertain

Many public speakers have given little or no attention to the speech to entertain; and consequently, when they attempt one, they only succeed in boring their audiences. On the surface, developing and presenting a good speech to entertain would seem easy, but this is far from the fact. Much practical experience, as well as a knowledge of certain principles and methods, is necessary if you intend to prepare and present a genuinely entertaining speech.

A common conception is that the speech to entertain must be funny, and certainly humor is a basic element in many speeches of this kind. Indeed, a sizable section of this chapter pertains to forms of humor. But it would be a misconception to hold that only humorous speeches are entertaining. Admittedly, they are popular with audiences; but speeches about travel experiences or about unusual people or events may also be highly entertaining. In fact, nearly anything that would provide interesting conversational material for the audience you are addressing may be appropriate content for a speech to entertain, because the purpose of such a presentation is not to impart a basic understanding of a subject but merely to provide a pleasant diversion.

Whether diversion is provided through humor or through novelty, it is definitely not confined to the speech to entertain, but may be equally appropriate in other types of speaking situations. For example, audiences that have been fatigued by a long program preceding a speech may require an abundance of entertainment along with the more serious discussion. Remember, therefore, that the suggestions offered here can be applied to other kinds of speeches, as well as to the speech to entertain.

TYPICAL SITUATIONS FOR SPEECHES TO ENTERTAIN

Speeches of entertainment are given on many and varied occasions, including: (1) *Club meetings.* Organized groups—religious, social, and political—may arrange sessions that are frankly for the purpose of diversion and amusement, and may include speeches. (2) *Dinners.* The after-dinner speech is undoubtedly the most common type of entertaining speech. Certainly it is the best known, the most abhorred when poorly done, and the most enjoyed when cleverly presented. (3) *Parties.* Social occasions, such as anniversary celebrations and reunions, sometimes offer the opportunity for an entertaining speech. When a gathering is to be large, a special program including speeches to entertain is frequently arranged.

THE PURPOSE: TO ENTERTAIN THE AUDIENCE

Even when your principal purpose in speaking will be to provide entertainment, it is often desirable to inject at least one serious idea or thought into your speech. Froth alone can become tiresome and may seem trivial. Underlying your humor, therefore, there may well be something a little more substantial—some sentiment of loyalty or appreciation for the group addressed, or a glance at the more serious side of the subject discussed. Similarly, speeches based upon novelty or adventure should contain serious elements if they are to be truly absorbing. These substantial or sobering elements, however, must never be allowed to predominate; they must be used only to provide a contrast to the entertainment.

SOME CHARACTERISTICS OF DELIVERY AND CONTENT

Remember that you want your audience to have a good time and that you cannot encourage enjoyment in others unless your manner suggests that you yourself are enjoying the situation. Be genial and good-natured—this is of great importance—but beware of appearing as though you were forcing merriment. Do not put on the sickly grin of the boy who vowed that the more he was thrashed the harder he would laugh. On the other hand, stay clear of the scowling determination of the overzealous reformer. As Mr. Dooley, a character created by Finley Peter Dunne, put it, "Let your spakin' be light and airy." Be quick and alert, lively and animated; above all, don't let your speech drag. Over three centuries ago, Milton expressed the proper mood for a speech to entertain in these lines:

. . . bring with thee
Jest, and youthful jollity,
Quips and cranks and wanton wiles,
Nods and becks and wreathéd smiles . . .
Sport that wrinkled care derides,
And laughter holding both his sides,
Come, and trip it as ye go,
On the light fantastic toe. . . .[1]

What you say ought to reflect the same mood as your delivery. Lightness, good humor, novelty, the spirit of fun—these are the elements of which the entertaining speech is built.

Be optimistic. This is not the place to unload your troubles, to be argumentative, or to paint a dark picture of the future—unless, of course, you are obviously doing it in jest. Be light hearted and let the troubles of tomorrow take care of themselves.

Avoid a complicated arrangement of ideas. Don't make your audience strain to understand you. Develop your speech around one or two simple ideas that can be grasped easily. Be very sure, however, that these few points have in them something novel, provocative, or original.

Sprinkle stories and illustrations liberally throughout your speech. Don't rely on "canned" jokes. Humorous anecdotes and tales of your own experiences or the adventures of someone else will serve best to illuminate your ideas and should be used generously. Unless you are clever at turning phrases, avoid too much discussion between your illustrations and descriptions; let one story lead naturally into another, each serving to bring out the theme around which your speech is built. But see that your tales are to the point; never "drag them in by the heels."

SOME USES AND FORMS OF HUMOR

Since humor is appropriate in many types of speeches on all kinds of occasions, the public speaker should learn to use it effectively. Reaction to humor, you will have observed, ranges all the way from the inward chuckle to the loud guffaw. You do not have to make your

[1]From "L'Allegro" by John Milton; lines 1-4, 7-10.

listeners roar with laughter, but at least try to loosen them up to the point of smiling. There are a number of ways to do this, but fundamental to all of them are a spirit of fun on the part of the speaker and an ability to see and portray the incongruity of situations, events, and ideas. It is *things out of their expected order* which cause us to laugh. A huge man on a big horse is not funny, but the same man astraddle a small, balky donkey is likely to bring a smile to the face of even the most matter-of-fact person.

But, you may ask, how can a speaker put into practice this principle of sensing and portraying the incongruous? He can begin by familiarizing himself with some of the characteristics of humor in order to understand its possible impact upon an audience. What is comic or witty can be analyzed in many different ways, but the public speaker may find it useful to note briefly some of the various forms in which humor manifests itself.[2] Characteristically, these forms include:

1. Exaggeration or overstatement.
2. Puns or plays on words.
3. Poking fun at authority or dignity.
4. Irony.
5. Burlesque or parody.
6. Unexpected turns.
7. Unusual or eccentric traits of people.

[2]Among the many collections of anecdotes and humor which may be of interest and use to the student speaker are Jacob M. Braude's *Speaker's Encyclopedia of Stories, Quotations, and Anecdotes* (Prentice-Hall, Englewood Cliffs, N.J., 1964); various compilations by Bennett Cerf, including *The Laugh's on Me* and *Laugh Day* (Doubleday, Garden City, N.Y., 1959 and 1962); *10,000 Jokes, Toasts, and Stories*, edited by Lewis and Faye Copeland (Doubleday, Garden City, N.Y., 1965); Maxwell Droke's *Speaker's Handbook of Humor* (Harper & Row, N.Y., 1956); William R. Gerler's *Executive's Treasury of Humor for Every Occasion* (Parker, West Nyack, N.Y., 1965); *The Best Jokes of All Time and How to Tell Them* by George Q. Lewis and Mark Wachs (Hawthorn Books, N.Y., 1966); *The World's Funniest Offbeat Humor* (Paul B. Lowney, Seattle, Wash., 1966); *New Speaker's Treasury of Wit and Wisdom* and *A Dictionary of Wit, Wisdom, and Satire* by Herbert V. Prochnow and Herbert V. Prochnow, Jr. (Harper & Row, N.Y., 1958 and 1962).

Among the numerous magazines and periodicals which carry witty sayings, entertaining anecdotes, and human interest stories are *Saturday Review, Reader's Digest, The New Yorker, Saturday Evening Post, Changing Times, Diner's Club Magazine, The American Legion Magazine, Farm Journal, Time, Newsweek, Coronet, Pageant,* and *Look.* Similar material will also be found in the press reports, editorial pages, and feature sections of such newspapers as *The New York Times, The Chicago Tribune, The Chicago Daily News, The St. Louis Globe-Democrat, The Los Angeles Times,* and *The Garden City (N. Y.) Newsday.* A number of the examples in this chapter have been adapted from items found in these newspapers, magazines, and books. To pinpoint the precise origin of a pun, joke, or anecdote is often difficult if not impossible; but in those instances where it has been possible to make note of the source, this has been done.

Exaggeration or overstatement

Often you can add humor to your speech and at the same time put your point across to the audience by a skillful use of exaggeration or overstatement. For example, a sadly underpaid worker cryptically complained to his tight-fisted boss: "I'm so underpaid I'm the only man I know who can cash his pay check on the bus." *(St. Louis Globe-Democrat.)* Pride of ancestry is a frequent prompter of overstatement. A well-to-do society matron was inordinately fond of tracing her lineage back to William the Conqueror. After listening patiently and at some length, a skeptical friend interrupted sarcastically, "Actually, I suppose your ancestors were with Noah on the Ark." "Certainly not," retorted the dowager disdainfully. "My family had a boat of its own."

Exaggeration is, of course, the basis of humor in many "tall tales." In *The Jokeswagen Book*, edited by Charles Preston, there is the instance of the distinctly different Texan who preferred to drive a Volkswagen instead of a Cadillac. An affluent colleague asked scornfully if the Volks was air-conditioned. "No," shrugged the Texan, "but I always keep a couple of cold ones in the refrigerator." And Harry Karns *(Garden City, N.Y., Newsday)* calls attention to the enterprising photographer who took a picture of the mythical monster of Scotland's Loch Ness. He swirled down over the creature and shot the photo from his flying saucer.

Puns and plays on words

"Show me a squirrel's home," says the punster, "and I'll show you a nutcracker's suite." ("Trade Winds," *Saturday Review.*) Frequently, laughter may be provoked by using words which have a double or extended meaning or which sound like other words with a different meaning. John Ciardi describes a girl as "certainly the best idea any boy has had to date."[3] And you have probably heard of the human cannonball who informed the proprietor of the circus that he had decided to retire from the act. "But you can't quit now," protested the disconcerted owner. "After twenty years—where would I ever find another man of your caliber?"

Sometimes, to give punch to the pun, the speaker may embroider the build-up a bit. Consider, for instance, the high cost of living. The soaring price of meat has put the finer cuts beyond the reach of many a family budget, and countless cost-conscious wives have had to invent innumerable ways to cook what is euphemistically called "ground beef." One harried husband insists that his mate has pre-

[3]*Saturday Review*, October 8, 1966, p. 16.

pared hamburger in so many different ways—and disguised it so ingeniously—that every night at dinner his four hungry children peer suspiciously at the meat course and solemnly intone, "How *now*, ground cow?" And finally there is the lenient lexicographer who defines a *braggart* as one who enters all conversations "feat" first, but adds that even though most of us cannot boast of moving mountains, we still may have to throw an occasional bluff.

Poking fun at dignity or authority

People like to see someone take a dig at those who are on top and, even more, at those who mistakenly think they are. It is human nature to resent insincerity or affectation and to enjoy pricking the balloon of pomposity. Cornelia Otis Skinner tells of a giddily garrulous countess who, in trying to impress the French actor Lucien Guitry, burbled, "You know, I simply talk the way I think." "Yes," replied Guitry wearily, "but more often."[4] A story making the rounds in political circles involves Sargent Shriver when he was handling both the Peace Corps and the Poverty programs. Paul Bell, head of the Corps' office in Central America, sent Shriver a memo asking him to approve the nomination of a Washington attorney to direct activities in Guatemala. Not knowing the lawyer and uncertain of his qualifications, Shriver returned Bell's request with a pointed question: "What does your man know of Guatemala?" Equally pointed was Bell's second memo to the millionaire administrator: "Very little, Sarge. But what do you know about poverty?" Politicians have, of course, always been fair game for jokesters. Senator Leverett Saltonstall describes a New England town meeting which was being held to consider the purchase of a chandelier. A venerable citizen stood up to protest the expenditure. "In the first place," he said, "there ain't one of us that can spell it. In the second place, there ain't nobody here that can play it. And in the third place, we need a new light fixture a whole lot more than we need a chandelier."[5]

There are times when this form of humor is neatly reversed, and the dignitary or "authority" turns the barb back upon the belittlers or fun-pokers, thus delivering the climactic *bon mot* himself. Eugene Exman relates the incident of a farewell dinner given in honor of a crusty, cantankerous British publisher who, at seventy, was about to retire. There were the usual testimonial speeches; and the old fellow's associates, overjoyed at the prospect of his departure, outdid each

[4]Cornelia Otis Skinner. *Elegant Wits and Grand Horizontals* (Boston, Mass.: Houghton Mifflin, 1962), p. 117.

[5]Walter Trohan, "Washington Scrapbook," *The Chicago Tribune*, November 20, 1966, p. 11.

other in voicing elaborate—but insincere—praise. When the moment came for the aged gentleman to acknowledge the empty accolades, he rose, gazed shrewdly around at the assembled guests, and innocently remarked, "I had no idea I was held in such high esteem. I shall stay on."

On occasion, the public speaker may find it useful to poke fun at his *own* dignity. In addressing a graduating class at the University of Iowa, W. Willard Wirtz, Secretary of Labor, commented that "commencement speakers have a good deal in common with grandfather clocks: standing usually some six feet tall, typically ponderous in construction, more traditional than functional, their distinction is largely their noisy communication of essentially commonplace information."

Irony

Say something in such a way that the opposite meaning—or at least a very different one—is clearly implied. A striking example can be seen in the title of Adlai Stevenson's speech "A Funny Thing Happened to Me on the Way to the White House" (pages 365-367). Its irony was especially significant to listeners who, a few weeks earlier, had heard him concede defeat in the 1952 election, when with a heavy heart he had said he was like the boy who had stubbed his toe: "too big to cry . . . but it hurt too much to laugh." Here, as is so often the case, ironic reaction represented one of the key ingredients of humor—the triumph of the objective viewpoint over subjective gloom.

In fact, underlying nearly all irony is an element of disappointment, disillusionment, or difficulty. Sam Levenson, humorist, lecturer, and author of *Everything but Money*, warns parents: "Insanity is hereditary. You can get it from your children." It may have been one of these parents who, while struggling with his income-tax forms, ruefully complained that under the "new math," 2 and 2 sometimes make 22 and added that the new mathematics has obviously been invented for figuring out the "new economics." (Harry Karns.) The perennial Old Grad philosophizes that a class reunion is "where you get together to see who is falling apart." (Roger Allen in *The Grand Rapids Press.)* And an astute geriatrician declares that *age* is something that makes antiques worth more—and people less.

Often, great wits have used irony to impale their enemies or make their listeners squirm. Obviously that kind of ironic thrust has no place in the speech to entertain, when your purpose is to create good humor in your audience. Avoid trying to be clever at the expense of someone else, and invariably include yourself among the victims of adversity, perplexity, or absurdity to whom you wryly refer.

Burlesque or parody

The chief characteristic of burlesque consists of treating absurd situations seriously or serious situations absurdly. Matty Simmons tells what happened when two middle-aged society women—overfed, overdressed, and overexpansive—met on a street in fashionable Palm Beach. One pointed to the enormous gem glittering at her throat and gushed grandly, "My dear! This is the world-famous Plotkin diamond." "I've heard of the Hope diamond," exclaimed her dazzled and envious friend, "and the curse that goes with it. I've also heard of the Koh-i-noor diamond. But of the Plotkin diamond—never." "Not only is this one of the biggest and most expensive diamonds in the world," persisted its proud possessor, "but it has its own curse that goes along with it—Mr. Plotkin!"[6]

A frequently used variation of burlesque is the *parody* or *take-off* on an idea or situation which is ordinarily treated with seriousness. A sense of incongruity can be developed by describing absurdities in the dignified language usually reserved for serious subjects, or by treating minor problems as if they were complicated and important. Despite the fact that nearly every eligible teen-ager is clamoring to enroll in an institution of higher learning, public relations officials continue to feel compelled to describe their colleges and universities in the most glowing and utopian terms. According to prevalent press agentry, the ideal college ought to be both rural and urban, both small and large, and stand upon a hill near a river or a lake—from which eminence it can look fondly back upon the traditions of a glorious past and eagerly forward to the experimental joys of the future. In parodying this picture, the late president of Vermont's Bennington College, William Carl Fels, wrote of his institution as follows: "It is a small, rural, private, experimental women's college of high quality which emphasizes the development of the individual. It shares the cultural advantages of New York, Boston, and Montreal. Its hill is moderately high. From it on a clear day, you can just see, beyond the toilet-paper factory, the historic Walloomsac River flowing northward away from Williamstown, where there is a small, rural, private, experimental college of high quality for well-rounded men."[7]

Unexpected turns

Lead your audience to believe that you are going to say the normal or anticipated thing; then say the opposite—or at least that which your listeners could not possibly expect. Paul Lowney tells of a man who

[6] *Diner's Club Magazine*, May 1965, p. 23.

[7] From *The Columbia University Forum*, II (Spring 1959), 41.

was bitten by a dog and was later informed by the physician that he had rabies. The victim snatched pencil and paper and began to scrawl rapidly. The doctor, hoping to reassure him, said soothingly, "Don't worry about making out your will. I'll pull you through." "This isn't my will," snapped the man. "It's just a list of the people I'm going to bite."[8] In the Soviet Union, where the unexpected seems to occur but rarely, they are telling this story: When Stalin realized he was dying, he summoned his successor, Khrushchev, clutched his hand, and whispered conspiratorially, "I've prepared two letters. When you find yourself in hot water over domestic difficulties, open the first one. When you're in real trouble—when your enemies are plotting against you and demanding your life's blood—open the second." Later, when Nikita found himself in the throes of an economic crisis, he opened the first letter. It read: "Blame everything on me." Khrushchev promptly denounced Stalin as a murderer and a tyrant. In 1964, when the bitter struggle for power raged anew and the big showdown came in the Kremlin, Khrushchev opened Stalin's second letter. Its pointed instruction: "Prepare two letters." (Matt Weinstock in *The Los Angeles Times.)* Equally illustrative of the unexpected twist is the comment of the fashion designer who declared, "Nothing can replace the modern swimsuit—and it practically has." Or the coed who insisted: "What I really want is to be swept off my feet by someone I can dominate."

Repartee that is truly witty is a genuine rarity; but when it does occur, it is almost sure to hinge upon a sudden or unexpected turn of phrase. Marshall McLuhan, widely heralded for his authorship of *The Gutenberg Galaxy* and *Understanding Media* and for his trenchant but not always closely connected comments on modern communication, recently lectured on these matters at Kendall College. In introducing the "Media Man," Charles Benton, president of Encyclopaedia Britannica, Inc., referred to one of the lecturer's books as "a string of pearls without the string." Retorted McLuhan, "Pearls are a great deal harder to come by than string."[9]

Unusual or eccentric traits of people

Describe some person's idiosyncracies, or illustrate peculiarities which seem to be characteristic of certain classes of people. It has been said, for instance, that a politician is a man with an answer for everything—and everybody. Asked at a press conference what he thought of the proposal to limit to one quart the amount of liquor

[8]*The World's Funniest Offbeat Humor* (Seattle, Washington: Paul B. Lowney, 1966).

[9]Virginia Kay, "Dateline Chicago," *Chicago Daily News,* November 25, 1966, p. 25.

American tourists may bring back from foreign countries, an Illinois senator replied, "I'd make it a pint. We have a big distilling industry in my state, and it pays a million dollars a day in revenue tax." "But, Senator," his questioner protested, "foreign countries don't have pints." "Then let them buy pint bottles from us," countered the politician. "We also have a big glass-making industry in my home state."[10]

The traits, trials, and triumphs of children provide a limitless source of humor. The *Associated Press* recently carried the report of the floor nurse in a Salt Lake City hospital. She was trying to speak via the intercom to a patient in the children's ward—a youngster who had never been hospitalized before and was unfamiliar with the electronic device. After several attempts failed to produce an answer from the child's room, the nurse spoke rather firmly, "Answer me, Jimmy. I know you're there." A few seconds later, a tiny, quavering voice responded, "Wh-what do you w-want . . . Wall?"[11] From Dorchester, England, *United Press International* relayed this story of a child's-eye view of a tonsillectomy: "When they wheeled me into this big room, I saw two lady angels, all dressed in white. Then two men angels came in. One of the men angels looked down my throat and said, 'Lord! Look at this child's tonsils!' And the Lord looked and said, 'My heavens! I'll take them out at once!' "[12]

Somewhat more precocious, perhaps, was the six-year-old who had just completed his first day in the second grade at a very progressive school. At dinner that night, the boy abruptly asked his parents, "What is sex?" Startled, the mother and father managed to stammer out a somewhat involved explanation of the birds and the bees. The puzzled youngster pulled a school questionnaire from his pocket and asked, "But how am I going to put all that information in this tiny little square marked 'Sex'?" This may have been the same youth who, when he became a high-school student, was asked by his exasperated teacher if he ever listened to the voice of conscience. Came the reply: "I don't know. What channel is it on?" (Earl Wilson.)

Mothers and little old ladies, too, have endearing and enduring charms for an audience. Florence Horner tells this story about her mother. "While others were busy at various household activities of debatable importance, my mother began washing walls. 'Well,' she announced to the rest of the family at suppertime, 'I've got four walls done and a little start on the ceiling.' We craned our necks dutifully,

[10]From *The Chicago Tribune*, July 4, 1965, p. 7.

[11]As reported in *Reader's Digest*, June 1966, p. 171.

[12]*Reader's Digest*, March 1966, p. 158.

and there on the gray ceiling, spelled out in spick-and-span white, was the message: 'HELP!'"[13]

Many young people of college age are getting married these days, and they seem to undertake the financing of the combined marital and educational ventures with a courage that borders on the breathtaking. *Changing Times, The Kiplinger Magazine*[14] recently carried a story illustrating this point. The mother of a married coed was asked by a neighbor how the newlyweds were getting along. "Oh, they're ecstatically happy," the mother declared with pardonable pride. "They've just returned from a month in Nassau, and they've leased a new apartment. My daughter's buying all new furniture for it, of course. And as soon as she and her husband are settled, they're going to buy a car." "Goodness," exclaimed the neighbor, "your son-in-law must be doing awfully well!" "He certainly is," agreed the mother. "He's getting straight A's."

In the foregoing pages we have described only a few of the many ways in which the incongruities and absurdities of life can be presented adeptly and meaningfully. Your ability to use the humorous, the novel, and the exciting in your speeches depends in large measure upon your ability to see the contrasts, the inconsistencies, and the incompatibilities of people and events around you. Watch the unexpected and strange things that happen. Often the little mishap of word or action before you speak will furnish you with spontaneous bits of humor and human interest. And if you don't take your speech too seriously—if you throw off your cares and proceed to enjoy the experience—even as you speak you will probably think of appropriate quips, novel touches, and exciting anecdotes you can introduce.

ORGANIZATION OF THE SPEECH TO ENTERTAIN

A speech to entertain may be organized in a number of ways, but there are two methods which have proved helpful to beginning speakers. The first is to employ the pattern for the one-point speech, as described in Chapter 11; and the second is to burlesque the entire motivated sequence.

Using the pattern of the one-point speech

When you use this method, your speech will consist of a series of illustrations, anecdotes, or humorous contrasts following one another

[13] *Reader's Digest*, January 1966, p. 98.
[14] October 1965, p. 35.

in rapid order. Each item, however, should refer in some way to one central idea. For the one-point type of organization, this simple step-by-step procedure will prove practical:

1. Tell a story or give an illustration.
2. Point out the essential idea or point of view expressed by it, and around which you intend to unify the details of your speech.
3. Follow with a series of additional stories and illustrations, each of which amplifies or illuminates this central point. Arrange these items so as to maintain a balance of interest or humor. Avoid grouping all of the funniest or most appealing material in one spot, and particularly beware of a letdown at the end. Save an especially striking, humorous, or novel anecdote for the last.
4. Close with an unusual restatement of the central idea which you have elaborated or illuminated. At this point also bring in whatever serious or sobering statement you may wish to make.

By developing your speech in this way, you not only will entertain your audience but also will make it easy for them to remember the ideas in your talk. "A Case for Optimism," on pages 360-362, follows this one-point pattern, as do "The Babies" by Mark Twain and "A Toast to Sir Thomas Lipton" by George Ade in the list of *Speeches for Collateral Study*, page 371.

Burlesquing the entire motivated sequence

When you use this second method of organizing a speech to entertain, the structure of your talk will contain all five steps of the motivated sequence; but most of the steps will burlesque those steps as used in serious persuasion.

Attention step. Begin your speech in one of four ways: refer to the occasion; allude to some recent humorous incident; poke fun at the chairman (do not, however, be mean or vicious; make it obvious that you are not serious); or tell a story or anecdote. Then in some way relate the beginning of your speech to the rest of the speech.

Need and satisfaction steps. Either present a serious problem (such as the difficulties of making income meet expenditures), but exaggerate the seriousness of it beyond all proportions, and then offer an absurd solution or show how the actual solution is absurd; or present an absurd problem (such as the danger caused by brushing one's teeth with an electric toothbrush), detail a number of fictitious stories illustrating it, then launch into an equally preposterous method of solving this problem. Incorporate a series of amusing or unusual anecdotes to amplify the incongruity.

Visualization step. By adding a more exaggerated picture of the conditions, heighten the absurdity already developed in the preceding steps.

Action step. Close your speech swiftly by burlesquing an exorbitant demand for action, by telling a story to illustrate the irony of your argument, or by summarizing the "vital" points in your speech. Make this final touch short and amusing.

A good example of a speech that burlesques the motivated sequence is Will Rogers' "Settling the Corset Problem of This Country," on pages 362-364.

Two final cautions: First, *don't talk too long.* Nothing spoils humor so much as dragging it out. Bring your speech to a point; illuminate that point brilliantly for a moment; then sit down. Unless you are the only speaker, five or ten minutes ought to be your limit. Second, *be sure your humor is in good taste.* If it leaves a sting or a feeling of embarrassment or shame, you will not create good feeling.

SAMPLE SPEECHES

A CASE FOR OPTIMISM[15]

Douglas Martin

I'm sure you have heard the verse that runs:

'Twixt optimist and pessimist
The difference is droll:
The optimist sees the doughnut,
The pessimist, the hole.

Poem embodying analogy used as opening

The longer I live, the more convinced I am of the truth of this poem. Life, like a doughnut, may seem full, rich, and enjoyable, or it may seem as empty as the hole of a doughnut. To the pessimist, the optimist seems foolish, but who is

Statement

[15]Based in part on material taken from *Friendly Speeches* (Cleveland: National Reference Library).

foolish—the one who sees the doughnut or the one who sees the hole?

Somebody else pointed out the difference between an optimist and a pessimist this way: An optimist looks at an oyster and expects a pearl; a pessimist looks at an oyster and expects ptomaine poisoning. Even if the pessimist is right, which I doubt, he probably won't enjoy himself either before or after he proves it. But the optimist is happy because he always is expecting pearls.

Analogy

Pessimists are easy to recognize. They are the ones who go around asking "What's good about it?" when someone says "Good morning." If they would look around, they would see *something* good, like the merchant did whose store was robbed. The day after the robbery, a sympathetic friend asked about the loss. "Lose much?" he wanted to know. "Some," said the merchant, "but then it would have been worse if the robbers had got in the night before. You see, yesterday I just finished marking everything down 20 per cent."

Anecdotes

There is another story about a shoemaker who left the gas heater in his shop turned on overnight and upon arriving in the morning struck a match to light it. There was a terrific explosion and the shoemaker was blown out through the door almost to the middle of the street. A passerby who rushed up to help inquired if he were injured. The shoemaker got up slowly and looked back at the shop which by now was burning briskly. "No, I ain't hurt," he said, "but I sure got out just in time, didn't I?"

Some writers have made fun of that kind of outlook. You may recall the fun Voltaire made of optimism in *Candide:* "Optimism," he said, "is a mania for maintaining that all is well when things are going badly." A later writer, James Branch Cabell, quipped: "The optimist proclaims that we live in the best of all possible worlds; the pessimist fears this is true."

Testimony pro and con

These writers, I suppose, couldn't resist the urge to make light of optimists, but I, for one, refuse to take *them* seriously. I like the remark by Keith Preston, literary critic and journalist, "There's as much bunk among the busters as among the boosters."

Optimism, rather than the cynicism of Voltaire, is the philosophy I like to hear preached. There was a little old lady who complained about the weather. "But, Melissa,"

Illustrations

said her friend, "awful weather is better than no weather." So quit complaining, I say, and start cheering; there is always something to cheer about. And quit expecting the worst. An optimist cleans his glasses before he eats his grapefruit.

Give in to optimism; don't fight it. Remember the doughnut and, as Elbert Hubbard advised: Restatement

As you travel on through life, brother,
Whatever be your goal,
Keep your eye upon the doughnut
And not upon the hole.

The following speech was given by Will Rogers at a banquet of the Corset Manufacturers of America at the Waldorf-Astoria Hotel in New York City. Note that it includes all five steps of the motivated sequence, each step a burlesque of serious persuasion.

SETTLING THE CORSET PROBLEM OF THIS COUNTRY[16]

Will Rogers

Attention Step

There has been an awful lot of fashion shows and all their by-products held here in New York. All the out-of-town buyers from all over have been

[16]Reprinted from Wilbur D. Nesbit, *After Dinner Speeches* (Chicago: Reilly and Lee, 1927), p. 197 ff.

here. So, on behalf of New York City, I had to help welcome them at their various banquets. There was the Retail Milliners' big fashion show at the Astor Ballroom where they showed 500 hats and me. Some of the hats were just as funny looking as I was.

Well, I settled the Hat-and-Dress business to the satisfaction of everybody but the Milliners. So the next night at the Commodore Hotel I mingled with those Princes of Brigands, the Leather and Shoe men, and later I want to tell all you people just how they operate. For we never paid more for our shoes and were nearer barefooted than we are today, so don't think that I am bought off this week by those pasteboard highbinders: it's only that I want to talk to the ladies today.

During this Reign of Indigestion I was called on to speak to the Corset Manufacturers. Now that only shows you what a degrading thing this after-dinner speaking is. I want to get out of it in a few weeks and back to the movies.

This speaking calls on a fellow to learn something about articles that a self-respecting man has no business knowing about. So that's why I'm going to get away. If a man is called on to tell in a public banquet room what he knows about corsets, there is no telling what other ladies' wearing apparel he might be called on to discuss. So me back to the morals of Hollywood before it's too late.

Need Step

I am, at that, mighty glad to appear at a dinner given by an essential industry. Just imagine, if you can, if the flesh of this country was allowed to wander around promiscuously! Why, there ain't no telling where it would wind up. There has got to be a gathering or a get-together place for everything in this world, so, when our human bodies get beyond our control, why, we have to call on some mechanical force to assemble them and bring back what might be called the semblance of a human frame.

These Corset Builders, while they might do a whole lot to help civilization, are a tremendous aid to the eyesight. They have got what you would call a Herculean task, as they really have to improve on nature. The same problem confronts them that does the people that run the subways in New York City. They both have to get so many pounds of human flesh into a given radius. The subway does it by having strong men to push and shove until they can just close the door with only the last man's foot out. But the Corset Carpenters arrive at the same thing by a series of strings.

Satisfaction Step

They have what is known as the Front Lace. This is known as a One-Man Corset. Now the Front Lace can be operated without a confederate. By judiciously holding your breath and with a conservative intake on the diaphragm, you arrange yourself inside this. Then you tie the strings to the door knob and slowly back away. When your speedometer says you have arrived at exactly 36, why, haul in your lines and tie off.

We have also the Side Lace that is made in case you are *very* fleshy, and need two accomplices to help you congregate yourself. You stand in the middle, and they pull from both sides. This acts something in the nature of a vise. This style has been known to operate so successful that the victims' buttons have popped off their shoes.

Of course, the fear of every fleshy lady is the broken corset string. I sat next to a catastrophe of this nature once. We didn't know it at first, the deluge seemed so gradual, till finally the gentleman on the opposite side of her and myself were gradually pushed off our chairs. To show you what a wonderful thing this corseting is, that lady had come to the dinner before the broken-string episode in a small roadster. She was delivered home in a bus.

They have also worked out a second line of control, or a place to park an extra string on the back. You can change a string now while you wait, and they have demountable strings.

Visualization Step

Now, of course, not as many women wear corsets as they used to, but what they have lost in women they have made up with men. When corsets were a dollar a pair, they used to be as alike as two Fords. A clerk just looked you over, decided on your circumference and wheelbase, and handed you out one. They came in long boxes, and you were in doubt at first if it was a corset or a casket.

Nowadays, with the Wraparound and the Diaphragm-Control, and all those things, a corset manufacturer uses more rubber than a tire company.

Action Step

Men have gone down in history for shaping the destinies of nations, but I tell you this set of Corset Architects shape the destinies of women, and that is a lot more important than some of the shaping that has been done on a lot of nations that I can name offhand.

No statesman or diplomat of recent years has been better known for his wit than the late Adlai Stevenson. On December 13, 1952, he delivered to the Gridiron Club in Washington this speech in which he commented humorously upon the first of his two unsuccessful campaigns for the Presidency:

A FUNNY THING HAPPENED TO ME ON THE WAY TO THE WHITE HOUSE[17]

Adlai Stevenson

A funny thing happened to me on the way to the White House!

The fact was, of course, that the General[18] was so far ahead we never even saw him. I was happy to hear that I had even placed second. But no one will say, I trust, that I snatched defeat from the jaws of victory.

Which reminds me that four years ago, occupying the seat I occupy tonight, was another great governor[19]—excuse me, the governor of another great state—some say the second greatest state in the Union. What just happened to me had just happened to him. In fact, it had just happened to him for the second time.

But did he despair? He did not. He said to himself—if I may take a newspaper man's license and tell you what a man says to himself—he said: "If I cannot be president myself, I can at least make somebody else president." Which, blast his merry heart, he proceeded to do. Look at him now. He's as contented as the cat that swallowed the canary, or should I say, the Cabinet.

At that Gridiron dinner just four years ago, the newly elected governor of Illinois[20] sat down there with you common people—which reminds me that I

[17]Reprinted by permission of Harold Ober Associates, Inc.

[18]President Dwight D. Eisenhower.

[19]Governor Thomas E. Dewey of New York, unsuccessful Republican candidate for President in 1944 and 1948.

[20]Stevenson had been elected governor of Illinois in November 1948.

rather enjoy talking over your heads—at last! I was happy and carefree and had nothing to worry about; nothing except the organization of a new Administration to clean up the state of Illinois after the long years of the usual Republican misrule.

I, a Democrat, had just been elected governor by the largest majority ever received in Republican Illinois. And here I am, four years later, just defeated by the largest majority ever received in Democratic America.

I had not planned it that way. I had wished to continue as governor of Illinois, there to erect a shining temple of administrative purity and political probity. But the gods decreed otherwise—after meeting in the Chicago Stockyards.[21] Mindful of the Chinese maiden's philosophical acceptance of unwanted and aggressive attentions, I concluded to accept my fate gallantly and joyfully.

Now I content myself that it is all for the best. After all, didn't Socrates say that the duty of a man of real principle is to stay out of politics? So you see I'm delighted that the sovereign people have put an even higher value on my principles than I did.

I am happy that almost 27 million voted for me. I was a little baffled by the emergence of that word "egghead" to describe the more intelligensiac members of that lunatic fringe who thought I was going to win. I am happy to note you have refrained from saying of the eggheads that the yolk was on them.

I enjoyed the campaign—in spots. There were times, I confess, when I was afraid I wouldn't die, times when I felt I wouldn't do it to a dog. Let me add, by the way, that, like every red-blooded American patriot, I own a dog.[22] It was not a campaign contribution. And I think the General would say to me that there are times when he wishes he was in my shoes—you see I had them fixed.[23]

As to my future: Well, there are those like the man who changed the sign on his car after the election from "Switched to Stevenson" to "Switched, Bothered and Bewildered," who feel that I should devote my classic talents to the welfare of mankind by frequent talking.

Then there is another smaller group who insist that God and/or the election has appointed me the scourge of the Republican Party. And finally there is the much smaller group that feels that it is not wholly unworthy or improper to earn a living. My sons are numbered in the latter group.

But despite anything that you may have read or written, there are some plans of action that I have definitely rejected. I have declined an invitation to become

[21]Site of the 1952 National Democratic Convention.

[22]In a speech defending himself from charges of having received unreported campaign funds, Richard Nixon, the Republican candidate for Vice-President in 1952, referred poignantly to his dog Checquers.

[23]A widely circulated photograph of Stevenson with his legs crossed showed a hole in the sole of one of his shoes.

president of the National Association of Gagwriters. And I will not go into vaudeville. It is equally definite that I will not become manager of the Washington Senators—I mean Clark Griffith's, not Mr. Taft's.

I have great faith in the people. As to their wisdom, well, Coca-Cola still outsells champagne. They may make mistakes. They do sometimes. But given time they correct their mistakes—at two- or four-year intervals.

I have faith in the people—and in their chosen leaders: men of high purpose, good will and humble hearts, men quite prepared to stand aside when the time comes and allow even more humble men to take over.

Some of the most enjoyable works of the American humorist Mark Twain are the speeches to entertain which he delivered at banquets and on other public occasions. The speech reprinted below was presented at the Seventy-first Annual Dinner of the New England Society, held in New York City in 1877. Appropriately enough, it deals with a subject of much concern to New Englanders—the weather.

THE NEW ENGLAND WEATHER[24]

Mark Twain

I reverently believe that the Maker who made us all makes everything in New England but the weather. I don't know who makes that, but I think it

[24]Reprinted by permission of Chamberlain & Willi, Trustees of the Estate of Samuel L. Clemens.

must be raw apprentices in the weather-clerk's factory who experiment and learn how, in New England, for board and clothes, and then are promoted to make weather for countries that require a good article, and will take their custom elsewhere if they don't get it.

There is a sumptuous variety about the New England weather that compels the stranger's admiration—and regret. The weather is always doing something there; always attending strictly to business; always getting up new designs and trying them on the people to see how they will go. But it gets through more business in spring than in any other season. In the spring I have counted one hundred and thirty-six different kinds of weather inside of four-and-twenty hours. It was I that made the fame and fortune of that man that had that marvelous collection of weather on exhibition at the Centennial, that so astounded the foreigners. He was going to travel all over the world and get specimens from all the climes. I said, "Don't you do it; you come to New England on a favorable spring day." I told him what we could do in the way of style, variety, and quantity. Well, he came and he made his collection in four days. As to variety, why, he confessed that he got hundreds of kinds of weather that he had never heard of before. And as to quantity—well, after he had picked out and discarded all that was blemished in any way, he not only had weather enough, but weather to spare; weather to hire out; weather to sell; to deposit; weather to invest; weather to give to the poor.

The people of New England are by nature patient and forbearing, but there are some things which they will not stand. Every year they kill a lot of poets for writing about "Beautiful Spring." These are generally casual visitors, who bring their notions of spring from somewhere else, and cannot, of course, know how the natives feel about spring. And so the first thing they know, the opportunity to inquire how they feel has permanently gone by.

Old Probabilities has a mighty reputation for accurate prophecy, and thoroughly well deserves it. You take up the paper and observe how crisply and confidently he checks off what today's weather is going to be on the Pacific, down South, in the Middle States, in the Wisconsin region. See him sail along in the joy and pride of his power till he gets to New England, and then see his tail drop. *He* doesn't know what the weather is going to be in New England. Well, he mulls over it, and by and by he gets out something about like this: Probable northeast to southwest winds, varying to the southward and westward and eastward, and points between, high and low barometer swapping around from place to place; probable areas of rain, snow, hail, and drought, succeeded or preceded by earthquakes, with thunder and lightning. Then he jots down this postscript from his wandering mind, to cover accidents: "But it is possible that the program may be wholly changed in the mean time."

Yes, one of the brightest gems in the New England weather is the dazzling uncertainty of it. There is only one thing certain about it: you are certain there is going to be plenty of it—a perfect grand review; but you never can tell which end of the procession is going to move first. You fix up for the drought; you leave your umbrella in the house and sally out, and two to one you get drowned. You make up your mind that the earthquake is due; you stand from under, and take hold of something to steady yourself, and the first thing you know you get struck by lightning. These are great disappointments; but they can't be helped. The lightning there is peculiar; it is so convincing, that when it strikes a thing, it doesn't leave enough of that thing behind for you to tell whether—Well, you'd think it was something valuable, and a Congressman had been there. And the thunder. When the thunder begins to merely tune up and scrape and saw, and key up the instruments for the performance, strangers say, "Why, what awful thunder you have here!" But when the baton is raised and the real concert begins, you'll find that stranger down in the cellar with his head in the ash-barrel.

Now as to the *size* of the weather in New England—lengthways, I mean. It is utterly disproportioned to the size of that little country. Half the time, when it is packed as full as it can stick, you will see that New England weather sticking out beyond the edges and projecting around hundreds and hundreds of miles over the neighboring states. She can't hold a tenth part of her weather. You can see cracks all about where she has strained herself trying to do it.

I could speak volumes about the inhuman perversity of the New England weather, but I will give but a single specimen. I like to hear rain on a tin roof. So I covered part of my roof with tin, with an eye to that luxury. Well, sir, do you think it ever rains on that tin? No, sir; skips it every time.

Mind, in this speech I have been trying merely to do honor to the New England weather—no language could do it justice. But, after all, there is at least one or two things about that weather (or, if you please, effects produced by it) which we residents would not like to part with. If we hadn't our bewitching autumn foliage, we should still have to credit the weather with one feature which compensates for all its bullying vagaries—the ice-storm: when a leafless tree is clothed with ice from the bottom to the top—ice that is as bright and clear as crystal; when every bough and twig is strung with ice-beads, frozen dewdrops, and the whole tree sparkles cold and white, like the Shah of Persia's diamond plume. Then the wind waves the branches, and the sun comes out and turns all those myriads of beads and drops to prisms that glow and burn and flash with all manner of colored fires, which change and change again with inconceivable rapidity from blue to red, from red to green, and green to gold—the tree becomes a spraying fountain, a very explosion of dazzling jewels; and it stands there the acme, the climax, the supremest possibility in art or nature, of bewildering, intoxicating, intolerable magnificence. One cannot make the words too strong.

Problems

1. Identify the various forms of humor used in the sample speeches on pages 360-369.
2. Listen to three of the more popular comedy programs on television and compare the types of humor that are employed. In what respects are the same methods or devices used to get laughs? What, in each case, seems to be unique about the program? To what extent are humorous effects dependent on the personality of the "star" and upon the particular way in which he delivers his lines? By watching these programs what may the public speaker learn *not to do* when giving a humorous talk?
3. Consider the following topics for entertaining speeches:

   You can't take it with you.
   How to swallow a pill.
   What this country really needs——.
   Gentlemen prefer blonds—and brunettes and redheads.
   There's many a slip 'twixt the cup and the lip.
   Professors I have known.
   Campus traditions in the year 2000.
   My solo flight in an automobile.

   For which of these topics would you recommend the one-point method of organization? For which would you recommend a burlesque of the motivated sequence? Why?
4. List three advantages of introducing humorous or entertaining material into speeches on serious subjects. Then list three dangers which must be avoided when doing this. Explain each advantage and danger briefly.
5. It is frequently said that the single most important rule to observe when presenting a humorous speech is to be sure that the audience laughs *with* you and not *at* you. Explain this rule and tell why it is important. How may the speaker see to it that he is laughed *with* rather than *at*?

Speaking assignment

1. Prepare and present a four- or five-minute speech to entertain on one of the following topics, on one of the topics listed in Problem 3 above, or on a similar topic of your choice. Either use the one-point pattern of organization, or burlesque the motivated sequence as explained in this chapter. Work particularly for a light and amusing style and manner of delivery. Exaggerate ideas as much as you like, inject quips and anecdotes, and poke fun at others, but also be certain of two things: (1) that your humor is relevant to the central idea of the speech and is in good taste, and (2) that in poking fun at people, you are not cruel or malicious.

   Life in the army (at camp, on the farm).
   The art of "reaching" for the check.

Seeing our friends at the zoo.
Measuring up to a too-good first impression.
Counting sheep and other sleep-inducing devices.
Rediscovering Tom Swift (or other fictional character).
Parkinson's Law works in colleges, too.
Out of step with the "in" crowd.
Love at first sight.

Speeches for collateral study[25]

1. George Ade, "A Toast to Sir Thomas Lipton," in Wilbur D. Nesbit, *After Dinner Speeches* (Chicago: Reilly and Lee, 1927), p. 180 ff.

2. Robert Benchley, "The Treasurer's Report," in *Benchley Beside Himself*, 3rd ed. (New York: Harpers, 1943), p. 193 ff.

3. Edward C. Elliott, "The Qualifications of a College President," in W. N. Brigance, *Classified Speech Models* (New York: Crofts, 1928), p. 305 ff.

4. Cornelia Otis Skinner, "A Toast from the Ladies of America," in Charles Hurd, *A Treasury of Great American Speeches* (New York: Hawthorn Books, 1959), p. 311 ff.

5. Mark Twain (Samuel L. Clemens), "The Babies," in Nesbit, *After Dinner Speeches*, p. 108 ff.

Suggestions for further reading

George Campbell, *The Philosophy of Rhetoric*, ed. Lloyd Bitzer (Carbondale: University of Southern Illinois Press, 1963), pp. 8-32, "Of Wit, Humor, and Ridicule."

Max Eastman, *Enjoyment of Laughter* (New York: Simon and Schuster, Inc., 1936).

Wilma Grimes, "The Mirth Experience in Public Address," *Speech Monographs*, XXII (November 1955), 243-255.

Kenneth G. Hance, David C. Ralph, and Milton J. Wiksell, *Principles of Speaking* (Belmont, California: Wadsworth Publishing Company, Inc., 1962), Chapter XV, "Speaking to Entertain."

Stewart Harral, *When It's Laughter You're After* (Norman, Okla.: University of Oklahoma Press, 1962).

Ralph A. Micken, *Speaking for Results* (Boston: Houghton Mifflin Company, 1958), pp. 198-199, "To Make an After-Dinner Speech."

Willard Hayes Yeager, *Effective Speaking for Every Occasion* (New York: Prentice-Hall, Inc., 1940), Chapter X, "How to Make Entertaining Speeches."

[25]The speeches for collateral study listed here and in following chapters are selected principally from books of collected speeches because they contain a variety of speech types and because they are found in nearly every college library. Many other excellent examples of these speech types may, of course, be found elsewhere. Some of the listed speeches overlap into other classifications besides the one under which they are named; their subsidiary function, as well as the primary one, should be observed in reading them.

CHAPTER TWENTY-ONE

The speech to inform

An important function of speech is to provide man with a means of communicating knowledge. Through speech one person is able to give others the benefit of his learning and experience. In this chapter we shall discuss how to inform clearly, interestingly, and meaningfully.

TYPES OF INFORMATIVE SPEECHES

Informative speeches take many forms. Three forms occur so frequently, however, that they merit special mention: (1) *Oral reports*—scientific reports, committee reports, executive reports, and similar informational accounts. Experts who engage in special research announce their findings. Committees carry on inquiries and report the results to the organization of which they are a part. Teachers, representatives of fraternal organizations, and businessmen attend conventions and later report to others the information they have obtained. (2) *Oral instructions*—class instructions, job instructions, and instructions for special group efforts. Teachers instruct students in ways of preparing assignments and performing experiments. Supervisors tell their subordinates how a task should be carried out. Leaders explain to volunteer workers their duties in a fund-raising drive or a cleanup campaign. For convenience, such instructions are often given to a group of persons rather than to single individuals and, even when written, may need to be accompanied by oral explanations. (3) *Informative lectures*—luncheon club lectures, class lectures, and lectures at meetings, study conferences, and institutes. People often are invited to share information or knowledge with groups interested in receiving it. Many informative talks are given each week before businessmen's luncheon clubs and women's study groups. Instructors present lectures daily on every college campus, and visiting speakers appear before church groups, conventions, and business and professional institutes.

THE PURPOSE: TO SECURE UNDERSTANDING

As you will recall from the discussion in Chapter 7, the main purpose of a speech to inform is to make certain that the audience understands clearly and fully the ideas presented. Hence, you should not view such a speech as an opportunity to parade your knowledge. You should not try to see how much ground you can cover in a given time; rather, you should try to help others grasp and remember the essential facts or ideas you present.

But while its primary purpose is to teach, an informative speech need not be dull and dry. Because people absorb information more easily when it interests them, a secondary purpose of such a speech is to make your information interesting to your audience. Be sure, however, that this secondary purpose is really secondary. Too often a speaker rambles from one interesting point to another without specifically relating them to each other or to his central theme. Remember that your principal duty is to make the conclusions of your report clear, to have your instructions understood, or to ensure a proper grasp of the content of your lecture.

THE MANNER OF SPEAKING

The manner in which you deliver an informative speech will depend almost entirely upon your subject and your audience. In general, talk slowly enough to be understood and rapidly enough to hold interest. Too fast a rate will confuse your listeners; too slow a rate will put them to sleep. The more difficult the information is to grasp, the more slowly you should proceed; but on the first sign of inattention, speed up a little.

CHARACTERISTICS OF CONTENT

Clear organization is the first essential. To be sure your speech is organized clearly, remember the following rules: *(a)* Do not have too many main points. If possible, reduce your ideas to three or four principal topics, and then group the remaining facts *under* these main headings. *(b)* Make clear the logical relation between your main points. Keep moving in the same direction; don't jump back and forth from one point to another. *(c)* Make your transitions obvious. As you pass from one main topic to the next, let your audience know about it. In a discussion of several different sports, for example, if you start to talk about baseball, say so definitely; or your hearers may think that you are still talking about football. If necessary, enumerate your points, "First, second, third," etc.

Use concrete data; don't be abstract. As the second essential, your speech not only must have a clear structure but must also be meaty. There are, of course, many different ways of presenting facts; but, above all, present them clearly and strikingly. Two cautions need to be kept in mind: *(a)* In your concern for accuracy of detail, do not sacrifice clarity. Nearly every rule has exceptions, but do not endanger your listeners' understanding of a rule by an excessively detailed discussion of the exceptions. As we said when treating statistics (see pp. 166-169), present figures in round numbers in order that the smaller digits may not prevent a comprehension of the larger one. Say "a little over two million" rather than "2,001,397." If extreme accuracy is essential, as in a financial statement or engineering survey, accompany your speech with a written report in which the detailed figures and facts are presented. *(b)* Use charts, graphs, and printed material whenever appropriate and helpful. Your audience will often understand a point better if they can see it at the same time they are hearing it. A diagram of a machine makes its operation easier to explain; columns and pied circles render proportions clearer; drawings and photographs may speak a hundred words. (At this point, review the discussion of visual aids, pp. 172-178.)

Avoid dullness by the occasional use of humor and of figures of speech. There is a limit to any person's capacity for absorbing facts. Recognizing this, the wise speaker uses vivid phrasing and includes occasional bits of humor to enliven, humanize, and enrich his factual materials.

Connect the unknown with the known. People learn new things by associating them with what they already know. If you are talking to a group of physicians, for example, compare the facts you are presenting to objects, procedures, or situations with which they are familiar because of their profession. An educator talking to a group of manufacturers on the problem of higher education presented his information in terms of *raw material, casting, machining, polishing,* and *assembling.*

ORGANIZATION

First of all, remember that in a speech to inform, you must not develop your major points too rapidly or sketchily. You must lead the thoughts of your listeners rather than force them. Nor can you expect your listeners to fill in the gaps with information they do not have. Moreover, instead of plunging into the middle of your subject, in most instances you will need to prepare your listeners' minds for what you are going to say. To do this, you must first gain their *attention* and show them why they *need* to know about your subject.

Attention step

When you are sure that the subject of your speech is of interest to the audience, you usually can attract attention simply by referring to your theme. But when your listeners are not vitally concerned with the subject or are not aware of its importance to them personally, you may have to use a startling statement, an unusual illustration, or one of the other proven methods for catching attention at the beginning of a speech (see pp. 241-251).

Need step

Although it should be short, the need step in a speech to inform is exceedingly important. Informative speakers often fail because they assume that their listeners are waiting to seize the "pearls of knowledge" which their speeches contain. Unfortunately, this is not always the case. You must show your audience that the information you are to present is valuable to them—that it is something they need to know or even to act upon. If you suggest how your information will help them get ahead, save money, or do their work more quickly and easily, they will be more ready to listen.

Develop the need step of the speech by including these elements:

1. *Statement.* Point out the importance of the subject and the need to be better informed upon it.
2. *Illustration.* Present one or more stories or examples which illustrate the importance of the need or demonstrate its significance and timeliness.
3. *Reinforcement.* Provide as many additional facts, figures, or quotations as are required to make the need convincing and impressive.
4. *Pointing.* Show how your subject directly relates to the interests, well-being, or success of your hearers. Point out, in effect: "This vitally concerns *you* because . . ."

There are times, of course, when the information in your speech is not of a practical or workaday variety. When this is the case, you can use the factor of suspense and build your need step on curiosity. Most people like to find answers to interesting problems or to understand curious or unusual facts. Take advantage of this trait by outlining a situation that contains mysterious elements and suggesting that you are about to make the mystery clear. A noted chemist, for example, began a speech by telling of an unusual murder case. He made his audience wonder who the guilty man was and then proceeded to show how, through the use of certain chemical tests, the man was identified and convicted.

Satisfaction step: the information itself

Having captured the attention of your audience and shown them why they "need" the information you are about to present, you are ready to offer the information itself. This is done in the satisfaction step—the step in which you answer or "satisfy" the need you have created.

Select and arrange your points systematically. The satisfaction step usually is the longest part of a speech to inform, and may comprise from three fourths to nine tenths of the whole. In this step you must exercise the greatest care to make clear your organization of ideas and materials, for nothing is quite so confusing as information presented in a careless, unsystematic, or improperly related manner.

Review the methods of selecting and arranging the main points of a speech as described in Chapter 14, and follow faithfully one of the plans there suggested. The *time sequence*, you will recall, arranges items in the order in which they actually occurred; the *space sequence* uses location or position as the basis for arrangement; the *cause-effect sequence* explains conditions and then the forces that created them, or mentions the forces and then points to the conditions they will produce; the *problem-solution sequence* describes a difficulty and the method or methods that may be used to correct it; and the *special topical sequence* utilizes the special divisions by which a certain sort of information customarily is cataloged.

Develop your satisfaction step in three phases. In order to unify the presentation of your information and to make it easier to understand and follow, you often will want to begin with an *initial summary*, provide the *detailed information*, and briefly restate or sum up your main points in a *final summary*.

1. *The initial summary.* As its name suggests, the initial summary consists of a brief enumeration of the main points you expect to cover. Its purpose is to help your hearers grasp the plan of your discussion as a whole, as well as see the relation which one idea bears to another. For example, if you were going to explain the organization of athletic activities on your campus, you might begin your satisfaction step in this way:

> In order to make clear the organization of athletic activities on our campus, I shall discuss, first, the management of our intercollegiate sports; second, our intramural program; and third, the class work in physical education.

Note how such a preview was used by Whitney J. Oates, chairman of the Council of Humanities at Princeton University, in an address on "Philosophy as the Center of Liberal Education":

> I propose first to sketch briefly the role of philosophy, as I see it, in history, in literature and the arts, the social sciences and the natural sciences, in other words, those subjects which constitute, broadly speaking, the traditional content of liberal education. And I shall conclude with a discussion of other ways in which philosophy reveals its significance in the intellectual life.[1]

The order in which you list the main points in your initial summary obviously should follow the same sequence you intend to use in your detailed discussion; otherwise you will confuse your listeners by setting up a guidepost which points in a direction different from the road you actually will take. Properly developed, an initial summary will help your audience follow your discussion and will help them see the relation of each point to the whole.

2. *The detailed information* is presented next, covering in order the main points enumerated in your initial summary. Explanations, facts, comparisons, and other information should be grouped around each main point in a systematic fashion and, when possible, amplified and illustrated by maps, pictures, tables, demonstrations, or other visible aids to understanding. As you move from one main point to the next, be sure you make clear that you are doing so. Use connective sentences or phrases freely to emphasize the shifts (see pp. 330-331). At all times be sure that your audience knows where you are and in what direction your discussion is heading. Follow a consistent plan of arrangement as you proceed, and amplify your points with an abun-

[1] *Liberal Education,* ed. F. L. Wormald (Washington, D.C.: *Bulletin of the Association of American Colleges),* L (May 1964), 213.

dance of supporting material, both verbal (p. 156) and visible (pp. 172-173).

A few suggestions are in order here about the detailed content of some common types of informative speeches. The presentation of *reports,* of course, was discussed in Chapter 3 (pp. 40-41). *Research reports,* you will recall, usually contain the following items: first, a clear statement of the hypothesis to be tested or the problem to be investigated; second, a brief review of previous research upon the subject; third, an explanation of the materials used, the apparatus employed, or the literary or historical sources investigated; fourth, a statement of the procedure followed in the study; and finally, a summary of the facts or results obtained. *Other types of reports*—such as those resulting from committee discussions, financial operations, travel, or direct observation—vary a great deal but nearly always include: first, a statement of the nature or scope of the subject to be covered; second, the sources from which material was gathered: discussion, observation, written records, etc.; and third, a review of the salient points discovered as a result of the inquiry.

When the purpose of an informative speech is to *give instructions,* it usually contains: first, an overall statement of the nature and purpose of the operation to be performed; and second, an explanation of each step in that operation in the order in which it is to be taken. The discussion of each step also may include the reason for it, the materials or tools or special information required, and the precautions to be observed. Frequently, in giving such talks, the speaker pauses after explaining each step in the process, inviting questions from his listeners or testing their understanding as he goes along.

The detailed development of an *informative lecture* varies so much with the subject that no single list of items would suffice to describe it. In the main, its substance is organized in the manner natural to the subject matter, as explained in Chapter 17.

Regardless of the subject or specific purpose of an informative speech, or how it may be treated in the satisfaction step, remember that its main objective is to secure a clear and thorough understanding on the part of your audience. The detailed information, therefore, must be clearly organized and fully amplified with concrete and specific supporting material.

3. *In the final summary* you tie together the information you have presented, in order to leave your audience with a unified picture. It consists of a restatement of your main points, together with any important conclusions or implications which have grown out of your discussion. It is similar to the initial summary but is usually some-

what longer. Notice the difference between the following final summary and the initial summary (see p. 377) for the speech on athletic activities.[2]

From what I have said, you can readily see that the three main divisions of our athletic system are closely related to one another. The intercollegiate sports serve as the stimulus for developing superior skill as well as a source of revenue for financing the rest of the program. Our intramural system extends the facilities for physical recreation to a large part of our student body—three thousand last year. And our physical education classes not only serve in training men to become the coaches of the future, but also act in systematically building up the physical endurance of the student body as a whole and in giving corrective work to those who have physical defects. The work of these three divisions is well organized and complete.

DEFINITIONS

In addition to the initial summary, the detailed information, and the final summary, the satisfaction step of a speech to inform sometimes requires a fourth item—the *definition of important terms.* There is no fixed point at which such definitions should be introduced; but when they relate to the whole body of information to be presented, they are most frequently given either just before or just after the initial summary.

The purpose of a definition is to clarify an obscure term or to establish a special meaning which you wish to attach to a particular word or phrase. Therefore, any means which will accomplish such an end may be employed. Usually, however, you will find yourself employing one of the following methods:

Dictionary definition. Put the term or concept to be defined into a general class or category and then carefully distinguish it from the other members of this class. ("An apple is a *fruit* that is *red* and *round* and *hard* and *juicy.*" "Man is a rational animal.")

Etymology. Clarify meaning by telling the history of a word—the elements from which it is derived. ("*Propel* comes from the Latin *pro* meaning *forward* and the Latin verb *pellere* meaning *to drive.* Therefore, a propeller is an instrument which drives something forward.")

[2] See also pp. 253-254 for examples of final summaries.

Negation. Clarify the meaning of a term or concept by telling what *it is not.* ("By socialism I do not mean *communism*, which believes in the common ownership of all property. Instead, I mean . . . .")

Example. Clarify by mentioning an actual example or instance of what you have in mind. ("You all have seen the Methodist church on Maple Street. This is what I mean by English Gothic architecture.")

Use in a sentence. Occasionally the best way to clarify the meaning of a term or concept is actually to use it in a sentence. ("*Hopping* is a slang term for *very* or *exceedingly.* For instance, if I say, 'He was *hopping* mad,' I mean that he was angry indeed.")

Study the four passages that follow. In each, the speaker attempts to define a word or concept which he is going to use in his speech. Which of the methods outlined above do you find employed? What additional methods are used?

When I speak of "speech" this morning, I have always in mind the full range of Man's speech behavior—the act of utterance, the symbol system of spoken language, the integration of matter and manner in spoken discourse, and dramatic communication in which discourse among characters is a central means of furthering the dramatic action.[3]

By "provincial" I mean here something more than I find in the dictionary definitions. I mean more, for instance, than "wanting the culture or polish of the capital" . . . and I mean more than "narrow in thought, in culture, in creed. . . ." I mean also a distortion of values, the exclusion of some, the exaggeration of others, which springs, not from lack of wide geographical perambulation, but from applying standards acquired within a limited area to the whole human experience; which confounds the contingent with the essential, the ephemeral with the permanent.[4]

What is this thing called hemophilia? Webster defines it as "a tendency, usually hereditary, to profuse bleeding even from slight wounds." Dr. Armand J. Quick, Professor of Biochemistry at Marquette University and a recognized world

[3]Carroll C. Arnold, "Speech as a Liberal Study," in *The Speaker's Resource Book*, ed. Carroll C. Arnold, Douglas Ehninger, and John C. Gerber, 2nd ed. (Glenview, Ill.: Scott, Foresman, 1966), p. 2.
[4]T. S. Eliot, *On Poetry and Poets*. Copyright 1945, 1957 by T. S. Eliot (New York: Farrar, Straus and Giroux, Inc.; and London: Faber & Faber, Ltd.), "What Is a Classic?"

authority on this topic, defines it as "a prothrombin consumption time of 8 to 13 seconds." Normal time is 15 seconds. Now do you know what hemophilia is?[5]

Most people use the word *Blues* to mean any song that is "blue" or torchy or lowdown or breast-beating—like "Stormy Weather," for example. But "Stormy Weather" is not a Blues, and neither is "Moanin' Low," nor "The Man I Love," or even "The Birth of the Blues." They are all popular songs.

The Blues is basically a strict poetic form combined with music. It is based on a rhymed couplet, with the first line repeated. For example, Billie Holiday sings:

"My man don't love me, treats me awful mean;
Oh, he's the lowest man I've ever seen."

But when she sings it, she repeats the first line—so it goes:

"My man don't love me, treats me awful mean;
I said, *my man don't love me, treats me awful mean;*
Oh, he's the lowest man I've ever seen."

That is one stanza of Blues. A full Blues is nothing more than a succession of such stanzas for as long as the singer wishes.[6]

CONCLUDING THE INFORMATIVE SPEECH

When you have presented your information and secured an understanding of it, you will have accomplished your purpose. Ordinarily, therefore, the final summary given at the end of the satisfaction step concludes an informative speech. There are times, however, when you may wish to encourage further interest in the subject you have been discussing—that is, when you want to actuate as well as simply inform. In such cases, add to the summary a few words suggesting how valuable this knowledge will be to your listeners, or recommend books and articles in which they can find a further consideration of the matter. Then close quickly with a sentence of appreciation for their attention or a few remarks aimed at motivating the additional study you recommend.

[5]Ralph Zimmermann, "Mingled Blood," in *Winning Orations of The Interstate Oratorical Association* and in *The Speaker's Resource Book*, ed. Carroll C. Arnold, Douglas Ehninger, and John C. Gerber, 2nd ed. (Glenview, Illinois: Scott, Foresman, 1966), p. 98. Reprinted by permission of The Interstate Oratorical Association.

[6]From *The Joy of Music*, copyright © 1959 by Leonard Bernstein, p. 109. Reprinted by permission of Simon and Schuster, Inc. The quoted lyrics are from "Fine and Mellow" by Billie Holiday.

SAMPLE OUTLINE

The following outline suggests one way to organize materials in a speech designed to inform or instruct:

THE BIRTH OF THE MOVIES[7]

Gaining attention

I. No form of entertainment is more widely popular than the movies.
   A. Throughout the world, people flock to watch movies.
   B. In the United States, despite the inroads of television, movies are still popular.
II. My purpose is to sketch developments which made this form of entertainment possible.

Showing the listeners why they need to know

I. The story of the movies' birth is worth telling.
   A. It forms an interesting chapter in the history of science and invention.
   B. It anticipates the development of an art form.
   C. It shows how far the modern sound and color film has advanced from humble beginnings.
II. As college students who frequent the movies, you should have a special interest in their early history.
   A. This knowledge will enable you to gain a better perspective of the motion picture industry as it exists today.
   B. This knowledge also will deepen your appreciation of the motion picture as an art form.

Satisfying the need to know: presenting the information (Initial summary)

I. I shall discuss five developments which, together, are responsible for the movies as we know them today: a new theory of human vision, the beginnings of the science of photography, improved methods and materials for action photography, the devising of projection technics, and the utilization of movies to tell a story.

(Detailed information)

   A. Explorations into the nature of vision were made by Peter Mark Roget.
      1. Roget's theory, presented before the Royal Society in London in 1824, maintained that "the image of a moving object is retained by the eye for a frac-

[7]Prepared by Douglas Nigh; assembled from material in the *Encyclopaedia Britannica*, *Encyclopedia Americana*, and *Collier's Encyclopedia*.

tion of a second longer than it actually appears" [*Collier's Encyclopedia*].

2. Roget developed this theory after observing actions through a Venetian blind.
3. Roget's theory led to experiments in viewing rapid movement of still images.
4. Mechanisms based on Roget's theory were limited to the animation of hand-drawn phases of motion.

B. The development of the science of photography led to attempts to view photographs of subjects in phases of motion.
   1. In 1861, Coleman Sellers patented a machine that mounted posed action photographs on a paddle wheel for viewing.
   2. In 1870, Henry R. Heyl showed a series of action photographs through a "magic lantern" projecting device.
   3. In 1877, two other Americans used a battery of 24 cameras in sequence to photograph a race horse in action.

C. Better methods and materials for action photography next were developed.
   1. In 1899, George Eastman developed a celluloid film strip.
      a. It was flexible and would not break or buckle.
      b. Its high-speed emulsion permitted photography of continuous action by one camera.
   2. Thomas A. Edison used Eastman's film in his camera, the Kinetograph.

D. Projection technics to permit viewing of the motion pictures were devised.
   1. The earliest and most important of these was Edison's Kinetoscope, a peep-show device, patented in 1891.
      a. The Kinetoscope was first used publicly in penny arcades in 1894.
      b. A customer saw a loop of filmed moving picture lasting about 50 seconds.
   2. Another important projector was Thomas Armat's Vitascope, presented publicly in a New York music hall in 1896.
      a. An entire audience was permitted to see films at the same time.

        b. Some of the films shown were those used in the penny arcades.
    E. Movies as we know them were born when they began to tell a story.
        1. In early moving pictures, the story was non-existent.
            a. Films were bits of vaudeville action or examples of trick shooting.
            b. Some pictures, taken with portable hand-cranked cameras, showed fire engines or trains in motion, or crowds out for a stroll.
        2. By 1899, George Méliès of France began to link brief scenes to form a narrative.
        3. In 1903, Edwin S. Porter produced *The Great Train Robbery*.
            a. It introduced disjunctive editing; events did not follow strict chronological sequence.
            b. It transformed movies into a widely accepted form of entertainment.
            c. It was on the program at the opening of the first moving picture theater—a nickelodeon in Pittsburgh.

II. The history of the birth of the movies is the history of five major developments: (Final summary)
    A. Roget supplied the theory of vision.
    B. The development of photography spurred other men to apply Roget's theory to the new science.
    C. George Eastman and Thomas Edison gave us the film and camera needed for action photography.
    D. Projection technics enabled us to see moving pictures on a screen.
    E. *The Great Train Robbery* ushered in an era of moving pictures as entertaining narratives.

From the sample outlined above, you will observe that the organization of a speech to inform or instruct will have a skeleton outline somewhat like this:[8]

[8]Note that the skeleton outline provides for details under supporting statements. Such details, although generally omitted from the streamlined outline on "The Birth of the Movies," are essential to the complete development of your speeches.

SUBJECT: ____________________

Specific purpose: ____________________

I. (Opening statement) ____________________. — Gaining attention
  A. (Support) ____________________.
    1, 2, etc. (Details) ____________________.
  B. (Support) ____________________.
II. (Statement of purpose) ____________________.

I. (Statement of need for information) ____________________. — Showing the listeners why they need to know
  A. (Support) ____________________.
    1, 2, etc. (Details) ____________________.
  B. (Support) ____________________.
    1, 2, etc. (Details) ____________________.
II. (Pointing statement relating to audience) ____________________.
  A, B, etc. (Support) ____________________.

I. (Statement of subject, including initial summary) ____________________. — Satisfying the need to know: presenting the information
  A. (Statement of first main division of the subject) ____________________.
    1. (Support) ____________________.
      a, b, etc. (Details) ____________________.
    2. (Support) ____________________.
      a, b, etc. (Details) ____________________.
  B, C, etc. (Statements of other main divisions of subject, supported by subordinate ideas and details ____________________.
II. (Final summary statement) ____________________.
  A. (First main division of subject summarized) ____________________.
  B, C, etc. (Other main divisions of subject summarized) ____________________.

SAMPLE SPEECHES

In the following two informative speeches, observe how the methods suggested in this chapter have been employed. The first speech, "Your Story Must Be Told" by Dean F. Berkley, is provided with relatively full comments and analysis; the second, "The Influence of Public Speaking in America" by Robert T. Oliver, pages 399-404, has been reprinted without marginal comments. Using the technics illustrated in the analysis of the first speech, you may wish to attempt an analysis of the Oliver address.

Preliminary comments on Dr. Berkley's speech

On February 23, 1960, Dr. Dean F. Berkley, of the School of Education at Indiana University, delivered the following speech at the annual convention of the National Institute of Drycleaning meeting in Chicago. Later published in *Vital Speeches of the Day* under the title "Your Story Must Be Told," Dr. Berkley's address reveals many of the qualities of a good informative talk as described in this chapter.

Adhering strictly to the three steps of the motivated sequence applicable to speeches to inform—attention, need, and satisfaction —Dr. Berkley quickly arouses interest at the outset by presenting two familiar examples. He then states and clarifies the central idea of his talk and defines the crucial term *communication*. The need step is given more extended development than is customary in informative speeches and contains an abundance of concrete material. Moreover, it is specifically pointed to the interests and concerns of operators of drycleaning establishments (see paragraph 9). The satisfaction step presents a number of well-chosen ideas in a clear and orderly fashion. Each idea is effectively explained and supported by several stories, examples, illustrations, or analogies. Although the satisfaction step lacks an initial summary, the information presented in the speech is adequately previewed in the attention step (see sentence 4 of paragraph 4). A restatement of the leading ideas offered and a story epitomizing and reinforcing them conclude the satisfaction step. As is usually the case in informative speeches, both the visualization and the action steps are omitted.

Throughout his talk, Dr. Berkley not only introduces a great deal of concrete data but frequently uses material of a humorous nature, thus enlivening the subject and giving the speech a verve and sparkle it would otherwise lack. In addition, interest is stimulated and important ideas emphasized by the use of striking phrases or figurative language (see, for example, the expression "penetrate beyond . . . walls" in paragraphs 1-3; the first sentence of paragraph 7; the last three sentences of paragraph 25).

Consistently, Dr. Berkley relates his remarks directly to his hearers. Drycleaners and their shops or equipment are specifically mentioned no less than five or six times, and the "pocketbook motive" is repeatedly stressed. By these references to the drycleaning business, the speaker not only brings his remarks directly home to his hearers but also fortifies the learning process by relating the new or unknown with the familiar. Learning is further facilitated by the use of an especially memorable story or clear summary to conclude each major point, and by the uniformly clear and simple style in which ideas are expressed.

A single major criticism of Dr. Berkley's talk is the absence of badly needed transitions at several places. It should be pointed out in the speaker's defense, however, that some of the transitions present in the oral version were necessarily omitted in condensing the speech for publication.[9] Moreover, at least two examples of effective transitions remain (see paragraphs 11 and 34); and the major divisions of the talk—the attention, need, and satisfaction steps—are clearly set off (see, for example, paragraphs 5 and 11).

Dr. Berkley, a native of South Dakota, received his bachelor's degree from Dakota Wesleyan University and his M.A. and Ed.D. from the University of Denver. For a number of years he was a teacher of speech and coach of debate in various South Dakota high schools; and from 1955 to 1957, he served as assistant to the Superintendent of Schools in Sioux Falls, South Dakota. Since 1957, he has been Director of College and University Placement and Professor of School Administration at Indiana University. He delivers on the average of a hundred speeches a year in all parts of the country.

YOUR STORY MUST BE TOLD[10]

Dean F. Berkley

I was ready to tuck the children into bed. As I went over to open the window, I noticed the next-door neighbor was practicing the piano. I could hear his music clearly though

Attention step.

Familiar examples which,

[9]Letter to the authors.

[10]From *Vital Speeches of the Day*, XXVI (May 1, 1960), pp. 424-428. Reprinted with permission of the author.

I knew his windows were closed. It had never occurred to me that perhaps my own practicing penetrated beyond my walls. The most amazing walls are penetrated. We go back hundreds of years and see a man seated at a bare writing table behind blocks of stone and bars of steel. In order to consume the burden of time and release nervous energy, he jotted down some of his thoughts. John Bunyan would have been the last to have presumed that what he did at that bare writing table would penetrate beyond those walls and result in one of the three or four most influential books in the history of Western Christendom. /1

by implication, support the central idea of the speech

In Frauenberg there is a drab two-story house. On the second floor is a small workroom, which in the sixteenth century was the workroom of a monk named Copernicus. In imagination we can see him peering into the heavens at night and jotting down his observations. Copernicus would have scoffed at the suggestion that what he did in that little room would create one of the major scientific revolutions in the history of mankind. Some time later, another man used his astronomical telescope to prove that the earth rotated daily upon its axis. Galileo had no reason to believe that he too had penetrated beyond the span of history by proving the Copernican theory. /2

One of the illusions of life is that we can choose to penetrate beyond our walls or not. There is an axiom as old as the human race which says that irrespective of what we do in our political, social, economic, or physical endeavors we penetrate beyond our walls. Far-fetched? Not for a moment. You might observe that the manager of a shop might lock himself in the office and he wouldn't penetrate beyond his walls. But you cannot isolate the influence of that man and the lives he touches. Put your drycleaning machine in a soundproofed room behind opaque glass. You can push a button to start it, but you have no way to know whether the machine is operating. Now, an electrician would have a light to indicate whether all was well within. Even in automation there is provision for feedback—for penetration, if you please. In a small operation, the reliance is more on verbal communication for this penetration, and we penetrate whether we like it or not. Our only choice is the kind and the quality of penetration. It is not a case of your story being told, but rather that it must be told in terms of degree and quality. /3

Central idea of speech stated figuratively

Central idea clarified and its truth impressed upon audience by direct reference to drycleaning business

One of the first questions we must ask ourselves is what is meant by communication? By telling your story? Someone has said that communication is the art of telling people who don't want to listen something they don't want to hear, doing it in such a way that they will do something they didn't want to do before—and leaving them pleased with themselves and with you. In that statement, facetious or not, are the ingredients of communication: listening, persuading, responding, promoting, and telling. Our concern, therefore, is to tell our story by using the elements of communication to convey our intention—always remembering that good intentions are not enough. What a man intends to communicate is not the determinant, but rather the ultimate interpretation. Herein is the first lesson of human relations: penetrating beyond our walls in terms of communication. /4

Communication defined, first facetiously and then seriously

We must now pause for a moment and examine the need for more effective communication in telling our story. We must first consider the need before we assess the communication strategy applicable in telling the story. /5

Need step.

Need for effective communication stated and illustrated by examples, analogies, and humorous stories

An early biblical account relates the activities of a group of men building a high tower. The Lord decided these men had evil purpose so he "smote them with a confusion of tongues" and project, Tower of Babel, went out of business. Think what a bit more confusion of tongues would do to our airline flight schedules, drycleaning deliveries, repair orders, or our choices in a restaurant. Apparently men have always been impressed with the importance of being able to pass the word along—or have they? A classic illustration takes us back to the late 1700's when Captain John Paul Jones found things going against him out on the Atlantic. This prompted a Captain Pearson of the British Navy to pose the question, "Sir, do you give quarter?" Jones retorted with the classic statement, "I have not yet begun to fight." But that isn't the end of the story. Behind Jones, on that bloody deck, lay a wounded Marine who, when he heard that remark, lifted himself up on one elbow and cried out in anguish, "Always somebody don't get the word!" /6

As an educator, I see first-hand some of the caustic, critical, and cantankerous questions raised about American education. Many of these questions are raised by people who are well-intentioned but either misinformed or uninformed. As a result, thousands of Americans are raising questions simply because they didn't get the word. A cursory examination will direct one to view many professions—beset with internal and external issues—simply because someone either in the ranks or on the outside didn't get the word. The labor movement today, the greatest of its kind in the history of man, has recently revealed some insidious practices prompting us to wonder whether somebody didn't get the word. American business, having risen to a pinnacle never before evidenced in the history of man, is beset with leaders who are unable to relate articulately the role of private enterprise in a democracy. This, in some quarters, prompts one to ask whether capitalism has gone soft. The cry raised by millions of Americans regarding the inroads of socialism may well have resulted because somebody didn't get the word. Scientists, engineers, skilled technicians, and many of our professional people are trapped in the prisons of their specialized language. This has resulted in misconceptions, open hostility, needless controversies, and even defeat—stemming from a lack of understanding. /7

There are some at this point who might wonder why we should get so concerned about this problem. Many would infer that business is going well and there is no reason for such concern. Typically, these same people also proclaim that anybody can talk. Such a statement is not false—it's just half true. Your little daughter or granddaughter who cuts out paper dolls cannot cut out an appendix. To follow this line of reasoning to its logical conclusion would indicate there are degrees of speaking just as there are degrees of cutting, ranging all the way from elementary chatter to the formal discipline of speech. /8

Those who would mix the charms of sound with nonsense by proclaiming communication as not being important, ignore twenty-three centuries of history and its obvious lesson that speech-making is inherent in human relations and a free society cannot exist without it. To reduce it to simple terms, we have the choice today to either shoot it out or talk it out. This was so succinctly related by Vice-President Nixon upon his return from Russia when he said, "We have the alternative of either talking with the Russians or someday we may be shooting them." What we must make clear is that the ability of men to live together, to coordinate their efforts, to avoid destructive conflicts, is determined by and large by their skill in communication. This is true on the international scene; this is true in your state drycleaners association; this is true in your shop at home. No matter how much skill you need in your job, no matter how varied your activities, no matter how large or small the organization—in the final analysis the biggest single task you have is one of communication. In the normal course of a day's work you may speak between forty and fifty thousand words. These cannot be words of indecision, of an inarticulate nature, or of vacillation if we are to sustain effective human relations. Perhaps there is a message in the incident of a mother of ten children in southern Indiana. Her husband divorced her because he didn't like her any more. Her only comment was, "Well, what would have happened if he really loved me!" What would happen to the effect of your story if you really became concerned about those forty to fifty thousand words each day? /9

Need "pointed" by relating importance of communication directly to drycleaning business

We dare not forget that man's first great human invention was the power to communicate. From this power he designed the mastery of man over nature and, more important, man over himself. The need for more effective communication is perhaps summarized adequately in these lines of Will Carleton:

Need step summarized and concluded

"Boys flying kites haul in their white-winged birds;
But you can't do that way when you're flying words.
'Careful with fire,' is good advice, we know;
'Careful with words,' is ten times doubly so.
Thoughts unexpressed may sometimes fall back dead,
But God Himself can't kill them, when they're said." /10

Let us turn our attention to *how* the story must be told. Some of the dimensions of communication, if you please. /11

Transition from need to satisfaction step

Recently I returned home betore the neighborhood bridge party at our house had been adjourned. After all had left, I posed this question to my wife, "Who listens?" This is a legitimate question for all of us. There is increasing evidence of both the relationship of listening to communication and our failure to be effective listeners. One of the things that we must do to tell our story is to develop an acuity in listening. It was my opportunity some time ago to assess the

Satisfaction step.

Detailed information starts immediately. Initial summary appears in the attention step.

listening effectiveness of workers in an industrial installation. We were shocked to find that about fifty per cent of the time of the white-collar workers was spent in listening. /12

Story and statistics introduce first major point of satisfaction step.

Dr. Ralph Nichols, of the University of Minnesota, has done much research in this area and variously estimates from forty to eighty per cent of the time of the typical worker is spent listening. I also know, on the basis of research, that in the period of a week you will only recall about twenty-five per cent of the central ideas of this talk! I also know that as soon as you leave this meeting you will be able to recall only one half of the central ideas! This implies that we must penetrate beyond our walls through effective communication, for it can be translated into a dollar-and-cent handicap. On the basis of typical adult communication habits, it was found, in a Detroit study, that we devote nine per cent of our time to writing, sixteen per cent to reading, thirty per cent to talking, and forty-five per cent to listening. No, it was no coincidence that the University of Minnesota, in advertising evening courses, related the following in sequence: *Effective Listening* and *Preparation for Marriage!* /13

Importance of listening further emphasized by relating it to "pocketbook" motive

Point clinched by humor

We typically graduate from school as rather good readers into a world of telephones, television, radio, conferences, and trial by jury. Does this apply to us? Think for a moment of the importance of your seamstresses', spotters', route-salesmen's, and countergirls' ability to listen. /14

Importance of listening directly related to drycleaning business

Think for a moment how the story can be told by the girl at the receiving counter who listens effectively—and then translates what she has heard into written or verbal orders easily understood in the back room. The importance of this certainly doesn't minimize the necessity for the manager to listen when an employee has a suggestion, relates a complaint, or wants a day off. Just as applicable is the necessity to listen when a salesman comes to call, or we hear the ideas of a competitor, or have research related to us by the National Institute of Drycleaning. /15

One of the most interesting communication experiments I have encountered is one suggested by Dr. Carl Rogers. He suggests that when you get into a disagreement with your wife, employees, or friends, just stop the discussion and apply this rule. "Each person can speak up for himself only *after* he has first restated the ideas and feelings of the previous speaker accurately and to the speaker's satisfac-

A practical suggestion for using listening to help solve disagreements

tion." Can you see what this would do in employer-employee discussions? Think what would happen were this applied to labor-management negotiations! This implies that before you can continue you must *really* see the other point of view. Try it sometime. You will find it extremely difficult; but if you are successful in seeing and feeling the other point of view, your own communication will be modified considerably. /16

A little boy once asked how he might become a good conversationalist (what he meant was to be effective in human relations). The wise old sage, who was asked the question, responded, "Listen, my son . . ." and paused then momentarily. "Yes, yes," cried the boy, "Go on." "That is all. Listen, my son," responded the wise man. This then becomes our first method of telling our story. /17

A final story to sum up and clinch importance of listening

There is no substitute for a person-to-person approach. We cannot forget that the "climate" is important—and we create it. The "climate" is created more by the face-to-face approach than in any other way. /18

Begins discussion of second major factor in communication —the "face-to-face" approach

A recent discussion with an advertising director for a large Ohio firm brought this point home to me rather emphatically. He indicated that there is a concerted effort at present to find out how we can complement advertising via mass media by a more personalized method. It was his contention that unless we make provision for effective communication on a person-to-person basis, the effects of the gimmicks, techniques, slick ads, and advertising psychology would be rendered impotent. When one stops to consider that during the ensuing year you will influence nine hundred persons (either negatively or positively—and we hope the latter), this becomes a matter of paramount importance. You see, the penetrating beyond our walls we render in terms of those nine hundred people will be on the basis of a person-to-person contact! /19

Stories and examples to show importance of the face-to-face approach

Some of you may have noted the recent innovation on some of our toll roads whereby, if you have the appropriate change, you merely toss it into a receptacle and proceed. Such is the case on one of the routes into Chicago. Frankly, I refuse to use that automatic lane! Why? Because I refuse to submit to such a grim reminder of an increasingly impersonal and mechanical world. You see, I prefer to be able to hear the attendant say "thank you." He creates a "climate" by this personal contact. How well I recall my first day at school! Upon entering that one-room rural school, with fear and trepidation, the teacher in a very gracious and courteous manner merely said, "We've been waiting for you." I began to wonder how she knew I was coming! I am still amazed at the "climate" she created in her person-to-person communication. Frankly, I must admit that the following year when I entered the schoolroom she stood there to meet me. But this time, with hands on her hips and no evidence of a smile, she said, "We've been *waiting for you.*" You see, I had created a "climate"! */20*

I know a high school principal in one of the largest schools in the country who practices the person-to-person method effectively. He listens well enough to pick up bits of information about various pupils each day. Armed with this information, he "accidentally" meets the appropriate students and asks them how their father feels after his illness, congratulates them on election to an office, pats them on the back for a better term mark, or wonders how the new baby sister is getting along. You would be amazed at the morale in this building, all a result of a man who is convinced the story must be told personally. */21*

Face-to-face principle directly applied to dry-cleaning business

A "climate" is in evidence in every shop we enter. In some it is bright and sunny; in others, cold and cloudy. This is true simply because we create a "climate" through a person-to-person relationship. This is the most important single reason why I go to a particular drycleaner and, on the basis of a limited survey of my friends, the reason for their choosing a plant. This is the reason one gasoline station gets over a thousand-dollars-a-year business from me. It all happened one rainy afternoon. With one windshield wiper out of commission, I pulled into a station and asked for a new wiper blade. The young fellow on duty said, "I'm sorry we're out, but I'll get one for you in fifteen minutes." He created a "climate"—an attitude—an image simply because of what he said and the way he said it. This decision was accentuated all the more because the man in the station across the street, where I had first asked for assistance, responded in terms indicating this was a most inconvenient request on that busy afternoon. */22*

Poem summarizing and clinching face-to-face point

This is nothing new or different, but it represents a constant challenge in telling our story. Examples and illustrations are numerous, but perhaps the following lines by a little-known poet say it more effectively than can I:

If I possessed a shop or store, I'd drive the grouches off my floor!
I'd never let some gloomy guy offend the folks who come to buy;

I'd never keep a boy or clerk—with mental toothache at his work,
Nor let a man who draws my pay drive customers of mine away.

I'd treat the man who takes my time—and spends a nickel or a dime
With courtesy, and make him feel that I was pleased to close the deal,

Because tomorrow, who can tell? He may want stuff I have to sell,
And in that case, then glad he'll be to spend his dollars all with me.

The reason people pass one door—to patronize another store,
Is not because the busier place—has better silks, or gloves, or lace

Or special prices, but it lies—in pleasant words and smiling eyes;
The only difference, I believe, is in the treatment folks receive! */23*

One of the troubles in running a business is that it is full of human beings! The presses never sulk; the drycleaning machine doesn't get jealous; and the tumbler may run for a whole year without affecting its willingness. Men are not so constituted. As a result, there are problems of preventative maintenance, premature obsolescence, and even complete operational failure! These factors, however, are much harder to solve and thus necessitate looking at some of the techniques of telling the story. */24*

Third major idea of satisfaction step introduced

In considering the how of communication, it is imperative to recognize the importance of the psychological climate. This factor is as variable as the atmospheric pressure. Unless our communication takes into account the basic drives for recognition, acceptance, accomplishment, and the need to belong, the reactions to your story will become evident.

Specific technics stated and explained

Creating the proper psychological climate can decrease both the unavoidable social barrier between employer-employee and the business house and its clientele. The average person wants to matter, and he glows with pride when you communicate your compliments to him. This factor probably accounts for someone indicating that the five most important words are: I am proud of you; the four most important: What is your opinion?; the three most important: If you please; the two most important: Thank you; and the least important word: I. Of the more than 600,000 words in the English language, we use one word 450 times more than any of the others and that word is *I*. Such overuse of this word does not, by and large, bring about an appropriate psychological climate. /25

Another important factor is that communication must be active. This means a two-way process. View your discussions with people as you might a tennis game. Unless they are able to field the ball and return it, there is no two-way activity. Communication experts call this "feedback"—for it is the only way we can arrive at mutual understanding. The fundamental phase of training by one of the Roman speech teachers centuries ago was boxing and fencing. His reasoning is now apparent to us, and we too must view communication as a two-way street. /26

The list would not be complete without mentioning some factors in communicating that might help tell your story —other than the mass media. /27

The "grapevine" is operative in every organization and can have a real value in building team spirit if properly cultivated. It can become highly destructive if there is ineffective and impersonal communication on the part of the boss. Often new employees must turn to the more experienced workers to get their information and have ideas and orders interpreted. If communication is restricted, then one has only to wonder, speculate, and give vent to rumors. /28

Such factors as social events, time schedules, written employment policies, punctuality, extending greetings to an acquaintance, and taking time for social amenities over the telephone are all important channels that tell your story. /29

A word of warning: danger

When we overuse any one avenue, it may lose its effectiveness. This is well illustrated in the story of the woman who brought a dress into the cleaners and asked that she have immediate service, and the clerk said it would be ready late that afternoon. She wrote on the ticket the word RUSH. Now what does this word mean? It went to the back room, and one of the employees said, "When shall I do it? I am all tied up." The response by another employee went something like this, "Just do the best you can. They always mark everything rush!" /30

in the overuse of any one avenue of communication

You see, this represented a communication failure because the word had lost its meaning. It used to mean to do it first. Apparently the current meaning is, don't put it at the bottom of the pile. The "rush" order lost its meaning because that particular line of communication was overloaded by overuse. We must be aware of alternate lines and channels to use in the event of overloading. /31

The communication channels are important. So important that if they aren't recognized the boss can easily become a prisoner of his own organization. The decisions you make are no better than the information you use to make the decision. Should you want to arrive at decisions regarding expansion of the building, new equipment, re-arranging facilities, or employee needs, it forces us to ask the following questions:

How good is that information?
Is any omitted?
How much is swept under the rug?
Have the elements of fear, jealousy, insecurity, ambition, flattery, and incompetence influenced the information which comes to you? /32

Point summarized and made specific by outlining questions the employer can ask himself

Finally, mention must be made of telling the story through your leadership in association work and in the home community. As people in positions of responsibility, we must think of the leadership role and the fact that self-expression is the first step in assuming that role. A great deal of time should be devoted to discussing this factor alone. A multitude of avenues are open to tell your story in the community, at state or regional meetings of your associations, and with your civic friends. We cannot deny that others will judge the quality of your shop by the quality of your telling the story—not by direct account, but through association of your leadership capacity to the type of business you operate. /33

Last major idea of the satisfaction step introduced and explained

In summary, what then are the key words or phrases related to this discussion so that you might best tell the story? /34

Transition to summary of satisfaction step

We penetrate beyond our walls and control only the matter of degree and quality—recognize the need for effective communication—effective listening—person-to-person—channels of communication—leadership. /35

Final summary of points in detailed information of satisfaction step

If you recall nothing else, take these words with you, and perhaps your story will be told a bit better. /36

The conversation of two receiving clerks in a drycleaning establishment may have a final message for us. At the end of a busy day one commented: "What a day. Sometimes I think I hate people." The response by her co-worker went like this: "Oh, I like people all right, but sometimes I forget that I do." /37

Story epitomizing central idea

Sometimes we might not like the effort it takes in telling our story, but we dare not forget its importance. Your survival in business depends on it. /38

Final appeal to "pocketbook" motive

Asked to comment on his philosophy of effective speaking, Dr. Berkley replied as follows:

It is my belief that in the preparation of a speech there must be (1) adequate analysis of the group, (2) identification of the areas that will have some "take home value" for such a group, (3) organization of the ideas into a discussion of three or four points, and (4) the statement of these points in language that is easily understood and simple enough to remember. I normally surround each point with a catchy phrase and sufficient illustrations, anecdotes, and humor so that the serious thesis of the talk becomes palatable. Effective speaking necessitates a physical delivery that is restrained, yet vigorous in its overall effect; gestures and vocal variety that are viewed as means of punctuation; and eye contact *cannot* be established if one must constantly refer to notes or manuscript—this implies familiarity with the material and sufficient enthusiasm about the topic to develop the necessary confidence to speak with conviction uninhibited by copiously written notes.[11]

The following speech was delivered by Professor Robert T. Oliver of Pennsylvania State University at the Annual Convention of Toastmasters International held in New York City on August 20, 1965. After a combined attention and need step, Professor Oliver developed his

[11]Letter to the authors.

subject in a roughly chronological order, and concluded his speech with a direct reference to the audience. Throughout, the information presented is animated and enlivened in such a way that the speech impresses and inspires at the same time that it informs.

Professor Oliver is a Past President of the Speech Association of America and the author of many books and articles in the fields of speech and international relations.

THE INFLUENCE OF PUBLIC SPEAKING IN AMERICA: BUILDING BLOCKS IN A FREE SOCIETY[12]

Robert T. Oliver

We meet together today as fellow workers in the development of one of the greatest of human arts—the realm of public speaking. Just as has always been true since ancient times, we recognize the enormous importance of the spoken word in the development of individual personality and in the effective functioning of democratic society.

Man is above all a languagized mammal. Individuals and communities are at their civilized best when there is a free and skilled development of public discourse. We all have moods, of course, when speech seems cheap and we insist that we prefer deeds to words, action to talk. But we realize this means preferring what one man can do by himself to what many can accomplish when working together in a cooperative enterprise. Language, and especially oral language, is the great instrument of human cooperation. *Community, communion,* and *communication* are inevitably closely related.

[12]From *Vital Speeches of the Day,* XXXI (October 1, 1965). Reprinted with permission of the author.

Winston Churchill, with a rifle in his hands crouched behind an earthen rampart along the Dover Coast, might have repelled two or three Nazi invaders. But this same Winston Churchill, speaking with his matchless oratory, was able to marshal the global resources and inspire the will to victory that toppled Hitler's empire and preserved the democratic civilization of the Anglo-American world.

In American history, public speaking has been important in two closely related achievements—the development of individual leaders and the growth of the ideas, ideals, and institutions which characterize our nation.

The debating societies, the Friday afternoon programs in our public schools, and such special occasions as Fourth of July celebrations did much to awaken and enlarge the minds and the spirits of men and women who arose to leadership throughout our history. Henry Ward Beecher, America's greatest preacher, traced his intellectual awakening to the speech class taught by John Lovell in Mt. Pleasant Academy, in Amherst, where for the first time he encountered a kind of teaching that was less concerned with the input of information into his mind than with the outflow of influence from his whole personality. Henry Clay attested that whatever he was and whatever he achieved he owed to his early and constant training in the art of public speaking. Andrew Johnson could not even read and write at the time of his marriage, but he educated himself by hiring a boy to read aloud to him the great orations of Burke, Fox, Erskine, and Pitt while he worked busily at his sewing in his tailor shop. Lucy Stone left her farm home to enter Oberlin College where, as a mere girl, she was not allowed to give speeches but prepared herself for leadership as an eloquent advocate of women's rights by sitting as a mute auditor in a young men's public speaking class. Woodrow Wilson wrote his first published essay on oratory and organized a debating society because he was convinced that skill in speech was the basic requirement for intellectual development and personal leadership. Such examples could be multiplied from the whole scope of our national history.

The earliest immigrants came to our shores from European homelands that were described by the French émigré Michel Guillaume de Crèvecoeur, in his *Letters from an American Farmer,* as "a continual scene of sore affliction or pinching penury." They came as debtors and peasants, as political refugees and religious dissenters. They came in poverty but in hopefulness and with pride. And while they built their homes and laid out farms, they also constructed meeting houses and invented the Town Meeting as a place in which to talk out their community problems through discussion and debate.

It was in these Town Meetings, and in the churches which preached spiritual individualism, and in the colonial legislatures—especially those in Massachusetts and Virginia—that our new nation was born.

We read with proper pride of the courage of the Minute Men at Concord and Lexington, but the doughty and eloquent John Adams raised the right question and proposed the right answer when he said: "What do we mean by the American Revolution? Do we mean the American War? The Revolution was effected before the war commenced. The Revolution was in the minds and hearts of the people . . . . This radical change in the principles, opinions, sentiments, and affections of the people was the real American Revolution."

In a real sense, the American Revolution was talked into being. It began in the homes, and taverns, and churches, and town meetings of the thirteen colonies—where our ancestors were learning to solve their own problems in their own way, rather than to await directions from overseas.

It began in the legislature of Massachusetts, where James Otis and Sam Adams were pouring out "inflammatory speeches" to support a propaganda principle that Adams well understood: "Put your adversary in the wrong and keep him there."

It began in St. John's Church, in Richmond, where the Virginia colonial assembly was in session on March 23, 1775, when a red-headed farmer-lawyer from the backwoods arose and electrified the delegates with a torrent of eloquence—reminding his listeners that "We have petitioned, we have remonstrated, we have supplicated . . . . and we have been spurned, with contempt, from the foot of the throne." Then Patrick Henry launched into his memorable peroration: "What is it that gentlemen wish? What would they have? Is life so dear, or peace so sweet, as to be purchased at the price of chains and slavery? Forbid it, Almighty God! I know not what course others may take, but as for me, give me liberty or give me death!"

A listener reported that "When he sat down, I felt sick with excitement. Every eye yet gazed entranced on Henry. It seemed as if a word from him would have led to any wild explosion of violence." There was no applause when this, one of America's greatest speeches, was finished. Only silence; no reply—just the vote, which set Virginia by the side of Massachusetts and assured the Revolution of eventual success.

Without eloquent and effective speech, this nation would never have been formed. Then through discussion and debate our basic institutions were devised and our guiding national policies were developed. This is how it was —through the democracy of free speech, skillfully used.

The Constitution was formulated in the course of a long summer of group discussion. Sometimes the delegates were so discouraged that they might have gone home with their task uncompleted, but George Washington quietly addressed them, saying: "If we offer to the people something that we do not ourselves approve, how can we afterward defend our work? Let us raise a standard to which the wise and the honest may repair. The event is in the hands of God."

The Constitution was ratified in a series of State Conventions, in the thrust and parry of great debate. We now had our fundamental instrument of government; but any nation needs more than laws. We needed also a sense of greatness and a dedication to the purpose courageously established by our founding fathers. We needed to create traditions and to establish high goals. This function of nation-building was performed with great artistry and effect largely through the oratory of Daniel Webster.

Webster was a public speaker of wide range and great skill, who was effective in the Congress, in the law courts, at public gatherings, and on ceremonial occasions. He became the greatest interpreter of the Constitution and the chief defender of the federal union against the threats of nullification and secession. But his greatest role was interpreting the meaning of Americanism in the early years of our history when the American people had not yet savored the magic of the phrase, "our pioneer ancestors." It was Webster who imprinted the glories of our frontier heritage so vividly in our national consciousness that it is personal and real even to our most recent immigrants.

One of Webster's greatest speeches was given at Plymouth, in December, 1820, while he was still a young man, to celebrate the courage and idealism of the Pilgrims. In it he explained the commemorative function which great public speaking may perform:

> It is a noble faculty of our nature [he said] which enables us to connect our thoughts, our sympathies, and our happiness with what is distant in place or time; and, looking before and after, to hold communion at once with our ancestors and our posterity. Human and mortal though we are, we are nevertheless not mere insulated beings, without relation to the past or the future. Neither the point of time, nor the spot of earth, in which we physically live, bounds our rational and intellectual enjoyments. We live in the past by a knowledge of its history; and in the future, by hope and anticipation. By ascending to an association with our ancestors, by contemplating their example and studying their character; by partaking their sentiments, and imbibing their spirit; by accompanying them in their toils, by sympathizing in their sufferings, and rejoicing in their successes and their triumphs, we seem to belong to their age, and to mingle our existence with theirs.

After Webster had concluded his depiction of the deeds and personalities of our New England forebears, the hardheaded publisher George Ticknor, who was in the audience, reported that he returned to his room, "never so excited by public speaking before in my life. Three or four times I thought my temples would burst with the gush of blood. . . . When I came out I was almost afraid to come near him. It seemed to me as if he was like a mount that might not be touched and that burned with fire. I was beside myself, and am so still."

By great oratory the reform movements of abolitionism, and women's suffrage, and prohibition, and internationalism were launched. By still other oratory the Southern States propagated their theories of state rights. And such great speakers as Webster, Henry Clay, William Henry Seward, Stephen

A. Douglas, and Abraham Lincoln sought to prevent, and did in fact delay, the advent of Civil War.

One of the most effective speeches from this period in our history was delivered in the relatively remote confines of the Pennsylvania Assembly, and its actual words were not reported or preserved. The speaker was Thaddeus Stevens, a club-footed, beetle-browed, dark-haired lawyer-legislator from Lancaster. The year was 1835, and Pennsylvania was about to repeal the free public school system, which had been in effect for a year. Newspapers and the public opposed free schools because they meant higher taxes. The Senate had already voted to abolish them, and the Assembly was about to concur.

Then Thaddeus Stevens arrived, late for the session, from Lancaster. He found himself almost alone in favor of free schools. Nevertheless, in a torrent of ironic eloquence, in which he charged that Pennsylvanians were more solicitous for their hogs than for their children, he proved so persuasive that the Senate reversed its earlier vote, and the Assembly ratified the free school system by a two-thirds vote. As the historian Richard N. Current attested, "No one questioned that Stevens' eloquence was responsible for this about-face."

One of the most courageous speeches in American history was not immediately successful, but in retrospect it proved to have a great and beneficent influence. This was the address by Thomas Corwin of Ohio in the Senate of the United States. On February 11, 1847, he denounced the war with Mexico and demanded that the United States make peace on the basis of returning to Mexico all the southwestern territories which our arms had won.

"It is idle, Mr. President," he thundered, "to suppose that the Mexican people would not feel as deeply for the dismemberment and disgrace of their country as you would feel for the dismemberment of this Union of ours . . . . If I were a Mexican, I would tell you, 'Have you not room enough in your own country to bury your dead men? If you come into mine, we will greet you with bloody hands, and welcome you to hospitable graves.'"

It is not surprising that now, more than a hundred years after Corwin's death, his name and his eloquent plea for generous justice, remain a strong pillar supporting the friendship of Mexico and the United States.

Of all the many orators who have pleaded and planned for the unity and harmony of the diverse groups which comprise this far-flung nation, none has spoken with greater eloquence or has left a finer heritage of leadership than Abraham Lincoln. One of the greatest of his statements, spoken just a few days before his death, is needed today as it was needed then, to heal sectional bitterness and to unite bitter adversaries in the common cause of national loyalty. The passage to which I refer is the conclusion of Lincoln's second inaugural:

> With malice toward none, with charity for all, with firmness in the right as God gives us to see the right, let us strive on to finish the work we are

in, to bind up the nation's wounds, to care for him who shall have borne the battle and for his widow and his orphan, to do all which may achieve and cherish a just and lasting peace, among ourselves, and with all nations.

From the long roll of distinguished American orators, there are many to choose, and I must omit them only with regret. There are Robert Green Ingersoll and Henry Ward Beecher, iconoclast lecturer and liberal preacher, who together did much to free American religion from the fear of hellfire and to substitute love and service. There are the great lawyers, Rufus Choate, Jeremiah Black, William Evarts, and Clarence Darrow, who humanized the law and who helped to extend its protection to broader spheres and to every class. There are the great reformers, Frederick Douglass, Theodore Weld, Ralph Waldo Emerson, John B. Gough, Lucretia Mott, and Frances E. Willard, who fought for human freedom, and temperance, and women's rights. There are the evangelical political leaders like William Jennings Bryan, Theodore Roosevelt, Robert M. LaFollette, and Woodrow Wilson, who raised the moral tone of political campaigning.

No other nation in history has matched the United States in platform eloquence. And the reason is clear. We have needed free and skilled public speaking in order to develop and deepen our self-governing democracy. The free platform is even more important than the free ballot box as a bastion for personal and public liberties.

There is one more thing I should like to say in conclusion. It is not only the great and splendid orations that signalize the true contributions of public speaking in American life. All through our history, in local communities, in Friday afternoon programs in the country schools, and in the many debating societies, ordinary men and women learned as they acquired skill in speech that their own opinions and their own feelings were matters of weight and influence in their communities.

The teaching and the learning of public speaking have been among the principal building blocks in the structure of our free society. And so it remains today. The man or woman who gains the understanding and ability to stand erect and to communicate deeply held convictions on matters of public concern is a better human being and a more constructive citizen.

This is the true measure of the influence of public speaking in the history of the United States. It has made and it still is making multiple thousands of us to be more effective human beings than we otherwise could hope to be.

To this ideal, Toastmasters International, with its scores of thousands of members, has made and is making and will continue to make an enormous contribution. Toastmasters Clubs and members deserve the gratitude of all who value democracy and treasure individualism, and of all who believe in the disciplined and liberal values of the study of effective speech.

Problems

1. List at least ten different situations in which informative speeches are called for. To what extent do you think the same principles of content and organization apply in each of these situations, and to what extent must special modifications or adaptations be made? Prepare a paper reporting your conclusions.

2. Make a study of one particular type of informative speaking—the classroom lecture, the expository sermon, the oral report, the informative radio or television address. After listening to a number of talks of this kind, prepare a paper in which you comment on any special problems of organization or presentation which appear to be present. How were these problems solved in the speeches you studied?

3. Outline an informative speech reprinted in a recent issue of *Vital Speeches* and note the compositional devices employed by the speaker. What method is used to gain attention? Does the speaker show the listeners why they need to know the information he is going to present? Is there an initial summary? Would you classify the talk as abstract or concrete? What *order* is followed: time, space, cause-effect, special topical, or some other sequence? What type of conclusion is used?

4. Find two other informative talks in *Vital Speeches*, in a recent issue of *Representative American Speeches* (ed. Lester Thonssen, New York: The H. W. Wilson Company), or some similar source. Compare the methods of organization employed and comment on the suitability of each method to the subject matter being discussed.

5. Analyze the use made of the factors of attention in at least three informative speeches. Are some of the factors used more frequently than others? Which seem to you to be most effective? Can you infer any rules or cautions to be observed when using the factors of attention?

6. Drawing upon your observations as a listener, discuss the role that the speaker's delivery plays in conveying information clearly and interestingly. Can you cite examples where delivery definitely helped or hindered the speaker in these respects?

7. Select a principle of physics, chemistry, biology, or a similar science. How might you relate this principle to concepts familiar to: (a) a farmer, (b) an automobile repairman, (c) a twelve-year-old newsboy, (d) a lawyer? Write a paragraph making this principle clear to one of the above.

8. Recall several informative speeches (classroom lectures, instructional talks given at military reserve unit meetings, directions to groups of employees, etc.) in which the speaker used visual aids to help communicate his ideas. What sort of visual aid (chart, map, working model, etc.) was employed? What type of material (statistics, operational procedures, etc.) was the aid used to present? Was the aid used separately or simultaneously with oral explanation? Was it effectively handled? Did it help to communicate

the idea it was intended to develop, or did it distract from that idea? If the aid was poorly chosen or ineffectively handled, how could its use have been improved? (For a discussion of various sorts of visual aids and rules governing their use, review pp. 172-178 of Chapter 10.)

Speaking assignment

1. Prepare a speech to inform for presentation in class. Select and narrow your subject from one of the topics suggested below, or from a similar topic. Use whatever visual aids you think will improve your presentation. (See pp. 172-178.) Follow the rules of organization and development set forth in this chapter.

New wonder drugs
Contemporary American writers (artists, musicians)
Teaching machines and programed learning
The Federal Communications Commission
How to learn through better listening
The use of visual aids in speaking
How television programs are selected
Cosmetics and beauty aids: a big business
Agencies of the United Nations
Alaska: our newest state
The Common Market
Advances in automation
The Poverty Program: aims and objectives
Medical problems of space travel
Recent advances in automotive engineering (or design)
The role of the federal government in urban renewal

Speeches for collateral study

1. Leonard Bernstein, "The World of Jazz," *The Speaker's Resource Book*, ed. Carroll C. Arnold, Douglas Ehninger, and John C. Gerber, 2nd ed. (Glenview, Illinois: Scott, Foresman, 1966), pp. 67-76.

2. T. S. Eliot, *On Poetry and Poets*. Copyright 1945, 1957 by T. S. Eliot (New York: Farrar, Straus and Giroux, Inc.; and London: Faber & Faber, Ltd.), "What Is a Classic?"

3. Thomas Henry Huxley, "The Method of Scientific Investigation" (with an analysis by Walter Blair), *The Speaker's Resource Book*, ed. Carroll C. Arnold, Douglas Ehninger, and John C. Gerber (Glenview, Ill.: Scott, Foresman, 1966), pp. 264-269.

4. Karl Menninger, "Healthier Than Healthy," *Contemporary American Speeches*, ed. Wil A. Linkugel, R. R. Allen, and Richard L. Johannesen (Belmont, Calif.: Wadsworth, 1965), pp. 26-36.

5. Lauralee Peters, "What Is Totalitarianism?" *Ibid.*, pp. 69-72. (Student speech.)

6. Carl Rogers, "What We Know about Psychotherapy," *Ibid.*, pp. 36-44.

7. Guy Suits, "Polymers, Crystals and Plasmas," in Alan H. Monroe and Douglas Ehninger, *Principles of Speech*, 5th ed. (Glenview, Illinois: Scott, Foresman, 1964), pp. 286-294.

8. Maxwell D. Taylor, "The Problems Confronting Us," *Vital Speeches of the Day*, XXXII (February 15, 1966), pp. 264-268.

9. Athlestan Spilhaus, "The Concept of a Sea-Grant University," *Vital Speeches of the Day*, XXXII (January 15, 1966), pp. 212-216.

Suggestions for further reading

Donald C. Bryant and Karl R. Wallace, *Fundamentals of Public Speaking*, 3rd ed. (New York: Appleton-Century-Crofts, 1960), Chapter IX, "Outlining the Informative Speech."

Nathaniel F. Cantor, *The Teaching-Learning Process* (New York: Holt, Rinehart and Winston, Inc., 1953).

John E. Dietrich and Keith Brooks, *Practical Speaking for the Technical Man* (Englewood Cliffs, N.J.: Prentice-Hall, Inc., 1958), Chapter VII, "Make Your Information Clear"; Chapter VIII, "Make Your Information Interesting."

Paul F. Douglass, *Communication Through Reports* (Englewood Cliffs, N.J.: Prentice-Hall, Inc., 1957), Chapter I, "The Information-Decision Process"; Chapter III, "Case History: Organization of Ideas"; Chapter IV, "Clear Statement."

L. O. Guthrie, *Factual Communication* (New York: The Macmillan Company, 1948), Chapter II, "Characteristics of a Factual Message"; Chapter III, "Making a Factual Talk"; Chapter IV, "Speaking and Writing Problems"; Chapter V, "Essentials of Understanding."

Herbert Hackett *et al.*, *Understanding and Being Understood* (New York: Longmans, Green & Company, Ltd., 1957).

Kenneth G. Hance, David C. Ralph, and Milton J. Wiksell, *Principles of Speaking* (Belmont, California: Wadsworth Publishing Company, Inc., 1962), Chapter XIII, "Speaking to Inform."

Roy Ivan Johnson, Marie Schalekamp, and Lloyd A. Garrison, *Communication: Handling Ideas Effectively* (New York: McGraw-Hill Book Company, 1956), Chapter X, "Making Reports: Materials and Methods."

Phillip K. Thompkins, "Organizing the Speech to Inform," *Today's Speech*, VII (September 1959), 21-22.

CHAPTER TWENTY-TWO

The speech to convince

We live today in a complex society. No longer can one man alone accomplish a task of any magnitude; he must first convince others that the task is worth while—must secure their consent or active support so that they will be willing to combine their efforts with his to achieve a common goal. The preceding chapter explained how a speaker may organize and present his ideas when his purpose is to increase the knowledge or understanding of his listeners. This chapter will explain how a speaker may organize and present his ideas when his purpose is to convince others—when his task is not only to inform others but also to change their existing beliefs or to instill new ones.

SITUATIONS REQUIRING SPEECHES TO CONVINCE

Speakers frequently are faced with the problem of convincing an audience. Consider for a moment three typical situations: *(a) Business meetings.* The executive committee of a small club as well as the board of directors of a large corporation regularly must make decisions concerning the welfare and the management of the organization they represent. At the meetings of the executive committee or the board of directors, officers present reports and urge their acceptance; committee chairmen offer recommendations for future actions; individuals propose policies and improvements. In each case the speaker wants the group to agree with his conclusion or to endorse the belief he recommends. *(b) Public meetings.* Countless speeches to convince are given at political rallies and mass meetings. Here the speaker attempts to change beliefs or to secure acceptance of his platform or program. Commercial policies likewise are debated at public meetings; for example, an officer of a company may try to convince the stockholders that they should favor a bond issue or reorganization plan. Such proposals may also be presented to church congregations and to social or study groups. *(c) Debates.* In a debate, whether it is an intercollegiate contest or an argument in a legislative body or courtroom, the clash of opinion grows out of conflicting efforts to convince. These are only a few of the typical situations in which speeches to attain belief are called for.

THE PURPOSE: TO SECURE BELIEF

Since your ultimate goal in every speech to convince is to persuade your listeners to believe as you wish, you must help them *want* to believe. For this reason, you should keep two subsidiary purposes in mind: *(a)* to provide your listeners with a *motive* for believing—for instance, self-preservation, power, profit, pleasure, or pride; and *(b)* to convince them of the logical soundness and hence of the intrinsic desirability of the conclusion or proposal you advance. Sometimes you may also need to arouse or to strengthen one or more of their basic emotions, such as fear, anger, or sympathy, in order to encourage belief in your proposal. When this is the case, your speech, while still aiming primarily at conviction, will have many of the characteristics of a speech to stimulate—a type of speech discussed in detail in the next chapter.

ANALYZING THE PROPOSITION

Before you begin to construct a speech to convince, you must be certain that you understand thoroughly the nature of your proposition—just what you want your audience to accept. There are three general kinds of propositions which you may present for approval or may argue against. They are called *propositions of fact, propositions of value,* and *propositions of policy.*

Propositions of fact and value

If you were attempting to get an audience to believe that "most Russian farmers dislike collectivism" or that "large government expenditures for the alleviation of poverty tend to maintain high prices artificially," you would in each case be presenting a proposition which asserts something to be a "fact." The analysis of such a factual statement involves two steps:

1. *Determine the criteria, or standards, upon which a judgment concerning the truth or validity of the proposition should be based.*

If you were asked to determine a man's height, you would immediately look for a yardstick or other measuring instrument. Some standard of measurement also is useful in judging the validity of the factual propositions concerning which men argue. In the first of the propositions listed above, for example, before you could prove that most Russian farmers dislike collectivism, you would have to define the term "dislike"; in the case of the second proposition, you would have to establish at what point prices may be said to be "high."

2. *Apply the criteria one at a time to the available evidence.* Just as you would determine whether tuition costs at your college are high or low by comparing them with an established average, so you must judge the truth or validity of a proposition of fact by measuring it against the standards or criteria you have set. Later, when you speak, if you can first get your audience to agree to the standards for judgment and can then present evidence which shows that your proposition measures up to each of these standards, you will find it much easier to win their belief.

Definite criteria also are important when you are analyzing propositions of value, which assert that something is good or bad, desirable or undesirable, justifiable or unjustifiable. Is desirability to be judged by economic or moral standards, by both, or by still other criteria? Often it is well to pick out two or three different kinds of criteria which cover all possible bases for judgment. For example, to determine the quality of a particular college, you might consider such factors as the distinction of its faculty, the adequacy of its physical plant, the success of its students in graduate and professional schools, and the reputation it enjoys in its region.

Propositions of policy

You would be dealing with typical questions of policy if you were urging your audience to approve of the following propositions: "The United States government *should adopt* a plan of direct financial aid to all low-income families." "Expenditures for foreign aid *should be* reduced." "The student senate *should have the authority* to dismiss students from the university." In each instance you would be urging your audience to endorse a policy or course of action. To analyze such a proposition properly, you must answer four subsidiary questions, each of which involves a proposition of fact or value and, therefore, must itself be analyzed individually.

1. *Is there a need for such a policy or course of action?* If an audience cannot be convinced that a change is needed, they will not approve a new policy.

2. *Is the proposed plan practicable?* If you cannot show the audience that your plan has a reasonable chance of being adopted—and that it will *work* if adopted—they can hardly be expected to endorse it.

3. *Are the benefits the proposal will bring greater than the disadvantages?* People will not approve a proposal that seems likely to create conditions worse than the ones it promises to correct. The benefits and disadvantages of a plan must be carefully weighed along with the probability of its being adopted.

4. *Is this proposal better than any other plan or policy?* Your listeners will not endorse your proposal if they believe some other way of meeting the need has fewer disadvantages or greater benefits.

In analyzing a policy or course of action, then, consider each of these four subsidiary questions (sometimes called "stock issues"). Determine the criteria by which each is to be examined; study the evidence you have collected; see how the facts lead you to answer the questions. Observe the way this process was applied in developing the outline, "Our Plenty Is Not So Plentiful," in Chapter 17 (pp. 298-303).

Remember also that you must later answer these four fundamental questions for your audience. Sometimes you will have to present proof for all four of them; sometimes your audience will already agree with you on the answer to one or two, and you can then concentrate on answering the remaining ones.

From what has been said about the three types of propositions, you can readily see how important it is that you completely understand the nature of the proposition you present. Frame it into a clear, concise statement and be able to explain it clearly to your audience. Unless you can make your hearers understand exactly *what* you propose, there is little reason to try to get them to see *why* you propose it. Moreover, you will often find it important to have a thorough grasp of the historical background of your subject and particularly of any recent events which have made its consideration important.

ORGANIZATION OF THE SPEECH TO CONVINCE

Seeking endorsement of a proposition of policy

The motivated sequence, as outlined in Chapter 16, provides a pattern for a speech to convince on a proposition of policy. In speeches of this sort, the speaker (1) secures the audience's *attention;* (2) shows that because of existing deficiencies or evils there is a *need* for some action; (3) provides *satisfaction* for this need by presenting a remedy which will remove the evils or deficiencies; (4) *visualizes* the benefits to be obtained from believing or acting as he proposes; and (5) requests *action* in the form of an endorsement of the proposal he advances.[1]

Opposing endorsement of a proposition of policy

On the other hand, the speaker who opposes a policy ("We should *not* deprive freshmen of the right to own and drive cars") will also try to capture attention, but he will then proceed by denying any or all of the contentions embodied in steps *(2)*, *(3)*, and *(4)*. Thus he may argue: (2) There is no need for such a policy; things are perfectly all right as they are. (3) The proposal is not practicable; it could not be made to work. (4) Instead of bringing benefits or advantages, the proposed policy would actually introduce new and worse evils; it would be unfair, difficult to administer, etc.

Sometimes you will be able to use all three of these contentions in developing a speech in which you oppose a policy. On other occasions you will find that only one or two of them apply, and your speech will be limited accordingly. Proof beyond reasonable doubt on any of the three, however, will cause an earnest listener to reject a proposal, since obviously he will not want to adopt a policy that is unneeded or impracticable or productive of new problems and evils. Proof beyond reasonable doubt on all three contentions would, of course, constitute the strongest possible case against the endorsement of a proposed change.

Here is a skeleton outline of the main points of a speech in which a proposed action is opposed on the grounds that it is unneeded, impracticable, and undesirable. For purposes of simplification, the attention step and supporting material have been omitted.

THE PROPOSED TURNPIKE

I. The turnpike from Ashton to Waterton, proposed by the Governor's Committee on Highways, is not needed. — Unneeded
   A. The existing highway connecting the two cities is only three years old and is in excellent condition.
   B. Automobile traffic between Ashton and Waterton,

[1]At this point you should carefully review pages 267-283 of Chapter 16, where these steps are explained and illustrated.

instead of increasing, has actually decreased six per cent during the last decade.

II. Even if the proposed turnpike were needed, it could not be built at this time. — Impracticable
   A. State funds for road construction are at an all-time low.
   B. Borrowing for road construction is difficult and costly in the present bond market.

III. Finally, even if such a turnpike were both needed and possible, its construction would be undesirable. — Undesirable
   A. It would impose a serious hardship on owners of motels, filling stations, restaurants, and other businesses along the present highway.
   B. The suggested route would spoil the Ashton State Park.

Seeking belief or disbelief in a proposition of fact

Rather than arguing for or against propositions of policy, many speeches seek to prove that something is or is not so; that is, they concern what we have called statements of fact ("Good study habits result in good grades").

Questions of whether or not something is true or correct may, of course, often be settled by personal observation, by conducting a controlled experiment, or by looking up the answer in a reliable printed source. Thus it would be absurd for men to argue whether it is raining outside, or whether the fruit in a certain basket is contaminated, or whether a particular train is the fastest one traveling between Chicago and New York. The first of these questions of fact could be settled by glancing out the window, the second by making appropriate chemical tests, and the third by referring to a timetable.

But now consider these questions: "Is Russia ahead of us in the missile race?" "Do the countries of Latin America resent United States interference in their affairs?" "Is knowledge a virtue?" "Is Jones guilty of embezzlement as charged?" Because they inquire whether something is or is not so, these too are questions of fact. But in answering them, a speaker must realize that none of the methods mentioned in the preceding paragraph would be conclusive. While observation or experimentation or printed data may help us arrive at a decision, in the end we must depend upon our own informed judgment—upon reasoning from the best facts available to what appears to be the most accurate or fairest answer; upon bringing together as much evidence as possible, establishing criteria by which to judge the evidence, and then testing the evidence by the criteria. On factual questions of this sort, men can and do make speeches trying to convince others that the opinion they are presenting is a correct judgment and should therefore be accepted.

How should speeches on factual questions be organized and developed? As in the case of speeches on questions of policy, the motivated sequence furnishes the basic pattern, needing only to be adapted to meet the special requirements imposed by the nature of the subject matter.

1. Secure the *attention* and interest of the audience.

2. State clearly the question that is to be decided, and show your listeners why a decision is *needed.* Do this by pointing out either *(a)* why the question concerns them personally or *(b)* why it concerns the community, state, nation, or world of which they are a part.

3. *Satisfy* the need developed in the preceding step by advancing what you believe to be the correct answer to the question under consideration and by offering evidence and argument to support your view.[2]

4. *Visualize* for your listeners the advantages they will gain by accepting the answer you recommend or the evils and dangers they will incur by rejecting it.

5. Appeal for *action*—for acceptance of your proposed answer and a determination to adhere to it.

These steps are illustrated in the following skeleton outline:

OUR STUDENT GOVERNMENT

I. State University has one of the oldest and most widely imitated systems of student government in the entire nation. — Attention

[2]Sometimes a question of fact involves a term or set of terms which the audience may not immediately understand. In such cases, develop the satisfaction step in two separate stages. First define the crucial term or terms, and then show how the facts or circumstances peculiar to the present case fall within the definition thus established. For example, if a lawyer wished to prove to a jury that a certain person was mentally incompetent, he would first make clear the legal definition of *mental incompetence* and then would demonstrate how the person's behavior justified describing him as mentally incompetent. Usually, however, the procedure outlined above (advancing your view and supporting it directly with evidence and argument) will be sufficient.

A. It was founded in 1883, when student government was almost entirely unknown.
B. Many of the leaders of our state and nation gained their first practical administrative experience as campus officers.
C. Representatives of many other colleges and universities have visited State to study how our student government is organized and to watch it in operation.

II. Has our student government, once a free and powerful institution, become a mere tool of the dean of men and the university administration? — *Statement of question*

I. This is a question of vital importance to each of us. — *Need*
A. The prestige of the university is at stake.
B. Our freedom as students to govern ourselves and conduct our own affairs is endangered.

I. In recent years the dean of men and other administrative officers of the university have encroached upon the rights and powers of our student government. — *Satisfaction: Answer to question*
A. All actions of the Student Senate must now have administrative approval. — *Supporting evidence*
B. The budgets of student organizations must be approved and their accounts audited by the university treasurer's office.
C. The election of class officers is conducted under the supervision of the dean.

I. Unless we are all aware of these serious encroachments upon our traditional rights as students and consider steps to oppose or counteract them, further encroachments will almost certainly occur. — *Visualization: Warning of future evils*

I. Make these facts known to your fellow students. — *Action*
II. Resolve that student government will once again be a strong and vital force on this campus.

If your purpose is to uphold the negative position on a question of fact (in this case, to prove that the administration has *not* infringed upon student rights and privileges), proceed in exactly the same way, except to offer a negative rather than an affirmative proposition at the beginning of the satisfaction step and present evidence and argument that justify this stand.

Seeking belief or disbelief in a proposition of value

Whereas propositions of fact assert that something is so, propositions of value, you will recall, assert that something is good or bad.

Typical propositions of value are: "Progressive education is undesirable." "Big-time athletics are detrimental to the best interests of college students." "Harry Truman was one of our greater presidents."

When advancing a proposition of value, with a view to convincing your listeners that they should agree with your estimate of a man, practice, institution, or theory, you may adapt the basic pattern of the motivated sequence as follows:

1. Capture the audience's *attention* and interest.

2. Make clear that an estimate concerning the worth of the man, practice, or institution is *needed.* Do this by showing either *(a)* why an estimate is important to your listeners personally or *(b)* why it is important to the community, state, nation, or world of which they are a part. With the *need* made clear, set forth the criteria upon which an appropriate estimate must rest.

3. *Satisfy* the need developed in the preceding step by advancing what you believe to be the correct estimate and by showing how this estimate meets the criteria specified.

4. *Visualize* the advantages that will accrue from agreeing with the estimate you offer or the evils and dangers that will follow from endorsing an alternative estimate.

5. Appeal for *action*—for acceptance of the proposed estimate and a determination to retain it.

Each of these basic steps is present in the following skeleton speech outline:

THE VALUES OF INTERCOLLEGIATE DEBATING

I. In recent years intercollegiate debating has come under strong attack from many quarters. — Attention
   A. Philosophers and social scientists charge that debate is a poor way to get at the truth concerning a disputable matter.
   B. Educators charge that debate teaches the student to approach a problem with an "either-or" attitude, thus causing him to develop habits of contentiousness

and dogmatism rather than of fact-centered objectivity.

I. How we evaluate debate is important to each of us for at least two reasons: — *Need: Evaluation necessary*
   A. As students we help support the debate program on this campus because a portion of our activity fee is allocated to the Debate Society.
   B. As citizens in a democratic society we are concerned because the method of decision-making employed in intercollegiate debating is essentially the same as that employed in the courtroom and the legislative assembly.

II. As is true of any extracurricular activity, there are two important criteria by which debate can be evaluated: — *Criteria*
   A. Does it develop abilities and traits of mind which will aid the student in his course work?
   B. Does it develop abilities and traits of mind which will be of value in later life?

I. The experience of many years has shown that debate is valuable. — *Satisfaction: Evaluation provided*
   A. Debate helps the student do better work in his courses.
      1. It teaches him to study a subject thoroughly and systematically.
      2. It teaches him to analyze complex ideas quickly and logically.
      3. It teaches him to speak and write clearly and convincingly.
   B. Training in debate is of value in later life.
      1. It teaches courtesy and fair play.
      2. It develops self-confidence and poise.

I. Picture the serious student of debate in the classroom and in his post-college career. — *Visualization*
   A. As a student he will know how to study, analyze, and present material.
   B. As a business or professional man he will be better able to meet arguments and to express his views in a fair and effective manner.

I. Remember these facts whenever you hear the value of intercollegiate debating questioned. — *Action*
   A. The contribution debate training makes to business or professional success has been eloquently affirmed by many thousands of prominent men and women who were themselves debaters in college.

B. We should encourage and support this worth-while activity in every way we can.

A negative speech on a question of value (for instance, a speech intended to prove that debating does *not* provide desirable and useful training) may be developed according to the same general pattern. But instead of showing that the practice or institution in question meets the criteria outlined in the need step, you will show that it *fails* to meet them. The visualization step would probably attempt to show that college debate experience was not merely useless to a person in his business or profession after college but even harmful.

THE MANNER OF SPEAKING FOR A SPEECH TO CONVINCE

To recommend any uniform style of delivery for the speech to convince is impossible. Your delivery will depend upon the situation in which you find yourself—upon the occasion and the audience. Your manner in talking to a small group of businessmen in an executive meeting will, of course, be different from your manner in addressing a large audience at a public gathering. Moreover, your delivery before an apathetic audience will differ from your delivery before either an interested group or a hostile one. In general, however, a straightforward, energetic presentation that suggests enthusiasm without seeming to be overemotional is most effective in securing conviction.

CONTENT OF THE SPEECH TO CONVINCE

Concrete facts and vivid illustrations

As in every other type of speech, you should avoid generalities and abstractions in a speech to convince. Use facts and figures that are within the experience of the audience. Incidents that are recent, common, or particularly striking are most powerful in attaining conviction. No other single factor is so important in this type of speech as presenting facts, pertinent facts—and then more facts. Review the forms of support discussed in Chapter 10 and use them constantly throughout your speech.

Sound, logical reasoning

Regardless of how much detailed and concrete evidence you present, however, a speech will not carry strong conviction unless your reasoning also is sound. A brief consideration of the three most frequently used forms of reasoning is therefore important.

Reasoning from example. This form of reasoning consists of drawing conclusions about a general class of objects after studying one or more individual members of that class. For instance, if a housewife is in doubt about the flavor of the apples in a bushel basket, she may bite into one of them to test its flavor. If it tastes all right, she reasons upon the basis of this example that all the apples in the basket have a good flavor. Or perhaps, if she is skeptical, she may dig down to the bottom to find out if all the apples seem to be the same. This sort of reasoning is employed in much of our thinking, whether the point at issue is big or little. Scientific experiments, laboratory tests, the determination of social trends—all these are based upon reasoning from example. Reasoning of this sort should be tested by asking the following questions:

1. *Is the sampling extensive enough to support the conclusion offered?* One robin does not make a spring; nor can two or three examples prove that a general proposition is incontestably true.
2. *Are the examples chosen fairly?* To show that something is true in New York, Chicago, and Boston—all large cities—does not prove it also is true in smaller towns all over the country.
3. *Are there any outstanding exceptions?* One well-known instance which differs from the general conclusion you urge may cause doubt unless you can show that this instance is the result of unusual circumstances.

Reasoning from axiom. This form of reasoning consists of applying an accepted rule or principle to a specific situation. For example, it is generally conceded that by buying in large quantities one may get merchandise more cheaply than by buying in small lots. When you argue that chain stores save money by purchasing goods in large quantities, therefore, you are merely applying this general rule to the specific instance—the chain store. Reasoning from axiom may be tested as follows:

1. *Is the axiom, or rule, true?* For many years people believed the world was flat. Many high-sounding assertions which pass for the truth are merely prejudices or superstitions. Before applying an axiom, make sure of its validity. And remember also that no matter how true a principle may be, you cannot base an argument upon it unless you can first convince your audience of its truth.
2. *Does the axiom apply to the specific situation in question?* A perfectly true or valid rule may be improperly applied. For instance, to argue, on the basis of the principle mentioned at the beginning of this

section, that chain stores buy goods more cheaply than individual merchants is warranted; but to argue on this same basis that the customer can always buy goods from chain stores at lower prices is not valid. Some additional form of proof would be required to establish this further contention.

Reasoning from causal relation. When something happens, we assume that it must have had a cause; and when we see a force in operation, we realize that it will produce an effect. A great deal of our reasoning is based on this relationship between cause and effect. The rate of violent crime goes up, and we hasten to lay the blame on war, on bad housing, on public apathy, on inept public officials. We hear that the star on our football team is in the hospital with a broken ankle, and we immediately become apprehensive about the results of Saturday's game. We reason from known effects to inferred causes, and from known causes to inferred effects. There is perhaps no other form of reasoning so often used by public speakers, nor is there any form of reasoning which may contain so many flaws. Test causal reasoning for soundness by asking:

1. *Has a result been mistaken for a cause?* When two phenomena occur simultaneously, it sometimes is hard to tell which is the cause and which the effect. Do higher wages cause higher prices, or is the reverse true?
2. *Is the cause strong enough to produce the result?* A small pebble on the track will not derail a passenger train, but a large boulder will. Be careful that you don't mistake a pebble for a boulder.
3. *Has anything prevented the cause from operating?* If a gun is not loaded, pulling the trigger will not make it shoot. Be certain that nothing has prevented the free operation of the cause which you assume has produced a given situation.
4. *Could any other cause have led to the same result?* Four different possible causes were listed at the beginning of this section for the increase in violent crime, each one urged by some persons as the sole cause. Be sure that you diagnose a situation correctly; don't put the blame on the wrong cause nor all the blame on a single cause if the blame should be divided among several causes.
5. *Is there actually a connection between the assumed cause and the alleged effect?* Sometimes people assume that merely because one thing happens immediately after another, the two are causally connected. Developing a severe chest pain shortly after you have had a bad fall doesn't necessarily mean that the pain was a result of the fall. Do not mistake a coincidence for a true cause-effect relationship.

SPECIAL TECHNICS OF THE SPEECH TO CONVINCE

The most important characteristic of a good speech to convince—indeed, more important than all the other characteristics put together—is that it is *audience-oriented.* Therefore, you should always speak with your audience's standpoint in mind. You cannot sell a man an automobile just because you like it; you must approach him on the basis of his own needs and desires. Nor can you induce a group of people to believe or act as you want them to unless you understand how they view your proposal. In no other type of speech is a thorough analysis of your listeners quite so important. You must find out all that you can about them: their likes and dislikes, their attitude toward your proposition, their habits, and patterns of thought. Put yourself in their place and look at the problem as they look at it. With the standpoint of the audience constantly in mind, utilize to the utmost the following special methods or technics:

Appeal to the dominant motives of the audience

Your speech not only must exhibit sound, logical reasoning and include many concrete facts and vivid illustrations, but also must contain effective appeals to the motives for human action (see Chapter 12). You must convince your audience that their basic desires will be better satisfied if they do what you propose. You may prove that they are losing money under present conditions or that they will save money by approving your plan, but underlying all this proof is the appeal to the motive of acquisition or saving.

Identify your proposal with existing beliefs

Find out what your listeners' attitudes and beliefs are; and, if possible, show that your proposal embodies these values. For example, if they believe that advertising is important, show how your proposal will act as advertising. If they believe in reciprocal trading in business, show that your plan embodies this idea. If they are opposed to communism, show how your proposal will serve to combat it. You will usually be able to find ways of linking your proposition with at least some of your audience's fixed opinions. Even when your plan is in exact opposition to an existing belief, you may be able to offset the disadvantage by balancing against this belief some equally strong opinion that is in your favor.

Use the "yes-response" technic

Do not begin your speech with an idea your listeners will find difficult to accept. Instead, start with ideas you think they will approve of. If you can first draw them into a pattern of agreeing with you and put them into a receptive and positive state of mind, you will reduce their resistance to less favorable arguments. Don't begin by saying, "I know you have a lot of objections to this plan, but you're all wrong about it," as did a man trying to persuade a group of stockholders to vote for a mining merger. A better beginning would have been, "You are interested in getting the greatest return on your investment consistent with safety." He could then have shown how the merger would produce this result.

Use the "this-or-nothing" technic

Try to show the impossibility of believing or doing anything other than what you propose. People often reject a proposition because they do not realize that it is the best one possible. By showing that there are only (let us say) three available courses of action, two of which are undesirable, you will cut off all avenues of escape save the one you advocate. Thus, if you explain that the only alternatives to bankruptcy are heavy borrowing and curtailment of operating expense, you may—by showing the impossibility of further extension of credit—secure approval for your program of reduced expenditure.

If you speak from the standpoint of your listeners, present concrete facts and vivid illustrations which are within their experience, use sound reasoning, appeal to their dominant motives, identify your proposal with their existing beliefs, employ the "yes-response," and use the "this-or-nothing" technic, you will be better able to secure the decision you seek.

But while people are—or should be—convinced chiefly through logical reasoning and evidence, they often *act* in a certain way largely because they wish or desire to do so. Most of us, for example, are concerned for the safety of our families and ourselves, but we seldom take any active steps to insure this safety until we experience an actual threat to our well-being—an epidemic, fire, flood, or shortage of water supply. Together with logic and evidence, therefore, you must employ vivid descriptions which appeal to the basic desires and emotions which underlie your hearers' logic.

Appeals of this sort are particularly important in the visualization step; in fact, this step should always be descriptive and should usually contain strong emotional inducements. Elsewhere in your speech, an occasional vivid example will add a dynamic quality to your argument which sound logic alone will not produce. Except in the visualization step, however, do not substitute emotional appeals for logic and evidence—use both. Make your logical arguments vivid and compelling, and you will have the essence of an effective speech to convince.

ADAPTING ORGANIZATION TO AUDIENCE ATTITUDE

Earlier in this chapter we examined several of the more common forms of the speech to convince, and we saw that in each case the five-step structure of attention, need, satisfaction, visualization, and action provided a suitable general organization. The detailed development of any particular speech to convince as it will actually be delivered, however, must depend on the audience's attitude toward the speaker's proposal. Let us, therefore, as a final step in our study of speaking to convince, consider some of the attitudes an audience may display toward a proposition, and the adaptations which the speaker must make to each.[3]

Audience interested in the situation but undecided

Some audiences are conscious that a problem or a need for decision exists, but they are uncertain as to what belief they should adopt or what course of action they should pursue. In such cases, your primary purpose is to get them to agree that your proposal is the best one possible.

Attention step. Since the audience already is interested in the situation, the attention step may be brief. Often it consists of a direct reference to the question or problem to be decided. At other times it may provide a short example or story illustrating the problem. When using this second method, however, take care to center your listeners' attention on the heart of the matter rather than on side issues or irrelevant details. Focus their thinking on fundamentals by excluding all but the central issue under consideration.

Need step. Review briefly the basic problem out of which the question or necessity for decision has grown. Summarize its causes and historical development if this will help your hearers understand the problem more clearly. Also, restate in a few words the scope and nature of the existing situation, and show why an immediate decision is imperative. Finally, set forth the standards or criteria which a sound decision must meet.

Satisfaction step. This will be the most important, and probably the longest, part of your speech. State the proposition or plan of action you wish your hearers to adopt, and define any vague or ambiguous terms. Show specifically how your proposal will satisfy the criteria outlined in the need step—why it will provide a practicable and de-

[3] See chart on pp. 628-629, where these methods of adaptation are summarized.

sirable answer to the problem under consideration. Proceed to demonstrate the benefits of your proposition and its superiority to any alternative proposal. Prove each of your contentions with an abundance of facts, figures, testimony, and examples.

Visualization step. Make this step rather brief in relation to the rest of the speech. Be vivid and persuasive, but don't exaggerate. Project the audience into the future by painting a realistic picture of the desirable conditions which will be brought about by approving your proposition or the evils that will result from rejecting it.

Action step. Restate in clear and forceful language your request for belief or for endorsement of the plan you advocate. Recapitulate briefly the principal arguments presented earlier in the speech.

Audience interested in the situation but hostile to the proposal

Sometimes audiences are conscious that a problem exists or that a question must be decided but are opposed to the particular belief or plan of action you wish them to accept. Often this hostility is based either on a fear that some undesirable result will accompany the proposed action or on a positive preference for an alternative belief or policy. Sometimes the hostility is a reflection of deeply ingrained prejudices. In any case, your goal must be to overcome existing objections and secure the acceptance of your ideas.

Attention step. This step is similar to that developed for the undecided audience. However, since you know there will be hostility toward your proposition, you should try, first of all, to conciliate your audience and win a hearing. Approach your proposal indirectly and gradually. Concede whatever you can to your audience's point of view; establish common ground by emphasizing areas of agreement; minimize or explain away differences. Make your listeners feel that you are genuinely interested in achieving the same results they are.[4]

Need step. Secure agreement on some basic principle or belief, and use this principle as the criterion by which to measure the soundness of the proposition you advance. Otherwise, develop this step as you would for an audience that is interested but undecided.

Satisfaction step. Show specifically how the proposed belief or plan of action meets the criterion established in the preceding step. Offer

[4]Review the discussion of common ground on pp. 131-132 of Chapter 8.

strong and extensive proof of the superiority of your proposal to any other proposition which you have reason to believe your listeners may favor. (But do not imply that you know they favor an alternative plan, or you may have to combat their embarrassment in admitting they have made a mistake.) Otherwise, develop this step in the same way you would if you were addressing an undecided audience.

Visualization and action steps. If you have been successful thus far, your audience should be in the same frame of mind as the audience discussed previously—that is, interested in the question but undecided about what to think or do. The development of your speech from this point on, therefore, will follow the pattern outlined for that audience but will provide special emphasis on the visualization, or benefits, step.

Audience apathetic to the situation

In contrast to the two audiences just discussed—the undecided and the hostile audiences—apathetic audiences are not interested in the problem at all. They say, "What's it to me?" "I should worry about this? That's up to George." Obviously, with such persons your main object is to make them realize that the problem *does* affect them—that they must assume a direct responsibility for arriving at a proper decision concerning it.

Attention step. Overcome apathy and inertia by touching briefly some matter which is related to your listeners' self-interest. Present one or two striking facts or figures, and use vivid phraseology to show how their health, happiness, security, prosperity, chances for advancement, and other personal concerns are directly involved.

Need step. With interest thus aroused, proceed to demonstrate fully and systematically how the question under discussion affects each individual member of the audience. Relate the problem to them by showing: *(a)* its direct and immediate effect upon them; *(b)* its present effects on their families, friends, business interests, or the social and professional groups to which they belong; *(c)* its probable future effects.

In showing these effects, employ the strongest possible evidence—specific instances and illustrations, striking statistics, strong testimony—and emphasize little-known or startling facts and conditions. This step will nearly always need to be longer in a speech to an apathetic audience than in a speech directed to an interested but undecided audience or an audience interested in the situation but hostile to the proposal. It will also require more impressive proof and more energetic delivery. From this point, however, you may develop your speech in the same manner as for an audience that is interested but undecided.

Audience hostile to belief in the existence of a problem

If an audience is hostile because they don't believe a problem exists, you must combat this disbelief at the outset, or your speech will have little chance of success. Your listeners are unaware of any danger or threat that confronts them and, therefore, will resist any proposed change in belief or policy.

Attention step. Place yourself on a common footing with the audience in the first few minutes by the use of common ground or the yes-response. Recognize their point of view, and admit whatever merits it may have, without in any way degrading your own. As early as possible, gain agreement on an acceptable criterion by which to judge the belief or policy you intend to advance. Support this criterion by quoting the testimony of persons who are respected by members of the audience—if possible, persons from among their own number.

Need step. Show at some length exactly how your audience's present belief or existing situation violates the criterion laid down in the preceding step and therefore must be corrected. Since this is the point concerning which your hearers are skeptical or uninformed, use powerful facts, figures, and especially testimony to establish your argument. Be careful, however, that you do not exaggerate. Instead of stilling opposition, stretching the facts will only strengthen resistance.

After convincing your hearers that their present belief or condition violates the criterion agreed upon, you may develop the rest of your speech as you would if you were addressing an audience that is interested in the question but hostile to the proposal.

Real-life audiences, obviously, are seldom as clear-cut and uniform in their attitudes as the foregoing discussion would seem to suggest. But if you can determine the attitude of the majority or the more influential part of an audience, you can usually develop an effective speech by following one of the four plans outlined or by employing a combination of them.

Remember, too, that there are times when it will be helpful to develop the need and satisfaction steps of a speech in parallel order, as explained on page 281 of Chapter 16. When this method is used, the various aspects of the need are discussed one at a time, together with that particular part of the plan or proposal which will satisfy each one. The division of points may often be made according to the criteria advanced as a basis for judgment. Thus, you might first consider the "cost" criterion—that is, the desirability of adopting a proposal that will prove as economical as possible—and then show how your proposition meets this test. Next, you might present certain social or cultural criteria, and demonstrate that the proposal satisfies each of these also. Finally, you might indicate the desirability of having a plan that is flexible enough to meet changing conditions, and show that your proposal has this quality. In this way, a complete case for your proposal may be developed in appropriate segments. Whatever method of organization you employ, however, always keep in mind the attitude of your listeners toward your proposition; you must always talk from the point of view of the people who are sitting before you. Notice how the student in the outline (Chapter 24, pp. 472-474) supporting a proposition of policy or a course of action adapted his organization to an interested but undecided audience. Notice also how Mrs. Luce skillfully adapted her arguments to a potentially hostile audience (in the first of the sample speeches printed at the close of this chapter).

SAMPLE SPEECHES

In the following two speeches, observe how the technics suggested in this chapter have been employed. The first speech, "What's Wrong with the American Press?" pp. 429-439, is provided with relatively full comments and analysis; the second, "A Question of Attitudes" (pp. 439-442), by Eugene Parks, a student at the University of Wisconsin, also explores a subject of considerable import for the era in which we live. Using the technics illustrated in the analysis of the first speech, you may wish to attempt a similar analysis of the second.

PRELIMINARY COMMENTS ON MRS. LUCE'S SPEECH

Few women have achieved distinction in so many different fields of endeavor as has Clare Boothe Luce, author, editor, playwright, war correspondent, lecturer, congresswoman, and ambassadress. In 1935, after her marriage to Henry Luce, founder of Time, Inc., publications, she expanded her literary and journalistic activities to include the writing of books and plays; and during World War II, she served as a correspondent on both the European and Asiatic fronts. In 1942, Mrs. Luce was elected to Congress, where she served until 1947. President Eisenhower appointed her ambassadress to Italy in 1953, a post which she filled with distinction until forced to retire four years later because of ill health. As a playwright, Mrs. Luce's most notable success was *The Women,* produced on Broadway in 1937 and later made into a highly successful motion picture.

Many of the talents which enabled Mrs. Luce to attain high rank in these varied pursuits are evident in the following speech which she delivered on April 21, 1960, to the Women's National Press Club at a dinner in honor of the American Society of Newspaper Editors. Defending a proposition of value before an interested but potentially hostile audience (see page 430), Mrs. Luce displayed not only a thorough command of her subject combined with sound reasoning and common sense but also the equally important qualities of tact, fairness, and courage. These qualities were all needed because Mrs. Luce attempted to frankly tell a group of journalists and editors what she believed was "wrong" with them and with the American press in general.

As you will see when you study her talk, Mrs. Luce approaches her central idea indirectly and gradually. During the first few moments she repeatedly uses the technics of concession, conciliation, and compliment to help her win a hearing and pave the way for her major contentions. Once she reaches these contentions, she states them boldly and explains and defends them at length.

Considered in terms of the motivated sequence, Mrs. Luce's speech falls into four major divisions. First comes a combined attention and need step some eighteen paragraphs in length. In this step, contact is made with the audience, the subject of the talk is disclosed and clarified, and an atmosphere of good will is established by Mrs. Luce's full recognition of what is admittedly "right" with the press. The step concludes with a clear statement of the abstract standard or criterion by which Mrs. Luce believes the quality of American journalism must ultimately be measured (last two sentences of paragraph 18).

The satisfaction step, beginning with paragraph 19, also works by indirection, employing examples and explanation to show how the press falls short of the ideal desired. Not until this step is well advanced are the speaker's two specific charges against the press openly stated (paragraph 28).

A relatively short visualization step is introduced by means of a humorous anecdote (paragraph 47) and developed by the method of contrast. An even shorter action step (paragraph 51), couched in the form of a challenge and containing an idealistic and patriotic appeal, concludes the talk.

While supporting material is present in considerable quantities throughout the speech, it is interesting to note that relatively little of it is concrete. Instead of massing incidents, cases, stories, and statistics to substantiate her contentions, Mrs. Luce usually depends upon explanation or generalized references or examples to support her views. Moreover, she artfully employs her own prestige as a journalist and public figure to help underwrite her criticisms of the press and bolster her proposed remedies.

A second interesting feature of the speech is that, except in the action step, relatively little use is made of motivation or emotional appeal. Consequently, the total impression one receives is that of an intelligent and sensible woman presenting in a tactful, good-humored, and yet courageous way ideas that are the result of her own careful study and reflection on the problem.

The style of Mrs. Luce's talk is especially worthy of study. Not only is the expression consistently clear and facile, but, without at any time becoming obtrusive, it is often made vivid by striking phrases and figures of speech—especially rhetorical questions, used both as a means of emphasis and as transitions linking major ideas. From this point of view, the speech provides a good example of how a style may contribute to the general end of persuasion.

WHAT'S WRONG WITH THE AMERICAN PRESS?[5]

Clare Boothe Luce

I am happy and flattered to be a guest of honor on this always exciting and challenging occasion. But looking over

Attention and need steps

[5]From *Vital Speeches of the Day,* XXVI (June 15, 1960), pp. 538-541. Reprinted by permission of Mrs. Luce.

this audience tonight I am less happy than you might think and more challenged than you could know. I stand here at this rostrum invited to throw rocks at you. You have asked *me* to tell *you* what's wrong with *you*—the American press. The subject not only is of great national significance but also has, one should say, infinite possibilities—and infinite perils to the rock thrower. /1

Potential hostility of audience recognized

Conciliation through humor

For the banquet speaker who criticizes the weaknesses and pretensions, or exposes the follies and sins of his listeners—even at their invitation—does not generally evoke an enthusiastic—no less a friendly—response. The delicate art of giving an audience hell is always one best left to the Billy Grahams and the Bishop Sheens. /2

But you are an audience of journalists. There is no audience anywhere who should be more bored—indeed, more revolted—by a speaker who tried to fawn on it, butter it up, exaggerate its virtues, play down its faults, and who would more quickly see through any attempt to do so. I ask you only to remember that I am not a volunteer for this subject tonight. You asked for it! /3

Conciliation through compliment to audience

Appeal for a fair hearing

For what is good journalism all about? On a working, finite level it is the effort to achieve illuminating candor in print and to strip away cant. It is the effort to do this not only in matters of state, diplomacy, and politics but also in every smaller aspect of life that touches the public interest or engages proper public curiosity. It is the effort to explain everything from a summit conference to why the moon looks larger coming over the horizon than it does when it has fully risen in the heavens. It is the effort, too, to describe the lives of men—and women—big and small, close at hand or thousands of miles away, familiar in their behavior or unfamiliar in their idiosyncrasies. It is—to use the big word—the pursuit of and the effort to state the truth. /4

A basic truth or principle with which audience will probably agree readily

No audience knows better than an audience of journalists that the pursuit of the truth, and the articulation of it, is the most delicate, hazardous, exacting and *inexact* of tasks. Consequently, no audience is more forgiving (I hope) to the speaker who fails or stumbles in his own pursuit of it. The only failure this audience could never excuse in any speaker would be the failure to try to tell the truth, as he sees it, about his subject. /5

A second appeal for a fair hearing

In my perilous but earnest effort to do so here tonight, I must begin by saying that if there is much that is wrong

Transition introducing the

with the American press, there is also much that is right with it. /6

major idea of the combined attention-need step

I know, then, that you will bear with me, much as it may go against your professional grain, if I ask you to accept some of the *good* with the bad—even though it may not make such good copy for your newspapers. /7

Conciliation through humor

For the plain fact is that the U. S. daily press today is not inspiringly good; it is just far and away the best press in the world. /8

To begin with, its news gathering, news printing, news dissemination techniques and capacities are without rivals on the globe. /9

Explanation and support of proposition advanced in paragraph 8

The deserving American journalist himself enjoys a far more elevated status than his foreign counterpart anywhere. And this, not only because Americans passionately believe that a free press is vital to the preservation of our form of democracy, but because the average American journalist has, on the record, shown himself to be less venal, less corrupt, and more responsible than the average journalist of many foreign lands. /10

Conciliation through compliment to audience

No capital under the sun has a press corps that is better equipped, and more eager to get the news, the news behind the news, and the news ahead of the news, the inside—outside—topside—bottomside news, than the Washington press corps. /11

I must add only half-jokingly that if the nation's dailies are overwhelmingly pro-Republican in their editorial policy, then the Washington press corps is a large corrective for this political imbalance. Not because Washington reporters are *all* Democrats. Rather because they place on the administration in power their white-hot spotlight of curiosity and exposure. So that no one—Republican or Democrat—can sit complacently in office in this capital unobserved by the men and women of the press who provide the news and information that can make or break an elected or appointed office-holder. /12

Conciliation through humor

Certainly no press corps contains more journalists of competence and distinction, zeal and dedication. What minds regularly tap more "reliable sources" in government, politics, diplomacy? What breasts guard and unguard more "high level" confidences more jealously? What hearts struggle more conscientiously and painfully to determine to what extent truth-telling, or shall we say "leaking," will

Ideas emphasized and style enlivened by use of rhetorical questions serve or unserve the public interest? What typewriters send out more facts, figures, statistics, views, and opinions about great public questions and great public figures? /13

And in what other country of the world are there so many great newspapers? Who could seriously challenge the pre-eminence among the big-city quality press of *The New York Times*? Where in the world is there a "provincial" newpaper (I use the term only in its technical sense) greater than, to take only one outstanding example, *The Milwaukee Journal*? Even the biggest and splashiest of the foreign English-language press, *The London Daily Mirror*, cannot touch in popular journalism *The New York Daily News*. (And since we are talking in superlatives—good and bad—is there a worse paper in England, Japan, France or India than *The New York Sunday Enquirer*?) /14

While the range between the best and the worst is very wide, America's some 1800 newspapers nevertheless average out a higher quality, variety, and volume of information than any other press in the world. /15

Emphasis by negation

Certainly no other press has greater freedom, more freely granted by the people, to find the news and to print it as it finds it. The American press need not be caught in the subtle toils of subsidies by groups or interests. It does not have to fight government newsprint allocations—that overt or covert censorship exercised in many so-called "free countries." Except as the American press is guided by the profit motive, which is in turn guided by the public demand for its papers, it is an unguided press. /16

Summary of major idea of attention-need step

All this is what is right with the American press. And the result of this situation is that our people have more ways to be well informed about issues and events near and far than any people in the world. And they are, by and large, better informed. /17

Transition introducing central question of speech

Criterion by which question must be judged

But now let us come to the question of the evening: "What is wrong with the American press?" We cannot answer this question unless we will voluntarily abandon our relative measurement of it against the press of *other* countries. We must measure it, in absolute terms, against its own highest ideal of freedom, responsibility—and let us not forget, success. /18

Satisfaction step

It is easy to point to many instances in which the American press—especially its individual members—tend to abuse their freedom and shirk their responsibility. /19

Supporting material
Examples and explanation

For example, one could note that nowadays the banner of press freedom is more often raised in matters of printing crime, sex and scandal stories, than it is in matters of printing the truth about great national figures, policies and issues. Or that too many members of the working press uncritically pass on—even if they do not personally swallow—too much high-level government and political cant, tripe, and public relations; or that there are too many journalists who seem willing to sell their birthright of candor and truth in order to become White House pets, party pets, corporation pets, Pentagon or State Department or trade union or Governor's Mansion pets; who wistfully yearn after Grey Eminency, or blatantly strive for publicity for themselves, on lecture platforms or political rostrums. */20*

While agreeing with most journalists that people are not as much interested in the issues as they should be, one could at the same time note that neither are many journalists. One could mention that such journalists seem to have forgotten that *men, not names* alone, make news, and that men are made by the clarity with which they state issues, and the resolution with which they face them. One could express the hope that more journalists would encourage rather than avoid controversy and argument, remembering that controversy and argument are not the enemies of democracy, but its friends. One could wish for fewer journalist prodigies of the well-written factual story, and more gifted talents for drawing explanations from the facts, or that working pressmen would be more creative in reporting the news, or that they would reflect less in themselves of what in this decade they have so roundly condemned in American leadership: apathy, cynicism, luke-warmness, and acceptance of the *status quo* about everything, from juvenile delinquency to nuclear destruction. One could pray, above all, for journalists who cared less about ideologies, and more about ideas. */21*

But such criticisms and complaints—important as they may be—cover only one area of the American press. It is, alas, a relatively small area. A large, unmeasurable percentage of the total editorial space in American newspapers is concerned not with public affairs or matters of stately importance. It is devoted instead to entertainment, titillation, amusement, voyeurism, and tripe. */22*

The average American newspaper reader wants news,

but he wants lots of things from his newspaper besides news: he wants the sports page, the comics, fashion, home-making, advice-to-the-lovelorn, do-it-yourself psychiatry, gossip columns, medical, cooking and decorating features, TV, movie and theater coverage, Hollywood personality stories, Broadway and society prattle, church columns, comics, bridge columns, crossword puzzles, big-money contests. Above all, he wants news that concerns not a bit the public weal but that people just find "interesting" reading. /23

Criticisms in paragraphs above softened by declaration that public must share part of the blame

I confess to enjoying much of this myself. And I do not mean to suggest that every newspaper must read like *The London Times.* But the plain fact is that we are witnessing in America what Professor William Ernest Hocking and others have called the debasement of popular taste. /24

Concession on the part of the speaker

Is it necessary? An editor of my acquaintance was asked recently whether the new circulation rise of his increasingly wild-eyed newspaper was being achieved at the expense of good journalism. He replied: "But you don't understand; our first journalistic need is to survive." I submit that a survival achieved by horribly debasing the journalistic coin is short-lived. The newspaper that engages in mindless, untalented sensationalism gets caught up in the headlong momentum it creates in its readers' appetites. It cannot continue satisfying the voracious appetites it is building. Such journalism may suddenly burn brightly with success; but it will surely burn briefly. /25

Rhetorical question used as transition

Style enlivened by direct discourse and metaphor

We have the familiar example of television closely at hand. The American press has rightly deplored the drivel, duplicity, and demeaning programming that has marked much of television's commercial trust. A critic, of course, need not necessarily always have clean hands. The press is right to flail what is wrong in television just as it is obliged to recognize the great service television has provided in areas where its public affairs, news, and good programs have succeeded in adding something new and enriching to American life. /26

Support by analogy or comparison

But if the press criticizes what is wrong in television without recognizing the moral for itself, it will have missed a valuable and highly visible opportunity for self-improvement. /27

The double charge against the American press may thus

Speaker's double

be stated: its failure to inform the public better than it does is the evasion of its responsibility; its failure to educate and elevate the public taste rather than following that taste like a blind, wallowing dinosaur is an abuse of its freedom. /28

charge against the press specifically stated

In view of the river of information which flows daily from the typewriters of American correspondents at home and abroad, why are the American people not better informed? Whose fault is it? At first glance it would seem to be the fault of the publishers, and especially editors. But the publisher or editor who does not give his readers plenty of what they want is going to lose circulation to a competitor who does. Or if he has a news monopoly in his city, and feels too free to short-change them on these things, he is going to lose circulation as his reader-slack is taken up by the radio, the TV, and the magazines. /29

Conciliation and concession by partial shifting of the blame

Add that even the news the reader wants in most cities, especially the smaller cities throughout the United States, is primarily local news. He remains, even as you and I, more interested in the news of his neighbors, his community, and his city than he is in the news out of Washington, Paris, or Rome. /30

Can we quarrel with this? We cannot. The Declaration of Independence itself set the pattern of the American way, and with it American reading habits. Life, liberty and the pursuit of *happiness* were to be man's prime and legitimate goals. /31

Rhetorical question used as transition

Perhaps the history of our country would have been better —and happier—if "the pursuit of truth, information and enlightenment" had been his third great goal. But that was not the way our Founding Fathers saw things. And that is not the way the American public sees them now. /32

Emphasis by contrast

The fact is that while "man" is a rational animal, *all* men and *all* women are not pre-eminently rational, logical, and thoughtful in their approach to life. They do not thirst, above all, for knowledge and information about the great domestic and international issues, even though these issues may profoundly affect not only their pocketbooks, but their very lives. /33

Today, as yesterday, people are primarily moved in their choice of reading by their daily emotions, their personal, immediate, existential prejudices, biases, ambitions, desires, and—as we know too well in the Freudian age—

by many subconscious yearnings and desires, and irrational hates and fears. /34

Very well then: let us accept the fact. /35

Should the American press bow to it? Accept it? Cater to it? Foster it? /36

Rhetorical questions used as transition

What else (the cynical and sophisticated will ask) is there to do? /37

The American press, no less than the TV and radio, is Big Business. It is now, as never before, a mass medium. As Big Business, it faces daily vast problems of costliness and competition. As a mass medium, it cannot handle these problems without seeking to satisfy the public's feelings, desires and wants. It publishes in the noisiest and most distracted age in our history. It seems doomed to satisfy endlessly the tastes of the nation—pluralistic, pragmatic, emotional, sensuous, and predominantly irrational. By its Big Business mass media nature it seems compelled to seek ever more and more to saturate the mass markets, to soak the common denominator reader-sponge with what it wants. /38

Explanation

Certainly we must face this fact: if the American press, as a mass medium, has formed the minds of America, the mass has also formed the medium. There is action, re-action, and inter-action going on ceaselessly between the newspaper-buying public and the editors. What is wrong with the American press is what is in part wrong with American society. /39

Concession

Is this then to exonerate the American press for its failures to give the American people more tasteful and more illuminating reading matter? Can the American press seek to be excused from responsibility for public lack of information as TV and radio often do, on the grounds that after all, "We have to give the people what they want or we will go out of business"? /40

Rhetorical questions used as transition and for emphasis

No. Not without abdicating its own American birthright, it cannot. The responsibility *is* fixed on the American press. Falling directly and clearly on publisher and editor, this responsibility is inbuilt into the freedom of the press itself. The freedom guaranteed by the Constitution under the First Amendment carries this responsibility with it. /41

Despite earlier concessions, speaker courageously places blame primarily on press itself

"Freedom," as Clemenceau said, "is nothing in the world but the opportunity for self-discipline"; that is to say, voluntarily to assume responsibility. /42

There are many valiant publishers, editors, and journalists in America who have made and are making courageous attempts to give readers a little more of what they *should* have, and a little less of what they want—or, as is more often true, what they only *think* they want, because they have no real knowledge of what is available to them. America owes these publishers and editors and journalists an incomparable debt of gratitude. /43

Concession and more specific assignment of blame (i.e., the criterion—responsibility—is not fully or well met at present)

What is really wrong with the American press is that there are not enough *such publishers and editors.* There is hardly an editor in this room who could not—if he passionately would—give every day, every year, a little more honest, creative effort to his readers on the great issues which face us—the issues which, in the years to come, must spell peace or disaster for our democracy. A beginning would be to try courageously, which is to say *consistently,* to keep such news (however brief) on the front page, playing it in some proportion to its real importance. For a newspaper which relegates to the back pages news which is vital to the citizenry as a whole, in favor of sensational "circulation-building" headlines about ephemeral stories of crime, lust, sex and scandal, is *actively* participating in the debasement of public taste and intelligence. Such a newspaper, more especially its editor, is not only breaking faith with the highest of democratic journalism, he is betraying his nation. And, you may be surprised to hear me say, he may even be courting commercial failure. /44

A specific recommendation for improvement

For there is enough in American life in these exciting sixties to keep interested and absorbed many of the readers who have been written off as impossible to reach except through cheap sensationalism. The commercial challenge is not to achieve success by reaching backward into cliché-ridden ideas, stories, and situations. It is rather to recognize that uniquely now in this country there is natural and self-propelled drive toward a better life, more sustaining and relevant interests. There is, in sum, an infinity of new subjects that make exciting, inviting, and important exploration for the American press. /45

Support by explanation

There can be no doubt that honorable and patriotic publishers and devoted and dedicated editors can increase little by little, in season and out, the public's appetite for better information. There can also be no doubt that they can also decrease, little by little, in the rest of their papers

Principal recommendation of satisfaction step restated and summarized

the type of stories which appeals to the worst in human nature by catering to the lowest-common-denominator taste in morals and ethics. /46

Teddy Roosevelt once said that a good journalist should be part St. Paul and part St. Vitus. /47

Visualization step

A good editor today must be part Santa Claus, part St. Valentine, part St. Thomas (the doubter), part St. Paul, and certainly he must be part St. Jude. St. Jude, as you know, is the patron saint of those who ask for the impossible. /48

Visualization step introduced by humorous allusion

It is not impossible to ask that the American press begin to reverse its present trend, which Dean Ed Barrett of the Columbia School of Journalism calls "giving the public too much froth because too few want substance." If this trend is not reversed (which it can be only by your determined effort), the American press will increasingly become the creature, rather than the creator of man's tastes. It will become a passive, yielding and, curiously, an effeminate press. And twixt the ads for the newest gas range, and the firmest girdle, the cheapest vacuum cleaner, and the best buy in Easter bonnets; twixt the sports page, the fashion page, the teenage columns, the children's comics; twixt the goo, glop, and glamour hand-outs on Elvis Presley and Elizabeth Taylor, and above all twixt the headlines on the sexiest murders, and the type of political editorializing which sees the great presidential issues of the day as being between the case of the "boyish forelock" versus the "tricky ski-jump nose," the press will lose its masculine prerogative which is to educate, inform, engage the interest of, and guide the minds of free men and women in a great democracy. /49

Visualization step developed by method of contrast

Negative phase

As I know that the American Society of Newspaper Editors holds hard to the belief in masculine superiority in the realm of the intellect, and could only view with horror the picture of the Fourth Estate as the "kept man" of the emotional masses, I—for one—am certain this will not happen. /50

Positive phase

Let us watch then, with hope, for the signs of a new, vigorous, masculine leadership in the American press. For if you fail, must not America also fail in its great and unique mission, which is also yours: to lead the world towards life, liberty, and the pursuit of enlightenment—so that it may

Action step

Challenge in form of idealistic and patriotic appeal

achieve happiness? It is that goal which the American press must seize afresh—creatively, purposefully, energetically, and with a zeal that holds a double promise: The promise of success and the promise of enlightenment. /51

A QUESTION OF ATTITUDES[6]

Eugene Parks

For almost 400 years the conscience of the United States has been faced with the problem of granting to the Negro the right to live as an American with equal opportunity to participate in this society. This has been a political problem in that Negroes have been denied the right to vote; it has been an economic problem in that Negroes have been forced to live in the slums of our cities and to do so with little or no education and little or no chance to escape; it has been a social problem in that the plight of the Negro has become a great concern for the entire nation.

For all of us, discussion of the "Negro problem in America" is nothing new. The national press, radio, and television have given considerable attention to civil rights. Each year countless conventions, with speakers and discussion groups, are held to inform the public about the plight of the Negro and discuss possible solutions.

I could speak of the slayings and bombings that have occurred in the South, and this would enable us to realize the injustice and brutality of the segrega-

[6]Presented in The Northern Oratorical League Contest, 1966. Text supplied through the courtesy of Mr. Parks; his instructor, Dennis Day; and The League.

tionist attitude. I could paint a picture of the Negro slums in Milwaukee or Chicago or New York. I could attempt to describe my thoughts about the years and years of deliberate efforts to suppress an entire race, but the important discussion of our human relations problem should deal with the attitudes of our population.

With the passage of federal civil rights legislation, the enactment of fair housing ordinances, and with the War on Poverty program in addition to other programs, the need for laws and funds to combat discrimination is being met. And yet there is evidence across the United States that legislation and money can do only so much.

In 1963 the late President John Kennedy stated that the Negro youth has one half as much chance of completing high school as his white counterpart; one third as much chance of completing college; and twice as much chance of becoming unemployed.

In 1964 the Department of Labor reported that nationally the American unemployment was 4.6 per cent of the total population, and among Negroes it was 9.2 per cent. Among Negro teenagers the unemployment rate was more than twice as high as for the rest of the nation.

All an individual need do is attend a NAACP or CORE or an Urban League meeting. Listen to the discontent voiced by group leaders. Listen to the charges that the War on Poverty Program is not working. President Johnson's Great Society is not producing what he said it would. In some instances there is a need for more money, or more legislation, or better management of programs; but the ultimate solution lies in another area.

I am not saying that discrimination in jobs, housing, and education has disappeared, but I believe the United States has progressed to the time when we must deal directly with the attitudes of the people. Until we do so, from this time on, progress in eliminating discrimination is going to be very slow and very slight. Perhaps we can indirectly legislate attitudes. And people, if they are forced to live and work together, do change their prejudices; but they do so very slowly.

I am looking for a means of speeding up this process by which the Negro will supposedly be fully accepted into this American way of life. I am impatient because I am young, and it is hard to be patient with a nation and a world that has taken so long to progress to this point.

The human relations problem is becoming one in which the Negro is being forced to analyze himself and the white person is being forced to analyze himself. And it is the attitudes of the Negro and the white person toward themselves that affect their attitudes toward each other.

What kind of attitudes am I talking about? The Negro urban birth rate is 40 per cent higher than that of whites, and it is estimated that one fifth of all Negro children are illegitimate. Many of these statistics come from cities with social services available, with welfare and hospital care provided. What kind of attitudes produce these figures which don't seem to be affected by legislation or money?

One attitude is that of the Negro male toward family life. Some sociologists believe that before any real progress can be made in human relations, the family structure must be strengthened. Because the Negro in this nation was forced for hundreds of years to watch his family separated, his women and children mistreated, and stand by powerless to do anything, the Negro male must now meet the responsibilities of being a husband and parent without the social background or economic opportunities to satisfy the demands placed upon him.

This theory is not true in all cases; but growing up in a Negro family and having contact with the Negro community, I can say that the family structure tends to be very weak. As long as this situation remains, then many of the economic and social problems of the Negro will remain.

How do you deal with an individual who has had no real family guidance? How do you deal with an individual whose parents and grandparents have lived with segregation and poverty? How do you deal with an individual who expects nothing of himself or of society?

I know, perhaps through experience, that the civil rights movement involves more than the elimination of overt discrimination and segregation. It involves persuading people that the times have really changed and persuading people to change with the times. It also involves getting people to admit attitudes that they really believe.

Edwin Berry, Director of the Chicago Urban League, once spoke of a project designed to convince Negro teenagers that job opportunities do exist. The teenagers are taken to the business district of Chicago and are shown Negroes who have assumed positions of leadership—jobs that are more challenging than being a porter or a janitor. The project seeks to persuade these teenagers that they can live productive and useful lives.

Another attitude I have often heard expressed is the idea that the civil rights movement is a Negro movement. But this is not a race problem. This is an economic, a political, a social problem caused by the black and the white. This perspective, in which we approach a human relations problem as a Negro problem, defeats any possible solution, because we perpetuate the segregationist style of thinking. We see all of our efforts as designed to help just the Negro race.

The civil rights movement is an effort to assimilate the Negro population into the same way of life with the same set of values as the rest of the population. It involves values dealing with the structure of the family—values dealing with sex, education, and politics. It involves changing opinions that families have held for generations. The means of significantly changing attitudes has not been found; but as people begin to examine themselves and do so earnestly, we can find the tools to deal with this situation.

I am concerned with the attitudes of the Negro population because I happen to be a member of the Negro race. It is important for me to find out how I am contributing to this human relations problem. It is important for each one of us to find out what we really believe and how we are contributing to this problem.

There are many people who tend to talk about other persons' prejudices without dealing with their own. Perhaps this is why a common statement about the North is that the Negro never really knows how much progress in eliminating discrimination has been made. Maybe this is why, despite legislation and broad new programs, many Negroes still feel that they are being denied something which they shouldn't have to ask or bargain for.

Perhaps one attitude toward this problem might be to agree with Julian Bond that, despite the precedents the United States has set in the last decade, an enormous human relations problem still exists, and there are still many prejudiced people in this nation. I tend to agree with Martin Luther King, who continually works for progress and seeks a solution from both Negro and white man. Sometime ago he wrote:

> We ain't what we gonna be.
> We ain't what we want to be.
> We ain't what we ought to be.
> But thank God we ain't what we was.

Problems

1. Recall a speech to convince that you have heard recently. Reconstruct as completely as possible the speech and the situation in which it was delivered. Describe the nature and purpose of the gathering, the initial attitude of the audience, the type of proposition the speaker advanced, the methods he used to develop his talk, and the adjustments he made to the audience's standpoint. Finally, estimate the probable effect the speech had in influencing the beliefs of the listeners.
2. If a suitable opportunity presents itself, attend with several of your classmates a meeting at which one or more speeches to convince are presented (an intercollegiate debate, a political rally, or a meeting of the student senate); and prepare a joint report covering the items listed in Problem 1.
3. Find in the Speeches for Collateral Study or elsewhere a speech on a proposition of policy, a speech on a proposition of fact, and a speech on a proposition of value. Outline each of these speeches carefully. How do they compare in structure with the patterns of development recommended on pages 411-416?

4. Turn in to your instructor four propositions of fact which cannot be settled by observation, experimentation, or direct recourse to printed data and which therefore would make suitable subjects for speeches to convince.
5. Make a list of five of your personal beliefs or convictions that might provide suitable subjects for speeches on propositions of value. Compile a similar list for speeches on propositions of policy.
6. Be ready to explain the function of each of the steps of the motivated sequence in a speech on a proposition of fact, a speech on a proposition of value, and a speech on a proposition of policy.
7. Comment on the speaking manner or delivery used for a speech to convince that you have recently heard delivered in a face-to-face situation or over television. Did the speaker's delivery aid him in achieving conviction, or did it hinder him? Why?
8. Which of the two following methods do you think is more likely to result in full and lasting conviction: *(a)* impressing your listeners with a motive for believing what you want them to believe or *(b)* showing them the logic of your proposal by presenting facts and reasoning? Be able to discuss your choice.
9. Prepare a written or oral report on the ethics of persuasion. Consider such questions as these: What methods and appeals may legitimately be used in effecting conviction? What methods and appeals should always be avoided? Are there any circumstances in which a man not only has the right but the obligation to undertake to convince others?
10. Find in the Speeches for Collateral Study as many instances as possible of the special technics of the speech to convince discussed on pages 421-422. Evaluate the effectiveness with which these devices are used.
11. Find in the Speeches for Collateral Study several instances of each of the forms of reasoning described on pages 418-420. How well does each piece of reasoning meet the tests listed on those pages?
12. Study several newspaper editorials to determine the forms of reasoning used in them. In each case, apply the appropriate test to determine how valid the reasoning is. Do the same for several advertisements clipped from magazines and for several television commercials.
13. Have your instructor help you locate a historically important speech that was delivered to an audience exhibiting one of the attitudes described on pages 423-427 (interested but undecided, interested but hostile to the proposal, etc.). Study the speech to determine the means the speaker employed to adapt his arguments and appeals to this audience attitude. How well would you say he succeeded? Speeches which you might study for this purpose include: Henry Ward Beecher, "Address Delivered at Liverpool, England, October 16, 1863," *Classified Speech Models*, edited by W. N. Brigance (Appleton-Century-Crofts, N.Y., 1928), p. 40 ff.; Henry W. Grady, "The New South," *Select Orations Illustrating American Political History*, edited by Samuel Bannister Harding (Macmillan, N.Y., 1930), p. 489 ff.;

Richard Nixon, "Address to the Russian People," *The Speaker's Resource Book*, edited by Carroll C. Arnold, Douglas Ehninger, and John Gerber, (Glenview, Illinois: Scott, Foresman, 1966), pp. 241-246.

Speaking assignment

1. Present in class a five- to seven-minute speech supporting or attacking one of the following propositions or a proposition suggested by one of these. In developing your talk, adhere to the structure and employ the methods and technics recommended in this chapter.

The United States leads the world in the space race.
Federal research grants are an important source of income for our college.
Good grades are an accurate barometer of future success.
You are safer in an airplane than on the highway.
Tax relief stimulates business activity.
Football has replaced baseball as our national sport.
A liberal education is to be preferred to professional or technical training.
Modern art is degenerate.
The seniority system in Congress hampers the effectiveness of that body.
Our facilities for treating the mentally ill are inadequate and outmoded.
Present federal legislation in the field of civil rights is ineffective.
Trade barriers between nations should be removed.
Intercollegiate athletics (or fraternities) should be abolished.
The federal government should operate on a balanced budget.
The jury system should be abolished.
We should have pay-as-you-view or government-supported television.
All states should require periodic re-examinations of persons holding drivers' licenses.
Strikes should be outlawed.
College professors should be promoted upon the basis of teaching rather than research.
The voting age in all states should be lowered to eighteen years.
The several states should adopt a uniform system of marriage and divorce laws.
R.O.T.C. should be abolished.

Speeches for collateral study

1. Dean Acheson, "Ethics in International Relations Today," *The Speaker's Resource Book*, ed. Carroll C. Arnold, Douglas Ehninger, and John C. Gerber, (Glenview, Illinois: Scott, Foresman, 1966), pp. 229-233.

2. M. M. Chambers, "Higher Education: Who Should Pay?" *Vital Speeches of the Day*, XXXII (May 1, 1966), 447-448.

3. J. W. Fulbright, "Education and Public Policy," *Representative American Speeches, 1964-1965*, ed. Lester Thonssen (New York: Wilson, 1965), 157-169.

4. Richard M. Jackson, "U. S. International Aviation Policy: A New Look Needed," *Vital Speeches of the Day*, XXXII (April 15, 1966), pp. 398-400.

5. John F. Kennedy and Hubert H. Humphrey, "The Kennedy-Humphrey Television Debate in Charleston, West Virginia," *Speeches for Illustration and Example*, ed. Goodwin F. Berquist, Jr. (Glenview, Illinois: Scott, Foresman, 1965), pp. 156-177.

6. Robert F. Kennedy, "Address at Law Day Exercises, University of Georgia," *Rights for Americans: The Speeches of Robert F. Kennedy*, ed. Thomas A. Hopkins (Indianapolis: Bobbs-Merrill, 1964), pp. 13-26.

Suggestions for further reading

Aristotle, *Rhetoric*, 1397a-1400b, "Lines of Proof and Disproof."

Ernest G. Bormann, "An Experimental Approach to Certain Concepts of Logical Proof," *Central States Speech Journal*, XIII (Winter 1961), 85-91.

Winston Brembeck and William S. Howell, *Persuasion: A Means of Social Control* (Englewood Cliffs, N.J.: Prentice-Hall, Inc., 1952).

Robert S. Cathcart, "An Experimental Study of the Relative Effectiveness of Four Methods of Presenting Evidence," *Speech Monographs*, XXII (August 1955), 227-233.

Douglas Ehninger and Wayne Brockriede, *Decision by Debate* (New York: Dodd, Mead & Company, 1963), Chapter VIII, "The Unit of Proof and Its Structure"; Chapter IX, "Evidence"; and Chapter X, "Substantive Proof."

Carl I. Hovland, Irving L. Janis, and Harold H. Kelley, *Communication and Persuasion* (New Haven, Conn.: Yale University Press, 1953), Chapter IV, "Organization of Persuasive Arguments."

Carl I. Hovland, Arthur Lumsdaine, and Fred D. Sheffield, "The Effects of Presenting 'One Side' versus 'Both Sides' in Changing Opinions on a Controversial Subject," *Experiments on Mass Communication*, by the same authors (Princeton, N. J.: Princeton University Press, 1949).

Daniel Katz, ed., *Public Opinion Quarterly*, XXIV (Summer 1960). Special issue on attitude change.

Wayne C. Minnick, *The Art of Persuasion* (Boston: Houghton Mifflin Company, 1957), Chapter I, "Persuasion and Society."

Robert T. Oliver, *The Psychology of Persuasive Speech*, 2nd ed. (New York: Longmans, Green & Company, Ltd., 1957).

Giles St. Aubyn, *The Art of Argument* (New York: Emerson Books, Inc., 1962).

CHAPTER TWENTY-THREE

The speech to stimulate

This chapter will discuss the speech to stimulate or inspire—the speech which attempts to reaffirm the ideals or to arouse the ambitions of the listeners. Sometimes such a speech has inspiration as its only purpose. Often, however, the speaker tries to stimulate the audience in the hope that they will enter upon a prescribed course of action. In this situation he attempts to create among his listeners a feeling of mutuality or agreement primarily through emotional arousal. (See chart, "The Five General Ends of Speech," Chapter 7, p. 115.)

TYPICAL SITUATIONS REQUIRING SPEECHES TO STIMULATE

Occasions for speeches to stimulate or inspire are frequent. *Memorials, dedications,* and *commencement exercises* typically require such talks. At these times it is customary for speakers to recall the traditions and ideals—patriotic, religious, and social—which people esteem but which need periodic revivification if they are to be retained as powerful forces in daily life. Moreover, such occasions offer a speaker the opportunity to deepen the reverence and enthusiasm of the audience for the lives and principles of great men.

At *conventions,* the wise program committee sees that an inspirational speech is presented early in the proceedings; the delegates must be made to feel that their presence is important and that the convention is worth while. Indeed, the primary function of many conventions is to inspire the delegates with greater loyalty and zeal for the cause or occupation which the convention represents. Under such circumstances, a keynote address, specifically intended to inspire or stimulate, is essential. At any meeting or series of meetings, however, the opening speaker not only may acquaint his listeners with the purpose of the occasion but also may endeavor to generate their enthusiasm and establish an appropriate mood for the business at hand.

Nearly all *meetings of sales or promotional organizations* require speeches to inspire. Salesmen are likely to become self-satisfied or disheartened and hence to need repeated stimulation, while promotional groups—particularly volunteer ones, such as a committee handling a community chest drive—require frequent encouragement. A good sales manager or committee chairman, then, not only should be able to criticize when criticism is needed but also should be able to arouse the latent enthusiasm of the people under his direction. *Organization banquets or meetings* afford similar opportunities. More than mere argument is required to get most people to try anything new or to persuade them to work for an organization.

If you attempt to start a club, an improvement association in your local community, or even a baseball team in your club or fraternity, you will always need to arouse enthusiasm. Usually you will find that everyone approves of the idea but suddenly becomes very busy when he is asked to help. People need to be inspired to do their part. *Campaign rallies* present the same problem. During any campaign—political, sales, membership, or financial—the staff of workers must be inspired frequently if they are to carry through their work to a successful conclusion. Teachers, ministers, and parents also at times need to stimulate their charges to greater devotion or more vigorous effort.

These are by no means all the situations in which speeches to stimulate or inspire are appropriate. Wherever there is a problem of spurring men, women, or children to greater activity or higher ambitions, the principles discussed in this chapter will be useful.

THE PURPOSE OF THE SPEECH TO STIMULATE

Obviously the purpose of a speech to stimulate is primarily to arouse enthusiasm or to deepen respect or feeling. But it should not end there. Enthusiasm or deep emotion without direction is like a steam engine running wild. The speaker not only must endeavor to stimulate his listeners but also, whenever possible, must direct them toward a definite course of belief or action. He should not merely arouse the audience but should arouse them about something definite and, if possible, give them something specific to do—a path to follow. Then, if he is to obtain the best results, he should also strive to make the enthusiasm or emotion endure. To inspire men while you are talking to them is one thing; to build the inspiration upon a strong enough foundation so that it lasts long after you have finished speaking is quite another. A sales manager, for example, may arouse a group of salesmen momentarily by picturing expansion of the business or telling of the ease with which someone else has made large sales; but unless he builds in each salesman a sincere belief in his goods, a confidence in his own capacity, and an assurance of personal gain from his work, all the talk of loyalty to the company and of its future will melt away on the first hot summer day. High-pressure methods may stimulate temporarily, but they seldom have a lasting effect.

THE MANNER OF SPEAKING

In presentation, a speech to stimulate should be dynamic, but it should also be obviously earnest and sincere. The outward expression of these qualities will, of course, vary with your specific purpose and with the nature of the occasion. If you wish to stir your listeners to strong enthusiasm, be enthusiastic yourself. Be vigorous both in mind and body; move about; use your arms and hands to emphasize your ideas. On the other hand, if you wish to instill a feeling of reverence or devotion, let your voice and manner suggest the depth of your feeling. At an athletic rally, your speaking may be free and vigorous; at a commencement exercise it may be just as dynamic but more formal and controlled. A sales meeting calls for brisk and decisive utterance, while a dedication ceremony requires dignity and polish. Above all, be well enough prepared so that you will not have to hesitate or use notes; you will have difficulty stimulating people if you falter or if you must constantly refer to a sheaf of papers.

CHARACTERISTICS OF CONTENT

In most situations calling for a speech to stimulate, the chances are strong that your listeners already agree with you in principle; therefore, do not argue with them. Your job is to jar them loose, to stir them up, to move them. The following suggestions can help you accomplish these ends.

Use striking phraseology. In the sample speech at the end of this chapter, notice the effectiveness of such statements as these: "If you cannot gather grapes from thorns, or figs from thistles, neither can you gather golden sentences from an empty mind. The reason why most of us do not say more is just because we have nothing more to say. We cannot speak in public because we do not think in private." Sentences cast into figurative or epigrammatic form make ideas vivid and hence tend to stimulate the imagination as well as to remain in the memory.

Whenever possible, use a slogan as your keynote. Of course, slogans are not always appropriate; but if the gist of your speech can be expressed in a slogan, use it to dramatize your central idea or to tie together your subordinate points. To be effective, a slogan must have many or all of the following qualities: brevity, rhythm, vividness, alliteration, contrast, and strong suggestion. Observe many of these qualities in the phrase, "Millions for defense, but not one cent for tribute!" or in the advertising slogan, "Progress is our most important product."

Be concrete and specific. Instead of saying, "a certain great astronaut," call him by name. Instead of referring to "huge sums of money," say "a hundred and twenty-three million," or "enough money to buy everyone in our whole town a new Lincoln Continental." Don't reiterate abstract principles; your audience agrees with them already. Use vivid examples and stories and incidents to make those principles come alive. Notice in particular the effectiveness of the illustrations in the speeches at the end of this chapter.

Use contrast. Follow an example of failure with one of success. Contrast humor with seriousness, and seriousness with humor. Stand the "big and little of it" side by side for your audience to see. Through carefully drawn contrasts you can achieve the exact focus and emphasis that you desire.

Use strong motivation. Be striking and colorful, but at the same time be sure that your speech is not all glitter. Build it upon the foundation of a strong appeal to fundamental human desires. Touch pride, sympathy, fighting spirit, family affection, desire for self-advancement, or any of the other motives of human action. Be careful, however, not to appeal to selfish motives alone. Although people often do act for selfish reasons, they usually are reluctant to admit that fact. Therefore, couple any self-serving motives with loftier ones, such as loyalty or patriotism.

Use vivid imagery. In every way possible, stir the imagination of your audience. Especially, use vivid descriptions which call up sharp, compelling images in your listeners' minds. Read again the discussion of imagery on pages 321-328, and note the importance of reference to experience and use of detail in creating vivid word pictures. You will find the effective use of imagery one of the most important means for stimulating the emotions of your audience.

ORGANIZATION OF THE SPEECH TO STIMULATE

A short speech to stimulate sometimes is organized simply as a one-point speech. When your purpose is merely to intensify your listeners' feelings about the seriousness of a problem, you may—in order to gain attention at the start—begin with a striking statement of that problem, and then explain it further, using many incisive and vivid examples. If, on the other hand, the audience already recognizes the seriousness of a problem, you may begin your speech with a vivid statement of the attitude or action which you urge, then present a series of descriptions and illustrations to visualize the desirable results which will follow that action, and close with a compelling restatement of your recommendation. Thus your first sentence is the attention, need, and satisfaction steps combined; the bulk of your speech is visualization, and the final statement is the action step.

For those occasions requiring longer or more complex speeches or speeches in which both problem and solution must be developed, all of the steps in the motivated sequence may be employed as follows:

Attention step

A keynote speech or the opening speech of a presiding officer at a meeting or convention usually begins with a reference to the occasion. In other types of speeches, the attention step may consist of an unusual statement or telling illustration. In his attention step in the sample speech on page 453, Dr. Tittle employed an unusual combination of quotation, personal reference, and statement of theme.

Need step

In the need step, stress the importance of greater activity or enthusiasm or a deeper feeling of respect or appreciation. This is done by showing how the present situation is unsatisfactory in contrast to what has been or to what is possible. Frequently the audience is awakened to a consciousness of present weaknesses merely by a vivid picture of possible improvements; thus the contrast between the present and the future is implied rather than stated. In the sample speech "Learning to Speak," for instance, observe how Dr. Tittle, by calling attention to the achievements of great speakers of the past, probably created in his student audience a feeling of the importance of speech and a need for further self-development to make similar accomplishments possible. Remember that a feeling of need cannot be created effectively merely by argument or assertion. Illustrations, narratives, startling facts, vivid phrases and sentences—these are essential. Keep the picture active and moving; and, above all, keep your audience at a high pitch of attention. Sometimes the need step may be short; but more often, particularly when the audience is apathetic or hostile, it is fairly long—comprising from a third to more than a half of the speech.

Satisfaction step

In a speech to stimulate, the satisfaction step is usually short unless it is combined with the visualization step (as in Dr. Tittle's speech). Ordinarily, it proposes one of two things: *(a)* a general attitude or state of mind which the audience is to assume, such as enthusiasm, anger, reverence, devotion, loyalty, renewed activity; or *(b)* a definite plan of action briefly outlined. If the second method is used, some device, such as a slogan or memorable saying, is helpful to impress the plan on the minds of your listeners. Thus, a speaker making a health talk to middle-aged businessmen suggested that they "sleep more; stuff less; and see a doctor often." When a definite course of action is proposed, state it positively but don't argue; argument sometimes convinces, but it seldom inspires.

Visualization step

Ordinarily the greater part of a speech to stimulate is the visualization step. The development of this step nearly always will be of the positive type mentioned in Chapter 16, page 283. Picture conditions as they will be when your plan is put into operation, or heighten the desirability of the feeling or attitude you are urging upon the audience. Here you can even afford a bit of mild exaggeration; everyone usually is with you in principle, and, therefore, overstatement will not seem unnatural. Again, avoid the abstract—be vivid, concrete, and specific; make the picture you draw both lively and realistic. Fill your speech with imagery. Use illustrations and narratives profusely.

Parallel development of need, satisfaction, and visualization steps

Frequently a parallel development of the need, satisfaction, and visualization steps is effective (see Chapter 16, page 281). If the need has more than one main aspect, each aspect may be followed through the need and satisfaction steps separately and drawn together in the visualization step; or more frequently, the need may be treated as one unit, and then its various aspects separately followed through the satisfaction and visualization steps. This latter method is used in the first sample speech: first the need for great speakers is pointed out; then qualities required for greatness are mentioned (satisfaction) and vividly pictured (visualization) one by one. In rare instances, all three steps—need, satisfaction, visualization—may be developed in parallel. When parallel structure is used, however, take care to limit the number of points you develop; too many units followed through individually will result in a stringy, ill-formed speech.

Action step

In a speech to stimulate an audience, no definite action step is required unless your central purpose is to request a specific behavior. Requests for generalized activity or for a certain feeling or attitude are usually implied rather than stated. If the visualization step is adequately developed, the implication will be clear. When an action step is included, it is usually developed in one of three ways: by a *rapid summary* of the specific action required, by a *quotation* which vividly suggests the action or attitude urged, or by a *challenge* which requires personal commitment on the part of the audience—a show of hands, signature, or vocal assent. The last method should never be used unless you are sure the audience is sufficiently aroused to react without hesitation or inhibition; if, however, people do commit themselves publicly, they will feel a certain additional obligation to keep their pledge.

Experience doubtless will suggest many variations of the methods advanced here for preparing and presenting speeches to stimulate; moreover, each individual occasion will dictate modifications. The suggestions presented here, however, provide an effective groundwork for a speech of this nature. Study the sample speeches which follow and also the speeches recommended for collateral study to see what modifications and adaptations are possible.

SAMPLE SPEECHES

The first of the two speeches that follow was a commencement address delivered to the graduates of the Northwestern University School of Speech in June 1924. The speaker was at the time of the speech pastor of the First Methodist Church of Evanston, Illinois, a church which a majority of the audience regularly attended. The occasion allowed for the full development of the speaker's ideas and required a relatively polished style. Note especially the wealth of illustrations, the parallel development of the satisfaction and visualization steps, and the absence of any definitely stated request for action.

LEARNING TO SPEAK[1]

Ernest Fremont Tittle

Attention step

One day, without any very definite outline in mind, Robert Burns sat down to write a poem and frankly confessed:

> Which way the subject theme may gang
>   Let time and chance determine;
> Perhaps it may turn out a sang—
>   Or probably a sermon.

I wish—how I wish tonight—that I might produce a song. But, if I succeed in producing anything, it will probably be a sermon. When Coleridge asked Lamb, "Did you ever hear me preach, Charles?" Lamb replied, "I n-never heard you do anything else." The bearing of this famous retort upon the present instance is, I am afraid, only too obvious.

But be it a "sang," or be it a "sermon," the theme which I have chosen for this occasion is Learning to Speak. And I marvel at my own temerity. I can only hope that some of you will consider it pertinent. You need not suggest—I already know—that it is also impertinent!

Need step

Everybody ought to learn how to speak. First, because speaking clarifies thought. I am going to suggest further on that clear thinking is the primary

[1]Reprinted by special permission of Mrs. Ernest F. Tittle.

requisite for good speaking; but just now I should like to suggest that honest effort to express thought usually results in clarifying it.

When someone complains, "I know what I want to say but cannot say it," you may not confess your well-founded suspicion that he doesn't quite know what he wants to say; but you may, perhaps, tactfully suggest that if only he will try to say what he knows, he will even better know what he is trying to say.

Once you have got your thought expressed you have a clearer understanding of the thought that you have wanted to express. Everybody, therefore, ought to learn how to speak if for no other reason than for the purpose of clarifying his own thinking.

But is it not also true that "a word fitly spoken is like apples of gold in pictures of silver"? It gives pleasure. Listening to good English, like listening to good music, is one of the most satisfying enjoyments of life. The brilliant conversationalist is a social asset even though it must be said of him, as it was said of W. T. Stead, that "his idea of good conversation is to have another man to listen to him."

And is not the clever after-dinner speaker a public servant? There is, to be sure, a vast difference between post-prandial orators. Once upon a time a mayor of Chicago introduced Chauncey Depew by suggesting that he was like an automatic machine—"You put in a dinner and up comes a speech." When Mr. Depew gained his feet, he suggested that the difference between his after-dinner speaking and the chairman's was that his Honor, the Mayor, "puts in a speech and up comes your dinner." But you will, I think, agree with me that the accomplished after-dinner speaker is a public servant. If he adds but little—and he usually does—to the sum total of the world's knowledge, he adds considerably to the sheer enjoyment of life.

Moreover, the pleasure which may be given by a gifted speaker is by no means the only service which he is able to render. For, as Walter Savage Landor once remarked, "On a winged word hath hung the destiny of nations." The speeches of Demosthenes in Athens, of Cicero in Rome, of Pitt and Burke and Gladstone in England, of Webster and Lincoln and Wilson in America, were not only utterances; they were events. They not only appealed to history. They made history. And this, at least to some extent, has been true of speeches made by far lesser men.

History used to be written as though it were merely a string of great men's biographies. This, as you remember, was the method of Plutarch. It was the method, also, of Carlyle, who once said of England that she boasted twenty-seven millions of people—mostly fools; and of the United States, "They have begotten with a rapidity beyond recorded example eighteen million of the greatest bores ever seen in this world before."

History for Carlyle was simply a succession of great men's biographies. He worshiped the hero and despised the crowd.

But the crowd, as we are beginning to realize, is not to be despised.

Think of the reformers before the Reformation: the unnumbered thousands who prepared the way for Luther; who helped to create the intellectual and moral environment of which Luther availed himself when he nailed his ninety-eight theses to the door of the old church in Wittenberg, and carved for himself a conspicuous place in the memory of mankind. Think of the unpictured, unpraised persons who fanned the fires of conviction which lighted the way for Abraham Lincoln to move into immortality as the emancipator of four million slaves. Think of the unfamous persons in every country in the world today who are forging the demand that war shall be placed in the same category with dueling, piracy, and human slavery.

It has been said that "The frail snowflake has sculptured continents." Is it not equally true that the spoken thought, not only of great men, but of millions of ordinary men, has molded the lives of nations and determined the course of civilization? How important, then, it is that everybody should learn how to speak. The voice of the ordinary man may not carry very far. All the more reason why, as far as it does carry, it should be made as clear and compelling as possible.

Satisfaction and visualization steps in parallel

Everybody may learn how to speak. By learning to speak, of course, I mean something different from learning to talk. Not long ago I heard an American Indian suggest that when the White man says to the Red man, "Why don't you talk more?" the Red man would like to reply to the White man, "Why don't you say more?" A vivacious representative of the gentler sex once asked Henry James whether he did not think that American women talk better than English women. "Yes," he replied, "they are more ready and much more brilliant. They rise to every suggestion. But," he added reflectively, and with rare tactfulness, "English women so often know what they are talking about." And has not Christopher Morley sententiously remarked that "The unluckiest insolvent in the world is the man whose expenditure of speech is too great for his income of ideas"?

By learning to speak one wishes to mean something more than learning to vocalize. The latter accomplishment is not beyond the reach of a parrot.

But everybody who is not an idiot may learn not only how to talk but how to speak. Ability to speak, like ability to swim or to drive a golf ball or to play the piano, may be cultivated. You may never develop into a Wendell Phillips or a Frances Willard, any more than you may develop into a Sybil Bauer or a Bobbie Jones or a Paderewski; but you need not go stuttering and stammering through life. As a biological descendant of Adam and Eve, you have a tongue and some teeth, and a modicum at least of intelligence. As a linguistic descendant of Shakespeare and Milton, you have nine parts of speech and a possible vocabulary of more than three hundred thousand words to choose from. If, therefore, you do not learn how to speak, it is your own fault. It is not because you cannot learn. It is merely because you will not go to the trouble of learning.

What, then, are some of the essential requirements for learning to speak as over against the mere ability to vocalize in a half-dozen languages? Let me mention, first, the ability to think. The man who has something to say can and will find some way to say it. If any man remains a "mute inglorious Milton," it is not because he cannot say what he thinks; it is rather because he has never thought anything worth saying.

If you cannot gather grapes from thorns, or figs from thistles, neither can you gather golden sentences from an empty mind. The reason why most of us do not say more is just because we have nothing more to say. We cannot speak in public, because we do not think in private.

A somewhat distinguished English preacher, who was naturally fluent, once declared that he could always go on saying something until he had something to say. But a far safer guide for most of us to follow is that deservedly famous stump speaker who advised, "Fill yourself with your subject, then knock out the bung and let nature caper."

Remy de Gourmont has remarked that "Works well thought out are invariably well written." Allowing for the inevitable exceptions, he has, I suspect, stated the rule—a rule which applies not only to effective writing but to effective speaking. Works well thought out are almost invariably well written; and ideas well thought out are almost invariably well spoken. A poor speech may be the result of a number of causes, including, perhaps, milk-fed chicken, vanilla ice cream, and French pastry; but it is even more likely to be the result of sloppy thinking. The ambitious speaker would do well to spend more time in clarifying his thought than in choosing his words.

Yet words, too, are important. There are colorful words that are as beautiful as red roses; and there are drab words that are as unlovely as an anaemic-looking woman. There are concrete words that keep people awake, and abstract words that put them to sleep. There are strong words that can punch like a prize-fighter; and weak words that are as insipid as a "mama's boy." There are warm, sympathetic words that grip men's hearts; and cold, detached words that leave an audience unmoved. There are noble words that lift every listener, at least for a moment, to the sunlit heights of God; and base words that leave an audience in the atmosphere of the cabaret. And so, other things being equal, including abstemious eating and clear thinking, the most effective speech will be the speech that contains the greatest number of colorful, concrete, strong, sympathetic, and inspiring words. Provided . . . what?

Very much of the effectiveness of public speaking depends upon the technic employed by the speaker.

An exasperated parishioner, who felt it incumbent upon him to protest against the feebleness of the clerical profession, remarked to the Reverend Sidney Smith, "If I had a son who was an idiot, I would make him a parson." To which the Reverend Sidney Smith replied, "Your father evidently was of a different opinion." Some protest, no doubt, needed to be made; but the gentleman who ventured to make it had not developed the right technic.

There are, as I have discovered, two very different ways of calling someone's attention to the fact that he has taken certain unwarranted liberties with the truth. If you employ the wrong way, the response is very likely to be, "You're another!" But if you employ the right way, the response may be, "Perhaps I have; and I shall endeavor hereafter to confine myself strictly to facts."

I was present some time ago at a meeting at which two speeches were made on the same theme. Both speakers, as it happened, took substantially the same position. But when the first speaker sat down, the audience was distinctly unfriendly; and when the second speaker sat down, the same audience vigorously applauded him. Both had said the same thing; but the first had said it in a way that merely irritated his audience, whereas the second had said it in a way that had convinced his audience. Many a speaker has met with opposition not so much because of what he said as because of the way in which he said it.

There is, of course, the exactly opposite danger that a man may say something that needs to be said, but say it so cautiously that no one will realize that he has said it. He will get it out, but he will not get it over; and if he fails to get it over, he has made an ineffective speech.

Not long ago, in the course of an address, I repeated the deservedly famous story of the merchant who hung out a sign reading, "I am a One Hundred Per Cent American: I hate Jews, Catholics, Negroes, and foreigners"; whereupon his competitor across the street hung out a sign reading, "I am a Two Hundred Per Cent American: I hate everybody." At the close of the meeting, an ardent member of the local Ku Klux Klan came forward and warmly congratulated me! I had gotten it out; but I had not, apparently, gotten it over.

One way to get something out without getting it over is to confine yourself to glittering generalities. Almost any audience will applaud glittering generalities, especially if they are couched in familiar rhetorical phrases.

Some one gets up and affirms, with the air of Christopher Columbus discovering America, that what this country needs is a good old-fashioned revival of religion. Shouts of Amen! from the Methodist corner. Decorous cries of Hear! Hear! from the Presbyterian corner. Smiles of approval from the Congregational corner. Slight intimations of approval from the Episcopalian corner. Even the out-and-out pagan in the audience feels an impulse to applaud! A good old-fashioned revival of religion sounds harmless enough. To the traditionalist it suggests the theology on which he was brought up. To the dogmatist it suggests the truth—as he sees it. To the emotionalist it suggests a perfectly wonderful opportunity to enjoy the luxury of inexpensive tears. To the pious profiteer and the orthodox exploiter, it suggests a type of religion which raises no embarrassing questions, makes no inconvenient demands, but leaves men undisturbed in the enjoyment of the fruits of other people's labor, and furnishes a divine sanction for the maintenance of the status quo. And so, as a sonorous platitude, almost any audience will endorse the statement that what this country needs is a good old-fashioned revival of religion.

But suppose the speaker feels under some obligation to descend from the pleasant heights of glittering generalities to the arduous lowlands of particular applications. Suppose he feels impelled to suggest that a good old-fashioned revival of religion would involve, as it did in the days of John the Baptist, an urgent, unflinching demand that the rough ways of industry shall be made smooth; and that the crooked ways of politics shall be made straight; and that every mountain and hill of unearned wealth shall be brought low; and that every valley of undeserved poverty shall be filled; and that all flesh shall be given equality of educational and economic opportunity; and that nothing less than this shall be termed the salvation of God. Having made a suggestion of this sort, would not the preacher discover a sudden drop of at least forty degrees in the temperature of the audience?

To be effective, a public speaker must develop a technic which will enable him to get out what needs to be said without needless and fruitless irritation, and at the same time to get it over.

But if much depends upon the technic of speaking, much more depends upon the life of the speaker. You cannot make silken purses out of sows' ears; nor can you get a big speech out of a little speaker. Schools of speech may give you a faultless technic. But what shall it profit a speaker if he acquire a faultless technic but fail to develop his mind and to enrich his soul?

When Senator Hayne had delivered, in the United States Senate, his famous speech defending the right of a sovereign state to withdraw from the Union, there were men of no little discernment who declared with heavy hearts that his argument was unanswerable. But, on the following day, Senator Hayne's unanswerable argument was brilliantly answered by Daniel Webster; and the Senate chamber had witnessed probably the most wonderful burst of pure oratory yet heard on the continent. Afterwards, Webster was asked how long he had been in the preparation of his great Reply. His answer was, "Twenty years." Said he, "When I stood up in the Senate Chamber and began to speak, a strange sensation came to me. All that I had ever thought, or read in literature, in history, in law, in politics, seemed to unroll before me in glowing panorama; and then it was easy, whenever I wanted a thunderbolt, to reach out and take it as it went smoking by."

Great speeches are not born in a day. It may require as long as twenty years to bring them forth. For they come out of the slowly nourished minds of men. They come out of the slowly maturing souls of men. They come very often out of suffering and heartache and loneliness and all but despair. They never come out of shallow minds and sordid secular souls.

How fearfully flat mere declamation falls. "Give me liberty or give me death," cries the school boy; and his declamation may be rhetorically impeccable. Yet somehow it is unconvincing. The words appear; but they are like wax figures in a museum. Only the flaming soul of a Patrick Henry could give them life.

I do not mean to suggest that it is beyond the power of a great actor to give convincing expression to words that another has written or spoken. I do mean to suggest that, in order to do so, the actor himself must, as a man, be great enough actually to experience the sentiment he is expressing.

Carlyle used to insist that "Sincerity is the first characteristic of all men in any way heroic. All the great men I have ever heard of," he declared, "have [sincerity] as the primary material of them."

Can you think of any permanently effective public speaker who was not deeply and even passionately sincere? I except, of course, the mere rhetorician: the popular preachers, the political spell-binders, the matinée idols, and every other kind of vocalizing idol whose feet are of clay. They have, to be sure, their little vogue, their little coterie of worshipers. But if they go up like a rocket, they come down like a stick, leaving no permanent light in the sky. It is not of such, but only of men who, being dead, yet speak, that I am thinking when I ask: Can you recall any single permanently effective public speaker who was not deeply and even passionately sincere?

In preparation for the important speech which he was to deliver on the occasion of his nomination to the United States Senate, Mr. Lincoln read that famous classic to which I have already referred, Webster's "Reply to Hayne." It begins, as you may remember, in this fashion:

"Mr. President: When the mariner has been tossed for many days in thick weather, and on an unknown sea, he naturally avails himself of the first pause in the storm, the earliest glimpse of the sun, to take his latitude, and ascertain how far the elements have driven him from his course. Let us imitate this prudence, and before we float farther on the waves of this debate, refer to the point from which we departed, that we may at least be able to conjecture where we now are."

But the sonorous sentences of the silver-tongued orator of the East were not natural to the plain-speaking lawyer of the West; and when Lincoln sat down to compose his speech, he began:

"Mr. Chairman: If we could first know where we are and whither we are tending, we could better judge what to do, and how to do it."

And, having before him, as I cannot but believe, these two classical examples, Woodrow Wilson began his own last published article in this fashion:

"In these doubtful and anxious days, when all the world is at unrest, and, look which way you will, the road ahead seems darkened by shadows which portend dangers of many kinds, it is only common prudence that we should look about us and attempt to assess the causes of distress and the most likely means of removing them."

In this last introduction one finds neither the ponderous oratory of a Webster

—quite natural to him; nor the homespun speech of a Lincoln—equally natural to him; but just that peculiar combination of embroidered Latinity and Anglo-Saxon simplicity which was natural to Woodrow Wilson.

Webster, Lincoln, Wilson—three Americans whose speeches became historical events. And different as they were in many respects, they were alike in this respect that Webster, during his great days, and Lincoln and Wilson during all their days, were passionately sincere.

Whosoever would be permanently effective as a public speaker must be sincere. If a personal confession be allowed, I may say that no man, however brilliant or eloquent, can move me to anything save anger if I have reason to believe that what he is contradicts what he says.

Is it not also true that whosoever would move his audience must lose sight of himself?

An old schoolmate of Joseph Parker once came to him in great distress. Joseph Parker was, at that time, one of the greatest of living preachers. The schoolmate was an undistinguished country curate.

"Parker," he said, "what is the matter with me? I have got a brain that is just as good as yours is; but for some reason, I am not able to get anywhere with it."

"Well," said Joseph Parker, "let me see what you do. Stand at the other end of this room and deliver for me your last Sunday's sermon."

The undistinguished curate did so, and received this criticism: "My old friend, the trouble with you is that you are trying to get something off instead of trying to get something in."

In the year 1858, the eyes of the American people were fixed upon two men. These men were engaged in a series of debates. And they were debating the greatest question of the age. One of them was trying to be eloquent; the other was trying to be honest. One was endeavoring to get something off; the other was endeavoring to get something in. One was seeking to win an election; the other was seeking to win a cause.

When Judge Douglas finished speaking, men shouted themselves hoarse, and exclaimed, "What a wonderful speech!" When Mr. Lincoln sat down, they said to one another, "Old Abe is right."

Douglas won the election. Lincoln said in a letter to a friend: "I am glad I made the late race. It gave me an opportunity to be heard on the greatest question of the age such as I could have gotten in no other way; and now, though I sink out of sight and become forgotten, I think I have made some marks which will tell for the cause of Liberty after I am gone." But, Abraham Lincoln did not sink out of sight or become forgotten. The American people—a determined portion of them—were looking for just such a man. It now appears that God Almighty was looking for just such a man. And when He found him, He highly exalted him and gave him a name that is above every name in American history.

When Douglas died, he moaned, "I have failed." When the spirit of Abraham Lincoln returned to the God who gave it, Edwin M. Stanton remarked, "And now, he belongs to the ages."

How everlastingly true it is even of public speakers: whosoever would save his life shall lose it; but whosoever will lose his life in devotion to a great cause will save it.

(No stated action step—the general attitude and course of action are implied.)

The following speech by the Reverend Martin Luther King, Jr., was delivered to a large outdoor audience gathered about the Lincoln Memorial in Washington, D.C., on the afternoon of August 28, 1963. It came as the climax of an all-day freedom march and demonstration which had brought some 200,000 persons to the capital city. As the text of the speech clearly shows, its purpose was to stimulate the listeners to carry on with renewed vigor the struggle to secure equal rights for persons of all races.[2]

I HAVE A DREAM[3]

Martin Luther King, Jr.

I am happy to join with you today in what will go down in history as the greatest demonstration for freedom in the history of our nation.

Five score years ago, a great American, in whose symbolic shadow we stand today, signed the Emancipation Proclamation. This momentous decree came as a great beacon light of hope to millions of Negro slaves, who had been seared in the flames of withering injustice. It came as a joyous daybreak to end the long night of their captivity.

But one hundred years later, the Negro is still not free. One hundred years later, the life of the Negro is still sadly crippled by the manacles of segregation and the chains of discrimination. One hundred years later, the Negro lives on a lonely island of poverty in the midst of a vast ocean of material prosperity. One hundred years later *(Applause)*, the Negro is still languished in the corners of American society and finds himself an exile in his own land. So we have come here today to dramatize a shameful condition.

[2]For a description of the speaking situation and an analysis of the structure of the address itself, see Carroll C. Arnold, Douglas Ehninger, and John C. Gerber, *The Speaker's Resource Book*, 2nd ed. (Glenview, Illinois: Scott, Foresman, 1966), pp. 152-154.

[3]Reprinted by permission of Dr. King.

In a sense we've come to our nation's Capitol to cash a check. When the architects of our republic wrote the magnificent words of the Constitution and the Declaration of Independence, they were signing a promissory note to which every American was to fall heir. This note was a promise that all men—yes, black men as well as white men—would be guaranteed the unalienable rights of life, liberty, and the pursuit of happiness.

It is obvious today that America has defaulted on this promissory note in so far as her citizens of color are concerned. Instead of honoring this sacred obligation, America has given the Negro people a bad check; a check which has come back marked "insufficient funds" *(Applause)*. But we refuse to believe that the bank of justice is bankrupt. We refuse to believe that there are insufficient funds in the great vaults of opportunity of this nation. So we've come to cash this check—a check that will give us upon demand the riches of freedom and the security of justice *(Applause)*. We have also come to this hallowed spot to remind America of the fierce urgency of *now*. This is no time to engage in the luxury of cooling off or to take the tranquilizing drug of gradualism. *Now is the time* to make real the promises of Democracy. *Now is the time* to rise from the dark and desolate valley of segregation to the sunlit path of racial justice. *Now is the (Applause) time* to lift our nation from the quicksands of racial injustice to the solid rock of brotherhood. *Now is the time* to make justice a reality for all of God's children.

It would be fatal for the nation to overlook the urgency of the moment. This sweltering summer of the Negro's legitimate discontent will not pass until there is an invigorating autumn of freedom and equality. Nineteen sixty-three is not an end, but a beginning. Those who hope that the Negro needed to blow off steam and will now be content will have a rude awakening if the nation returns to business as usual *(Applause)*. There will be neither rest nor tranquility in America until the Negro is granted his citizenship rights. The whirlwinds of revolt will continue to shake the foundations of our nation until the bright day of justice emerges.

But that is something that I must say to my people who stand on the warm threshold which leads into the palace of justice. In the process of gaining our rightful place we must not be guilty of wrongful deeds. Let us not seek to satisfy our thirst for freedom by drinking from the cup of bitterness and hatred *(Applause)*.

We must forever conduct our struggle on the high plane of dignity and discipline. We must not allow our creative protest to degenerate into physical violence. Again and again we must rise to the majestic heights of meeting physical force with soul force. The marvelous new militancy which has engulfed the Negro community must not lead us to a distrust of all white people, for many of our white brothers, as evidenced by their presence here today, have come to realize that their destiny is tied up with our destiny *(Applause)*. And they have come to realize that their freedom is inextricably bound to our freedom. We cannot walk alone.

And as we walk, we must make the pledge that we shall always march ahead. We cannot turn back. There are those who ask the devotees of civil rights, "When will you be satisfied?" We can never be satisfied as long as the Negro is the victim of the unspeakable horrors of police brutality. We can never be satisfied as long as our bodies, heavy with the fatigue of travel, cannot gain lodging in the motels of the highways and the hotels of the cities *(Applause)*. We cannot be satisfied as long as the Negro's basic mobility is from a smaller ghetto to a larger one. We can never be satisfied as long as our children are stripped of their selfhood and robbed of their dignity by signs stating "For Whites Only" *(Applause)*. We cannot be satisfied as long as a Negro in Mississippi cannot vote and a Negro in New York believes he has nothing for which to vote *(Applause)*. No, no, we are not satisfied, and we will not be satisfied until justice rolls down like waters and righteousness like a mighty stream *(Applause)*.

I am not unmindful that some of you have come here out of great trials and tribulations. Some of you have come fresh from narrow jail cells. Some of you have come from areas where your quest for freedom left you battered by the storms of persecution and staggered by the winds of police brutality. You have been the veterans of creative suffering. Continue to work with the faith that unearned suffering is redemptive.

Go back to Mississippi, go back to Alabama, go back to South Carolina, go back to Georgia, go back to Louisiana, go back to the slums and ghettos of our northern cities, knowing that somehow this situation can and will be changed. Let us not wallow in the valley of despair.

I say to you today, my friends *(Applause)*, so even though we face the difficulties of today and tomorrow, I still have a dream. It is a dream deeply rooted in the American dream.

I have a dream that one day this nation will rise up and live out the true meaning of its creed: "We hold these truths to be self-evident; that all men are created equal" *(Applause)*.

I have a dream that one day on the red hills of Georgia the sons of former slaves and the sons of former slaveowners will be able to sit down together at the table of brotherhood; I have a dream—

That one day even the state of Mississippi, a state sweltering with the heat of injustice, sweltering with the heat of oppression, will be transformed into an oasis of freedom and justice; I have a dream—

That my four little children will one day live in a nation where they will not be judged by the color of their skin but by the content of their character; I have a dream today *(Applause)*.

I have a dream that one day, down in Alabama, with its vicious racists, with its governor having his lips dripping with the words of interposition and nullification, one day right there in Alabama little black boys and black girls will be able to join hands with little white boys and white girls as sisters and brothers; I have a dream today *(Applause)*—

I have a dream that one day every valley shall be exalted, every hill and mountain shall be made low, the rough places will be made plane and crooked places will be made straight, and the glory of the Lord shall be revealed, and all flesh shall see it together.

This is our hope. This is the faith that I go back to the South with. With this faith we will be able to hew out of the mountain of despair a stone of hope. With this faith we will be able to transform the jangling discords of our nation into a beautiful symphony of brotherhood. With this faith we will be able to work together, to pray together, to struggle together, to go to jail together, to stand up for freedom together, knowing that we will be free one day *(Applause)*.

This will be the day *(Applause)*. . . . This will be the day when all of God's children will be able to sing with new meaning "My country 'tis of thee, sweet land of liberty, of thee I sing. Land where my fathers died, land of the pilgrim's pride, from every mountainside, let freedom ring," and if America is to be a great nation—this must become true.

So let freedom ring—from the prodigious hilltops of New Hampshire, let freedom ring; from the mighty mountains of New York, let freedom ring—from the heightening Alleghenies of Pennsylvania!

Let freedom ring from the snowcapped Rockies of Colorado!

Let freedom ring from the curvaceous slopes of California!

But not only that; let freedom ring from Stone Mountain of Georgia!

Let freedom ring from Lookout Mountain of Tennessee!

Let freedom ring from every hill and mole hill of Mississippi. From every mountainside, let freedom ring, and when this happens *(Applause)*. . .

When we allow freedom to ring, when we let it ring from every village and every hamlet, from every state and every city, we will be able to speed up that day when all of God's children, black men and white men, Jews and Gentiles, Protestants and Catholics, will be able to join hands and sing in the words of the old Negro spiritual, "Free at last! Free at last! Thank God almighty, we are free at last!" *(Thunderous applause.)*

Problems

1. List all of the situations you can think of which call for speeches to stimulate. Then classify these situations as to type (situations calling for the arousal of enthusiasm, the deepening of a feeling of respect or reverence, the rededication to fundamental principles, etc.). Finally, describe the manner of presentation or delivery which you think would be appropriate to each type of situation.
2. Compare the speech to stimulate with the speech to convince, basing your comparison on the following points: *(a)* characteristics of content, *(b)* allover structure or organization, *(c)* attitude of audience to which it is presented, and *(d)* preferred manner of style or expression.
3. Consider the church sermon as a species of the speech to stimulate. To what extent might an effective sermon follow the principles and methods outlined in this chapter? What special modifications or adaptations would need to be made?
4. A special type of speech to stimulate is the keynote address given at a national political convention. With the aid of your instructor, locate in *Vital Speeches of the Day* or elsewhere such a keynote address and analyze it in terms of the principles and criteria set forth above. (William Jennings Bryan's "Cross of Gold" speech listed in the Speeches for Collateral Study may be used for this purpose.)
5. Outline the sample speech "I Have a Dream," printed at the end of this chapter and compare its structure with the plan of organization recommended on pages 450-452.
6. Note in this same speech examples of striking or memorable phrases and expressions, of contrast, and of motive appeal. Does the speaker use a slogan? To what extent do you think the style of the speech, as distinguished from the ideas presented, served the end of stimulation? Defend your answer.
7. Consider the problems presented by the typical high school or college commencement address, conceived of as a speech to stimulate. In your judgment, is it easy or difficult to construct an effective commencement address of this sort? What specific advantages does the speaker have in such a situation? What specific difficulties must he overcome? What are some of the ways

in which these difficulties might be surmounted? Should a commencement address which seeks to stimulate be directed to the graduates, to the general audience, or to both? Explain.

8. Contrast as to *(a)* purpose, *(b)* suitable content, *(c)* probable organizational pattern, *(d)* style, and *(e)* manner of delivery a speech to stimulate given at a pep rally preceding the homecoming football game and a speech to stimulate given at Memorial Day services.

Speaking assignment

1. Prepare and present to the class a five- or six-minute speech to stimulate, suitable for one of the following occasions (or a similar occasion). Use one of the patterns of organization outlined on pages 450-452, and pay particular attention to the problem of adapting your style and manner of delivery to the subject matter of your speech and to the assumed speaking situation.

The first meeting of a group of volunteer workers for a community chest drive.
An athletic pep rally.
A student-government sponsored Veterans' Day or Memorial Day service held on campus and open to both students and faculty.
A meeting held to commemorate the anniversary of the founding of your college.
A sales meeting of the advertising staff of the college newspaper or yearbook.
The opening meeting of a two-day student study conference on some current national or international problem (civil rights, United States foreign policy, labor relations, etc.).

(*Note:* Either you or your instructor should announce in advance of the speech the nature of the speaking situation and/or of the audience you assume.)

Speeches for collateral study

1. William Jennings Bryan, "Cross of Gold," *Famous Speeches in American History*, ed. Glenn R. Capp (Indianapolis: Bobbs-Merrill, 1963), pp. 119-131.
2. Russell Conwell, "Acres of Diamonds," *American Forum: Speeches on Historic Issues, 1788-1900*, ed. Ernest J. Wrage and Barnet Baskerville (New York: Harper & Row, 1960), pp. 263-275.
3. Jonathan Edwards, "Sinners in the Hands of an Angry God," *American Speeches*, ed. Wayland Maxfield Parrish and Marie Hochmuth (New York: Longmans, Green, 1954), pp. 73-90.
4. Samuel B. Gould, "A Flavor for Our Daily Bread," *Representative American Speeches, 1962-1963*, ed. Lester Thonssen (New York: Wilson, 1963), pp. 122-128.
5. Herbert Hoover, "Leadership for a Free World," *Vital Speeches of the Day*, XIV (July 1, 1948), 548 ff.
6. Bryan McEntegart, "A Totality of Outlook," *Contemporary American Speeches*, ed. Wil A. Linkugel, R. R. Allen, and Richard L. Johannesen (Belmont, Calif.: Wadsworth, 1965), pp. 175-178.

7. Bryon Dehaan, "Enlisting Community Support for Civil Rights." *Vital Speeches of the Day,* XXXII (February 15, 1966), pp. 272-275.

8. M. I. Prichard, "Across the Potomac on London Bridge." *Vital Speeches of the Day,* XXXII (May 15, 1966), pp. 464-466.

9. M. J. Warnock, "A Stretch of the Imagination." *Vital Speeches of the Day,* XXXII (February 1, 1966), pp. 234-237.

Suggestions for further reading

Wilbur E. Gilman, Bower Aly, and Loren D. Reid, *The Fundamentals of Speaking* (New York: The Macmillan Company, 1951), Chapter XIV, "Impressing."

Giles Wilkeson Gray and Waldo W. Braden, *Public Speaking: Principles and Practice,* 2nd ed. (New York: Harper & Row, 1963), Chapter XXI, "The Stimulating Speech."

Richard E. Hughes and P. Albert Duhamel, "Rhetorical Qualities of Words," in *Selected Readings in Public Speaking,* ed. Jane Blankenship and Robert Wilhoit (Belmont, California: Dickenson Publishing Co., Inc., 1961), pp. 130-156.

James H. McBurney and Ernest J. Wrage, *The Art of Good Speech* (New York: Prentice-Hall, Inc., 1953), Chapter XVI, "The Methods of Evocation."

Ralph A. Micken, *Speaking for Results* (Boston: Houghton Mifflin Company, 1958), pp. 157-164, "The Inspirational Speech."

Robert T. Oliver, *The Psychology of Persuasive Speech,* 2nd ed. (New York: Longmans, Green, 1957), Chapter XX, "The Speech to Stimulate."

William Phillips Sandford and Willard Hayes Yeager, *Effective Business Speech* (New York: McGraw-Hill Book Company, 1960), Chapter XIII, "Speeches to Inspire People and Organizations."

Richard M. Weaver, "Ultimate Terms in Contemporary Rhetoric," *The Ethics of Rhetoric* (Chicago, Illinois: Henry Regnery Company, 1953), pp. 211-232.

CHAPTER TWENTY-FOUR

The speech to actuate

The speech to convince, you will recall, attempts to influence the beliefs of an audience (Chapter 22); and the speech to stimulate attempts to arouse enthusiasm or to deepen a feeling of respect or reverence (Chapter 23). As distinguished from these, the speech to actuate, which we are now to consider, seeks an immediate overt response from the listeners. It attempts to persuade them to commit themselves on the spot by signing a petition, making a contribution, standing up to be counted, going out on strike, or engaging in some other sort of observable public act.

SITUATIONS REQUIRING SPEECHES TO ACTUATE

Any situation which calls for immediate action, rather than mere mental resolution or an intention to act in the indefinite future should a suitable situation arise, requires a speech to actuate. Hence such speeches frequently are given in *deliberative or legislative bodies* by a person who wishes other members to vote for a motion he has introduced or to support a program he favors. They are common at *political rallies* aimed at enlisting party workers and at *mass meetings* called to plan protest marches or public demonstrations. *Lawyers' pleas* before juries and the *sermons of an evangelist* such as Billy Graham, of course, are classic examples. On the campus, any meeting of a club or organization at which listeners are asked to accept membership on working committees, to make financial contributions to a cause, to sell tickets, to enter contests, or to go out after new members calls for one or more speeches to actuate. The characteristics of *immediacy* and of *overt action* by the audience, then, distinguish the speech to actuate.

THE PURPOSE OF THE SPEECH TO ACTUATE

While the purpose of a speech to actuate is to elicit from the audience some specific behavior, the request for this action usually will fall on deaf ears unless the listeners first are convinced of the need and the practicability of the proposal and are moved to act upon it. Therefore, the two secondary or intermediate purposes of a speaker giving a speech to actuate are (1) to convince and (2) to stimulate his audience.

In those cases where the behavior requested must continue over a period of days or weeks, it is especially important that the speaker convince the audience of the need and practicability of his proposed course of action. The determination and enthusiasm which the listeners feel as the speaker concludes his remarks may dissipate rapidly when they come out on the cold street corner where they are to demonstrate or when they encounter the rebuffs of the first persons to whom they attempt to sell tickets. In all types of persuasive speaking, the speaker has the moral obligation to support his recommendations with sound evidence and arguments. In a speech to actuate, however, such support is more than a question of ethics; it is indispensable for securing the action which the speaker seeks.

THE MANNER OF SPEAKING

A speech to actuate, like a speech to stimulate, calls for a forceful and dynamic manner of delivery. This does not mean that you must shout or wave your arms wildly. It does mean, however, that your delivery must be animated and must mirror an inner intensity of belief and feeling. Obviously, you cannot stir an audience to action unless your own enthusiasm and commitment to the cause are evident.

Above all, avoid the actions of a demagog or rabble rouser. A speaker's most important personal asset is the respect his listeners have for his integrity and sincerity and for his qualities of mind and judgment. Make it evident that you have thought long and carefully about the course of action you recommend, be honestly enthusiastic, pattern your vocal and physical delivery on the model of a well-informed and responsible individual who is genuinely aroused. A delivery of this type is the most effective in moving men to action.

CHARACTERISTICS OF CONTENT

As we already have suggested, the speech to actuate is closely related both to the speech to convince and to the speech to stimulate, differing only in the fact that it attempts to translate belief or feeling into immediate overt behavior (see page 468). For this reason, its content will be similar to the contents of those types of speeches. Like the speech to convince, the speech to actuate must contain strong evidence and sound logical reasoning; and like the speech to stimulate, it must infuse this evidence and reasoning with powerful motivation and vivid imagery. Moreover, as in the speech to stimulate, striking phraseology and concrete language are essential, and no opportunity should be overlooked to cast one's proposal into a catch phrase or to throw ideas into striking contrast. (At this point, review carefully the characteristic content of the speech to stimulate, as described on pages 448-449.)

ORGANIZATION OF THE SPEECH TO ACTUATE

In its organization, the speech to actuate makes full use of each of the steps in the motivated sequence, the ideas being developed and arranged in accordance with the following considerations:

Attention step

Although the attention step of a speech to actuate is usually short, it is extremely important. If people are to be motivated to act, everything in your speech, from the very first words to the very last, must drive strongly at impelling the behavior you desire. Moreover, what you say as you begin should contribute directly toward clarifying the action you propose. Do not waste time by telling a funny story that has only a marginal bearing on your purpose, or by reading a quotation which—though timely and interesting—might point the audience in an alternative direction. Be brief, but be direct and forceful; from your very first minute on the platform, begin to build toward the exact response you eventually will request.

Need step

If the audience already is aware of the need for the action you are going to recommend, review that need briefly, perhaps adding one or two illustrations which show its urgent nature, and remind your listeners of ways in which it affects them. When, on the other hand, the audience is unaware of the need or does not recognize its full scope and importance, develop the need step at some length and with strong emphasis. Use the four points explained in Chapter 16 on the motivated sequence (see page 281):

1. *Statement.* State clearly the specific need or problem which requires action.

2. *Illustration.* Give one or two examples which further clarify this need.

3. *Ramification.* Employ as many forms of support as may be required to make this need convincing and impressive.

4. *Pointing.* Show how your listeners are involved—how their health, security, happiness, etc., are directly affected.

Satisfaction step

Combine solid proof of the practicability of your proposed action with strong motivation and suggestion. Show that it actually will raise the money, result in the improvement, or remove the evils that you claim it will. Support your contention by showing that similar actions have had these results in the past, or are having these results in other states or communities. Give facts and figures. In addition, take full advantage of the human wants or desires described in Chapter 12 (pp. 191-204). Show how the action you propose will be easy to perform, or relatively cheap, or will bring prestige to the person or group performing it. Fit your motive appeals to the particular audience you are addressing. If security is their dominant motive, stress that; if they value self-enhancement or freedom of action, emphasize those drives. Be ethical in your use of motive appeals, and always aim at man's nobler desires rather than his baser ones; but within these limits, motivate your audience as strongly as you can. Logical arguments produce the conviction that sustains action once it is under way; strong motive appeals, however, arouse people out of their apathy and prompt them to action in the first place.

Visualization step

Use the positive or joint rather than the negative method for developing the visualization step (see pp. 283-284). If you tell an audience how bad things will be if they do not act, your description does not support your proposal directly, and may sometimes crystallize negative or inhibitory ideas in their minds. On the other hand, a positive description of benefits, especially when it is projected in vivid and compelling language, clarifies the goal toward which the proposed action is directed and is itself a strong motivating factor.

Action step

Besides continuing the strong motivation present in the satisfaction and visualization steps and reviewing the arguments which prove your proposed action necessary and practicable, the action step should contain one very important additional element. This is a clear and sufficiently detailed statement of what to do or where to go in order to perform the action you recommend. All too often speakers get their audiences aroused and determined to act, but fail to give them precise directions for carrying out the action. Sometimes the listeners do not know exactly where to go to register or to vote, or the hours at which the polling places will be open; they may not know the exact street address to which to send their contributions or how to address the envelope; they are sometimes left with only a vague impression concerning the corner on which the mass rally is to be held, or the hour at which the protest marchers are to assemble.

Even with the best of intentions, most people are remiss about initiating the inquiries which will bring them the needed information. They tend to say, "Yes, I must find out that address, but I am so busy today that I will wait until tomorrow." The trouble is that one "tomorrow" follows another, and the matter continues to drift. To help ensure action, then, make such inquiries unnecessary. Before concluding your speech, state fully and explicitly—repeating information you have given in earlier steps if necessary—exactly what it is you want done, and exactly where, when, and how to do it. Remember: *what, where, when, how*—and *now*. When your hearers are armed with this information, they are much more likely to act as you want them to.

In the outline and speech that follow, note how the principles and methods described in this chapter have been used in an effort to move an audience to action.

SAMPLE OUTLINE

The following outline is of a student speech given by Howard Brown before an audience presumed to be the board of directors of the Central Fibre Products Company. As the company's production engineer, Mr. Brown urged the purchase of new equipment.

FILTERING OUR INDUSTRIAL WASTE

Attention step

I. The decision we reach today can mean greater profit for Central Fibre or a continuation of our practice of literally throwing money down the drain.

Need step

I. Our present waste disposal method is seriously inadequate.
   A. We need to diminish the amount of stream pollution caused by the waste water of our plant.

1. Pressure has been brought under National Law #3972 and a corresponding state law by the State Board of Sanitation.
2. The pollution we cause is equivalent to that of a city of 60,000 population.

B. We are letting substantial profits drain into the Wabash River.
1. Every minute we discharge water containing from three to twelve pounds of minute usable fiber.
2. Every day we pump 15,500,000 gallons of water which we heat, use, and discharge into the river.
a. This water carries with it countless B.T.U.'s we have added.

II. In short, our disposal is both illegal and inefficient.

III. We need a practical solution of this problem that will meet the following requirements:
A. The discharged water must be brought within the standards required by state and national laws.
B. The system must be reliable in operation.
C. It must be economical.
D. It should reduce our present waste.
E. If possible, it should help improve the quality of our product.

Satisfaction step

I. The installation of an Oliver Vacuum 8 x 10 Saveall in our mill will solve our problem.
A. The Saveall would be conveniently located at the west end of the machine room in our mill.
1. Here it would be close to the machines, screens, digestors, and beaters.
B. Here is the way it operates:
1. This oversize flow sheet shows the simplified operation of the Saveall in paper mill use. (Show and explain chart.)
2. These detailed working drawings and actual photographs of the Saveall show how it has been installed at other mills. (Show drawings and pictures.)
C. The Saveall will meet the requirements of a practical solution:
1. It will reduce our stream pollution below the legal limits allowed by statute. (Read specifications and guarantee.)
2. The Oliver Filter Company is a very reliable firm of world-wide reputation.
a. The Saveall was designed for paper mill use.
b. Savealls are being used successfully by 1300 paper mills in all parts of the world.
3. The plan is economical.
a. The original cost of the Saveall will be $75,000.

   b. Since servicing is done by the Oliver Company, upkeep will be small.
   c. Added labor costs will be nil.
4. The Saveall in a short time will pay for itself in the amount of fiber recovered.
   a. The Terre Haute Paper Company reports a saving of 660 tons of fiber last year.
   b. The Tama, Iowa, mill has shown a 900-ton saving per year.
5. By reusing the "white" or clear water processed by the Saveall, higher grade products can be made.
   a. The Terre Haute mill has produced better products.
   b. The Tama mill also improved the quality of its products.

II. The Oliver Saveall is a practical and economical solution to our problem.

Visualization step

I. By installing an Oliver Saveall, we can save an average of 5 pounds of fiber per minute—7 tons a day.
   A. At $15 a ton, in one day our saving would be $105.
   B. In less than two and one-half years the Saveall will have paid for itself. (Show graph of cumulated savings vs. cost.)

II. The clear water we use will be free of river refuse.
   A. This will speed up production.
   B. It will give us a better grade of product.

III. We shall be free from danger of legal action because of stream pollution.

Action step

I. I recommend we order the Oliver Saveall immediately.
   A. The law demands action on our part.
   B. An Oliver Saveall will meet that demand and at the same time will end the flow of thousands of our dollars down the Wabash.

SAMPLE SPEECH

The following speech asking that Congress declare war on Japan was composed by President Franklin D. Roosevelt early on the morning of its delivery, December 8, 1941.

Although he spoke for only six minutes, President Roosevelt clearly outlined the reasons for the action he requested and established the fact that Japan rather than the United States had been the aggressor. The speech was greeted with tumultuous applause, and so promptly did Congress respond that within two and one half hours after its delivery the formal declaration of war had been signed by the President.

A REQUEST FOR A DECLARATION OF WAR[1]

Franklin Delano Roosevelt

Yesterday, December 7, 1941—a date which will live in infamy—the United States of America was suddenly and deliberately attacked by naval and air forces of the Empire of Japan.

The United States was at peace with that nation and, at the solicitation of Japan, was still in conversation with its government and its Emperor, looking toward the maintenance of peace in the Pacific. Indeed, one hour after Japanese air squadrons had commenced bombing in Oahu, the Japanese ambassador to the United States and his colleague delivered to the Secretary of State a formal reply to a recent American message. While this reply stated that it seemed useless to continue the existing diplomatic negotiations, it contained no threat or hint of war or armed attack.

It will be recorded that the distance of Hawaii from Japan makes it obvious that the attack was deliberately planned many days or even weeks ago. During the intervening time the Japanese Government has deliberately sought to deceive the United States by false statements and expressions of hope for continued peace.

The attack yesterday on the Hawaiian Islands has caused severe damage to American naval and military forces. Very many American lives have been lost. In addition American ships have been reported torpedoed on the high seas between San Francisco and Honolulu.

Yesterday the Japanese government also launched an attack against Malaya.

Last night Japanese forces attacked Hong Kong.

[1]Reprinted by permission.

Last night Japanese forces attacked Guam.

Last night Japanese forces attacked the Philippine Islands.

Last night the Japanese attacked Wake Island.

This morning the Japanese attacked Midway Island.

Japan has, therefore, undertaken a surprise offensive extending throughout the Pacific area. The facts of yesterday speak for themselves. The people of the United States have already formed their opinions and well understand the implications to the very life and safety of our nation.

As Commander-in-Chief of the Army and Navy, I have directed that all measures be taken for our defense.

Always will we remember the character of the onslaught against us.

No matter how long it may take us to overcome this premeditated invasion, the American people in their righteous might will win through to absolute victory.

I believe I interpret the will of the Congress and of the people when I assert that we will not only defend ourselves to the uttermost but will make very certain that this form of treachery shall never endanger us again.

Hostilities exist. There is no blinking at the fact that our people, our territory, and our interests are in grave danger.

With confidence in our armed forces—with the unbounding determination of our people—we will gain the inevitable triumph—so help us God.

I ask that the Congress declare that since the unprovoked and dastardly attack by Japan on Sunday, December 7th, a state of war has existed between the United States and the Japanese Empire.

Problems

1. Radio and television commercials, as well as advertisements in newspapers and magazines, are aimed at actuating listeners or readers. Compare the methods used by the mass media in an effort to achieve this result with the methods recommended in this chapter. What similarities do you detect? What differences? What special modifications or adaptations are present in the advertisements and commercials? What additional methods are employed?
2. How would you evaluate the ethical standards to which advertisers adhere in their attempts to actuate buyers? Do they usually give the full and unbiased information upon which intelligent action should be based? If not, in what respects do they sometimes fall short? Would you agree with this statement: "Those attempts to actuate which are guided by high ethical and moral standards in the end always are more persuasive than those which are not." Why do you answer as you do?
3. A leader of the French Revolution is reported to have looked out of the window one day and said: "There goes the mob on their way to the palace. I must hurry to place myself at their head, for I am their leader." What implications does this statement have for speakers who seek to actuate audiences?

4. If you were presenting a speech to actuate, would you encourage questions and comments from the audience at its completion or would you discourage them? Defend your answer.
5. What motive appeals would you employ if you were attempting to induce an audience of college students to take the following actions: *(a)* contribute to the community chest, *(b)* enlist in the army, *(c)* study harder, *(d)* give up their automobiles, *(e)* have an annual physical examination, *(f)* learn to speak Russian, and *(g)* drop out of college?
6. Comment on this statement: "Most men act out of desire rather than reason; they only use reason to justify to themselves what they want to do anyway."
7. Devise a slogan or catch phrase which you might use in a speech to actuate on each of the following subjects:

The citizen's duty to vote
The bond-a-month plan
Clean-up, paint-up week
Dental checkups
A speed-reading course

Speaking assignments

1. Present a five-minute speech to actuate, the purpose of which is to persuade the members of your speech class to sign a petition requesting the alteration of an unpopular rule or the correction of an undesirable situation on the campus or in your community. Select a rule or situation which actually exists—not an imaginary or fictional one. Show your listeners why they should be concerned, explain why a petition of this sort has a good chance of influencing the authorities in charge, point out the advantages to be gained from acting as you recommend, etc. Use carefully reasoned arguments, strong motivation, and vivid and compelling language. Let your delivery conform to the suggestions offered in this chapter. At the close of your speech, pass the petition among the members of the class for signatures. You might urge your audience to sign a petition requesting one of the following changes:

That graduating seniors be excused from final examinations.
That the student government be given complete control over "activity fees."
That freshmen be allowed to drive cars.
That campus food service be improved.
That men students be allowed to visit women students in their rooms.
That parking meters be installed on X Street.
That local merchants stay open one evening a week.
That city garbage pickup be put on a twice-a-week schedule.
That advertising sound trucks be prohibited in the area of the campus.

That the college establish a cooperative bookstore (or grocery, or gasoline station).
That landlords renting to students conform strictly to antidiscrimination laws.
That the community enter at once upon a plan of urban renewal.

2. Select a specific, overt action which you wish to elicit from the members of your speech class. Then prepare a five-sentence speech designed to secure that response. Devote one sentence, and one sentence only, to each of the steps in the motivated sequence. Frame these sentences in the most striking and impelling language you can devise, and deliver them so as to achieve the maximum effect with each.

Speeches for collateral study

1. Patrick Henry, "To the Convention Delegates" ("Give me liberty . . ."), *Modern Eloquence*, ed. Thomas B. Reed (Philadelphia: Morris, 1903), XIII, pp. 1178-1181. (This speech has been reconstructed by Henry's biographer, Weems.)
2. Lyndon Baines Johnson, "Remarks to a Joint Session of the Congress," *Representative American Speeches, 1963-1964*, ed. Lester Thonssen (New York: Wilson, 1964), pp. 37-42.
3. Franklin Delano Roosevelt, "Four Freedoms." Message to Congress, January 6, 1941. *Classic Speeches*, ed. Richard Crosscup (New York: Philosophical Library, 1965), pp. 384-392.
4. Woodrow Wilson, "Declaration of War Speech" (April 12, 1917), *Famous Speeches in American History*, ed. Glenn R. Capp (Indianapolis: Bobbs-Merrill, 1963), pp. 147-159.

Suggestions for further reading

Herbert L. Abelson, *Persuasion: How Opinions and Attitudes Are Changed* (New York: Springer Publishing Company, Inc., 1959).
Martin P. Anderson, Wesley Lewis, and James Murray, *The Speaker and His Audience* (New York: Harper & Row, 1964), Chapter XVIII, "Speaking to Create Change."
Gary Lynn Cronkhite, "Logic, Emotion, and the Paradigm of Persuasion," *Quarterly Journal of Speech*, L (February 1964), 13-18.
B. J. Diggs, "Persuasion and Ethics," *Quarterly Journal of Speech*, L (December 1964), 359-373.
Franklyn S. Haiman, "Democratic Ethics and the Hidden Persuaders," *Quarterly Journal of Speech*, XLIV (December 1958), 385-392.
Ralph Micken, *Speaking for Results* (Boston: Houghton Mifflin Company, 1958), "To Move an Agreeable Audience to Action," pp. 173-174.
Wayne C. Minnick, "The Philosophy of Persuasion," *Speech Teacher*, IX (September 1960), 211-215.
Robert T. Oliver, "Ethics and Efficiency in Persuasion," *Southern Speech Journal*, XXVI (Fall 1960), 10-15.

Robert T. Oliver, *The Psychology of Persuasive Speech*, 2nd ed. (New York: Longmans, Green, 1957), Chapter XIX, "The Speech to Actuate."

Paul E. Ried, "A Spectrum of Persuasive Design," *Speech Teacher*, XIII (March 1964), 87-95.

Floyd L. Ruch, *Psychology and Life*, 7th ed. (Glenview, Illinois: Scott, Foresman, 1967), Chapter XVI, "Communication and Persuasion."

Arleigh B. Williamson, *Speaking in Public* (New York: Prentice-Hall, Inc., 1930), Chapter XVII, "The Speech for Action, I—General Considerations," and Chapter XVIII, "The Speech for Action, II—Special Considerations."

CHAPTER TWENTY-FIVE

Answering questions and objections

When he has completed a speech, a speaker often is confronted with questions and sometimes with objections from his listeners. Rather than resenting them, he should welcome these questions and even objections as an indication of the interest he has aroused. Moreover, in responding, he has an opportunity to establish a closer contact with individuals in his audience than would otherwise be possible and to elaborate upon those points which affect the group most vitally.

THE PURPOSE OF THE REPLY

When someone asks a question or raises an objection to something you have said, the *ultimate aim* of your answer should be to further the particular purpose of your speech. Thus, if the purpose of your speech is to raise funds for a new building, raising funds should still be uppermost in your mind as you answer questions. The *immediate aim* of your answer, however, should be to satisfy your questioner, to satisfy others in the audience, and to retain your own prestige.

To satisfy your questioner. Questions are asked for one of two reasons: to secure additional information or to object to what has been said. To satisfy your questioner, therefore, you must either give him additional facts or convince him that his objection is invalid.

To satisfy others in the audience. Sometimes you may not care what the person who questioned you thinks, but the point he has raised may be important to other members of your audience. Therefore, your answer must be directed not only to the questioner but also to the others in the audience whose objection he may have voiced.

To retain your own prestige. Sometimes a question is asked or an objection raised merely to put you on the spot, to place you on the defensive, or to grab the spotlight. When this happens, your answer will have as its immediate object the retention of your own prestige; to retain it, you must keep control of the situation.

Although one of these purposes will usually predominate, you should keep them all in mind as you phrase your answer to a question.

METHODS OF ANSWERING

Your method of answering questions or objections must depend upon the real motives of those who raise them. You will answer the mere troublemaker in one way and the sincerely interested questioner in another. Let us consider some of the methods which speakers have found useful.

Give additional information

Very frequently objections are raised because people do not know enough about your subject. When this is the case, present additional information on the point in dispute. The added facts will not only answer the question raised but also will add weight to what you have already said. Do not present the bare facts alone, however; connect the unknown with the known. Make sure that the audience understands the significance of your information. In general, organize your facts in the following way:

1. Repeat the question (so that everyone can hear it).
2. Present the additional information.
   a. Use time order, space order, etc. (See pp. 228-230).
   b. Connect what you now say with what you have already explained.
3. Draw a conclusion from this information.
4. Show how this conclusion answers the question and, if you can, how it supports some point in your original speech.

Make a comparison

A listener may raise a valid objection to your proposal. When this occurs, two courses are open to you: either you may modify your proposal to meet the objection; or, if this is impossible, you may weigh the objection against the benefits you have shown. In the latter case, make your reply somewhat as follows:

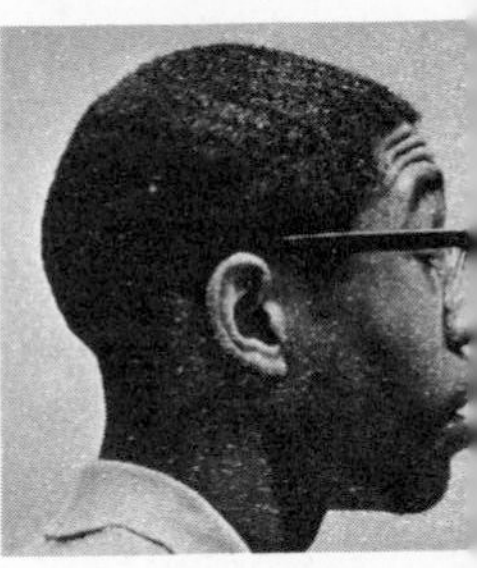

1. Repeat the objection.
2. Admit its validity, but minimize its importance.
3. Remind the audience of the benefits of your proposal by restating them in summary form.
4. Point out that the benefits outweigh the disadvantages.

Develop a counterargument

Sometimes a listener will ask a question, not because he seeks more information or wishes to voice a valid objection, but because he has not reasoned soundly or has some personal prejudice about the subject. In this event you must deal with either *(a)* a line of reasoning at variance with your own or *(b)* a strong personal motive or established belief. These may be handled thus:

To attack a line of reasoning at variance with your own:
1. Repeat the question or objection.
2. Point out its underlying logic or assumption.
3. Show the fallacy in reasoning or the invalidity of the assumption. (Cite facts, figures, testimony.)
4. Deny or definitely modify the questioner's point on the basis of what you have just shown.
5. State the correct conclusion and, if possible, connect it with some point in your speech.

To counter a personal motive or established belief:
1. Repeat the question or objection.
2. Point out the underlying belief or motive for this objection, and show—if you can—that your proposal is really in line with it, or at least does not oppose it.
3. Present some new aspect of the situation which will identify your proposition with the questioner's belief or motive.
4. Emphasize some stronger motive or some more firmly established belief than that on which the objection is based, and show that

Marshall McLuhan, author of *Understanding Media*, is questioned by a member of his audience during one of several events in a "McLuhan Symposium" at Kendall College. At McLuhan's right in the photographs is Studs Terkel, Chicago author and radio personality, who interviewed the media expert for Station WFMT-FM.

your proposal is in line with this stronger motive or more widely held belief. (Steps 2 and 3 are sometimes omitted and Step 4 relied upon entirely.)

5. Draw a definite conclusion and, if possible, connect it with some point in your speech.

You will notice that the fundamental technic used in both methods outlined above is that of finding a basis for agreement with the questioner upon some point of logic, motivation, or belief and then putting the objection in opposition to this point and your proposal in agreement with it.

Answer a question with a question

Sometimes one question can best be answered by another. Such a counterquestion often puts the questioner on the defensive, and he must either answer your question or admit defeat. Frequently his answer to your question will give you the cue for answering his original question. Even if he is not completely appeased, he may be quieted and the rest of the audience satisfied. Be careful, however, to be tactful when you reply in this way.

One example will illustrate this method. A speaker who was advocating home rule for one of the British dependencies was interrupted by a listener who asked whether he didn't think "these people are too illiterate to govern themselves." The speaker rejoined by asking, "Do you know what the percentage of literacy was in the United States when we declared our independence?" The questioner did not, and sat down. The point was so obvious that it was almost needless for the speaker to proceed, as he did, to compare the figures between the dependency of which he spoke and the American colonies in 1776.

Inject humor

If you consider the point raised by a question or objection to be unimportant, you may be able to meet the difficulty by using humor. Be careful, however, that the point you consider unimportant is not considered important by your audience. Handle the situation thus:

1. Sidetrack the point with genial humor. Show the funny side of the objection, but beware of sarcasm or ridicule.
2. Shift the attention of the audience to another point by taking up a more serious objection that has already been raised or by re-emphasizing an important point made in your original speech.

On rare occasions, it may even be allowable to take an ironical dig at the person asking the question or making the objection. By poking fun at him, you please the sporting tendency in men and reduce the effect of his objection. This is particularly true if the questioner is a bombastic, self-important individual who is known as a chronic objector. Be especially careful, however, not to use sarcasm on someone who is respected by the audience, or your attack will boomerang.

Rely on personal prestige

Sometimes you can rely upon the weight of your own word to answer the objection. A simple statement that "I have not found it so in my experience" will occasionally be sufficient. This is particularly true if the audience regards you as an authority upon the subject; your own prestige will outweigh that of the person raising the question. However, do not overestimate your own reputation. Usually a far better plan is to take the extra time for presenting the information or argument upon which your conclusion is based.

Admit ignorance

Far from reducing your prestige, your admission that you do not know the answer to a question will often raise you in the audience's esteem. Such an admission labels you as a conscientious person who sticks to the facts and refuses to go beyond them. You avoid being thought a bluffer or a know-it-all. This does not mean that you never need to know the answer to what is asked. Before you begin to speak, you should be thoroughly informed upon your subject, but you cannot be expected to be able to answer everything that may be asked. However, if you cannot answer a question, combine your admission of ignorance with a valid reason for it. Proceed in this way:

1. Restate the question.
2. Admit your ignorance.
3. State definitely where the information can be found, or demonstrate why it is inaccessible.
4. Direct attention to some other point in your speech.

ORGANIZATION OF ANSWERS

The methods for organizing your answers have been discussed in the preceding pages. Note that every method includes these three essentials:

1. Restatement of the question or objection.
2. Statement of your conclusion on the matter.
3. Some connection with your original speech.

The first of these is important to show the audience just what you are talking about; the second, to make your position clear; and the third, to keep your original purpose in the foreground and to prevent wandering. Interspersed among these three essential elements in the manner outlined above will be your information, argument, humor, etc.

As you frame your replies, remember above all that you are not conducting a tea-table conversation—that you have spoken for a purpose and that the discussion must not be allowed to digress from that purpose.

SAMPLE QUESTIONS AND ANSWERS

Following his address to the Royal African Society of London on "Nigeria in 1965," Sir James Robertson answered questions from members of the audience. Sir James, a former governor-general of Nigeria, had devoted most of his talk to describing his impressions of that colony upon returning to it after several years' absence. In the answers that follow, how closely does Sir James follow the suggestions in this chapter? What criticisms, if any, do you have of his methods of answering questions?

QUESTION: Will the speaker give us his impression on whether the other governments in other countries are heading the same way as Nigeria?

SIR JAMES: Well, I think this a very difficult question. I don't know. I find it not very easy because I don't know much about what's happening in the Sudan now. One reads very different accounts. It doesn't seem to me that they've got away from their original difficulty there of so many little bits of parties not being able to get together. And the position now seems to be very much the same as it was in 1958—was it?—when the military coup took place, and President Abboud came in, in order to make a stable government instead of all these little warring political parties. And at the present moment these warring political parties seem to be all there again and no strong government. But I don't know. The Sudan was always my first love, having spent thirty-one years there, and knowing it much better than Nigeria; so it's rather tragic to have to say that I am not at all sure what the future there is going to be. The other countries that were mentioned—in Kenya, Uganda—I think Uganda's pretty stable. I think that Kenya is remarkably stable, considering what it might have become. Tanganyika I don't know anything about. President Nyererc came and stayed at Government House once at Lagos, and I thought that he was a pretty sensible man, so one has a little bit of hope there. Zanzibar is in darkness. One doesn't know what has happened, and what is happening, so that I wouldn't like to say anything about that.

QUESTION: Is it possible for an ordinary citizen, not sponsored by a bank, to travel around Nigeria today without being bankrupt in the first week by enormous accommodation charges?

SIR JAMES: As far as I am concerned this is a hypothetical question, because I was sponsored by a bank, and I don't know what other people have to do. I was very kindly looked after, and to this moment I don't know how much the bank had to pay for the pleasure that I and my wife had going around sponsored by them. I only hope that what I did in Nigeria was worth it to the bank. I don't know.

QUESTION: I want to ask Sir James what he thinks can be done in this country to get better knowledge of the African continent spread among the people.

SIR JAMES: When I was in Africa, I used to come home on leave sometimes, and I'd meet someone and they'd say: "Oh, you're in Africa. Where do you live?" And so I'd say: "Well, I live near Khartoum." And they said: "Oh, you must know our cousin who lives in Johannesburg." And when you said to them that Johannesburg was further from Khartoum than Khartoum was from London, they wouldn't believe you. Many people in this country look on Africa as a little country where one would know everybody. And I think that this questioner has a very good point. When anything happens in Africa, in the Congo or South Africa, or if there's trouble somewhere, it means that it's more difficult to get money or loans or investment in Nigeria, or in places which are hundreds or thousands of miles away. And this is due to ignorance. Well, a lot of us are trying all we can to dissipate this ignorance. I belong to a body—the Commonwealth Institute—out at Kensington. We are every year teaching in the schools with lectures and so on about Africa. This Institute here—the Royal African Society, the Royal Commonwealth Society, the Overseas League—all these bodies are doing their best to explain and teach about the problems. But I think the fact is that most people are only interested in their own little personal affairs, and maybe this is true also in Africa—that if you live in a village somewhere out at Okenni, or somewhere like that, Mr. Chairman, you don't really care very much what's happening in New York, or down in Alabama, where the Negroes may be getting a bad time. The human brain is small. It can't cope with everything. But I agree with you very much that we must all try to spread information about Africa, so that people will understand that what happens in the Congo doesn't necessarily mean that it's going to happen in Nigeria or in Ghana or anywhere else.[1]

The following questions were asked of Mr. James M. Landis, Special Assistant to President Kennedy, shortly after Mr. Landis presented his conclusions about needed reforms in federal regulatory agencies. Observe how he answers each question directly and then adds explanation to make his viewpoint clear.

QUESTION: Does a federal agency have any role in trying to improve the quality of an industry, such as radio and TV?

MR. LANDIS: I think it does. It certainly should. There, incidentally, is another slight advance that's been made by the Federal Communications Commission. I think I criticized the Commission for not doing a job on the renewal of its licenses.

When a licensee seeks a license, one of the criteria in determining who should be the licensee with regard to a particular frequency is the nature of the programs he says he's going to put on. And an element in evaluating the quality of the programs is the emphasis that it places on, let's say, the public-interest aspect of its programs.

If that is a true criterion, when that licensee comes up for renewal in three years' time, he ought to be asked, "Have you done what you promised you'd do, or what you said you'd do?"

QUESTION: Does that amount to censorship?

MR. LANDIS: That is not censorship. It isn't censorship in any sense. Censorship is really preventing somebody from saying or speaking what they want to say. Now here, because of the "nature of the beast," there is only one frequency available. You have to award that to some applicant who comes along.

Now, obviously, you have to have criteria as to whether you pick A, B or C. You pick A, rather than B, because A promises to do so-and-so. I don't think it's a matter of censorship. I think it's a matter of how that frequency can be used best in the public interest.[2]

Soon after he took office as Secretary of State in 1961, Dean Rusk was interviewed on the "Today" show over NBC-TV. Martin Agronsky of NBC asked Mr. Rusk for his interpretation of the role the Secretary of State should have in formulating foreign policy.

[1]From *African Affairs*, LXIV (October 1965), 258-260. Published by the Royal African Society, London, and reprinted with the Society's permission.

[2]From *U.S. News and World Report*, L (March 27, 1961), 85-86.

MR. AGRONSKY: Mr. Secretary, you noted once that Harry Truman had defined the President's relation to foreign policy in five words. He said, "The President makes foreign policy." What does the Secretary of State make? What is the function of your job? How do you see it?

MR. RUSK: The primary responsibility of the Secretary of State is to help the President carry one of the most awesome responsibilities that is known to man. That means that the Secretary of State must be a principal, perhaps the primary, adviser to the President on foreign policy, but it also means that the Secretary must administer and lead the Department of State so that a great department can be of maximum help to the President. It means that the Secretary must help to represent the administration's point of view with the Congress and with congressional leaders and also help explain to the country what we are trying to do in foreign policy. Because, although the Constitution gives very heavy responsibilities to the President, our Constitution also gives the President a license to lead, and, in exercising that leadership in a country which moves by consent, the President must have the help of a great many others, including his principal Cabinet officers. The Secretary of State's role is to help in every way possible the President carry out his far-reaching and extremely complicated and difficult responsibilities in the foreign policy field.[3]

A QUESTION-AND-ANSWER INTERVIEW

Although the following exchange did not grow directly out of a public-speech situation, it does demonstrate a number of the technics discussed in this chapter. Employing a light and rather informal approach, Author Leslie Lieber questions Mr. Cerf in such a way as to bring out some provocative views on the subject of speechmaking in general and the use of language, eloquence, and showmanship in particular.

WHITE HOUSE SLANG?[4]

An Interview with Bennett Cerf, Writer and Publisher

QUESTION: Mr. Cerf, as a lifelong watchdog of our English language and publisher of a monumental dictionary, do you feel that the English spoken by modern U.S. Presidents is on a par with their exalted office? For instance, Presi-

[3]From *The Department of State Bulletin*, XLIV (February 27, 1961), 306.

[4]Reprinted from *This Week Magazine*, September 25, 1966, p. 2. Copyright 1966 by the United Newspapers Magazine Corporation.

dent Johnson recently told critics of his Vietnam policy to "cool it"—the first time a slang word of dubious ancestry has crept into a major Presidential address. Do you approve?

MR. CERF: It's fine with me. Now's not the time for the President of the United States to worry about the King's English. After all, we're living in an informal age. Politicians don't go around in top hats anymore. There's no reason why the English language shouldn't wear sports clothes, too. I don't say the President should speak like an illiterate. But "cool it" is folksy, and the Chief Executive should be allowed to sound human. You can't be too corny for the American people—all the decent sentiments in life are corny. But linguistically speaking, Disraeli is dullsville.

QUESTION: Then you're satisfied with the way they have been handling the language?

MR. CERF: The Presidents aren't handling it enough for us to form much of a judgment. Who really knows how Presidents would talk without their ghost writers? When you ask me to compare the Presidents, it boils down to comparing the men who wrote their stuff. FDR was the verbal relay-man for speechwriters Robert Sherwood and Sam Rosenman. Bob wrote informal ones, Sam wrote legal ones—but they all came out as FDR. Truman was the sound-box for political lyrics turned out by Bill Hillman. Eisenhower "finalized" the prose of Malcolm Moos and Emmet Hughes. Kennedy's addresses were largely written by those two sibilant scribes, Sorensen and Schlesinger. And the men who put much of the Great Society vocabulary in LBJ's mouth are ex-journalist Bill Moyers and others. So how can we judge our Presidents' mastery of language? All we know is how well they recite what's on the cue cards.

QUESTION: But wouldn't you say that eloquence is still a great Presidential asset?

MR. CERF: More important than eloquence today is delivery. This shows class. Delivery can get you elected. Of our last five Presidents only Roosevelt and Kennedy had it. Dewey took some emergency delivery lessons from Lowell Thomas in the 1948 Presidential campaign. But it was too late.

QUESTION: Why do you feel that Presidential oratory has lost its effectiveness—that eloquence is as dead as yesterday's newspaper?

MR. CERF: Because words—the inspirational, high-sounding ones that leaders once deployed to move the masses—have lost their meaning. I mean words like "justice" and "liberty" that once stirred men's souls and brought audiences cheering to their feet. The 20th Century does not fall for those words so easily. "Freedom—let's bring 'freedom' to the Vietnamese." What does that mean? The Vietnamese don't want that word. They want something to eat. That's why people have begun to suspect words.

QUESTION: How would you rank our last five Presidents for their effective use of the English language?

MR. CERF: Roosevelt first, then Kennedy—although I believe Kennedy would have acquired the polish to surpass FDR had he lived. I'd place Truman third on the list for the vigor and saltiness of his delivery—with a special gold star for showmanship in his priceless imitation of H. V. Kaltenborn. Next comes Johnson. My nomination for last place would have to go to Dwight D. Eisenhower, a lovely man who resisted like a true soldier all of actor Robert Montgomery's valiant attempts to inculcate in him a flair for the dramatic.

QUESTION: Mr. Cerf, you seem to rank showmanship and a "flair for the dramatic" even above rhetoric as prime Presidential assets. Where will all this emphasis on showmanship lead?

MR. CERF: It could even lead people like Ronald Reagan and George Murphy a lot closer to the White House than anyone at Actors Studio perhaps even dreamed possible.

Problems

1. Attend a speech or lecture following which the audience is given an opportunity to ask questions or raise objections. Report on the following: *(a)* the various sorts of questions or objections that were raised, *(b)* the point or points in the prepared address to which the majority of the questions referred, *(c)* how fully or clearly these points had been developed during the course of the address, *(d)* how the speaker organized his replies, *(e)* whether in your judgment the question period was useful in supplementing or clarifying the original address, *(f)* what question, if any, seemed designed to embarrass the speaker rather than to elicit additional information.
2. Let the class as a whole read the printed transcript of a speech or lecture which was followed by a question period, and discuss together the items indicated in Problem 1. (See, for example, the lecture by Colin Legum, "Pan-Africanism, the Communists and the West," in *The Speaker's Resource Book,* 2nd ed., Carroll Arnold, Douglas Ehninger, and John Gerber [Glenview, Illinois: Scott, Foresman, 1966], pp. 255-263. This lecture originally appeared in the magazine *African Affairs,* LXIII [July 1964], 186-196.)
3. Phrase three imaginary questions or objections that might have been raised concerning your most recent classroom speech and, using one of the methods suggested in this chapter, work out suitable replies.
4. In a general class discussion, suggest and evaluate various ways in which a

speaker may handle questions that obviously are intended to embarrass him or to undermine his position.

Speaking assignments

1. Prepare and present a seven-minute speech to inform or convince on a subject approved by your instructor. After the speech, answer such questions or objections as your classmates may raise concerning it. Appoint for each class period a student chairman, whose duty it will be to introduce the speakers and preside over the question periods.
2. Prepare and present an eight-minute speech to convince, during the course of which you may be interrupted by questions or objections from the audience. In this assignment, the following rules will apply: (1) You will have two minutes of uninterrupted speaking time to get started. (2) For the next four minutes you will be subject to questions and objections. (3) Finally, you will have two minutes of uninterrupted speaking time to conclude your speech. (4) A student chairman, aided by the instructor if necessary, will see to it that only one questioner speaks at a time, that the questions or objections are stated in a courteous manner, and that they are germane to the speaker's remarks. (5) The instructor or an appointed timer will indicate, through appropriate signals, when the questions and objections may begin and when they are to cease.

Suggestions for further reading

Douglas Ehninger and Wayne Brockriede, *Decision by Debate* (New York: Dodd, Mead & Company, 1963), Chapter XVI, "Attack and Defense."

Halbert E. Gulley, *Discussion, Conference, and Group Process* (New York: Holt, Rinehart & Winston, Inc.), "Leading a Forum Period," pp. 300-302.

James H. McBurney and Glen E. Mills, *Argumentation and Debate*, 2nd ed. (New York: The Macmillan Company, 1964), Chapter XVI, "Fallacies and Stratagems," and Chapter XVII, "Refutation and Rebuttal."

James H. McBurney and Kenneth G. Hance, *Discussion in Human Affairs* (New York: Harper & Row, 1950), Chapter XXI, "The Forum." See especially pp. 321-326.

Ralph Y. McGinnis, "Refutation and Rebuttal," Chapter XI of *Argumentation and Debate*, rev. ed., ed. James H. McBath (New York: Holt, Rinehart & Winston, Inc., 1963).

Elbert R. Moses, "The Art of Questioning," *Today's Speech*, VIII (November 1960), 21-22.

PART SIX

SPECIAL TYPES OF SPEECHES

How to preside at a meeting and introduce speakers

Speeches for courtesy

Speeches to generate good will

Speeches of tribute

Adapting speech to radio and television

CHAPTER TWENTY-SIX

How to preside at a meeting and introduce speakers

Whether the occasion is a public lecture, a planned entertainment for a dinner meeting of a business or professional group, or a series of speeches at a conference, the success of any program is often largely determined by the effectiveness with which the chairman or toastmaster presides. A good chairman does not say much and does not parade his personality, yet his presence is felt. The audience senses his unobtrusive control of the situation and appreciates the efficiency with which the meeting proceeds. Sincerity, energy, and decisiveness —these are the personal qualities which mark him.[1]

COMMANDING THE SITUATION

The first duty of a chairman or presiding officer is to take charge, to command the situation, to be boss without being bossy. He has three very important obligations: *(a) To make the audience feel that all is going well.* People like to see that things are smoothly organized and running efficiently and to know that someone is in control. *(b) To hold the audience's attention by keeping the program moving.* If the chairman is uncertain or hesitant, people become fidgety, and the meeting invariably drags. But if the chairman is decisive and keeps things moving, they usually will be attentive and orderly. *(c) To discourage opposition.* Persons occasionally come to a meeting for the purpose of creating trouble or opposing the plans to be presented. If they feel that the presiding officer really is in command and if there are no unnecessary or awkward delays in the program, they may be discouraged from carrying out their intention.

[1]The special duties of the chairman of a meeting conducted according to the rules of parliamentary procedure are discussed in Chapter 34.

BASIC PROCEDURES

To command a situation, however, you must prepare yourself in advance of the meeting. Do not trust to the inspiration of the moment merely because you are not the principal speaker. As chairman, your preparation must often be just as thorough as that of the main speaker. The following procedure is basic:

1. *Determine the purpose of the meeting.*

2. *Acquaint yourself with the program.* Know who is going to speak or sing or play; know the title of each speaker's talk and the name of each artist's selection; understand the function of each part of the program in advancing the purpose of the whole.

3. *Make a time schedule.* Determine how long the meeting or program should last; apportion the time among the various persons who are scheduled to appear; and before the meeting begins, tell each participant tactfully exactly how much time he will have at his disposal.

4. *Carefully prepare the remarks you will need to make.* Know what you are going to say in calling the gathering to order and also in your later remarks. You may have to modify your commentary according to the turn of events, but you must always be ready with something.

5. *Start the meeting promptly.* Be on time yourself and see that the others on the program are, too; then keep things moving as nearly on schedule as possible.

If you prepare yourself in this way, the meeting will not automatically be assured of success, but the chances for its effectiveness will be greatly improved.

INCIDENTAL DUTIES

In addition to commanding the situation as a whole, the presiding officer frequently has three incidental responsibilities: *(a)* setting the keynote, *(b)* performing duties of courtesy, and *(c)* preserving order.

Setting the keynote

At the beginning of a program, it is sometimes difficult to get people settled down and ready to listen. Your first duty, of course, is to establish order and to direct the attention of the audience to the platform. Then, however, with a few carefully chosen remarks, you should proceed to set the mood and the keynote for the meeting.

If the occasion is to be one of fun and good humor, let your opening statement reflect this fact. Speak as though you yourself expected to have a good time and expected everyone else to enjoy himself also. If, on the other hand, the occasion has a serious, businesslike purpose, speak quietly and to the point. Remember that the purpose of your remarks is not to enhance your own reputation for wit or intelligence but to put the audience into the proper frame of mind for what is to follow. Mention the aim or objective of the meeting and the organization under whose auspices it is being held. Refer to the background of events that have led up to the gathering, and review any special rules or procedures that will prevail. Be careful, however, not to say too much and thereby steal the thunder of the speakers who are to follow you. Merely set the stage for them; do not occupy it yourself.

Nor does your duty of setting the keynote end with your opening remarks. Each time you introduce a new speaker or make any comment at all, you should try to maintain and enhance the mood of the meeting. Do not inject facetious comments which will destroy the serious arguments of a preceding speaker; and in introducing the talk to follow, do not laboriously analyze the intended subject and thus mar the good humor which the next speaker may hope to create. If, however, one of the speakers falls down on his job, you must attempt to bring the meeting back to its proper tone or spirit. Experience will make you better able to judge the mood of an audience and the probable effect that your incidental remarks will have upon it. But from the first, common sense combined with alertness to what is happening will provide a reasonably sure guide.

Performing duties of courtesy

A presiding officer is frequently expected to perform acts of courtesy for the group he represents. There may be visitors to welcome; or, if he is himself a visitor, he may wish to express appreciation for his hosts' welcome. At the close of a convention the presiding officer is expected to express the thanks of the group he represents for the courtesies extended by those responsible for entertaining his organization. Similarly, he must sometimes express appreciation for the services of a visiting speaker or entertainer. (A more complete discussion of this problem will be found in the following chapter.)

These acts of courtesy should never take the form of long and elaborate speeches. They may often be incorporated in the chairman's opening remarks or in a brief comment at the close of the meeting. Above all, such expressions of courtesy should be sincere. Do not try to exhibit the size of your vocabulary or the fertility of your imagination. Express a genuine welcome or an honest appreciation in simple language, mention one or two pertinent facts, and proceed with the program. Your attitude and the tone of your voice will express your feeling as fully as any words you can say.

Preserving order

If the chairman sets the appropriate keynote at the beginning of the meeting and keeps the program moving rapidly and smoothly, he will seldom have trouble preserving order. Disorder is more often the result of restlessness than of bad intentions. Therefore, if you notice a disturbance in the audience, do not immediately bark at the offenders; instead, increase the tempo of the program and make your own remarks more lively. You will find in most cases that the commotion will cease.

Occasionally, however, an individual in the audience will attempt to interrupt or heckle the speaker. Usually, an experienced speaker can handle such matters himself; but if you see that he is becoming annoyed or the audience is becoming distracted, you may have to intervene. Suggest to the heckler that he wait until the speech is finished and that he will then be given an opportunity to ask questions. Ordinarily this will satisfy him, and frequently his question will be answered in the course of the speech. If, during the question period, several people start objecting and questioning at the same time, ask them to speak in turn and to state their questions as briefly as possible. When the speaker has answered one objection, call on another person before the first objector has a chance to grab control of the situation by making a long speech or asking a protracted series of questions.

Such action on the part of the chairman should be prompt and decisive but at the same time tactful. Coercion may result in greater disorder or in sullen hostility. On the other hand, firmness combined with dignified courtesy will usually quell any unruly person and simultaneously keep the respect of the other listeners.

On rare occasions, as chairman you may have to administer a reprimand to the entire audience or to someone in it. Do this only as a last resort; but if you are forced to such an extremity, do not be half-hearted about it. In no uncertain terms, let the person know that he is disturbing the meeting by his actions; then if he persists, have him ejected by the ushers or the police. It is much better to go through with this unpleasantness than to lose command of the situation entirely. After such an incident has occurred, however, do or say something which will quickly and forcibly call the attention of the audience back to the program, and make no further reference to the disturbance.

INTRODUCING SPEAKERS

In addition to controlling the situation and performing these incidental duties, the chairman must introduce the speaker or speakers. Performing this duty effectively is not so simple as it may seem. Too often the introductions are long and rambling and bore rather than enlighten the listeners. Although extremely important, the speech of introduction should be brief and to the point.

If someone else is better acquainted with the main speaker than you are, you may request that person to introduce him. An arrangement of this kind must be made well before the meeting; don't call upon him without warning. And be sure he understands that he is to introduce the speaker and not to tell a long series of anecdotes about their acquaintanceship.

The purpose of the speech of introduction

The main objective of a speech of introduction is to arouse the audience's desire to hear the speaker; everything else must be subordinated to this aim. Your duty is to introduce, not to make a speech yourself or to air your own views on the subject. You are only the advance agent; your job is to sell the speaker to your audience. This carries a twofold responsibility: *(a)* You must arouse curiosity about the speaker or his subject; by doing this, you will make it easier for him to get the attention of the audience. And *(b)* you must make the audience like or respect the speaker—or both; in this way you will make his listeners more likely to accept what he says or to do what he asks.

The manner of speaking

When you give a speech of introduction, your manner of speaking should be suited to the nature of the occasion, the closeness of your acquaintance with the speaker, and the prestige of the speaker himself. If you are introducing a justice of the United States Supreme Court, for instance, it would hardly be appropriate to poke fun at him. Nor would this approach be tactful if the speaker were a stranger to you or if the occasion were serious and dignified. On the other hand, if you are presenting an old friend to a group of your associates at an informal occasion, a solemn, dignified manner would be equally out of place. The difficulty for most people is that they know only *one* method: either they present every speaker with ponderous dignity regardless of the occasion, or they introduce him by telling a joke about him. Neither of these methods is bad in itself, but each should be used in its proper place.

Regardless of the formality or informality of the occasion, however, a speech of introduction should always reflect sincere enthusiasm. Suggest by the way you talk about the speaker that you yourself are eager to hear him. Be careful, however, not to overdo it. Your audience will quickly sense if your enthusiasm is counterfeit or forced. If you have no real interest in the speaker, develop one—or ask someone else to introduce him.

Characteristics of content

In planning a speech of introduction observe these general principles:

Be brief. To say too much is worse than to say too little. Shailer Matthews' introduction of President Wilson might be considered the ideal introductory speech; he said, "Ladies and Gentlemen: the President." The prestige of the man you introduce will not always be great enough for you to be so brief, but it is better to err in this direction than to speak too long.

Don't talk about yourself. There is always an understandable temptation to present your own views on the subject or to tell anecdotes about your own experiences as a speaker. Resist this impulse; call attention to the speaker—not to yourself.

Tell about the speaker. Who is he? What is his position in business or government? What experiences has he had that qualify him to speak on this subject? Beware, however, of emphasizing what a good *speaker* a man is. Such comments may embarrass him. Let him demonstrate his own speaking ability; you tell who he is and what he knows. Never introduce a man as "a distinguished orator."

Emphasize the importance of the speaker's subject unless the audience already realizes its importance. Briefly point out the *value* of the information the speaker is about to offer; let him provide the information itself. For example, "All of us drive automobiles in which we use the products made from petroleum. A knowledge of the way these products are manufactured and marketed is therefore certain to be interesting and valuable to us. . . ."

Mention the appropriateness of the subject or the speaker if possible. If a country club is considering the construction of a new golf course, a speech on types of grass is especially timely. Or if the occasion is the anniversary of a firm, it is appropriate that the founder should be one of the speakers. Factual statements of this kind serve to connect the speaker more closely with the audience.

Use humor if it suits the occasion. Nothing puts an audience at its ease and creates a friendly feeling better than congenial laughter. Take care, however, that your humor is in good taste. Do not inadvertently destroy the prestige of the speaker or run the risk of offending him.

Organization

In a very long and formal speech of introduction all five steps in the motivated sequence might possibly be employed, but usually the entire sequence is not needed. In most instances, one of the following abbreviated forms will suffice.

Secure attention and arouse interest by plunging directly into the:

1. *Need step:* a statement of the importance of the subject to the audience.
2. *Satisfaction step:* a sharply abbreviated statement of the speaker's special qualifications to talk on this subject.
3. *Action step:* the presentation of the speaker.

When the speaker may be considered more important than his subject, secure attention by beginning with the:

1. *Satisfaction step:* a statement of facts about the speaker, especially facts that are not ordinarily known or those that are of particular significance to the occasion.
2. *Action step:* the presentation of the speaker and a brief announcement of his subject.

When time is short or the speaker is so well known that extreme brevity is desirable, gain attention by your salutation—"Ladies and Gentlemen," "Members of the Izaak Walton League," etc.—and proceed at once to the:

1. *Action step:* a brief announcement of the speaker's name, position, and subject.

Usually, the better known and respected a speaker is, the shorter your introduction should be; the less known he is, the more you will need to arouse interest in his subject and build up his prestige. But always remember the four primary virtues of a speech of introduction: *tact, brevity, sincerity,* and *enthusiasm.*

SAMPLE INTRODUCTIONS

W. H. Auden, lecturing at the University of Iowa on March 13, 1963, on "The Poet and His Poems," was introduced by Professor John C. Gerber, chairman of the Department of English. In his introductory remarks, Professor Gerber combined humorous references to the local scene with serious information concerning Mr. Auden's life and accomplishments. As a result, he created a desire on the part of the audience to hear what the speaker had to say and, at the same time, gave the speaker a warm and sincere welcome.

INTRODUCING W. H. AUDEN[2]

John C. Gerber

Good evening, ladies and gentlemen.

For the Committee on University Lectures I welcome you to another lecture in our 1962-63 series—a lecture to which we have all been looking forward.

I think you will agree with me that the arrival of a poet in Iowa City is not necessarily an unusual event. Happily we have come to expect poets to migrate here. We rejoice in the fact that Iowa City probably has more poets per city block than any other city in the country. We have tall poets and short poets, good poets and better poets, bearded poets and even a few clean-shaven ones. And we welcome them all and feel fortunate that they are here.

Yet despite our familiarity with poets, the arrival of a particular poet who is

[2]Text furnished by Professor Gerber and used with his permission.

on the platform with me is an extraordinary event for us all. And the reason is quite obvious. Mr. W. H. Auden is one of the truly great poets of our time.

When Emerson spoke of the poet he meant a man of highest insight; the mode of his writing was incidental. Mr. Auden is a poet in this broad sense, for his work has taken many forms. He has been an editor, a translator, a playwright, a librettist, a critic, and an essayist—and in all of these guises he has shown the same shrewd awareness of the dilemmas of our age. His last book of essays, *The Dyer's Hand and Other Essays,* has been called by Alfred Kazin "the most telling collection of critical essays published in this country for a very long time." Mr. Kazin finds in it "the driving quality of a man who feels compelled to define as sharply as possible . . . the poets' predicament in a fallen world."

But it has been in poetry, of course, that Mr. Auden has given us his sharpest and most moving perceptions. Beginning with a volume of poems published in 1930, his influence spread so quickly and so firmly that we still refer to his group as the Auden Circle or the Auden generation. In 1937, with seven books already to his credit, Mr. Auden was awarded the King's Gold Medal for the best poetry of the year.

His move to America in 1939 was followed by what many consider his finest period. At least it was during this period that he wrote many of his most frequently anthologized poems, such as "In Memory of W. B. Yeats," "September 1, 1939," and "Herman Melville."

Since the publication of his *Collected Poetry* in 1945, there has been no doubt that Mr. Auden is one of the few major poets of our age. His more recent works, like *The Age of Anxiety* in 1947, *The Shield of Achilles* in 1955, and *Homage to Clio* in 1960, have simply strengthened this view.

As any thoughtful man inevitably must, Mr. Auden has tried to face up to the question of what we must do to be saved. His earlier poems suggested that regeneration might come from without, that is, through reform of social and political institutions. In his later poems he has suggested the opposite, namely, that a meaningful change can come only from within. Many feel that this change has greatly enriched Mr. Auden's poetry. One of these is our own Professor McDowell, who in a recent essay wrote that under Christian influence Mr. Auden's vision deepened and his technical resources have grown more ample.

Originally an English subject, Mr. Auden is now an American citizen. Naturally we are proud of this fact. But his nationality is really incidental. What is important is that he is one of the great spokesmen for our times and to our times. And it is as such that I now present him to you. He will speak on the subject, "The Poet and His Poems."

Mr. Auden, we are glad to have you here.

A speech of introduction developed in a consistently humorous vein was made by Thomas R. Mulroy when presenting actress Ilka Chase to The Executives' Club of Chicago. The occasion was a weekly luncheon meeting, and approximately 1200 members and guests were present. Mr. Mulroy, who was then president of the organization, is a member of The American Bar Association, The International Academy of Trial Lawyers, The Board of Directors of the Lyric Opera of Chicago, and is associated with numerous other professional and civic groups. In your opinion, does this speaker follow the precepts of this chapter in making his introduction? What changes, if any, would you make if you were giving this speech?

INTRODUCING ILKA CHASE[3]

Thomas R. Mulroy

It is a tradition for this club, Miss Chase, that the president in introducing an artiste such as you must attempt to be satiric and sardonic—but not today! You, my dear lady, are a dangerous woman, and I would not think of letting you have the last laugh.

You know, there is an old adage that God made women without a sense of humor so that they could love men instead of laughing at them. Our guest is a devastating exception to that rule.

Anyway, it is too hard to introduce women. You have to select your words with such infinite care. For example, you may call a woman a kitten, but you must not call her a cat.

[3]Guy R. Lyle and Kevin Guinagh, *I Am Happy to Present: A Book of Introductions* (New York: Wilson, 1953). Reprinted by permission.

You may call a woman a mouse, but definitely not a rat!

You may call a woman, as a term of endearment, "duck," but you simply must avoid "goose!"

You may—and I recommend it to you, gentlemen—greet your wife in the morning with a cheery: "My dear, you certainly are a vision," but, please, oh, please, never say, "My dear, you certainly are a sight!"

Miss Chase is a fashion expert. She has exquisite taste, always knowing the right thing to wear at the right time. Not so, all women. I was in Florida this winter, and all the slacks I saw on women reminded me of the Lucky Strike advertisement: "So round, so firm, so fully packed!"

But men are queer, too. They say the main difference between man and beast is man's brains, but there the difference ends, because man is lion-hearted, chicken-livered, pigeon-toed, busy as a bee, sly as a fox, blind as a bat, gentle as a lamb, drunk as a hoot owl, stubborn as a mule, strong as an ox, vain as a peacock, happy as a lark, or crazy as a loon—depending upon your particular point of view.

Miss Chase gained stage fame on Broadway by her portrayal of the part of the brazen cat, and I don't mean kitten, in the play entitled *The Women.* She is now a scintillating movie star.

Miss Chase is the author of two successive best sellers, *Past Imperfect* and *In Bed We Cry.* I read *Past Imperfect* and liked it very much. I read *In Bed We Cry* . . . period!

Abraham Lincoln once wrote a review of a book—not Miss Chase's, of course—from which I wonder if I might adopt his comments as my own view of *In Bed We Cry.* Mr. Lincoln wrote:

"For those who like this kind of book, this is the kind of a book they will like."

Miss Chase has always been years ahead of her time, a genuine prodigy.

At the tender age of fourteen, she was valedictorian of her graduating class in a secluded convent school, and on the occasion of her address she delivered this sweet, idealistic, and unsophisticated philosophy of true love (with my own apologies to Dorothy Parker):

> Dear fathers, mothers, and classmates, I would like to recite a poem about true love:
>
> When you finally swear you're his,
> Shivering and sighing,
> And he vows his passion is
> Infinite, undying,—
> Classmates, make a note of this:
> One of you is lying!

Here is indeed the truly soft-spoken woman's woman, incorrigible romanticist, shy rosebud, as we next find her at the age of twenty-five. One evening an old friend of the family rushed in to her and said, sobbing: "Ilka, some man has taken my car and run away with my wife!"

"No! No!" exclaimed Ilka, "Not your *new* car!"

Now that all my bad jokes are concluded, let me say in all earnestness that this huge gathering today is a dramatic tribute to Ilka Chase, one of America's brilliant women.

I do now present to you, with a genuine feeling of privilege, the one and only Ilka Chase.

Problems

1. Assume that you are to act as toastmaster or chairman on one or more of the following occasions (or on some similar occasion):

a. A special assembly called to celebrate the completion of a successful football season.

b. A student-government awards banquet.

c. A program meeting of a club to which you belong.

d. A student-faculty mass meeting called to protest a regulation issued by the Dean's office.

Plan a suitable program of speeches, entertainment, etc.; allocate the amount of time to be devoted to each item on the program; outline suitable speeches of introduction; prepare for publicity releases; and arrange for press coverage. In short, work out a complete plan which you might show to a steering committee or a faculty sponsor.

2. Select one of the speeches reprinted at the end of Chapter 20, 21, 22, or 23, and assume that you are to introduce this speech and speaker to a campus audience. Outline or write out a suitable speech of introduction.

3. With the aid of your instructor, find five speeches of introduction of varying length and quality. Compare and contrast these speeches critically. Which one is most effective? Which is least effective? Why? What general rules and cautions concerning the speech of introduction may be inferred from this study?

4. Interview the faculty member who serves as chairman of your campus lecture committee, or some faculty member who frequently introduces visiting lecturers or artists. Ask him his conception of a good speech of introduction and what rules or principles he tries to follow when introducing speakers.

5. Select an imaginary subject, speaker, audience, and occasion; then write what you would consider the worst possible speech of introduction for this situation.

Speaking assignments

1. For the remainder of the semester, let appointed student chairmen preside over successive rounds of classroom speeches. Each student should act

as chairman for one day. The chairman's duties will include arranging the speeches in a suitable order, introducing the speakers, keeping the program moving on time, preserving order, presiding over question periods, etc. He will be graded on how well he performs these tasks.

2. Let each member of the class interview another member and then present a speech introducing him and some imaginary subject upon which he might speak.

Suggestions for further reading

William Albig, *Modern Public Opinion* (New York: McGraw-Hill Book Company, 1956), Chapter VII, "The Leader and Personal Symbolism."

John E. Baird, *Guide to Conducting Meetings* (Nashville, Tennessee: Abingdon Press, 1965).

Virgil L. Baker and Ralph T. Eubanks, *Speech in Personal and Public Affairs* (New York: David McKay Co., Inc., 1965), Chapter XXI, "Presiding at a Meeting."

Kenneth G. Hance, David C. Ralph, and Milton J. Wiksell, *Principles of Speaking* (Belmont, California: Wadsworth Publishing Company, Inc., 1962), Chapter XVIII, "Leading a Meeting."

E. J. Hegarty, *How to Run Better Meetings* (New York: McGraw-Hill Book Company, 1957).

Guy R. Lyle and Kevin Guinagh, *I Am Happy to Present: A Book of Introductions* (New York: H. W. Wilson Company, 1953).

William Phillips Sandford and Willard Hayes Yeager, *Effective Business Speech* (New York: McGraw-Hill Book Company, 1950), Chapter VII, "How to Plan and Conduct Informal Meetings."

C. W. Wright, *Better Speeches for All Occasions* (New York: Crown Publishers, Inc., 1948), Chapter IV, "Introducing a Speaker," and Chapter V, "Thanking a Speaker."

CHAPTER TWENTY-SEVEN

Speeches for courtesy

Most speakers, at one time or another, will have occasion to give a speech for courtesy either on behalf of themselves or on behalf of an organization they represent. The ability to say the appropriate and effective thing on such an occasion is a valuable asset.

TYPICAL SITUATIONS REQUIRING SPEECHES FOR COURTESY

Speeches for courtesy most frequently are given to fulfill one of three obligations: (1) *To welcome visitors or new members.* Customarily, the presiding officer of the organization or one of its prominent members will voice a greeting and extend a welcome to guests and newcomers. At a convention, the mayor of the city or the president of the local branch of the organization usually welcomes the visiting delegates; or at a local meeting, the presiding officer usually is expected to extend greetings to any guests who may be present. (2) *To respond to a welcome or greeting.* An individual or organization thus welcomed is often expected to express appreciation for that greeting. (3) *To present or accept a gift or award.* If an individual is given a gift or award for some accomplishment or for some service he has rendered, the person making the presentation is expected to review at least briefly what this accomplishment or service was, and to express the appreciation of the organization or group on whose behalf the award is made. The recipient, in turn, is usually expected to express his appreciation in a brief speech of response.

THE PURPOSE OF THE SPEECH FOR COURTESY

The speech for courtesy has a double purpose: first, to express a genuine sentiment of gratitude or hospitality and, second, to create good feeling in the audience. The success of such a speech, therefore, often depends upon whether the listeners feel that the appropriate thing has been said. When guests are present or acknowledgments are due, the audience expects the proper courtesies to be extended. Just as the courtesies of private life put people at ease, so the public acts of courtesy create good feeling in an audience.

THE MANNER OF SPEAKING

In no other type of speech is the temptation so great to repeat with oratorical flourish a series of flowery platitudes. Resist this temptation always. Do not try to overdo yourself in graciousness. Speak sincerely and honestly, but let your manner—serious or jovial, brisk or tranquil—fit the spirit of the occasion. Usually a note of optimism is appropriate. In accordance with the circumstance, suggest by your manner that you are pleased by the presence of the guest, that you appreciate the award, or that you are genuinely glad to be present.

CHARACTERISTICS OF CONTENT

Remember that your duty is to perform tactfully and sincerely an expected act of courtesy, and keep the following points in mind:

Indicate why you are speaking. Identify the circumstances, mention the visitors you are greeting and the guests you are welcoming. Then describe briefly the accomplishment or service for which the award is being made.

Indicate for whom you are speaking. If you are the spokesman for a group, make clear that the greeting or acknowledgment comes from the whole group, not from you alone. For example, "It is a privilege to be here this afternoon to accept in the name of the Markham Hospital Board the ambulance your organization has so generously contributed to our community." References to yourself or to the group you represent should, of course, be modest.

Present complimentary facts about the person or group to whom you are extending the courtesy. Your emphasis should be on the achievements or good qualities of the person or group you are greeting or to whom the award is being made rather than on yourself or the group you represent.

Avoid points of disagreement. Be particularly careful that your remarks offend no one. Let the incidents and facts you present illuminate the importance of the occasion or group you are addressing or of the guest you are welcoming. Suppose, for example, that a prominent judge were a guest at a meeting of your local club. In welcoming him, it would be bad taste to talk about the red tape in legal procedure or the organized strength of criminal gangs. Instead, relate complimentary incidents involving the judge and his accomplishments, and show that you are genuinely glad he is present.

ORGANIZATION

The speech for courtesy should seldom include more than three of the steps in the motivated sequence. At times, only the satisfaction step—the actual greeting—is required. Obviously no need step is used, for the situation itself implies the audience's consciousness of the need for an act of courtesy; and just as obviously no action is required. If all of the three remaining steps—attention, satisfaction, and visualization—are included, they may be arranged in the following fashion:

Attention step

The opening may consist of a reference to the occasion, to the person or group addressed, or to the group for which you are spokesman. If you are presenting or accepting a gift or award, you may appropriately begin by referring to the donor of the gift or to the conditions under which the award is made. Such references at the beginning of your speech should be brief and should lead directly into the satisfaction step.

Satisfaction step

The bulk of the speech is the satisfaction step—the performance of the actual act of courtesy. The greeting, presentation, or response may be illuminated and amplified by one or more of the following elements:

1. Complimentary facts about the host, guest, or donor.
2. Facts about the group you represent, indicating the warmth or extent of your greeting—for example, the number of people who join with you in this welcome, the earnestness of their efforts in preparing for the occasion, and the eagerness with which they have looked forward to it.
3. Plans for the future, giving tangible evidence of the *practical* nature of your hospitality or appreciation—for example, plans made for the accommodation or entertainment of the guests welcomed, plans you as a guest have for the period of your stay, or plans you have for the use of the award you have just received.

Visualization step

Again depending upon the circumstance, the function of the visualization step in the speech for courtesy is to suggest anticipated pleasure in having the guests present, in being present as a guest, or in using the gift or award and remembering the donors of it. Many times, instead of forming a separate aspect of the speech, visualization is included in the discussion of the various points of the satisfaction step—a kind of parallel treatment. In either case, an expression of anticipated pleasure always should be included. At the end of the visualization step, close with an emphatic and sincere reiteration of the greeting or acknowledgment.

The organization suggested above is, of course, intended to be quite inclusive; ordinarily, not all of the listed elements will be used in every speech of this kind. Necessarily, the steps to be followed will vary with each situation. For example, a student to whom a prize is awarded may not be expected to say more than "Thank you" or to show his appreciation by smiling or nodding an acknowledgment. The ensuing speeches illustrate a few of the various ways in which a speech for courtesy may be developed.

SAMPLE SPEECHES

On February 12, 1964, British Prime Minister Sir Alec Douglas-Home arrived in Washington with a party of advisers for talks with President Johnson and members of his cabinet. As he alighted from a helicopter on the White House lawn, President Johnson greeted him with a brief speech of welcome and the Prime Minister replied.

THE PRESIDENT'S WELCOME[1]

Lyndon B. Johnson

Mr. Prime Minister, you do this land and this house great honor by your visit. Mrs. Johnson and I welcome you, Lady Douglas-Home, the Foreign Secretary, Mrs. Butler, and other members of your party to the United States and to the White House.

This visit only continues a tradition that is both spacious and warm. Meet-

[1]Texts of this speech and the following one have been supplied by the White House Press Secretary and the British Embassy.

ings between American Presidents and British Prime Ministers were first firmly established by our great President, Franklin Roosevelt, and your legendary Prime Minister—and now our fellow American—Sir Winston Churchill.

No matter the political complexion of our two Governments, this tradition has remained happily unbroken for more than a quarter of a century.

During these years we have had our differences, but these differences have passed away. They have passed away because of a very special reason: There is between our two countries the invisible cords of a mingled respect and understanding and affection, much as two brothers who may differ but whose ties are too strong to ever break.

So we meet today as Presidents and Prime Ministers of two countries, as they have always met, with friendship and high resolve to face our common problems and to try to settle them for the common good. Together our nations are secure. They are strong enough to win any fight, and we hope they are wise enough to prevent one. Together we search for tolerance, we search for hope, we search for peace.

In that spirit and with that aim, Mr. Prime Minister, we welcome you. We welcome you to this house and to this land, and may God bless our work together.

THE PRIME MINISTER'S REPLY

Sir Alec Douglas-Home

Mr. President, I would like to thank you very much for the warmth of your welcome to my wife and myself and to the Foreign Secretary and Mrs. Butler, and to say how much we are looking forward to our exchange of views with you.

We are engaged, as you have so clearly and graphically put it the other day, in the pursuits of peace, and much of our talks will undoubtedly be concerned with how we can improve the situation in a difficult and dangerous world, and we in Britain are particularly conscious now of its difficulties and its dangers because we are engaged, as you know, far afield in trying to help to maintain stability and order which is, I know, your concern, too, as a great power.

Since, as you say, this is one of a sequence of meetings which have always been of great benefit to our own countries, I would like you to know that my firm desire is to keep as close as we can to the United States as partners and as allies and as two countries upon which the peace of the world may well depend.

So, Sir, I would like once more to thank you. We are going to enjoy ourselves in Washington, and we brought the sun with us and that may be a good omen.

I would once more only say that anything that I can do in our talks and my Government can do to help to keep the relations between Britain and the United States close and harmonious will be done with the full support of all of our countrymen.

Thank you very much.

Three days after the completion of the first successful orbital flight by an American, President John F. Kennedy presented the National Aeronautics and Space Administration's Distinguished Service Medal to the astronaut, Lieutenant Colonel John H. Glenn, Jr. Although brief and extremely simple in style, President Kennedy's speech and Colonel Glenn's response are marked by grace as well as sincerity.

PRESENTING THE DISTINGUISHED SERVICE MEDAL[2]

John F. Kennedy

Colonel Glenn, will you step forward. Seventeen years ago today, a group of Marines put the American Flag on Mount Suribachi, so it is very appropriate that today we decorate Colonel Glenn of the United States Marine Corps, and also realize that in the not too distant future a Marine or a Naval man or an Air Force man will put the American Flag on the moon.

I present this Citation. The President of the United States takes pleasure in awarding the National Aeronautics and Space Administration's Distinguished Service Medal to Lieutenant Colonel John H. Glenn, Jr., United States Marine

[2]Texts of this speech and the following one have been furnished by the White House Press Secretary.

Corps, for services set forth in the following: For exceptionally meritorious service to the government of the United States in a duty of great responsibility as the first American astronaut to perform orbital flight. Lieutenant Colonel Glenn's orbital flight on February 20, 1962, made an outstanding contribution to the advancement of human knowledge of space technology and in demonstration of man's capabilities in space flight.

His performance was marked by his great professional knowledge, his skill as a test pilot, his unflinching courage, and his extraordinary ability to perform most difficult tasks under conditions of great physical stress and personal danger. His performance in fulfillment of this most dangerous assignment reflects the highest credit upon himself and the United States.

Colonel, we appreciate what you have done!

We have Mr. and Mrs. Glenn, who launched Colonel Glenn originally—they are right here in the front row—and also Mrs. Glenn and David and Lynn.

And we would like to have you say a word to everybody.

ACCEPTING THE MEDAL

John H. Glenn, Jr.

All right—fine, thank you. Sit down, please—it's hot.

I can't express my appreciation adequately, to be here accepting this, when I know how many thousands of people all over the country were involved in helping accomplish what we did last Tuesday—and knowing how, particularly this group here at the Cape, and many of the group here on the platform, our own group of astronauts who were scattered all around the world who performed their functions here at the Cape also—we all acted literally and figuratively as a team. It was a real team effort all the way.

We have stressed the team effort in Project Mercury. It goes across the board—I think sort of a cross-cut of Americana, of industry, and military, and Civil Service—government work—contractors. It's almost a cross-cut of American effort in the technical field—I think it wasn't specialized by any one particular group. It was headed up by NASA, of course, but thousands and thousands of people have contributed, certainly as much or more than I have to the Project.

I would like to consider that I was sort of a figurehead for the whole big, tremendous effort. And I am very proud of the Medal I have on my lapel here, for all of us—you included—because I think it represents all of our efforts —not just mine.

Thank you very much. And thank you, Mr. President.

Problems

1. Make a list of all the occasions you can think of that occur on your campus during the course of a school year which call for a speech for courtesy. Compare the frequency of these occasions with the frequency of occasions requiring speeches to entertain, inform, convince, stimulate, or actuate.
2. Describe the speaking manner that you think probably would be most appropriate for each of the following occasions for courtesy:

a. The presentation of letters to a basketball team that has not won a game all season.

b. Responding to an award for high scholarship presented by the president of the college at spring commencement.

c. Welcoming delegates from other campuses to a convention of student-government leaders.

d. Welcoming new faculty members to the campus at a coffee hour sponsored by the interfraternity council.

e. Responding to an award for having worn the most original costume at the annual Halloween dance.

3. Find a printed speech of welcome or of presentation. Outline this speech and prepare a written report commenting on its general content and organization.
4. Outline what you believe would be an appropriate speech of response to the welcome or presentation studied in Problem 3. Indicate not only the ideas you would develop, but also the probable order in which you would arrange them.

Speaking assignment

Prepare a three-minute speech for courtesy suitable for one of the following occasions:

a. Welcoming a distinguished alumnus to a fraternity banquet.

b. Welcoming newly initiated members into an honorary society.

c. Responding to a speech welcoming your group or delegation to a neighboring campus.

d. Accepting an award for athletic or scholastic achievement.
e. Accepting an office to which you have been elected.
f. Presenting a gift to a faculty member on his retirement.

Speeches for collateral study

1. Dwight D. Eisenhower, "This Continent a Single Entity," *Vital Speeches of the Day,* XX (December 1, 1953), 98 ff.
2. William Faulkner, "The Writer's Duty," *The Speaker's Resource Book,* ed. Carroll Arnold, Douglas Ehninger, and John Gerber (Glenview, Illinois: Scott, Foresman, 1966), pp. 52-53.
3. John F. Kennedy, "Inaugural Address," *The Speaker's Resource Book,* ed. Carroll Arnold, Douglas Ehninger, and John Gerber (Glenview, Illinois: Scott, Foresman, 1966), pp. 225-227.
4. Douglas MacArthur, "On Accepting the National Football Foundation's Gold Medal Award," *Footballer,* II (January 1960), 2-4.
5. Adlai E. Stevenson, "Address of Welcome," in *Major Campaign Speeches of Adlai E. Stevenson* (New York: Random House, 1953), p. 3 ff.
6. U Thant, "Accepting the Post of Secretary General of the UN," Alan Monroe and Douglas Ehninger, *Principles of Speech,* 5th ed. (Glenview, Illinois: Scott, Foresman, 1964), pp. 323-324.

Suggestions for further reading

W. Norwood Brigance, *Speech: Its Techniques and Disciplines in a Free Society,* 2nd ed. (New York: Appleton-Century-Crofts, 1961), pp. 494-499, "The Address of Welcome," "The Response," "The Presentation," "The Acceptance," "The Farewell."

Giles W. Gray and Waldo W. Braden, *Public Speaking: Principles and Practice,* 2nd ed. (New York: Harper & Row, 1963), pp. 398-408, "Speeches of Courtesy."

Robert T. Oliver and Rupert L. Cortright, *New Training for Effective Speech,* rev. ed. (New York: Dryden, 1951), pp. 503-505, "Speeches of Welcome . . . Response . . . Presentation . . . Acceptance . . . Farewell."

Eugene E. White, *Practical Public Speaking,* 2nd ed. (New York: The Macmillan Company, 1964), pp. 354-361, "The Speeches of Courtesy."

C. W. Wright, *Better Speeches for All Occasions* (New York: Crown Publishers, Inc., 1948), Chapter VIII, "An Address of Welcome"; Chapter IX, "Responding to an Address of Welcome"; Chapter X, "The Formal Address of Welcome"; Chapter XI, "Presenting A Gift"; Chapter XII, "Accepting a Gift."

Willard Hayes Yeager, *Effective Speaking for Every Occasion* (New York: Prentice-Hall, Inc., 1940), Chapter V, "How to Make Speeches of Response and Farewell."

CHAPTER TWENTY-EIGHT

Speeches to generate good will

Either directly or indirectly, nearly every speech seeks the good will of the audience. In this chapter, however, we are concerned with the type of speech which has as its *primary* aim the generating of the listeners' good will. In one sense, the purpose of the good-will speech is to *inform*—to tell about the organization or enterprise for which good will is sought; in another sense, its purpose is to *persuade* (to convince or stimulate or actuate)—though it cannot be too argumentative or overtly persuasive because its appeal for direct support must be subordinated or even hidden. Viewed in terms of its purpose, then, the good-will speech is a hybrid: *an informative speech which attempts to persuade.*

Within recent years, speeches for good will have begun to play a significant role in the public relations of many business firms. For example, the representatives of one large Chicago corporation made more than 1800 speeches of this type in one year. And, of course, business firms are not alone in this practice. Governments, professional and charitable organizations, institutional enterprises, schools, churches, financial foundations—all endeavor to generate public support through this kind of speaking.

TYPICAL SITUATIONS FOR SPEECHES FOR GOOD WILL

Four of the most common situations in which good-will speeches are given are luncheon club meetings, educational programs, special demonstration programs, and conventions. *Luncheon club meetings* present an excellent opportunity for such talks because the typical audience, composed of leading men and women from all types of businesses and professions, is usually interested in governmental affairs and in the way other businesses operate. Since such meetings are semisocial in nature, the good feeling of the audience is practically guaranteed. Gaining the good will and support of such an audience is not only relatively easy but also extremely valuable. *Educational programs* are often arranged by schools, clubs, and church groups to make it possible for the young people to hear a speaker tell about his business or profession and explain the opportunities it affords and the training it requires. By tactful reference, a speaker may create much incidental good will for the particular organization he represents. *Special demonstration programs* are frequently presented by corporations and by university extension departments. *Conventions* sometimes offer opportunities for good-will talks, particularly at their banquets and luncheons. A typical good-will speech was given at a recent convention of bankers by an official from an airplane manufacturing concern who spoke on commercial aviation, showing its relation to banking.

THE PURPOSE OF THE GOOD-WILL SPEECH

Although the real purpose of the speech is to generate good will, this must not be *apparent.* As far as the audience is concerned, the purpose must appear to be primarily informative; only rarely may it be overtly persuasive—for example, when a speaker is urging joint action toward a common goal. Moreover, to secure his listeners' good will, the speaker must present his information so that they will understand and be favorably disposed toward his organization, his government, or whatever venture he may represent. In short, the speaker's purpose in a good-will speech is to provide information about his profession or enterprise in such a way that he will unobtrusively gain good will and support for it.

THE MANNER OF SPEAKING

Three qualities—modesty, tolerance, and good humor—characterize the manner of speaking required for good-will speeches. Although the speaker will be talking about his own vocation and trying to make it seem important to his audience, he should beware of bragging. In giving a good-will speech, let the facts speak for themselves. Moreover, show a tolerant attitude toward others, especially competitors. The railroad representative who violently attacks the truck companies and bus lines gains more ill will than good. A courteous, positive attitude accompanied by a tactful presentation of the forward-looking and beneficial things his company has done will be much more effective. Finally, exercise good humor. The good-will speech is not for the crusader. Take the task more genially. Don't try to cram your talk down people's throats; instead, show so much good feeling toward your listeners that they will spontaneously respond to your manner of speaking.

CHARACTERISTICS OF CONTENT

There are four useful guides to consider when shaping the content of the speech to create good will:

Present novel, interesting facts about your organization, enterprise, or profession. Make your listeners feel that you are letting them in on the inside; give them first-hand information about things that are not generally known. But avoid talking about what is common knowledge.

Show some definite relation between your organization, enterprise, or profession and the lives of your listeners. Make them see how your activities are related to their prosperity or happiness. For example, the official from the airplane manufacturer who spoke to a convention of bankers showed how the rapid transfer of commercial paper resulted in a great saving to banks.

Avoid a too-definite request for approval; assume that you already have it. Don't make the mistake of telling your listeners outright that they don't know anything about your organization and that you are trying to get their good will. Instead, suggest that they already know a good deal about it (if they don't, they will probably think they ought to), and then proceed as suggested above.

Offer some definite service. This may be in the form of an invitation to visit your plant or office, the distribution of samples or souvenirs, the offer of some special service to the members of this particular audience, or the suggestion that your organization will join theirs in solving a common problem. The important thing is not *what* you offer them but the impression that *you are at their service.*

ORGANIZATION

Let us see how these guidelines can be of use in organizing a well-rounded good-will speech.

Attention step

The purpose of the beginning of your speech is to establish a friendly feeling and to arouse the audience's curiosity about your profession or the institution you represent. You may gain the first objective by a tactful compliment to the group or a reference to the occasion that has brought you together. Follow this with one or two unusual facts or illustrations concerning your organization. For instance, "Before we began manufacturing television parts, the Lash Electric Company confined its business to the making of phonograph motors. We succeeded so well that we almost went bankrupt! That was only fifteen years ago. Today our export trade to foreign countries is over one hundred times as large as our total annual domestic business in those days. It may interest you to know how this change took place." It is important that, in some such way, you arouse the audience's curiosity about your organization.

Need step

Point out certain problems facing your audience with which your institution or profession or government is vitally concerned. For instance, if you represent an air line, show the relation of transportation to community business. By so doing, you can establish common ground with your audience. Ordinarily the need step will be relatively brief and will consist largely of suggestions briefly developed with only an occasional illustration. However, if you intend to suggest joint action in meeting a common problem, the need step will require a fuller development.

Satisfaction step

The meat of your speech will be in the satisfaction step. Here is the place to tell the audience about your institution, profession, or business and what it does. You can do this in at least three ways:

Relate interesting events in the history of the institution. Pick those events which will demonstrate its humanity, its reliability, and its importance to the community, to your country, or to the world of nations.

Explain its organization and operation. Pick out those things that are unusual or that may contain beneficial suggestions for your audience. This method often helps impress upon them the size and efficiency of your operation or enterprise.

Tell what your organization does. Explain its products; point out how widely they are used; discuss the policies upon which it is run —especially those which you think your audience will agree with or admire; point out what your company has done for this particular community: people employed, local purchases made, assistance in community or national enterprises, improvement of real estate. Don't boast, but see that your listeners realize the value of your work *to them.*

Visualization step

Your object here is to crystallize the good will that your presentation of information has created. Do this by giving your hearers a bird's-eye view of the importance of your work to them. Look to the future. Make a rapid survey of the points you have covered in your satisfaction step, or combine them in a single story or illustration. Or, to approach this step from the opposite direction, picture for them the vacancy or loss that would result if the organization you represent should leave the community or go out of business. Be careful, however, not to leave the impression that there is any real danger that this will occur.

Action step

It is here that you make your offer of service to the audience—for example, invite the group to visit your plant, your city, your state; or point out the willingness of your organization to assist in some common enterprise.

SAMPLE SPEECH

The plan outlined above will have to be modified, of course, to suit the needs of your institution, organization, or profession and the occasion on which you speak. But never lose sight of one fact: you must indirectly demonstrate to your listeners that the business, entity, or mission you represent is of value to them. Analyze how this has been done by Her Excellency Indira Gandhi, Prime Minister of India, in her speech to the National Press Club, Washington, D.C., on March 29, 1966.

INDIA IN PERSPECTIVE: UNITED STATES COOPERATION[1]

Her Excellency Indira Gandhi

Mr. President, Ladies and Gentlemen: I am delighted to be here today in this gathering of newsmen and representatives of mass communication media.

[1]From *Vital Speeches of the Day,* XXXII (May 1, 1966), 423-425. Reprinted by permission of Her Excellency.

Need I say that I am especially happy that the women members of the profession are also present.

I am grateful to the President and to Mrs. Johnson, the members of the United States Government, and the people of this country for their kindness, hospitality and warmth of welcome to me. I have had frank and friendly talks with President Johnson and have profited from an exchange of views on many matters. We have asked nothing of each other. However, I am confident that as a result of these talks the understanding between our two countries has been immeasurably increased.

This afternoon I should like to speak to you, and through you, to the American people. I should like to speak about India: an old country, a new country, a fast-developing country. India, where many centuries are telescoped into one. In our historical situation, we have learned to live with internal strains and tensions. These we consider growing pains.

This year, we are also confronted with a difficult food situation caused by an unprecedented drought. There is acute scarcity in parts of the country, but no famine or starvation as we understood the words in pre-independence days. We may have averted deaths, but continued malnutrition is as dangerous. We are making every effort to ensure equitable distribution of available cereals including the wheat and other supplies which America and other countries are generously providing.

Nevertheless, 1966 will be a hard year. To the casual observer, the Indian scene, political and economic, might appear distressing, even ominous. Such a conclusion, however, would be wrong.

I do not underrate India's problems. It is an ancient country, reborn and striving courageously to make the tremendous transition from a traditional to a modern society. It is an effort which represents one of the most significant human experiments of our time.

Consider India. It is only one third the geographic size of the United States. But when you talk of India, you are talking of a country with more people than all the Americas, North and South. You are talking about one seventh of the entire human race.

Obviously, what happens to India is of profound importance. Not because of the vote India casts in the United Nations. Not because of any military prowess. Not because of its rich culture. But because it constitutes a society of nearly 500 million people. Many faiths, languages, races live side by side. India is the largest composite society in the world. This is an essential fact to which I should draw your attention.

India, like the United States, is wedded to the democratic ideal. Early next year, an electorate of some 250 million people will go forth to elect freely, and without fear, their chosen representatives for the fourth time since Indian independence.

But what does democracy mean in the mid-twentieth century? Does it merely mean the right to vote, the rule of law, freedom of speech, association and worship? Or does it mean more than that? I suggest it does. Today, democracy inescapably implies social welfare, equality of opportunity, reasonable living standards, the dignity of the individual. Man does not live by bread alone. But equally he needs bread to enjoy liberty.

This is the remarkable feature of democracy in India. It represents a striking historical reversal. Political democracy as we know it today was for the most part, certainly in Europe, the end-product of a long revolutionary process of industrial development and educational and social change. In India, democracy has been made the instrument of such a change. We firmly believe that democracy and development can and must go hand in hand and that the human being cannot be sacrificed in the name of material development.

Nonetheless, with the grant of political rights to a huge and increasingly social and politically conscious electorate, the people—like Oliver Twist—want more. They are right to want more—and better.

This revolution of rising expectations, as it has been called, generates its own pressures. India has not escaped from these pressures and is subject to them. The rapid rise in population has aggravated our problems. We have added largely to our numbers since Independence. Every month there are a million more Indians to care for. We have, however, launched a vast family-planning programme. The magnitude of our effort will be evident from just two statistics: 18,000 family-planning centers are actually operating in the country today; we have also increased the budget for family planning 20-fold.

Poverty is our basic problem. It is our principal enemy. The per capita income of the average Indian is no more than $70 per annum. If a per capita monthly consumption of $4 is regarded as a bare minimum, then half the population of India lives below the breadline. This lends urgency to development.

I find it difficult to understand the concern of those of our friends who feel that India's plans are too ambitious. Time is not with India, but against it. With the increase in population we have to run fast to stand still.

There was a 40 per cent increase in national income in the first decade of Indian planning. Of this only 16 per cent went into higher living standards. The rest was absorbed by population growth.

Many of our problems are problems of growth, and often the result of success. Even the population increase is wholly rooted in improved health, better nutritional standards, and the eradication of diseases like malaria. In 1951 we had 100 million cases of malaria; in 1965 only 100,000.

We have a foreign-exchange crisis because we have a large and diversified industrial economy that just did not exist a decade ago. Today we make jets and computers and export machine tools to Western Europe. We have supplied heavy water to Belgium. We are among the leading nations in the development of nuclear energy for peaceful purposes. If India faces a crisis today it is largely a crisis of development.

I do not say this in extenuation of our mistakes or failures. I am conscious of the fact that we should and could have done better. But, taking the record as a whole, what has been achieved is quite remarkable, especially as it has been achieved in conditions of peace and political stability. In an unstable world, India stands out as a rock of stability. We may quarrel among ourselves. But in times of crises, the nation has time and again risen as one to face the challenge. Basically India is united and strong. There is an underlying strand of Indianness that cannot be torn asunder.

The impatient observer often gets an exaggerated sense of disunity on account of our regional, caste, and communal pulls. These negative forces are there. They are manifestations of an unfortunate but only too natural desire to secure as large a slice of the all-too-small cake of opportunity that we can yet provide our people. They do not represent any fundamental division. And they are weakening with every passing year, although a contrary impression might be created by the violence of their death struggle.

Indeed, considering the size of India, the diversity of its people, and the immense problems of poverty with which it is grappling, the wonder is not that there have been strain and internal tension, but that there has been such an extraordinary degree of stability and orderly progress.

This achievement should not be underestimated. It is useful to recall that even such old and prosperous countries as the United States, Canada, and Belgium have problems of race, language, and religion—by-products of history —which they are trying to solve in their own way.

Development with democracy in conditions of stability has been a major Indian contribution to world peace and human welfare. Yet poverty remains our main enemy. We are dedicated to victory in this struggle, and we are convinced that we shall win.

In the task of economic development we have received crucial assistance from the United States, other friendly nations, and various international agencies. We are grateful for this act of faith.

Although India may have received substantial foreign assistance in absolute terms, our own effort has been four to five times as large. The aid received by India in per capita terms is also about the lowest on the international scale. Given a modest step-up in foreign assistance, better terms in trade, opportunities of repayment in kind, a re-scheduling of external debts, and improved plan-implementation on our part, India can attain a stage of self-generating growth within the next decade. Even today, I might add, India is also a donor nation and has aided and is aiding a number of countries in Asia and Africa.

The present economic difficulties confronting India constitute a passing phase. If our third plan has not done as well as we had hoped, there are some external reasons for this, quite apart from any failures on our part: the Chinese attack in 1962 which resulted in a substantial diversion of resources and materials from development to defense; the Indo-Pakistan conflict, the pause in aid that followed and still continues, and—most recently—the unprecedented drought that has affected large parts of the country and created problems of food, rising prices, and balance-of-payments difficulties.

All these, I am convinced, are temporary difficulties, and the Indian economy should resume its forward momentum within the year. Meanwhile, there is much that has been achieved that does not enter into the cold statistics of growth. Most important of these gains are changing attitudes and values, a changing social structure, the spread of education and health services, child care, including a fairly large and expanding school-feeding programme, the development of many new skills—intellectual and scientific—the rise of a new class of managers, technicians, and entrepreneurs, and technological progress.

We have only made a beginning and have a long road to travel. We are conscious of this. But we are not deterred. We have adopted planning in a mixed economy as the means of attaining the objectives we seek, namely, the well-being of the individual, 500 million individuals, members of a composite, democratic society. If India succeeds, the world will be a happier and a safer place for us all. If India were perchance to fail, then the world will have cause for anxiety. But we shall not fail.

Over the past eighteen years of freedom, we have sought to evolve a purposeful and meaningful national consensus, based upon the principles of secularism and democratic socialism. We interpret these principles in the context of the Indian reality. We are at the same time conscious of living in an interdependent world. We want peace for its own sake, as a human necessity. We also know that India's development can go forward as fast as we would like, only in a peaceful world. This outlook has influenced our independent foreign policy.

We no longer live in a bi-polar world. There have been significant shifts in alignment both in the East and the West. The Sino-Soviet rift, the proliferation of nuclear weapons, and the decolonisation of large parts of Asia and Africa have resulted in material changes in the international situation.

China's ideology cannot push outwards if its neighbours and other nations possess strong, independent, nationalist governments. They must also see a viable alternative to China. India can be that Asian alternative, an alternative model for economic and social change, a democratic, socialist model. It is by its effort to develop in democratic socialism that India poses the most serious challenge to China. It is for this reason again that Peking tries to undo India's non-alignment.

The Sino-Indian problem, in this context, is more than a boundary question. It is a wider problem of relations between two giant Asian States and their future role in South and Southeast Asia. We seek no spheres of intluence, but if the intention is to weaken us, to erode us politically, or to disrupt our federal unity, we shall not oblige.

We are, like others, deeply concerned about the future of Viet Nam, a near Asian neighbour. We share the world's regret that a peaceful solution has eluded that troubled land thus far despite many and varied efforts. Nevertheless, we are convinced that all of us must keep trying. The Geneva Conference could offer a way out and might yet provide the machinery for a return to the negotiating table. India is Chairman of the International Control Commission, and we have been and are always ready to play a constructive role in the continuing quest for peace in Viet Nam. I have been in my talks with Mr. Johnson impressed by the sincerity of the President's desire for a peaceful settlement in that war-torn country.

The real battle in Southeast Asia and indeed in other areas of the developing world is one of development in conditions of social equality, freedom, and stability. We believe that Asian development through the individual efforts of each country and through regional cooperation with friendly assistance from outside is eminently desirable. The Mekong river project and the Asian Development Bank, in both of which our countries are participating, are pointers.

Though we have rejected Communism for ourselves, we do believe in peaceful co-existence. As your President has said, "No man or nation is wise enough to prescribe a single economic system or a single set of political institutions to meet the needs of more than a hundred countries, each with its own history, its own resources, its own culture, and its own proud spiritual tradition." An idea can only be opposed by a better idea freely chosen by those concerned. Hence our friendship with the Soviet Union, Yugoslavia, and other countries of Eastern Europe. It is because we genuinely desire to promote peace and co-existence that we have not sought to join the nuclear arms race, despite the fact that we possess the necessary technical capability. Here is testimony to our *bona fides* as a non-aligned nation.

I move nearer home to India. Only two months ago we signed an agreement with our neighbour Pakistan. Through the Tashkent Declaration both our countries proclaimed their faith in peace and in peaceful methods to resolve differences between nations. Since that January day, we on our side have moved with sincerity and speed to deepen and enlarge the Tashkent spirit. It pains me to hear accusations made that India is not reconciled to the very existence of Pakistan. We want Pakistan to live and prosper. We want Pakistan to be stable and devoted to the path of peace. To this end we are prepared to open frontiers, to work out joint economic projects, and to heal the wounds of partition.

I have spoken for longer than I had intended. But it was my desire to put India in perspective. Let me repeat that the fate of India is of the greatest concern to the world and that a stable, democratic and prosperous India will by itself be a force for peace and stability.

India desires the friendship and cooperation of the United States. Though sometimes misunderstandings arise, I believe there is a far wider area of agreement than of disagreement between our two countries.

Both India and the US need one another's friendship and cooperation in this troubled world. India is as important to the US as the US is to India. Let us both recognize this cardinal truth.

Problems

1. Describe briefly at least three groups or organizations to which you belong and on whose behalf you might deliver a good-will speech to the members of your speech class or to some other audience. These groups may include church organizations, clubs, associations of hobbyists, trade groups, professional societies, political parties, and the like.
2. List as many occasions as you can think of on which a good-will speech might be appropriate. Include meetings of luncheon clubs, professional groups, and conventions.
3. You were told on page 516 that the good-will speech is a "hybrid type," combining elements of the speech to inform and the speech to persuade. Describe various circumstances under which you think the informative element should predominate in a good-will speech and then describe other circumstances under which the persuasive element should be emphasized. In the second case, at what point would you say that the speech becomes openly persuasive in purpose?
4. After reading several of the Speeches for Collateral Study listed at the end of this chapter, write a short paper entitled "Methods for Developing the Good-Will Speech." Emphasize methods and technics which you discover in the speeches but do not find specifically mentioned in the preceding chapter.
5. After delivering the classroom speech described in the Speaking Assignment below, tell what specific changes you would make in order to adapt this speech to at least three of the following audiences:

a. A group of junior high school students.
b. A convention of dentists, doctors, or some other professional group.
c. A county farmers' institute.
d. A parent-teacher association.

e. A labor union meeting.
f. A group of local merchants.
g. The residents of an old people's home.

Speaking assignment

1. Present to the class a six- or seven-minute good-will speech on behalf of (1) a group or organization to which you belong, (2) an interest or hobby which you enjoy, or (3) the profession you intend to enter—for example, "The Lawyer in the Modern World," "The Doctor and Humanity," or "How the Engineer Makes Our Lives Better." Be sure that you incorporate in your talk each of the four special "characteristics of content" for a speech of this type. (For these characteristics, see again p. 518.)

Speeches for collateral study

1. Richard J. Babcock, "The Dynamic Future of Agriculture," *Vital Speeches of the Day*, XXVII (February 15, 1961), 269 ff.

2. Winston Churchill, "Address to the American Congress," *Congressional Record*, LXXXVII (Proceedings for December 26, 1941). Printed also in *Representative American Speeches, 1941-1942*, ed. A. Craig Baird (New York: Wilson, 1942), p. 19 ff.

3. G. C. Brewer, "A Business Career." *Vital Speeches of the Day*, XXXII (March 1, 1966), pp. 297-302.

4. Leroy Collins, "Industrialization of the South," *Vital Speeches of the Day*, XXVI (July 1, 1960), 564 ff.

5. Liaquat Ali Khan, "A Century of Great Awakenings," in Liaquat Ali Khan, *Pakistan, The Heart of Asia* (Cambridge: Harvard University Press, 1950), p. 227 ff.

6. Robert W. Sarnoff, "Television's Role in the American Democracy," in Alan H. Monroe and Douglas Ehninger, *Principles of Speech*, 5th ed. (Glenview, Illinois: Scott, Foresman, 1964), pp. 301-307.

7. Glenn T. Seaborg, "The Scientist as Human Being," *Representative American Speeches, 1964-1965*, ed. Lester Thonssen (New York: Wilson, 1965), pp. 129-137.

8. Robert C. Weaver, "The Negro as American," *Representative American Speeches, 1963-1964*, ed. Lester Thonssen (New York: Wilson, 1964), pp. 58-70.

Suggestions for further reading

Elizabeth G. Andersch and Lorin C. Staats, *Speech for Everyday Use* (New York: Holt, Rinehart & Winston, Inc., 1950), Part Two, Chapter VIII, "Good-Will Speech."

Ralph A. Micken, *Speaking for Results* (Boston: Houghton Mifflin Company, 1958), pp. 143-153, "To Secure Goodwill."

William Phillips Sandford and Willard Hayes Yeager, *Effective Business Speech* (New York: McGraw-Hill Book Company, 1960), Chapter X, "Speeches to Build Good Will."

Eugene E. White, *Practical Public Speaking*, 2nd ed. (New York: The Macmillan Company, 1964), pp. 351-354, "The Speech of Good Will."

Willard Hayes Yeager, *Effective Speaking for Every Occasion* (New York: Prentice-Hall, Inc., 1940), Chapter VIII, "How to Make Good-Will Speeches."

CHAPTER TWENTY-NINE

Speeches of tribute

On many occasions a speaker is called upon to present a brief address in which he commends the qualities or achievements of others. When this is the case, he is said to be presenting a speech of tribute.

TYPICAL SITUATIONS REQUIRING SPEECHES OF TRIBUTE

The more common forms of the speech of tribute are the eulogy, the dedication, the farewell, and the nomination.

Eulogy

By definition, a eulogy is a speech which praises highly an individual or group for their traits or accomplishments. Although it may be delivered while the persons concerned are still alive, more often it is presented after they are deceased and may, in fact, follow their death by many years—witness the many eulogies which still are given to honor the humanity of Lincoln, the fortitude of the Pilgrim Fathers, or the bravery of our Marines on Iwo Jima.

Dedication

When a building or memorial is erected to honor the memory of some person or group, as part of the dedication ceremony it is appropriate that a speech be given honoring the persons to whom the memorial is dedicated.

Farewell

When an executive with whom a group of men have long been associated retires or leaves to enter another field or when anyone generally admired is about to leave the community in which he has lived or the office he has held, public appreciation is often expressed for his fellowship and work.

Nomination

When an individual is nominated for an office, it is customary to pay tribute to him in order to show his fitness for the position. In most respects, a speech of nomination is similar to other speeches of tribute; but since there are some fundamental differences, it will be discussed separately at the end of the chapter.

THE PURPOSE OF THE SPEECH OF TRIBUTE

The basic purpose of a speech of tribute is to evoke appreciation of the commendable traits or accomplishments of the person being honored. If you can move your audience to feel deeply the essential worth or importance of the man, you will have succeeded. But you may go further than this. *(a)* You may, by honoring him, arouse a deeper devotion to the cause he represents. Did he give all that he had for his company? Then strive to make your audience feel a deeper loyalty to the company for which he worked. Was he known as a friend of boys? Then try to arouse a feeling that boys' work deserves the support of all. Finally, *(b)* you may create a desire in your listeners to emulate the person being honored—to follow in his footsteps, to develop the same virtues, to achieve the same renown.

THE MANNER OF SPEAKING

A farewell banquet usually blends an atmosphere of merriment with a spirit of sincere regret. Dignity and formality are on the whole characteristic of memorial services, the unveiling of monuments, and similar dedicatory ceremonies, while enthusiasm is usually the keynote of the nominating address. Regardless of the general tone of the occasion, however, in a speech of tribute avoid high-sounding phrases, bombastic oratory, and obvious "oiliness"; these things will kill its effect more quickly than anything else. A simple, honest expression of admiration is best.

CHARACTERISTICS OF CONTENT

Too often speeches of tribute merely enumerate a long list of achievements, and in this sense are little better than obituaries. Remember the impossibility of telling everything about a man or group in the brief time during which you are to speak. Instead, pick out a few qualities and emphasize them. Focus the content of your speech on one or more of the following factors:

Dominant personal traits. Select those aspects of the man's personality or of the group's behavior which are the most worthy of admiration and then relate incidents which will illustrate these traits. Show how they affected decisions, removed obstacles, or influenced others.

Outstanding achievements. Select a few particularly outstanding accomplishments. Tell about them in detail to show how valuable they were and how influential in achieving results. Let your speech say, "Here is what this man or group has done; see how important it is."

Influence on his associates. The importance of a man lies not so much in any material personal accomplishments as in the influence he has had on the lives of his fellow men or on the shaping of events. Since, of course, you will mention individual traits and achievements in showing what that influence has been, this approach differs from the other two mainly in emphasis or in the point of view you prefer to take.

Keep in mind, then, that these three sources are not mutually exclusive. Every speech of tribute probably will contain ideas and details drawn, in part, from each of them. In the interest of unity and effect upon the audience, however, emphasize only one and subordinate the other two.

In developing your central ideas, beware of complicated statistics and long enumerations. Do not name organization after organization to which a man belonged. The few traits, accomplishments, or impacts you do tell about, narrate in an impelling, human way. In describing the group to whom praise is due, speak in general rather than detailed or specific terms. After all, you are not engaged in giving a precise technical report on their output, but in relating events that will arouse admiration and cause others to emulate them. Let each event become a story, living and personal. Only in this way will you be able to achieve the effect you desire.

ORGANIZATION

Ordinarily you will have little difficulty in getting people to listen to a speech of tribute. The audience probably already admires the man or group about whom you are to speak and is curious to know what you are going to say concerning them.

Attention step

Your task, therefore, is to *direct* the attention of the audience toward those characteristics or accomplishments which you consider most important. There are three commonly used ways to do this:

1. Make a straightforward, sincere statement of these commendable traits or achievements or of the influence they have had upon others.
2. Relate one or more instances which vividly illustrate them.
3. Relate an incident which shows the problems faced by your subject, thus leading directly into the need step.

Need step

The speech of tribute contains no real need step in the sense of demonstrating a problem confronting the audience. The tribute subsequently paid in the satisfaction step may be heightened, however, by emphasizing obstacles overcome or difficulties faced. This serves to throw into sharp relief the traits or achievements which you wish to commend. John Kennedy's energetic accomplishments, for example, become the more noteworthy when contrasted with some of his severe illnesses and the physical reverses of his earlier career.

A slightly different method is that of pointing out, not the personal problems of a person to whom tribute is paid, but the problems of the organization which it was his official responsibility to meet or, in a still larger sense, the problems of society which his accomplishments helped solve. Thus, an account of the former seriousness of diabetes might precede a tribute to the men who isolated insulin.

Satisfaction step

The largest part of a speech of tribute will be the satisfaction step, for it is here the tribute is actually paid. Relate incidents which show how the problems, personal or public, which you have outlined in the need step were met and surmounted. In doing this, be sure to demonstrate at least one of three things:

1. How certain admirable traits—vision, courage, and tenacity, for example—made it possible to deal successfully with these problems.
2. How remarkable the achievements were in the face of the obstacles encountered.
3. How great the influence of the achievements was on others.

Visualization step

In the preceding step you will have enumerated the traits or achievements of the person or group being honored. In this step, try to bring all of these together so as to create a vivid composite picture of their accomplishments.

Introduce an apt quotation. If you can find a bit of poetry or literary description which fits the man or group to whom you are paying tribute, introduce it here. If you use this method, however, commit the passage to memory so that you do not falter, and be sure the quotation is not too long or flowery.

Draw a picture of a world (community, business, or profession) inhabited by such persons. Suggest how much better things would be if more people had similar qualities.

Suggest the loss which the absence of the individual or group will bring. Show vividly how much he or they will be missed. Be specific: "It's going to seem mighty strange to walk into Bob's office and not find him there ready to listen, ready to advise, ready to help."

Action step

Frequently, no action step is used in a speech of tribute. When it is, it will vary with the occasion somewhat as follows:

Eulogy. Suggest that the best tribute the audience can pay the person they are honoring is to live as he did or to carry on what he started.

Dedication. Suggest the appropriateness of dedicating this monument, building, etc., to such a person or group, and express the hope that it will inspire others to emulate their accomplishments.

Farewell. Extend to the person or persons who are going away the best wishes of those you represent, and express a determination to carry on what they have begun.

By following these principles and procedures with reasonable care and discernment, you should be able to devise a useful framework upon which to build. To create a complete speech of tribute you will need to fill it with vivid, illustrative materials and develop it sensitively to suit the mood of the occasion.

NOMINATION: A SPECIAL FORM

The nomination is a special type of speech of tribute. Here your primary purpose will be to get a man nominated and later elected; the tribute will be secondary, used as a means of securing approval of your nominee. Your manner of speaking will generally be less formal and dignified than when giving other speeches of tribute. It should, however, be businesslike and energetic. In general, the content of your speech will follow the pattern already described, but the illustrations should be chosen to show the nominee's qualifications for this particular office. Although it has special requirements, fundamentally the nominating speech is a speech to actuate through conviction. Organize it as follows:

Attention step. Announce that you are going to nominate a man for this office.

Need step. Point out the qualifications the nominee will need. Enumerate the problems that will face him or the problems facing the organization which he will serve.

Satisfaction step. Present evidence that your nominee has necessary qualifications to solve these problems. Emphasize especially his past experience and the policies to which he has adhered.

Visualization step. Picture the probable success of his term in office and the value the organization and community will derive from it.

Action step. Formally place his name in nomination and urge your audience to vote for him.

Sometimes the man is named at the very beginning of the attention step. This is good practice if the audience is already favorable toward his nomination. But if there is some doubt about the attitude of the audience, wait until the satisfaction step to reveal his name. In this way, by showing the particular fitness of the man before he is actually named, you will avoid unnecessary hostility.

In political conventions the name of the proposed candidate is often withheld until the very end of the nominating speech to avoid premature demonstrations. This practice, however, should not be used elsewhere. Before the concluding phase of the speech, everyone will guess who the man is, and the device is too obviously a mere trick of rhetoric.

Obviously, not all nominations need to be supported by a speech. Frequently, the person nominated is well known by the audience, and his qualifications appreciated. The mere statement "Mr. Chairman, I nominate John Citizen for the office of treasurer" is all that such a situation requires. The organization outlined above, therefore, is recommended not for a purely routine nomination, but for those special occasions when some explanation or proof is needed to support your proposal.

SAMPLE SPEECHES OF TRIBUTE

In the two speeches which follow, you will find illustrated many of the ideas presented in this chapter. The first example is a *eulogy;* the second is a *dedicatory address.*

Eulogy

On October 25, 1964, President Herbert Clark Hoover was buried on a low hill overlooking the small frame house in which he had been born ninety years before at West Branch, Iowa. As a part of the simple funeral service, Dr. D. Elton Trueblood—a Quaker theologian, author, professor of philosophy at Earlham College, and a friend of the late President—delivered the following speech of tribute.

HERBERT CLARK HOOVER[1]

D. Elton Trueblood

We have gathered today to honor one of the great men of the twentieth century. His is the story of what is best in the American heritage. He bears witness to a way of life which we seldom demonstrate, but which is infinitely precious in that it provides a standard by which we may judge our relative failures, as well as our relative successes. In so far as his is the kind of life we truly prize, the basic orientation of the Republic is likely to be sound. Therefore, we perform a service when we try to make clear the nature of the heritage which Herbert Clark Hoover, the thirty-first President of the United States of America, has represented with unusual fidelity.

First, there is the beginning which combines reverence, frugality, and toil. Herbert Hoover belongs to the procession of hard-working and God-loving Quaker pioneers who crossed the nation in great steps, establishing strong communities at each point. West Milton, Ohio, and West Branch, Iowa, were important stopping places as the Hoovers moved from the Atlantic to the Pacific. The Quaker cemetery near the west branch of the Miami River and the simple frame birthplace at West Branch, Iowa, are potent symbols of something precious in

[1]Text furnished by Dr. Trueblood, with permission for this reprint.

American history. They are symbols of men close to the soil and close to Almighty God who made it. It is important to remember that the life of toil and reverence led naturally to the life of learning, so that schools were set up at each stopping place along the way. That Herbert Hoover, as a boy of seventeen, should be attracted to Stanford University in its opening year was, therefore, in no way surprising.

The expectation of hard work carried over into the life of learning in those glorious years when Stanford was new. By amazing good fortune, the Quaker boy was guided not only into the study of geology but into the study of Latin under a man as remarkable as Professor Augustus T. Murray. The result was an unending spiritual influence, which reached its climax in the days in the White House.

Herbert Hoover's work as a geologist and mining engineer was brilliantly successful, but the public judgment is right in thinking of this vocational chapter as only a preparation for larger public work. The great days at the end of the First World War and immediately afterward, when Herbert Hoover, in his mission of compassion, was the most influential man in Europe, constituted, not an interlude in Herbert Hoover's career, but a logical fulfillment.

All along, the heritage to which he was being faithful was one in which public service is intrinsic. The consciously nourished ideal required every Christian to find, on his pilgrim-way, the life to which God had called him, whether humble or exalted. It included a conception in which duty could be mentioned without self-consciousness and without apology. It required of each person that he should show diligence in his calling, that he should practice frugality and simplicity, and that he should accept responsibility for some unique contribution to the total community.

The most important thing to say about Herbert Hoover is that he has demonstrated an ethic which is identical with that which made America great.

There are some who suppose that we have outgrown it, or that we ought to outgrow it, but a life like that which we honor today is the best refutation of their position.

It is not unreasonable to see Herbert Hoover's life in six major chapters. These six are as follows: 1, Boy in Iowa and Oregon; 2, Student at Stanford; 3, Engineer in various countries; 4, Director of relief; 5, Statesman; 6, Elder.

It might be supposed that the last of these chapters would be an anticlimax, but it has not been so. Instead, his influence has gone on from strength to strength. He became the very idea of the elder statesman, writing much, speaking seldom, counseling untold numbers of men and women and standing as a symbol of moral strength.

All knew that there was at least one great man in America who stood above the possibility of corruption and self-seeking. All recognized that he was one who had never sought personal gain or even payment for his public service. As the years went on, after the end of the White House days, through the great depression, through the Second World War, and through the years which succeeded that war, there was probably no thoughtful person in the United States who did not come to see the unfairness of the judgment of those who had blamed Mr. Hoover for what was in reality a world-wide economic storm. In his magnificent patience Mr. Hoover did not even worry about the outcome. He knew that he had been right, he knew that he had been unjustly blamed, and by a wonderful grace he lived long enough to see the time when what had been a problem was a problem no longer. Indeed, as we see the events of thirty-five years ago in perspective, it is obvious that the critics have been more hurt than the criticized. This is particularly true of those who tried to raise their own public stature by seeking to harm that of Mr. Hoover. These critics now stand out clearly for all to see, and the public has made its judgment.

The six chapters are now over, and in one sense the volume is complete, but there is another sense in which it is still going on. Herbert Hoover will be remembered as long as the American dream is cherished because he is, to such a great extent, the last of the famous pioneers. He represents the westward trek; he represents dignified simplicity; he represents to a remarkable degree the unity of a faith which expresses itself in compassionate service to mankind. He has worked hard; he has been very brave; he has endured. How appropriate that what is mortal of him should finally rest, after all his struggles and his victories, in his native soil, mid-way in the western trek and near the middle of North America! He never wavered from the living faith in Jesus Christ which was indigenous to his heritage, and in which he lived and served and died.

The story is a great one and it is a good one. It is essentially a story that is triumphant. Therefore, it is reasonable that today our mood should be one of rejoicing. This is not a time for tears. This corruption has put on incorruption; this mortal has put on immortality; death is swallowed up in victory. Thanks be to God, which giveth us the victory through our Lord, Jesus Christ.

Speech of dedication

Brotherhood House, on the northwest corner of Seventh Avenue and Fortieth Street in New York City, provides free office and meeting facilities for one hundred volunteer social agencies operating in the metropolitan area. When the cornerstone of the building was laid on September 12, 1962, Governor Nelson A. Rockefeller of the State of New York delivered this dedicatory address.

REMARKS AT THE CORNERSTONE LAYING OF THE BROTHERHOOD-IN-ACTION BUILDING[2]

Nelson A. Rockefeller

It is with more than official pleasure that I take part in these cornerstone-laying ceremonies today. For if there are two words in the English language which have, for me, specific and urgent meaning, they are "brotherhood" and "action."

Too often, one is used thoughtlessly, the other as a symbol rather than the deed itself. But the vision which inspired the Honorable George J. Beldock in 1945 and which will soon take physical form in the useful and inspiring edifice whose cornerstone is laid today was neither.

In today's world of surging, conflicting, and threatening interests, a realistic appreciation of human brotherhood and what a true understanding of its strength can contribute is morally comforting and reassuring.

Such an understanding may well be the priceless product hammered out in the rooms and meeting places of this Brotherhood Hall, a structure combining the monumental and the functional.

[2]Text furnished by Governor Rockefeller and used with his permission.

This is purposeful action. It is a characteristic of programs which we have initiated and activated during these past four years in New York State.

I would especially like to commend the type of action which is proposed here. For it is a practical step to bring about greater mutual understanding among the more than one hundred organizations carrying the banner of brotherhood in this great city.

Such voluntary groups have, quite properly, specific objectives, but many share common aims. It is to provide a place where the common aims—not the differences—may be discussed, defined, and hardened into effective programs that this Hall is being constructed.

Just as the skilled workers are bringing their individual talents to bear on the common objective of erecting this beautiful and useful building, so may the users of it find in their common interest in brotherhood an objective to which they may devote their individual talents.

Brotherhood House, with its six stories, all-glass front, and tastefully landscaped setting, will provide the physical facilities to encourage the conversations, discussions, debates, and informal talks needed. Its large library, meditation and music rooms, auditorium, seminar and conference rooms, radio and TV studio are all tangible aids.

But what will make this endeavor shine with the lustre of good deeds accomplished is the spirit of the House. It will be a symbol of brotherhood, to be sure, but much more. Judge Beldock has defined its function as "a vision for all to share; a challenge for all to meet." With these sentiments, I am in complete accord.

Today is in fact a beginning. But there is great promise for good in an unfolding, action-packed future. Taking part in these ceremonies is, of course, pleasant. But the real joy will come to me—as to all—when Brotherhood Hall is functioning effectively as a continuing influence for realization of that brotherhood of man under the Fatherhood of God which fulfills our highest traditions and heritage as a people.

Problems

1. Select as an example of a speech of tribute either Lincoln's "Gettysburg Address" (dedication) or Pericles' "Funeral Oration" (eulogy). Both have been reprinted countless times; your instructor will help you locate a reliable text. Make a list of the major ideas each speaker chose to present, describe the organization of his speech, and the language or style which he employed. To what extent is each speech addressed directly to the audience? To what extent is it addressed to all men in all ages? What rules concerning a speech of tribute may be inferred from studying these examples?
2. If you were to classify the speech of tribute under one of the five general purposes—entertain, inform, convince, stimulate, or actuate—which would you choose? Why?

3. Would you say that a speech of tribute is an easy or difficult type of speech to present effectively? What specific advantages does a speaker have when developing and delivering such a talk? What specific obstacles must he surmount?
4. In your opinion, which of the following elements is most important in assuring the success of a speech of tribute: the ideas presented, the language in which they are expressed, or the manner in which they are delivered? Defend your answer.
5. From your study of this chapter, of some of the suggested readings, and of the sample speeches found on pp. 535-539, make a list of ten "thou-shalt-not's" or faults to be avoided when giving a speech of tribute.

Speaking assignments

1. Prepare a five-minute speech paying tribute to:

a. A man important in national or world history.

b. Someone in your home community who, though he never gained fame, contributed in a significant way to the welfare or happiness of many.

c. A group of volunteers who participated in a charity drive.

d. A team of scientists who completed a successful program.

e. A faculty member who has long served as a fraternity or campus activity advisor.

f. The highest ranking student in your class.

g. An outstanding athlete or team which has received state or national recognition.

h. An officer of a student organization who has served long and well.

i. Founders of an organization for civic betterment.

2. Assume that your public speaking class is to elect the following officers: a president, a vice-president, a secretary, and a sergeant at arms. Interview the student whom you would like to nominate for one of these offices in order to find out as much as you can about his background, interests, and qualifications. Then prepare and present a two- or three-minute speech in which you nominate him for this post. Assume that the president will preside over class meetings, that the secretary will keep a record of attendance and grades, and that the sergeant at arms will preserve order and decorum.

Speeches for collateral study

1. Bernard Baruch, "Woodrow Wilson," *Representative American Speeches: 1956-1957*, ed. A. Craig Baird (New York: H. W. Wilson, 1957), p. 141 ff.

2. Winston Churchill, "King George VI," *Vital Speeches of the Day*, XVIII (March 1, 1952), 290 ff.

3. Irving M. Ives, "Tribute to the Late Senator Robert Taft," *Congressional Record*, XCIX, Proceedings for August 3, 1953.

4. John F. Kennedy, "Portraits of Five Senators in the Senate Reception Room," *Representative American Speeches: 1957-1958*, ed. A. Craig Baird (New York: H. W. Wilson, 1958), p. 83 ff.

5. Adlai E. Stevenson, "Eulogy on Eleanor Roosevelt," in Alan Monroe and Douglas Ehninger, *Principles of Speech*, 5th ed. (Glenview: Illinois: Scott, Foresman, 1964), pp. 318-321.

6. Richard Cardinal Cushing, "Eulogy to John Kennedy," *Vital Speeches of the Day*, XXX (December 1, 1963), 100-101.

7. Robert S. Emrich, "The Greatness of Lincoln," *Representative American Speeches: 1958-1959*, ed. A. Craig Baird (New York: H. W. Wilson, 1959), pp. 169-177.

Suggestions for further reading

Martin P. Anderson, Wesley Lewis, and James Murray, *The Speaker and His Audience* (New York: Harper & Row, 1964), pp. 442-443, "The Commemorative Speech."

Aristotle, *Rhetoric*, 1366a-1368b, "The Objects of Praise and Blame."

W. Norwood Brigance, *Speech: Its Techniques and Disciplines in a Free Society*, 2nd ed. (New York: Appleton-Century-Crofts, 1961), pp. 498-502, "Speeches of Commemoration."

Kenneth G. Hance, David C. Ralph, and Milton J. Wiksell, *Principles of Speaking* (Belmont, California: Wadsworth Publishing Company, 1962), pp. 269-270, "Tribute and Response."

Ralph A. Micken, *Speaking for Results* (Boston: Houghton Mifflin Company, 1958), pp. 165-172, "To Speak in Praise."

Quintilian, *Institutio Oratoria* iii.vii, "Of Panegyric."

Willard Hayes Yeager, *Effective Speaking for Every Occasion* (New York: Prentice-Hall, Inc., 1940), Chapter IV, "How to Make Speeches of Praise and Blame," and Chapter VI, "How to Make Speeches of Celebration."

CHAPTER THIRTY

Adapting speech to radio and television

A thorough consideration of all of the types of speech which are electronically transmitted—newscasts, dramatic productions, market reports, commercials, travelogues, and many others—would be far beyond the scope of this volume. Excellent books devoted entirely to this subject are available, and you should read them if you expect to do specialized work in radio or television.[1] But every speaker today needs at least a general knowledge of the technics involved in using these two electronic media. Any man or woman in business or in a profession or in a position of community leadership can expect to be called upon at times to speak from the local radio or television station. The aim of this chapter, therefore, is to point out the most important differences between face-to-face speaking and speaking over the air to an unseen audience, and to suggest briefly how the principles and procedures previously presented may be adapted to the broadcasting situation.[2] You will observe that, although important differences do exist, many of the same fundamental principles apply; and, more often than not, what is good speech before a visible audience also is good speech over the air.

THE PURPOSE OF A BROADCAST SPEECH

Television and radio speakers hope, of course, to reach a larger audience than could be gathered together in person at one place. This motivation aside, however, there is no great difference between the pur-

[1]A number of these books are listed at the end of this chapter.

[2]Note: For purposes of this discussion, the term "broadcast" will be used inclusively to mean *both* the "telecast" and the "radiocast."

poses of broadcast speeches and of the types of speeches discussed in the preceding chapters. Like other speakers, radio and television speakers attempt to entertain, to inform, to convince, to stimulate, or to actuate; they introduce other speakers, express welcomes, debate public issues, pay tributes, and attempt to gain good will. Your purpose in talking before a visible audience may also be your purpose when you broadcast. And with some modifications, the same characteristics of speech content and delivery and the same methods of speech organization are used.

THE RADIO AND TELEVISION AUDIENCE

Since anyone who has a radio or television set within the transmitting range of the broadcasting station can tune in, the audience for a broadcast speech will normally be comprised of individuals of both sexes and of all ages, creeds, occupations, interests, and degrees of intelligence. There is no such thing as a television or radio audience composed entirely of young men, or of Democrats, or of Baptists, or of union members. This fact puts an additional premium upon the speaker's tact and his ability to endow a subject with universal interest and far-ranging appeal.

Factors in audience modification

The hour of the broadcast and the location of the station may, however, modify the nature of this audience somewhat. Surveys have shown that women audiences predominate during the morning and early afternoon hours when husbands are away at work and children are at school. Children listen to the radio or watch TV screens mainly in the late afternoon and early evening and only rarely in the late evening. Men are more likely to give attention during the evenings and on Sundays and holidays, since they are usually not working then. At mealtimes, probably more people listen to the radio than watch telecasts; but in either case the audience for a speech may be small because most people prefer musical programs or brief announcements about the weather, news, and markets at this time.

Sometimes the location of the station also affects the constituency of the audience. On the whole, a metropolitan station tends to draw a larger urban audience; and usually a station in a smaller city attracts a larger rural audience. This is less true, however, of large, powerful stations and network broadcasts, which usually reach every kind of community. Moreover, some radio stations cater to certain types of listeners, and certain program series on both radio and television are frankly pointed to specialized groups. If you speak from such a station or on such a program, many of your listeners and viewers will be those who have tuned in because of their particular interest in that kind of program. College and university stations, for example, usually specialize in various types of educational and public service presentations.

An important characteristic of radio and television audiences is that they are not all assembled in auditoriums, theatres, or similar meeting places; instead, they ordinarily listen or view *as separate individuals* or *as small, intimate, informal groups* wherever they happen to be at a given moment. In spite of the fact that the audience as a whole may be quite large, the individuals will not be gathered in a mass but will be scattered about in living rooms, offices, hotel rooms, automobiles, and similar surroundings. Thus, while the listener or viewer is no doubt aware that others are also receiving the same program, he is primarily influenced by his own intimate environment and ordinarily expects the speaker to talk in an informal, conversational manner suited to that environment.

The noncaptive audience

Two further facts need to be remembered: listeners and viewers customarily have numerous distractions, and they can easily turn off a broadcast at any time. In a public gathering, people hesitate to make themselves conspicuous by getting up and leaving an audience which a speaker is addressing in person; but the individual in a radio or television audience feels no hesitation at all about tuning the speaker out with a twist of the dial. In fact, he may be compelled to do so because he is likely to be surrounded by household noises: the baby's crying, the ringing of a telephone, the clatter of dishes, a conversation at the other end of the room—all of which compete with the broadcast for his attention. Both of these facts require that electronic speechmaking create a high degree of interest.

TWO TYPES OF BROADCAST SPEECHES

Environmentally, there are two principal types of broadcast speeches: (1) those which are made in the television or radio studio without an audience present, and (2) those which are given before actual audiences in the studio or are broadcast from the speaker's stand in an auditorium. In the former, the speaker faces an *unseen audience;* in the latter, he confronts *two audiences:* one which is physically present, and another which he imagines to be "out there somewhere" but which is invisible to him.

Broadcasts without an audience present

When you speak directly from the studio for the broadcast audience alone, your style of speaking should be quite informal and conversational. The novice tends to think of the composite "millions" of persons in his audience and to make an oration to them, forgetting that he is talking directly to only one, two, or three persons in each highly personalized environment. A better plan is to imagine that you are talking with someone over a very clear-toned telephone or that you are conversing in a relaxed, friendly fashion with an acquaintance who is sitting across the room from you. Indeed, some speakers bring a friend into the studio with them and direct their remarks to him or to the announcer if he is in the same room. You needn't shout; the transmitter is sufficiently powerful to carry your voice over many miles. Do not strain for dramatic effects either; remember that your invisible audience will be gathered in small groups and that your manner should therefore be natural and informal. Now and then glance at the engineer in the control room; he hears how your voice sounds over the air waves and can use prearranged hand signals to tell you if you are doing anything wrong in a technical sense.

At first, perhaps, talking in a soundproof room may seem strange to you. Do not be surprised if your voice sounds a little flat or the pauses between phrases seem a little long; these things are natural results of studio acoustics. Nor is the microphone a deadly instrument, as some novices seem to fear; it is simply a substitute for the ears of your listeners—a sort of mouthpiece for a multiple telephone circuit. Talk to it naturally as you would in talking over the telephone to a close acquaintance.

Broadcasts with an audience present

Sometimes a speech for a particular audience or occasion—for instance, an anniversary banquet, a political rally, or a dedication—is of sufficient public interest to justify broadcasting it. On nearly all such occasions the speaker's primary duty is to the audience immediately before him; radio listeners and television viewers are allowed, as it were, "to look in through the window." When your broadcast audience knows that an actual audience is confronting you, they do not object to your talking formally as a public speaker rather than as an intimate conversationalist. They use their imaginations to project themselves into your presence and, in a sense, become a part of the crowd at the dinner or in the auditorium. If you are speaking over radio only, you can bolster their imaginations by occasionally referring pointedly to the specific audience you are addressing or to the occasion which has brought the group together. Of course, an occasional ripple of laughter, as well as applause or called-out questions, will help remind your unseen audience of the other audience at the scene of the broadcast. Although your primary duty is to your immediate audience, you must be reasonably concerned with the needs and comprehension of your broadcast audience, too; even in this situation, the content and structure of your speech and, to some extent, your manner of speaking should be somewhat modified in the interest of those invisible people with whom you are trying to communicate.

A great many programs are broadcast from a studio with listeners present. Quite often a group of twenty or thirty people (in large stations, even more) are invited to participate as a special audience. Then, after the scheduled speech or discussion is concluded, they ask questions or make comments. In the broadcast of a formal panel discussion, even when no studio audience is present, a panelist may use the other panel members as his audience and join them in the discussion following the prepared speeches. This kind of broadcast, with a specially invited "studio audience," differs from those discussed in the preceding paragraph because the primary consideration here is for the *broadcast* audience; the studio audience is present only to represent this larger audience and to give a greater sense of reality to the situation. Hence, although the speaker must talk directly to the actual audience and seek responses from it, he must remember that his primary purpose is to reach the *outside* audience. He must beware of letting the studio audience run away with the show; he must spend more time answering questions of general interest and cut short his replies to unrepresentative queries. His manner of speaking, however, will be governed by the presence of an actual audience.

THE MANNER OF SPEAKING FOR RADIO

In presenting a radio talk, remember that your listeners cannot see you and therefore are robbed of all the visual cues so useful to speaker and audience. Gestures, for example, may rid you of excess energy or emphasize points in your own mind (and many radio speakers use them for these reasons), but your invisible listener cannot see them, and their visual emphasis will be lost on him. Moreover, as stressed in Part Two, a great deal of meaning is also conveyed by facial expression; but again, your listener cannot see it. You must make up for this loss of visual clues in some other way. Furthermore, you will be unable to use visual aids in trying to explain a point in a radio speech. All meaning must be conveyed by sound alone: attention must be created and held, ideas made clear, and action impelled merely by the use of your voice.

Note the positioning and types of microphones used by Secretary of State Dean Rusk in an appearance before the Foreign Relations Committee.

In both television and radio speaking, your voice passes through the microphone, transmitter, and receiver before reaching your listener. Regardless of the perfection of the equipment, some distortion will occur. In certain instances, this distortion is beneficial, making the speaker's voice sound better than it is naturally; but it is far more likely that many little faults may be exaggerated with ruinous effect. Moreover, failure to use the microphone properly may result in indistinctness or even in disagreeable noises. Let us first, then, study the correct use of the microphone in order that we may handle it effectively and avoid unwanted distractions.

Using the microphone

Many different types of microphones are available for radio and television use. Some pick up sound equally well from all directions; others pick up more effectively the sound made directly in front of them, and tend to "lose" sound that is made at the side or above or behind them. Ask the studio announcer or the technician how far from the microphone you should stand or sit, and from what angle you should direct your voice toward it. Also experiment to determine how loudly you should speak, because microphones differ in their sensitivity.

With most microphones the loudness of the picked-up sound varies in approximate geometric ratio to its distance from the *source* of the sound. That is, if you speak with the same degree of force, the vocal sound picked up by the microphone at a distance of one foot will be four times as loud as at a distance of two feet. Therefore, to make sure that your voice does not fade or unintentionally increase in volume, *you should always stay approximately the same distance from the instrument.* Especially when you have both an actual audience and a microphone in front of you, remember not to move about too freely. Hand, lapel, and chest microphones have been developed in order to give the speaker more mobility in such circumstances, but you may still produce uneven volume if you turn your head too often or too far aside. In the studio, the temptation to move about is not so great; if you are seated or standing comfortably, you are likely to remain stationary. Even so, if you are reading from a manuscript, you must be careful not to alter the angle of your head too greatly or too suddenly as you look up at the microphone and down at the script, because this movement may sharply change the volume.

Reduce extraneous noises to a minimum. Because radio equipment is so very sensitive, sudden increases in volume tend to produce "blasting," an effect similar to what would happen if you were to hit the keyboard of a piano with a sledge hammer—a crash of sound rather than a clear tone. This makes it imperative that you refrain from shouting or abruptly increasing the force of your voice. The man in the control room can—within reasonable limits—modify the volume of your voice, building it up or toning it down; but he cannot anticipate every change you may make. Seek your vocal variety through differences of rate or pitch, therefore, and keep the degree of force reasonably constant.

This same sensitivity in broadcasting equipment intensifies the effects of two mistakes commonly made by amateurs. The first is rattling or rustling papers close to the microphone. The actual noise in the studio is slight; but as amplified over the air, it can be very distracting to the listener. At its worst, it may sound like the rapid firing of a gun, the flapping of an awning in an angry wind, or the crushing of an orange crate into kindling. At the very least, it will make your audience keenly aware that you are reading, thereby destroying the illusion of direct spoken communication. The second mistake is tapping the microphone or table. This distraction, like the first, may be heard only faintly in the studio but loudly over the air. Take care, then, to avoid drumming on the table or thumping it for emphasis; let your gestures be noiseless.

Handle notes or manuscripts quietly. In preparing your notes or manuscript, select soft paper, unclip the pages before you approach the microphone, and lay each sheet aside carefully and quietly when you have finished reading it. In general, you will make less noise if you leave your manuscript on the table or speaker's stand rather than hold it in your hand. It is exceedingly important, of course, to check the pages of your manuscript before the broadcast to make sure they are in the correct order. No pause seems as long as the moment when you turn to page three and find page four instead.

Speak distinctly and pronounce words accurately. Both because the microphone is so sensitive and because your listeners focus their attention entirely upon your voice, the distinctness of your speech and the accuracy of your pronunciation are especially important. Errors and crudities that might pass unnoticed on the platform will stand out over the air. A little effort on your part, however, and attention to the suggestions concerning intelligibility made in Chapter 6 will help you avoid such faults. Of course, in your efforts to combat carelessness, do not go to the opposite extreme. Do not speak so carefully and with such slow deliberation that your speech sounds stilted and artificial. Particular care should be exercised in the utterance of the sibilants—sounds such as *s, z, th, sh.* While some microphones minimize the problem, the high frequencies characteristic of these sounds tend to produce a whistling or hissing noise if they are given too much emphasis. If you have trouble with sibilants, use sparingly words in which these sounds occur in stressed positions—or better, learn to subdue your production of them.

Keep your vocal pitch moderately low, your tones lively. There is no question that the quality of the speaker's voice is changed in transmission. In general, high-pitched voices are less pleasant over the radio, while those of moderately low pitch are sometimes improved in the process of broadcasting. The only way to check the effect of transmission on your own voice is to have an audition or a reliable recording made so that you can listen to yourself talk. In general, speak in the lower part of your pitch range. The fact that you can talk conversationally before the microphone and do not have to project to an audience should improve the quality of your voice, since most people use better quality when they speak quietly than when they apply force. Retain your liveliness and flexibility, however; keep the resonating passages open, and use them. Do not let the quietness of the studio deceive you into allowing your voice to become flat and colorless.

Compensating for the lack of visual cues

Use a fairly rapid rate and avoid long pauses. Since your radio listeners cannot see you, you must use your voice to fill in the gaps that would otherwise be filled by visible cues. You must, therefore, speak at a fairly rapid rate. This does not mean that you have to rush, but it does mean that you cannot allow your speech to drag. Long pauses make it difficult to follow the ideas in a speech. On a platform where the audience can see you, you can sometimes emphasize a point by standing silent, holding your listeners' attention by the earnestness of your facial expression and the apparent tension of your body; but all this is lost on the radio listener—he gets only the silence. Pauses can, of course, sometimes be used effectively in radio speaking; but they must be employed sparingly and be of short duration. Again, on the platform a speaker may pause to search for the exact word to express his thought; he is thinking it out with his audience, and they see him doing it. On the air, however, such pauses are empty and may suggest that the speaker is ill at ease and unprepared.

Strive for vocal variety. The visual cues a speaker gives his audience do more, of course, than fill in the gaps left by pauses in his voice. They also serve to give emphasis, to convey additional meaning, and to hold attention. When, as in a radio speech, this burden is thrown entirely on the voice, variety of vocal expression is more than a valuable asset—it is a primary essential. As stressed in an earlier paragraph, develop a high degree of vocal skill and flexibility, and use it to the utmost whenever you are broadcasting.

Write your speech and practice reading it. Groping for words is a major sin when talking on the radio. Since the audience cannot see the speaker, most people write out their speeches word for word and read them from manuscript. This procedure also ensures that you will be able to finish your speech within the allotted time. There is one disadvantage: some persons cannot write with the informality of oral style; and even when they can, they have difficulty in reading aloud in a natural, easy, conversational manner. This disadvantage, however, can be overcome with practice. The almost unanimous advice of experts is to use a manuscript for a radio speech and to learn how to read it naturally.

Make your speech sound like you. This procedure requires, first of all, that you write your manuscript in an informal, direct style. Avoid sentences with complex subordinate clauses and stilted or inverted expressions. Instead of saying "Only two runs did the team score," say "The team scored only two runs." Insert connective phrases and summary sentences that sound the way you talk. A helpful procedure is to make a recording of your speech, using notes; transcribe the recording; edit the resulting manuscript for errors of fact or wording; and then cut it down in length if necessary, being careful to *retain its spoken style.*

When you have prepared the manuscript, practice reading it aloud. Don't read it for the first time as you stand before the studio microphone. Become familiar enough with each passage so that you can ad-lib if you happen to lose your place or misplace a page. Above all, *practice reading your material with a mental image of your listener before you*—make it sound as if you were presenting an extemporaneous speech. Don't overstress the unimportant words like *the, of,* and *to.* Use a normal, conversational manner, avoiding equally a droning monotone and an artificial overemphasis or stagy inflection. Read again the comments in Chapter 1 (p. 9) concerning conversational mode, and strive for sincere and natural communication even in your practice reading.

THE MANNER OF SPEAKING FOR TELEVISION

Unlike radiocasting, telecasting permits your audience to see you while you talk. Hence your physical behavior—your appearance, facial expression, and movement—may help convey your thought just as it does when you are addressing an audience in person. At the same time, irritating mannerisms are magnified by the camera and will annoy your listeners; and a monotonous, dead-pan expression or slavish dependence on a manuscript will cause them to lose interest. Indeed, the way in which the camera lens picks up your image—especially in close-ups—and the intimacy with which your audience views that image on the television screen make your appearance and movement even more important than when an audience sees you in person.

In television speaking, therefore, you cannot concentrate on voice alone as you do in radio broadcasting. Neither can you talk as you would if you were facing a live audience. Your voice and action must conform to the limitations imposed by the microphone and the television camera. Thus the suggestions offered earlier in this chapter regarding microphone technic and the avoidance of distracting noises are equally pertinent to television broadcasts. In addition, you must adapt yourself to the distractions of the dazzle and heat of the lighting equipment, to the shifting of cameras on their booms or dollies, and to the restriction of your movement within the area upon which the lights and cameras are focused. And, moreover, you must make this adaptation seem easy and natural, avoiding equally a stunned or disconcerted appearance and the tendency to overact, to play to the gallery.

The technical aspects of television are changing rapidly, and the facilities at different stations vary considerably. Hence, each time you telecast a speech you will need special advice from the directors and technicians in order to adapt your presentation to the prevailing conditions. For this reason, detailed instructions would be inappropriate here, and the following suggestions are limited to matters which are fairly universal in their application.

Adapting to the television camera

Like the ordinary camera, the television camera takes a picture. And, like the ordinary camera, its lens adjustment and its distance determine the audience's view of the speaker: face only, head and shoulders, full view, etc. It likewise limits the amount of background and demonstration materials that can be visible on the screen. Moreover, the angle from which the picture is taken can be varied—front, side, above, or below. Usually the camera angles and distances are changed during the broadcast to provide variety. Often two or more cameras are used, with the telecast pick-up shifting from one to another so that the picture changes from a distance view to a close-up, or from a front view to an angle shot; or one or more of the cameras may be moved on a boom or dolly so that the angle is shifted gradually from panoramic to close-up, and then the reverse. If an actual audience is present, the eye of the camera may go from speaker to audience and back again. Find out ahead of time, therefore, where you are to stand or sit, how far you may safely move without going beyond the focal depth or angle of the camera or outside of the lighted area; and if you intend to use visual aids, such as maps and models, arrange in advance for their proper placement.

A further adaptation is necessary because of the sensitivity of the television camera to various colors. For instance, under the bright lighting the normal reddish color of the lips fades out and the natural shadows of the face may disappear, leaving it with a flattened appearance. Hence, special facial make-up must be applied in order to make the picture look natural. Shiny objects such as jewelry or even beads of perspiration on the face or a bald head may glitter or glare distractingly in the brilliant light unless toned down with dull paint or panchromatic powder; and without basic make-up, a man's shaven face may appear dirty and unkempt. Clothes also must be carefully chosen for color and pattern to give life to the image without creating bizarre effects. Technical developments may reduce or eliminate the necessity for some of these adaptations, but it is always a sound practice to inquire what the studio or local situation demands.

Adapting appearance and movement to the type of broadcast

An earlier part of this chapter discussed the difference between broadcasts in the studio without an audience and broadcasts before an actual audience. In television, this difference is particularly important. If you are speaking to an actual audience, you will be expected to talk to it, not to the camera. Your posture, movements, and gestures must fit the real audience before you. Use enough action to keep the scene alive but avoid overdramatic gestures, for these will amuse rather than impress your television viewers.

The studio telecast without an audience is, of course, a much more intimate thing. Here you must think of yourself as if you were talking to each viewer in his own living room. You may stand up to speak, especially if you have something to point out or demonstrate, but quite as often you will be seated at a desk or even in an easy chair. Your movements should be those natural to easy, informal, animated conversation. Do not sit stiffly, but change your position occasionally, and use your hands to emphasize and clarify your points. You may lean forward to stress important statements or move your head to bring out a transition. The sweep of your gestures, however, should be somewhat restrained, involving only the movement of the hand and forearm in a relatively small arc; avoid declamatory gestures entirely.

To give the impression of eye contact with your viewer, look directly at the camera frequently, but don't glare at it continuously or you will seem unnatural. Occasionally, look away at not too great an angle and then look back again. Avoid darting your glances abruptly or aimlessly hither and yon. And above all, don't rely too heavily on a manuscript or notes. If you must read all or part of your speech, you may be able to arrange for the use of a teleprompter. This device reproduces a copy of your speech in large type and positions it near the camera but out of range of its lens. Thus, even though you are reading, you can maintain fairly good eye contact with the audience in a pictorial sense at least.

Using visual aids in television

The photographic technics of television make possible the use of a wide choice of visual aids to illustrate and substantiate the content of a speech. Indeed, the use of maps, graphs, charts, pictures, models,

"If you must read all or part of your speech . . . a teleprompter reproduces a copy in large type and positions it near the camera but out of range of its lens. Thus, even though reading, you can maintain fairly good eye contact with the audience. . . ."

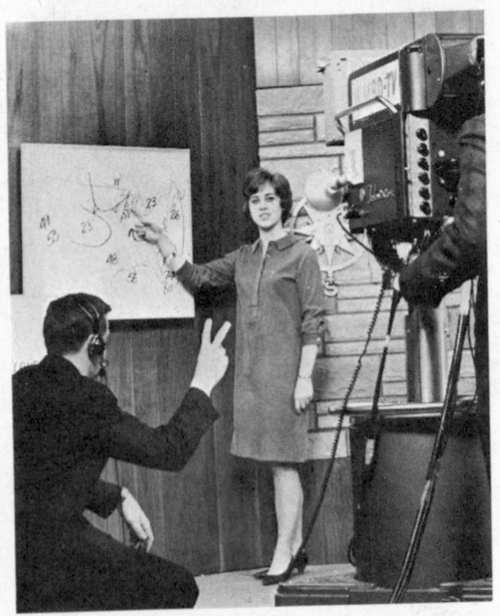

A glimpse of some of the equipment in general use in telecasting, as well as the manner of speaking for television with the assistance of teleprompters, is shown in two of these photos, while a teleprompter is clearly visible in the third. TOP: Lucille Ball watches as the camera is on Henry Fonda narrating a scene from a television special. ABOVE LEFT: In the close-up is a teleprompter used by President Lyndon B. Johnson for an address delivered out of doors. Note the large type of the passage being read, and the underlining of a portion for emphasis. Compare this marked script with another read by the President from a notebook, a photo of which is on page 29. ABOVE RIGHT: A Bradley University student gives the weather report at a local television station. A more extensive view of a studio may be found on page 174.

and even short sequences involving motion pictures and animated cartoons adds variety and life to a television speech, for people tire of looking steadily and only at the image of the speaker for long intervals. Sometimes large-scale visual aids are placed beside or behind the speaker so that he can point to them as he talks. Frequently, small pictures or miniature models are picked up by a separate camera. When speaking to a large face-to-face audience, you will not be able to use these devices often; but in the intimate studio broadcast, you can. In fact, sometimes you may best organize a television talk around a series of visual aids especially devised to portray your ideas.

Adapting vocal delivery to television

While most of the vocal requirements of radio broadcasting apply to television also, there are a few important variations. Since the audience sees as well as hears the speaker, he can speak more slowly and can pause longer for transitions or emphasis. In fact, fairly long pauses accompanied by the pointing out of pertinent details on maps or charts are perfectly natural. When the same program is broadcast over both radio and television, however, the speaker must not pause too long or slow down his rate of speaking too drastically.

In telecasts, the speaker should be particularly careful to avoid overemphatic vocal delivery, and should maintain a quiet, conversational manner. Variety and emphasis are needed; but an excessively excited tone, too fast a rate, or an overassertive inflection is likely to be in bad taste. Especially in the intimate studio telecast, you must remember that you are conversing with your listeners as a guest in their homes and should therefore keep your voice within the limits of reasonably animated conversation.

CONTENT AND ORGANIZATION OF THE BROADCAST SPEECH

Although the principles of speech development presented in previous chapters apply to radio-tv speech as well, some of them deserve special emphasis. In particular, bear the following suggestions in mind:

Remember that the time limit is exact. Nearly all television and radio broadcasting stations operate on a schedule that is adhered to within a thirty-seconds' leeway; if a program runs overtime, it will be cut off. Moreover, programs start on time; if the studio is up several flights of stairs, allow yourself time to get there and catch your breath before you have to begin talking. Although you may be scheduled for a fifteen-minute program, you will not have a full fifteen minutes available for your speech; you must make allowances for announcements and for an introduction. Ask how much time is actually yours, and find out from the announcer or technician the signals you will be given at intervals to alert you to the time which has elapsed and the time which remains. Since many people, without realizing it, find that they talk much faster in a studio than elsewhere, allow for this possibility by having an additional illustration or story prepared, one which can be conveniently inserted near the end of your talk if you see that you are getting through too early. In case you are "running slow," be prepared also to cut out a paragraph or two. To do this smoothly, "back time" your speech by noting on the manuscript or teleprompter copy at what point you have one or two minutes of material remaining to be delivered. If, then, near the end of the broadcast, the clock shows that you have too much or too little time, you are thus prepared to adjust your remarks accordingly.

Make your appeal as universal as possible. Remember that all sorts of people may be listening; try to interest as many as you can by making your illustrations, comments, and applications as varied and appealing as possible.

Use animated, colorful, concrete material. Avoid abstract theorizing; listeners will turn you off. Use a wealth of stories, illustrations, and comparisons—especially those of the "believe-it-or-not" type, those which contain plenty of action, and those which relate to the everyday experiences of your listeners.

Use as many of the factors of attention as possible. Review the factors of attention as presented in Chapter 13. Give special emphasis to the *vital*—relate your material to the important needs and desires of as many types of people as you can; to *activity and reality*—keep your speech concrete and full of movement; to *suspense*—early in your speech arouse curiosity, or promise that some valuable information will be given later.

Use simple (but not puerile) wording and sentence structure. Avoid technical terms when common terms will do; if you must use difficult or strange terms, explain them. In general, avoid flowery, over-elegant diction and long, involved sentences. Do not, on the other hand, talk down to your audience; even children like to be talked to as if they were grown up.

Use a simple form of speech organization. Avoid complex patterns of organization and lengthy chains of reasoning. Rarely will you have time to make such reasoning clear; and because you cannot see your listener, you cannot tell whether he understands it or not. A few main ideas, clearly related and simply developed, should serve as the main structure of your speech.

Mark your transitions clearly. When you move from one idea to another, be sure to indicate this fact by a word or two or by a distinct change of rate or pitch. On the platform or in a television broadcast, you can indicate such transitions by movement or gesture, but over the radio your voice alone must do this work. These transitions should not be stereotyped, however; vary them and keep them informal. Such phrases as "In the first place" and "Secondly" sound too stilted for the conversational mode of speaking called for in the studio. It is much better to say, "Now I want to tell you" or "But let's look at something else for a minute."

Give your speech a sense of continuous movement and development. Don't let your remarks bog down or ramble. Keep the audience aware that you are getting somewhere, that you have an objective and are moving steadily toward it.

Avoid profanity and remarks offensive to special groups. You must be extremely careful to avoid comments or allusions that could be interpreted as slurs upon any religious, racial, or occupational group. Remember that the air is public property and that all types of people may be listening. Profanity or risqué stories are never necessary to a good speaker; on the air they are absolutely taboo. To protect its license, the station will shut you off if you try to use them.

These are a few of the considerations you should keep in mind when you prepare a speech for broadcasting. You can observe their application every day by listening to some of the many talks given on radio or television.

THE AUDITION OR REHEARSAL

Many stations require an audition or rehearsal before a broadcast. Even if a station does not require a rehearsal, you would be wise to arrange for one if possible. In an audition you present your speech before the microphone just as you would if the program were on the air; the difference lies in the fact that the speech is recorded or is transmitted directly to a loudspeaker in an adjoining room. Similarly, television broadcasts may be rehearsed to check the lighting, camera locations, and movements of the speaker.

The audition serves to test your delivery—the rate, modulation, and quality of your voice, and the proper use of the microphone. Furthermore, an audition serves as an excellent check on the timing of your speech; if you find that it is too long or too short as given in the actual studio situation, you still have time to revise it. Finally, an audition will accustom you to the studio, to the deadened sound resulting from acoustically treated walls and ceiling, to the quiet movement of people, to the technical array of equipment, and to the sense of mystery with which broadcasting even yet affects so many people.

SAMPLE SPEECH

The following talk by Robert Gardiner, Executive Secretary of the United Nations Economic Commission for Africa, was broadcast over the facilities of the British Broadcasting Corporation as one of that network's Reith Lectures for the 1965-1966 season.

After an introduction which plunged the listener into the heart of the subject, Mr. Gardiner sketched the problem of race prejudice as he, a native of Ghana, viewed it, and then outlined the conditions which a satisfactory solution must meet. Note in particular the direct, simple style; the frequent use of the word "we" as a means of binding together speaker and audience; the several striking examples; and the objective, restrained handling of a potentially explosive subject. "A World of Peoples" is a good example of how a speaker may make a radio or television talk clear and interesting for the average listener, without sacrificing either significance of ideas or dignity of treatment.

A WORLD OF PEOPLES[3]

Robert Gardiner

As things are, no one would argue that there is no antipathy between races. What I want to do here is to analyse some of the attitudes which contribute to this antipathy. It can range from being ill at ease in strange company to open hostility and persecution of others because they differ from us. It is referred to variously as race-prejudice, colour-prejudice, colour-bar, racialism, and racism. I personally prefer the term racism. It seems to me a good clear

[3]*The Listener*, BBC Publications, LXXIV, No. 1911 (November 11, 1965), 739-742. Reprinted with permission of The British Broadcasting Corporation.

description of the antipathy and of the dangers it holds for us. The name was first given to a racial doctrine which began at the end of the nineteenth century. According to it, a man's worth was determined by the race to which he belonged. In due course, the notions which make up this doctrine served as the basis of Nazism: a good enough reason for making an examination of "racism" the starting point for a study of the problems of a world of peoples.

It is normal for us to feel more at ease in the company of the people we know: with our own sort, with our own people. What we really mean by the expression "our own people" is the people who are known to us, whom we can understand easily, and with whom we can get along without much difficulty: in short, people with whom we have a common background and a basically similar outlook. These people need not be just members of our family or immediate relations; but we sometimes express the idea of "our own people" by describing them as our kith and kin, and emphasize our close ties with them in such sayings as "blood is thicker than water." The mention of blood brings us to a meaning of the expression "our own people" which has special relevance to these talks. It suggests a link between the ability to get along together and racial affinity. But being able to get along with others does not depend solely on relationships of blood and race. There is a whole range of cultural and social factors which can be as effective as kindred relations in bringing and keeping people together.

As individuals we all tend to be loyal to the groups to which we belong, be it our family, school, neighbourhood, office, or factory. We tend to refer to people who belong to our group as "us" and to others who are outside as "them."

In its positive form, group loyalty or "team spirit" is an essential component in nation-building, and we of the newer nations are anxious to strengthen it within our own societies. It is a tremendously powerful emotional motor. But a motor will propel you only where you want to go; this particular one has been put to some devilish uses in our time, none more so than during the Nazi regime in Germany, when it was the motive and driving force for collective hostility against a whole people, the Jews.

Loyalties and hostilities among social groups often come to be regarded as unalterable and instinctive, and we tend to develop a belief in the superiority of the group to which we belong and the inferiority of other groups. When differences can be identified by so easy a criterion as skin colour, such beliefs can assume ugly and dangerous potentialities.

It is sometimes claimed that aversion to skin colour is inherent, innate, or instinctive. There are no facts to substantiate this claim. The nearest we can get to a reasonable explanation for it is that our likes and dislikes become imprinted on our minds so early in our lives that we tend to consider them part of our nature. But it is true that strangeness and unfamiliarity do frighten and momentarily repel. The typical reactions of white people to Africans are fully reciprocated by Africans when they first encounter white people. They are apt to mistake them for ghosts or for pale, sickly individuals.

Four hundred years ago a traveller in Mozambique described the reactions of Africans to white skin like this: "They take great pride, thinking there are no fairer people than they in all the world, so that when they see any white people, that wear apparel on their bodies, they laugh and mocke at them, thinking us to be monsters and ugly people; . . . they think and verily persuade themselves that they are the right colour of men and that we have a false and counterfeit colour." And yet it has been seriously suggested that the colour black, as such, has a special psychological significance for all races.

No. We like or dislike people or objects because we have learnt to, or because we have cultivated agreeable or disagreeable attitudes towards them. In most other instances we may be completely indifferent to the existence of other groups. For instance, contact with a remote Eskimo, if he is not involved economically or politically or socially in our lives, does not arouse any emotional reaction in us, except perhaps a distant human curiosity about his way of life. In general, the assumption that there is a race-repulsion instinct has not been supported by psychological studies. We all know that children adopt the attitudes that prevail in their homes and communities. What we do not so often realize is that children are not unique in this. Adults are influenced by the traditions of their community and the examples of others.

Strangeness and unfamiliarity may temporarily frighten and repel, but they do not necessarily elicit hostile reactions or lasting hostility. There are many instances in which complete strangeness has done just the opposite. Amerindians visiting Europe soon after the discovery of America were described as "a source of great interest to scientists; the portraits of many of them were painted by famous artists; kings and queens received them as fellow sovereigns, showering them with gifts of money, jewels, and clothing while entertaining them in royal style."

If repulsion is not instinctive, and strangeness is not the cause of antagonism, then why and how does racial antagonism arise? Prejudice is such an emotional thing that it is not easy to find rational explanations for it. All the same, one can sometimes see causes. It is found that some people will attribute undesirable characteristics to groups with whom they have little or no contact. Their hostility is based on hearsay or on isolated experience.

It is sometimes claimed that race antipathy stems out of the same order of cultural differences. But surely if this were the only basis of hostility it would disappear once the member of the alien race has been culturally assimilated. Cultural assimilation is possible when the groups coming together have developed relatively similar backgrounds. The West Indian from Martinique or any of the French islands can be more easily assimilated in France than an African who is still attached to tribal society. In the same way, a British West Indian who speaks English stands a better chance in England than a non-English-speaking Pakistani. But racist thinking, which attaches importance to obvious and striking differences such as colour, makes social assimilation difficult, even for those who have achieved cultural assimilation. No matter how assimilated a Negro may be, he is a Negro first and everything else later: even in France, where the claim is that the culture of a man is more important than his skin-colour.

One of the more ludicrous manifestations of "race-thinking" is also one of the most familiar. Have we not all been guilty at one time or another of saying, "I really can't tell one Chinese from another," "one Negro from another," "one white man from another"? There surely is a time when the sheer difference between a black face and a white face, between a yellow face and a black face, is so overwhelming that it prevents us from looking more closely. But it is a stage that we grow out of, or should grow out of, if we have the capacity to interest ourselves in human beings. The truth is that too many of us fall into the easy and lazy habit of going no further than the recognition of the obvious difference.

. . . .

It may be helpful to review the characteristics of racism: in racism we draw no distinction between the individual and the group to which he belongs. We cease to see the postman, the bus-conductor, the doctor, the shopkeeper, the office or factory colleague who is known to us. We forget the personal or human relations we may have had with him; they simply fade out of our minds. We are ready to attribute group characteristics to him. He becomes a typical black, or white, or yellow man—an easy target for race attacks. We proceed to form or accept theories about him. Once one gets into the race-thinking mood and the individual is forgotten, it is surprising how many sweeping generalizations can be remembered.

No section of any community is wholly immune against racism. It is wrong to assume that unfounded beliefs in race are confined to the uneducated masses. Sometimes, in fact often, they are more discerning than scholars who are wrapped up in obscure theories. The highly speculative game of race-theorizing in which some historians and philologists indulge can be fascinating; but it is a game which prepares the mind for group-hostility and nations for conflicts and wars. People who have been friendly and peaceful neighbours and co-workers can suddenly turn into enemies, joining in hostile attacks on their recent friends or standing by while others attack them. Racism is a hysterical phenomenon.

Fortunately, though, in every community the majority of the people accept popular views and current behaviour patterns; their attitudes are not fixed. On the other hand, there are people who hold so rigidly to false generalizations that even psychotherapy may not succeed in curing them. These are pathological cases and must be recognized as such. They are people who for various reasons feel their positions threatened, and who harbour feelings of insecurity and anxiety. To sum up, we may accept the view that "The cause of prejudice is in the subject, not the object of prejudice. It is an irrational, pathological phenomenon, rising from the individual's own inadequacies, and resulting in displaced aggression."

. . . .

Presenting facts in the hope of removing prejudices is a form of social therapy. But, as with most mentally ill people, success in refuting one false notion only makes room for another. Take the familiar allegation that one particular racial group is more prone to tuberculosis or some other social disease. Health statistics may disprove this. But if they do, the statistical evidence will be ignored, or the figures will be challenged. If statistical evidence supports the allegation, racists will ignore the fact that any group living in similar conditions would be prone to the same disease. The expression "a man convinced against his will is of the same opinion still" aptly describes the mentality and behaviour of racists. That is why I am inclined to agree with those who argue that it cannot be uprooted point by point. It is sometimes necessary to enact laws against racism as a first step towards breaking a vicious circle. Experience imposed may help to speed up the process of persuasion. How often has it not been said: "Until I met some of them," or "travelled with some of them," or "my child started inviting some of them to our home, I didn't know they could be so nice!" Legislation can at least create the conditions for such meetings.

The mistake is often made of describing a racial situation either as a Negro problem or a White problem. All racial groups in a situation are involved, in different ways. Recently the American magazine *Ebony* has come out with an issue on the "White Problem in America." It is an idea which fits in with contemporary ways of looking at the race question. But I feel it is wrong. There is both a Negro question and a White question.

Racism has its corollaries as well: there is what may be called "counter-racism," where the group which has been stigmatized as inferior reacts, humanly enough one might say, by stigmatizing other groups as inferior. This is as extreme a denial of the truth about human life as the denial of equality which gave birth to it. And then there is the phenomenon—I suppose it could be described as "inverse racism"—in which some members of a dominant group are moved by an exaggerated sense of guilt to offer themselves as scapegoats for their own groups. The answer to racism is neither abject submission nor counter-hostility.

I think it may be helpful to consider what we should expect in a healthy racial situation. Let us remember that members of other racial groups, whatever they are, are not potential angels; they are ordinary human beings with all the weaknesses of men. They seek an opportunity to lead their lives in peace and in harmony with their neighbours. As we do not normally make friends with every member of our own ethnic group, or even like them, so we should not expect to like all strangers indiscriminately. It is honest and healthy to allow for our personal likes and dislikes, without giving offence. It is not good to give special and privileged treatment to members of minority groups. All they ask for and should be given is their rights as human beings. To treat a person better than normal because of his race or colour is a form of discrimination, as much as treating him worse.

. . . .

Britain is the centre of an inter-racial Commonwealth. It is also one of the important world centres which until recently could boast of freedom from prejudice. Britain, like any other country, has a sovereign right to decide who may or may not enter her territory. British statesmen have been aware of Britain's inter-racial role in Commonwealth and world affairs, and to some extent the recent controversy in Britain about immigration has recognized it as an international problem and not just a national one. But it seems to me that problems of migration and the treatment of settlers, which are now within the exclusive jurisdiction of individual countries, will eventually have to be examined collectively in a world organization. Migration policies in the Pacific and Southeast Asia, the security of minority settlers in the newly independent states, the migration of workers into highly industrialized countries, and the way that automation may affect their future—all these issues pose problems which can easily inflame race feelings.

In a world with practically no distances between countries, such issues cannot be ignored. "All real living is meeting," a contemporary philosopher has said. In spite of the ideological barriers that man with perverse determination has erected in our time, we do live in an age of meeting. The television, the camera, and the fixed-orbit satellite are perhaps the advanced symbols of this fact. But seeing our neighbour—and everybody now is our neighbour—is not knowing our neighbour. Just as the brain interprets the messages of the optic nerve, we too must be equipped to interpret the messages about other peoples.

Racism has been described as a pathological state of mind, as a form of irrationalism and as an epidemic. These descriptions do suggest that there is a healthy state to be attained and preserved in a world of peoples. We have to use all the resources at our disposal and the skills we can command, consciously to enrich our living by making the meeting of peoples an open-hearted endeavour to understand and appreciate each other. To go no further, the horrors of the Nazi concentration camps should impress on us how urgent it is for all of us to learn habits of understanding and tolerance.

Problems

1. On three or four consecutive days, listen to a popular television newscaster and attempt to determine those aspects of vocal and physical delivery upon which his effectiveness appears to rest. Prepare a report on your findings.
2. Compare the newscaster studied in Problem 1 with another popular newscaster. Are the same factors of effectiveness present in both? If not, how do the two men chiefly differ? To what extent is it possible to recommend a single standard or ideal style of delivery which all television newscasters should follow?
3. Compare one of the television newscasters studied in Problems 1 or 2 with a well-known radio newscaster. How do the technics of the radio newscaster differ from those which are used by his colleague on television? If the two men were to exchange media, would either or both of them lose some of their effectiveness?
4. Analyze critically a speech delivered over radio or television, paying particular attention to *(a)* the suitability of the subject for a broadcast speech, *(b)* the speaker's diction and sentence structure, *(c)* the organization of the talk, *(d)* the variety and vividness of the supporting material.
5. Select a speech to inform or convince which you gave in class earlier this semester and, observing the rules of good television speaking as described in this chapter, reduce it to a manuscript suitable for a ten-minute television talk.
6. As a variation of Problem 5, rewrite for radio or television presentation one of the sample speeches given in this book at the close of the chapters on the speech to inform or the speech to convince.
7. Interview the manager or program director of a local radio or television station to get his ideas concerning the nature of an effective radiocast or telecast talk. Ask him also to explain to you some of the special rules and restrictions which a radio or television speaker must observe concerning libel and the ethical responsibility of public utterance. Write a report on the results of your interview.

Speaking assignments

1. Prepare and present from manuscript a ten-minute informative or persuasive speech especially adapted for radio or television. In choosing and developing a subject and in wording and delivering your speech, observe in so far as possible the various recommendations set forth in this chapter and check the timing.

If possible, deliver the speech over a closed-circuit radio or television hookup. In case the necessary equipment is not available, the radio-speaking situation can be roughly simulated by having the speaker talk from behind a screen.

2. Prepare in manuscript form a five or ten-minute summary of campus or community news suitable for broadcast. Present this news to the class either face-to-face while seated at a table or over a closed-circuit television or radio hookup. Ask your classmates to comment in particular upon your manner of delivery.

Suggestions for further reading

Waldo Abbot and Richard L. Rider, *Handbook of Broadcasting*, 4th ed. (New York: McGraw-Hill Book Company, 1957).

Samuel L. Becker and H. Clay Harshbarger, *Television: Techniques for Planning and Performance* (New York: Holt, Rinehart & Winston, Inc., 1958).

Hadley Cantril and G. W. Allport, *Psychology of Radio* (New York: Harper, 1935).

Giraud Chester and Garnet R. Garrison, *Television and Radio,* 3rd ed. (New York: Appleton-Century-Crofts, 1963).

Edward Stasheff and Rudy Bretz, *The Television Program,* 3rd ed. (New York: Hill & Wang, Inc., 1962).

Max Wylie, *Radio and Television Writing*, rev. ed. (New York: Holt, Rinehart & Winston, Inc., 1950).

PART SEVEN

PRINCIPLES OF DISCUSSION AND CONFERENCE

Preparing for discussion

Outlining the discussion plan

Leading and participating in discussion

Parliamentary procedure

CHAPTER THIRTY-ONE

Preparing for discussion

In our society more and more of the daily operations of business, education, and government are directed by groups of people meeting as committees, boards, or councils. As a result, businessmen, labor leaders, industrial workers, public officials, educators, and members of other professions spend much of their time participating in discussions of one sort or another. Often, indeed, a man's success in his job depends on how skilled a discussion leader or participant he may be.

DISCUSSION DEFINED AND PROJECTED

What do we mean by the term *discussion?* Although in daily conversation it is loosely used to cover almost any interchange of ideas or opinions, as we employ it here we mean *a cooperative and relatively systematic process in which a group of persons exchange and evaluate ideas and information about a mutual problem in order to understand or solve that problem.*

From taking part in discussions in the classroom or in campus, social, or church groups, you undoubtedly already have discovered that merely having a number of people talk over a problem together does not insure that a wise or expedient solution will be reached. Sometimes an informed individual can think through and solve a problem more rapidly and efficiently than can a group. A group, however, is more likely than an individual to be aware of and give attention to all aspects of a question. Moreover, a group decision is more democratic than an individual one; and, since people tend to support more strongly the decisions which they themselves have helped to make, a group consensus is more likely to produce satisfying and permanent results. Finally, although group discussions admittedly do take time, their efficiency can be increased if the participants prepare themselves carefully on the question to be considered and if they are familiar with effective methods of participation and leadership.

The purpose of this chapter and of the two that follow is to acquaint you with principles and methods for productive group discussions. Once we have explored some of the ways in which we can prepare ourselves to participate more constructively in this kind of group communication, we will move to a detailed consideration of "Outlining the Discussion Plan" in Chapter 32, and then examine—in Chapter 33—the technics of "Leading and Participating in Discussion."

In this initial chapter the following questions will be treated: What are the purposes of discussion? What are the types of discussion groups? What are the characteristics of effective discussion? How should an individual prepare to participate in discussion?

PURPOSES OF DISCUSSION

Discussions usually have one of two basic purposes: (1) to exchange information or ideas, or (2) to reach an agreement or decision.

To exchange information or ideas

The least a discussion can accomplish is to inform each participant of what the other members of the group know or think about the subject under consideration. Sometimes, as in the classroom, this may be the only purpose, but more often the exchange of ideas is merely preliminary to making a decision. In either case, the pooling of information and the expression of divergent views are valuable for gaining a broad understanding of the problem and, in addition, provide a sound basis for any decision that may be arrived at later.

To reach an agreement or make a decision

When the purpose of a discussion is to reach an agreement or to decide what the group as a whole should believe or do, conflicting facts are examined and differences of opinion are evaluated in an effort to arrive at a common judgment or consensus. In cases where a consensus proves impossible, at least the range of disagreement may be narrowed, and a clearer understanding of outstanding differences may be attained. Usually in such discussions the procedure is quite informal, although occasionally decisions may be determined by balloting.

TYPES OF DISCUSSION GROUPS

The four most common types of discussion groups are *study groups*, *decision-making groups*, *panels*, and *symposiums*. The last two are designed to take place before audiences, and may conveniently be adapted to radio or television.

Study groups

Study groups usually are quite informal. A lecture or film may be used at the beginning of the session in order to provide needed data or to stimulate thought, but the bulk of the time is devoted to the mutual exchange of information and ideas. The purpose of the participants is to learn something from one another or to correct or clarify their own thinking about the subject. A common type of study group is the college class. Another is the convention session at which men and women in the same business or profession meet to explain the results of research or to exchange experiences in dealing with common problems.

Decision-making groups

When the president of a business organization calls a meeting of his executive committee to decide on future policies, or the social chairman of a fraternity gathers the members to select an orchestra for the spring prom, the purpose of the discussion is not merely to exchange ideas but to arrive at a mutually satisfactory choice or decision. In every college and community, dozens of such decision-making groups meet every day. Occasionally, if the group is large or the problem an especially knotty one, the leader may invoke the rules of parliamentary procedure. Usually, however, less formal methods are used, and the members proceed in much the same way as they would in a study group.

Panels

When a group is too large to engage in effective discussion or its members are not well enough informed for such discussion to be profitable, three to five persons may be selected to discuss the topic for the benefit of the other members, who then act as an audience. The individuals in this small group—or panel, as it is called—are chosen either because they are well informed on the subject and can supply the facts needed for a sound judgment or because they are known to represent divergent points of view. The members of the panel discuss the subject among themselves, asking questions of one another and agreeing or disagreeing just as they would if they were in a small study or action group. Following the discussion by the panel members, questions or comments from the floor usually are in order.

Symposiums

Another type of audience or "public" discussion is the symposium. In this form, several persons—again usually three to five—give short

"The four most common types of discussion groups are study groups, decision-making groups, panels, and symposiums. . . . Various modifications of the panel and symposium are possible, and sometimes these forms may be combined. . . ."

Examine these photos of people talking together, and then determine (1) whether the definition of *discussion* at the opening of this chapter may be applied to their activity, and—when it may be so applied—(2) which of the four common types of discussion groups a photo in question represents. CLOCKWISE: An American history seminar at Amherst College; a group of students in a snack shop absorbed in serious conversation; doctors from Mayo Clinic participating in an international medical conference, in which they exchanged comments and questions with a group of surgeons in London; participants in a broadcast of the Northwestern Reviewing Stand; and teams representing the steel industry and labor at contract negotiations.

speeches, each presenting a different facet of the problem or expressing a different view concerning a possible solution. The symposium is a common procedure at large conventions or conferences, where experts are invited to speak on various aspects of a general topic. Like the panel discussion, it customarily is followed by questions or comments from the audience.

Various modifications of the panel and symposium are possible, and sometimes these forms may be combined, but the essential characteristic of each is that a group of experts or spokesmen do most of the talking while the larger group listens.

ESSENTIALS FOR PROFITABLE DISCUSSION

If a discussion is to accomplish anything, the individuals who take part in it must be capable of contributing worth-while ideas, and the conduct of the group must be such that an objective and systematic examination of the problem is possible.

Essentials for the group as a whole

The first requisite for profitable discussion is *orderliness.* This does not imply a high degree of formality; indeed, formality often is undesirable. Orderliness does require, however, that only one person talk at a time, that the discussants be consistently courteous, and that some fairly definite procedure be followed to prevent the group from wandering too far afield. A carefully drawn discussion plan (see Chapter 32) will help greatly in meeting this last requirement. In the second place, every member of the group must have *a cooperative rather than a competitive attitude.* If each person insists on having his own way, the discussion will get nowhere. Individuals must be willing to consider points of view other than their own and, instead of criticizing another member for any mistakes he may make in analysis or reasoning, should try to understand and assist him. Moreover, there must be *a willingness to compromise.* There are times, of course, when compromise is not desirable; but reasonable compromise usually hurts no one and sometimes is the only way of reaching an agreement or making a decision. If a general desire to "meet the other fellow halfway" prevails, there is likely to be a better feeling in the group and a more fruitful exchange of opinions.

Finally, the group should have *a sense of accomplishment.* Unless people feel that they are getting somewhere, their interest and enthusiasm soon diminish. Before the consideration of the problem actually begins, a definite goal should be set and the field of discussion limited. This can best be done by putting the problem into the form of a simple and impartially phrased question. A discussion on the problem of school dropouts, for example, might center in the question: "How can we keep young people in school?" Or a discussion on the problem of traffic deaths might ask: "What are the principal causes of death on the highway?" *In general, it is wise to avoid questions which present the group with only two alternatives or choices,* for such questions tend to split the group into competing factions and to make an impartial exploration of a problem very difficult. The question, "Should we raise the sales tax in this state to four per cent?" for instance, since it invites the answers "yes" or "no," might well lead to a two-sided argument or debate.

Essentials for the discussion participant[1]

First and foremost, it is imperative that the participant have *a thorough knowledge of the subject* being considered. If you know what you are talking about, other shortcomings will be more easily forgiven. The second essential is *an acquaintance with the other members of the group.* The more you know about them, the better you will be able to understand why they think as they do and to adjust your own views so as to help reach a consensus. Equally important is *close attention to the discussion* as it progresses. Unless you listen to what is going on, you may lose track of the direction the discussion has taken and will be likely to make foolish comments, to repeat points already made, or to entertain mistaken ideas concerning the positions taken by the other participants. Finally, *meaningful contributions to the discussion itself* are desirable. If you remain silent, you may learn a good deal, but you will not enhance the knowledge of others or help solve the problem with which the group is concerned. Develop the ability to present your ideas clearly and tactfully and learn to bring them in at the most strategic time.

Qualities required of the leader

The fruitfulness of a discussion depends a great deal on the leader's *capacity for rapid analysis.* He must be able to see in what direction the group is turning, to catch significant points even when they are buried in superfluous detail, to note essential agreements between points of view, and to strip controversial issues of unnecessary complexity so as to narrow the discussion to the basic issues. In short, he needs to be alert, quick-witted, and clear-thinking. Moreover, *a good*

[1]Note: In this chapter, the *qualities* of a good participant and leader are considered. The *methods* and *technics* of participation and leadership will be discussed in Chapter 33, "Leading and Participating in Discussion."

discussion leader must be able to state the results of his analysis clearly and briefly, and to make the essential points stand out before the group as vividly as they do in his own mind.

Just as important for the leader is *the quality of fairness or impartiality.* By seeing that minority views are allowed expression and by phrasing questions and summarizing contributions fairly, he can help maintain a spirit of cooperative inquiry among persons who may differ vigorously from one another. At the same time, however, the keenness of his analysis and the impartiality of his leadership must be tempered with *tact both in words and in manner.* There is no place in discussion for a leader who is easily irritated or who says things in a way that irritates others. A good rule is always to accept comments and to state them with the most generous interpretation possible; given a remark containing a reasonable argument and a sarcastic connotation, focus the discussion on the reason, and ignore the sarcasm.

What we have said thus far, about the purpose and function of discussion and the essentials for effective interpersonal communication of this kind, should have made clear the objectives of your preparation. Now let us turn our attention to the process of preparation itself.

GENERAL PREPARATION

Just how should the individual prepare himself to lead or to participate in a discussion? What should he do to ensure that he will be able to contribute to the best of his ability? Two fundamental steps are required: first, he must study and analyze the problem or subject which is to be considered; and, second, he must find out all that he can about the other members of the group.

Analysis of the specific subjects to be discussed

The more you know about the subject under discussion, the better. Don't rely on obsolete information, however; make sure that your facts are up-to-date. The broader and more ready the knowledge at your command, the better able you will be to take part in the discussion, no matter how it may develop or what course it may follow. Although many persons believe they do not need to prepare as carefully for a discussion as for a speech, the truth of the matter is just the opposite. In group communication of this kind you cannot arbitrarily narrow the subject or determine the specific purpose in advance, nor can you be sure of the exact direction the group will take. To be ready for any eventuality, therefore, you must have a flexibility born of broad knowledge. For each aspect of the problem that may be discussed, make the following analysis:

First, review the facts you already know. Go over the information you have acquired on the subject through reading or personal experience and organize it in your mind. Prepare as if you were going to present a speech on every phase of the entire subject; you then will be better qualified to discuss any part of it almost spontaneously.

Second, find out if recent changes may have affected the problem. Bring your knowledge up-to-date. Fit the newly acquired information into the outline of what you already have.

Third, determine a tentative point of view on the problem to be considered. Make up your mind as to what your attitude will be. Do you think that Hemingway was a greater writer than Faulkner? If so, exactly how and why? What can be done to attract new members into your club? Should cigarette smoking be declared illegal? Stake out a tentative position on each question that is likely to come before the group and have clearly in mind the reasons for your view. Be ready to state and substantiate this opinion at whatever place in the discussion seems most appropriate; but also be willing to change your mind if you are proved wrong by additional facts disclosed by other discussants.

Finally, anticipate the effect of your idea or proposal upon the other members of the group or on the organization to which they belong. Possibly what you propose will cause someone to lose money or to retract a promise he has made; forethought will enable you to understand his opposition if it arises and to make wise adjustment to it. If an audience will be present to hear and participate in the discussion, or if radio and television listeners are involved, extend your analysis to include an estimate of their probable knowledge of the problem and their possible attitude toward it. The more thoroughly you organize your facts and relate them to the problem and people involved, the more successful and influential will your contributions to the discussion be.

Analysis of the group

As a discussant, even though you are thoroughly familiar with the subject to be discussed, you will be handicapped unless you appreciate the relation between it and the objectives of your group. At the very beginning, then, determine the function of the group of which you are a part. Find out whether it has any official status or power. Is it brought together merely to investigate, or does it have authority to make decisions? What resources are at its command? Next, analyze the larger unit to which this group belongs. If you are a member of the student council, you must know not only the function of that council but also the policies and traditions of the college or university as a whole. Finally, make a detailed analysis of the individuals who compose the group. By doing so, you will know that X's comments are likely to be exaggerated and must be taken with a grain of salt, but that what W says will bear serious consideration. Furthermore, you will know that the best way of getting X to understand a point will be to use vivid illustrations or that substantial facts will be needed to convince W. In particular, answer for yourself as well as you can the following questions: What is the official position of each member of the group? What are each one's personal traits? What knowledge does each have of the subject to be discussed? What attitude will each probably show toward the interpretations or proposals which I plan to offer?

As a leader, your knowledge of the group—gained through careful analysis—becomes doubly important. It will be your responsibility to ascertain each discussant's special field of competence so that when questions arise which require a special type of information, you can immediately call upon the person who is able to supply it. Take note also of each person's prestige with the other members of the group. If, for example, an individual is considered an extremist, plan to limit or to counterbalance his contributions. An extremist often has good ideas, but they may be rejected merely because he advocates them. Let someone else follow up the points raised by such a person so that a more moderate statement may save those parts of the idea which are worth preserving. See to it also that other persons do not become disgusted because some garrulous crank monopolizes most of the discussion. Finally, find out about each participant's administrative abilities and special capacities. Groups often make decisions and determine policies but leave them to be carried out by individual members or a committee appointed by the chairman. The chairman's appointment of persons to administer the work may, therefore, cause a project to succeed or fail.

BROADCASTING A DISCUSSION

Of the various types of discussion listed on pages 569-572, the panel is most frequently broadcast on radio or television. Local stations present panel discussions by high-school students, clergymen, or civic leaders; networks regularly give time to the discussion of current events by groups of politicians, government officials, or news commentators. Although more formal than panels, symposium discussions also are convenient for broadcasting because the speeches of which they are in part composed can be more carefully planned and timed. The usual pattern for a broadcast symposium is for speakers with sharply differing views to present their opinions in short, uninterrupted statements, after which they engage in an informal question-and-answer period among themselves or with the audience participating.

All broadcasts of discussions have two characteristics in common: first, the discussion is carried on not so much for the benefit of the participants as for that of the listening or viewing audience whose informational background, attitudes, and interests must be kept constantly in mind; and second, the discussion is planned and controlled so as to focus on a single theme or problem of general interest to which the speakers attempt to contribute from their specialized backgrounds of knowledge or experience. Broadcasts such as "Meet the Press," which quiz or interview celebrities, do not constitute discussions in the sense in which the term is used here because they do not ordinarily provide for a mutual interchange of ideas among the participants.

Radio and television discussions, whether informative or argumentative, whether conducted as panels or symposiums, should be as much like other discussions as possible, differing only in so far as they must be adapted to the nature of the listening and viewing audience and to the strict time limits which broadcasting schedules impose. In televised programs, of course, the discussion group must be seated on only one side of the table or—depending upon the number and position of cameras employed—in some other manner so that the speakers' faces instead of their backs will be visible to the viewers. Within these limits, however, what is good discussion elsewhere is good discussion on radio or television also.

Preparing a broadcast discussion

Unlike the telecast or radiocast of a speech, discussions which are to be broadcast rarely are written out and read from a script. To do so would tend to rob them of their spontaneity and liveliness. Instead, both for radio or television presentation and for on-the-scene audiences, the discussion plan is carefully outlined in advance (see Chapter 32), the names of the participants who are to introduce each point are noted on this outline, and the principal ideas to be brought out during each phase of the discussion are itemized at the proper place. Then the leader, in order to lead the group to a conclusion within the time allotted for the broadcast or public discussion, notes the amount of time which can be spent on each section of the outline. Ordinarily, these matters of content and procedure can best be determined by a practice session or preliminary run-through of some kind.

The practice discussion

When the discussion is to be held before an audience or is to be broadcast, a preliminary warm-up period or even a complete practice session is not only essential but extremely useful. Whether it is scheduled in an auditorium or in a studio without "live" microphones, the pre-program practice takes the form of an experimental rehearsal of part or all of the planned discussion by the panel in private. It may occur immediately before the actual program begins, but more often it is held some time in advance. In either case, the ice is broken, and the participants are more likely to join quickly in a vigorous give-and-take before the audience, the microphones, or the cameras. Moreover, the discussants have a chance to verify each other's views, and therefore tend to make their comments more freely and pointedly. Finally, in this preliminary period, the leader not only can gauge the temper of his group and decide upon a method for handling certain participants, but he also has an opportunity to explain any special rules or details of procedure.

In a practice session the participants discuss the topic at some length and agree on those points that seem most important to include when the group later appears before the audience. And, as suggested above, often the entire agenda and discussion plan are worked out by the group as a whole, even to the detail of deciding which discussant is to introduce each phase of the problem and when. If these practice discussions are *recorded* on tapes or disks, they can be played back and thus provide the leader and his colleagues with an opportunity to analyze their remarks and to improve the manner in which they are eventually to be presented.

Care must be taken, of course, not to continue preliminary discussion until the participants become stale. Repeated rehearsals in which the same things are said in the same way soon become boring and lead to a final presentation that lacks freshness and life. Instead, limit the length and number of such practice periods, or make sure that new materials and fresh points of view are brought in at each succeeding session.

Preliminary practice of this kind is possible only for discussions which are to be held for an audience at the scene or those which are to be broadcast. All of the other aspects of preparation which we have discussed, however—both for the leader and for the individual participants—not only are possible but necessary if intelligent and fruitful discussion in study or decision-making groups is to follow. We shall see in the next chapters how careful preparation can lead to an orderly consideration of a subject and to effective participation in the discussion itself.

Problems

1. Compare and contrast *discussion* as defined in this chapter with each of the following types of oral interchange: social conversation, interviews, debates, class recitations, bull sessions.
2. Compare the preparation you made for your most recent classroom speech with the preparation that would be necessary for effective participation in a discussion on the same or a similar subject. In what respects would the two processes be alike? How would they differ? Do you agree with the statement made in the chapter that preparation for the discussion would be more difficult and time-consuming? Why or why not?
3. Listen to a discussion broadcast on radio or television and be prepared to answer the following questions concerning it: Was it a panel, a symposium, a combination of these types, or did it follow a different format? Was the audience allowed to participate? If so, when and how? Were the discussants well informed? Did they display an objective attitude toward the subject and a cooperative attitude toward each other? Were all aspects of the subject or all important points of view on the problem adequately represented? How, in your opinion, might the discussion have been improved?
4. List several situations other than radio or television broadcasts in which a panel discussion might be the most appropriate form to use. List other non-broadcasting situations in which the symposium probably would be more suitable.
5. Analyze a discussion as carried on in one of your classes. To what extent did the group as a whole conduct itself in a way consistent with the essentials for profitable discussion, as described on pp. 572-574? Keeping in mind the essentials for a good discussion participant as described on p. 573, comment in particular on the behavior of two or three individuals in the class—the one or two who best exemplified these essentials and the one or two who least exemplified them. To what extent did the instructor or discussion leader display the qualities outlined on pp. 573-574?
6. Analyze a discussion as carried on in some relatively small study or decision-making group of which you are a member (a church organization, student-government committee, etc.). How well did the group adhere to the purposes and methods of profitable discussion as described in this chapter? In what specific respects did the discussion fail to measure up to these criteria? Why?
7. Assume that as part of a mythical National Student Week you have been asked to arrange on your campus a panel or symposium discussion that is to

be open to all students and faculty. Select a subject that you think would be of interest to such an audience. Indicate whom you would invite to participate. Where and when would you hold the discussion? How long would it last? What sort of preliminary practice session, if any, would you plan? In each case be prepared to defend your answer.

8. What special problems or difficulties does a decision-making group face, which a study group does not need to worry about? Does the absence of these problems mean that it is easier to conduct a profitable study discussion than it is to conduct a productive decision-making discussion?

Speaking assignment

1. Drawing upon the sources listed under Suggestions for Further Reading at the close of this chapter, present to the class a seven- or eight-minute informative speech on the nature and purposes of discussion. In so far as possible, develop ideas not covered in the present chapter, so that you will be adding to the knowledge of the class concerning discussion and its aims. Follow in all respects the recommendations for an informative speech as outlined in Chapter 21. In fact, it would be a good idea to reread that chapter before beginning to prepare your speech. At the close of your speech ask for questions from the class and be prepared to clarify or supplement any point on which they desire more information.

Suggestions for further reading

Dean C. Barnlund and Franklyn S. Haiman, *The Dynamics of Discussion* (Boston: Houghton Mifflin Company, 1960), Chapter IV, "The Origin and Nature of Problems for Discussion."

Laura Crowell, *Discussion: Method of Democracy* (Glenview, Illinois: Scott, Foresman and Company, 1963), Chapter III, "The Discussion Question," and Chapter IV, "Gathering Information on the Question."

Halbert E. Gulley, *Discussion, Conference, and Group Process* (New York: Holt-Dryden, 1960), Chapter III, "Discussion Questions," and Chapter VII, "Becoming Informed."

William S. Howell and Donald K. Smith, *Discussion* (New York: The Macmillan Company, 1956), Chapter III, "Preparing a Discussion."

James H. McBurney and Kenneth G. Hance, *Discussion in Human Affairs* (New York: Harper & Row, 1950), Chapter XI, "Problems for Discussion," and Chapter XII, "Preparing for Discussion."

William M. Sattler, "The Use of the Case Method in College Discussion Classes," *Speech Teacher*, VII (September 1958), 216-225.

CHAPTER THIRTY-TWO

Outlining the discussion plan

In discussion, much time may be lost because of needless repetition or aimless wandering from point to point. A carefully developed discussion plan, however, will help to eliminate these problems.

Ideally, the entire group should work out the discussion plan together; but if this is impossible, the leader must take the responsibility for developing it. Even if you never serve as leader, you should understand the basic types of discussion plans because, as a participant, you will be able to follow the discussion more intelligently; and if the leader fails to prepare a plan, you sometimes can save the situation by "leading from the floor" with appropriately timed questions and comments.

Since there are several distinct types of discussion, this chapter will present separate plans for study groups and decision-making groups, and also will give suggestions for the discussion of a series of problems and for panels and symposiums. These plans can be used in most situations, though some modifications may be required because of the special interests or capacities of persons in the group or because of peculiarities of the subject under consideration. No separate plan for radio or television discussion has been included since broadcast discussions should follow as closely as possible the organization of other types of group discourse.

A PLAN FOR STUDY GROUPS

Often a study group discusses a book, or parts of it, and occasionally uses a study outline or syllabus prepared by an authority in a given field. When this is the case, the discussion usually should follow a sequence similar to the outline of the material studied. Your main task if you are leader will be to relate the points in that outline to the experience of the individual discussants in the group and to see that the more important facts and principles receive proper emphasis. If the prepared outlines are out of date or incomplete, the discussion plan should provide questions that will bring out the missing information or current points of view.

Usually, however, no prepared outline is available; or if it is, it is not suited to the needs of the particular group. In such situations, the leader or the group should determine the exact objective of the discussion and, as we pointed out in the preceding chapter, word it as a clear and impartial question—usually a question of fact or of value. Questions of fact, such as "What are the essentials for effective discussion?" or "What is our community doing to combat the increasing crime rate?" attempt to increase and clarify knowledge within the group; questions of value, such as "How successful is our community recreation program?" or "Is the United Nations the best means to ensure world peace?" seek judgments or appraisals. If you are evolving a procedure for a study group, the following suggestions should help you prepare a satisfactory discussion plan for questions of this kind.

Introduction

The introduction consists of a statement of the discussion question by the leader, together with one or two illustrative examples showing its general importance or its relation to the individuals in the group.

Analysis

After the leader's introduction, the group determines the importance of the subject and narrows the scope of the discussion to those phases which seem most important. They should consider such typical questions as:

1. What importance does the subject have for the group? Why?
2. Into what major topical divisions may the subject conveniently be divided? (See pp. 151 and 228-231 for suggestions.)
3. To which of these phases should the discussion be narrowed?
   a. Which topics are of the greatest interest and importance to the group?
   b. Upon which topics are the members of the group already informed so fully that further discussion would be fruitless?

Summary of analysis. At the conclusion of the analysis step, the leader or the group as a whole should summarize the list of topics to which the general subject has been narrowed, and suggest the order in which these might best be considered. (The patterns for informative speeches, as outlined on pp. 228-231, might be used.)

Investigation

In the investigative phase, the members consider systematically and in order each topic chosen as a result of Question 3 above. The ensuing discussion of *each topic* usually should be centered in questions such as:

1. What terms need definition? Is there agreement as to their generally accepted meanings? What definition does the group prefer?
2. What background material needs to be considered: historical, social, geographic, etc.?
3. What personal experiences of members of the group might illuminate and clarify the discussion?
4. What principles or causal relationships may be inferred from the information thus brought forth?

Summary of investigation. In summarizing the investigative phase of the discussion, the leader or group should recall the facts or principles upon which there seems to be general agreement and also those points for which information is lacking or conflicting.

Final summary

As a final step, the leader, with the aid of the group, should summarize briefly the most important matters covered in both the analytical and the investigative phases of the discussion. This concluding summary need not be exhaustive; its purpose is to bring together the more important points in such a way that they will be easily remembered, and their relationship to each other and to the general subject clearly recognized.

Obviously this plan for study groups is only a general one. For any actual discussion, it will need to be adapted to the subject under study and also developed in more detail. By thinking through this general plan in the light of your own knowledge of the subject, however, you will be able to prepare specific questions that will bring out information from different members; and by properly analyzing the interests and knowledge of the people in the group, you may predict the direction in which their interests will probably lead them during the discussion. A good method is to prepare a detailed outline of such a plan, phrased as a series of questions rather than as a series of statements. Remember, however, that the function of a discussion plan is to guide rather than to straitjacket the group; therefore, it should be kept flexible and be changed in any way that seems advisable as the discussion proceeds.

A PLAN FOR DECISION-MAKING GROUPS

Decision-making groups, as we said earlier, are concerned with more than the exchange of opinions and information; they are faced with situations requiring agreement on beliefs or on courses of action to be pursued. If the group is one which meets regularly, such as an executive committee, the members may not be aware of the problem prior to the meeting at which it is to be discussed. More frequently, the problem is known in advance, and at times a serious difficulty or conflict of interests may be the very reason for calling the group together. At any rate, the principal function of the decision-making group is to solve a problem; the objective is to reach a consensus on what to do about it and how to do it. Discussions having this purpose deal with so-called questions of policy—inquiries which ask what "policy" it would be best to follow now or in the future. (See pp. 411-413.) Two examples of such questions are: "What can be done to increase the number of participants in our activity?" and "How can our company meet the competition from foreign imports?" Of course, as we shall see in the following suggested procedure, the determination of a policy also requires the consideration of questions both of fact and of value.

One of the discussion plans commonly employed by decision-making groups is based on John Dewey's analysis of how we think reflectively when we are confronted with a problem.[1] This plan involves five steps: (1) defining the problem, (2) analyzing the problem, (3) suggesting solutions, (4) evaluating these solutions, and (5) putting the preferred solution into effect.

Defining the problem

This step should include:

1. Brief introductory remarks by the chairman touching on the general purpose of the discussion and its importance to the group.
2. The consideration of the following questions:
   a. How can the problem under consideration be phrased as a question? (*Note:* Usually the question will have been phrased by the leader or the group before the actual discussion begins. If not, it should be phrased at this time.)

[1]See *How We Think* by John Dewey (Boston, Mass.: D.C. Heath & Co., 1933), pp. 102-118.

b. What terms need defining?
   (1) What do the terms in the question mean?
   (2) What other terms or concepts will be encountered in this discussion that should be defined at this time?

Analyzing the problem

The analysis of the problem confronting the group consists of evaluating its scope and importance, discovering its causes, determining the essential matters that need correction, and setting up the basic requirements for an effective solution. The following sequence of questions is suggested:

1. What is the evidence that an unsatisfactory situation exists?
   a. Is the problem sufficiently serious to warrant discussion and action at this time? (If the answer to this question is negative, further discussion is obviously pointless.)
   b. Is the situation likely to improve itself, or will it become worse if nothing is done about it?
2. What caused this difficulty?
   a. Are its causes primarily economic, political, social, etc.?
3. What conditions in the present situation must be corrected? What demands must be met; what desires satisfied?
4. What satisfactory elements in the present situation must be retained?
5. In the light of the answers to Questions 3 and 4 above, what are the essential criteria by which any proposed plan is to be judged?
   a. What must the plan do?
   b. What must the plan avoid?
   c. What limits of time, money, manpower, or other restrictive circumstances must be considered?

Summary of the analysis. The leader, with the help of the group, should summarize the points agreed upon thus far. Particularly important is a clear statement of the agreements reached on Question 5, since these requirements will subsequently serve as the basic criteria for evaluating the proposed solutions. Moreover, a clear understanding regarding these requirements will tend to make further discussion more objective and will minimize the tendency to attack and defend proposals because of personal prejudices.

Suggesting solutions

In this step, the group should:

1. Bring forth all proposed solutions for the difficulty.
   a. Be sure that each proposal is defined or explained briefly but clearly.
   b. If many solutions are suggested, group them according to type for initial consideration.

2. Be sure that all the proposals are listed, preferably on a blackboard, so that the subsequent evaluations and comparisons can be complete.

Evaluating the solutions

The various proposals suggested for meeting the problem now should be examined and compared in an attempt to agree on a satisfactory plan. The following procedure is suggested:

1. Note the elements that are common to all the proposals and secure agreement for their retention.
2. Examine the differences in the proposals in the light of the criteria set up in Question 5 of the analysis step.
3. On the basis of this examination, eliminate the less desirable proposals and narrow the discussion to those which remain.
4. Examine the remaining proposals to see *(a)* whether one of them can be revised to eliminate objectionable features or to add desirable ones, or *(b)* whether the better parts of two or more plans can be combined into a new and more satisfactory one.

Summary of the solution-evaluation. When an agreement has been reached, the chairman—with the aid of the group—should sum up the principal features of the accepted plan. In groups which have no power or authority to act, this statement will normally end the discussion.

Putting the solution into effect

When a group is able to put its proposal into operation—to actuate it—the following steps should be considered:

1. Selection of persons or committees to be responsible for taking the action agreed upon.
2. Determination of the time, place, and other circumstances which govern putting the proposal into effect.
3. Taking official action, such as appropriating money or providing legal authorization whenever such action is necessary.

Summary of the actuative phase. The chairman should briefly restate the action agreed upon to be sure it is clear to the group. This statement normally ends the discussion.

ADAPTING THE DISCUSSION PLAN TO THE QUESTION

The foregoing plan for decision-making groups covers the whole deliberative process from the first analysis of existing conditions to the taking of final action. This entire process, however, is not always required. As Harrison Elliott points out in his book, *The Process of Group Thinking*, "A group may face a question in any one of five stages: (1) a baffling or confused situation; (2) a problem definitely defined; (3) alternatives specifically suggested; (4) a single definite proposal; (5) ways and means of carrying out a conclusion."[2]

How much of the decision-making process will need to be included in the discussion plan will depend, then, upon the stage at which the question comes before the group. If a proposal has already been approved at a previous meeting, or if the group finds itself in immediate agreement on it, all that needs to be discussed is the method of putting the proposal into effect. Similarly, if the group meets to consider the merits of a single definite solution to a recognized problem, the analysis of the problem, as outlined above, can be condensed to a brief discussion of the essential requirements for a satisfactory plan; or, following a brief, concise summary of those criteria by the chairman, the discussants may proceed immediately to an examination of the proposal in the light of those requirements. An essential part of preparing a discussion plan, therefore, is to determine at what stage the question is likely to come before the group; you can then prepare your outline to pick up the discussion at that stage without needless reconsideration of points already settled. The chairman, however, should study the entire outline so that he will be able to adapt accordingly if something he thought was settled turns out still to be in dispute.

A situation requiring a modified discussion plan of the type indicated above occurred on a university campus. Three student organizations had made preliminary plans to produce musical comedies on the campus during the same week. Obviously three such shows would conflict with one another, yet none of the organizations wanted to give up its plans entirely. All agreed that the best solution would be for the three groups to combine their efforts in a joint production; but differences in membership requirements, financial policies, and standards of skill required of the participants made it difficult for the organizations to agree on a definite plan. A preliminary meeting of representatives from the student organizations together with representatives of the faculty had disclosed that the final plan, to be acceptable, must provide for *(a)* skilled professional direction;

[2]Harrison Elliott, *The Process of Group Thinking* (New York: Association Press, 1932), 89 ff.

(b) opportunity for all students, regardless of organization membership, to try out for places in the cast or chorus or to work on the stage crew; *(c)* equal representation of the three student groups on the managing board; and *(d)* provision for an adequate financial guarantee.

Prior to the second meeting, the chairman secured from members of the joint committee several definitely outlined proposals; and copies of these proposals, with the names of the authors omitted, were placed before each member of the committee at the beginning of the meeting. The chairman opened the discussion by recalling the four general requirements listed above, and these were accepted by all. From this point on, the discussion focused upon the specific proposals before the group. It was found that the three plans had a number of common features; the differences were ironed out; some details were added and some dropped; a revised plan was found to be acceptable and was adopted; and provisions were made to put it into operation. Thus, beginning with the suggestion and evaluation of solutions, the procedure described in the preceding section of this chapter was followed almost exactly. Similar abridgments of the complete discussion plan can often be adapted to the actual stage at which the question comes before the group.

PLANNING FOR THE DISCUSSION OF A SERIES OF PROBLEMS

Executive committees, governing boards, and similar groups are often faced with the necessity of discussing several problems during the same meeting. Some of these problems may be related to one another, while others are quite distinct. Obviously, related questions should be discussed together or in immediate sequence, but the order in which unrelated questions should be considered requires some thought by the chairman. The following procedure, or a similar one, may be helpful in arranging the agenda for such a meeting:

Make a list of all the items to come up for consideration. Include both important and less important matters, those which need immediate attention and those which can be postponed.

Reduce this list to fit the time limit. Determine how much time is available for the discussion, and cross off enough of the less important items to bring the list within that limitation. The deleted items can be put on a supplementary list to be used in case the primary items are disposed of in less time than expected.

Arrange the items to be discussed in an orderly sequence. Some matters are dependent upon others. Suppose, for example, that the managing board of a college newspaper is meeting to decide upon the size of the editorial staff but that a proposal is also under consideration for issuing the paper daily instead of weekly. Obviously the second item would have to be settled before the first. If you are to lead the discussion efficiently, you must arrange the items for consideration so that there will be no need to duplicate or double back.

Outline the subsidiary questions involved in each major problem to be discussed. In the proposal to issue the college paper daily, a number of subordinate points will need to be considered: What will be the added cost of printing and distributing? Can enough advertising space be sold to meet this added expense? What will be done about existing advertising contracts based on the weekly plan? Is there enough local news to provide copy for a daily paper? Should an attempt be made to carry national as well as local news? The leader must have such points as these well in mind so that none of them will be overlooked. A mimeographed or blackboard outline of these points will often help keep the discussion centered on the problem and moving in an orderly fashion.

Finally, determine the questions which will arise from each decision that is made. If it is decided to publish the paper daily, a procedure must be agreed upon for getting the approval of the college authorities; a date must be set for instituting the change; and plans must be laid for putting the proposal into effect. As each decision is reached, the leader must be ready to lead the discussion on to the next one. Leadership of this sort will make the discussion orderly and productive.

PLANNING FOR PANEL AND SYMPOSIUM DISCUSSIONS

Develop a detailed discussion plan. For a panel discussion before an audience, the discussion plan should be prepared in great detail. If the purpose is to be informative only, the study-group type of plan can be used; if a problem or a proposed course of action is to be discussed, the plan for decision-making groups will be more suitable. As explained in the preceding chapter, it often is desirable that the speakers run through the discussion in private before their public appearance; for such preliminary practice may suggest how the discussion can be compressed, what less important points can be omitted, and how the whole plan can be made more coherent.

Make use of discussants' specialized knowledge. Whatever type of discussion plan is used, it should provide for utilizing the specialized information of all the panel members. Although no one should limit his remarks to his special field of knowledge, he should at least be given the first opportunity to discuss questions relating to that field. Unless something of this sort is done, the very purpose of selecting a panel to conduct the discussion for the audience is likely to be defeated.

Partition topic among symposium speakers. If the discussion is to be a symposium—a series of speeches followed, perhaps, by an open forum—the plan may be a simple partition of the topic among the speakers, with a different phase being assigned to each. Or one person may present the problem, and each of the other speakers suggest and evaluate a different type of solution. After the speakers have completed their formal remarks, the meeting may be opened for questions from the audience, the chairman referring to the various symposium speakers those questions which relate most closely to the points they have made.

Adapt the plan to the personnel. Any type of discussion plan must be adapted to the personnel of the group. The discussion leader must not assume that everyone will be logical, clear-thinking, and unemotional. He should be aware of prejudices and strong feelings and plan how to deal with them. If certain points are not vital to the issue and are likely to cause bitterness or unnecessary controversy, they may deliberately be excluded. If a certain person is known to have considerable prestige with the other members of the group, the discussion plan must be arranged to include the consideration of beliefs other than his in order to avoid a too-hasty acceptance of his point of view. In short, the plan must be developed not only to cover the subject but also to direct people in their discussion of it.

Be flexible. None of the suggestions presented in this chapter will take the place of the discussion leader's good sense or experience in planning and conducting the discussion. The better informed you are on the subject or problem to be considered, and the better you know the members of the group, the better able you will be to outline a discussion plan. When good sense or experience or special knowledge indicates that a procedure different from that suggested in this chapter would lead to more rapid progress and more fruitful results, do not hesitate to devise a completely different type of plan. In the beginning, however, you will be wise to follow rather closely the procedures suggested in this chapter, which are based on the advice of experienced discussion leaders.

SUGGESTED DISCUSSION QUESTIONS

The first list includes both questions of fact and questions of value, suitable for use in study groups. The second list contains questions of policy for decision-making groups. Panels and symposiums, of course, may use questions of either type.

For study groups:

1. How effective is our freshmen-orientation program?
2. What benefits does the undergraduate gain from participating in extracurricular activities?
3. What part should religion play in the life of the college?
4. How well are high school students prepared for higher education?
5. How do Russian and Chinese communism differ in philosophy and purpose?
6. What was Shakespeare's greatest play?
7. How have expressways affected American cities?
8. In what ways does the federal government support research in science (or the humanities)?
9. What is the present foreign policy of the United States?
10. How does civil rights legislation attempt to secure political (or social) equality for minority groups.

For decision-making groups:

1. What can be done to increase the effectiveness of student government in our college?
2. How can the colleges and universities better meet the problem of increased enrollments?
3. What can be done to increase the number of qualified teachers in our public schools?
4. Should the college student pursue a liberal or a practical education?
5. How can we best fight poverty in the United States?
6. How can labor and management increase their understanding of each other's problems?
7. How can the quality of television programs be improved?
8. How can we reduce the number of traffic deaths?
9. What policy should the United States pursue toward the underdeveloped countries of Asia and Africa?
10. Should we have governmental censorship of the arts?

Problems

1. Assume that you are to be the leader of a discussion on one of the study-group questions listed above, or on a similar question. Work out a plan for this discussion, following the steps outlined on pp. 581-584, or making such modifications of these steps as may seem wise.
2. Divide the class into groups of five to seven students each. Let each group appoint a leader, and under his direction work out together a plan for a discussion on some question suitable for a study group. Reduce this plan to an outline which the leader and participants might keep before them during an actual discussion on the question. Your purpose in this assignment is not to engage in a discussion on the question itself, but merely to devise a plan which might be used in such a discussion. You will have ample opportunity later to engage in actual discussions.
3. If you were planning a discussion on the first, fourth, or tenth questions for decision-making groups as listed on p. 591, what specific subquestions or issues would you want to be sure to include? In what order do you think these issues might best be considered by the group? Why?
4. If you were planning a decision-making discussion on the third, fifth, or ninth subjects in the same list, what information in the nature of facts, figures, etc., would you want the group to have at its disposal? Why would each of these different kinds of information be crucial to an intelligent decision?
5. Remembering that a good question for discussion should be stated briefly, clearly, and objectively, frame a question on each of the following subjects suitable, *(a)* for a study group and *(b)* for a decision-making group.

School drop-outs
The military draft
Space travel
Governmental support of the arts
Civil defense
Safety features in automobiles
Intercollegiate athletics
Business and government
Modern architecture
Urban renewal

6. Take the discussion plan as worked out in Problem 1 above and adapt it to a panel discussion to be held before one or more of the following audiences: the students in your speech course, a women's club, a labor union meeting.
7. State some of the criteria which you think a decision-making group should employ in evaluating proposals for:

A new superhighway between your town and the state capital.

A plan for having the students in your college grade the faculty members on the effectiveness of their teaching.

A law requiring periodic re-examination of each automobile driver's knowledge of traffic laws and driving skill.

Raising the sales tax in your state.

Speaking assignment

1. Divide the class into groups of five students each. Let each group present a symposium on the subject or problem of its choice. One member of the group should act as leader or chairman. It will be his duty to introduce the other speakers, to make appropriate transitional remarks between their speeches, to summarize the discussion at its close, and to preside over a question-and-answer exchange with the audience. The other members of the group may present different aspects of the selected subject; or if they are considering a problem, one speaker may explain what that problem is, and the others present various solutions. Each group should plan to use an entire class period to present its symposium.

Suggestions for further reading

Dean C. Barnlund and Franklyn S. Haiman, *The Dynamics of Discussion* (Boston: Houghton Mifflin Company, 1960), Chapter V, "Organizing Group Thinking."

Rupert L. Cortright and George L. Hinds, *Creative Discussion* (New York: The Macmillan Company, 1959), Chapter III, "The Management of Meetings."

Laura Crowell, *Discussion: Method of Democracy* (Glenview, Illinois: Scott, Foresman and Company, 1963), Chapter VI, "Outlining the Problem-Solving Question," and Chapter VII, "Organizing for an Enlightenment Discussion."

Henry Lee Ewbank, Jr., and J. Jeffery Auer, *Discussion and Debate*, 2nd ed. (New York: Appleton-Century-Crofts, 1951), Chapter XVI, "Organizing and Leading Discussion."

Halbert E. Gulley, *Discussion, Conference, and Group Process* (New York: Holt-Dryden, 1960), Chapter X, "Discussion Patterns."

R. Victor Harnack and Thorrel B. Fest, *Group Discussion: Theory and Technique* (New York: Appleton-Century-Crofts, 1964), Chapter IV, "Problem Solving: The Pattern of Thought."

William S. Howell and Donald K. Smith, *Discussion* (The Macmillan Company, 1956), Chapter IV, "A System of Problem Solving."

CHAPTER THIRTY-THREE

Leading and participating in discussion

Having studied the nature and purpose of discussion and outlined various plans according to which discussions may proceed, you now are ready to consider in detail the role of the leader and of the participant in the discussion process.

THE LEADER'S DUTIES

Even the most carefully developed discussion plan is not a guarantee that the members of the group will be motivated to consider the problem or, if they are, that they will have the skills and attitudes to enable them to reach a wise decision. It is the duty of the leader to stimulate and guide the group in these respects. Specifically, his tasks are six in number: (1) to get the discussion started, (2) to keep it from wandering, (3) to bring out the essential facts, (4) to see that all have an opportunity to participate, (5) to help resolve any conflicts that may arise, and (6) from time to time to survey and summarize the progress that the group is making. Of course, not all of these tasks need to be performed in every discussion, for sometimes—without any guidance from the leader—the group itself will fulfill the required functions. He must, however, stand ready to aid the discussants if needed; and by constantly studying the interplay of opposing views or factions, he must keep in broad perspective the progress of the discussion as a whole.

Get the discussion started

The leader should begin the discussion, as suggested in Chapter 32, by stating the question to be discussed and pointing out its importance, especially as it is related to the audience or to the members of the discussion group. This statement, while brief, should be made with vigor and earnestness, suggesting the vital nature of the subject; and it should be expressed in concrete terms supported by specific instances. It should, moreover, lead into a series of provocative questions designed to pull members of the group into the discussion. You might, for example, ask, "In what way have you, personally, met this problem recently?" Or better, "Bob told me that he ran into this problem in the following way. . . . [Briefly describe.] Have any of you had a similar experience; or, if not, how did your experience differ?" If such questions fail to draw forth discussion, call on individuals by name to relate their experiences or to tell how they analyze the problem. Ask someone for specific information that you know he has: ask the treasurer for a statement of the cash on hand, or the secretary for the size of the membership, or a fraternity man for the attitude of the members of his chapter. Or go to the board and start a list—of causes of the problem, of types of people or groups whom it affects, of terms needing definition, of proposed courses of action, of anything which fits into your discussion outline and calls for enumeration. Curiously enough, people who hesitate to begin a discussion seldom hesitate to add to a list once it has been started.

Still another method is to bring out, at the beginning, one or more extreme points of view on the question. You can relate these views yourself or, better, call on members of the group who hold them. Nothing seems to stir people into active discussion quite so readily as an extreme statement with which to disagree. The danger of this method, of course, is that it may start a verbal battle which leads the discussion astray or stirs up personal animosity. Judiciously used, however, it is an unusually effective "starter."

Keep the discussion from wandering

The tendency of a group to stray from the central issue can be greatly diminished if the leader writes a skeleton outline of the discussion plan on a blackboard. If a blackboard is not available, he may supply each participant with a dittoed or mimeographed copy of the tentative outline. When people can see what points are to be taken up and in what order, they are more likely to follow them systematically. Unless something important has been omitted from the outline, the leader can direct attention to the various items in it, one after another, and thus keep the discussion progressing steadily. Using the outline as a skeletal framework, many leaders also fill in the details on the blackboard as they are brought up in the discussion, thus providing the group with an ever-present visual summary of what has been said or decided. If, then, the discussion takes an irrelevant turn, all the leader usually needs to do is call attention to the irrelevancy and refer again to the outline. This kind of reference is also useful when someone doubles back to a point already covered or jumps ahead to a point not yet discussed. Of course, the leader must be sensible and fair in holding the group to the discussion plan, and sometimes he will find that the fault is in the outline rather than in the speaker who moves away from it. In general, however, he will do well to hold the group to the outline as it has originally been developed.

Bring out the facts

Normally, if the preceding suggestions are followed, the facts needed to solve the problem or to cover the subject of the discussion will be brought out. If the participants are fair minded and well informed and the discussion plan is complete, no special effort beyond that already indicated will be required. Unfortunately, discussion groups do not always function so smoothly and efficiently, and the leader sometimes needs to ensure that important data or views are not ignored and that opinions are not mistaken for proven facts.

When he believes that something important has been overlooked, the leader may tactfully inquire, "Has anyone noticed that . . .?" adding the missing fact himself. Or he may say, "Mary called my attention yesterday to the fact that . . . . Has anyone else noticed this to be true?" It is even better, of course, to ask some individual in the group a question designed to bring out this fact. Similarly, if there seems to be a tendency to dwell on one point of view to the exclusion of an equally important one, the leader may call attention to the neglect by suggesting, "Perhaps we should ask John to express his view of this" or "I have heard this other point of view expressed, too. . . . What do you think of it?"

While the leader should never directly accuse a discussant of twisting facts or making unsupported statements, it is also his duty to make certain that such remarks do not pass unchallenged. He may handle instances of this sort tactfully by asking the speaker for further details or for the evidence on which the statement is based. Thus he may say, "I wonder if you would tell us, Helen, what has led you to this conclusion?" or "Is that a statement of your own opinion, Henry, or have you observed it to be true in actual practice?" By skillful questioning, a good discussion leader can ensure that all points of view are considered, that the important facts are made available, and that the group does not uncritically accept assertions for which supporting evidence is lacking. However, he should, whenever possible, draw the necessary facts and opinions out of the group and do so without appearing to dominate the discussion.

Ensure participation

At times one or two persons in the group may begin to monopolize the conversation. Not infrequently such persons have a great deal to contribute, but there is also a very strong possibility that they will repeat themselves or expand obvious points needlessly. When this occurs, the leader may avoid recognizing a talkative member by not looking directly at him. Or he may call upon other members of the group, by name if necessary, asking them questions which will lead the discussion forward and away from the overworked point or the overtalkative person. In extreme cases it may be necessary for him to suggest in a tactful manner that if the discussion is to be profitable, all must have an opportunity to participate; or he may even have to invoke a limit on the number of times any one member can speak. If the time for the close of the discussion is drawing near, sometimes a statement of that fact will spur into action members who hitherto have remained silent. Remember that while the discussion leader does not have the right to tell the group what to think, he does have the obligation to maintain an atmosphere in which it can think most productively; and such an atmosphere will not be possible unless all feel that they have an equal chance to participate.

Resolve conflict

Vigorous conflict among ideas is essential to productive discussion; but occasionally, on problems concerning which the members of the group have deep feelings or ingrained biases, the conflict becomes emotionalized and bitter. In such cases, the leader usually must act to ease the situation.

Sometimes it is sufficient merely to restate the emotionalized comments in neutral language, and thus bring the discussion back to a more rational or objective level. If this fails, the leader may tactfully point out that unless the discussion is kept fact centered and rational a wise or workable decision cannot be reached. In cases where conflict persists and opposing factions seem unable or unwilling to compromise their views, he can call for a vote and ask the group to abide by a majority decision on the disputed matter. And finally, he may even decide that for the good of all it would be advisable to adjourn the discussion for a period of hours or days and to tackle the problem again later when tempers have had a chance to cool. It is surprising how often such a cooling-off period re-establishes friendly relations and a willingness to attack the difference anew. This kind of heat-reducing interim has, in fact, been employed frequently in labor-management negotiations.

Provide summaries

Often a group becomes so concerned with the details of a problem or so engrossed in the consideration of one or two isolated points that it fails to realize how much ground it has covered in its discussion of the subject or how much yet remains to be done. For this reason, the leader, from time to time, should summarize the progress which the group has made, recalling the matters that have already been agreed upon and pointing to the major differences of opinion that remain to be solved. Such summaries, obviously, should reflect what the group has said or decided, and not what the leader himself thinks about the subject. Moreover, the members always should have an opportunity to correct or to add to the summary as the leader presents it. Without such summaries injected into the discussion at appropriate points, it is almost impossible for a group to keep aware of its progress.

At the conclusion of the discussion, the leader—either alone or with the aid of the group as a whole—should summarize the discussion in its entirety, making clear exactly what has been agreed upon and specifying any problems or disagreements that remain to be resolved. This final summary, like the internal summaries made earlier, should reflect the conclusions of the group rather than those of the leader, and should give attention to all important points of view. In addition, it may remind the members of the methods which they have chosen to put their decision into effect and single out such provisions as are necessary to make sure that the decision is carried out.

THE PARTICIPANTS' DUTIES

Evaluate the opinions of others

One of the greatest differences between a public speech and a group discussion lies in the obvious fact that in the latter, one person does not do all the talking. Each member will do some speaking, but during the greater part of the time he will be listening. While you are listening, your principal task will be to evaluate what the speaker is saying so that you may weigh his opinions against your own and against those expressed by other members of the group. By asking yourself the following questions, you will be able to make your judgments more thorough and systematic:

1. *Do the training and experience of the speaker qualify him to express an authoritative opinion?* Is he an expert on the subject under discussion?

2. *Is his statement based on first-hand knowledge?* Did he observe the evidence, or is he merely reporting a rumor?

3. *Is his opinion prejudiced?* Is it influenced by personal interest? Does he stand to profit personally from some decision the group may reach?

4. *Does he usually state his opinions frankly?* Does he reveal all the facts known to him, or is he in the habit of concealing facts unfavorable to his cause?

5. *Are the facts or opinions he presents consistent with human experience?* Do they sound plausible? Could they reasonably be true?

6. *Are the facts or opinions he presents consistent with one another?* If two reports contradict each other, which seems more substantial and trustworthy?

7. *What weight will other members of the group give to this person's opinion?* Is his prestige so great that the group will agree with him in the face of conflicting evidence, or is he so little respected that he will not be believed unless someone else supports his opinion?

If you ask yourself these questions about each participant and his contribution, you will be able to evaluate his remarks more accurately, and also to reach more easily and objectively a decision concerning the problem as a whole.

When to take part in discussion

There is no dogmatic answer to the frequently asked question, "When should I talk and when should I keep quiet?" In general, the longer you have been a member of a group, the freer you may be with your comments. Newcomers do well to speak rarely and only when they have something really contributive to say. In most cases, however, the following suggestions will apply:

Speak directly to the point. If what you have to say does not bear directly on the discussion at the moment, keep quiet. Too often someone digresses to discuss another point which is far removed and thus impedes the progress of the group. No matter how important an idea may seem to you, wait until the particular matter under discussion is settled before you shift to a different one. Remember that only one thing must be considered at a time.

Speak when you have a report to present. Frequently reports are made to a group by officials or committee chairmen. The treasurer's report, for instance, is an important part of a business meeting. The purpose of such reports usually is either to present information or to suggest some action; sometimes, of course, these purposes are combined. In any case, the report should be brief and to the point and should emphasize at the end, in summary fashion, those facts or conclusions which are important to the group.

Speak, of course, when you are asked a direct question. Do not, however, give a long-winded reply. Unless you can contribute a new point of view or additional information, cut your answer short.

Speak when you have an intelligent comment or suggestion to make. Frequently some aspect of the subject has been neglected, or some important idea has slipped by unnoticed. Even when you have no tangible information upon this particular point, a brief comment or question may stimulate others to contribute the needed information.

Speak when you can clarify a point which another participant has badly muddled. Quite often someone else may make an important point but express it so vaguely that the group fails to appreciate its significance. If you can tactfully make the point clear, you will have performed a valuable service.

Speak when you can correct an error. In correcting an error, you must exercise a great deal of tact to avoid starting a fruitless argument. If the point is important, however, and you know the other discussant is mistaken, by all means make the correction. If you are courteous and modest, avoiding any suggestion of officiousness, you should be able to correct the error without offense.

Speak when you can offer added information upon the question. No one person knows everything. Only on the combined information of the entire group can a sound judgment be based. If, therefore, you can illuminate the problem by an apt illustration, if you can cite accurate figures bearing upon it, or if you can relay the testimony of someone outside the group, by all means do so. Be very sure of one thing: that what you say has a direct bearing upon the point at issue.

Remember that nothing is so disconcerting as to have someone inject information which is entirely beside the point.

Speak when you can ask an intelligent question. If you are in doubt about something and are fairly sure that others are also in doubt, find out about the matter at once; do not allow a decision to be made until your doubt is resolved. Obviously, you should not ask questions continually, but a question asked at the proper moment will often save a great deal of muddled thinking and discussion. Moreover, when the discussion has wandered, a question will frequently bring it back to the main issue. Finally, whether you are the leader or only one of the discussants, ask questions to bring out the facts behind unsupported opinions.

Speak when you can inject humor into an otherwise dry discussion. This suggestion needs to be followed with extreme caution. Once in a while, however, a little humor will enliven a tired group and quicken the pace of the discussion. Moreover, if strong disagreement should reach the point of personal animosity, a little good-natured humor will often serve to relieve the tension that has built up.

How to take part in discussion

Delivery. Your manner of speaking should, of course, vary according to the type of discussion being conducted. Informal groups permit an easier and more familiar manner than do public panels or formal business meetings. Members of a panel or a symposium also must talk loudly enough to be heard by the audience as well as by the other discussants. In radio and television discussion, the participants should be seated equally distant from the microphone to help ensure that their voices will go out over the airways with comparable volume and force. The comments made in Chapter 30 about microphone technic, especially those about rustling paper and tapping the table, apply even more to discussion than to single speeches since the more people there are, the more chance there is for inadvertent noise and other distractions.

Presentation of your point of view. Participation in discussion should always have one basic aim: to help the group think objectively and creatively in analyzing the subject or solving the problem at hand. To this end, it is generally desirable that you organize your contribution not assertively or persuasively in an attempt to win other people to your point of view, but rather in the fashion that will best stimulate others to think for themselves. Therefore, instead of stating your conclusion first and then supplying the arguments in favor of it, let your contribution recount how and why you came to think as you do. Begin by stating the nature of the problem as you see it; outline the various hypotheses or solutions that occurred to you as you were thinking about it; tell why you rejected certain of them; and only after all this, state your own opinion and explain the reasons that support it. In this way, you give other members of the group a chance to check the accuracy and completeness of your thinking on the matter and to point out any deficiencies or fallacies that may not have occurred to you. At the same time, you will also be making your contribution in the most objective and rational manner possible.

Sincerity and objectivity. Above all, remember that a serious discussion is no showplace for prima donnas or an arena for verbal combatants. When you have something to say, speak modestly and sincerely, and always maintain an objective attitude. Accept criticism with dignity and treat disagreement with an open mind. Your purpose is not primarily to get your own view accepted, but to work out with the other members of the group the best possible choice or decision that all of you together can devise.

SAMPLE DISCUSSION

In the following discussion, broadcast over Station WGN in Chicago on June 1, 1952, James H. McBurney and Irving J. Lee, teachers of speech; Maynard Krueger, an economist; and Herbert Thelen, a psychologist, considered the uses and limitations of the discussion method as a way of arriving at collective choices and decisions.

WHAT CAN TALK SETTLE?[1]

Moderator: James H. McBurney
Panelists: Maynard Krueger, Herbert Thelen, and Irving J. Lee

MR. McBURNEY: Gentlemen, I think it is most appropriate that we raise the question: "What can talk settle?" here on this Reviewing Stand. We have been conducting weekly discussions for some eighteen years, and we frequently meet the criticism: What do you ever settle? One letter puts it this way: "You talk, talk, talk and talk some more; blah, blah, blah, but you never settle anything and nothing ever happens." How would you answer that kind of criticism, Krueger?

MR. KRUEGER: I would say, McBurney, that if talk were all blah, it isn't

[1]Printed by permission, The Northwestern University Reviewing Stand, Evanston, Illinois.

going to settle anything, but talk doesn't have to be blah, and an awful lot of talk is not blah, and that by and large the world is suffering more from lack of talk than it is from too much talk.

MR. McBURNEY: Thelen, what would you say on that criticism?

MR. THELEN: I would say the man shows the criticism is unjust because he has already reached one conclusion from the talk, namely, talk is all blah, blah, blah. The question I would have is whether there are other conclusions in addition to that one being reached.

MR. LEE: Sometimes the general feeling that talk doesn't get anywhere comes because the man who listens starts out by expecting simple answers, and easy solutions to great big problems; and when, after twenty or thirty minutes of talk, you don't have one of these nice package solutions, he has the feeling that the talk didn't settle anything.

MR. McBURNEY: Of course, there are a number of things we do know about the outcomes of discussion. How applicable they are to the kind of program we conduct here every week is an open question, but we do know that the attitudes of people who participate in discussion change significantly; and we do know, secondly, that the dispersion of attitudes is significantly reduced as a result of discussion. In other words, we know that people get closer together. And we know, thirdly, that they reach a consensus or approach a consensus at least on attitudes significantly superior to those held at the outset of the discussion, if you can judge by the opinion of experts. I object very strongly to the notion that talk in the form of discussion is futile. Things do happen.

MR. KRUEGER: I would say, McBurney, as a dean of a school of speech, you probably have to say something like that. On the other hand, I think it's also true that the whole educational process—not quite the whole of it, but most of the educational process—is conducted on the assumption that communication, verbal and written communication between people, can result in their arriving at some joint conclusions as to what it's proper to think and what it's proper to do.

MR. THELEN: I think a special problem for programs of this sort is that the people who write the letters are eavesdropping on a conversation rather than taking part in it, and I think this factor of participation and the quality of it make it different.

MR. McBURNEY: As a matter of fact, the conclusions I reported apply to a situation in which there is, I take it, a little more participation than listeners to a program of this sort would engage in.

MR. LEE: I shouldn't want to take our correspondent's point of view as a means by which we generalize about all kinds of talking, because it seems to me that away from the radio studio and the microphone there are all sorts of occasions when the opportunity to talk with other people provides a protection against making a fool of yourself. That is, a supervisor, a boss, an administrator who has a plan or a program or who thinks he has a way of functioning, will discover one of the most useful ways he can protect himself against acting foolishly is to find a group of people who will listen to him, who will check on the very conclusions and points he makes.

MR. KRUEGER: You mean, then, in the talk process, the talker at any given time is actually getting a service performed for him by the people who consent to talk with him.

MR. LEE: Krueger, you phrase what I think is one of the ultimate justifications or one of the ultimate reasons why a man ought to look for such opportunities. Namely, here is a way to see whether or not the wisdom he has arrived at joins with or goes along with the collective wisdom.

MR. McBURNEY: Of course, when you ask the question, "What can talk settle?" you really have a somewhat ambiguous term in that word "settle." What do you mean by settle? How do you have to settle things by talk in order to make talk useful, Lee?

MR. LEE: You, I take it, are raising a kind of distinction between talking and acting: that is, as if talk merely leads to more talk and then you stop and engage in some sort of function. I am not sure that putting the problem in those terms clarifies it. Thelen, you ought to give us your view about that distinction. Do you see it that way? Let me open it by saying for myself, I don't see it that way. I know of no social action which doesn't require talk in the very process of working something out.

MR. THELEN: I think you are putting talk in the context of a total experience in which talking is only one kind of action that goes on, that basically our problems are always ones of communicating experience and talk plays a part in doing this. I think the important thing that talk does more explicitly than any other form of action is to allow people to know they are at the same place or have the same feelings or start from the same points of view so that they can then coordinate their activities.

MR. KRUEGER: When you say, Thelen, talk is one of the means people have of communicating with each other, wouldn't you be willing to go a little further than that and say that talk is one of the most important ways of communicating?

MR. THELEN: Surely, because of its greater specificity. That, any classroom teacher knows. There are a lot of other means, too, such as showing a person how to do it himself, sometimes without saying a word about it. A very effective science-teaching method, for example, involves carrying through a demonstration completely silently and then discussing with the class what were the points one was trying to demonstrate, but the talk does help as a guide to reflection and drawing conclusions.

MR. McBURNEY: Let me ask, if I may, a number of somewhat more specific questions in this area. I am trying to find out how you have to settle things in order to make talk significant. Do you have to reach an agreement in order to have a significant outcome?

MR. LEE: Sometimes, I should suppose, if you didn't have an agreement as a result of thirty minutes of talk, that would be useful. It's so easy to approach a problem with the feeling that the little answer I come up with is enough, and it may be that the most educational, the most therapeutic thing that could happen to a participant is to realize that maybe we have to disagree at present in terms of the way we have experienced or defined the problems we have to face.

MR. KRUEGER: But it is quite possible for people to disagree about what ought to be done. They may continue to disagree about what ought to be done but, nevertheless, agree that having gone through this process of deciding what ought to be done, they will go ahead and do this until they change their minds about it. So if the action to be taken is regarded as of a temporary character, if it is not a death sentence that is being passed, then it becomes quite possible for people, as a result of talk, to clarify their differences and yet to have sufficiently substantial unity of action for all the practical purposes that men face.

MR. THELEN: I agree with you on that. I think that one of the problems of talk is that there are certain kinds of talk we don't have that we should have. For example, a group can agree that it has no confidence in any ideas so far suggested instead of simply fighting over the alternatives that have been suggested until somebody gives way, but once a group knows it has no particular confidence in the alternatives suggested, then it can begin to raise the question of why it doesn't have confidence. What could they do to get more confidence in these actions or some other action?

MR. McBURNEY: I should like to suggest, in answer to my own question, that there are many areas in which talk can be conducted without reaching any agreement, and conducted most profitably. If you reach an agreement to disagree, you have a significant agreement—if that agreement is reached in mutual understanding. I think *understanding* is one of the more important outcomes of talk, and I would hope that such understanding or contribution to such understanding would be one of the more important outcomes of discussions of the kind we are having here today.

MR. LEE: Think of a business situation in which you have a series of supervisors or foremen or office managers. His mere adherence to the usefulness of discussion will move him to bring people together to tell them all sorts of things that, without the discussion, he and they may never hear about or learn about. In other words, the mere recognition that all talk isn't designed to settle something is important. It is often designed to let you know what I am doing, let you know what I am thinking.

MR. KRUEGER: I would wager, Lee, if it were permitted, that when anybody raises the question: "What can talk settle?" he is thinking primarily about problem solving. That is, he is thinking primarily of situations in which there is a problem to which a solution is sought and it is expected that out of the talk process will come some sort of solution to the problem. Now, the solution to the problem may be to decide that the problem isn't what they thought it was. The solution may be to decide that there really isn't any problem by the time they get through talking. The therapeutic value of the talk itself may have caused the problem to disappear, but there are a great many tough problems that don't disappear simply because people talk about them, and where it's reasonable to expect that out of the talk process, there will come an action solution to a problem.

MR. THELEN: I am particularly impressed by that point, Krueger, the notion that while a group doesn't seem to agree on the things that it was trying to agree on, it is actually reaching agreement on other things that are much more important to it. I would like to throw in a little example here that I happened to bring along with me for this occasion. Consider a couple of club women, for example, on a nominating committee, and somebody suggests, "Well, how about Mrs. Smith? She would make a fine president." So the dowager in the group says, "Such a lovely person, so completely devoted to her family." And somebody else says, "Yes, and so sweet; why, she is on good terms with all the right people." Now, it looks as though they have reached an agreement that this is a fine person, but actually, I would submit, what they have reached an agreement on is that she is not going to be the next president.

MR. McBURNEY: Gentlemen, however futile or efficacious talk is in resolving human problems, what are the alternatives to it?

MR. KRUEGER: Let me take the first crack at that, McBurney, because I am not an expert in this field at all. I am strictly a lay practitioner. It seems to me —what the experts here leave of me when they get through, I don't know— but it seems to me that in the broad civilizing process that has gone on among men for a long period of time, the heart of the business is that men learn to settle their problems by discussion rather than by what seems to me to be the major alternative to settling problems by discussion, that is, trying to settle them by clouting each other over the head. The civilizing process consists to a very considerable extent in developing our ability to settle problems by talk rather than by sticking bayonets in people's backs.

MR. McBURNEY: I personally agree with that. I think that's the ultimate alternative.

MR. LEE: I don't find any point or anything in what you said, Krueger, that would lead any expert to take issue, whether at this table or any other. Quite apart from its civilizing influence, I again go back to that notion that there is in many minds perhaps more wisdom than in any one mind; and if you don't have talk, then you have solutions imposed by individuals. You have one man in the family. You have one man in the state, and you have one man on the team; and if you don't have talk, one of the alternatives, to me, is action by individuals without concern for the people at the receiving end of the action.

MR. KRUEGER: In this sense then, Lee, political democracy consists essentially of government by talk, whereas a totalitarian setup minimizes the role of discussion in the government process.

MR. THELEN: I would have a small difference on that, that it isn't so much government by talk, but government in terms of the data that are necessary to reach good decisions. Some of these data have to be gotten by talk, but I think there are other ways to get data, too, in the surveys of various kinds. Even examination of objective facts, like how many people go to what kinds of movies, is also involved.

MR. LEE: In a dictatorship or in any fascist or other monolithic society there is talk, but it's only one way. I suppose the peculiar character of talk in a democratic community is that it is two-way, that even if an individual makes a decision, someone—unless we feel that talk is useless—has the opportunity to raise a question. And when you raise a question, then you introduce talk, and you make settlements broader. You make them responsible in terms of many people.

MR. McBURNEY: All of this leads me to ask: What are the conditions and requisites for significant talk? In other words, Lee, how should we talk with people in order to get something accomplished?

MR. LEE: Well, I suppose the quickest beginning point at that question is to say we have to learn to talk together. We all learn to verbalize. We all learn to wave our lower jaws, but, it seems to me, there is a very special kind of skill which requires certain kinds of attitudes to learn to talk with people productively.

MR. KRUEGER: Learning to discuss then, you say, is something more than simply learning to talk.

MR. LEE: That's right. The child can do it one way. Now, it is only as we grow up and learn a different set of skills that we get this thing which is talking between and with people.

MR. McBURNEY: Do you agree with that, Thelen?

MR. THELEN: Yes, I think we are seeing the beginning of the development of the technology of social problem solving in which talk will be the basic instrument of communication. This technology is going to have included in it such skills as the skills of knowing what kind of data a group needs to reach a decision at any given time, the skills of knowing what the group is talking about, what it says it's talking about—instead of something else—the skills of knowing how to break down a problem so that the first action step you take can test what the next step ought to be, and that kind of thing. I think healthy progress is being made, but we have a long way to go.

MR. LEE: And I should also add that there are all sorts of other skills we need. Think, for example, of learning how to listen. Any kind of survey you make of any controversy between small groups of people reveals—or at least, those we have made reveal—that people make a stab at listening. That is, we hear with one ear, but we aren't giving the man full, undivided, receptive attention.

It takes some skill, and it takes learning to understand, not merely to hear the words a man says, but to listen with a view to understanding what he is trying to say.

MR. McBURNEY: Now, you have given one requisite of significant talk which might be summed up as a more or less conscious methodology in which you have had some experience. Are there any other requisites of good talk?

MR. KRUEGER: I think there are, McBurney. At least, there is one that I think I can mention. Apart from these skills that Lee and Thelen have mentioned, and knowing the methodology of productive discussion, it seems to me there is something a bit less tangible than that. I don't know that there are any formal ways of teaching it to people, but I don't see any reason for expecting that talk would develop into discussion of the problem-solving sort unless you are able to assume a simple elementary kind of honesty on the part of people who are engaging in the discussion. That is, if somebody talks with somebody else, and there is no relationship between what he says and what he really thinks, then I see no reason for that kind of talk to arrive at—any kind of talk to arrive at—any kind of productive decision. Therefore, it seems to me that simple, ordinary bourgeois honesty of the sort which I think the totalitarian systematically repudiates—both the fascists and communists—is a prerequisite for expecting talk of the two-way variety to result in any kind of satisfactory settlement of any problem.

MR. THELEN: I think the problem of honesty, however, has to be hit at two levels. There is the level of deliberately saying something other than what you mean—this is that elementary kind of thing. But many times one is in a situation where he says something which at that moment he believes and means, but shortly after he realizes he didn't mean that at all. There are all kinds of conditions in groups that lead to this kind of thing happening.

MR. LEE: And another one of these conditions for good talk which is not a denial of this one, but perhaps a different one, is that we need to learn a kind of patience, a kind of capacity to sit with a tough problem.

MR. McBURNEY: With the world burning up around you, you want patience?

MR. LEE: Yes, I do. With the world burning up, we need the best kind of reflection and the best kind of looking at the problem, because the thing that worries me most when people talk together is the kind of impatient leader that says: Let's get done with the talk and do something.

MR. McBURNEY: This impatient leader may face deadlines of all sorts; that is, the work of the world has to get done, and you can't sit around and talk indefinitely. We get hungry. We meet all sorts of practical emergencies.

MR. LEE: McBurney, I have at least one answer to that. It would be very useful if sometimes administrators foresaw the kinds of problems they have. I sometimes wonder whether one of the most useful tactics of the administrator is to indicate that a deadline exists as a way of preventing the kind of patient cross-talk that I want more of.

MR. THELEN: Right. The amount of energy that gets spent in trying to get out of a mess that could have been prevented with much less energy earlier is phenomenal.

MR. LEE: That's my point.

MR. KRUEGER: I could give you an illustration, however, that doesn't quite check with your description. Last year when the Administration in Washington sent over to Capitol Hill way in advance of the end of the fiscal year a string of budgetary messages, Congress got to work on the appropriation bills, and on some of the major ones, it was more than four months after the expiration of the fiscal year; that is, four months of the next fiscal year had already passed, before Congress had got through with its discussion, so-called, of the appropriation bills. Now, that wasn't a problem of the administrator. There was a problem of the policy-making branch of a government getting itself organized in such a way that it could get its talking done in time.

MR. LEE: And it becomes a technique or a problem of planning the talk rather than of putting the onus on the difficulty of getting a decision. In other words, if we are dealing with a tremendous problem—and budgetary ones are tremendous, I take it—then it may be that we have to take a brand new attitude toward talk and say if it takes three times as long, let us set up the machinery so that we have three times as much time. I suspect that much of that discussion that went on so long was not discussion over the dollars and cents, but discussion of the policy that should have been made long before anybody talked about spending the dollars and cents.

MR. KRUEGER: That's undoubtedly true. That's why I called it "so-called" discussion.

MR. LEE: I should like to offer as a kind of generalization, maybe, that talk which ends in a hurry, with quick, packaged conclusions, may in the long run create as many problems as it is supposed to solve.

MR. McBURNEY: I would like to ask another question in this area. How expert does a man have to be to engage in significant talk, Lee? How much do you have to know?

MR. LEE: I met some people recently who were a little afraid to talk about the steel crisis and the Korean problem and so on because they said that the only people who really can talk about these are the people who are responsible for making decisions. I would like to tell those people that you ought to engage in talk, and you ought to engage in talk at the level at which you are able to engage in the discussion, but you mustn't pretend or presume to come to conclusions that go beyond your experience or knowledge and ability with respect to the problem. The talk may be at a low level in terms of solutions, but it seems to me there are still values in getting people to do the talking.

MR. McBURNEY: Of course, if you are dealing with a problem which requires a solution at a fairly high intellectual level and the people engaging in the talk are essentially uninformed, how patient does one have to be?

MR. KRUEGER: May I make a suggestion on that, McBurney? My opinion is that when most of the questions of policy that come out, on which people feel an answer has to be given right away, we are in a hurry to get an answer. There is nothing substantially wrong with the administrator going ahead and giving an answer to the question—the president of the steel corporation, the President of the United States—provided the answer given by the experts to the question is then subject to review. Now, if an election comes up again in four years, if there is an opportunity to make what they call a post-audit and decide whether they want more of the same kind of action or less of it, then I see no objection to not having quite so much of a pre-audit of their actions. In other words, if the action that is taken is regarded as a continuing part of the discussion process and is subject to criticism, I think the overwhelming bulk of the population is possessed of the capacities for making the simple kind of judgment as to whether they want more or less of the sort of thing that has been going on.

MR. McBURNEY: We have been in the process here of spelling out some of the requisites and conditions of good talk. I am sure none of you men would wish to take this as a definitive list, but perhaps it will be helpful. I should like to introduce some applications if I may. How about political talk? We are in for a lot of it in the next few months, Krueger. Do you think it will do any good? Will it change any votes? Will it bring any enlightenment?

MR. KRUEGER: Since I think that the basic questions that are shaking the world apart . . .

MR. McBURNEY: Of course, you have done a lot of that talking yourself.

MR. KRUEGER: I have done my share. Since I think that those basic questions that are shaking the world apart, like economic stability and the war and peace questions, are questions that have to be solved through the political process, my only hope for getting them solved is through political talk. However, I think there is a big distinction between the kind of political talk that goes on in the heat of an electoral battle which is an infighting sort of job, the sort you are going to see during the next several months, and the kind of political talk that goes on during, say, the three and a half years that are not years of campaigning. I see far more that is productive in the political discussions between campaigns than I do in the political discussions during campaigns.

MR. THELEN: But those political campaigns serve a very useful purpose, don't they, in getting people wrought-up and involved and in becoming sensitive to issues that during the three and a half years when there is no particular pressure one is not sensitive to, nor even aware of? So I would see the hot political campaign as a shot in the arm to being a citizen at the national level, and becoming identified with large questions. We probably all need this.

MR. McBURNEY: Some people suggested, you know, that President Truman talked himself through the last election and that Mr. Dewey withdrew from talk at his own peril. Is there anything in that analysis, Krueger?

MR. KRUEGER: I think there may be in the sense that he showed that he was a vigorous fighter by his talk. The number of whistle stops and the vigor of the adjectives used showed a lot of people that Mr. Truman was really a candidate, which some of them might not otherwise have thought. It also probably meant that some people who were inclined to vote for him, but might have stayed home, instead, actually turned out and got their vote cast.

MR. LEE: There was a brief indication a minute or two ago that maybe talk doesn't change votes. Well, it may be that a Republican campaigning may not bring many Democrats across the line, but campaigning does tend to keep the boys who are already sold in line. That is, if you eliminated talk by any standard bearer, there would be great danger that you would lose the people already committed to any political party.

MR. McBURNEY: May I ask another question? Do you think the steel crisis is an evidence of a breakdown in talk, Krueger?

MR. KRUEGER: I would say, McBurney, that it's an evidence that there hasn't been enough talk going on on the question. This country has got a basic question of what its policy ought to be with regard to the continuity of operations in industry that it cannot afford to have stopped. I haven't heard much sensible talk about that. For my money, I would look forward to a period of eight or ten years of serious discussion of this question with the President acting on it, with Congress acting on it, with the Supreme Court acting on it, all their decisions being taken as temporary; and if after ten years of public discussion of that question, we could arrive at something like a policy for this country, I would consider that success.

MR. McBURNEY: You are really placing a premium on patience, I would say. Of course, I could ask, too, about the Korean situation. Is that an evidence of a breakdown of talk? What do you think of that?

MR. LEE: No, McBurney, it seems to me it has taken a long time, and the issues are complicated and involved, and it may be that what we have in Korea is a slightly different version of the discussion process. It seems to me you have to make a distinction between a situation in which people meet with a view to getting an answer and the kind of power political situation that we have in Korea in which each of the participants has already decided what is the answer. But even in that kind of stalemate situation, I still wouldn't give up on talk because the very process tells the participants how far the other man is likely to go. I still wouldn't give up. Indeed, I would counsel patience on Korea even though every impulse is to cut it off and do something else. . . .

ANNOUNCER: I am sorry to interrupt, but our time is up.

Problems

1. Study carefully the sample discussion printed above. What particular devices, if any, did the leader use to stimulate the discussion and get it

started? Was he called upon at any time to keep the discussion from wandering or to resolve emotionalized conflict? Did he have to act to bring out needed facts or neglected points of view? Did he summarize frequently enough? Were his summaries fair and comprehensive? If you had been leading this discussion, what, if anything, would you have done differently? Why?

2. Select from this printed discussion the participant whom you believe best exemplifies the qualities of a good discussant and the participant who seems to exhibit these qualities least. Defend your choices.

3. Evaluate the question with which this discussion deals? Is it too broad or too narrow? Is it suited to the participants and to the audience? Is it clearly and fairly stated?

4. Assume that you are leading a discussion on some subject or problem of current interest. Frame several tactful questions or comments which you might use if some participant were (*a*) monopolizing the discussion, (*b*) remaining silent, (*c*) wandering from the point, (*d*) failing to back up his opinions with facts, (*e*) making comments that threaten to result in emotionalized conflict.

5. What, in your opinion, is the best way to become a good discussion leader? What part does a knowledge of discussion method and the rules printed in books and manuals play in the process? How important is actual practice in leading? Under what conditions should this practice be carried on? How and by whom should it be evaluated or criticized? What may one learn from observing good discussion leaders in action?

6. Write a paper on one of the following topics: (*a*) The Ideal Discussion Leader, or (*b*) The Ideal Discussion Participant. Let your paper reflect the fact that you have read extensively in the sources suggested at the close of this chapter or the two preceding ones.

Discussion assignments

1. Divide the class into groups of five or six students each. Let each group select a leader; and on a topic approved by the instructor, plan and conduct a study or decision-making discussion that consumes at least one and preferably two or three class periods. If the discussion extends beyond one class period, select a new leader for each succeeding meeting. Evaluate the leader and participants according to the recommendations and criteria set forth in this chapter. Or as a variation, let the group have an opportunity to evaluate itself after the discussion is over. (Since these discussions are not to be overheard by other members of the class, they may be conducted simultaneously in different rooms or in the different corners of a large room.)

2. After each group has discussed its chosen subject in private for the time allotted, let it rework the material for a thirty-minute panel discussion to be conducted before the entire class. Such reworking will entail two principal

tasks: (1) selecting from the discussion as a whole those parts or aspects which are most interesting or important, and (2) adapting the selected portions to the specific audience at hand.

Suggestions for further reading

Dean C. Barnlund, "Consistency of Emergent Leadership in Groups with Changing Tasks and Members," *Speech Monographs*, XXIX (March 1962), 45-52.

Robert S. Cathcart, "Leadership as a Secondary Function in Group Discussion," *Speech Teacher*, XI (September 1962), 221-226.

Milton Dickens, "'Spread-of-Participation' in Discussion," *Speech Monographs*, XXII (March 1955), 28-30.

R. Victor Harnack and Thorrel B. Fest, *Group Discussion: Theory and Technique* (New York: Appleton-Century-Crofts, 1964), Chapter XI, "Becoming a Better Participant."

Franklyn S. Haiman, *Group Leadership and Democratic Action* (Boston: Houghton Mifflin Company, 1951).

Franklyn S. Haiman, "A Measurement of Authoritarian Attitudes toward Discussion Leadership," *Quarterly Journal of Speech*, XLI (April 1955), 140-144.

Franklyn S. Haiman, Gale E. Jensen, and William E. Utterback, "The Specialization of Roles and Functions in a Group," *Quarterly Journal of Speech*, XLIII (April 1957), 165-174.

Irving J. Lee, *How to Talk with People* (New York: Harper, 1952).

Jack Matthews and A. W. Bendig, "Measuring the Outcome of Discussion," *Speech Monographs*, XXII (March 1955), 39-42.

Calvin D. Mortensen, "Should the Discussion Group Have an Assigned Leader?" *Speech Teacher*, XV (January 1966), 34-41.

Stanley F. Paulson, "Pressures Toward Conformity in Group Discussion," *Quarterly Journal of Speech*, XLIV (February 1958), 50-55.

Thomas M. Scheidel and Laura Crowell, "Idea Development in Small Discussion Groups," *Quarterly Journal of Speech*, L (April 1964), 140-145.

William E. Utterback, "The Influence of Style of Moderation on the Outcomes of Discussion," *Quarterly Journal of Speech*, XLIV (April 1958), 149-152.

William E. Utterback and Wallace C. Fotheringham, "Experimental Studies of Motivated Group Discussion," *Speech Monographs*, XXV (November 1958), 268-277.

Richard R. Wischmeier, "Group and Leader-Centered Leadership," *Speech Monographs*, XXII (March 1955), 43-48.

CHAPTER THIRTY-FOUR

Parliamentary procedure

The formality with which a deliberative body proceeds depends upon its nature, traditions, and purposes. Legislative assemblies follow detailed and somewhat complicated rules, while many informal groups employ very few, if any. Organizations which have more than ten or twelve members, however, usually find it advisable to transact business according to the principles of parliamentary procedure. The detailed rules of parliamentary procedure may be found in such manuals as *Robert's Rules of Order Revised.*[1] Our purpose here is to present only some of the basic principles—those which are useful even in relatively informal situations.

If you wish to participate properly in meetings of groups which observe the principles of parliamentary procedure, you should know these principles and how to apply them. This is especially true if you must assume the duties of chairman. The various rules or principles will seem clearer and more understandable if you recognize the reasons behind them. They have as their objective the furtherance of the aims of the group, the implementation of the will of the majority, the protection of the rights of minority members, and the efficient expedition of business. Applied knowledgeably and legitimately, then, these principles will enable you to protect your interests and to guard against misuses of parliamentary procedure by unscrupulous individuals.

THE CHAIRMAN

If the president of an organization has already been chosen, he automatically becomes the group's presiding officer. When no such

[1](Glenview, Illinois: Scott, Foresman and Company, 1951).

officer has been selected, the first order of business is to elect a chairman from the membership by majority vote.

The most important duties of the chairman are to preserve order and to see that all parties receive a fair hearing. In order to ensure that only one person speaks at a time, the chairman must recognize members before they begin their remarks. In addition, he customarily has certain appointive powers, including the naming of committees. In informal groups the chairman may enter the discussion; in more formal bodies, however, he usually presides without voicing his opinions on the subjects considered and does not vote unless the vote is by ballot or his vote would clearly affect the outcome, as in making or breaking a tie.

ORDER OF BUSINESS

Nearly every organization has a regular order of business which it follows at each meeting. But when no such predetermined order exists, a group may use the following plan or such parts of this plan as may fit its purposes:

1. Minutes of the last meeting—to be read, corrected when necessary, and approved.
2. Reports of officers and of standing committees.
3. Reports of special committees.
4. Consideration of unfinished business from the previous meeting as indicated in the minutes.
5. Consideration of new items of business.
6. Determination of the time and place of the next meeting, unless this is regularly established.
7. Adjournment.

Sometimes a question for discussion is so important that it is made a special order of business for the next meeting. When this is done, the question is taken up immediately after committee reports, and all other questions are omitted or postponed. Occasionally an important question arises, the settlement of which cannot wait until the next meeting, nor even for its regular place in the order of business for that meeting. In such cases a question may be considered in advance of its regular place in the order of business by the vote of two thirds of the group.

THE SUBJECT FOR DISCUSSION[2]

Introducing the subject

At times, plans are made in advance to take up a question for discussion; for example, a question may be made a special order for the next meeting, or it may be referred to a committee with instructions to report and make recommendations at a specified meeting. Usually, however, a subject is introduced for consideration simply by a member's making a motion in regard to it when new business is in order. Such a motion (a main motion) is made by saying, "Mr. Chairman, I move that . . . " In order to prevent consideration of a proposal that interests only one member, the rules require a second person to support the proposal by seconding it. To second a motion you say, "Mr. Chairman, I second the motion," or "I second the motion."

Discussion of a new subject—except when relaxation of the rules may be in the interests of the group—must be withheld until the motion regarding it is made and seconded. In any case, when a main motion has properly come before the group (is pending), no other main motion may be considered until the pending motion is disposed of.

Dividing or amending a motion

A motion up for consideration may be modified in two principal ways: by dividing the question and by amending.

Dividing the question. Sometimes a motion contains two or more parts, each of which can stand alone, although they are related to the same subject. It can be divided into questions to be discussed and voted on separately through the motion to divide the question. In making this motion, the member should state specifically the manner in which the motion should be divided. Each part of the divided motion must be sufficiently independent of the others to be carried out if the other parts are not adopted. If a motion contains several parts or resolutions which relate to different subjects, it must be divided upon the request of one member.

Amending the motion. There are times when some part of the motion is undesirable or not clearly stated. The motion then may be

[2]You will note that in this treatment of "the subject for discussion," attention is focused primarily on the manner of introducing and handling a *main* motion. There are other kinds of motions—for example, subsidiary, incidental, and privileged motions. For information about other kinds of motions, see *Robert's Rules of Order Revised* and the table of parliamentary motions on pages 620-621 of this chapter.

changed—for example, by striking out or adding certain words. Any such action requires a motion to amend, which must itself be seconded and passed by a majority vote before it can alter the wording of the original motion. The motion to amend may itself be amended or discussed, but it must be voted on before the main question can be decided. If the motion to amend is adopted, the discussion will return to the original motion *as amended;* if the amending motion fails, the discussion will return to the original motion *as made.*

A motion to amend must be germane; that is, it must be on the same subject as the original motion, even though it may conflict with the original motion's purpose entirely. In addition, the amending motion must embody a real change. Merely to change the original motion from an affirmative to a negative statement is not permissible. Thus, you could not move to insert "not" after "we" in the motion "that we reduce dues by $5.00." You could, however, move to strike out "reduce" and insert "increase" in the motion. Though conflicting with the purpose of the original motion, such an amendment is germane. The following example indicates a proper use of the motion to amend:

1. Original motion: ". . . that an expenditure of $500 be authorized for repairing the clubhouse roof."
2. Motion to amend: "I move to amend the motion by striking out ('$500') after ('expenditure of') and inserting ('$750')."
3. Motion as amended: ". . . that an expenditure of $750 be authorized for repairing the clubhouse roof."

Discussing the subject

Any member who is recognized by the chairman may discuss a motion which is before the group, but he must limit his remarks to that motion. As soon as the motion has been settled or disposed of, no further discussion on it is in order. Discussing a subject already disposed of requires that another motion, such as a motion to reconsider or to rescind the decision, be made and adopted. A motion to reconsider must be made by a member who voted with the prevailing side but who wishes to change his vote, and a majority must favor reconsideration. A motion to rescind can be made by any member for the purpose of reversing a decision which has not been carried out. When no advance notice is given, the motion to rescind requires a two-thirds vote.

Certain types of motions, of which the following are well-known examples, cannot be discussed at all but must either be complied with, as in No. 1, or be put to a vote at once:

1. Motions to follow the correct order of business ("call for the orders of the day"—no vote taken if chairman complies, which he is bound to do if it is the will of the assembly. If he suspects that it is not the will of the assembly, he can put the question of proceeding to the orders of the day to a vote.)
2. Motions for immediate vote—"previous question."
3. Motions to table—"lay on the table."
4. Motions to adjourn (usually, but not always).

Disposing of motions

A motion can be disposed of—that is, removed from discussion finally or temporarily—in three principal ways: (1) by a vote on the motion, (2) by adoption of another motion to postpone or to table it, and (3) by adoption of a motion to refer the proposal to a committee.

1. *Vote on the motion.* A majority vote is needed for adoption of a main motion. Usually the time for taking the vote comes about naturally: the important points having been discussed, the group is ready to make a decision. When the chairman senses this attitude, he may suggest a vote; and if there is no objection, he may put the question to a vote. At times, however, discussion may continue even after all the important arguments seem to have been presented. In such situations, a member may wish to make a motion to stop the discussion and take a vote. Such a motion is called the "previous question." This motion cannot be discussed; it must be voted on at once, and it must receive a two-thirds vote for adoption. If adopted, it stops discussion on the main motion and requires that a vote on the main motion be taken at once. (In less formal groups, the motion to stop discussion sometimes is made by a member's calling out "Question!" If no one objects, the chairman puts the pending motion to a vote at once. An objection, however, necessitates a vote on the "previous question." If the call obviously is counter to the will of the assembly, the chairman may rule it out of order.)

2. *Motions to postpone and to table.* The motion to postpone to a certain time and the motion to table remove a proposal from discussion for the time being. The motion to postpone indefinitely, however, kills a proposal—stops all discussion on it.

The motion to postpone to a certain time is made by saying, "Mr. Chairman, I move that the question be postponed until . . ." Adoption of this motion, by majority vote, permits consideration of the proposal at a more convenient or suitable time.

The motion to table is made by saying, "Mr. Chairman, I move that the question be laid on the table." Adoption of this motion, by majority vote, removes the proposal from consideration until a motion to take it from the table is made and adopted. Thus, tabling often results in ignoring a proposal or forgetting about it.

The motion to postpone indefinitely is made by saying, "Mr. Chairman, I move that the question be postponed indefinitely." Adoption of this motion, by majority vote, defeats a proposal indirectly; that is, by voting against consideration of a proposal, the group indicates its attitude toward the proposal without committing itself on it directly. This motion is often used to test the support or opposition a proposal has; adoption prevents discussion of the proposal unless a motion to reconsider the decision to postpone is made and adopted.

3. *Motion to refer to a committee.* A motion to refer a proposal to a committee, if adopted, has the effect of removing the main motion from consideration by the group at that time and passing it on to the committee indicated. Occasionally the motion of referral authorizes the committee to take final action, but usually the group itself decides which action to take after it has received the committee's report. Sometimes the motion refers the matter to a standing committee, or names a special committee, or authorizes the chairman to appoint a committee. The motion may refer the proposal to a committee without instructions, or it may include instructions to be followed in the investigation or deliberations.

The form for stating a motion to refer to committee varies with its maker's intent. A few of the forms frequently used are: "Mr. Chairman, I move that the question be referred to the __________ committee," or "to the __________ committee, with instructions to report at __________ [a definite time]," or "to the __________ committee, with power to act." When a special committee is needed to consider a proposal, provision for creating that committee should be included in the proposal, as follows: "Mr. Chairman, I move that this question be referred to a committee of __________ members to be appointed by the chair," or "__________ members, namely, Mr. __________, Miss __________, Mrs. __________ [etc.]," the remainder of the motion continuing as indicated above.

ADJOURNMENT

The meeting may be concluded at the close of business by the adoption of a motion to adjourn. In its simple form this motion may be introduced at any time, even interrupting discussion on a motion, provided that another meeting has been scheduled. The motion to

PARLIAMENTARY PROCEDURE FOR HANDLING MOTIONS

Classification of motions	*Types of motions and their purposes*	*Order of handling*	*Must be seconded*	*Can be discussed*	*Can be amended*	*Vote required*[1]	*Can be reconsidered*
Main motion	(To present a proposal to the assembly)	Cannot be made while any other motion is pending	Yes	Yes	Yes	Majority	Yes
Subsidiary motions[2]	To postpone indefinitely (to kill a motion)	Has precedence over above motion	Yes	Yes	No	Majority	Affirmative vote only
	To amend (to modify a motion)	Has precedence over above motions	Yes	When motion is debatable	Yes	Majority	Yes
	To refer (a motion) to committee	Has precedence over above motions	Yes	Yes	Yes	Majority	Until committee takes up subject
	To postpone (discussion of a motion) to a certain time	Has precedence over above motions	Yes	Yes	Yes	Majority	Yes
	To limit discussion (of a motion)	Has precedence over above motions	Yes	No	Yes	Two-thirds	Yes
	Previous question (to take a vote on the pending motion)	Has precedence over above motions	Yes	No	No	Two-thirds	No
	To table (to lay a motion aside until later)	Has precedence over above motions	Yes	No	No	Majority	No
Incidental motions[3]	To suspend the rules (to change the order of business temporarily)	Has precedence over a pending motion when its purpose relates to the motion	Yes	No	No	Two-thirds	No
	To close nominations[4]	[4]	Yes	No	Yes	Two-thirds	No
	To request leave to withdraw or modify a motion[5]	Has precedence over motion to which it pertains and other motions applied to it	No	No	No	Majority[5]	Negative vote only
	To rise to a point of order (to enforce the rules)[6]	Has precedence over pending motion out of which it arises	No	No	No	Chair decides[7]	No
	To appeal from the decision of the chair (to reverse chair's ruling)[6]	Is in order only when made immediately after chair announces ruling	Yes	When ruling was on debatable motion	No	Majority[1]	Yes
	To divide the question (to consider a motion by parts)	Has precedence over motion to which it pertains and motion to postpone indefinitely	[8]	No	Yes	Majority[8]	No

	To object to consideration of a question	In order only when a main motion is first introduced	No	No	No	Two-thirds	Negative vote only
	To divide the assembly (to take a standing vote)	Has precedence after question has been put	No	No	No	Chair decides	No
Privileged motions	To call for the orders of the day (to keep meeting to order of business)[6,9]	Has precedence over above motions	No	No	No	No vote required	No
	To raise a question of privilege (to point out noise, etc.)[6]	Has precedence over above motions	No	No	No	Chair decides[7]	No
	To recess[10]	Has precedence over above motions	Yes	No[10]	Yes	Majority	No
	To adjourn[11]	Has precedence over above motions	Yes	No[11]	No[11]	Majority	No
	To fix the time to which to adjourn (to set next meeting time)[12]	Has precedence over above motions	Yes	No[12]	Yes	Majority	Yes
Unclassified motions	To take from the table (to bring up tabled motion for consideration)	Cannot be made while another motion is pending	Yes	No	No	Majority	No
	To reconsider (to reverse vote on previously decided motion)[13]	Can be made while another motion is pending[13]	Yes	When motion to be reconsidered is debatable	No	Majority	No
	To rescind (to repeal decision on a motion)[14]	Cannot be made while another motion is pending	Yes	Yes	Yes	Majority or two-thirds[14]	Negative vote only

[1]A tied vote is always lost except on an appeal from the decision of the chair. The vote is taken on the ruling, not the appeal, and a tie sustains the ruling.

[2]Subsidiary motions are applied to a motion before the assembly for the purpose of disposing of it properly.

[3]Incidental motions are incidental to the conduct of business. Most of them arise out of a pending motion and must be decided before the pending motion is decided.

[4]The chair opens nominations with "Nominations are now in order." A member may move to close nominations, or the chair may declare nominations closed if there is no response to his inquiry, "Are there any further nominations?"

[5]When the motion is before the assembly, the mover requests permission to withdraw or modify it, and if there is no objection from anyone, the chair announces that the motion is withdrawn or modified. If anyone objects, the chair puts the request to a vote.

[6]A member may interrupt a speaker to rise to a point of order or of appeal, to call for orders of the day, or to raise a question of privilege.

[7]Chair's ruling stands unless appealed and reversed.

[8]If propositions or resolutions relate to independent subjects, they must be divided on the request of a single member. The request to divide the question may be made when another member has the floor. If they relate to the same subject but each part can stand alone, they may be divided only on a regular motion and vote.

[9]The regular order of business may be changed by a motion to suspend the rules.

[10]The motion to recess is not privileged if made at a time when no other motion is pending. When not privileged, it can be discussed. When privileged, it cannot be discussed, but can be amended as to length of recess.

[11]The motion to adjourn is not privileged if qualified or if adoption would dissolve the assembly. When not privileged, it can be discussed and amended.

[12]The motion to fix the time to which to adjourn is not privileged if no other motion is pending or if the assembly has scheduled another meeting on the same or following day. When not privileged, it can be discussed.

[13]A motion to reconsider may be made only by one who voted on the prevailing side. It must be made during the meeting at which the vote to be reconsidered was taken, or on the succeeding day of the same session. If reconsideration is moved while another motion is pending, discussion on it is delayed until discussion is completed on the pending motion; then it has precedence over all new motions of equal rank.

[14]It is impossible to rescind any action that has been taken as a result of a motion, but the unexecuted part may be rescinded. Adoption of the motion to rescind requires only a majority vote when notice is given at a previous meeting; it requires a two-thirds vote when no notice is given and the motion to rescind is voted on immediately.

adjourn requires a majority vote. When it interrupts discussion of another motion, it is said to be privileged; under such circumstances it may not be discussed and must be voted on at once. If adjournment would have the effect of disbanding the group entirely with no provision for reassembling, the motion to adjourn is not privileged—it may not interrupt pending business and is subject to discussion. Without this safeguard, business might be left unfinished with no provision for ultimate settlement.

When a group wishes to schedule another meeting on the same or the next day and has made no provision for such a meeting, a motion to fix the time to which to adjourn must be made and adopted by majority vote. The motion is privileged in these circumstances; that is, it may be introduced and voted on without discussion while another question is pending.

MODIFYING THE RULES OF ORDER

In small informal groups, not all of the rules presented in this chapter may be necessary. As mentioned earlier, parliamentary procedure is designed to expedite the orderly and democratic conduct of business, not to complicate it with unnecessary dogmatism and detail. Larger and more formal groups, on the other hand, usually require more detailed rules than are presented here. Sometimes the situation calls for the adoption of rules not even specifically contained in manuals of parliamentary procedure, but fitted to the needs of a particular group. A group may formulate—in addition to its constitution or bylaws—certain special or standing rules. In any event, apply the principles of parliamentary procedure as fully as required to preserve order and to expedite business in your group, but only to that degree.

STRATAGEMS IN PARLIAMENTARY PROCEDURE

Although the purpose of parliamentary procedure is to enable groups to transact business in a fair and democratic manner, it can be misused by certain individuals to gain unfair advantage for the cause they favor. Such practices are indefensible; yet when they are successful, their success is due as much to the indifference or ignorance of the victims as to the skill of the strategists. The best protection against such methods is knowledge of the rules and the ability, acquired through practice, to apply them correctly. Some of the stratagems to guard against are as follows:

Selection of biased officers and committees

The ultimate disposition of a proposal often depends as much upon the attitude of officials or committees as upon the attitude of the whole group. A chairman who is partial to one side may skillfully give that side the advantage in discussion even when seeming to keep within the letter of the rules—for example, by calling upon the best speakers on his own side and the worst on the opposing side. In his rulings and committee appointments, too, he may favor one side over another. The effect of such practices should be obvious.

Committees are often more important, so far as decision-making is concerned, than the organization as a whole; complicated problems are generally referred to them for study and report. This practice saves a good deal of time; but if the committee happens to be biased, the report will be prejudiced, and its influence upon the whole group will therefore be one-sided.

Thus, if a proposal is referred to a committee composed of members known to favor it, the chances of ultimate adoption are greater than if it is referred to a committee known to oppose it. Usually the subject matter of a proposal determines the committee to which it is referred; but many proposals extend within the possible jurisdiction of more than one committee so that a choice between them is possible. Sometimes an entirely new (special) committee is elected or appointed to deal with the proposal. When this is done, the make-up of this committee is exceedingly important. For all of the above reasons, then, it is important to scrutinize the nominations for the office of chairman or president and the selection of committees very carefully.

Changing the order of business

A change from the regular order of business may be used strategically. In this manner, the strategists watch for a time when absence has depleted the ranks of the opposition; then, while those who support the measure are preponderant, the order of business is changed (by a two-thirds vote), the item in question is introduced, and it is pushed through. A measure may be defeated in somewhat similar fashion by injecting another item ahead of it. Thus, consideration of the first measure can be delayed until greater opposition to it can be marshaled. This particular type of strategy is often applied so subtly that it is detected only with difficulty.

Division of the majority by use of amendments

Strategic use of amendments is for the purpose of dividing the majority. Suppose that the minority favors a proposal and the majority opposes it. The minority may offer an amendment that will please part of the opposing group. If and when the motion is so amended, the opposition to it will be split and the motion may be passed.

Now reverse the situation. Suppose that the minority oppose the motion. They may offer an amendment which, if passed, will split the majority and draw support away from the original proposal. If enough votes are gained from the majority to help the minority group pass the amendment, when the motion *as amended* is put to a vote, the minority may be helped in defeating it by the votes of those who opposed the amendment and who prefer to see the whole proposal fail rather than have it approved in its amended form.

Of course, the strategy of using amendments to divide the opposition is seldom as simple as indicated above. Amendments cause shifts in both directions—from the minority to the majority as well as from the majority to the minority. Strategists, therefore, may defeat themselves if they do not neatly calculate the resulting balance of power. They also may defeat themselves at the outset if they let it become obvious that they are making an amendment for strategic purposes. Dangerous and doubtful as it is, however, this type of strategy may be employed with success. The best defense against it is an informed and alert membership.

Postponement of action by adjournment

Sometimes in the general fatigue at the end of a long meeting, the proposal for adjournment is welcome. When such is the case, a minority may successfully use the motion to adjourn to cut short discussion and prevent unfavorable action on a pending proposal; this proposal would then carry over to the next meeting. This method is most often used when many absentees are known to favor the proposal and their vote might be counted on at the next meeting, or when subsequent events probably will afford additional arguments.

There are, of course, many other stratagems of parliamentary procedure which are employed. These few, however, are frequently used. To protect oneself from such tactics, it is not enough to examine the *obvious* reason for some move; the scrutiny must extend to the motive behind the move and to the consequences, should it be successful.

Be sufficiently familiar with the common stratagems so that you can guard against them. Most importantly, resolve to know the rules of parliamentary procedure so well that you can use them to accomplish their real purpose: to make sure that the majority's judgment prevails and, at the same time, to protect any fair and reasonable attempt of the minority to modify that judgment.

Problems

1. After consulting *Robert's Rules of Order Revised,* or a similar manual, prepare an oral or written report on one of the following subjects: privileged motions, incidental motions, subsidiary motions, voting, bylaws, constitution, meetings. If your report is oral, give the class an opportunity to ask questions or engage in a few moments of discussion on the subject covered. Ask them to use the table of parliamentary motions on pages 620-621 as a reference guide during this discussion.
2. Assume that you are a member of the student council of your college. Frame four main motions on matters that might come before this body—a proposed change in women's curfew hours, reorganization of the board in control of student publications, programming on the campus TV station, etc.
3. Phrase a possible amendment to each of the motions you have prepared for Problem 2. Be sure that your amendments are germane and that they embody a real change.
4. Taking one of the main motions prepared for Problem 2, phrase correctly *(a)* a motion to postpone to a certain time, *(b)* to table, and *(c)* to refer to a special committee. (Consult *Robert's Rules of Order Revised* for the proper phrasing.)
5. State a motion that has more than one part and show how it might be divided in order to be discussed properly.
6. Observe critically the operation of parliamentary procedure in some deliberative body—the student council, the board of aldermen, the state legislature, etc. Prepare a report, with special attention to *(a)* parliamentary procedure as a fair and orderly means of transacting the business of that body, *(b)* the use of stratagems to delay or obstruct decisions, and *(c)* the role of the chairman.

Parliamentary-procedure practice

1. Organize the class into a hypothetical meeting of some organization—the student council, the women's self-governing association, the dramatics club, etc. Following the rules of parliamentary procedure, select a chairman and proceed to introduce and transact business. Let either the instructor or some student specially appointed for the task act as parliamentarian, to aid in the solution of any problems that might arise in the use of the rules.

Suggestions for further reading

J. Jeffery Auer, *Essentials of Parliamentary Procedure,* 3rd ed. (New York: Appleton-Century-Crofts, 1959).

Giles Wilkeson Gray, "Implementing the Philosophy of Parliamentary Procedure," *Speech Teacher,* X (January 1961), 13-21.

John W. Gray and Richard G. Rea, *Parliamentary Procedure: A Programed Introduction* (Glenview, Illinois: Scott, Foresman and Company, 1963).

Paul Mason, "The Legal Side of Parliamentary Procedure," *Today's Speech*, IV (November 1956), 9-14.

Henry M. Robert, *Robert's Rules of Order Revised* (Glenview, Illinois: Scott, Foresman and Company, 1951).

ADAPTATION OF THE MOTIVATED SEQUENCE TO TYPICAL

General end	Audience attitude	Attention step	Need step
To Entertain	*(A)* Interested	1. Mention subject. 2. Use series of anecdotes and illustrations to amplify your viewpoint. 3. Use humor. *(Normal End of the Speech)*	*Sometimes:* Burlesque the development of the entire motivated sequence as if for one of the other general ends. Exaggerate obviously if you use this method.
	(B) Apathetic	1. Relate subject to the experience and interests of the audience. 2. Proceed as above.	Proceed as above.
To Inform	*(C)* Interested in Subject	1. Reference to subject. 2. Narrow scope of subject to limits of the speech.	Briefly mention its importance to the listeners—why they need to know.
	(D) Apathetic to Subject	Overcome inertia; arouse curiosity by the use of: 1. Unusual illustration. 2. Striking facts.	Demonstrate the importance of the subject to the audience by: 1. Explanation of its importance. 2. Illustrations.
To Convince	*(E)* Apathetic to Situation	Relate subject to listeners' personal concerns by use of: 1. Striking facts or figures. 2. Vivid phraseology.	1. Use powerful factual evidence—*specific instances, striking statistics, testimony*—to show how question vitally affects audience. 2. State requirements as below.
	(F) Interested in the Situation but Undecided	1. Reference to need (or) 2. Brief illustration of some unusual aspect of it. 3. Narrow attention toward basic aspect of the problem which underlies the need.	1. Point out basic nature of problem: *(a)* Historical background. *(b)* Basic causes. 2. Ramifications of present bad effects. 3. Point out what *requirements* an effective solution must meet to satisfy this need.
	(G) Interested in the Situation; Hostile to Proposal	1. Establish common ground by emphasizing point of agreement with audience: *(a)* Attitudes. *(b)* Beliefs. *(c)* Common experiences. 2. Continue as above.	1. Secure agreement on some basic principle or belief. 2. Continue as above, relating entire discussion to this principle. 3. Establish requirements of the solution on this basic principle.
	(H) Hostile to Belief in Existence of Problem	1. Begin as above. 2. Establish agreement as soon as possible on an acceptable principle to use in basing judgment of present situation: *(a)* Quote persons respected by audience.	1. Show that present conditions violate this principle. *(a)* Use facts, figures, and especially acceptable testimony. *(b)* Beware of exaggeration. 2. Continue as above.
To Stimulate	*(I)* Favorable but not Aroused	Intensify interest: 1. New angles of situation. 2. Vivid illustrations. 3. Personal challenge.	Make the need *impressive:* 1. Vivid illustrations; imagery. 2. Unusual comparisons and contrasts. 3. Striking factual disclosures. 4. Point out effect on audience.
	(J) Apathetic to Proposal	Same as above, but more *striking*. Especial emphasis on *vital* attention factor.	Same as above with special stress on the vital effect of problem on the audience. Apply strong personal motive appeals.
To Actuate	*(E)* to *(J)* Same as above.	Develop as above, depending on attitude of the audience. Follow methods in proper row *(E)* to *(J)* as indicated.	Develop as above, using methods as indicated in rows *(E)* to *(J)*, depending on the attitude of the audience.

AUDIENCE ATTITUDES TOWARD THE SUBJECT OR PURPOSE

Satisfaction step	Visualization step	Action step
Sometimes: Continue burlesque as suggested.	*Sometimes:* Continue burlesque as before.	*Sometimes:* Continue burlesque as before.
Proceed as above.	Proceed as above.	Proceed as above.
1. Begin with initial summary. (*a*) Define terms if necessary. 2. Present details of information. (*a*) Be concrete and specific. (*b*) Retain interest with factors of attention. (*c*) Follow: time order, space, etc. 3. Close with final summary.	*Sometimes:* Suggest pleasure to be had from knowledge of this information.	*Sometimes:* Suggest places for a further study or application of this information.
1. State the proposed belief or plan of action to be approved. 2. Explain it clearly. 3. Show logically how it will meet the requirements laid down in the need step. 4. Offer proof that the proposition will work: (*a*) Facts. (*b*) Figures. (*c*) Testimony of experts. (*d*) Examples of successful operation. 5. Demonstrate its benefits.	Use *Positive, Negative,* or method of *Contrast.* 1. Project audience into the future. 2. Picture desirable (or undesirable) conditions. 3. Use vivid imagery. 4. *Be brief.* 5. *Don't exaggerate!*	1. Restate request for belief or approval of plan of action. 2. Recapitulate reasons for its adoption: (*a*) Summary. (*b*) Illustration. (*c*) Quotation. (*d*) Personal intention.
1. Show relation of the proposal to the basic principle laid down in the need step. 2. Show its superiority on this basis to any other proposal. 3. Otherwise, proceed as above.	Proceed as above.	Proceed as above.
Proceed as above.	Proceed as above.	Proceed as above.
Make a brief statement of the attitude or future action desired. 1. Make it short. 2. Use dynamic phrasing.	Use *Positive* method. 1. Project audience into future. 2. Picture desirable conditions. 3. Use *mild* exaggeration. 4. Use vivid imagery.	1. Use challenge to commit listeners to proposal (or) 2. Use suggestion to assume they are already so committed.
Develop as above, using methods as indicated in rows *(E)* to *(J)*, depending on the attitude of the audience. Stress importance of *definite action by the audience.*	Develop as indicated in appropriate row above.	Develop as indicated in appropriate row above. Place responsibility for overt action on the individual members of the audience.

INTERNATIONAL PHONETIC ALPHABET

Symbol	Key Word	Pronunciation	Symbol	Key Word	Pronunciation
Vowels					
[i]	flee	[fli]	[ɔ]	thaw	[θɔ]
[ɪ]	sit	[sɪt]	[o]	no	[no]
[e]	mate	[met]	[ʊ]	good	[gʊd]
[ɛ]	fed	[fɛd]	[u]	suit	[sut]
[æ]	hat	[hæt]	[ɝ]	mercy	[ˋmɝsɪ] (*r* sounded)
[a]	ask	[ask] (as heard in the East)	[ɜ]	mercy	[ˋmɜsɪ] (*r* silent)
			[ɚ]	mother	[ˋmʌðɚ] (*r* sounded)
[ɑ]	part	[pɑrt]	[ə]	rather	[ˋræðə] (*r* silent)
[ɒ]	wad	[wɒd] (as heard in New England)		attack	[əˋtæk]
			[ʌ]	annul	[əˋnʌl]
Diphthongs					
[aɪ]	mile	[maɪl]	[ju]	union	[ˋjunjən]
[aʊ]	cow	[kaʊ]		mute	[mjut]
[ɔɪ]	employ	[ɪmˋplɔɪ]	[ɪu]	mute	[mɪut]
Consonants					
[p]	post	[post]	[h]	hat	[hæt]
[b]	bat	[bæt]	[tʃ]	chat	[tʃæt]
[t]	tale	[tel]	[dʒ]	jest	[dʒɛst]
[d]	duty	[ˋdjutɪ]	[m]	mute	[mjut]
[k]	cow	[kaʊ]	[m̩]	keep ’em	[ˋkipm̩]
[g]	gap	[gæp]	[n]	union	[ˋjunjən]
[f]	face	[fes]	[n̩]	mutton	[ˋmʌtn̩]
[v]	vine	[vaɪn]	[ŋ]	bang	[bæŋ]
[θ]	both	[boθ]	[l]	mile	[maɪl]
[ð]	then	[ðɛn]	[l̩]	handle	[ˋhændl̩]
[s]	sit	[sɪt]	[w]	wet	[wɛt]
[z]	zero	[ˋzɪro]	[hw]	when	[hwɛn]
[ʃ]	push	[pʊʃ]	[j]	yellow	[ˋjɛlo]
[ʒ]	measure	[ˋmɛʒɚ]	[r]	red	[rɛd]

IPA: Explanatory notes[1]

As a student of speech, you should become aware of the International Phonetic Alphabet (IPA) and the ways in which it can assist you in improving your speech. Basically, a symbol is assigned to each speech sound; and these symbols, individually and in combination, are useful tools for analyzing pronunciation and articulation—your own as well as others'. Properly employed in listening, transcribing, and speaking, this phonetic guide can help you make certain that the nature and quality of your speech meet established norms.

On the preceding page is an abridged version of the IPA. As you can see, the alphabet is divided into symbols for the *vowel*, *diphthong*, and *consonant* sounds. Many more symbols are required to represent and distinguish between individual speech sounds than are available in our conventional alphabet, particularly among the vowels. Sounds, for example, which are represented in spelling by the letter "a" require several phonetic symbols so that each may be distinguished. Another point that might be cited is that in the sounds which are represented by "er" or "uh" the distinction must be made between accented and unaccented forms; therefore you will note that [ɝ], [ɜ], and [ʌ], which are used only in accented syllables, are regarded as separate sounds from [ɚ] and [ə], which appear only in unaccented syllables.

Diphthongs are here considered as single speech sounds. Diphthong symbols, and such consonant symbols as [tʃ] and [dʒ], are regarded as single phonetic symbols. The diphthongs [ju] and [ɪu] often alternate (as in [mjut] and [mɪut]), with the same speaker sometimes using both forms. The symbol [ju] is a rising diphthong (the second element stressed more than the first), whereas [ɪu] is either a falling diphthong (first element stressed) or a level-stress diphthong.

As you study the accompanying chart, observe that key words containing sounds represented by specific symbols are transcribed into phonetic symbols in the pronunciation column. Accent marks are included with transcriptions of words of more than one syllable. Note, too, that the accent mark always *precedes* the accented syllable.

[1]For a more complete explanation of the phonetic alphabet, see John S. Kenyon and Thomas A. Knott, "Introduction," *A Pronouncing Dictionary of American English* (Springfield, Mass.: G. and C. Merriam Co., 1951). Also see Ralph R. Leutenegger, *The Sounds of American English* (Glenview, Ill.: Scott, Foresman and Company, 1963). For demonstrations of the phonemes, listen to Demonstration Exercises 1–3 in *Voice and Articulation: Recorded Exercises,* by Donald H. Ecroyd, Murray M. Halfond, and Carol Chworowsky Towne (Glenview, Ill.: Scott, Foresman and Company, 1966).

INDEX

A

D

E

N

O

P

S

2 3 4 5 6 7 8 9 10 11 12 13 14 15 16 17 18 19 20 21 22 23 24 25 P 75 74 73 72 71 70 69 68 67

CHECKLIST AND INDEX FOR EVALUATION AND IMPROVEMENT OF STUDENT SPEECHES

(revised and updated)

This chart can be used by instructors and students in evaluating outlines, manuscripts, and speeches as delivered. It lists most of the factors contributing to effective communication, with references to relevant pages. Instructors will find it useful in checking and correcting students' work. They may, for example, write symbols keyed to specific items in the checklist **(Outl., 5, etc.)** on a student's outline or manuscript, or they may record the symbols on a card when listening to a speech. A plus sign **(+)** with the symbol will indicate work well done; a minus sign **(−)**, that it is unsatisfactory. Written at the top of a page, the symbol will pertain to the work in general; written in the margin, it will pertain to material immediately opposite.

In correcting errors, students will be helped by the page references provided with this checklist. It will also be useful to them in the preparation of their assignments, both in reviewing principal items to be covered and in locating information bearing on a particular problem.

OUTL. / Factors of outline form

1 Indentation proper (292-293)
2 Subordination of points proper and logical (291-292)
3 Symbols properly used (293)
4 Satisfactory number of items per unit (291)
5 Sentences complete (294)
6 Neatly written
7 Wording of main points clear and concise (225-227, 298)
8 Sources cited (294)

AN. / Factors in analysis

9 Audience specified (138)
10 Audience diagnosis complete (129-139)
11 Primary interests and fixed beliefs of audience indicated, and correctly stated (130-131)
12 Audience attitude correctly analyzed (131-134)
13 Occasion well analyzed (128, 139-140)
14 Subject appropriate (112-113)
15 Subject sufficiently narrowed (31, 113)
16 General end appropriate (115-118)
17 Purpose specific, and possible to attain (31-32, 119-122)

CONT. / Factors in content

18 Adequate support for proof or illumination of ideas
- A Good use of explanation (157-159)
- B Good use of analogy or comparison (159-161)
- C Good use of illustration (161-164)
- D Good use of specific instances (164-166)
- E Good use of statistics (166-169)
- F Good use of testimony (169-171)
- G Good use of restatement (171)
- H Good use of visual aids (172-178)

19 Sound reasoning (418-420)
20 Good use of special technics
- A Good use of "yes-response" (421-422)
- B Good use of "this-or-nothing" (422)

21 Adequate motive appeal (193-202)
- A Proper motive appeals for audience (202-204)
- B Strong appeal (202-204)
- C Tactful appeal (204)

22 Good use of factors of attention (209-214)
23 Effective wording (318-331)
- A Meaning adequately expressed (318-320)